PROCEDURES FOR THE
CANADIAN LEGAL OFFICE

PROCEDURES FOR THE CANADIAN LEGAL OFFICE

Seventh Edition

M. Louise Winterstein
Centennial College

NELSON / EDUCATION

NELSON / EDUCATION

PROCEDURES FOR THE CANADIAN LEGAL OFFICE, SEVENTH EDITION
by M. Louise Winterstein

**Associate Vice President,
Editorial Director:**
Evelyn Veitch

**Editor-in-Chief,
Higher Education:**
Anne Williams

Marketing Manager:
Shannon White

Developmental Editor:
Tracy Yan

Permissions Coordinator:
Bhisham Kinha

Content Production Manager:
Imoinda Romain

Production Service:
GEX Inc.

Copy Editor:
Holly Dickinson

Proofreader:
GEX Inc.

Indexer:
GEX Inc.

**Senior Manufacturing
Coordinator:**
Charmaine Lee-Wah

Design Director:
Ken Phipps

Interior Design:
VISUTronx

Design Modifications:
Peggy Rhodes

Cover Design:
Dianna Little

Cover Colour Modifications:
Emilie Cook

Cover Image:
iofoto/Shutterstock

Compositor:
GEX Inc.

Printer:
WebCom

**Library and Archives Canada
Cataloguing in Publication**

Winterstein, Louise, 1957-

Procedures for the Canadian legal office / M. Louise Winterstein. — 7th ed.

Includes index.

Seventh ed. published under title: Procedures for the legal offices / Elsie E. Swartz, Louise Winterstein. First-6th eds. published under title: Procedures for the legal secretary.

ISBN 978-0-17-644071-8

1. Legal secretaries—Canada—Handbooks, manuals, etc. 2. Forms (Law)—Canada. I. Swartz, Elsie E., 1924- . Procedures for the legal office. II. Title.

KE353.W55 2008
651'.93400971   C2007-907321-2

KF319.W55 2008

ISBN-10: 0-17-644071-2
ISBN-13: 978-0-17-644071-8

This textbook is intended as a procedural guide only; it does not offer legal advice. A lawyer should be consulted whenever expert legal advice is required.

Please note that all names of law firms, clients, and other individuals in this text are fictional and are not based on any real-life individuals; any similarities are entirely coincidental.

To my family:

My husband Ed, for his support and encouragement in all my endeavours
My children Lee, Shannon, and **Amanda,** for the joy they bring
And in memory of **my parents, Adam** and **Mabel Grant**

Standynge Fæste

BRIEF CONTENTS

CONTENTS

PREFACE

This seventh edition of *Procedures for the Canadian Legal Office* has been completely updated and revised and reflects changes current to January 1, 2008, in the areas of general and civil litigation, family, real estate, and corporate and estate practice and procedures. Many small but important changes have been made throughout this text to incorporate any statutory amendments in legal procedures and the procedural changes resulting from the impact of technology on the legal profession, especially in the area of electronic filing and registration in corporate and real estate practice. The new format allows for a more user-friendly text, with the figures, charts, and tables close to the text to which they pertain to facilitate understanding of the material. The document precedents have been placed at the end of the chapters, as was traditionally done, to retain the format of the documents and to provide for easy reference by the reader. The accompanying assignment book reflects the suggestions from various instructors over the years, namely, a focus on terminology and document production, including transcription material, allowing students the opportunity for the hands-on exercises that simulate the law office environment that have been a continuing mainstay for this text.

Acknowledgments

This text could not have been completed without the support of many individuals from the legal profession and various court, land registry, and government offices. I hesitate to name them all individually lest I inadvertently omit someone, but to each I extend my sincere thanks.

I would like to acknowledge the assistance of some of my colleagues at Centennial College: Patti Ann Sullivan of the Ontario Bar, a valued colleague who helps make teaching a pleasure and who graciously reviewed parts of this text and provided valuable feedback; Barb Saipe, also of the Ontario Bar, for her input on estates practice; and Brian Bradley, for the benefit of his wealth of conveyancing knowledge.

To Kevin Smulan, Nelson Education Ltd., thank you for encouraging the development of this book; and to Tracy Yan, Developmental Editor, Nelson Education Ltd., thank you for encouraging me. To Gini Henderson, a valued friend, thank you for providing a quick software solution when time was of the essence.

My appreciation also goes to the following people and legal software companies for their support for this text and for facilitating the learning goals of the community colleges: Mark Harris and Ann Volpe (DIVORCEmate); Mitchell Brown and Zorina Mohammed (Do Process Inc.); Catherine Bowes and James Picano (Korbitec Inc.); Alan Tuback (PCLaw™); and Laura Micks (Teranet Inc.). I would also like to extend my gratitude to the following individuals who gave of their time and expertise to review this text and provide valuable comments and suggestions: Chris Gigler (Sheridan College), Virginia Harwood (Durham College), Carmen Burt (Okanagan College), and Patricia Lee (Camosun College).

Last, but certainly not least, my appreciation to my students, who provide insights and inspiration in the classroom and after they graduate. In particular, I would like to thank Pearlamina Jerome, an exceptional student and legal assistant who was a pleasure to teach and a wonderful resource after graduation and who assisted in the preparation of the updated glossary for this edition.

Any comments on or suggestions for this text would be gratefully appreciated by the author.

Best wishes for success as you pursue your career in the legal field.

About the Author

Louise Winterstein is a faculty member in the School of Business at Centennial College in Toronto, where she teaches legal procedures and software in the Law Clerk and Office Administration–Legal programs. Louise is a community college graduate herself, who also has a bachelor of arts in history from the University of Waterloo. She worked in the legal field for 10 years before becoming a corporate trainer and then a college instructor, and firmly believes that not only did curiosity not kill the cat, but that lifelong learning keeps it alive and well.

PART 1

General Legal Office Procedures and Documentation

CHAPTER 1

The Legal Environment

OBJECTIVES:

- Describe the different professions and careers in a law office
- Demonstrate an understanding of the structure of law firms
- Describe the general purpose and procedure for applying for legal aid
- Discuss the performance guidelines for legal assistants
- Demonstrate an understanding of the ethics of legal advice and confidentiality

The legal profession is one of the oldest in the world. Its terms and customs are a reflection of the fact that law itself is of great antiquity. With the adoption of English common law in most of the Canadian provinces, the basic customs and traditions of the English legal profession were inherited, but with modifications to suit the particular circumstances of Canada.

LAWYERS

The individuals who make up the legal profession are known as lawyers or members of the bar. In Canada, a lawyer is both a **barrister and solicitor** and may be known as a **counsel** if his or her practice largely involves court work.

To become a lawyer, individuals attend law school and complete a bachelor of laws (LL.B.) degree. They then spend a period, known as **articling**, working under a lawyer's supervision. This is followed by a special course preparing them to be *called to the bar*—the term used in the legal profession to indicate that an individual is eligible to practise law.

QUEEN'S COUNSEL

Lawyers may also be appointed Queen's Counsel (Q.C.) or King's Counsel (K.C.) (if the monarch is a king) as a mark of recognition for exceptional service to the legal profession. Such designations were done annually by the Attorney General or Minister of Justice of a province or by the Justice Minister of Canada. The practice of making such appointments has been discontinued federally and in the provinces of Ontario and Quebec but is still done annually in the remaining provinces. For those lawyers who have received such a designation, the Q.C. notation appears after their name on all documentation.

COMMISSIONER AND NOTARY PUBLIC

A lawyer is automatically a **commissioner** for the purpose of administering oaths to persons coming before him or her to swear or affirm to the truth of statement and a **notary public** to affirm under notarial seal the execution of certain legal writing or the authenticity of a copy of a document or writing.

LAW SOCIETIES

Each province has it own law society that sets the requirements for admission to the bar; these are administered by the governing body of the legal profession in that province, examples of which are The Law Society of British Columbia, The Law Society of Upper Canada (Ontario), The Nova Scotia Barristers' Society, and

Le Barreau du Québec. All practising lawyers of a province must belong to the provincial law society, pay annual dues, including professional liability insurance, and follow the rules of professional conduct laid down by the society.

ASSOCIATIONS

Many lawyers belong voluntarily to the Canadian Bar Association (CBA), which has provincial branches that provide educational and networking opportunities for its members. The CBA meets annually to discuss matters relating the legal profession and the administration of justice in the country.

In some provinces, there are also county or district law associations that, among other activities, maintain law libraries for the use of the profession and set the tariff (fee) that may be charged for performing certain types of legal work.

LEGAL AID

Legal aid is an assistance plan that provides access to legal services for people who might otherwise not be able to afford a lawyer.

Each province has its own legal aid plan and its own criteria for eligibility. In some provinces, the plan has staff lawyers (often known as public defenders) who act for eligible clients; in other provinces, the majority of legal aid work is done by lawyers from private practice. Over half of all cases handled under legal aid concern criminal charges, and the balance involve civil disputes, mostly in family law.

To ensure that no person accused of a criminal offence is unaware of his or her rights in court, legal aid operates a duty counsel system in most provincial courts. Duty counsel are lawyers who advise on legal rights, help in applications for bail, and assist in application for legal aid. Duty counsel also work in many of the provincial family court systems.

Legal aid is funded by both the provincial and federal governments and in some cases by contributions from provincial law societies. Lawyers who do legal aid accept a lower fee than would be charged to a private client and are, in effect, donating part of their time to assist such clients.

Any resident of a province can apply for legal aid. On application, the resident's financial circumstances and the nature of the help required are assessed. Each province has its own eligibility guidelines. Income, disposable assets, indebtedness, maintenance obligations, and other expenses are usually considered. Depending on the assessment, free legal services may be approved for the applicant, or he or she may be asked to pay part of the costs of the legal help provided. If the assessment shows that the applicant can pay his or her own legal costs, legal aid is not granted.

When legal aid is granted, a legal aid certificate is issued and forwarded either to the individual or to the solicitor selected by the applicant from the panel of lawyers. If the solicitor is prepared to accept the applicant as a client, he or she completes the solicitor's acknowledgement and undertaking portion of the certificate and returns it to the legal aid office.

LAW FIRMS

Law firms may vary in size from a single office with one lawyer (known as a **sole practitioner**) to a suite of offices with several hundred lawyers. Lawyers may limit their work to one specific area of legal services, such as real estate, litigation, estates, corporate, criminal, family, environmental, immigration, taxation, intellectual property, entertainment, or labour law. Alternatively, they may be involved in a general practice, where they undertake to perform legal services in any number of areas of legal work.

Traditionally, a law firm is not a company, and the word *Company* or *Limited* does not appear in its name as it is a partnership in which the partners share in the profits of the law firm, although the profits may not always be equally distributed between the partners. Founding or senior partners of a law firm may receive a larger percentage than junior partners, whose percentage may increase with years of partnership in the firm. The firm may consist of partners only, or it may employ other lawyers to be associated with it (known as **associates**).

The name of the law firm is determined by the partnership agreement and is traditionally composed of the last name of some or all of the partners arranged in agreed order, often by seniority of admission in the partnership. The name of the law firm may also include names of former partners who are deceased or retired. The modern trend, however, is toward shorter names that are easily recognizable by the public. The firm name appears on its letterhead, and depending on the number or preference of the law firm, the letterhead may or may not show the names of all the partners and lawyers in the firm. For large law firms, the usual practice is for the name of the law firm to appear at the top, with the name of the individual lawyer and his or her direct telephone number and e-mail address shown below. Figure 1.1 (p. 6) contains some examples of legal letterheads.

In some provinces, including Ontario, law firms are allowed to enter into a **limited liability partnership**. Under this type of structure, partners are limited in their liability (legal and/or financial responsibility) to their own debts, obligations, and negligent acts and to those members of the law firm who are under their direct control or supervision, such as associate lawyers, legal assistants, or articling students. In other words, partners are not held liable for the debts, obligations, or negligent actions of other partners or employees of the firm over which they had no knowledge or responsibility. Law firms that have become limited liability partnerships display the acronym "LLP" after their firm name.

LAW OFFICE STAFF

A wide range of legal support staff is found in the law office. Such staff will have varying levels of experience and responsibility and will perform a wide variety of functions to assist the lawyers. In addition to the positions described in detail below, there may also be administrative and human resource managers, computer programmers and systems analysts, receptionists, switchboard operators, accountants and accounting personnel, and mailroom personnel that take care of deliveries, printing, and large photocopying projects. All legal office staff require the

Figure 1.1 Examples of Legal Letterheads

Hill, Johnston & Grant
Barristers & Solicitors

Suite 2501, 17 Princess Street South
Toronto, Ontario, M8Y 3N5
Canada

Our Reference No.

www.hilljohngrant.com

Telephone: (416) 354-9900
Facsimile: (416) 354-9909

Peter T. Grant
Direct Line: (416) 354-9898
E-mail: ptgrant@hilljohngrant.com

SMITH, FRASER, HAMID & LEE LLP
Barristers and Solicitors

Douglas L. Smith, Q.C.	Aaron P. Fraser, Q.C.	Facsimile (416) 233-9980
John A. Hamid, Q.C.	John M. Lee, Q.C.	Telephone (416) 233-9985
Martin J. Chen	Leonard A. Blackwell	
Mary J. Spencer	Maria P. Gallaro	Suite 503
Shelley A. Colangelo	Harold R. Stauffer	75 Victoria Street
Gregory H. Swartz	Carol E. Irvine	Toronto, Ontario M5C 2B1
Arturo A. Himayla	Amar G. Singh	Canada

Please Refer to File No.

www.smithfraser.com

McCAFFERY & LEHMAN
Barristers & Solicitors

3500 Upper Water Street, Suite 400
Halifax, Nova Scotia, B3J 2X2
Canada

Our Reference No.

www.mccafferylehman.com

Telephone: 902-226-6000
Facsimile: 902-226-6060

WYSOCKI & WARSH
Barristers and Solicitors

Paul Wysocki, Q.C.   Sandra P. Warsh, Q.C.
John B. Tsubouchi   Michelle P. Lee

www.wysockiwarsh.com

1050 West Georgia Street
Vancouver, British Columbia
V6C 4R1
Canada

Telephone: (604) 689-4000
Facsimile: (604) 689-4040

characteristics of adaptability, cooperation, courtesy, dependability, flexibility, initiative, and tact, as well as the ability to work under pressure and to work well with others in addition to the specialized education and training required for their particular position.

Law Clerks/Paralegals

In most provinces of Canada, a law clerk and a paralegal are considered the same, with slight variations in job descriptions, and may be referred to by a variety of titles, such as law clerks, paralegals, legal assistants, or conveyancers (those individuals who conduct real property title searches). These are individuals who have successfully completed the courses required by their provincial association and gained experience in the legal field. To register in such courses, an individual must be actively engaged in work of a legal nature. Alternatively, law clerks may be individuals who have successfully completed a program at a community college. In either case, the law clerk/paralegal will have acquired some theoretical knowledge of the law, experience in the legal field, and computer proficiency in legal document production and specialized legal software. In most provinces, law clerks/paralegals are required to work under the supervision of a lawyer and in all provinces are not allowed to represent themselves to the public as lawyers.

In Ontario, a distinction is made between a law clerk and a paralegal. A law clerk is an individual who works under the supervision of a lawyer. However, a paralegal is an individual who does *not* work under the supervision of a lawyer and is often a self-employed individual or sometimes individuals who group together to provide a limited range of legal services to the public or under contract to law firms. Paralegals usually have a combination of education and previous experience in a specialized legal or a quasi-legal field. An example of a paralegal enterprise would be the services offered by former police officers who specialize in assisting individuals fighting traffic offences. The legal work that paralegals are allowed to carry out is limited by government legislation and is also currently under review in Ontario.

Although the functions of a law clerk and legal secretary sometimes coincide, the law clerk has more extensive knowledge of the theory of law in order to draft standard legal documents, conduct legal research, interview witnesses, collect client information in family law or estate matters, search title to real property, carry out the steps to close a real estate transaction, or appear in court on behalf of the lawyer.

Legal Secretaries/Administrative Assistants

A legal secretary may also be referred to by a number of titles, such as legal administrative assistant, legal assistant, or, quite often now, "legal admin." A legal administrative assistant is an individual who works under the supervision of a lawyer to provide a variety of legal support services. These individuals are usually graduates of a two-year diploma program from a community college. Excellent written and verbal language skills, along with computer literacy in word processing, spreadsheets, databases, and presentation software applications, as well as knowledge of general and legal office procedures and terminology, are required to be successful in this position.

For expediency purposes in this textbook, the term "legal assistant" will be used to refer to the role of law clerks, paralegals, or legal administrative assistants in describing legal office procedures and the preparation of legal documentation unless specifically stated otherwise.

TECHNOLOGY IN THE LAW OFFICE

In most law offices today, the lawyers and all legal support personnel have a desktop or laptop computer, often in a networked computer environment, with access to the major software application packages, as well as e-mail, fax modems, and online search capabilities. Specialized legal accounting and time management software involving time docketing, diaries, and tickler systems are also commonly used, as well as software programs specifically designed for real estate, corporate, estates, litigation, and family law document production.

The extent of the use of computer information technology in the practice of law varies from office to office. Some law offices are highly automated; others are less so. Almost all, however, have at least the computer technology to produce documents, maintain computerized accounting records, and perform electronic searches and/or filing where available. For the purposes of this text, familiarity with common word processing software applications, e-mail, and the Internet is assumed. References in the text to document production and office procedures will reflect this.

PERFORMANCE GUIDELINES

A legal assistant must try to aim for complete accuracy at all times. Even a simple error in keyboarding may be both costly and embarrassing. To achieve a high level of performance, keep the following points in mind:

- Proofread and check all keyboarded material. Check dates, amounts, and the spelling of names and places. Work that contains material copied from another source should be proofread or compared with someone else. Check the new copy carefully as that other person reads aloud from the original material.
- Be sure that the material reads sensibly. Even though the dictator may have said something that sounds like, "Please let us know when it will be can be it...," the finished material should read, "Please let us know when it will be convenient..." As a new legal assistant, you will find that some of the material you prepare will not make sense at first. Legal terminology has traditionally been very formal, and although there is a growing trend to simplify legal language, there are still some Latin and traditional terms that convey a precise meaning that has been developed over many years. As you gain experience in your field, this traditional phrasing will become familiar.
- Be sure that what is prepared is grammatically correct. You should correct an error in grammar provided that the correction does not in any way alter the meaning of the sentence. Do not edit or rewrite material given you by a lawyer. For example, it might appear that the phrase "remise, release, and forever discharge" contains

unnecessary words, but the words have special meaning in legal work when used in this form, and the omission of one of them would be questioned.

- Maintain an alphabetical index of the names, addresses, telephone and fax numbers, and e-mail addresses of clients, law firms, and other individuals frequently written to or contacted. This index should be maintained on your computer, but a paper copy as a backup should also be available.
- Clarify anything you are uncertain about before you begin your work. Write down any verbal instructions given to you. Do not guess; ask questions if you do not understand any instructions or look it up in a reference text. Both time and money are wasted when work must be redone or corrected because of errors made by you. A lawyer would prefer to be given two pages of work done correctly rather than four pages that each contain errors requiring the work to be corrected or redone.

Precedents

- Compile a set of examples or precedents. When a form or document is prepared for the first time, make an extra copy and place it in a binder to create an alphabetical precedent file to which you can refer in the future. Make a note in the upper right-hand corner of the face page of the precedent of the minimum number of copies required and what happens to each of those copies.
- One of the key skills that a legal assistant needs to develop is the ability to take the information provided by the lawyer or the client and, using a document precedent, create a document that is correct in content and format.

In this text, all precedent examples have been placed at the end of the chapter to which they correspond in order to retain the correct formatting and for ease of reference.

LEGAL ADVICE AND CONFIDENTIALITY

Only lawyers may give legal advice; in fulfilling your duties as a law clerk or legal administrative assistant, you must never under any circumstances offer legal advice, and all work must be done under the supervision of a lawyer.

A lawyer is a **fiduciary**, a word of Latin origin meaning *one who is entrusted*. The information that a lawyer receives is a privileged communication to be held in strict confidence and used as necessary in the matter being handled for the client.

You are an employee of the law firm that employs you and are bound by the same code of ethics as the lawyer. The lawyer must be able to rely on your discretion to keep confidential any information you may learn and to resist any temptation to mention outside the office, even in passing, any detail of a case or matter. *Nothing* may be discussed outside the office. There are no exceptions to this rule, and most law firms will require you to sign a confidentiality agreement stating that you understand this rule and will keep confidential all client information.

In a very real sense, a legal assistant contributes to the success of a law firm. Adaptability and flexibility in a time of rapid continuing advances in technology will enhance your value to your employers and contribute to the prompt service of the clients' needs. Your courtesy, diplomacy, and tact in dealing with clients and all those with whom you come in contact set the atmosphere for your office and create goodwill for your firm. In a real sense, you do not work for a lawyer; you work with a lawyer to provide the legal services to those who come for assistance. Each of you contributes in a special way to meet that need; you may indeed be proud of the part you have to play.

Terms and Concepts

barrister and solicitor
counsel
articling
Queen's Counsel
commissioner
notary public
Canadian Bar Association
legal aid
law firms
sole practitioner

associate
limited liability partnership (LLP)
law clerk
legal administrative assistant
paralegal
performance guidelines
precedent
fiduciary
confidentiality agreement

Review Questions

1. A lawyer may be referred to by other terms, such as a member of the bar. Name three other terms that may describe a lawyer.

2. In what area of law would a lawyer be said to be practising if his or her practice solely involved acting for clients who
   a. were charged with assault, murder, and similar offences?
   b. were buying and selling land, houses, condominiums, etc.?
   c. wanted to come to this country to make it their permanent home?
   d. were involved in suing someone to resolve a dispute between them?

3. What is meant when a client is a "legal aid" client?

4. Hill, Johnston & Grant is a "law firm." What is meant by that term? What would it mean if the firm was named Hill, Johnston & Grant LLP?

5. In what ways do law clerks/legal administrative assistants help the lawyer?

6. Why is it necessary for a legal assistant to have good proofreading skills?

7. How much of what you learn of the affairs of a client can you discuss outside the office? Why or why not?

8. Why should you maintain a set of precedents?

9. **Internet Research:** What is the name of the governing body in your province for
   a. lawyers?
   b. law clerks?

CHAPTER 2

Procedures and Practices in the Law Office

OBJECTIVES:

- Describe diary procedures and the various delivery methods used in the legal office

- Apply knowledge of mail, e-mail, telephone, and voice-mail systems

- Discuss the use of photocopiers and reference sources in the legal office

- Describe the various methods of preparing legal material

- Demonstrate an understanding of the use of and style for punctuation, numbers, and quotations in producing legal documentation

This text does not detail general office procedures; there are many excellent general office procedures handbooks published in Canada that are devoted to a presentation of these procedures, such as the *Gregg Reference Manual* (McGraw-Hill Ryerson) and the *Pitman Office Handbook* (Copp Clark Pitman Ltd.). You should note, however, how some of these procedures are carried out in a law office.

DIARIES/CALENDARS

When a person arranges to consult the lawyer, the appointment is noted in both the lawyer's and the legal assistant's diaries or calendars. A diary records all time commitments for the lawyer and may also show notations of work performed as well as reminders of things to be done on or by specific dates.

The lawyer's diary may be maintained in a book or often now on a calendaring system on the computer. In a networked computer environment, other authorized individuals, such as the legal assistant, may have access to view and/or create appointments on the lawyer's calendar. This reduces the difficulty of arranging suitable conference times for a number of the firm's lawyers.

When the diary is maintained in a book or desk calendar, both the lawyer and the legal assistant should maintain diaries. Notations in the lawyer's diary may be made by you, the lawyer personally, or another member of the firm with whom the lawyer works closely. Check each day to ensure that the entries in your diary are identical to those in the lawyer's diary.

DELIVERY METHODS

Law offices use many methods to deliver mail, messages, and materials. The facilities of the post office are still widely used, as are facsimile transmissions, e-mail, messengers, and commercial courier services, as described below.

Fax

An actual copy of material—letters, documents, graphs, pictures, etc., whether printed, typed, or handwritten—may be electronically transmitted directly from one office to another through a fax machine (short for facsimile). The material that is sent or received is also referred to as "a fax," and the procedure is known as "faxing."

Material is transmitted by inserting a page or pages into the fax machine, dialling the fax number of the office to which it is to be sent (using the telephone keypad that is part of the fax machine), and pressing the start button.

It should be noted that the number for a fax machine is different from the regular office telephone number. Law firms indicate their fax numbers on their letterhead and websites and in legal directories. If the regular number is used instead of the fax number, the material will not be transmitted. You should be very careful to key in the correct fax number as the material to be faxed is often confidential. Many law firms include a standard paragraph at the bottom of their fax cover sheet to cover such circumstances, but any errors in transmission could be costly and embarrassing. It is also possible to fax directly from computer to computer if both computers have fax modems.

Material that is sent by fax requires a cover page, which sets out the name and fax number of the person or office to which it is being sent, information on the sender, and the number of pages being transmitted (including the cover page). Figure 2.1 illustrates a typical cover page for a fax transmission.

Figure 2.1 Fax Cover Page

HILL, JOHNSTON & GRANT
Barristers & Solicitors
Suite 2501, 17 Princess Street South, City, Province Postal Code
Telephone: (000) 354-9900   Facsimile: (000) 354-9909

FAX COVER PAGE

Date: File No.

To: From:

Fax: Fax:

Phone: Phone:

Pages

(including cover page)

If pages are missing, please contact:

COMMENTS:

This fax is confidential and is intended only for the person(s) named above. Its contents may also be protected by privilege, and all rights to privilege are expressly claimed and not waived. If you have received this fax in error, please call us immediately and destroy the entire fax. If this fax is not intended for you, any review, distribution, copying, or disclosure of this fax is strictly prohibited.

Courier Services

There are many commercial courier services that deliver material in Canada, the United States, and other parts of the world. They ensure delivery within a set period—usually 24 hours for North America or by 9 a.m. the next day. The law office will either have a supply of forms or a customer access number for the website of the courier service it uses regularly. When the paper or electronic form has been completed, either the legal assistant or the designated person in the office will call the courier service to have the material picked up or taken to a central clearing point by certain times each day.

Staff Messengers and Taxicabs

Frequently, material addressed to another law firm or business located in the same area is personally delivered by an employee of the law firm or is sent by taxicab, if distance does not permit easy personal delivery. When sending material by taxicab, the taxi company will usually indicate the delivery charges when you place the call, or if the service is regularly used, the company will provide charge slips and bill the law firm later.

File Number

When material is sent using special postal or delivery services, write the file number on the charge slip or receipt. The accounting department can then allocate the charge for the delivery. This is discussed in more detail in Chapter 5.

HANDLING THE MAIL

Faxes

Most large law offices have one employee whose responsibilities include sending and receiving fax material. In smaller offices, each legal assistant may be responsible for transmitting faxes and for delivering fax material as it is received.

All fax messages should be regarded as confidential material for the recipient and treated accordingly. No one should read material addressed to another unless specifically authorized to do so.

Incoming Mail

In small law offices, one member of the support staff may be assigned the responsibility to receive, open, and distribute the mail received each day and to distribute material delivered by messengers. Each piece of material is usually date stamped to record its receipt date. In other law offices, all mail from the post office is received by mailroom personnel and sorted and distributed directly to the appropriate lawyer or to his or her legal assistant. Material received during the day through deliveries is distributed by the messenger or receptionist to the lawyer to whom it is addressed.

When the mail is distributed to the lawyer's legal assistant, it should be sorted into categories: letters and memoranda, documents, and newspapers and publications. Business envelopes marked "Personal" or "Confidential" should be opened only if such an action has been authorized by the lawyer; plain envelopes marked "Personal" or "Confidential" should never be opened. Each item should be date stamped and sorted by priority so that the lawyer may review only the most urgent mail, if busy.

In some law offices, legal assistants are expected to read the incoming mail, highlight any important points in the material, secure any relevant files, and process material, such as a cheque in payment of an account. The incoming mail should be placed in a specific location on the lawyer's desk. Many legal assistants place each category of mail in a different coloured file folder; this not only makes it easier for the lawyer to identify urgent items but also ensures that material left on the lawyer's desk remains confidential.

When the lawyer is out of the office for a number of days, his or her mail will usually be delivered to his or her legal assistant. It should not be left to accumulate on the lawyer's desk but should be opened and sorted. Items requiring immediate attention are referred to the person delegated to handle the files in the lawyer's absence; items that require the lawyer's personal attention may be acknowledged, depending on the length of time the lawyer will be out of the office. Figure 2.2 illustrates a sample response that could be sent during the lawyer's absence.

Figure 2.2 Sample Response during Lawyer's Absence

In Mr. Grant's absence from the office, I acknowledge receipt of your letter of September 4, which will be brought to his attention on his return next week.

Yours very truly,

HILL, JOHNSTON & GRANT

Sylvia Sharp
Legal Assistant to Peter T. Grant

Sort the mail that is left for the lawyer's attention into categories: *Requiring Attention*, *For Your Information*, and *At Your Convenience*. Place the material for each category in labelled file folders of different colours. The day before the lawyer's return, prepare an alphabetical summary of the material in the *Requiring Attention* file (Figure 2.2) to permit the lawyer to quickly review the material. You might also wish to prepare a similar summary of items in the *For Your Information* file, as illustrated in Figure 2.3 (p. 16).

Figure 2.3 Summary of Mail Requiring Attention

REQUIRING YOUR ATTENTION

File	Information
1. ANDERSON, R.C. Re: Peterson	Letter from Mr. Campo offering to settle this matter at $270,000 plus costs
2. PENMAR INVESTMENTS Re: Corporate Affairs	Letter from Mr. Pearl asking your opinion on advisability of changing number of directors
3. PRINCESS HOMES LTD. Re: Annual Meeting	Letter from Mr. MacLeod asking you to draft amendments to the by-laws to increase number of directors. The meeting is next Wednesday.
4. WINSTON, M.B. Re: Partnership Agreement	Letter from Mr. Winston with suggestions for changes in the draft partnership agreement

Outgoing Mail

In most law offices, you usually fold the signed mail, insert it in its envelope, and put it in specific locations for processing by a mail clerk. In a small law office, you may be responsible for processing the outgoing mail and putting it through the postage meter. Mail should be processed at regular intervals during the day rather than only at the end of the day. If special postal or other delivery services are used, make sure you meet the specific time limits for submitting mail.

E-MAIL

Electronic or e-mail is used extensively by law firms to communicate internally (instead of interoffice memorandums) or externally (instead of letters) with other law firms, the government, and clients. Documents may also be e-mailed by including them as attachments to the e-mail message, which has led to the almost universal use of Microsoft Word so that everyone can open document attachments. Although general office procedural handbooks cover e-mail, several important guidelines are worth emphasizing here:

- All e-mail is sent and received via the Internet but resides on the law firm's network server, and there is no guarantee of privacy. Some law firms employ encryption software, but this works only if the other party has the software to unencrypt it. Much of what is sent and received is not encrypted, so discretion should be used in what is said. In other words, do not say anything in an e-mail that you do not wish to be made public.
- Always complete the subject portion of the e-mail. Not only is this proper business etiquette, but also many people will not open an e-mail if the subject line is not completed as it may be construed as junk mail or spam.

- Use appropriate language and grammar. Do not use offensive language, slang, acronyms, or instant messaging (IM) language without proper capitalization for business related e-mails. Not only is it unprofessional, it could also easily be misinterpreted by the receiver.
- Keep your e-mail succinct and to the point. Before sending, re-read your message carefully to ensure that it is saying what you intended or providing the correct information in a clear, concise manner. Proofread carefully and use the Spell Check feature.
- E-mail is an efficient communication tool, but if the matter is complicated or ambiguous, consider whether an in-person meeting or a telephone conversation would be more appropriate.
- Check your e-mail regularly and respond promptly to any e-mails you receive that are business related. Any personal e-mail should only be sent during your break or lunch time. Remember that law firms (and most other businesses) may monitor e-mail and Internet use.

TELEPHONE

The telephone systems found in law offices are often highly sophisticated, permitting the lawyer to block incoming calls, to transfer calls to another number, to be aware that another call is waiting, or to conference with several people simultaneously.

In many law offices, each lawyer is assigned a separate telephone number that allows callers to dial him or her directly. The law firm usually maintains a central number that is answered by a telephone operator to assist callers who are not aware of the direct-dial numbers of law office personnel. This operator may also answer any separately assigned numbers if that telephone is not answered after a specific number of rings.

Answering the Telephone for the Lawyer

If you answer the telephone for the lawyer, identify his or her office and yourself, for example: "Peter Grant's office. Romona Khan, legal assistant, speaking." If the lawyer is free to receive calls, announce the name of the caller. If the lawyer is not free to speak, advise the caller that the lawyer is "not available at the moment," that he or she "is in conference," "is with a client," or even "not in the office." Do not disclose with whom the lawyer is in conference; the name of the client; where he or she is, if not in the office; or why he or she is not available. It is acceptable to say that the lawyer "is in court today." It is not acceptable to say that the lawyer "is at a meeting in the Smith Fraser office" or "is not back from lunch yet." Ask whether the caller would like to leave a message on the lawyer's voice mail or leave it with you. If you are taking the message, promptly record it on a telephone message form (Figure 2.4 p. 18). Note that the lawyer's name is shown as initials only. This is a common practice in many legal offices. Some offices have the form completed in duplicate; one copy is given to the lawyer, and a second copy is retained for a chronological record of incoming calls.

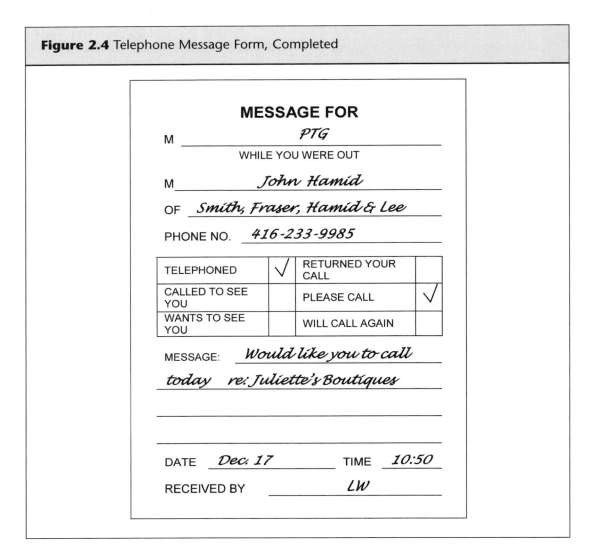

Figure 2.4 Telephone Message Form, Completed

Urgent Messages

If you receive an urgent message for the lawyer when he or she is in conference with clients or other lawyers, or if you receive such a message for the client or other lawyers, you cannot hold it until the meeting has concluded. Messages that are not urgent should be delivered to the individual for whom they are intended following the meeting. Prepare any urgent message and take it to the conference room. Lightly knock on the door, wait for a moment, and then enter quietly, place the message before the person for whom it is intended, and leave the room. If the message is for a client or lawyer you cannot identify, give it to your lawyer to distribute.

Returning Calls

Once you have taken a message from a caller and have given it to the lawyer, it is his or her responsibility to respond to the message. The caller may wish to speak to the lawyer; do not tell the caller that you "will have the lawyer call you." That will be taken as a promise that the lawyer will call. Only indicate that you "will give the lawyer the message." The message can indicate that the caller is anxious to speak to the lawyer; that information will help the lawyer to determine which messages should be dealt with first if time is limited.

VOICE MAIL

Most law offices have an electronic telephone answering service ("voice mailbox") that can be used to leave a message if the directly dialled number is busy or is not answered. Voice mail messages should be retrieved and replied to as soon as possible in case they are of an urgent nature and to provide prompt service to clients and other callers. Sometimes the legal assistant will be asked to key out a voice mail message, exactly as it is received, and then place the printout in the file to provide written confirmation of an important voice mail message.

When you are creating your own recorded voice mail message on your telephone, it should contain the following information presented in a clear and pleasant voice:

- your name, title, and the name of any lawyer(s) you are a legal assistant to
- where you are (for example, "I'm away from my desk right now, but please leave a message, and I will return your call promptly when I return")
- whom they can turn to if the matter is urgent (for example, "dial 0 for reception")
- if you are going to be absent for several days, your voice mail message should reflect this and advise of any person who may be covering for you (for example, "I am away from the office until November 15; please contact Jonathan Chen at extension 223 in my absence")

If you are leaving a voice mail message on someone else's voice mail, keep in mind the following guidelines:

- say your name and telephone number clearly (do not mumble or go too quickly)
- provide the date and time of your call
- leave a brief message that either requests information or provides information in a clear and concise manner
- state when you will be available if they wish to call you back

PHOTOCOPIES

Law firms make extensive use of photocopiers for documentation. Most models can collate and staple sets of copies; others can adjust for wrinkled paper, adjust for light or dark originals, ignore lines caused by the edges of tape, provide variable reductions or enlargements, allow automatic double-sided copying, reproduce colours, affix cover sheets, and have continuous-run capabilities, as well as automatic multipage feeding of originals. Many law offices have a main photocopying centre, equipped with the most modern equipment and run by support staff to handle large and complex reproduction requirements. Other photocopiers are located throughout the office for legal assistants to use. When you are employed by a law firm, become acquainted with its reproduction facilities and procedures. Most law offices exercise strict control over the use of reproduction equipment. In some offices, a user card must be inserted in the machine or a code number must be keyed in before copies can be made. The cost of the photocopying is then automatically recorded. The client is expected to reimburse the law firm for reproduction expenses, as discussed in Chapter 5.

REFERENCE SOURCES

Although all word processing programs have a spell-checking feature, and there are also online dictionaries, a legal assistant should have a good dictionary that not only gives information about word meanings but also demonstrates appropriate word division. Many of the other traditional reference materials may be accessed from the Internet, such as a telephone directory (http://www.Canada411) or a postal code directory (http://www.canadapost.ca).

Legal directories are available on a national or provincial level in either hard copy, such as the *Canada Legal Directory* (Thomson Carswell) and the British Columbia, Alberta, or Atlantic *Legal Telephone Directories* (CLB Media Inc.), or in both hard copy and electronic format, such as the *Martindale-Hubbell Canadian Law Directory* (LexisNexis) and the *Ontario Legal Directory* (University of Toronto Press). The electronic format is installed on individual personal computers or on the network server, and then all members of the firm can electronically search by area of legal practice, location (province, city, etc.), firm name, or the individual lawyer's name to obtain contact information. Many of these legal directories also provide contact information for law clerks/paralegals and the various government ministries, courthouses, and land registry offices. Alternatively, you should become familiar with the websites for these various government agencies and bookmark them in your web browser directory.

You will also encounter various other Internet and resource publications that relate specifically to a particular area of legal procedure. These are discussed in later chapters when the specific procedures to which they relate are considered.

PREPARING LEGAL MATERIAL

A legal assistant prepares a great variety of correspondence, memoranda, and legal documents. Many legal documents must be prepared to conform to the format and content established by the provincial or federal government. In this text, we refer to these as **prescribed forms.** Such forms are available from legal stationers in printed paper form or in electronic format and require that the necessary information be inserted in blank spaces. Many law firms have the format and content of the prescribed forms keyed in by a legal assistant or document production specialist for storage in the computer memory bank.

The lawyer may draft material on his or her computer and then revise and edit until he or she is satisfied with the draft or alternatively make handwritten changes to be done by the legal assistant. In some offices, computers are linked so that material prepared on one computer may be downloaded onto the hard drive of another computer or e-mailed to another computer in the office. In either situation, the legal assistant can then electronically cut and paste the material into a document or do the final formatting of the complete document.

Methods of Preparing Material

1. Key the entire document into the memory of a computer. One copy can be printed and reviewed by the author; the document can be recalled and corrected as necessary and then printed. Copies can be obtained by photocopying the original or printing out the required number. This method is referred to as "fully keyed."
2. Recall to the screen the shell of a prescribed form that has been stored in the computer. The style and content of prescribed forms are set out in government statutes and can be recorded. Once recalled to the screen, the form can be prepared by inserting the necessary specific information in the various fields that must be completed.
3. Assemble a document by stringing together stored standard paragraphs and merging them with personalized, customized paragraphs to produce a complete document. Many legal documents, such as wills, contain standard paragraphs and clauses that are used frequently when a new document is prepared. Such material is often referred to as "boilerplate."
4. Use the facilities of a commercial automated document assembly programs such as Divorcemate or The Conveyancer (Do Process). For example, The Conveyancer is a real estate program for residential transactions of real property in Ontario. All the necessary documents, including file opening cards, tickler slips, correspondence, required forms, and final correspondence, can be created through this program once the required client information has been inserted.
5. Use the features of your word processing program to reduce repetitive keyboarding of standard sections of correspondence and documents by creating templates or macros. For example, the ending of a letter is usually identical, and many keystrokes are saved if this part of a letter is recorded for recall and used as letters are prepared.

Subsequent chapters of this text outline the various procedures and documents encountered in the main areas of legal practice. Regardless of the method used to prepare such material, the principles outlined in those chapters must be followed. Where appropriate, your attention will be drawn to special preparation guidelines that you may find useful.

Original and Copy

In this text, the term *original* refers to a completed page or pages that are signed or are to be used as the main copy of the document; the page or pages may be fully keyed, may be printed out on a printer attached to a computer, or may be a photocopy of the page or pages. The term *copy* refers to a photocopy or computer printout that is intended to be a reproduction of an original document. For example, a photocopy of a signed will would be referred to as a copy.

Drafts

Many legal documents are prepared in draft form and may be revised several times. Identify each draft in turn by inserting a header or footer with the draft number and/or date. For example:

Draft No. 1 January 15, 20__
Draft No. 2 January 21, 20__

Microsoft Word has a reviewing toolbar that has functions that allow for any changes (whether additions or deletions) to be shown (by strikethroughs or highlighted text) and the ability to add comments to the margins of the document. These features allow the various parties involved in creating and editing the document to see and review each other's changes without having to reread the entire document and are frequently used in creating and editing legal documentation. Once all parties have made their revisions and accepted all changes, the editing and commenting functions can be easily "turned off" to produce a finished document.

Margins

When using word processing equipment to prepare material, you have a choice of either a ragged right margin or a justified right margin. Full justification produces even lines, although on some of them there may be large gaps between words. There is a growing trend to produce material with flush left margins and ragged right margins (left justified). Additionally, the default margin settings in Microsoft Word are 1.25" for the right and left margins. Many law firms change the default setting to the more traditional left and right margins of 1". Material in this text illustrates both practices. As a legal assistant, you should follow the preference of your law firm.

Spacing

With the widespread use of automated keyboarding equipment, traditional spacing principles are changing. Use the following as a guideline:

Line Spacing and Fonts

Traditionally, most legal documents were double-spaced and in 12-point font. However, single- or 1.5-line spacing and 10-point font are being more frequently used. Most firms use either Arial or Times New Roman font, and all bolding of words is considered optional. Some prescribed documents specify the required spacing and font size, but, otherwise, you should follow the preference of your individual lawyer or your law firm, remembering always to be consistent in the use of spacing and fonts throughout a document so that it appears professional.

After Periods

There has been a recent trend toward leaving only one space after a period. However, the traditional practice of leaving two spaces following a period is still the accepted practice for all legal correspondence and documentation.

USE OF INITIAL CAPITALS

The modern trend in capitalization—and the practice usually followed by legal publishers and in published statutes, rules of practice, and law reports—is to keep initial capitals to a minimum. Many lawyers and law firms follow this trend; others prefer that an initial capital be used on the first letter of the names of legal documents and on the first letter of the descriptive labels given to parties in legal papers. Whatever practice is followed in the law office that employs you, be consistent in its use. This is much easier to do if initial capitals are kept to a minimum.

General office procedure textbooks outline rules for capitalization. Table 2.1 provides guidelines and examples of the current trend in the use of initial capitals in preparing legal documentation. Special capitalization requirements for specific legal papers are discussed in subsequent chapters.

Table 2.1 Capitalization Guidelines for Legal Documentation	

Descriptive terms for parties	Omit initial capitals on terms used to describe parties in matters, such as executor, vendor, or plaintiff, when the name appears in the body of typed correspondence or other legal paper. For example:
	
	    A meeting of shareholders will be held after the directors' meeting.
	    The plaintiff and defendant have agreed to settle the case.
	
	In some legal documents, such as agreements, this guide is not always followed. This is discussed in Chapter 7.

Titles of legal papers	Omit initial capitals on the names of legal documents, such as will, mortgage, deed, affidavit, or statement of claim, when the name appears in the body of documents. For example: When the vendor comes in to sign the deed, he also wishes to consult us about a new will.

Government officials	Use an initial capital on the names of courts and phrases but not on the word *court* when it is used later in the same legal document. For example:
	
	    Superior Court of Justice
	    but the court

Table 2.1 Continued	
Titles	Initial capitals appear on titles that precede a name but not on titles used alone. This practice is also followed in the body of legal documents. For example: His Honour Judge Smith *but* the judge Initial capitals are used for references to government officials when such office has been defined in that form in an act or regulations. For example: Attorney General Director Official Guardian Public Trustee Registrar General
Proper names	Use an initial capital on words such as province, city, act, or department, when they are part of a proper name. Usually, you omit the initial capital when such words are referred to later in the same document. For example: I have read the *Income Tax Act*. In s. 48 of that act.... In legal work, however, you may see an initial capital on the word when it is used in a specific, rather than a general, reference. For example: I have read the *Income Tax Act*. In s. 46 of that Act.... *but* What does the act indicate in regard to property rights? Follow the preference of the law office in the use of initial capitals. If the decision is yours, it is suggested that you follow the traditional practice and omit the initial capital.

USE OF NUMBERS

General office procedure handbooks outline the rules for the expression of numbers. Table 2.2 provides guidelines and examples of special formatting rules that apply to numbers appearing in legal documents.

Table 2.2 Number Formatting Guidelines for Legal Documentation	
Monetary amounts	If expressing monetary amounts in figures, use a decimal point and key the decimal amounts even if they are zeros. Large monetary amounts are shown with commas; the metric number style, which separates groups of large amounts with a space, is not usually seen in legal work. For example: Preferred: $1,068.00 not $1 068 or $1068

Legal correspondence and court documents	Monetary amounts and other quantities are shown in figures only. For example:
	      The doctor's account will be $350.00.
	      There were 12 affidavits filed in support of the motion.
	 Percentages are shown in figures followed by the word *percent*. For example:
	      9 percent

All other legal instruments or commercial documents	Monetary amounts, distances, dimensions, percentages, and number of days, months, or years are expressed in words and then figures. Place the figures in parentheses following the words. When the number or amount is followed by a word that can be shown by a single keyboard symbol, such as $ for dollars, or % for percent, express the number or amount first in words, followed by the word, and then by the figure and symbol in parentheses. For example:
	      Twenty-five dollars ten cents ($25.10)
	      seven percent (7%)
	 When the number or amount is followed by a word that cannot be represented by a single keyboard symbol, such as days, months, etc., express the number or amount first in words, followed by the figures in parentheses and then the word. For example:
	      seven (7) days' notice
	      ten (10) dozen
	      two hundred (200) units

Numbers preceded by a noun	In all legal documents and correspondence, numbers preceded by a noun are expressed in figures only. For example:
	      paragraph 7
	      Lot 7
	      Licence No. 5987432
	      Plan No. 5689

Table 2.2 Continued	

Time	In all legal documents and correspondence, use figures with the abbreviations a.m. and p.m. and words with o'clock. For example:
	    7:30 a.m. ten o'clock
	The ciphers used with even hours are omitted unless non-even times are also included in the same reference. For example:
	    9 a.m. to 1 p.m. *but* 9:00 a.m. to 12:30 p.m.

Dates	In all legal documents and correspondence, use numerals only when the day follows the month; use numerals and the ordinals (*st*, *nd*, *rd*, or *th*) ending when the day precedes the month. For example:
	    January 23, 20__
	    23rd January, 20__
	    or 23rd day of January, 20__
	When using figures to represent a date, express the numbers in day, month, and year sequence, separated by a slash. For example:
	    January 31, 20__ would be 31/01/00__

QUOTATIONS

You will find quotations from legal and other sources in all areas of legal practice. These are prepared according to the following rules:

1. Type quotations of three lines or fewer as part of the text, with quotation marks at the beginning and conclusion of the quoted material. For example:

   The judge's decision indicated that "there will be no costs." The judge also indicated that the matter was now concluded.

2. Set off quotations of more than three lines separately, single spaced, and indented 5 or 10 spaces from both the left-hand and right-hand margins. Opening and closing quotation marks are omitted. If used, they appear at the beginning of each paragraph and at the end of the last paragraph.

   In the *Ontario Reports*, published weekly by The Law Society of Upper Canada, quotations appear in a reduced print size and are indented only from the left margin.

3. Indent the first line of a quotation an additional five spaces if the quoted material starts a paragraph. If the quoted material contains a second paragraph, also indent the first line of that paragraph. For example:

> Unless courts protect their process from abuse, they will become mere debating forums. Their primary function in civil matters is to bring disputes to a timely and final end after giving both sides a full opportunity to present all proper points that are reasonably available.
> I would dismiss this application with costs, if demanded.

4. Show omissions from quoted material by three equally spaced ellipsis dots (or periods) if the omission is from the body of the sentence and by four ellipsis dots (the fourth is the period of the sentence) if the omission concludes the sentence. For example:

> The insured shall not bring an action to recover the amount of a claim under this contract . . . until the amount of the loss has been ascertained . . . by a judgment against the insured after trial. . . .

5. Show omissions of several sentences or paragraphs by three or four asterisks between the quoted portions. For example:

****

6. Use double quotation marks for a quotation that is not enclosed in quotation marks in the original material. For example, in the illustration shown under item 1, the judge's words did not appear in quotation marks in his decision but are shown in quotation marks when quoted in other typed material.
7. Use single quotation marks for a quotation within a quotation that itself appears in quotation marks. If the second quotation comes at the end of the entire quotation, use both sets of quotation marks at the conclusion of the quotation. For example:

> ,. . .'private park preserve.'"

8. Use the word *sic* in parentheses to indicate that an error in a quoted word appeared in the original material.
9. Put only those punctuation marks that actually form part of the material being quoted inside quotation marks. In non legal work, periods and commas are shown as part of the quotation inside the quotation marks; in legal material, this might result in a major change in meaning of the quoted material. In this text, a punctuation mark appears inside the quotation marks only when it is part of the quoted material.
10. If the first word of a sentence had no initial capital in its original form, show the first letter of the quotation with a capital in parentheses. For example:

> "(M)urder is a term defined in the *Criminal Code*."

Terms and Concepts

diary/calendar procedures

delivery methods

facsimile (fax)

mail procedures

e-mail guidelines

telephone procedures

voice mail guidelines

photocopies

reference souces

legal material preparation guidelines

prescribed forms

original and copy

drafts

margins

spacing

capitalization

numbers

quotations

Review Questions

1. What is the purpose of requiring a cover page for material that is being faxed?

2. Assume that you receive your lawyer's mail each day. How would you handle it?

3. What is the purpose of requiring users of photocopy equipment to record the number of copies prepared on the equipment?

4. In dealing with callers on the telephone when the lawyer is in conference, why would you not indicate the name of the party with whom your lawyer is in conference?

5. You have printed out four sets of documents. Which one will be called the "original"? What is meant by the term *copy*?

6. The lawyer is in conference with a new client. He has indicated that they are not to be disturbed. What would you do if you received an urgent message for the client?

7. If you are asked to "highlight" changes in a new draft of a legal agreement, what are you being asked to do? What is the purpose of this procedure?

8. If the law firm that employs you follows an office procedure that differs from that discussed in this chapter, what would you do?

9. **Internet Research:** Locate an online Canadian legal dictionary, become familiar with using it, and bookmark it for future use.

CHAPTER 3

Client Records

OBJECTIVES:

- Identify and describe the steps taken when acting for a new client
- Discuss different file naming and client identification systems used in legal offices
- Explain the importance of and procedures for conflict of interest searches and tickler systems
- Prepare file opening documents such as retainer and authorization
- Discuss record management procedures for client files

When a client has asked the law firm to act for him or her in a legal matter, certain procedural steps are taken:

1. The matter is given a file name.
2. The matter is assigned a **file** or **matter number**.
3. Correspondence and document files are opened to keep the letters, memoranda, and other material provided by the client or written and received during the course of the matter. A **new matter form** is completed and filed with the accounting department, and a copy is inserted into the client file. These records are known collectively as client files.
4. Accounting records are opened to document the work done and the time spent on the client's matter. These records are called **dockets** and are discussed in detail in Chapter 5.
5. A search of the law firm's clients is conducted to ensure that the law firm does not act for any other party in connection with this client that may result in a **conflict of interest**.
6. The legal assistant's client index is brought up to date to include relevant information on the new matter.
7. If applicable, **tickler** notations are prepared to remind the lawyer of dates by which certain steps must or should be taken to protect the client's legal position.
8. A **retainer** and possibly an **authorization** may be signed by the client to permit the law firm to have access to some privileged information.
9. The file and the docket are closed when the work for the client has been completed and the lawyer's account has been sent to the client and paid.

The impact of changing technology is evident in the method by which some of these steps are carried out. In some law offices, these steps may still be done manually; however, in most law firms, computer software programs allow them to be carried out electronically. Client files are still usually kept in folders; tickler slips and calendars may still be paper records; and hard or paper copies of client indices are still maintained, although they may be generated using a software program. **Practice management software** programs such as Amicus (Gavel and Gown Software), ProLaw (Thomson Elite), and one of the most widely used in Canada, PCLaw™ (LexisNexis), manage all accounting functions, including time and billing, as well as records management, calendaring, and tickler systems, and perform conflict of interest searches. Very large Canadian law firms have programmer analysts develop their own in-house software to perform these functions. The degree of software use varies from firm to firm, and the legal assistant's degree of access to individual functions of the software may also vary as well. For example, in many medium and large firms, legal assistants still complete paper copies of new file or matter forms, tickler slips, or accounting requisitions, which are then entered into the system by accounting or records management personnel.

NAMING NEW CLIENT FILES/MATTERS

The words *file* and *matter* are often used interchangeably to mean both the client file folder and the legal matter the file is concerned with, and this is the practice in this text. However, you should be aware that in some legal practices, the word *file* is used in reference to the actual physical client file folder ("Please leave the Smith v. Jones file on my desk") and *matter* is used to refer to the legal matter itself (Which lawyer is responsible for the Smith v. Jones matter?").

When records are set up for a new file or matter, there are two main parts: the word name, which identifies the file for easy recognition and for alphabetical indexing systems; and the file or matter number, which identifies the file for accounting purposes and for numerical indexing systems. The word name is further divided into two parts:

1. The name of your law firm's individual client or clients or the name of a company, which should appear in file indexing order, that is, the surname of an individual first. Depending on how common the name is or the area of law, the surname may be followed with a given name or initials.
2. The name(s) of the opposing party or parties or the nature of the matter.
3. These two parts are separated by *v.*, *ats*, *re*, or *and*, depending on the circumstances:

Use	Type of Matter	Example
v. (versus)	When your client believes he or she has a claim against another party that may require a lawsuit (i.e., court proceedings)	Smith v. Jones 45667
ats (at the suit of)	When another party believes he or she has a claim against your client and is suing your client	Martin ats Crane 94260
and	When your client is involved in application proceedings or certain business proceedings	Chan and Chan 94260 Re: Separation Agreement
re or Re (depending on preference of law firm)	For all other legal matters. Note that the word name can continue on additional lines if necessary.	Podoba, Ken 67768 Re: Power of Attorney

(Continued...)

et al. (and others)	If the name of the client or opposing party includes several names, use the name of one of the clients or opposing parties followed by either *et al.* or *and others* depending on the preference of your law office

> Martinet et al. v. Craig   6221

> Martinet and others   6221
> v. Craig

p/f (purchase from) or s/t (sale to)	In real estate files, these terms or abbreviations may be used as well as the address of the property being bought or sold

> Smith, John R. p/f Garvin 2241
> 178 Salisbury Road, Barrie

> Smith, J. R. sale to Garvin 2241
> 178 Salisbury Road, Barrie

ASSIGNING FILE/MATTER NUMBERS

In addition to the word name, all files are assigned a **matter number** or **file number**, which identifies that particular client and the legal proceedings for that client. This number will be used to maintain all accounting records for this matter and may also be used for indexing purposes.

The usual practice is for the next consecutive number to be assigned to the new matter by the accounting or practice management software that the law firm uses. In a small law office, a legal assistant may use the software to make the assignment; however, because of the necessity to ensure consistency, most law offices make one individual in the accounting or records department responsible for

1. assigning not only new matter numbers but also all client numbers or alphabetical designations and
2. maintaining the appropriate records for these processes, including the actual physical opening of the file in a standard manner.

In some law offices, the practice is to assign consecutive numbers on a yearly basis. At the beginning of each fiscal year, the numbering starts again at 1, and the year forms the first or last portion of the number. For example, 682/08 would indicate that this was the 682nd file opened in the year 2008. The initials of the lawyer handling the matter may also be included with the matter number. For example, a new matter opened for a client of Peter T. Grant could be identified as 3680/PTG or 3680/08/PTG.

Many legal offices use a client identification system, whereby each client is assigned a fixed numerical identification (referred to as a **client number**) and each matter for that client is assigned a different number (referred to as a **matter number**), which are separated by a slash (/) or a hyphen (-). These two numbers together then compose the file number. In this system, each matter for which the law firm is acting for a client will therefore have a different matter number but the same client identification. Some firms put the client number first; others put the file number first. For example, assume that Gregory Gelon is a client of the law firm and his client identification number is 0567. If we act for him in connection with several matters, the file labels would appear as follows:

Client Number First:

> Gelon, Gregory   0567/04749
> Re: Podoba

> Gelon, Gregory   0567/04875
> Re: Will

File Number First:

> Gelon, Gregory   04749/0567
> Re: Podoba

> Gelon, Gregory   04875/0567
> Re: Will

The file numbering system, including the number of characters making up the file or matter number, and the way information is shown on the file label will vary from law office to law office, depending on the records management system followed in each office. You will need to become familiar with it to open new files and access existing files.

FILE FOLDERS

Although many records are now maintained electronically, it is still necessary to have a client file folder to hold correspondence and legal documentation, including any material provided by the client, such as photographs or a signed cheque. Any such material provided by the client is usually kept in a separate folder and is returned to them when the matter is completed.

Special File Folders

Special file folders for use in various areas of legal practice are available from legal stationers. The front covers of these files are preprinted and contain checklists of many of the required steps in the particular area of law related to the client's matter. Some law firms use ordinary file folders and staple a similar checklist to the inside cover of the file.

Many client files become quite large and are often divided into sections, with the sections kept in an expandable accordion file. Such sub- or inner files are frequently colour-coded. For example, the correspondence file might be buff coloured; the memoranda file, green; the document file, blue; and so on. Alternatively, in many offices, each type of legal work is maintained in a different file folder. For example, all real estate files might be in green folders, all estate files in blue, and so on.

File Organization

Although main and subfiles are often set up by the records management personnel, in a smaller office this may be the legal assistant's responsibility, and you should be aware of some common practices in document management for files:

1. The file or matter number will be shown on the label and on the front cover of the file folder. Alternatively, some law firms use special folders that attach the file number on the outside edge of the folder so that it is very visible when put in the file cabinet.
2. Many law firms attach a file brad to the front and back cover of the file folder for documents to be attached to or a separate correspondence brad for correspondence only.
3. The inside of the front cover usually has the new file/matter form (discussed below) attached to the file brad.
4. The back of the file folder will have all other documents attached to it, with the most recent document on top.
5. Note that original documents (that is, signed copies of material, photographs, cheques, etc.) will not be hole punched and placed on the file brad. They may be paper clipped together or placed in an envelope within the file for safekeeping.

New File/Matter Form

Practices vary among offices on methods of recording new matter information. Some offices simply prepare a memorandum to file, others prepare a new matter form, and many use practice management software that allows information to be entered, as illustrated in Figure 3.1, which shows the Open Matter dialog box for PCLaw™.

Whichever method is used, the information required is much the same and may come from verbal instructions, rough notes, or a tape of the first interview. If a new matter form is used, a template is recalled to the screen and then completed. Figure 3.2A illustrates an example of a template for a new matter form with instructions for completion. Figure 3.2B on page 36 illustrates a completed new matter form.

Note that all the boxes on the form, except those concerned with the file number (provided by accounting), the closed date, and closed file number, are filled in from information provided by the client or the lawyer. The other boxes are filled in when work on the file is completed and the file is closed. One copy is then sent (either electronically or by hard copy) to the accounting or records department, which will open the new matter and assign it a file number. Another copy is then usually attached to the inside of the front cover of the client's file for easy reference.

A code number or abbreviation to indicate the area of legal practice that is the subject of the file is required, and firms maintain an internal law office index for this purpose for accounting and records management purposes.

There is also a section where the legal assistant indicates with his or her name or initials and the appropriate date that a conflict of interest search (discussed on the following pages) has been successfully completed.

Figure 3.1 New Matter Dialog Box, PCLaw™

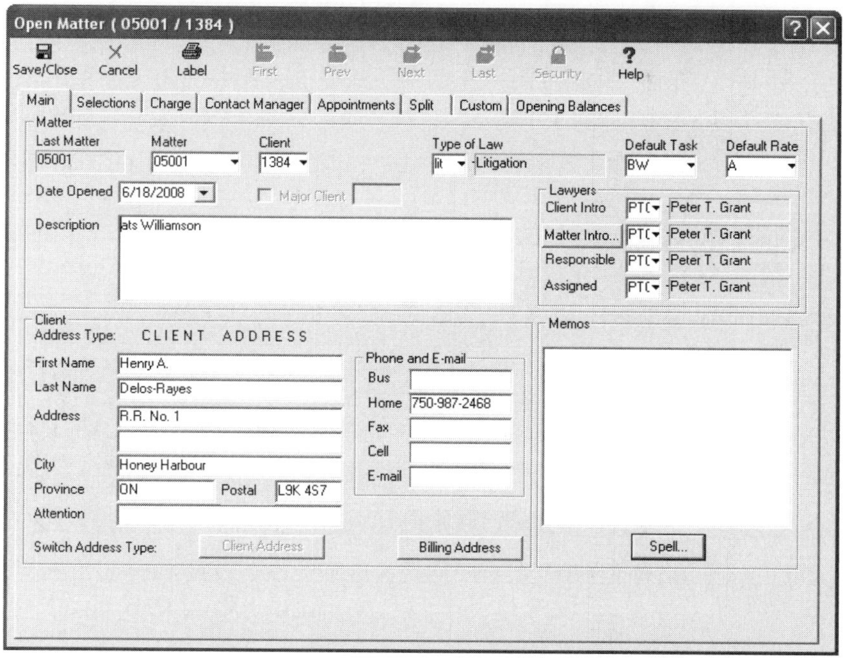

Source: PCLaw™ screen shots used with the permission of LexisNexis Practice Management Systems Inc.

Figure 3.2A New Matter Form, with instructions for completion

NEW MATTER FORM		
CLIENT:	*Name of client(s), in filing order*	**FILE NO.** *Include client & matter numbers*
MATTER:	*Name of other/opposing party or description of legal matter*	**CODE NO.** *Area of Legal Practice Code No.*
BUSINESS ADDRESS: *Contact information for our client at their place of business (if available) OR If a corporate client, contact information (including name and title of contact person)*		**HOME ADDRESS:** *Contact information for our client at home address* *Not applicable for a corporate client*

Tel:		**Tel:**	
Fax:		**Fax:**	
E-mail:		**E-mail:**	

LAWYER(S) RESPONSIBLE: *Names or initials of lawyer(s) who will be handling the file*

OTHER SOLICITORS: (if applicable) *Contact information for other party's solicitors (include name of individual lawyer if available)*	**Tel:**	
	Fax:	
	E-mail:	
	Other:	

FEES				DATE	
Tariff	**Estimated Fee**	**Time Value**	**Retainer Paid**	**Date Opened**	**Date Closed & Closed File No.**
Insert "X" (if applicable)	*Insert amount (if applicable)*	*Insert an "X" (if applicable)*	*Insert amount (if applicable)*	*Insert date file opened*	*Insert date file closed & closed file no.*

Notes:
Any special notes or instructions from lawyer (if applicable)

File Folder Label(s):

Name of client, in filing order *Subject line*	*File No.*	*Optional file label*

Figure 3.2B New Matter Form, Completed

NEW MATTER FORM		
CLIENT: DELOS-RAYES, Henry A.		**FILE NO.** 05001/1384
MATTER: ats WILLIAMSON, John J.		**CODE NO.** 05

BUSINESS ADDRESS:		HOME ADDRESS: R.R. No. 1 Honey Harbour ON L9K 4S7	
Tel:		**Tel:**	705-987-2468
Fax:		**Fax:**	
E-mail:		**E-mail:**	hdelos@mail.com

LAWYER(S) RESPONSIBLE:

OTHER SOLICITORS: (if applicable) HARE, ROSS & WILKINSON 94 Wimbleton Crescent Barrie ON L4V 5X2 Patricia M. Cochrane		**Tel:**	705-975-4891
		Fax:	705-975-4892
		E-mail:	pcochrane@hrw.com
		Other:	Assistant: Sue Martin

FEES				DATE	
Tariff	**Estimated Fee**	**Time Value**	**Retainer Paid**	**Date Opened**	**Date Closed & Closed File No.**
		X	$500.00	Oct. 24, 20__	

Notes:
Superior Court action as a result of a collision with cow

File FolderLabel(s):

DELOS-RAYES, Henry A. ats WILLIAMSON	05001/1384	

INDEX OF FILES AND DOCKETS

In addition to the index of frequently written names and addresses mentioned in Chapter 1, a legal assistant should maintain an index of current files and dockets. In a law office that has automated office management and record systems, this index may be generated regularly from the computer records. This index will allow the legal assistant to access matter numbers for accounting purposes and provide a way to quickly access the status of open files.

CONFLICT OF INTEREST

A law firm is not allowed to act for both sides or parties in a legal proceeding. Thus, when a new client retains the law firm, a **conflict of interest** search will be carried out to ensure that another lawyer in the firm does not represent the other party or parties. In a small firm, this search may be conducted by circulating an internal memorandum or e-mail to all the lawyers listing any new clients. In larger firms, with many lawyers and new clients, software such as PCLaw™ is used to conduct the search. An example of the PCLaw™ conflict search dialog box is shown in Figure 3.3.

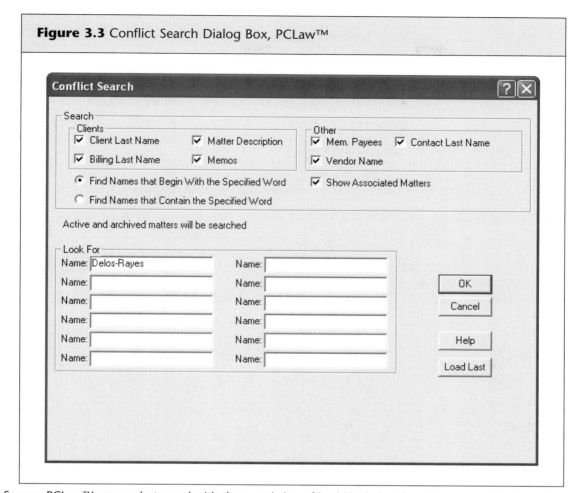

Figure 3.3 Conflict Search Dialog Box, PCLaw™

Source: PCLaw™ screen shots used with the permission of LexisNexis Practice Management Systems Inc.

TICKLER SYSTEM

Law firms are required to ensure that matters involving a major degree of responsibility on the part of the lawyer are not overlooked and are completed by required dates. This requirement is met through the maintenance of a **tickler system**, which may also be referred to in some provinces as a **bring forward system**. It may be maintained manually or through practice management software. A manual system maintains the tickler system in a file tray or box, which is indexed by years, months, and days. Whether the tickler system is computerized or manual, the information required to be completed is usually similar. Figure 3.4A (p. 38) illustrates an example of a template for a tickler slip with instructions for completion. Figure 3.4B (p. 38) illustrates a completed tickler slip.

The legal assistant completes a tickler slip (either manually or electronically) from information provided by the lawyer. The tickler slip is filed under the tickler date. In some offices, a duplicate copy is also filed under the due date, and a third copy is filed alphabetically by client to permit easy verification of the number and location of each tickler slip relating to that particular client.

Figure 3.4A Tickler Slip Template with Instructions for Completion

	Month	Day	Year		Month	Day	Year
TICKLER DATE	*Date lawyer to be __reminded__ in order to complete action*			DUE DATE	*Date by which certain action must be taken*		
FILE NO.	*File No.*						
CLIENT:	*Client name, in filing order*						
MATTER:	*Name(s) of other party OR subject line of file*						
LAWYER(S) RESPONSIBLE:	*Lawyer responsible for file (may be initials only)*						
COMMENTS:	*State what action is to be taken*						
	Month	Day	Year		Month	Day	Year
LIMITATION DATE	*The date by which action must be taken or right to do so may be lost—may be the same as the DUE DATE*			DATE INITIATED	*Date the tickler slip is prepared*		
APPROVED BY:	*The signature of the lawyer on whose instructions the tickler slip is being prepared*						

Figure 3.4B Tickler Slip, Completed

	Month	Day	Year		Month	Day	Year
TICKLER DATE	Nov.	28	20__	DUE DATE	Nov.	30	20__
FILE NO.	05001/1384						
CLIENT:	DELOS-RAYES, Henry A.						
MATTER:	ats WILLIAMSON, John J.						
LAWYER(S) RESPONSIBLE:	PTG, LCR						
COMMENTS:	Either notice of intent to defend or statement of defence to be filed						
	Month	Day	Year		Month	Day	Year
LIMITATION DATE	Nov.	30	20__	DATE INITIATED	Nov.	20	20__
APPROVED BY:							

Each day, the person responsible for the tickler system removes from the tickler tray or box all slips bearing that date and distributes one copy to the lawyer responsible as a reminder of what is to be done. In an automated system, the reminder would appear on the lawyer's and the legal assistant's computer screens on the particular tickler or due date.

Although the actual procedures for the tickler system vary from office to office, they are all basically very similar, and whatever system is used, it must be diligently followed.

RETAINER AND AUTHORIZATION

Retainer

A client seeking the services of a lawyer or law firm may be asked to sign a **retainer**, a document that states the nature of the services to be performed and the specific authority to carry out those services. Although a retainer is requested in many types of legal services, it is most frequently used when the client is asking the law firm to act in a legal problem that may lead to court proceedings. The form of a retainer is not prescribed by statute; law offices have developed many acceptable forms for this document. Precedent 3.1A illustrates a sample template and Precedent 3.1B shows the template when completed.

The word "retainer" also refers to a payment that may be made by the client to the law firm at the time the law firm is engaged to act for the client. This money is used to cover anticipated expenses incurred on behalf of the client. How such payments are dealt with is discussed in Chapter 5.

Authorization

If the matter for which the law firm is to provide services involves information such as medical reports or employment records that are privileged or confidential, the client is also requested to sign an **authorization**. This directs the person or company to whom it is addressed to release such information to the lawyer or law firm. There are many acceptable forms of authorizations, a sample template for authorization is illustrated in Precedent 3.2A; a completed authorization is illustrated in Precedent 3.2 B.

Number of Copies

Prepare a minimum of two copies of retainers and authorizations; the original, signed copy is for the law firm, and the second copy is for the client. If the authorization is to be used to secure information from a number of sources, prepare a master copy, photocopy or print the required number, and request the client to sign each individual copy, each of which is then addressed to the appropriate source.

RECORDS MANAGEMENT

Alphabetical Indexing Guidelines

With the introduction of computerized record-keeping systems, numerical filing systems are now widely used in law offices. The rules of alphabetical filing, however, are used in the manual maintenance of many indices, such as an index of clients, or in a decentralized filing system.

The following are the basic indexing rules that have particular application to a law office:

1. Index according to the first word in the file name. When the first word is the same for two or more files, index according to the second word or initial, then according to the third, and so on. For example:

> Smith, J. re Brown
> Smith J.A. re Will
> Smith, John, Motors Limited and Harrison

When indexing, keep in mind the guide "nothing before something." Listings in the telephone directory are an example of the application of this.

2. When indexing names, note the following guidelines:
   a. Disregard articles, prepositions, and conjunctions (for example, a, the, of, &, v., ats, and re).
   b. Treat hyphenated names as one indexing unit.
   c. Treat compound names containing prefixes, such as De, la, Mc, Mac, Von, etc., as one unit.
   d. When the name contains a number as the first "word," there are two different practices:
      • either index as if the first number of the name was spelled out (for example, 3rd Street Grill would be indexed according to the word "third")

      or

      • index in numerical order before the alphabetical character filing
      Follow the preference of your law firm
   e. Disregard titles, such as Dr., Count, Prince, etc., unless the title appears before a given name or surname alone:

   > Dr. Henry Jones is indexed as Jones, Henry (Dr.)
   > Prince William is indexed as Prince William
   > Father Herman is indexed as Father Herman
   > Father John Grey is indexed as Grey, John (Father)

   f. Treat abbreviations, such as CBC, C.N.R., or Chas., as if they were spelled in full; for example, CBC is indexed as Canadian Broadcasting Corporation.
   g. Treat individual letters that are not an abbreviation, as in XYZ Company Limited, as separate units.

3. When indexing a company name, follow these additional guidelines if the company or business name contains the surname and given name or names of an individual:
   a. Index by the surname when the company or business is commonly known by that name. For example:

   > William Neilson Ltd. is indexed as Neilson, William Ltd. because
   > the company is commonly referred to as "Neilsons."

b. Index by the given name when the company or business is commonly known by both the given name and surname. For example:

Laura Secord Inc. is indexed and commonly known as "Laura Secord."

4. Traditional filing rules set out that names of government departments and ministries are indexed first by the name of the province or government. This traditional rule is followed when the government is that of Canada. For example:

Canada, Health and Health, Department Old Age Security

However, because it is unusual for law firms to act for a provincial government, other than that of the province in which their offices are located, the traditional filing rule is usually not followed. The practice then is to index provincial government departments and ministries under the name of the department or ministry. For example:

Highways, Ministry of re: Oshawa Road Closing *rather than*
Ontario, Province of, Highways, Ministry of re Oshawa Road Closing

Follow the preference of your law office.

5. Index municipalities by name, followed by the status of the municipality. For example:

Barrie, City of re Tax Assessment
Essex, County of re Harper

6. When there are several files for the same client, the first word of the second part of the file name will determine the indexing order. For example:

Anderson, Ronald C. re Bank of Montreal
Anderson, Ronald C. re Marriage Contract
Anderson, Ronald C. re Will

Filing Systems

Alphabetical Filing

If the client records are filed alphabetically, they are maintained in the appropriate file drawer under the word name assigned to the new matter, keeping the above guidelines in mind. Note that all files will, however, still be assigned a file number for accounting purposes.

Numerical Filing

If client records are filed numerically, they are maintained in numerical order according to their file number so that the files for one client may be scattered among all the files, unless, as many firms do, each client is assigned a fixed numerical identification (the client number) and each matter for that client is assigned a different number (the matter number). This would ensure that all the files for one client would be filed together. A numerical filing system is considered an indirect filing system because an alphabetical index (either electronic or paper) must be created and used to locate any particular file.

Centralized Filing Systems

All files for the law office files are kept in one central location. This is usually a numerical filing system. Any files that are removed from the central location will have to be signed out by the legal assistant so that anyone else looking for the file will know where to locate it.

Decentralized Filing Systems

Files are kept in close proximity to the lawyer's or legal assistant's location. This is usually an alphabetical filing system by word name, regardless of the way they are identified, because it is easier to recall a name than a number and no index is required to locate the file.

Electronic File Management

The ability to be able to quickly and accurately retrieve electronic records is equally as important as retrieving client files. Lawyers and legal assistants often work in teams, and it is common for more than one person to work on the creation and editing of a legal document. To facilitate this, the legal assistant needs to set up and maintain an electronic file management system. Whereas some software, such as PCLaw™, Divorcemate, and The Conveyancer, do this for you, Microsoft Word does not, beyond defaulting to the My Documents folder or directory. Use the following guidelines in creating an electronic filing system:

1. When a new client comes to the firm, in addition to opening the physical file folder and assigning a matter number, a new folder or directory should be created in the My Documents folder of your computer. This is usually just the client's surname if an individual and the company name if a corporation. If the client's name is common, the first name or initial may be added after the surname. Thus, the directory might look like the example in Figure 3.5.
2. If the client has many matters with your law firm, then subfolders or directories will need to be created within the main client folder. For example, suppose that your law firm acts for Cornerstone Investments Ltd. on an ongoing basis dealing with a variety of corporate matters. This would require a number of subfolders according to each individual matter, as shown in the example in Figure 3.5.
3. Even with such an electronic filing system, over time, as you create a large number of documents and save them on your computer, it may become more difficult to find a specific document. To be able to quickly locate and retrieve a document, you therefore need to insert a document reference or identification showing the name and location of the document. Put this reference (usually in a smaller font size) in the footer portion of all or only the last page of the document using the Microsoft Word Insert Field function. Select the field for FileName and check off the box for "Add path to filename" so that the drive

and all folders and subfolders are shown. Many law firms also insert the initial of the author(s) of the document and the date (using the insert date field) into this footer so that if there are many revisions to a document, one can easily see which is the most recent version, as shown in the example here:

C:\MyDocuments\CornerstoneInvestmentsLtd.\LeasingMatters\City CentreLease.doc

PTG\May 20, 20__

It should be noted that some law firms have designed and implemented an electronic file management system along with a macro that will insert the document reference. Such a system may not be structured in the manner discussed here. As always, follow the preference of your law firm.

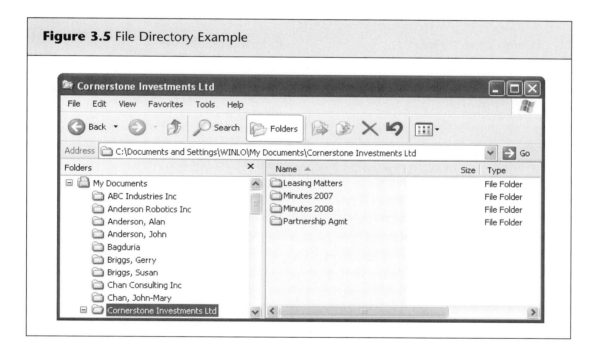

Figure 3.5 File Directory Example

CLOSED FILES

When work for a client is completed, the records previously set-up must be closed; this is known as closing the file.

Storage of Closed Files

Closed files are normally stored numerically in a specified location in the office, and from time to time, the oldest may be sent to outside (often referred to as off-site) storage. Increasingly, such files are scanned into electronic databases. An office alphabetical cross-index may be maintained or the database may be searched electronically from the legal assistant's computer if the file needs to be retrieved. The closed file number is not usually the number by which the file was identified while it was active; the closed number is usually a new number assigned so that all closed files are in consecutive order.

Destroying Closed Files

Most law firms have a retention policy requiring that closed files that need not be permanently retained be destroyed after a specified number of years. When a file is to be closed, the lawyer concerned should indicate the number of years the file is to be retained. At that time, the file is usually destroyed, or the lawyer is asked to review the file and indicate whether it should be destroyed or retained for a further period of time.

Terms and Concepts

file opening procedures	indexing guidelines
file or matter number	conflict of interest
new matter form	tickler system
dockets	bring forward system
conflict of interest	filing systems
tickler	alphabetical filing
retainer	numerical filing
authorization	centralized filing system
practice management software	decentralized filing system
matter number or file number	electronic file management guidelines
client number	document reference or identification
procedures for file folders	closed files procedures
records management	closed file number

Review Questions

1. You have been asked to set up the necessary records for a new client. What would you do?

2. What are the advantages of using coloured and/or subfile folders in client files?

3. The Hill, Johnston & Grant law firm requires a file opening form to be prepared when a new matter is undertaken for a client. What are the advantages of following this procedure?

4. Why is it so important for a law firm to maintain a tickler system?

5. The Hill, Johnston & Grant law office identifies matters numerically. Why do you feel it is necessary to also give the file a word name?

6. Many law firms maintain all files in a central location. Indicate one advantage and one disadvantage of such a system.

7. Why would a client be requested to sign
   a. a retainer?
   b. an authorization?
8. What happens to a file when the work for the client has been completed?
9. What is the benefit of maintaining an index of files and dockets?

RETAINER

TO: *Name of law firm to whom retainer is being given*
Barristers & Solicitors
Street Address
City, Province, Postal Code

Attention: (name of lawyer)

RE: *Nature of legal matter*

I/WE, *(NAME or NAMES of party/ies giving retainer in normal name order in all capital letters; bolding optional)*, of the *(name of city, and county, district, municipality, or province)*, do hereby retain and employ you as my/our solicitors to represent me/us in any matter concerning *(nature of legal matter),* and to take such steps and conduct such proceedings as you may consider necessary and proper.

I/We agree to provide along with this signed retainer a financial retainer in the amount of $00.00, which will be held in trust on my/our behalf.

I/We understand that I/we will be billed *(select one*: on an hourly basis/according to tariff/an estimated fee of $00.00) plus all disbursements made on my/our behalf will be charged to me/us on a cost basis.

I/We understand that during the course of this matter you may render interim accounts for fees and disbursements and that upon such account being rendered you may deduct the amount of the account from monies held by you on my/our behalf and agree that accounts paid more than 30 days after their date will bear interest at *(insert figure)* percent per annum from their date.

I/We acknowledge receipt of a copy of this retainer.

DATED at   , this   day of (*month*), 20__.

WITNESS:)
)
)
) _____
) *(name of client in normal name order)*
)
)
) _____
) *(name of second client, if applicable)*

RETAINER

TO: **McCAFFERY & LEHMAN**
      Barristers & Solicitors
      3500 Upper Water Street, Suite 400
      Halifax, Nova Scotia, B3J 2X2

      Attention: Seamus McCaffery

RE: Claim against Marswood Supplies Inc.

I, **JOHN PARKER WHITE,** of the Town of Middleton, in the County of Annapolis, Province of Nova Scotia, do hereby retain and employ you as my solicitors to represent me in any matter concerning a claim against Marswood Supplies Inc. of the City of Toronto, and to take such steps and conduct such proceedings as you may consider necessary and proper.

I agree to provide along with this signed retainer a financial retainer in the amount of $1,000.00, which will be held in trust on my behalf.

I understand that I will be billed on an hourly basis plus all disbursements made on my behalf will be charged to me on a cost basis.

I understand that during the course of this matter you may render interim accounts for fees and disbursements and that upon such account being rendered you may deduct the amount of the account from monies held by you on my behalf and agree that accounts paid more than 30 days after their date will bear interest at 6 percent per annum from their date.

I acknowledge receipt of a copy of this retainer.

DATED at Halifax, this   day of September, 20___.

WITNESS:)
)
)
)   _____
)   John Parker White

TO: *Name of person or company to whom authorization is to be sent*
        Street Address
        City, Province Postal Code

AUTHORIZATION

I, *(NAME of client in name order in all capitals; bolding optional)*, of the *(name of city, and county, district, municipality, or province)*, do hereby direct you to forward to my solicitors, *(name of solicitors, street address, city, province and postal code)*, any information that they may require in connection with *(details of circumstances and nature of information required)*.

DATED at   , this   day of *(month)*, 20___.

WITNESS:)
)
)
)   _____
)   *(name of client in normal signing order)*

TO: Dr. Anthony Tremblay
        400 6th Street, Suite 500
        Calgary, AB T2G 4J9

AUTHORIZATION

I, **MIYATA CAMP**, of the City of Red Deer, in the County of Red Deer, Province of Alberta, do hereby direct you to forward to my solicitors, Cookson, Oakville, Matthews & Palmer, Suite 73, Calgary-Dominion Centre, P.O. Box 90, Calgary, AB T2R 0B4, any medical information that they may require in connection with the injury I sustained at my workplace on January 15, 20___.

DATED at Calgary, this   day of April, 20___.

WITNESS:)
)
)
)   _____
)   Miyata Camp

CHAPTER 4

Legal Correspondence: Memoranda and Letters

OBJECTIVES:

- Identify and describe the different types of correspondence prepared in legal offices

- Use precedents to prepare memoranda and legal letters

In this chapter, we discuss the two main types of correspondence you will encounter in a law office: memoranda and letters. Information is presented on the various styles that may be used in preparing such material. Most law offices have adopted a standard style for correspondence and provide such information in an office manual. When you are employed as a law clerk or legal administrative assistant in such an office, you will, of course, be expected to prepare correspondence following those preferred styles.

MEMORANDA

Interoffice or file memoranda (or memorandums) are frequently used in legal offices. Although e-mail may be used for most interoffice communication, memoranda are still prepared to inform another lawyer about developments in a case or matter or record in the file details of a telephone conversation or a conference.

Some memoranda are very detailed and outline the law on certain issues or legal principles, with references to decided court cases. Such memoranda are known as **memoranda of law** and are usually prepared when the lawyer acts for a client in court proceedings. Memoranda of law are discussed in Chapter 6.

FORM OF MEMORANDA

Memoranda may be fully keyed (Precedent 4.1), prepared using the templates provided by word processing software, or using a template or macro created specially for the individual law firm. Such memoranda are usually single spaced, and when the subject of the memorandum is the name of a client file, you should include the file number in the Re or *Subject* section of the heading.

Continuation Pages

Continuation pages of a memorandum should be headed with the name or initials of the person to whom the memorandum is addressed, the page number, and the date. This information may be set out in consecutive lines at the left side of the page:

> Memo to PTG
> Page 2
> January 31, 20__

Alternatively, the information may be set out across the page similar to the style of heading on a continuation page of a letter.

Number of Copies

The number of copies of a memorandum depends on its purpose, but general guidelines are as follows:

1. Prepare a file copy of a memorandum addressed to another person only when it contains information that should be permanently in a file held by the sender.

2. Prepare one copy of a memorandum to file and place it in the file to which it relates.
3. If the law office maintains a chronological file of all outgoing correspondence and memoranda, prepare an extra copy and place it in that file as well.

LETTERS

A letter is often the first contact the law office has with a client, and both the contents and its professional appearance are a reflection of the firm and its employees, so care should always be taken in the preparation of all such correspondence.

Letter Format

The two letter formats most commonly used in legal correspondence are as follows:

1. **Modified block** has the date, the complimentary close, and signature line indented to begin at the centre point of the page (Precedent 4.2). If the paragraphs are indented, this style is often referred to as "semi block" (Precedent 4.3).
2. **Full block** has all components of the letter beginning flush with the left margin (Precedents 4.4 and 4.5).

Punctuation Styles

There are two main punctuation styles:

1. **mixed or two-point punctuation**, which has a colon after the salutation and a comma after the complimentary close (Precedents 4.2 and 4.3)
2. **open punctuation**, which has no punctuation following the salutation or complimentary close (Precedents 4.4 and 4.5)

Both letter and punctuation styles are used in legal practice. You should be familiar with both, but always follow the preference of your law firm.

DATE LINE

The format of the letterhead and the letter style govern the placement of the date. In modified block, it is placed where it will complement the letterhead; that may be in the centre or further to the right-hand side (Precedents 4.2 and 4.3). In full block, the date is placed flush with the left margin (Precedents 4.4 and 4.5).

A letter bears the date it is transcribed, not the date it was dictated, unless instructions are received to the contrary. If necessary, correct any references in dictation to "today," "tomorrow," or "yesterday." Ordinals are omitted when dates are shown in the traditional month, day, and year order.

SPECIAL NOTATIONS

On-Arrival Notations

Type the notations *Personal* or *Confidential* in capital letters, underscored or bolded (not both), flush left and between the date and the inside address on a letter (Precedent 4.2).

Without Prejudice

The notation **without prejudice** indicates that the contents of the letter may not be used against the person writing it in any court proceedings. It is shown in capital letters, underscored or bold (not both), between the date and inside address on the letter. It *never appears on an envelope.* Many lawyers require that this notation appear on all letters written to any person concerned in a matter in which litigation is pending (Precedent 4.3).

Type-of-Mail or Delivery Notations

Many law offices use both the facilities of the post office and of the other special delivery services, as discussed in Chapter 2, to forward mail and material. On outgoing correspondence being sent by other than regular mail, show the method being used in capital letters, underscored or bolded (not both), keeping the following points in mind:

1. The notation should appear between the date and the inside address.
2. If the material is to be delivered by a staff messenger or taxicab, mark all copies of the letter and the envelope *Delivered* (Precedents 4.3).
3. If the material is to be forwarded by fax, the notation should include the words *By Fax* or *Faxed To* and the fax number (Precedent 4.4).

INSIDE ADDRESS

Most software programs will print the envelope or label from the inside address keyed in for the letter; thus, the following requirements for both Canada Post and the US postal service should be considered when keying the inside address on the letter:

1. The preference is for envelope addresses to be keyed in full capitals with no punctuation, but both allow upper- and lowercase addresses as well, and this is usually the preferred method of preparation (Precedents 4.2, 4.3, 4.4, and 4.5).
2. The two-letter provincial or state abbreviation is to be used, followed by two spaces and then the postal or zip code on the same line (Precedents 4.2, 4.3, 4.4, and 4.5).
3. The # symbol or the word "No." should not appear in the address.

Courtesy Titles

There is a trend in business to omit courtesy titles when addressing an individual in correspondence. Some law firms use the title Mr. before the name of a male lawyer or Ms. before the name of a female lawyer, unless there is a stated preference for Miss or Mrs. The traditional practice of using Esq. (an abbreviation for Esquire—a traditional courtesy title for male lawyers) following the name of a male lawyer is outdated and rarely used as there is no feminine equivalent of Esq.

Q.C. (Queen's Counsel)

If a lawyer holds the designation Queen's Counsel, the abbreviation Q.C. is shown following his or her name (Precedents 4.3, 4.4, and 4.5). For example:

Mr. Gregory P. Drohan, Q.C.   Gregory P. Drohan, Q.C.
Ms. Mary C. Pagnello, Q.C.   Mary C. Pagnello, Q.C.

Barristers & Solicitors

The name of the law firm is shown in an inside address exactly in the form in which it appears on its letterhead, including the *LLP* notation (discussed in Chapter 2) if applicable. If it is a long name, it may appear on two lines; the second line should be indented two spaces. It is identified on the next line with the words Barristers & Solicitors or Barristers and Solicitors, followed on subsequent lines with the balance of the inside address (Precedents 4.3, 4.4, and 4.5).

Individual Lawyer

In a letter to a lawyer who is practising alone and who is not a Queen's Counsel, the designation Barrister & Solicitor or Barrister and Solicitor appears on the second line of the inside address. These words do not necessarily follow the name of an individual lawyer who is a Queen's Counsel since a lawyer must be a barrister and solicitor to be appointed a Q.C.

Attention Line

A letter to a firm of lawyers is frequently addressed to the law firm for the attention of a specific lawyer to ensure that, in his or her absence, it will be opened and any necessary action taken. Although the attention line is less frequently used in general business, it is still used in legal correspondence.

A number of traditional styles are used for the attention line, which is considered part of the inside address. The usual position is a double space below the inside address, flush with the left margin, with or without a colon, and in upper- and lower-case. Bolding the line is an optional practice (Precedent 4.3).

When correspondence is prepared on a computer and the software program prints the envelope or label from the inside address keyed in the letter, the attention line may be keyed in as part of the address, following either the name of the company or the Barristers & Solicitors line if the letter is addressed to a law firm. For example:

Hill, Johnston & Grant
Barristers & Solicitors
Attention Mr. Michael D. Colucci
17 Princess Street South
City, Province   Postal Code

SALUTATIONS

Firms of Lawyers

When writing directly to a firm of lawyers, use the salutation *Dear Sirs and Mesdames* (Precedent 4.3). The salutation *Ladies and Gentlemen* is not widely used but is still acceptable. When a letter is addressed directly to the law firm but marked for the attention of a specific lawyer, the salutation is still to the firm, not to the individual lawyer. The salutation is always to the person or firm set out in the first line of the inside address. For example, if a letter is addressed

Hill, Johnston & Grant
Barristers & Solicitors (Address...)

Attention: Peter T. Grant, Q.C.

the salutation is "Dear Sirs and Mesdames" (not "Dear Mr. Grant").
The colon after the word "Attention" is optional; as always, follow the preference of your law firm.

Individual Lawyers

When writing directly to an individual lawyer, the salutation is either formal (Dear Sir, Dear Madam, Dear Mr. Grant, Dear Ms. Ritchie) or familiar (Dear Peter, Dear Lynda), depending on the tone of the letter and the relationship between the lawyer and the addressee.

SUBJECT LINE

The subject line of a letter indicates the particular legal matter to which the correspondence relates, which is helpful to the recipient and assists in filing the correspondence. The subject line is usually the name of the particular file; thus, the name of your law firm's client appears first in any correspondence you prepare. When the law firm maintains its files numerically, a reference to the file number should be included in the outgoing correspondence. This reference may be in the last line of the subject lines, may appear a double space beneath the date line, or may follow the preprinted *Our Reference No.* or *Our File No.* wording on the letterhead. If the law firm to whom the letter is addressed has shown a file reference on its correspondence, that reference should also be included in the subject lines. Precedents 4.2, 4.3, 4.4, and 4.5 illustrate subject lines in legal correspondence.

The legal aid certificate number is included in the subject line of correspondence addressed to the Area Director or Legal Accounts Officer of the Legal Aid Plan but is omitted in correspondence addressed to any other individual or law firm.

The subject line is shown two lines beneath the salutation. Its placement on the line depends on the letter style followed. In the block style, the subject line is flush with the left margin (Precedents 4.4 and 4.5); in modified block, it is usually indented when paragraphs are indented (Precedent 4.2). The subject may be bolded or underlined, but not both, and the current practice is to bold it (Precedents 4.2, 4.3, 4.4, and 4.5).

If the subject matter is long, as is often the case in legal correspondence, divide it into logical groups and show each group as a separate line in block style and without end-of-line punctuation (Precedent 4.3).

Modern practice tends to omit the introductory notations Subject: or Re: because the placement of the subject line or lines below the salutation is an indication of its nature, but such introductions may still be used in legal correspondence. See the examples in Precedents 4.2, 4.3, 4.4, and 4.5. Follow the style preferred by your law firm.

BODY OF THE LETTER

Spacing

Letters are normally single spaced. Very short letters may be double spaced. Lengthy letters on legal questions, known as opinion letters, are sometimes double spaced.

Punctuation

Regardless of the style of punctuation used for the date line, inside address, etc., normal punctuation is used in the body of the letter itself.

Capitalization

A guide on the use of capitals and numbers in legal correspondence is set out in Chapter 2.

COMPLIMENTARY CLOSE AND SIGNATURE BLOCK

The complimentary close preferred will frequently be stated by the lawyer, but if this is not the custom, use *Yours very truly*. *Yours truly* may still be encountered in legal correspondence, but this form is now considered out of date. A letter is then ended in one of three ways, depending on the preference of the law firm:

1. Traditionally, the lawyer signed on behalf of the firm, and unless it was a personal letter, the name of the law firm was keyed a double space below the complimentary close in full capitals (Precedents 4.2, 4.3, and 4.4). Bolding of the law firm's name is optional. For example:

Yours very truly,

HILL, JOHNSTON & GRANT

Peter T. Grant

2. If the person signing the letter is an employee of the firm (law student, law clerk, legal administrative assistant, accountant, etc.), his or her position *must* appear beneath the name. Additionally, some firms previously required that any associate lawyer (not a partner) or any employee of the firm include the word *Per:* (which means on behalf of) below the name of the firm. For example:

For a law clerk: *For an associate lawyer:*

Yours very truly,   Yours very truly,

HILL, JOHNSTON & GRANT   **HILL, JOHNSTON & GRANT**

Per:

Amarjit Singh   Michael D. Colucci
Law Clerk

3. Some law firms are now omitting the name of the law firm altogether in the complimentary close (Precedent 4.5). However, the practice of having anyone who is not a lawyer include his or her title beneath the name is still followed. For example:

Yours very truly,

Margaret Aspin
Office Manager

If you are not told which form to follow, use the firm name with the name of the lawyer. This indicates clearly that the lawyer who signs is doing so on behalf of the law firm and not personally.

REFERENCE INITIAL NOTATIONS

Reference initial notations are not required on the original of a letter; however, they are usually shown. The standard location for reference initial notations is flush with the left-hand margin in line with, or one or two spaces beneath, the last line of the complimentary close. There are a variety of ways in which they are shown; however, in many law offices, the custom of showing both the initial of the author of the letter and the person who prepares it is still followed (Precedents 4.2, 4.3, 4.4, and 4.5).

ENCLOSURE

When a letter contains an enclosure, use the word *Enclosure* or the abbreviation *Enc.* flush with the left-hand margin, one or two spaces beneath the reference initial notation. If there is more than one enclosure, either indicate the number or specify the nature of the enclosure(s) (Precedent 4.2). For example:

PTG:ees
Enclosures 2
or
/ees
Enclosures: Account, Ledger Statement

If the letter is given to the lawyer for signature before you have the enclosure ready, flag the letter with a coloured paper clip or a post-it note reading *awaiting enclosure* or something similar, as a reminder that the enclosure is not yet included.

SECOND OR CONTINUATION PAGES

Second or continuation pages showing the name of the law firm are necessary when a letter runs to more than one page. Before the introduction of computers, many law firms had a printed second or continuation sheet. Many law firms now have a macro to insert the second page header. If such a page has not been stored, the second and other additional pages are prepared in the normal way.

The following information is required to be shown at the top of each continuation page:

1. Name of the addressee; if the letter is addressed specifically to a lawyer at a law firm, show the name of the lawyer followed by the name of the law firm; if the

letter is addressed to the law firm for the attention of a lawyer, show the name of the law firm followed by the attention line

2. Page number
3. The date

This information may be shown either across the page or on individual lines at the left-hand side of the page (Precedents 4.6 and 4.7).

If it is not possible to begin a new page with a new paragraph, carry over at least two lines of a paragraph. In addition, at least two lines of a carryover paragraph should appear at the end of the previous page. There should also be at least two lines of the body of the letter with the complimentary close and signature. Word processing features that prevent widows and orphans and protect blocks of text can be of assistance.

COPIES

Number of Copies

A minimum of two copies of outgoing correspondence are required: the original and a copy for the file. Many lawyers maintain a chronological file of all outgoing correspondence and memoranda, known as a **letter or day book**, and an additional copy is made for this purpose.

Copy Notations

When a copy of a letter is sent to another person in addition to the person to whom the letter is addressed, and the addressee is to be aware of that fact, show the abbreviation c for a copy on the original flush with the left-hand margin and two spaces beneath the last notation (Precedents 4.2 and 4.3). For example:

PTG:ees
Enclosures 2
c Mr. James Brown
  Ms. Mary Smith

Place a check mark after the name of the person who is to receive the copy. If the copy is to be sent by some special type of mail or delivery service, this information is shown following the name of the recipient (Precedent 4.3).

Blind Copy Notations

Often a copy of a letter is to be sent to another person *without* the knowledge of the addressee. This notation *never* appears on the original, signed copy of the letter. Once the original letter has been signed, photocopy a copy of the original and mark it with a "Copy for... " stamp, which your office will usually have available; write in the name of the person for whom the copy is intended. Be sure to indicate on your file copy that a blind copy was sent to (name of person).

ENVELOPES

A suitable-size envelope is required for each piece of outgoing correspondence that is delivered through the regular postal or other physical delivery services. Most software programs will print the envelope or label from the information keyed in for the inside address.

Special Notations

Method of delivery notations and on-arrival notations, such as Delivered or Personal and Confidential, are shown a double space beneath the return address or a double space above the address portion (Precedent 4.8).

Attention Line

The attention line may appear in the top left-hand portion or may be included as part of the address, following the name of the company or the Barrister and Solicitor line (Precedent 4.9).

Return Envelopes

When enclosing a self-addressed return envelope in outgoing correspondence, use a plain envelope with no return address printing and address it directly to the lawyer requesting the reply, not merely to his or her attention.

Correspondence prepared for illustrations in this text will reflect a variety of style practices.

Terms and Concepts

interoffice/file memoranda
memoranda of law
full block and modified block letter format
standard and open punctuation
mixed or two-point punctuation
date line
on-arrival notations
without prejudice
mail/delivery notations
inside address
addressing standards
Esquire
Queen's Counsel notations

attention line
salutations
subject line
body of letter
complimentary close
reference initials
enclosure
second or continuation pages
copy and blind copy notations
letter or day book
continuation page headings
envelope notations

Review Questions

1. What is the purpose of the memorandum to file?

2. What is the purpose of including the law office's file number as part of the letter?

3. How can you tell whether the salutation should be to the law firm or to an individual?

4. Why should the type of delivery being used be shown on the letter?

5. What would you do if a letter indicated that there is an enclosure, but the enclosure was not available at the time the letter is submitted for signature?

6. How do you know what form of letter ending to use in a letter if the lawyer only uses the words "Yours very truly, etc."?

7. Letters are frequently mailed. Name three other methods by which a letter can reach the addressee.

8. Give an example of two on-arrival notations. Where are these notations shown on the letter and on the envelope?

9. Assume that you are an employee of Hill, Johnston & Grant. How would the complimentary close and signature block appear for a letter that you are to sign?

Hill, Johnston & Grant

MEMORANDUM

TO: File

FROM: Lynda C. Ritchie

DATE: January 2, 20__

RE: Camp v. Miyata
Our File No. 04806/0614

I had a call today from Mr. Black stating that there is an indication that the date for this case will be set for the latter part of next month.

I suggested to him that we should carry on with the discoveries, and he said that we should either do that or settle the case. He indicated that he is realistic enough to know that they will not get $1,100,000 and that I should be realistic enough to know that they will not accept $400,000.

He said that the prior offer had been $725,000—I believe it was $700,000. He stated that he thinks the compensation should be $800,000 and that the case could be settled for $750,000.

I said I would speak to my client.

LCR/urs

Letterhead	
	# Hill, Johnston & Grant
	Barristers & Solicitors
	www.hilljohngrant.com
	Suite 2501, 17 Princess Street South
	City, Province Postal Code
	Telephone: (000) 354-9900
	Facsimile: (000) 354-9909
Date	February 10, 20__
On Arrival Notation	**P E R S 0 N A L**
Inside Address	Mr. Michael J. Daysworth
	95 Sherdale Valley Crescent
	Victoria BC V6E 3C9
Salutation	Dear Sir:
Subect Line including Reference Notation	**Humber Mountain Inn and Country Club**
	Our Reference No. 04582/1322
Body	We are the solicitors for Humber Mountain Inn and Country Club. We have been instructed that you are indebted to our client in the amount of $6,549.75 for accommodation and services provided by our client to you on the occasion of your daughter's wedding on November 21 last year, as set out on the enclosed statement.
	Please be advised that unless your certified cheque for this amount, payable to Humber Mountain Inn and Country Club, is received in this office on or before February 28, 20__, we have instructions to take such further and other action as may be necessary to protect our client's interests. This action may well involve additional costs, which may have to be borne by you.
Complimentary Close	Yours very truly,
	HILL, JOHNSTON & GRANT
	Per:
Signature Block	
Reference Initials	RLR/urs
	Paul L. Riverio
Enclosure Notation	Enclosure 1
Copy Notation	c Mr. James R. Hall
	Humber Mountain Inn and Country Club

Letterhead	# Hill, Johnston & Grant
	Barristers & Solicitors
	www.hilljohngrant.com
	Suite 2501, 17 Princess Street South
	City, Province Postal Code
Date	Telephone: (000) 354-9900
	Facsimile: (000) 354-9909
	February 14, 20__
On Arrival Notation	**DELIVERED**
Special Notation	**WITHOUT PREJUDICE**
Inside Address	Carson, Stephenson & West
	Barristers & Solicitors
	250 King Street North
	Hamilton ON L7W 2C9
Attention Line	Attention: Gordon P. West, Q.C.
Salutation	Dear Sirs and Mesdames:
Subect Line including Reference Notations	**Re: Milne and O'Grady – Milgrady Fine Foods Ltd.**
	Our File No. 04460/1079
	Your File No. 08/943/GPW

We have your letter of February 6. We do not think that Mr. Milne is prepared to make any proposal with respect to this case. He feels very strongly about the matter.

In addition, he has discovered that the accountant has treated as receipts of the new firm monies paid in respect of accounts rendered before there was such a firm. As you will recall from the partnership agreement, O'Grady did not acquire any interest in these accounts, and as a result he received a good deal of money to which he was not entitled.

If Mr. O'Grady insists on the matter going to court, we are afraid that there is nothing more we can do to prevent it.

Yours very truly,

HILL, JOHNSTON & GRANT

Mitra J. Bonilla

Body (label for the above paragraphs)

Complimentary Close · **Signature Block**

Reference Initials MJB:urs

Copy Notation c J. L. Milne - DELIVERED

Letterhead	# Hill, Johnston & Grant Barristers & Solicitors *www.hilljohngrant.com* Suite 2501, 17 Princess Street South City, Province Postal Code Telephone: (000) 354-9900 Facsimile: (000) 354-9909
Date	February 14, 20__
On Arrival Notation	**BY FAX (416) 233-9980**
Inside Address	Mr. John A. Hamid Smith, Fraser, Hamid & Lee LLP Barristers & Solicitors Suite 503, 75 Victoria Street Toronto ON M5C 2B1
Salutation	Dear Mr. Hamid:
Subect Line including Reference Notation	**Dees and Millar** **Our Reference No. 04327/1276**
Body	We have just received a letter from Mr. Dees in which he has advised me that his employer, East Hardware Limited, has informed him that arrangements have been made for him to take a special training course at Rochester, New York, from February 18 to February 25. He states that his employer has gone to considerable trouble to make these arrangements and is very anxious that he take this particular course. He indicated that it will not be offered again until next October. In view of the fact that you may not be able to proceed in February, would you kindly advise us at your earliest convenience whether you will agree to an adjournment, as it appears that it will be impossible for Mr. Dees to attend.
Complimentary Close	Yours very truly,
	HILL, JOHNSTON & GRANT
Signature Block including Job Title	Marie J. Armstrong Law Clerk
Reference Initials	MJA:urs

Letterhead

Hill, Johnston & Grant

Barristers & Solicitors

www.hilljohngrant.com

Suite 2501, 17 Princess Street South
City, Province Postal Code

Telephone: (000) 354-9900
Facsimile: (000) 354-9909

Reference Notation

Our Reference No. 04642/1218

Date

February 14, 20__

Inside Address

Marlene L. Shelson, Q.C.
Wahl, Prentice, Temple & Drohan
Barristers & Solicitors
75 Winterhaven Road
Calgary, AB T2T 5R6

Salutation

Dear Ms. Shelson

Subect Line

Re: Crenwood v. Staufferdale

Body

I received your notice of appointment for the examination for discovery of my client on February 28. As I advised you by telephone yesterday, my client will be unable to attend on that date. He has undergone emergency surgery for a perforated appendix and is expected to be hospitalized for at least a week or 10 days.

As requested by you, we have asked Mr. Crenwood's wife to secure a medical certificate from their family doctor. I will produce this as soon as it has been received.

I would expect that Mr. Crenwood would be available for discovery about the middle of March. In view of his age, I think you will agree that we should allow him some time to recover from the effects of what is a major illness.

Complimentary Close

Yours very truly

Signature Block

Peter T. Grant

Reference Initials

PTG:urs

Peter T. Grant, Q.C.
Hill, Johnston & Grant
Page 2
January 31, 20___

Ms. Lynda C. Ritchie
Hill, Johnston & Grant   - 2 -   January 31, 20___

Smith, Fraser, Hamid & Lee LLP
Attention: L. A. Blackwell
Page 2
January 31, 20___

Smith, Fraser, Hamid & Lee
Attention: L. A. Blackwell   2   January 31, 20___

Hill, Johnston & Grant
Barristers & Solicitors
17 Princess Street South, Suite 2501
Your City, Province Postal Code
Canada

PERSONAL

DELIVERED

Robert J. West, Q.C.
Carson, Stephenson & West
Barristers & Solicitors
250 King Street North
Hamilton, ON L7W 2C9

Hill, Johnston & Grant
Barristers & Solicitors
17 Princess Street South, Suite 2501
Your City, Province Postal Code
Canada

REGISTERED MAIL

Smith, Fraser, Hamid & Lee LLP
Barristers & Solicitors
Attention Miss Mary J. Spencer
75 Victoria Street, Suite 503
Toronto, ON M5C 2B1

CHAPTER 5

Client Dockets and Accounts

OBJECTIVES:

- Demonstrate an understanding of basic legal office accounting procedures, such as legal fees, dockets, and the application of GST to legal goods and services

- Demonstrate an understanding of disbursements

- Distinguish between the two types of bank accounts in a legal office

- Prepare various accounting documents such as cash receipts, cheque requisitions, and daily time record sheets

- Calculate and prepare client accounts

Maintaining proper books and records is a necessary part of the law office accounting operation. Such records are now usually maintained electronically, and information and paper records are printed out as required. The principles of accounting in a law office form a major area of study and therefore are not covered in this text. We consider only some of the basic accounting routines with which the legal assistant is required to be familiar, as illustrated in Figure 5.1 (p. 70).

LEGAL FEES

When a client initially retains a lawyer, a fee structure will be explained and agreed upon with the client, and this will be reflected in the retainer and new matter form discussed in Chapter 3. The most common fee structures for legal services are as follows:

Time Value or Hourly

This is the most frequent method used in billing for legal services and is calculated based on the amount of time the lawyer spends on the file. Lawyers may have a variety of hourly rates that are charged to their clients (usually based on the area of legal practice), and a reduced hourly rate may be charged for any work performed by a law clerk or paralegal. The work performed by legal administrative assistants, accountants, IT personnel, etc. may not be charged on an hourly rate to clients as this is considered part of the overhead or operating expenses of a law firm. Lawyers keep detailed records of their time so that clients may be charged for any time spent on their file, known as **billable time**. Work that is performed that is not charged to a client, such as the time a partner might spend in managing the law firm, is known as **unbillable** or **nonbillable time**.

Tariff

This is when a lawyer is paid his or her legal fees in accordance with a tariff, which is a schedule of fees established by a government authority, such as a provincial legal aid plan.

Estimated or Flat Fee

This occurs when a client is quoted a flat or estimated fee for the legal services when retaining the lawyer. It is usually applied when the legal work required is a routine or standardized service, such as the preparation of a will or the purchase or sale of residential real estate.

Contingency Fees

This fee arrangement allows lawyers and their clients to agree that the lawyer will be paid only if he or she is successful in the claim being pursued. A percentage of the monies awarded by the courts is paid to the lawyer as the fee. Contingency fees

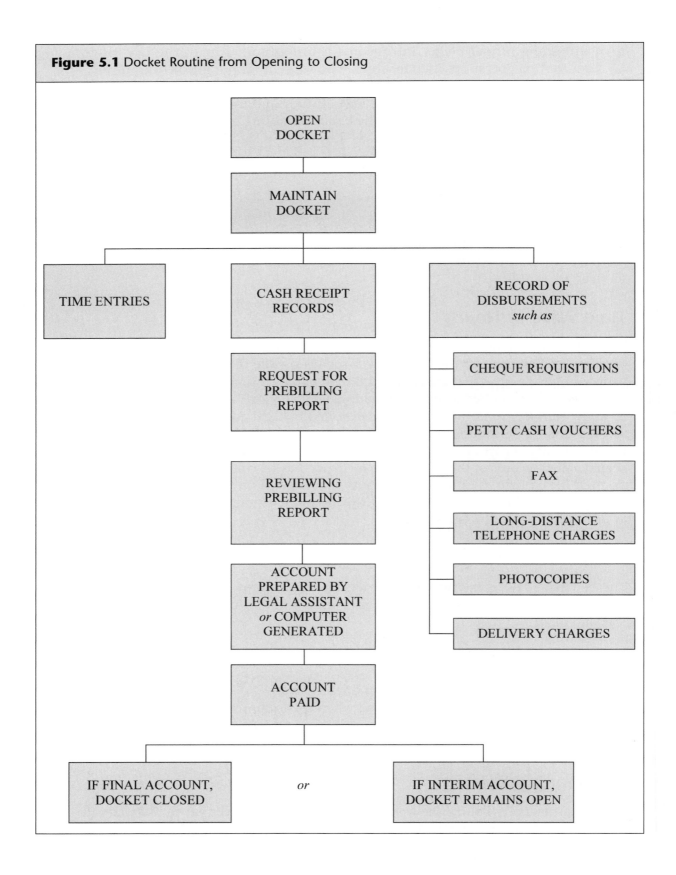

Figure 5.1 Docket Routine from Opening to Closing

are allowed only in certain provinces (currently Alberta, British Columbia, Ontario, and Quebec) and are not allowed in criminal, quasi-criminal, and family law matters. There are strict regulations governing contingency fees, including that it must be in writing and the method by which the fee is to be calculated must be clearly set out.

It should be noted that no matter which method of fee arrangement is used, the lawyer will still maintain a record of the number of hours spent working on a client file in order to have an accurate record of his or her time for internal accounting purposes.

A record of all expenses incurred on behalf of the clients, known as **disbursements**, is also maintained so that these may be recovered when the client is billed, and these are discussed in greater detail later in this chapter.

GOODS AND SERVICES TAX AND LEGAL SERVICES

The Goods and Services Tax (GST) is charged on all specified supplies under the *Excise Tax Act*; "supplies" means both goods and services. A law firm is considered a "supplier" under the act and is required to collect from its clients and remit to the government tax at the rate of 5 percent on fees charged for supplying most legal services to residents of Canada and to non-residents in specified circumstances. A law firm is required to register as a collector of the GST, is assigned a GST registration number (for example, R946802753), and is required to file periodic GST tax returns.

The legal assistant is usually involved in such procedures only to the extent that he or she ensures that the accounting department is given the information it requires to allow the proper accounting records to be maintained. However, as discussed later in this chapter, on occasion the legal assistant may be required to separate disbursements into those that are subject to GST and those that are not subject to GST while preparing an account to the client.

Harmonized Sales Tax (HST)

In the provinces of Nova Scotia, New Brunswick, and Newfoundland and Labrador, a harmonized sales tax of 13 percent replaces both the federal GST and the provincial sales tax (PST) and is applied on the same basis as the GST.

MAINTAINING ACCOUNTING PROCESSES

As discussed in Chapter 3, most law firms use practice management software that, among other functions, handles the computer accounting records of a law firm. These programs maintain the records of work in progress, billable hours, disbursements, and general cost data; further, they provide fast and efficient maintenance of account information, time diaries, and fee schedules. Such systems are capable not only of recording information but also of preparing final accounts, including the calculation of GST payable on both fees and the applicable disbursements.

Even with electronic accounting programs, many accounting records must begin as paper documents, either prepared on a printed form or from a recorded form. The data from such forms are either keyed into the system by accounting department personnel or may be keyed directly into the main computer accounting records by the legal assistant.

DOCKETS

As discussed in Chapter 3, a docket is opened at the time a new file is opened for a client. Dockets are usually maintained numerically; once a docket has been opened, all material prepared for it must be identified by the number and name under which it was opened.

The day-by-day record of work performed by a lawyer and any expenses incurred on behalf of a client are maintained on such client dockets, and the individual notations are known as entries or charges.

Dockets contain the following types of entries/charges:

Time Charges	Disbursement Charges	Receipts
A record of all time spent working on the matter for the client	A record of all expenses incurred on behalf of the client	A record of all monies received from or on behalf of the client

These entries/charges are discussed in detail below.

TIME CHARGES

All lawyers and often law clerks/paralegals who spend time considering a particular case or matter record the time spent in hours or tenths of an hour as follows:

Amount of Time	Decimal Amount
1–6 minutes	.1
7–12 minutes	.2
13–18 minutes	.3
19–24 minutes	.4
25–30 minutes	.5
31–36 minutes	.6
37–42 minutes	.7
43–48 minutes	.8
49–54 minutes	.9
55–60 minutes	1.0

The system of keeping time records is not standardized. The simplest way to maintain records of work on a file is through use of a lawyer's docket sheet, which is stapled to the inside front cover of each individual client file. As services are rendered or expenses incurred, notations are made on the form. This is rarely used anymore as most law firms have a centralized computer accounting system that requires the entry of daily time records.

Daily Time Records

Each time a lawyer or law clerk/paralegal works on a file, he or she keeps a record of what work was performed and how much time was spent on it. This may be accomplished in two ways:

1. A daily time record sheet is prepared; the style of this sheet varies from office to office. An example is illustrated in Figure 5.2. This form may be a paper document or may be recorded in the computer memory; in some offices, it is both. The lawyer may make handwritten or keyed entries on the sheet detailing the work performed for each client during the day. The legal assistant will then insert the file number and key the records into a computerized accounting system such as PCLaw™ using the Time Entry Screen illustrated in Figure 5.3 (p. 74).

Figure 5.2 Daily Time Record

Hill, Johnston & Grant

	Mo.	Day	Year
Date	09	20	20__

		No.	Initials
Lawyer		015	PTG

DAILY TIME RECORD

Page __1__ of __1__ Pages

FILE NO.	FILE NAME	NARRATIVE	TIME HRS	TIME 1/10
04856/0076	ANDERSON, Ronald re Accident Claim	MW CL RD liability; TT insurance company and LT insurance company	1	8
04893/0390	HARRISON re Marriage Contract	LT CL with draft agreement for review		3
04598/0798	HUNTER, Rex re Sale 48 Markwood	LT Smith, Fraser with draft DE and draft MG back for approval		3
04610/1010	HARVEY, Louise re Separation Agmt.	CW you re proposed agreement; TF Armstrong; CW FPH and LCR	2	5
04909/0482	JULIETTE'S BOUTIQUE re White	AT John Jason; TF Smith, Fraser, LT Smith, Fraser; TT CL; DR WR	1	0
04982/1087	WELBY, Alexandra re Welby, J. Estate	LT Glasgow Herald re advertisement for relatives; RD file and DR OD		6
		PAGE TOTAL	6	5

Figure 5.3 Time Entry Screen, PCLaw™

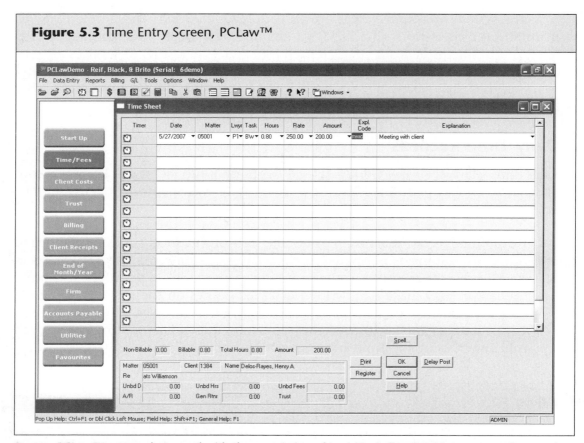

Source: PCLaw™ screen shots used with the permission of LexisNexis Practice Management Systems Inc.

Figure 5.4 Quick Timer, PCLaw™

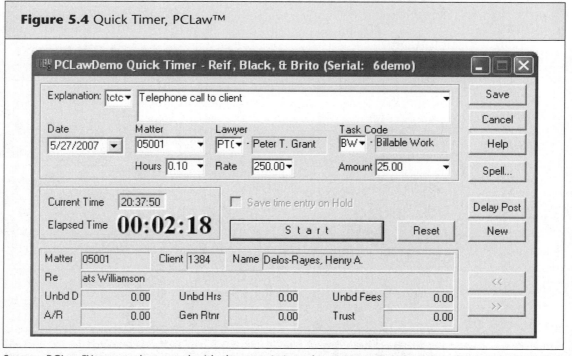

Source: PCLaw™ screen shots used with the permission of LexisNexis Practice Management Systems Inc.

2. Alternatively, the time spent and the work done may be entered directly into the computerized accounting system by the lawyer or law clerk/paralegal using a direct entry feature such as PCLaw™ Quick Timer, as illustrated in Figure 5.4.

It is essential that time entries be made on a regular, preferably daily, basis so that all work performed will be calculated into the client's account.

Figure 5.5 Daily Time Record Entry Codes, Sample List

Hill, Johnston & Grant

The following abbreviations should be used where possible in completing the narrative portion of the daily time record.

ACTIVITY CODES

AD	advising	EW	engaged with	RL	reading law
AE	amending	FL	filing	RS	revising
		FR	travelling from		
AF	arranging for	IS	issuing/issued	RT	reporting to
AM	attending meeting	LF	letter from	RV	reviewed/reviewing
AT	attending	LT	letter to	SV	serving
CW	conference with	MO	memo	TF	telephone call from
DR	drafting	MW	meeting with	TO	travelling to
DW	discussions with	PR	preparing	TT	telephone call to
EM	e-mail	PX	proofreading		

SPECIAL TERMS AND DOCUMENT CODES

GENERAL		LITIGATION		CORPORATE	
AV	affidavit/statutory declaration	AP	applicant	AA	art. of amendment
				AX	articles of incorporation
BR	brief	AS	affidavit of service		
BS	bill of sale	AZ	affidavit of documents	BL	by-laws
				DM	directors' meeting
CL	client	DF	defendant	IO	incorporating
				MI	corporate minutes
LC	licence	DJ	default judgment	RC	corporate records
PA	power of attorney	DS	discovery		
RE	release	FT	factum		
RN	retainer	JU	judgment	SA	shareholders' agmt.
SO	solicitor	MO	motion	SM	shareholders' mtg.
UN	undertaking	NA	notice of action		
		ND	notice of intent to defend		
ESTATES		NM	notice of motion	**REAL ESTATE**	
BF	beneficiary	NP	notice of application	DE	deed/transfer
ES	estate admin.				
		OR	order		
		PC	pre-trial conference	MD	mortgage discharge
		PD	petition for divorce		
		PF	plaintiff		
ET	estate trustee	PL	pleadings	ME	mortgage extension
		PT	petitioner	MG	mortgage/charge
WL	will			ML	mortgage renewal
XE	executor			RD	Reg/Land Titles Off.
		RP	respondent	TS	title search
		SC	statement of claim		
		SD	statement of defence	TZ	tax certificate

Preparing Docket Entries

If the lawyer does not complete the daily record sheet as the service is performed or do the computerized entry, the appropriate entries may be dictated or might have to be taken from his or her diary. The legal assistant may be expected to make the appropriate entries to record all outgoing correspondence. Many law firms require that the text of narrative be kept brief and concise and that activity codes be used to reduce the length of the narrative. Figure 5.5 (p. 75) illustrates an example of abbreviations that might be used in keying docket entries.

Note that these abbreviations are not standardized, and each firm will often develop its own abbreviations. Although the abbreviations appear on the daily time record or docket entries, the computer will convert them to plain English. In some law offices, the document narrative for entries is a brief description in plain English of the work performed. In either instance, the computer summary of the services may become the basis for the account to be rendered or may become the account itself, so great care should be taken that all inputs are accurate.

DISBURSEMENTS

In addition to entries for fees, dockets also record information relating to disbursements incurred on behalf of the client. In most accounting systems, the information that goes to the accounting department is on a paper form, which may have been printed out using a recorded form or may be completed on an existing printed form. Disbursements usually include items such as cheques in payment of supplies or services for the client, petty cash charges, long-distance telephone calls, photocopying charges, and so on.

Formerly, many law firms used a variety of forms of different colours to record these various types of disbursements. However, many disbursements, such as long-distance telephone calls and photocopying charges, may now be recorded automatically in computerized accounting systems; often, there is only one type of disbursement form for payment of money by cheque or from petty cash.

There are no prescribed disbursement forms; each law firm designs its own and will provide detailed instructions on their completion for the new legal assistant.

Classification of Disbursements

Disbursements incurred in supplying a service to a client for which the client reimburses the law firm are considered part of the consideration for the legal service and are therefore subject to GST, unless the expense was incurred by the law firm acting as an "agent" for the client. For example, disbursements made to government departments or agencies for filing of registration fees, land transfer taxes, licences, permits, and other government charges are tax exempt, and when the law firm pays such disbursements on behalf of the client, it acts as the client's agent. Therefore, the disbursement is not subject to GST when billed to the client.

It is therefore necessary to classify disbursements by code numbers to identify whether the disbursement is taxable (a non-agency disbursement) and subject to GST when billed to the client or tax exempt (an agency disbursement) and not subject to GST when billed to the client. The applicable code number is shown on the disbursement form and will be recorded when the disbursement is keyed into the computer records. Figure 5.6 illustrates a specimen index of such codes. Each law firm will have its own distinctive codes for use in its accounting system, and most accounting software systems are programmed (according to the codes) as to whether the disbursement is subject to GST or not subject to GST.

Figure 5.6 Disbursement Codes, Sample List

Hill, Johnston & Grant

DISBURSEMENT ACTIVITY CODES & GST STATUS

SUBJECT TO GST	CODE
Accident Report	012
Advertising Notices	080
Agency Fees	081
Billable Time	100
By-Laws	039
Corporate Name Search	032
Corporate Supplies (Box, Seal, Minute Book, Shares)	038
Courier	005
Status Certificate	053
Examination Fee	021
Fax	006
Legal Research Fees (Quicklaw)	092
Long-Distance Charges	008
Medical Reports	011
Photocopies	007
Postage	010
Serve Documents	015
Transaction Levy Surcharge	079
Transcript	017
Travel and Parking	009
Utilities Search (Hydro, Gas, Etc.)	052

NOT SUBJECT TO GST	CODE
Building Dept. Search	051
Certificates (Divorce, Status, Birth, Death, Marriage, etc.)	076
Filing Fees	027
Government Fees	034
Land Transfer Tax	061
Official Guardian	024
Payments to/from client (Proceeds, Retainers, etc.)	002
Real Estate Commission	073
Registration Fees	045
Search Fees	060
Summons/Subpoena	018
Tax Search/Certificate	050
Witness Fees	082

CHEQUE REQUISITIONS

When a cheque is required to pay for expenses incurred while acting for a client, the necessary cheque may be requested by preparing one copy of the appropriate disbursement form. This is usually a cheque requisition, duly completed and signed, and given to the accounting department, together with the invoice or account being paid. The accounting department requires all such documentation for information on the vendor's GST registration number to support a claim for an input tax credit when filing the periodic GST return. Figure 5.7 illustrates a sample cheque requisition.

In some law offices, the legal assistant may be authorized to sign requisitions up to a specific amount; all other requisitions would require the signature of the lawyer or the authorization of an individual in the office with the responsibility of approving requisitions for cheques over a specified amount.

When the cheque has been issued and signed, the accounting department will usually mail it, unless the lawyer or legal assistant has requested that the cheque be returned to him or her for their attention.

PETTY CASH EXPENDITURES

Small expenses incurred are paid out from the petty cash fund maintained by the accounting department. Prepare a disbursement form such as the petty cash voucher shown in Figure 5.8 (p. 80). Some offices may use a special petty cash form and will instruct you on its preparation.

LONG-DISTANCE TELEPHONE CALLS

Practice varies on the method used to record charges for long-distance telephone calls. As discussed in Chapter 2, advanced technology has made available telephones that have many electronic features. On such telephones, long-distance charges may be automatically recorded in the docket by a computer. This requires the person placing the call to code in the appropriate docket number before dialling the telephone number. Many law offices are equipped with these types of telephones.

In offices where long-distance telephone charges are not automatically recorded in the docket, some formal procedure will be followed to record the charges for long-distance charges from the office or from outside the office and charged to the office number. Follow the practice established in your law office. Note, however, that if long-distance calls are dialled directly and not automatically recorded in the docket, it is possible to determine the cost of the call. Dial "0" (zero), the area code, and the seven-digit number and then ask the operator to call you back with the time and charges after the call has been completed.

Figure 5.7 Cheque Requisition

CHEQUE REQUISITION

PAYABLE TO:	1	DATE:	11
VENDOR GST REGISTRATION NO.	2	AMOUNT $	12
		ADD GST $	13
COVERING	3	ADD PST $	14
DISBURSEMENT CODE	4	TOTAL $	15
TO BE CHARGED AS FOLLOWS:		Firm Account	16
Client/Matter No.	5	Trust Account	16
Matter:	6	Certified	17
Special Instructions:	7	**ACCOUNTING DEPT.**	
Requested by: 8	Lawyer No. 9	Cheque No.	18
Signature	10	Cheque Date	18

LEGEND

1. Party being paid
2. The GST No. of party being paid (if applicable)
3. What the payment is for—NOT THE MATTER
4. Disbursement Code (see Figure 5.6)
5. Client/Matter No.
6. The name of the matter
7. Any special instructions, e.g., if cheque required by certain date or time
8. The name of person requesting the cheque
9. Lawyer Code No.
10. The signature of lawyer or other person authorizing request
11. Date prepared
12. Amount payable, excluding GST
13. Amount of GST, if applicable
14. Amount of PST, if applicable
15. The total amount of cheque requested
16. The bank account on which cheque is to be drawn
17. Insert "x" if cheque to be certified
18. Completed by Accounting Department

CHEQUE REQUISITION

PAYABLE TO: Etobicoke Courier Services	DATE: Nov. 3, 20
VENDOR GST REGISTRATION NO. R99258461	AMOUNT $ 14.00
	ADD GST $ 0.70
COVERING Delivery Services	ADD PST $
DISBURSEMENT CODE 005	TOTAL $ 14.70
TO BE CHARGED AS FOLLOWS:	Firm Account X
Client/Matter No. 04172/1276	Trust Account
Matter: Growski re New Will	Certified
Special Instructions: Please mail cheque with attached invoice	**ACCOUNTING DEPT.**
Requested by: Michael D. Colucci Lawyer No. 007	Cheque No.
Signature *Michael D. Colucci*	Cheque Date

Figure 5.8 Petty Cash Voucher

PETTY CASH VOUCHER

CLIENT/MATTER NO. _____ 1 _____   DATE: _____ 2 _____

MATTER _____ 3 _____   AMOUNT $ 4

_____   ADD GST $ 5

                                                                ADD PST $ _____ 6 _____

PAID TO: _____ 7 _____   TOTAL $ 8

DESCRIPTION: _____ 9 _____

                 Office Expense _____ 10 _____   Disbursement Code _____ 11 _____

CASH RECEIVED BY: _____ 12 _____
                                                     Signature

LEGEND

1. Client/matter number	7. Name of the person who made the disbursement
2. Date of preparation	8. The total amount of the disbursement
3. Name of matter	9. Description of disbursement
4. Amount of disbursement	10. "X" if disbursement is not to be charged to the client
5. The amount of any GST	11. Indicate appropriate disbursement code (see Figure 5.7)
6. The amount of any PST	12. Signature of person receiving the cash

PETTY CASH VOUCHER

CLIENT/MATTER NO. _____ 04610/1010 _____   DATE: Mar. 17, 20___

MATTER _____ Harvey, Mary re Separation Agreement _____   AMOUNT $ 3.00

_____   ADD GST $ 0.15

                                                   ADD PST $ _____ 0.24 _____

PAID TO: _____ Pronto Print Shop _____   TOTAL $ 3.39

DESCRIPTION: _____ Photocopies _____

                 Office Expense _____   Disbursement Code _____ 007 _____

CASH RECEIVED BY: *Thomas Hussain*
                                                     Signature

PHOTOCOPIES

Practice varies from office to office on the method followed to ensure that charges for photocopying are recorded in the docket.

In offices where docket information is stored electronically, photocopying may be charged in a number of ways. A master daily sheet, recording the file number, client name, and number of photocopies, may be maintained at the copier. More commonly, the photocopier is linked to a computer and is activated only when a special card has been inserted or when the appropriate user and docket number have been keyed in. The appropriate docket is then electronically charged with the number of photocopies made.

RECEIPTS

When monies are received before a matter is completed or when it has been completed and an account rendered, a record of such monies is recorded in the docket. In many law offices, all mail is opened in a central mailroom and all cheques are given to the accounting department for processing. In other law offices, the cheque may first be received by the lawyer or the legal assistant and then forwarded to the accounting department with information about the matter to which it relates. Some law offices may use a cash receipt form similar to that illustrated in Figure 5.9 (p. 82).

BANK ACCOUNTS

A law firm is required by law to maintain two types of bank accounts: a **firm** or **general account** and a **trust account** and to reconcile them monthly.

Firm or General Account

Deposit in this account all money that

1. belongs entirely to the law firm;
2. is received on account of fees for which an account has been rendered or is received to reimburse the law firm for disbursements made or expenses incurred on behalf of a client; or
3. is received by way of an agreed retainer or is received as an agreed fee in advance, where the law firm is entitled to such money regardless of whether services are rendered or disbursements are made.

Trust Account

Deposit in this account all money that

1. is received by the law firm and belongs in whole or in part to a client or that is to be held on the client's behalf or to his or her or another's direction or order, including money advanced on account of fees for services not yet rendered or money advanced on account of disbursements not yet made or

Figure 5.9 Cash Receipts Form

CASH RECEIPTS

CLIENT/MATTER NO. _____ 1 _____ DATE: _____ 2 _____

MATTER _____ 3 _____

RECEIVED FROM: _____ 4 _____

AMOUNT RECEIVED $ _____ 5 _____

CREDIT FUNDS TO: Accounts Receivable _____ 7 _____   Cash _____ 6 _____

                     Trust _____ 7 _____   Cheque _____ 6 _____

                     Other: _____ 7 _____

PARTICULARS: _____ 8 _____

_____ 9 _____
Signature

LEGEND

1. Client/matter number
2. Date of preparation
3. Name of matter
4. Name of party making payment
5. Amount of payment received
6. Insert an "x" on appropriate line
7. Insert an "x" on appropriate line to indicate whether funds are in payment of a rendered account or deposited in trust (e.g., a retainer) or as specified by the lawyer
8. What payment covers or to be used for
9. Signature of lawyer forwarding funds. The legal assistant may sign lawyer's name on his/her behalf and include their initials.

CASH RECEIPTS

CLIENT/MATTER NO. _____ 04569/1139 _____ DATE: _Mar. 31, 20___

MATTER _____ Braidwood and Revelle, Purchase of 1097 Garydale Wood Road, Bolton _____

RECEIVED FROM: _____ Matthew and Melissa Braidwood _____

AMOUNT RECEIVED $ _42,397.07_

CREDIT FUNDS TO: Accounts Receivable _____   Cash _____

                     Trust _____ x _____   Cheque _____ x _____

                     Other: _____

PARTICULARS: _____ Funds provided by client to close real estate transaction _____

Lynda C. Ritchie
Signature

2. represents in part money belonging to a client and in part money belonging to the law firm, where it is not practicable to split the payment.

Money may be transferred from the trust account to the firm or general account only when authorized by the lawyer. Many law firms have a special account form for this purpose.

ACCOUNTS

Depending on the practice followed by the law office, accounts may be rendered to a client at intervals during the conduct of a matter or at the completion of a case or matter. Many law firms render accounts for disbursements at regular intervals, often monthly. Accounts may be prepared on letter- or legal-size paper using paper printed with the firm's letterhead or may be completed using a recorded account form. When prepared electronically directly from the computer docket information, the account is frequently set out on plain paper. Note that the law firm's GST registration number must appear on all accounts.

Billing Report

When an account is to be prepared, the lawyer will usually request a billing report from the accounting department showing a summary of time and disbursements to date. Such a report not only sets out the time spent by each lawyer or law clerk/paralegal working on the matter but also assigns a dollar value to that time, depending on the hourly rate established for each lawyer or law clerk/paralegal. These hourly rates vary, depending on the lawyer's experience and expertise, and do not represent the individual earnings for that person. Fees charged to a client belong to the law firm and are used not only to reimburse the lawyer who handled the matter but also to pay for the salaries of associate lawyers and support staff, rent for the office space, furniture and equipment, employee benefits, pensions and all contributory insurance plans, and various other costs of running the law office.

The form of the billing report varies from office to office. If the docket information is stored electronically, the lawyer will receive a computer printout setting out a chronological record of all time entries and disbursements, a summary of time expressed in both hours and dollar values, and disbursements by category (Figure 5.10, p. 84).

Style of Accounts

Law firms that have an electronic accounting system may use the software to create both the billing report and the final account once the billing report has been reviewed by the lawyer and any necessary amendments have been made.

Alternatively, a legal assistant may prepare the account, which may be set out on a form recorded in the computer memory. Precedent 5.1 illustrates a specimen recorded account template; each asterisk (*) represents a field where information

Figure 5.10 Prebilling Report Created Using PCLaw™

Amanda Robinson   March 30, 20___
429 Melrose Avenue
Toronto ON M4M 3G8
Attention: File #:   3445-001
                                                             Inv. #:   Sample

RE: Personal Injury

DATE	DESCRIPTION	HOURS	AMOUNT	LAWYER
Feb-01-xx	Correspondence to Dr. Singh	0.10	25.00	PTG
	Attendance at court to issue statement of claim	0.20	10.00	MJA
Feb-12-xx	Review documents from medical file	0.80	200.00	PTG
Feb-22-xx	Telephone call with adjuster	0.30	75.00	PTG
Mar-04-xx	Telephone call to client	0.20	50.00	PTG
Mar-10-xx	Drafting letter to insurance company re settlement	0.50	125.00	PTG
Mar-24-xx	Review of letter from Mars Insurance and discussing same with client	0.50	125.00	PTG
Mar-30-xx	Receipt and review of letter and settlement funds from insurance company; forwarding same to client	0.60	150.00	PTG
	Totals	3.10	$760.00	
	GST on Fees		$38.00	

FEE SUMMARY:

Lawyers	Hours	Effective Rate	Amount
Peter T. Grant	3.00	$250.00	$750.00
Jennifer Stauffer	.20	$50.00	$10.00

DISBURSEMENTS

		Disbursements	Receipts
Feb-01-xx	Photocopies	3.50	
Feb-12-xx	Issue Statement of Claim*	181.00	
Feb-12-xx	Transaction Levy: Statement of Claim	50.00	
	Totals	$234.50	$0.00
	GST on Disbursements	$2.68	

Total Fees, Disbursements, & GST	1,043.31
Previous Balance	$0.00
Previous Payments	$0.00
Balance Due Now	**$1,035.18**
AMOUNT QUOTED:	**$0.00**

Source: PCLaw™ screen shots used with the permission of LexisNexis Practice Management Systems Inc.

may be inserted. Precedent 5.2 shows a completed account using this template. There are many acceptable styles for accounts, depending on the preference of the law firm. Precedent 5.3 illustrates an alternative style.

Information in Accounts

The following information is usually included in an account rendered to a client:

1. Name and address of the person(s), company, or law firm to whom the account is to be sent for payment
2. Initials of the lawyer rendering the account as a traditional reference line
3. Docket or file number, shown either as part of the subject line or on an "Our Reference No." or "Our File No." line printed on the account form
4. A subject line containing information on the matter for which services were performed. If the subject line normally contains the name of the client to whom the account is addressed, that name may be omitted from the subject line on the account.
5. The period covered by the account, typed in a variety of locations:
   a. down the left-hand side of the account;
   b. after the introductory words of the body; or
   c. before the introductory words
6. The nature of the services rendered, described in the body of the account in the left two-thirds of the page and prefaced with opening words such as

   TO PROFESSIONAL SERVICES rendered during the period...
   TO OUR PROFESSIONAL SERVICES...
   TO OUR SERVICES HEREIN...

   The body of the account is either single or double spaced; there may be one running paragraph, or each subsection may be an individual paragraph. In some instances (for example, when rendering accounts to government departments), it is necessary to itemize chronologically each service rendered (Precedent 5.3).
7. The amount of fees plus applicable GST, the amount of taxable disbursements and the amount of GST, the amount of tax exempt disbursements, and the total of these items
8. The amount of any monies previously paid that apply to the account and the balance due when this amount is deducted from the total of the fees and disbursements
9. The date of the account, shown either in the heading or at the end on a line following the total amount of the account. Because the law firm is responsible from the date of rendering the account for the payment to the government of the GST charged to the client, many firms require that the account not be dated until the actual day it is to be sent out. Follow the preference of your law office in this matter.
10. A signature by the lawyer rendering the account on behalf of the law firm, if that is the firm's custom

11. The abbreviation *E. & O.E.* (errors and omissions excepted) at the end of the account, if that is the firm's preference
12. The law firm's GST registration number. This is frequently part of the printed or recorded account form.

Number of Copies

If the account is prepared electronically, the number of copies printed out will depend on the preference of the law office. For example, the computer may be programmed to print out not only the copies to be sent to the client but also copies for the accounting department and the billing lawyer, as well as a reminder copy to be sent to the client if payment is not received within a specified period of time.

If the account is fully keyed by the legal assistant, he or she should prepare a minimum of four copies. The original and one copy are sent to the client, one copy is for the accounting department, and one copy is for the office file. Additional copies are often required if the office requires that rendered accounts be approved before submission by the accounting department or a specified individual in the office.

Interest

A law firm has the right to charge interest on unpaid accounts. A statement similar to that illustrated in Precedents 5.1, 5.2, and 5.3 is included in the account, if that is the practice of the law firm.

Monies Received

If monies are received to apply against fees and disbursements before the account is rendered, the account is either marked "Paid in Full" or shows the amount of the account less the monies received and the balance still owing.

TRANSACTION LEVY SURCHARGE

In Ontario, law firms are required to pay a **transaction levy surcharge** in connection with real estate and litigation files. This levy is submitted to the Lawyer's Professional Indemnity Fund on a regular basis, and these funds are used in connection with real estate and litigation malpractice claims. The surcharge as of January 1, 2008, is $50.00 plus GST and is levied only for the first document that is filed with a government office (such as the registry or court office) in any real estate or litigation matter. Thus, if a deed and mortgage are both registered at the same time when a house is purchased, there would be only one transaction levy surcharge. The transaction levy surcharge is waived if title insurance (discussed in Chapter 20) is obtained by the purchasers. This transaction levy is billed to the client as a disbursement in the account. Note that it is not part of the filing or registration fee for the document but is charged separately to the client's account at the time of requisitioning the cheque for the filing or registration fee.

LEGAL AID ACCOUNTS

Legal aid accounts are submitted to the provincial legal aid plan and are settled by legal accounts officers. The account is submitted by the lawyer who accepted the legal aid certificate, not by the law firm with whom the lawyer is associated. It is the lawyer who is paid; if he or she has a commitment for the monies received by his or her law firm, that is not the concern of the legal aid plan. Legal aid accounts are prepared on standard special forms or electronically in accordance with detailed instructions set out by the legal aid plan for each province.

CLOSING THE DOCKET

When a matter is completed and the rendered account completes the work to be performed on behalf of a client, both the file and the docket are closed. The accounting department may automatically close the docket or may require notification to do so. The practice varies from office to office; follow carefully the procedure of the law office in which you are employed.

When payment of the rendered account is received, the cheque may go directly to the accounting department from the mailroom, and that department will advise the lawyer of the payment; alternatively, the cheque may initially be given to the lawyer concerned, who will forward it to the accounting department. Many law offices require that a cash receipt form be completed to accompany the cheque and any copy of the account returned by the client. The account is usually receipted and returned to the client.

It is courteous to write a short letter of acknowledgement of payment by a client; the receipted account can be included with it. Such a letter might follow this wording:

> *Dear (name):*
> *(subject line)*
> *Thank you for your letter of (date) enclosing your cheque for (amount) in payment of our account in the above matter. The receipted account is enclosed for your records.*

No docket entry is made, of course, for such a letter when the account is a final one; an entry is made only if the account was an interim one.

Terms and Concepts

legal fees	Goods and Services Tax (GST)
time value/hourly	Harmonized Sales Tax (HST)
billable and unbillable time	dockets
nonbillable time	docket entries
tariff	time charges
estimated/flat fee	disbursement charges
contingency fee	receipts
disbursements	daily time records

classification of disbursements
cheque requisition
petty cash voucher
cash receipts
firm or general account
trust account

petty cash
account calculation and preparation
billing report
E. & O.E.
transaction levy surcharge

Review Questions

1. Explain the following legal fee structures:
   a. time value/hourly
   b. tariff
   c. estimated/flat fee
   d. contingency fee

2. Name and explain the three types of docket entries.

3. Why do lawyers record the time spent working on a matter for a client?

4. Why should you endeavour to ensure that daily time entries are submitted promptly?

5. What types of bank accounts will a law firm maintain? Give an example of what monies would be deposited in such an account or accounts.

6. Why is it necessary to classify disbursements made on behalf of the client?

7. Give two examples of taxable disbursements and of exempt disbursements.

8. Explain and give an example of when the following accounting forms would be used:
   a. cheque requisition
   b. petty cash voucher
   c. cash receipt

9. Monies have been received from the client during the course of acting for him or her. How are such monies referred to when the account is rendered?

*

in account with
Hill, Johnston & Grant

17 Princess Street South, Suite 2501
City, Province Postal Code

GST Registration No. R964802753

Re: *
Our File No.   *

TO PROFESSIONAL SERVICES RENDERED for the period from
* to *, in connection with the above matter, including the following:

*

	OUR FEE:	$	*
	GST (5%)		*

DISBURSEMENTS

Subject to GST
* $ *
*   *
*   *
                                         *
      Subtotal   *
      GST (5%)   *   *

Not Subject to GST
* $ *
*   *
*   *   *

                                   Subtotal $ *
Less payment received from trust (date)   *

                                   BALANCE DUE: $ *

HILL, JOHNSTON & GRANT

                Per:

(date)
PTG/ri
E. & O.E.

*Payment due upon receipt.. In accordance with the Solicitors Act, interest will be charged at the rate of *% per year
on unpaid fees, charges, or disbursements calculated from a date that is one month after this statement is delivered.*

Miss Joyce Growski
400 Prince Henry Road
Edmonton AB T5A 3G2

in account with

Hill, Johnston & Grant

17 Princess Street South, Suite 2501
City, Province Postal Code

GST Registration No. R964802753

| Re: | New Will |
| Our File No. | 04172/1277 |

TO PROFESSIONAL SERVICES RENDERED for the period from January 5
to 10, 20___, in connection with the above matter, including the following:

Interview with you to receive instructions on the revisions to your present will;
drafting new will and forwarding to you for review; telephone conversation
with you in regard to changes; preparing revised will and telephone call to you;
attended on you to execute will.

| | | OUR FEE: | $ | 350.00 |
| | | GST (5%) | | 17.50 |

DISBURSEMENTS

Subject to GST
| Photocopies | $ | 6.50 | |
| Courier Services | | 14.00 | |

| Subtotal | 20.50 | |
| GST (5%) | 1.03 | 21.53 |

Not Subject to GST
| Deposit Will | 20.00 | 20.00 |

| | | Subtotal | $ | 409.03 |
| Less payment received from trust, January 30, 20___ | | | | 200.00 |

| | | BALANCE DUE: | $ | 209.03 |

HILL, JOHNSTON & GRANT

Per:

January 30, 20___
PTG/ri
E. & O.E.

*Payment due upon receipt.. In accordance with the Solicitors Act, interest will be charged at the rate of 10% per year
on unpaid fees, charges, or disbursements calculated from a date that is one month after this statement is delivered.*

Miss Joyce Growski
400 Prince Henry Road
Edmonton AB T5A 3G2

in account with

Hill, Johnston & Grant

Suite 2501, 17 Princess Street South
City, Province Postal Code

LAWYER'S INITIALS	DATE	GST REGISTRATION NO.	FILE NUMBER
PTG	January 8, 20__	R9646802753	04172/1276

New Will

TO PROFESSIONAL SERVICES RENDERED as follows:

2007
December 19   Interview with you to receive instructions on
the revisions to your present will;

December 20   Drafting of new will and forwarding to you
for review;

2008
January 4   Attending on you at your home to execute will

January 5   Attending to deposit will with registrar

OUR FEE		$ 350.00
GST (5%)		17.50

DISBURSEMENTS
Subject to GST

Photocopies		$ 6.50	
Courier Services		14.00	
Subtotal			
GST (5%)		20.50	
		1.03	21.53

Not Subject to GST

Deposit Will		20.00	20.00
BALANCE DUE			$409.03

HILL, JOHNSTON & GRANT

Per:

PTG/urs
E. & O. E.

*Payment due upon receipt. In accordance with the Solicitors Act, interest will be charged at the rate of 10% per year
on unpaid fees, charges, or disbursements calculated from a date that is one month after this statement is delivered.*

CHAPTER 6

Legal Citations

OBJECTIVES:

- Distinguish between statute law and case law and explain the significance of each

- Define and describe the various legal publications, such as acts, regulations, gazettes, and law reports, and how they may be located

- Prepare memoranda of law and letters incorporating citations

In their work, lawyers deal with problems and situations governed by principles of common law or statute law, and the ability of lawyers, law clerks/paralegals, and legal administrative assistants to accurately cite the law is an essential part of legal advocacy.

Common law is based on unwritten custom and long-established practices. Much of this law is based on court decisions made by judges; this is referred to as **case law** or **precedent**. The decision of a judge in a matter must be followed by all lower court judges dealing with similar matters, until the decision is changed by a higher court.

Statute law is based on the legislation passed by Parliament or provincial legislatures in the form of **acts**. This form of law has put into writing many common law principles and is sometimes referred to as written law.

When referring to a source of law, the lawyer is said to **cite** it, and the actual reference is called a **citation**. The citation provides a way to accurately locate the law (whether case or statute) that is being relied on in the legal situation being reviewed.

STATUTE LAW

The federal *Constitution Act* sets out the divisions of legislative power between the federal government and the provinces; this division was originally set out in 1867 in the *British North America Act*. Each province, in turn, may grant power to its municipalities (for example, to a city) to pass by-laws and ordinances.

Statutes

Legislation passed by the federal government or a provincial legislature is known as an act; all acts in effect in a province and in Canada are known as statutes.

Each year, Canada and each province publish volumes containing all new acts passed during the previous legislative year, as well as amendments to existing acts, and these are identified by year (for example, Statutes of Ontario 2007). These statutes are referred to by the following abbreviations:

Name of Statutes	Abbreviation
Statutes of Canada	S.C.
Statutes of Alberta	S.A.
Statutes of British Columbia	S.B.C.
Statutes of Manitoba	S.M.
Statutes of New Brunswick	S.N.B.
Statutes of Newfoundland and Labrador	S.N.
Statutes of Nova Scotia	S.N.S.
Statutes of the Northwest Territories	S.N.W.T.
Statutes of Nunavut	S.Nu.
Statutes of Ontario	S.O.
Statutes of Prince Edward Island	S.P.E.I.
Statutes of Quebec	S.Q.
Statutes of Saskatchewan	S.S.
Statutes of Yukon	S.Y.

Revised Statutes

At certain intervals, which vary provincially and federally, all existing acts of Canada and the provinces and territories are published, including all amendments made to them since the last publication, and are referred to as revised statutes. These are identified by the year of consolidation (for example, Revised Statutes of Canada 1985). The revised statutes are referred to by the following abbreviations:

Name of Statutes	Abbreviation
Revised Statutes of Canada	R.S.C.
Revised Statutes of Alberta	R.S.A.
Revised Statutes of British Columbia	R.S.B.C.
Revised Statutes of Manitoba	R.S.M.
Revised Statutes of New Brunswick	R.S.N.B.
Revised Statutes of Newfoundland and Labrador	R.S.N.
Revised Statutes of Nova Scotia	R.S.N.S.
Revised Statutes of the Northwest Territories	R.S.N.W.T.
Revised Statutes of Nunavut	R.S.Nu.
Revised Statutes of Ontario	R.S.O.
Revised Statutes of Prince Edward Island	R.S.P.E.I.
Revised Statutes of Quebec	R.S.Q.
Revised Statutes of Saskatchewan	R.S.S.
Revised Statutes of Yukon	R.S.Y.

Order of Acts in Statutes

In publications of both statutes and revised statutes, the acts appear in alphabetical order; each act is a numbered chapter. Several provinces, such as British Columbia, follow a straight numerical sequence, for example, Chapter 1, Chapter 2. Federal statutes and those of many other provinces, including Ontario, follow an alphanumeric sequence, for example, Chapter C-2 (federal) or Chapter C.2 (Ontario).

Names of Acts

When an act is passed, it is given a name that clearly identifies its main purpose; for example, the *Age of Majority Act* establishes the age at which an individual is deemed to be an adult and may vote in provincial and federal elections. The article "the" is part of the proper name of an act in the provinces of Manitoba and Saskatchewan, for example, *The Manitoba Hydro Act*. For all other provinces, territories, and federal acts, "the" is not part of the proper name of the act, for example, the *Trustee Act*.

Locating Acts

Although most law firms will maintain a copy of any statutes (including updates) that are applicable to the areas of law in which they practise, most federal and provincial statutes may also now be accessed electronically through government-sponsored websites, as well as the electronic databases discussed later in this chapter. Below is a list of applicable government websites:

Jurisdiction	Provider	URL
Canada	Department of Justice, Canada	http://laws.justice.gc.ca/
Alberta	Alberta's Queen's Printer	http://www.qp.gov.ab.ca/index.cfm
British Columbia	British Columbia Queen's Printer	http://www.qp.gov.bc.ca/statreg/
Manitoba	Queen's Printer for Manitoba	http://www.gov.mb.ca/chc/statpub/
New Brunswick	Queen's Printer for New Brunswick	http://www.gov.mb.ca/chc/statpub/
Newfoundland and Labrador	House of Assembly	http://www.hoa.gov.nl.ca/hoa/sr/
Nova Scotia	Nova Scotia Legislative Counsel	http://www.gov.ns.ca/legislature/legc/
Northwest Territories	Department of Justice	http://www.justice.gov.nt.ca/
Nunavut	Department of Justice	http://www.justice.gov.nu.ca/
Ontario	Ministry of Government Services	http://www.justice.gov.nu.ca/
Prince Edward Island	Legislative Counsel Office	http://www.gov.pe.ca/law/
Quebec	Publications Québec	http://www.publicationsduquebec.gouv.qc.ca
Saskatchewan	Queen's Printer	http://www.qp.gov.sk.ca/
Yukon	Department of Justice	http://www.justice.gov.yk.ca/

Although government websites may be considered reliable, remember to review any disclaimer on the website stating how comprehensive and current the site is. This should always be taken into consideration when conducting and relying on Internet research.

References to Acts

When any reference, or citation, to a statute is made, it must contain the following information:

1. the name of the act (in italics or underlined)
2. the abbreviation for the statute or revised statutes and year
3. the chapter number (including the alpha letter if applicable)
4. the section/subsections (if applicable)

Each part of the citation is separated by a comma. See the following examples:

Name of Act	Statute	Chapter	Section/Subsections
Canada Business Corporations Act,	R.S.C. 1985,	c. C-44,	s. 1(d)(iii)
Alberta Health Care Insurance Act,	R.S.A. 2000,	c. A-20	

If the act has not yet been consolidated, the year in which the act was passed is shown as part of the name of the act, in addition to the statute reference. For example:

Name of Act	Statute	Chapter	Section/Subsections
Ammunition Regulation Act, 1994,	S.O. 1994,	c. 20,	s. 4(1)

REGULATIONS

The acts of a province or of Canada stipulate the law on a particular topic; **regulations** are published to indicate how the law is to be carried out or administered. For example, the *Courts of Justice Act*, R.S.O. 1990, c. C.43, sets out the structure and jurisdiction of courts in Ontario. The *Rules of Civil Procedure* contain the regulations providing how the provisions of this act are to be carried out covering such matters as how a legal proceeding is commenced in the courts, the form of required documents, where proceedings are to be heard, and how orders of the court are to be enforced.

Periodically, all existing regulations are consolidated in volumes known as the revised or consolidated regulations, identified by the year of consolidation; for example, for Canada, consolidated regulations are identified as *Consolidated Regulations of Canada*, or C.R.C.; for Ontario, they are identified as *Revised Regulations of Ontario*, or R.R.O., with the appropriate year. In consolidations, the regulations are arranged in alphabetical order and are identified by consecutive chapter numbers.

Subsequent to the publication of the consolidated revised regulations, new regulations are published in the appropriate gazette, discussed below, and are usually identified by a regulations number, commencing at 1 for each calendar year, and the year it was passed. Note that some provinces show all four digits for the year; others use only two. For example:

O. Reg. 48/06: refers to the 48th consecutive regulation passed in Ontario in 2006

N.S. Reg. 83/2007: refers to the 83rd consecutive regulation passed in Nova Scotia in 2007

For Canada, regulations are identified by Statutory Orders and Regulations numbers commencing at 1 for each calendar year. For example:

SOR/2006-347

GAZETTES

The provinces and territories, as well as Canada, issue official publications entitled "gazettes" at regular intervals to provide information on statutory notices, royal assent to new acts, appointments, new regulations, etc. The following is a list of the gazettes that are available free to the general public in full-text versions online:

Name of Publication	Website
Canada Gazette	http://canadagazette.gc.ca/
Alberta Gazette	http://www.qp.gov.ab.ca/display_gazette.cfm
Ontario Gazette	http://www.ontariogazette.gov.on.ca/
Royal Gazette (Prince Edward Island)	http://www.gov.pe.ca/royalgazette/
Royal Gazette (New Brunswick)	http://www.gnb.ca/0062/gazette/index-e.asp
Newfoundland and Labrador Gazette	http://www.gs.gov.nl.ca/gs/oqp/gazette/
Nunavut Gazette	http://www.justice.gov.nu.ca/english/gazette/
Yukon Gazette	http://gazette.gov.yk.ca/home.html

Alternatively, copies of all provincial, territorial and federal gazettes may be subscribed to for a fee either electronically or in hard copy and may also be found in the law office or public library. These "gazettes" are important because once an act or regulation is published in a gazette, it is considered publicly and officially published.

CASE LAW

When a court decision is made that is thought to be of great interest to lawyers, it is reported in a **law report**, which is a published account of a legal proceeding. The report outlines the facts of the case, the arguments put forth by all parties involved, the judgment given by the court, and the reasons for that judgment. Lawyers are very interested in such decisions since the judgment arrived at in one case must be followed in another case where the facts are the same, until a higher court changes the decision. In acting for a client, the lawyer frequently wishes to know the decision of the courts in similar situations and will refer to previously decided cases.

LAW REPORTS

There are many published law reports. Lawyers subscribe to the series of reports published for the province in which they practise, as well as to the reports of cases decided in the Supreme Court of Canada. Many series are published weekly or monthly in booklet form or may be subscribed to electronically. At regular intervals (often after 10 booklets have been published), the booklets are sent out to be bound into a hardcover volume.

Abbreviations for Law Reports

Abbreviations for the more frequently encountered Canadian law reports are shown in Table 6.1. Not all series are still being published, but reference is still made to cases they reported.

References may also be made to English reports, some of which are listed in Table 6.2 (p. 102). When in doubt about the correct abbreviation for a law report not shown in Table 6.1 or 6.2, refer to the *Canadian Guide to Uniform Legal Citation*, 6th Edition (Thomson Carswell), a copy of which is usually available in the law office library.

Identification of Bound Volumes of Law Reports

Each series of law reports is contained in bound volumes, identified by the abbreviation for the law report and either by year or by consecutive volume number. Frequently, when a law report is identified by year, there are several published volumes of that law report in the year. It is necessary to indicate which volume for that year is being referred to; for example, including a 2 or a 3 indicates that it is the second or third volume in the year. Some law reports have been identified by volume alone at one time and by year at other times.

Table 6.1 provides a guide for determining whether a Canadian case is cited by year or by volume. When square brackets appear before the abbreviation for the law report, the report is cited by year.

Table 6.1 Guide to Citing Canadian Law Reports

LAW REPORT	PERIOD	ABBREVIATION
Alberta Law Reports	1908–1933	Alta. L.R.
	1976–1992	Alta. L.R. (2d)
	1992–	Alta. L.R. (3d)
Alberta Reports	1976–	A.R.
All Canada Weekly Summaries	1970–1979	[ ] A.C.W.S.
	1980–1986	A.C.W.S. (2d)
	1986–	A.C.W.S. (3d)
Atlantic Provinces Report	1975–	A.P.R.
British Columbia Reports	1867–1947	B.C.R.
British Columbia Law Reports	1977–1986	B.C.L.R.
	1986–1995	B.C.L.R. (2d)
	1995–	B.C.L.R. (3d)
Business Law Reports	1977–1990	B.L.R.
	1991–1999	B.L.R. (2d)
	2000–	B.L.R. (3d)
Canadian Bankruptcy Reports	1920–1960	C.B.R.
	1960–1990	C.B.R. (N.S.)
	1991–1998	C.B.R. (3d)
	1998–	C.B.R. (4th)
Canadian Cases on the Law of Torts	1976–1990	C.C.L.T.
	1990–2000	C.C.L.T. (2d)
	2000–	C.C.L.T. (3d)
Canadian Intellectual Property Reports	1984–1990	C.I.P.R.
Canadian Patent Reporter	1941–1971	C.P.R.
	1971–1984	C.P.R. (2d)
	1985–1999	C.P.R. (3d)
	1999–	C.P.R. (4th)
Carswell''s Practice Cases	1976–1985	C.P.C.
	1985–1992	C.P.C. (2d)
	1992–1997	C.P.C. (3d)
	1997–2000	C.P.C. (4th)
	2001–2005	C.P.C. (5th)
	2006–	C.P.C. (6th)

Table 6.1 Guide to Citing Canadian Law Reports (continued)

LAW REPORT	PERIOD	ABBREVIATION
Dominion Law Reports	1912–1922	D.L.R.
	1923–1955	[ ] D.L.R.
	1956–1968	D.L.R. (2d)
	1969–1984	D.L.R. (3d)
	1984–	D.L.R. (4th)
Eastern Law Reporter	1906–1915	E.L.R.
Estates & Trusts Reports	1977–1994	E.T.R.
	1994–	E.T.R. (2d)
Federal Court Reports	1971–	[ ] F.C.
Labour Arbitration Cases	1948–1972	L.A.C.
	1973–1981	L.A.C. (2d)
	1982–1989	L.A.C. (3d)
	1989–	L.A.C. (4th)
Manitoba Reports	1883–1961	Man. R.
	1979–	Man. R. (2d)
Maritime Provinces Reports	1929–1968	M.P.R.
Motor Vehicle Reports	1979–1988	M.V.R.
	1988–1994	M.V.R. (2d)
	1994–2000	M.V.R. (3d)
	2000–	M.V.R. (4th)
National Reporter	1973–	N.R.
New Brunswick Reports	1825–1928	N.B.R.
	1969–	N.B.R. (2d)
Newfoundland & Prince Edward Island Reports	1971–	Nfld. & P.E.I.R.
Northwest Territories Reports	1983–1998	[ ] N.W.T.R.
Nova Scotia Reports	1834–1929	N.S.R.
	1965–1969	N.S.R.
	1969–	N.S.R. (2d)
Ontario Appeal Reports	1876–1900	O.A.R.

Table 6.1 Guide to Citing Canadian Law Reports (continued)

LAW REPORT	PERIOD	ABBREVIATION
Ontario Law Reports	1901–1931	O.L.R.
Ontario Practice Reports	1850–1901	O.P.R.
Ontario Reports	1882–1900	O.R.
	1931–1973	[ ] O.R.
	1973–1990	O.R. (2d)
	1991–	O.R. (3d)
Ontario Weekly Notes	1909–1932	O.W.N.
	1933–1962	[ ] O.W.N.
Real Property Reports	1977–1988	R.P.R.
	1988–1996	R.P.R. (2d)
	1996–	R.P.R. (3d)
Reports of Family Law	1971–1978	R.F.L.
	1978–1986	R.F.L. (2d)
	1986–1994	R.F.L. (3d)
	1994–2000	R.F.L. (4th)
	2000–	R.F.L. (5th)
Reports of Family Law (Reprint Series)	1824–1970	R.F.L. Rep.
Saskatchewan Law Reports	1907–1931	Sask. L.R.
Saskatchewan Reports	1980–	S.R.
Canada Law Reports: Supreme Court of Canada	1923–1969	[ ] S.C.R.
Canada Supreme Court Reports	1877–1922	S.C.R.
	1970–	[ ] S.C.R.
Western Law Reporter	1905–1917	W.L.R.
Western Weekly Reports	1911–1916	W.W.R.
	1917–1950	[ ] W.W.R.
	1951–1970	W.W.R. (N.S.)
	1971–	[ ] W.W.R.

Table 6.2 Guide to Abbreviations for Some English Law Reports

REPORT	ABBREVIATION
All England Reports, 1936–	All E.R.
All England Law Reports, 1999–	All E.R.
Law Reports, Appeal Case	A.C.
Law Reports, Chancery Division	Ch.
Law Reports, King's Bench Division	K.B.
Queen's Bench Reports	Q.B.
Law Reports, Probate, Divorce, and Admiralty Division	P.

NOTE: The year is not an essential part of any English case having a date prior to 1891.

Preparing Citations of Law Reports

A keyed reference to a law report has the following elements:

1. Name of the case (referred to as the **style of cause** or **title of proceeding**) in italics or underscored
2. Year in square or round brackets depending on whether the year is "essential" or "non-essential" in order to locate the law report
3. Volume number (if any), abbreviated name of law report, series (if any)
4. Page number at which the case starts
5. Name of the court (in brackets) that decided the case if not obvious from the name of the report series

The **ONLY** comma is between the case name and the beginning of the reference to its location.

Example 1

Name of Case (Style of Cause)	Year	Volume Number (if any) Abbreviated Name of Law Report Series (if any)	Page Number	Name of Court (if required)
Hart v. Stone	(2001),	75 O.R. (3d)	101	(C.A.)

The following is an explanation of each element of Example 1:

Name of Case

- *Hart v. Stone* is the name of the case, which is also referred to sometimes as the "style of cause" and denotes that this is a lawsuit in which Hart is suing Stone. Only the last names of the first mentioned party on each side are shown; that is, *et al.* or *and others* is not included if there are additional parties on either side.
- The "v." is an abbreviation for versus. The names of the parties and the "v." are italicized or may be underlined (but not both).
- Note that a style of cause of *R. v. Stone* would be a reference to a criminal case against Stone. The "R" refers to the Latin word for queen—*regina*—in legal citations.
- Note that a style of cause of *Re Hart and Stone* would indicate a case that was an application to the court for its determination.

Year

- The year denotes when the judgment was handed by the court in this case, which is also the year in which it was published. If the decision and the publication date are different, then both may be shown, but this is not the usual practice.
- If the year is not required to locate the law report, then any reference to a year is said to be "non-essential" and appears in round brackets followed by a comma, as shown in this example. This is how most law reports are now organized, with the notable exception of the Supreme Court Reports, discussed below.

Volume, Law Report, Series

- 75 O.R. (3d) denotes that this case may be found in the 75th volume of the 3rd series of the *Ontario Reports*.
- Frequently, law reports identified by volume number have several series, each commencing with Volume 1 and continuing indefinitely until a new series is started. It is then necessary to indicate which series the volume is part of by including a (2d), (3d), or (N.S.) following the name of the law report to indicate the second, third, or new series of that report.

Page Number

- 101 denotes that this case is reported beginning on page 101 of the applicable volume of the report.
- Note that the word "page" is not included.

Name of Court

- (C.A.) refers to the Court of Appeal.
- This reference is included because the assumption might otherwise be made that this was a decision of a lower court.

Example 2			
Name of Case (Style of Cause)	Year	Volume Number (if any) Abbreviated Name of Law Report Series (if any)	Page Number
Re Hart Holding Ltd. and Stone,	[2006]	1 S.C.R.	46

The following is an explanation of each element of this second example:

Name of Case

- In this proceeding, one of the parties is a corporation, so the full name of the corporation is shown, along with just the last name of the second party, who is an individual.
- Note that the "Re" is included in the name of the case and denotes that it is an application proceeding with the names separated by *and* instead of *v.*

Year

- The year still denotes when the judgment was handed down by the court.
- The year, however, is now also "essential" because in this report series, the volume is designated first by year and then by volume within the year; that is, a new sequence of volume numbers begins each year.
- Square brackets are used to denote that the series is organized by year, and the comma now appears before the year following the style of cause.

Volume, Law Report, Series

- 1 S.C.R. denotes that this case may be found in the 1st volume of the Supreme Court Reports for 2006.

Page Number

- 46 denotes that this case is reported beginning on page 46 of the applicable volume of the report.

Name of the Court

- The name of the court is not included as it is obvious from the name of the report.

Pinpoint References

If a certain page or paragraph of the law report is being quoted or merits special attention, a **pinpoint reference** may be made to this section of the law report. If the reference is to a certain paragraph (which is becoming more common with electronic documents), the abbreviations "para." or "paras." should be used, followed by the applicable paragraph number or numbers. If the reference is to a certain page or pages, it is not preceded by the word "page" or "pages"; just the actual page number or numbers are keyed in. These references are always preceded by the word *at*, as shown in the following examples:

British Columbia v. Tenner (1985), 28 B.C.L.R. (2d) 241 at para. 41
R. v. Faid (1983), 3 W.W.R. 673 at 675–676

More than One Report Cited

Many decided cases are reported in more than one law report; these are referred to as **parallel citations**. When citing such cases, the name of the case is set out, followed by each law report in which it may be found. Note that the year of the decision does not need to be repeated with each report and that each parallel citation is separated with the comma. For example:

Fagan v. Emery Investments Ltd. (1986), 54 O.R. (2d) 615, 27 D.L.R. (4th) 257, 3 C.P.C. (2d) 101

NEUTRAL CITATIONS

Since 1999, some Canadian courts have started to assign a neutral citation to their judgments, most notably the Supreme Court of Canada. If the case being reported has a neutral citation, the neutral citation is cited first, followed by any print report citations. The print citation is still required as the neutral citation is only a case identifier and does not identify where the printed report of the case can be found. A neutral citation consists of three parts, as shown in the following example:

Year of Decision	Court	Ordinal Number
2005	SCC	29

The following example shows parallel citations of a case including the neutral citation:

R. v. Sharpe, 2001 SCC 2, [2001] 1 S.C.R. 45, 194 D.L.R. (4th) 1

This citation is of a criminal case that was appealed. The Supreme Court of Canada handed down its decision in 2001, which has the neutral citation of SCC 2, which means that it was the 2nd case decided in 2001. This is followed by the print citation, which was reported in Volume 1 of the Supreme Court Reports of 2001 beginning on page 45, and the parallel citation is in Volume 194 of the 4th series of the Dominion Law Reports beginning on page 1.

ELECTRONIC RESOURCE CITATIONS

Before the introduction of electronic technology, the only way to ascertain the cases related to a particular fact pattern was to determine the key word or phrases that described the legal situation, such as CONTRACTS: *Implied terms - Discretion*. The topical index of reported cases under that key word or phrase was searched, and the applicable cases were read to determine which best supported the current fact pattern. This method was slow and time-consuming. Although it is still necessary to read the applicable cases when they have been determined, electronic technology now permits the quick retrieval of a list of cases to be reviewed on a particular topic using much the same methodology but by using the electronic search engines of legal databases.

Traditionally, a law student or junior lawyer searched the law reports for the appropriate decided cases; however, legal assistants are now sometimes responsible for initiating computer retrieval searches and providing the necessary list or hard copies of appropriate cases or statutes to be reviewed. Subscription services such as LexisNexis Quicklaw™ (http://global.lexisnexis.com/ca) or WestlaweCARSWELL (http://www.westlawecarswell.com/home) or the open access database CanLII (http://www.canlii.org), managed by the Federation of Law Societies of Canada, provide searchable electronic databases of both statute and case law.

In citing these resources, keep the following points in mind:

1. Always cite a printed report first, if possible, in addition to the electronic reference
2. Include the style of cause (in italics) as in a traditional citation, followed by any citations from print reporters, and then key in the reference to the electronic database, which is usually shown at the top of the first page of the case. For example:

   Hebb v. Hebb (1991), 103 N.S.R. (2d) 147, CanLII 2523 (NS C.A.)

3. The URL address is not usually shown (as this may change) and is only used if citing an unreported case that is not available anywhere else. However, this is usually unnecessary as electronic databases have a case identifier or docket number that may be used, as shown in the following examples:

   Bovingdon v. Hergott, 2006 CanLII 31202 (ON S.C.)
   R. v. Shawon, [1995.] S.C.J. No. 9 (QL)

The "S.C.J." abbreviation here refers to Supreme Court Judgments; the abbreviation is also used for each of the provincial and territorial judgment databases. For example, O.C.J. would refer to Ontario Court Judgments, and B.C.J. would refer to British Columbia Judgments. The court identification is then followed by "No." and the identifying number in the Quicklaw database.

MEMORANDA OF LAW

Reference may be made to decided cases in legal correspondence, but the most frequent use is in a special type of memorandum, a **memorandum of law**, that is prepared most frequently for the use of lawyers who practise in the area of civil litigation. When a lawyer is retained to act for a client in a matter that may lead to court proceedings, the lawyer looks for previously decided cases (also called **authorities**) that support the client's position. The individual reading the law finds the names of cases dealing with a problem similar to that of the new client and then reads the cases in the law reports and prepares a memorandum setting out the information learned from the cases. An example of a memorandum of law is shown in Precedent 6.1. The memorandum is usually double spaced, many pages in length, and contains citations of and quotations from the decided cases that have been reviewed. A guide for typing quotations is provided in Chapter 2.

Reference to Judges

The memorandum of law usually indicates the last name of the judge or judges who gave the decision from which material is being quoted, followed by an abbreviation indicating the position of that judge or those judges. The following table lists the accepted abbreviations to be used, including some archaic references that may be encountered in older case law reports:

Abbreviation	Reference
C.J.C.	Chief Justice of Canada
C.J.A.	Chief Justice of Appeal
C.J.	Chief Justice, Chief Judge
J.A.	Justice of Appeal, Judge of Appeals Court
JJ.A.	Justices of Appeal, Judges of Appeals Court
J.	Justice, Judge
JJ.	Justices, Judges
Mag.	Magistrate
Co.Ct.J.	Judge, County Court
D.C.J.	Judge, District Court
Surr.Ct.J.	Judge, Surrogate Court
C.J.H.C.	Chief Justice, High Court

The abbreviation is keyed directly after the name or names of the judge or judges, and there is no comma inserted between the name of the judge and the office. For example:

Austin J.   Callaghan C.J.   Blair, Morden, and Tarnopolsky JJ.A.

Number of Copies

Prepare a minimum of two copies of a memorandum of law: one for the lawyer to whom it is addressed and one for the individual who did the research and prepared the memorandum.

Memoranda Subfile

Memoranda of law should be maintained in a separate subfile identified by the file name and the subname *Memoranda*. Other memoranda of information related to the legal matter are also kept in this file. Memoranda to file that merely record telephone messages or confirm the completion of some procedural step are maintained in the correspondence file.

Terms and Concepts

common law	essential and non-essential dates
case law	style of cause
precedent	title of proceeding
statute law	pinpoint references
acts	parallel citations
cite/citation	neutral citations
statutes	electronic resource citations
revised statutes	memorandum of law
reference to acts	authorities
regulations	reference to judges
gazettes	memorandum subfile
law report citations	

Review Questions

1. Why do lawyers review previous decisions in cases that dealt with a fact situation similar to that of the new client?

2. There are often new acts after the latest series of Revised Statutes of (name). How are such statutes referred to in a citation?

3. The statutes or acts of a province (and Canada) set out the law on a particular topic. What indicates the guidelines to carry out the law set out in that act or statute, and how are they referred to?

4. Bound volumes of published law reports may be identified in two ways. What are they?

5. When a series of law reports is identified by volume number, there may have been several series, each of which commenced with Volume 1. How are those different series identified?

6. What type of legal proceeding is being reported if the citation is
   a. *Re Johanssen and Green*
   b. *R. v. Green*
   c. *Johanssen v. Green*

7. What is meant by the following terms:
   a. pinpoint reference
   b. parallel citation

8. Cite each of the following in the proper format:
   a. Canada Elections Act Statutes of Canada 2000 chapter 9
   b. R. v. Latimer 2001 1 Supreme Court Reports 3 at paragraph 10
   c. Ballard v. Ballard (2001), 201 Newfoundland & PEI Reports 352 at page 355

9. **Internet Research:** Although there is a continuing trend away from Latin terms and specialized abbreviations, some are still used in legal practice, especially in memoranda of law. The following is a list of some of these terms that you should become familiar with. Some are defined in the glossary at the end of this textbook; others will require research on the Internet.

ad hoc	ff
aff'd	*non sequitur*
bona fide	*per se*
de facto	*per stirpes*
de jure	pp.
ex officio	*prima facie*
et seq.	rev'd
ibid	*scienter*
id est	*sine die*
in camera	*supra*
inter alia	*stare decisis*
intra vires	*status quo*
inter vivos	*ultra vires*

Hill, Johnston & Grant

MEMORANDUM

TO: PTG

FROM: AMZ

DATE: January 31, 20__

SUBJECT: Farrier v. Wyers   **File No.**   04973/1364

I have now read the old case which you asked me to review.

Ihde v. Starr (1909), 19 O.L.R. 471 (aff'd 21 O.L.R. 407)

Briefly, this case concerned a dispute between adjoining landowners, the plaintiff claiming that the defendant's buildings and premises were partially situate upon a right of way or "private park preserve," of which she (the plaintiff) and all other landowners in the area were entitled to the use and enjoyment of. The defendant contended that they were purchasers with notice, that the location of her buildings resulted from mutual mistake, and, finally, that the statute of limitations gave her a good defence.

Per Meredith C.J. at 477 et seq.:

> If it were necessary for the decision of the case to determine whether a case for the reformation of the conveyance was made out I would have great difficulty in coming to the conclusion that the respondent had made out such a case. Lord Thurlow's language is very strong on this subject: "The evidence which goes to prove that the words taken down in writing were contrary to the concurrent intention of all parties must be strong evidence."

****

> I find no evidence to support a finding that the appellant purchased with such notice of the respondent's equitable right . . . as is required to defeat the appellant's registered title.

AMZ/ri

CHAPTER 7

Introduction to Legal Documents

OBJECTIVES:

- Distinguish between commercial documents and court documents

- Demonstrate an understanding of municipal divisions and how this applies to legal documentation

- Demonstrate an understanding of the terminology associated with commercial documents

- Use legal precedents to prepare documents such as agreements, affidavits, declarations, notarial certificates, and releases

The tangible product of legal work for clients is often a carefully prepared legal paper. That legal document represents to the client the services that the lawyer has performed for him or her. Both the contents and the overall appearance or formatting of the finished product are a visible reflection of the law firm.

CLASSIFICATION OF LEGAL DOCUMENTS

All legal papers are classified as one of the following:

Commercial documents	Formal legal documents, such as agreements, wills, or real estate documents, that give formal expression to a legal act or agreement. May also be referred to as **legal instruments**.
Court documents	Legal documents prepared for use in legal proceedings brought before the courts or other administrative tribunals. These are discussed in later chapters.

PREPARATION OF LEGAL PAPERS

Certain legal procedures are common in all law offices, whether small or large and regardless of the area of law that is practised. These procedures involve formalizing in writing agreements between parties, verifying the authenticity of an executed legal document, or swearing to the truth of certain statements of fact. Many of these documents are not prescribed by statute, nor is specialized software or templates available. However, a document is sometimes used so frequently that the basic content and form have been recorded, and the document requires only the insertion of particular information to complete it. The clauses to be used in some documents are common to all documents of that type; these clauses have been recorded and are assembled along with the particular information necessary to complete the document. Follow any of the methods discussed in Chapter 2 when preparing such legal documents.

This chapter considers generally the preparation of commercial documents. As specific commercial documents are discussed in subsequent chapters, the special points to be followed in their preparation are noted.

MUNICIPAL DIVISIONS OF A PROVINCE

Before considering legal documents, it is necessary to review the municipal divisions of a province as well as how that information may be required to be set out for legal documents. Canada is currently divided into 10 provinces and 3 territories. The provinces and territories of Canada are, in turn, divided into municipalities that are legally incorporated and governed by councils elected by the voters of each municipality, as illustrated in Figure 7.1.

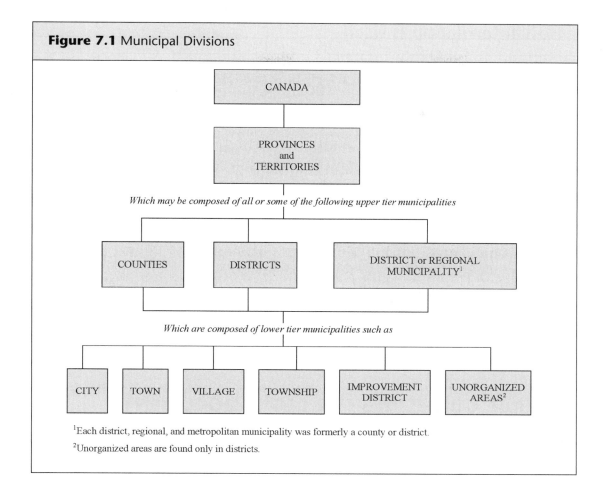

Figure 7.1 Municipal Divisions

Types of Municipalities

In most provinces and territories, there are two tiers or levels of municipalities: an upper tier and a lower tier. Examples of **upper tier municipalities** are counties and districts and regional or district municipalities. Examples of **lower tier municipalities** are cities, towns, villages, hamlets, and townships. Each of these municipalities has its own elections and governing councils. Some provinces have amalgamated several lower and upper tier municipalities into one municipality, for example, the City of Toronto.

Verifying the Status of a Municipality

It may be necessary to check on the upper tier status of a municipality or to determine in which upper tier municipality a lower tier municipality is located. A client may not know the status of the municipality in which he or she lives. This may be done through a government publication, such as a municipal directory, or through provincial government websites that list all upper tier municipalities, together with the lower tier municipalities located in each upper tier municipality, as well as changes in the status of municipalities as a result of annexations, amalgamations, dissolutions, or renamings that took place in previous years.

How Information Is Used

For many years, parties to a legal document were frequently identified by the lower and upper tier municipalities in which they lived, referred to as a general address. For example:

> ...of the City of Whitby, in the Regional Municipality of Durham...
> ...of the City of Halifax, in the Halifax Regional Municipality...
> ...of the City of Sault Ste. Marie, in the District of Algoma...

Alternatively, just the lower tier municipality or amalgamated municipality and the province may be used. For example:

> ...of the City of Brandon, Province of Manitoba...
> ...of the City of Toronto, Province of Ontario...

With the introduction of electronic filing of legal documents, there is a growing trend away from using general addresses. However, for the documents discussed in this chapter, many law firms still use general addresses. Both styles are reflected in the precedents illustrated in this text. As always, you should follow the practice of your firm.

GENERAL GUIDELINES FOR LEGAL DOCUMENT PREPARATION

These general guidelines apply to the preparation of all legal documentation, including the commercial documents discussed in this chapter.

Types of Paper and Margins

Traditionally, legal paper has meant paper measuring 8.5 by 14 inches. Commercial documents have usually been prepared on this size of paper, and many still are. However, many documents, including court documents, wills, and many contracts and agreements, are now prepared on letter-size paper (8.5 by 11 inches). Most law firms prepare all documents on one side of plain, good-quality white paper of the desired length. A 1-inch (25 mm) margin on all sides is the standard guideline, but allow for practice variations.

Document Reference

Commercial documents are often quite lengthy and go through many revisions, and the use of a footer containing a document reference and the date of preparation, as discussed in Chapter 3, is usually required.

Page Endings

A minimum of two lines of text should appear at the end of a page or at the beginning of a page. The widow/orphan function in word processing software facilitates this. Additionally, no signatory clause, whether in a legal document or correspondence, should be on a page by itself.

Bold Font

The use of bold font is always considered optional; however, it is frequently used in commercial documents to enhance the overall appearance of the document. It must, however, be applied consistently; for example, if you bold one section heading, then bold all section headings, etc.

Date

All legal documents must be dated either before or at the time of execution. The location of the date varies in different types of documents. If the date appears within the body or in the ending, it is the date on which the document is or will be signed. If the date is shown in the heading, it is one of the following:

1. the date on which the document was prepared;
2. the date on which the document is to be effective (this indicates that the document is being signed to take effect on a date other than the date of signing, and the heading will show the date "as of..."); or
3. the date on which the document is signed; in this event, the heading is prepared with the date left to be inserted when the document is signed.

Page Numbering

There are different ways to number pages:

1. In one continuous, self-contained document, pages after the initial page are numbered consecutively from 2 to the end of the given number of pages. The first page is not numbered. Numbers are usually centred at the top of the page. Numerical page numbering, such as 2., 3. or -2-, -3-, for example, is the most frequently used style.
2. In a document that consists of a number of individual sections, each of which is started on a new page, each section is treated as a self-contained document for the purposes of page numbering. For example, the first page of Section III would be 1, the second 2, and so on. Pages in self-contained sections are also frequently identified by the section to which they refer, with Arabic numbering used to refer to sections instead of Roman numerals. Each page is then

identified by section number and the appropriate page number; that is, 3-1 represents the first page in Section III; 3-2, the second page in Section III; and so on. The next section, Section IV, is then paginated as 4-1, 4-2, and so on.

Number of Copies

The general rule when preparing legal documents is to prepare one more copy than there are parties signing the document. Thus, if you prepare a release to be signed by one person, two copies would be required. If it is an agreement between four people, then five copies would be required. The extra copy is, of course, for the file.

In this text, the term *original* refers to a completed page or pages that are signed or used as the governing copy of the document; the page or pages may be printed out on a printer attached to a computer or may be a photocopy. The term *copy* refers to a photocopy of the signed or governing copy of the original document. A photocopy is always made of any executed document for the file.

COMMERCIAL DOCUMENTS

In this section, we basically consider the preparation of agreements and contracts; other documents are covered later. In this and subsequent chapters, any reference to an agreement also includes a contract.

Commercial documents usually have four main parts:

1. Heading (which may include the title of the document, the date, and the parties)
2. Body
3. Ending (including attestation and testimonium clauses)
4. Backsheet (also known as an endorsement or back)

Heading

The form of the heading of a commercial document usually briefly identifies the nature of the document, the date of the document, and the parties to it. For example:

> THIS AGREEMENT made the .... of ...., 20__
> KNOW ALL MEN BY THESE PRESENTS THAT I ...
> THIS (type of) CONTRACT made as of the .... day of ...., 20__

Or it may simply be the title of the document, for example, SEPARATION AGREEMENT.

Parties

It is necessary to list the party or parties to a legal document. As mentioned previously, the parties were traditionally listed by name and general address, followed by a descriptive label, and were additionally identified as being "of the first part, "of the second part," etc. (Figure 7.2). However, the current trend is to show the parties by name only, followed by the descriptive label (Figure 7.3).

Figure 7.2 Heading Showing Individual and Corporate Parties, with General Address Description, Name, and Party Label

THIS AGREEMENT made the 31st day of October, 20___

BETWEEN:

CONSTANCE PENELOPE GENTILI,
of the City of Toronto, Province of Ontario

hereinafter referred to as "Gentili"

OF THE FIRST PART

- and -

EAST HARDWARE LIMITED,
a corporation incorporated under the laws
of the Province of Ontario

hereinafter referred to as "East Hardware"

OF THE SECOND PART

Figure 7.3 Heading Showing Individual Parties and Using Name as Label

THIS AGREEMENT made as of the 1st day of February, 20___

BETWEEN:

ANDREW PATRICK CORMACK,
and ALICE ELIZABETH CORMACK

(herein "Cormack")

- and -

RONALD CRAIG ANDERSON

(herein "Anderson")

Follow the style preferred by your lawyer or law firm in listing the parties but note the following general guidelines:

1. The names of the parties are shown in capital letters and may appear in bold-face type if that is the preference of your law office. If additional information other than the names is included, show it in upper- and lowercase.

2. For an individual, show at least the first name, the initial or second name, and the surname.

3. For a corporation, show at least the full legal corporate name. Traditionally, the jurisdiction under which it was incorporated, or both the jurisdiction under which it was incorporated *and* the location of its registered office, is shown, although, again, this is now considered optional.

4. When two individuals are parties with a similar interest, they appear as a single party for the purposes of the descriptive label; however, they are considered two parties for the purposes of signing the legal document.

5. The descriptive label given to a party or parties is used throughout the document whenever reference is made to that party or parties. The parties are identified in this wording by their last name or by terms that define the parties' role in the legal matter. The quotation marks enclosing the last name or role term are omitted when the name or term is used in the body of the document. Some lawyers prefer that this line be enclosed in parentheses; others do not use parentheses. The line traditionally was worded *hereinafter referred to as "..."*, but the wording *herein called the "..."* or just *herein "..."* is now frequently used (Figures 7.2 and 7.3).

Body

The body of an agreement usually begins with **recitals**. These are clauses that provide background information on the parties to the agreement and the general purpose of the agreement itself and are not numbered. The traditional form of agreement has each of these clauses begin with the words "WHEREAS" and "AND WHEREAS," and the final recital begins with "NOW THEREFORE...," as illustrated in Precedent 7.1. Alternatively, any recitals may be shown as an introductory paragraph or paragraphs, as illustrated in Precedent 7.2.

The recitals are followed by paragraphs setting out the terms and conditions of the agreement. These paragraphs may be referred to as articles or clauses and are always numbered for ease of reference. They may also have descriptive headings or titles at the beginning of each new topic (Precedents 7.1 and 7.3).

Certain words or phrases may be delineated to have a specific meaning for that document, and such words are referred to as **definitions** and are shown in brackets with quotation marks, usually with initial capitalization, for example, John Smith and Mary Smith (the "Children"). Any further reference to such a defined term within the document is thus keyed exactly as shown in the bracketed term without the quotation marks (Precedents 7.1 and 7.2).

Note the following additional guidelines in formatting the body of an agreement:

1. Traditionally, the body of the document was double spaced, but single and 1.5 spacing are now also considered acceptable. Follow the preference of your law firm.

2. Leave a bottom margin of no more than 1 inch (or 25 mm) and try to end each page at approximately the same line.

3. Indent paragraphs one or two tabs in most styles; this may vary depending on the style of the body of the legal paper.

4. If a paragraph does not fit on one page, end the page with a minimum of two lines of the paragraph and begin the new page with a minimum of two lines of the carryover paragraph. If the paragraph contains only three lines and two lines will fit on the page within the normal bottom margin, include the third line on the page rather than carry over just one line, or carry over the entire paragraph to the next page. On carryover lines, one full line and part of a line are considered the equivalent of two lines.

5. Show at least two lines of the body of the legal paper on the page with the ending. Reformat your pages to achieve this if necessary.

6. Show amounts in commercial documents first in words and then in numbers in parentheses, as discussed in Chapter 2.

7. A number of variations from the traditional style may be followed when preparing fully keyed commercial papers. Always follow the preference of your lawyer or law firm but ensure that all formatting is consistently applied in order to prepare a professional-looking document. The "Styles" function is Microsoft Word is frequently used to ensure this.

Ending

The ending of a commercial legal document contains the testimonium and attestation clauses and signatures. When you are preparing legal documents, the testimonium and attestation clauses should not appear on a page without at least two lines of the body of the document. In the unusual instance where there are so many signatures that they require more than a full page, as many signatures as possible appear on the same page as part of the body of the document, and the others are carried over to the following page. Precedents 7.2 and 7.3 illustrate endings in agreements, which are discussed in greater detail below.

Note that although the ending usually indicates that the agreement is to be executed under seal, in practice, the actual seal itself is often omitted. Follow the preference of your law firm.

Testimonium Clause

The testimonium clause is the last clause of the body of a traditional commercial document, which were formerly worded in very traditional, formal legal language. Current practice has simplified that language. The testimonium clause commences with words such as IN WITNESS WHEREOF"" or the simpler wording TO EVIDENCE THEIR AGREEMENT"" and indicates which parties to the document are to sign or execute it; it may also indicate whether the document is to be witnessed and whether legal seals are required. In traditional-style endings, the introductory ending words are followed by the words "*SIGNED, SEALED AND DELIVERED*"; in simplified styles, those words may still be used, may be replaced by wording such as *IN THE PRESENCE OF*, or may be omitted. Follow the preference of your lawyer or law firm in this matter. If the document is not dated in the heading, the date appears in the testimonium clause and is the date of signing, not the date on which the document is prepared. Figure 7.4 (p. 120) illustrates examples of various testimonium clauses that may be used.

Figure 7.4 Sample Testimonium Clauses

A. ONE PARTY ONLY SIGNING

1. **IN WITNESS WHEREOF** the party hereto has signed this *(name of document)* before a witness.

2. **IN WITNESS WHEREOF** the *(descriptive label)* has signed and sealed this *(name of document)*.

B. TWO OR MORE PARTIES SIGNING

1. **IN WITNESS WHEREOF** the parties hereto have signed this agreement before a witness.

2. **IN WITNESS WHEREOF** the parties hereto have signed and sealed this agreement before a witness.

3. **IN WITNESS WHEREOF** this agreement has been signed by the parties hereto before a witness this _____ day of _____ , 20__, *or* as of the _____ day of _____ , 20__.

4. **TO EVIDENCE THEIR AGREEMENT** each party has signed this contract before a witness this _____ day of _____ , 20__.

5. **TO EVIDENCE THEIR AGREEMENT** the husband and wife have each signed this agreement.

Attestation Clause and Signatures

Many legal documents require that the signature of an individual who is executing in his or her personal capacity be witnessed to make the document valid. This is known as attesting, and the clause is called the **attestation clause**. The witness signs at the left-hand side of the page, after actually seeing the party or parties sign the document. The individuals who are parties to the document sign at the right-hand side of the page in the presence of each other and in the order set out in the heading of the document.

If two or more parties are to execute the document, include lines with their names beneath to indicate exactly where they are to sign. If the same witness is not expected to witness the execution of a document by all parties to it, include a line for a witness opposite the line for the signature of each executing party and, beneath the line, indicate whose signature will be witnessed (Precedent 7.2).

For a corporation, an impression seal showing the name of the corporation and the jurisdiction or the year of incorporation is used. The letters "CS" are keyed where the corporate seal will be impressed after the document has been executed (Figure 7.5).

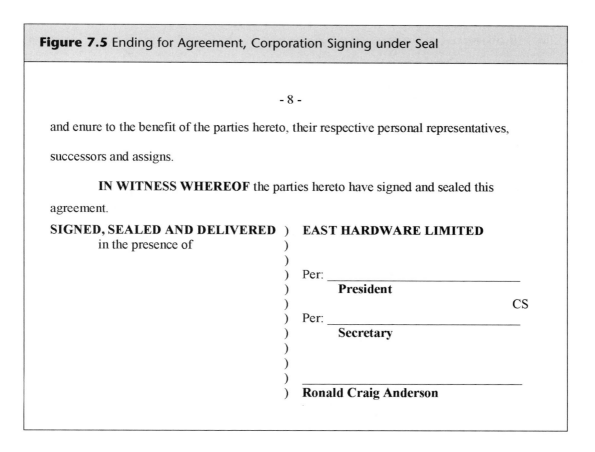

Figure 7.5 Ending for Agreement, Corporation Signing under Seal

- 8 -

and enure to the benefit of the parties hereto, their respective personal representatives,

successors and assigns.

> **IN WITNESS WHEREOF** the parties hereto have signed and sealed this

agreement.

SIGNED, SEALED AND DELIVERED) **EAST HARDWARE LIMITED**
    in the presence of   )

)
) Per: _____
)   **President**
)   CS
) Per: _____
)   **Secretary**
)
)
) _____
) **Ronald Craig Anderson**

Traditionally, every corporation executed documents under its corporate seal; however, in some provinces, the acts dealing with the operation of corporations state that a corporation may, but need not, have a corporate seal. For corporations that do not have a corporate seal, an additional statement must be included beneath the name of the signing party (Figure 7.6, p. 122). The by-laws of a corporation will indicate who may sign on its behalf. This will usually be any two of a given number of officers or directors. Information on the office held by those signing for the corporation is usually shown on the line beneath their signatures. No witness is required to signatures of officers or directors of a corporation who sign in their official capacity.

Figure 7.6 Ending for Agreement, Corporation with No Corporate Seal

- 9 -

26.   This contract shall be governed by and construed in accordance with laws of

Ontario and no other jurisdiction.

     IN WITNESS WHEREOF the parties hereto have signed and sealed this

agreement this   day of   , 20__.

SIGNED, SEALED AND DELIVERED)
     in the presence of   )
)
)
)   _____
)   **Katerina R. Veneracion**
)
)   **1359246 ONTARIO LIMITED**
)
)
)   Per: _____
)   **John J. Smith, Secretary**
)   I have authority to bind the
)   corporation

ENDORSEMENTS OR BACK OF LEGAL PAPERS

Legal documents have an identifying last page that is traditionally referred to as the **endorsement** but is more generally called the **back** or **backsheet**. The nature of the document determines what is shown there; usually, this includes the date or name of the court (if applicable), the names of the parties, the title of the document, and the name and address of the law firm preparing the document.

Precedents 7.4 and 7.5 illustrate the patterns of backs for legal documents. Note the following:

1. On legal-size paper, the page is considered to be divided into quarters and the endorsement is shown in the second quarter.
2. On letter-size paper, the page is considered to be divided in two and the endorsement is prepared on the right-hand half of the page.

AFFIDAVITS

One of the most common legal documents prepared is the **affidavit**. It forms part of the procedure in almost every area of legal practice. An affidavit is a written statement by an individual, referred to as the **deponent**, who voluntarily signs and swears or affirms before a person authorized to administer the oath or affirmation, referred to as a **commissioner**. The purpose of an affidavit is to establish or prove a fact or facts. An affidavit is usually made by only one person, although, in some circumstances, two people can join in a single affidavit. Affidavits prepared in connection with court proceeding may have material attached to support the statement of facts. These are called **exhibits** and are discussed in detail in Chapter 9.

Heading

The heading of an affidavit is determined by the manner in which it is to be used. Affidavits used in court work have a very distinctive heading common to all court papers and are considered in Chapter 9. Affidavits may be headed by the province and county or municipality in which they will be used or may simply be the title of the affidavit (Figure 7.7).

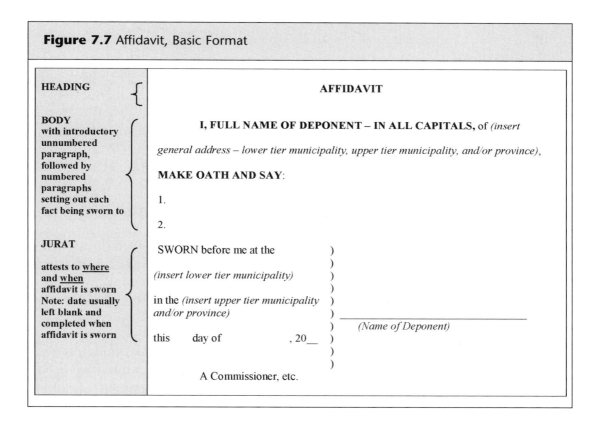

Figure 7.7 Affidavit, Basic Format

HEADING

BODY
with introductory unnumbered paragraph, followed by numbered paragraphs setting out each fact being sworn to

JURAT

attests to <u>where</u> and <u>when</u> affidavit is sworn
Note: date usually left blank and completed when affidavit is sworn

AFFIDAVIT

I, FULL NAME OF DEPONENT – IN ALL CAPITALS, of *(insert*

general address – lower tier municipality, upper tier municipality, and/or province),

MAKE OATH AND SAY:

1.

2.

SWORN before me at the)
)
(insert lower tier municipality))
)
in the *(insert upper tier municipality*)
and/or province))   _____
)   *(Name of Deponent)*
this   day of   , 20__)
)
)
    A Commissioner, etc.

Body

The first paragraph is not numbered and sets out the name (in full capitals) and general address of the person making the affidavit, followed by the statement "MAKE OATH AND SAY (or AFFIRM)." The person's occupation may be shown in this paragraph if applicable to the purpose of the affidavit.

The facts that the person wishes to swear to are then set out in paragraphs; each fact is usually set out in a separate paragraph. The paragraphs are numbered consecutively (1, 2, 3, etc.). When the deponent appears before a commissioner to complete the affidavit, he or she swears or affirms that the contents of the affidavit are true, to the best of his or her knowledge and belief.

Ending

The ending of an affidavit is known as the **jurat**. It attests that the affidavit was sworn or affirmed to at a stated time and in a stated place before an authorized person. The form of jurat is identical in every affidavit. It is typed on the left-hand side of the page and may be single or double spaced, with room left beneath it for the signature of the authorized witness, that is, a commissioner or notary public. The person swearing the affidavit signs on the right, as illustrated in Figure 7.7.

The "me" in the jurat refers to the commissioner, and this word is never changed. The place of swearing shown in the jurat represents the general address where the commissioner is located when the deponent or deponents appears before him or her.

The jurat may not appear on a page alone; at least two lines of the body of the affidavit must appear on a page with it. Unless you know the exact date on which the affidavit will be sworn, leave the date blank in the jurat; it will be filled in when the affidavit is being sworn or affirmed before the commissioner. The "A Commissioner, etc." wording is used in commercial legal documents. In court documents, as discussed in Chapter 9, the wording is "Commissioner for taking Affidavits" and may appear in full or initial capitals.

AFFIDAVIT OF EXECUTION

For many years, an affidavit was often included as part of legal documents such as agreements, contracts, powers of attorney, and many real estate documents. Such an affidavit was usually concerned with the legal capacity of the person involved to enter into a contract (affidavit as to legal age) or was a sworn statement of a witness, verifying that he or she had, in fact, seen the party or parties sign the document (affidavit of subscribing witness). Over the years, changes in prescribed documents have resulted in the omission of these affidavits in the new documents. As a result, they are no longer frequently prepared.

However, there are still a limited number of documents that do require the use of either of these sworn statements, which are now frequently combined into one affidavit of execution (Figure 7.8). You may not be asked to prepare such an affidavit very often, but you should be aware of how to do so.

This affidavit indicates

1. the name and general address of the witness;
2. the place (the city, town, or village) where the witness saw the document signed;
3. the name of the party or parties who signed in the presence of the witness; and
4. a statement that the person whose signature they witnessed is of legal age (18 or 19 years depending on the province).

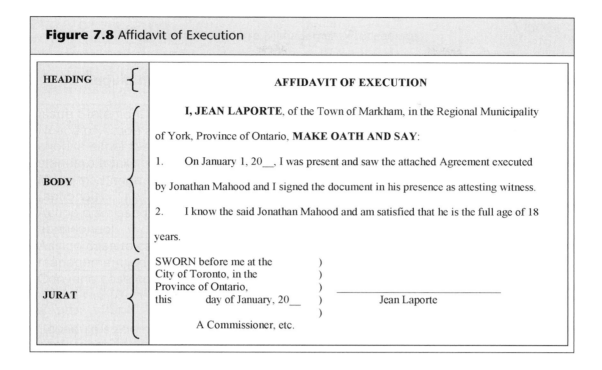

Figure 7.8 Affidavit of Execution

HEADING {

AFFIDAVIT OF EXECUTION

BODY {

I, JEAN LAPORTE, of the Town of Markham, in the Regional Municipality of York, Province of Ontario, **MAKE OATH AND SAY**:

1.   On January 1, 20__, I was present and saw the attached Agreement executed by Jonathan Mahood and I signed the document in his presence as attesting witness.

2.   I know the said Jonathan Mahood and am satisfied that he is the full age of 18 years.

JURAT {

SWORN before me at the   )
City of Toronto, in the   )
Province of Ontario,   )   _____
this   day of January, 20__)   Jean Laporte
)
        A Commissioner, etc.

If two or more persons executed the document, and a different witness was present when each person signed, each witness must complete an affidavit of execution.

This affidavit is never used alone. When required, it appears as part of the legal document and is inserted after the page on which the signature or signatures of the party or parties appear, but before the back. A copy of the affidavit is required for each copy of the legal paper, and these copies can be prepared in the same manner as the required copies of the full document.

STATUTORY DECLARATION

Frequently, an individual must provide proof of some facts when there is no action or matter in the courts or when no legal documents are involved. This person then completes what is known as a statutory declaration (Precedent 7.6). This is a prescribed form that is a formal statement of facts, declared before a commissioner. The person making the declaration is called the **declarant**.

Heading

The heading is divided into two parts: the province, in which the declaration is prepared, and the matter for which the declaration is made. The name, address, and occupation of the declarant are often included as well.

Body

The first paragraph is not numbered and contains the name of the declarant and his or her general address. Following the words "SOLEMNLY DECLARE THAT," numbered paragraphs set out the facts being declared. The body of a declaration may be single, 1.5, or double spaced.

Ending

The ending has a standard paragraph that begins with "And I make this solemn declaration...." It is always included just before the jurat, which is identical to that of a standard affidavit, with the exception that, instead of the word *Sworn*, the word *Declared* is used. The declaration requires the signature of, first, the declarant and, second, the commissioner and is dated at the time of execution.

Declaration by Two People

A statutory declaration is often made by two people simultaneously by deleting any reference to "I" and substituting the word "WE." Additionally, the word "SEVERALLY" is inserted before "DECLARE" at the end of the first paragraph and also before "DECLARED" in the jurat. Two lines are keyed to the right of the jurat so that both declarants may sign before the commissioner.

Back

Declarations require a back that must be completed with the following information: the date, the matter that is the subject of the declaration (the information for which appears in the heading of the statutory declaration), the name of the person whose declaration it is, and the name of the law firm in whose office the declaration is prepared (Precedent 7.7). Note that declarations may be prepared on letter- or legal-sized paper. Use the guidelines in Precedents 7.4 and 7.5 to format the back of any declaration.

NOTARIAL CERTIFICATES

A notarial certificate is a legal document, signed by a **notary public**, that certifies the authenticity of the copy of the paper to which it is affixed. Individuals may have to prove that a copy of a paper is indeed an exact copy of the original paper. They come to a lawyer who is a notary public and present the original and a copy of the paper. The notary public checks the copy with the original and, if satisfied that the copy is, in fact, a copy of the original, certifies this by completing and signing a notarial certificate, which is then affixed to the front of the copy. The copy is then said to be a notarial copy; that is, it has been proved to be an authentic copy of the original.

There are two styles of notarial certificates, one of which is identified as the short form and uses traditional legal language, which is discussed here. A special form of notarial certificate using simplified language is now used in estate work and is discussed in Chapter 34.

In many offices, a standard template is used to prepare the notarial certificate (Precedent 7.8), requiring only the specific information for each notarial document to be inserted, and then the required number of copies are printed out. A separate certificate is required for each copy that is authenticated (notarized), and each certificate is individually signed and sealed by the notary public. Notarial certificates are dated at the time of execution and do not require a back since the certificate is attached to the front of the paper being notarized.

RELEASE

A **release** is a legal document in which the person signing the release gives up all rights or claims in a legal matter involving the party or parties to whom the release is given. Releases are used in court work, in estate work, and in any situation in which it is necessary to have one party relinquish any legal rights he or she might have in a particular situation. For example, when a house is damaged by fire, the owner of the property will usually receive reimbursement from the company that insured the property. When the insurance company makes the payment, it will require the owner to sign a release to indicate that he or she has been fully reimbursed, has no further claim, and gives up any further rights he or she may have as a result of the fire under the policy of insurance.

As with the notarial certificate, most law firms have a template form that may be adapted for each matter as required. An example of a completed release is shown in Precedent 7.9. Sufficient copies should be prepared to provide an executed copy for both the party or parties giving and the party or parties receiving the release, as well as a copy for the lawyer's files.

In some instances, a release is given to be held in **escrow** pending completion of some condition (for example, receipt of a cheque). To hold in escrow means that a third party will keep the release until the person to whom the release is to be given has met some condition.

ASSEMBLING A COMMERCIAL DOCUMENT

To assemble a completed commercial document, follow these steps:

1. Arrange the pages in numerical order and make all the necessary photocopies.
2. Insert any affidavit of execution (discussed earlier in this chapter) after the signature page and before the back.
3. Put the back after all the numbered pages and any affidavit, with the printed side on the outside of the assembled pages. Ensure that the dated heading of the back is at the left side of the assembled document, that is, on the side on which the staple or paper clip will be affixed.
4. Assemble complete sets and staple each set in the upper left-hand corner. Often a blue cardboard triangular pocket, referred to as a **corner**, is used. Insert the left-hand corner of the assembled pages in the corner and staple through the combined corner and pages.
5. Do not fold the legal document until it has been executed.

Terms and Concepts

commercial documents	endorsement/back/backsheet
legal instruments	affidavit
court documents	deponent
municipal divisions	commissioner
upper tier municipality	exhibits
lower tier municipality	jurat
county	affidavit of execution
district	statutory declaration
regional municipality	declarant
legal document preparation guidelines	notarial certificate
recitals	notary public
definitions	release
testimonium clause	escrow
attestation clause	corner
corporate seal	

Review Questions

1. An agreement may show the date of preparation, the date of execution, or a date that is said to be "as of...." When might the last form of date be used?

2. If a corporation does not have a legal seal, how may it execute a commercial document?

3. There are four parties to an agreement. How many photocopies will be required? Which copy is considered the "original"?

4. What term is used to identify the ending of an affidavit, and what information appears in the ending? What other document has this form of ending?

5. What is the purpose of the following documents?
   a. affidavit
   b. affidavit of execution
   c. statutory declaration
   d. notarial certificate
   e. release

6. If a release is given in escrow, what does this mean?

7. **Internet Research**: What is the general address for
   a. where you live?
   b. the capital of your province/territory?
   c. the capital of Canada?

PRECEDENTS

Precedent 7.1 Sample Agreement, Traditional Style, First Page

HEADING

with date agreement to be effective

and

with parties described by name label

THIS AGREEMENT made as of the 1st day of January, 20___.

BETWEEN:

JONATHAN MAHOOD

herein called "Mahood"

and

MEDIA SOLUTIONS INC.

herein called "Media Solutions"

BODY

with traditional-style recitals

and

with articles (or clauses) with numbered side headings and numbered paragraphs

WHEREAS Mahood is the creator of, and owns all rights, title and interest including copyright, in and to, an interactive computer software game entitled "Arkiteks" (herein the "Game");

AND WHEREAS Media Solutions is in the business of distributing software products throughout the world;

AND WHEREAS Mahood wishes to retain the services of Media Solutions to distribute the Game.

NOW THEREFORE THIS AGREEMENT WITNESSETH that in consideration of the mutual covenants, provisos, and terms contained herein and other good and valuable consideration, Mahood and Media Solutions enter in this agreement (the "Agreement) with each other as follows:

Term and Territory

1.01   The Agreement shall be in effect for a period of five (5) years commencing on the date of the Agreement (the "Term"), unless terminated sooner in accordance with the terms and conditions of the Agreement, and upon expiry the contract between the parties automatically renews for another five (5) year term unless either party wishes to terminate upon giving written notice to the other not less than sixty (60) days prior to the date of the expiration of the Term.

2.01   The distribution rights granted herein shall be for the world (the "Territory").

HEADING with title of document and with parties described by role label	<div align="center">**SEPARATION AGREEMENT**</div> BETWEEN: <div align="center">**DARCY NATHANIEL MIDDLETON**</div> <div align="right">herein called "the husband"</div> <div align="center">and</div> <div align="center">**MORENA TRACEY MIDDLETON**</div> <div align="right">herein called "the wife"</div>
BODY with simplified recital and numbered paragraphs style	The husband and wife were married on September 1, 2000; separated on May 15, 2006; and entered into an agreement of separation on July 20, 2007 (the "Separation Agreement"). The husband and wife have agreed to amend the said Separation Agreement as follows: 1. Paragraph 4 of the Separation Agreement is rescinded and the husband and the wife agree the following shall be substituted therefor: 4. The husband agrees to cause the wife to be named as beneficiary for the value of Fifty Percent (50%) of the proceeds payable under Humber Life Insurance Policy No. 5961 2. The husband and the wife agree that all other terms of the Separation Agreement shall remain in full force and effect as amended notwithstanding the issuance of a certificate of divorce.

ENDING
 	
with testimonium clause that includes date of execution
 	
and
 	
attestation clause with individual signatories and witness lines
	TO EVIDENCE THEIR AGREEMENT the husband and the wife have each signed this agreement before a witness this day of , 20__.
	
	IN THE PRESENCE OF:)
	    )
	    )
	_____) _____
	As to the signature of:) **Darcy Nathaniel Middleton**
	    )
	    )
	_____) _____
	As to the signature of:) **Morena Tracey Middleton**

DOCUMENT REFERENCE	C:\PTG\middleton\separation agmt April 15, 20__

Page numbering at top of page and centred {

BODY Alternate style with centred paragraph headings {

ENDING

with

Testimonium Clause

and

Attestation Clause with individual and corporate signatories

Note that the parties are shown in the ending in same order as they appear in the heading

DOCUMENT REFERENCE {

- 8 -

ARTICLE TEN

TERMINATION

10.01   Pursuant to section 1.01, either party may terminate the Agreement upon written notice to the other to be given not less than sixty (60) days prior to the date of the expiration of the Term or any successive term.

10.02   Non-payment of Mahood's share of Gross or Adjusted Receipts or the bankruptcy or insolvency of Media Solutions shall be deemed grounds for termination of the Agreement by either Mahood or Media Solutions upon ten (10) days' written notice.

ARTICLE ELEVEN

ASSIGNMENT

11.01   Neither party may assign or otherwise transfer the Agreement without the written consent of the other party. The Agreement shall enure to the benefit of and bind the parties hereto and their respective legal representatives, successors or assigns.

IN WITNESS WHEREOF the parties hereto have executed this Agreement this   day of   , 20__ .

SIGNED, SEALED & DELIVERED)
    in the presence of)
)
)
) _____
)   **Jonathan Mahood**
)
) **MEDIA SOLUTIONS INC.**
)
) Per:_____
)   **President**
)   CS
)
) Per: _____
)   **Vice President**

Right half of 8.5" × 11" page

DATED: December 31,   20__

**RONALD CRAIG ANDERSON
and JOSEPH PETER KOWALSKI**

to

SAMUEL JOHN GOLDBERG

R E L E A S E

*With word processing software,
set the left margin at centre and the
top, bottom, and right margins
at 0. The computer will then
default to approximately ¼"
margins.*

**HILL, JOHNSTON & GRANT
17 Princess Street South, Suite 2501
City, Province, Postal Code**

------- 3.5 inches (1st quarter) -------

------- 3.5 inches (2nd quarter) -------

DATED: December 31,   20____

CONSTANCE JEAN GENTILI

- and -

EAST HARDWARE LIMITED

A G R E E M E N T

With word processing software,
select legal landscape paper size;
set left margin at 3.5 inches and
right margin at 7 inches.

HILL, JOHNSTON & GRANT
17 Princess Street South
Suite 2501
City, Province, Postal Code

HEADING

C A N A D A) IN THE MATTER OF
)
PROVINCE OF _____) _____
) _____
)
) AND IN THE MATTER OF
)
) _____
To Wit:) _____

BODY

with introductory unnumbered paragraph, followed by numbered paragraphs setting out each fact being sworn to

I, FULL NAME OF DECLARANT – IN ALL CAPITALS, of *(insert*

general address – lower tier municipality), in the *(upper tier municipality and/or*

province)

DO SOLEMNLY DECLARE, that:

1.

2.

3.

4.

ENDING

with standard last paragraph (unnumbered)

and

JURAT

And I make this solemn declaration conscientiously believing it to be true, and knowing that it is of the same force and effect as if made under oath.

DECLARED before me at the)
)
(insert lower tier municipality))
)
in the *(insert upper tier municipality*)
and/or province))
) _____
this   day of   , 20__)   *(Name of Declarant)*
)
)
       A Commissioner, etc.

------ 3.5 inches (1st quarter) ------   ---------- 3.5 inches (2nd quarter) ----------

DATED: *Month Day,*   20___

IN THE MATTER OF

AND IN THE MATTER OF

STATUTORY DECLARATION
of
NAME OF DECLARANT

With word processing software,
select legal landscape paper size;
set left margin at 3.5 inches and
right margin at 7 inches.

HILL, JOHNSTON & GRANT
17 Princess Street South
Suite 2501
City, Province, Postal Code

C A N A D A)

PROVINCE OF _____)

)

To Wit)

TO ALL WHOM THESE PRESENTS

MAY COME, BE SEEN, OR KNOWN

      I, NAME OF NOTARY PUBLIC, a Notary Public, in and for the Province of

_____, by Royal Authority duly appointed, residing at the *(general or postal*

address) in said Province, **DO CERTIFY AND ATTEST** that the paper-writing hereto

annexed is a true copy of *(insert description of document)*, dated *(insert date of*

document), the said copy having been compared by me with the said original document,

an act whereof being requested I have granted under my notarial form and seal of office to

serve and avail as occasion shall or may require.

      IN TESTIMONY WHEREOF I have hereto subscribed my name and affixed

my notarial seal of office, this   day of   , 20__.

_____

A Notary Public

in and for the Province of _____

KNOW ALL MEN BY THESE PRESENTS, that I, **HENRY MAURICE BLACKWOOD**, of the City of Mississauga, in the Regional Municipality of Peel, in consideration of the settlement of the action brought by me in the Superior Court of Justice against **WAYNE HOWARD COCHRANE**, and in consideration of the monies paid thereunder pursuant to such settlement (receipt whereof is hereby acknowledged), do hereby remise, release and forever discharge Wayne Howard Cochrane, his heirs, executors, administrators, successors and assigns, of and from all actions, causes of action, claims and demands which against Wayne Howard Cochrane I or my respective heirs, executors, administrators, successors or assigns hereafter can, shall or may have for or by reason of any matter or thing existing up to the present time, and in particular but without limiting the generality of the foregoing of and from all actions, causes of action, claims and demands in any way arising out of or relating to the distribution of the estate of Rosalie Cynthia Blackwood.

IT IS UNDERSTOOD AND AGREED that the said payment or promise of payment is deemed to be no admission whatever of liability on the part of the said Wayne Howard Cochrane.

IN WITNESS WHEREOF I have hereto affixed my hand this   day of January, 20__.

SIGNED, SEALED AND DELIVERED   )
    in the presence of   )
)
) _____
)   Henry Maurice Blackwood

PART 2

Civil Litigation and Family Law

CHAPTER 8

Introduction to Civil Litigation

OBJECTIVES:

- Demonstrate an understanding of the structure of the Canadian court system
- Demonstrate an understanding of the Rules of Court as they apply to civil litigation
- Identify and describe the court system in Ontario and its offices and officials
- Demonstrate an understanding of the application of Rule 3 (Time)
- Describe the process of opening and maintaining a litigation file

Many lawyers practise in the area of civil litigation, in which disputes between parties are resolved in court trials or hearings, or applications are made to the court asking for its advice, direction, or decision on a particular question.

COURT STRUCTURE OF CANADA

There are many courts in Canada and its provinces and territories. Some are courts of original jurisdiction, hearing cases for the first time, and are therefore known as **courts of first instance**. Others are courts of appeal, rehearing cases already decided in courts of original jurisdiction, and are therefore known as **appellate courts**. The following chart (Figure 8.1) shows the structure of the federal and provincial/territorial courts.

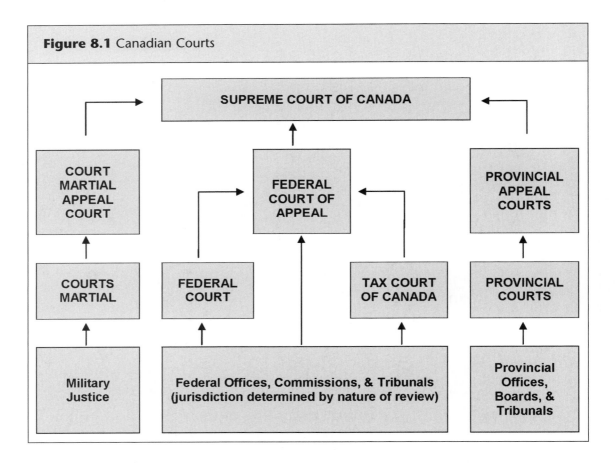

Figure 8.1 Canadian Courts

The highest court is the Supreme Court of Canada, and it has exclusive, final jurisdiction in both civil and criminal matters; it is an appellate court only. Beneath this is the federal, military, and provincial/territorial appeal court level. The Federal Court of Canada has both trial and appeal divisions to deal with matters involving the Crown and federally constituted commissions or tribunals in civil matters, including appeals from the Tax Court of Canada; it has no criminal jurisdiction. The Court Martial Appeal Court hears appeals regarding military justice only.

The provincial/territorial appeal courts hear appeals from the lower provincial/territorial courts. These provincial/territorial courts are where most cases are tried, and these courts have different names and structure variations in each of the provinces and territories. Some courts are concerned only with criminal cases; some deal only with civil cases; others deal with both criminal and civil cases. In some provinces, there are also *surrogate courts* that deal primarily with the processing of estates; *family courts* that deal with marriage, divorce, and children; and *county courts* and *provincial courts*, each with special civil and criminal trial jurisdiction. Figure 8.2 provides a comparative chart of the provincial and territorial courts in Canada and their Internet addresses.

Figure 8.2 Comparative Chart of Provincial/Territorial Courts and Internet Addresses

Provincial and Territorial Courts in Canada

Province/Territory	Highest Court of First Instance	Appellate Court
Alberta http://www.albertacourts.ab.ca/	Court of Queen's Bench of Alberta	Court of Appeal for Alberta
British Columbia http://www.courts.gov.bc.ca/	Supreme Court of British Columbia	Court of Appeal of British Columbia
Manitoba http://www.manitobacourts.mb.ca/	Court of Queen's Bench for Manitoba	Court of Appeal of Manitoba
New Brunswick http://www.gnb.ca/cour/index-e.asp	Court of Queen's Bench	Court of Appeal
Newfoundland and Labrador http://www.court.nl.ca/Default.htm	Supreme Court of Newfoundland and Labrador – Trial Division	Supreme Court of Newfoundland and Labrador – Court of Appeal
Northwest Territories http://www.nwtcourts.ca/	Supreme Court of Northwest Territories	Court of Appeal for the Northwest Territories
Nova Scotia http://www.courts.ns.ca/	Supreme Court of Nova Scotia – Trial Division	Supreme Court of Nova Scotia – Appeal Division
Nunavut http://www.nucj.ca/welcome.htm	Nunavut Court of Justice (Unified Court)	
Ontario http://www.ontariocourts.on.ca/english.htm	Superior Court of Justice	Court of Appeal for Ontario
Prince Edward Island http://www.gov.pe.ca/courts/	Supreme Court of Prince Edward Island – Trial Division	Supreme Court of Prince Edward Island – Appeal Division
Quebec http://www.tribunaux.qc.ca/mjq_en/index.html	Superior Court of Quebec	Court of Appeal of Quebec
Saskatchewan http://www.sasklawcourts.ca/	Court of Queen's Bench	Court of Appeal
Yukon http://www.yukoncourts.ca/	Supreme Court	Court of Appeal

RULES OF COURT

There are statutory acts, rules, and regulations that outline the procedures to be followed in civil procedures in the courts in each of the provinces. Although many of the documents, terms, and procedures are similar across Canada, the specific rules of court for the province and the court in which any civil matter is to proceed must be followed. For Ontario, these are the *Rules of Civil Procedure*, R.R.O. 1990, Regulation 194, as amended, which are used in explaining the documentation and procedures of civil litigation for this text. Each year, the *Rules of Civil Procedure*, as amended to date, are published in *Ontario Civil Practice* (Thomson Carswell) and *Ontario Annual Practice* (Canada Law Book) or may be accessed online at http://www.e-laws.gov.on.ca/index.html.

ONTARIO COURT SYSTEM

The following chart (Figure 8.3) provides an overview of the court system for Ontario, which is described in more detail below.

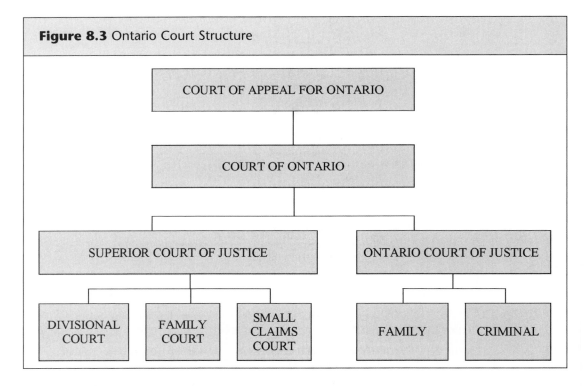

Figure 8.3 Ontario Court Structure

COURT OF APPEAL FOR ONTARIO

COURT OF ONTARIO

SUPERIOR COURT OF JUSTICE

ONTARIO COURT OF JUSTICE

DIVISIONAL COURT

FAMILY COURT

SMALL CLAIMS COURT

FAMILY

CRIMINAL

COURT OF APPEAL FOR ONTARIO

The Court of Appeal for Ontario is the highest court in the province. This court may hear both civil and criminal appeals from lower Ontario courts subject to provisions set out in the *Courts of Justice Act*. The court sits in courtrooms at Osgoode Hall in

Toronto. An uneven number of judges, not fewer than three, hear each appeal. An appeal from the Court of Appeal for Ontario may be made to the Supreme Court of Canada if leave (authorization) to commence an appeal is obtained.

SUPERIOR COURT OF JUSTICE

This court was previously named the Ontario Court (General Division), which name will appear in previous legal documentation and case law. This court hears all types of criminal and family law cases, civil law matters (including estates), and all trials of cases with a jury. The Superior Court of Justice sits in courtrooms in the court-house in the county centre and is presided over by a single Superior Court judge. There may be separate sittings for civil proceedings that are to be tried with or without a jury, as well as for the trial of certain criminal matters, such as murder. An appeal from a judgment (that is, a decision) of a proceeding heard in the Superior Court of Ontario may be to either the Divisional Court or the Court of Appeal for Ontario, depending on the nature of the proceedings.

Divisional Court

This branch of the Superior Court of Justice has original jurisdiction to hear applications for judicial review of decisions of administrative tribunals, such as the Ontario Municipal Board, the governing bodies of various professions, and certain departments of municipal and provincial governments that have the authority to regulate by issuing licences or granting permits. The Divisional Court has appellate jurisdiction to hear appeals in specified circumstances from the Superior Court of Justice and the Small Claims Court.

Family Court

This branch of the Superior Court of Justice incorporates the Unified Family Court that formerly operated in some regions and is sometimes still referred to by this name. Family Court can hear all types of family law cases. It currently operates only in certain areas of Ontario and is discussed further in Chapter 18.

Small Claims Court

This branch of the Superior Court of Justice hears claims not in excess of $10,000; however, this amount is currently under review and may be increased in the near future. There is at least one Small Claims Court for each county in Ontario; each is identified by the name of the area in which it is located. A person bringing a claim in this court may, but is not required to, employ a lawyer to act for him or her. The proceedings are heard by a judge, and the trials are more informal. The procedures and documentation for this court may be found at http://www.attorneygeneral.jus.gov.on.ca/english/courts/scc/.

ONTARIO COURT OF JUSTICE

This court was previously named the Ontario Court (Provincial Division), which name will appear in previous legal documentation and case law. There are two sections of the Ontario Court of Justice: Family and Criminal. They are presided over by Ontario Court of Justice judges. In this division, judges try traffic offences, hear criminal and certain family law cases, conduct bail hearings and preliminary hearings for accused people, and preside over offences under the *Young Offenders' Act.* There is at least one Ontario Court of Justice for each county in Ontario; each is identified by that name and the name of the area at which it is located (for example, the Ontario Court of Justice at Brantford). Proceedings are heard by one Ontario Court of Justice judge. With certain exceptions, an appeal may be made to the Superior Court of Justice.

COURT OFFICES

Ontario, like the other provinces and territories, has been divided into judicial regions composed of a number of upper tier municipalities. Information on the Ontario courts within each region may be found at the Ministry of the Attorney General website (http://www.attorneygeneral.jus.gov.on.ca/english/courts/cadaddr.asp). Each region has a regional senior judge for the Superior Court of Justice and a regional director, whose offices are located in the regional centre. In addition, each region has a full complement of Superior Court of Justice and Ontario Court of Justice judges and a special advisory committee, which advises on procedures to ensure the effective use of resources and personnel in court management.

There are many court offices with which you will be in contact in your work as a legal assistant. In most areas, all such offices are located in the courthouse in the upper tier municipality; this courthouse is usually referred to as the county courthouse whether or not the upper tier municipality is actually a county. The following are also usually located in the county courthouse: offices of the Superior Court of Justice, Small Claims Court, and Ontario Court of Justice; sheriff's office and judges' offices; court registrars and other court officials; and courtrooms.

COURT OFFICERS

There are several officers of the courts whose official titles you should know. If you need the name of the individual holding a particular office, such as a local registrar, refer to the appropriate county listing for the province in the *Canadian Law List* or the court websites listed in Figure 8.2.

Judges

Judges are lawyers appointed to hear cases in the court. They are said to "sit" or to be "on the bench." Judges of the Court of Appeal for Ontario and for the Superior Court of Justice are appointed by the federal government; judges of the Ontario Court of Justice are appointed by the provincial government.

A judge of the Court of Appeal is known as, for example, The Honourable Mr. Justice Smith or the Honourable Madam Justice Smith. The chief judge of the Court of Appeal is known as the Chief Justice of Ontario.

A judge of the Superior Court of Justice or the Ontario Court of Justice is known as, for example, Justice Judge Smith or Her Honour Judge Smith. They may also be addressed as Mr. or Madam Justice Smith. The chief judge of the Superior Court of Justice is known as the Chief Justice of the Superior Court of Justice; the chief judge of the Ontario Court of Justice is referred to as the Chief Justice of the Ontario Court of Justice.

Registrar of the Court

The **registrar** is the chief administrative officer of the court; local registrars may be appointed to assist in each county courthouse. Deputy local registrars may also be appointed to perform and exercise all the powers and duties of the local registrar.

Master

A **master** is an officer of the Superior Court of Justice who is a lawyer appointed to assist the judges. Masters do not try legal proceedings but may hear and dispose of certain matters brought to them for determination or referred to them by the judges.

Sheriff

The **sheriff** is an officer of the Crown appointed in each county in the province. His or her duties include the execution of certain documents issuing from the courts and summoning jurors for cases being tried with a jury.

LEGAL PROCEEDINGS

All proceedings in the Superior Court of Justice are either an **action** or an **application**. An action is when one party is suing another party, often referred to as a lawsuit. The party who starts the lawsuit is the **plaintiff**, and the party being sued is the **defendant**. In handwritten drafts prepared by lawyers, the Greek letter π (pi) is often used to symbolize the plaintiff, and the Greek letter Δ (delta) may be used to symbolize the defendant.

An **application** is a civil proceeding in which the advice or direction of the court is sought. The parties to an application are the **applicant** and the **respondent**.

Although parties to a legal proceeding may act in person, they usually conduct the proceeding through a lawyer. The same solicitors act for all parties who join together to originate a legal proceeding. The parties against whom a legal proceeding is originated may all act through the same solicitors, or each party may engage his or her own solicitor. This text assumes that all parties to a legal proceeding act through solicitors.

TIME

Many court procedures must be taken within certain prescribed time periods. Rule 3 (Time) *Rules of Civil Procedure* sets out how such time periods are to be calculated:

- In calculating the required number of days, *exclude* the day of service or filing and *include* the date on which the other event is to take place.
- Where a period of less than seven days is prescribed, do not count holidays, which include Saturdays, Sundays, and statutory holidays (New Year's Day, Good Friday, Easter Monday, Victoria Day, Canada Day, Civic Holiday, Labour Day, Thanksgiving Day, Remembrance Day, Christmas, and Boxing Day). For example, if a proceeding is to take place on Monday, November 25, and three days' notice must be given to the other parties, the document giving notice must be served by Wednesday, November 20.
- Where a period of seven days or more is prescribed, holidays are included when calculating the required number of days. For example, if a court procedure is to take place on November 25, and 10 days' notice must be given to the other parties, the document giving notice must be served by November 15.
- When the time for doing an act under the rules expires on a holiday, it may be done on the next day that is not a holiday, and if any document, other than an originating process (which is explained in Chapter 10), is served after 4 p.m., the document will be considered to have been served on the next day that is not a holiday.

ACTING FOR A LITIGATION CLIENT

When a client consults a lawyer about some problem that may require a legal proceeding to resolve it, the general procedural steps discussed in Chapter 3 are followed. The following outlines some of the specific requirements for a litigation file.

Retainer and Authorization

The client is usually asked to sign a retainer authorizing the law firm to act on his or her behalf and to take whatever steps are necessary to conduct or defend a legal proceeding. If the client has been injured or has suffered a wage loss, for example, he or she is asked to sign an authorization to permit the law firm to be given information about the injuries, the amount of money lost in wages, or other details that cannot be released without the permission of the client.

The client may be requested to provide money to cover disbursements that the law firm will make on his or her behalf. These funds are deposited in the trust account, following the procedures discussed in Chapter 5.

Tickler Slips

Tickler slips are prepared to remind the lawyer of the limitation dates for commencing and completing the steps in any legal proceeding. The limitation date is the date by which a legal proceeding must be commenced or a step must be taken, or the right to do so is lost. Limitation dates differ, depending on the type of problem; for example, in Ontario, legal proceedings must be commenced within two years of the date of a motor vehicle accident or within six years from the date of a breach of contract. The lawyer will advise you of the appropriate limitation date.

Once a legal proceeding is commenced, the rules set out the time limits within which certain steps must be completed. Failure to meet those time limits may cause serious problems for the client. For example, once an action is started, and the defendant is served in Ontario, the defendant usually has 20 days in which to take steps to dispute the proceeding. Failure to take these steps within the 20 days can result in the plaintiff being awarded judgment by default.

In preparing tickler slips, use a reminder date that provides sufficient time for the lawyer to comply with the time periods. For example, the lawyer should be reminded approximately one month before the limitation date, or about three or four days before a time limit.

Client File

A file and docket are opened for the new litigation client. At first, only one file folder may be required to maintain the correspondence; however, most litigation files require additional subfiles for the necessary documentation.

Correspondence File

The label on the correspondence file should indicate the name of the file and the subname *Correspondence*. Indicate the period covered by the material in the file. For example:

ANDERSON, R.C. v. PETERSON
Correspondence File No. 1
June 15, 2008 – October 13, 2008

When the first correspondence file becomes full, open a second file for correspondence. For example:

ANDERSON, R.C. v. PETERSON
Correspondence File No. 2
October 14, 2008 –

Additional Subfiles

If the lawyer is unable to settle the client's problem, it may be necessary to commence a legal proceeding in the courts. When that happens, additional subfiles are required. When the file consists only of the main correspondence file and one or two subfiles, these files may be maintained in an expansion folder. This folder should also be labelled with the file name.

The original court documents prepared for use in the legal proceeding and those served on your law firm by the other party are maintained in a separate subfile identified by the name of the file and the subname *Documents*. Photocopies of these court documents will be required for inclusion in a **record**, which is a booklet containing a copy of all relevant documents filed with the court for the use of the judge at the trial. If the lawyer acts for the party commencing the legal proceeding, a separate subfile labeled *Record* will be required. A photocopy of all court documents prepared by your firm, as well as any served on your firm by other parties to the proceeding, is placed in this subfile to facilitate the creation of the record discussed further in Chapter 14. As the litigation proceeding progresses, other subfiles may also be opened and maintained in the main expansion folder. As various steps in a legal proceeding are discussed in subsequent chapters, reference is made to additional subfiles that may be set up.

Large Files

If the litigation proceeding is a complex one, expansion folders may not be adequate to hold all the file material, and file boxes may be used. Each box is labelled to clearly indicate the files it contains. It is not unusual for the various subfiles to occupy a whole drawer in a filing cabinet. The subfiles in a litigation file are kept in alphabetical order within the main file.

SETTLEMENT

When a client requests the lawyer to act for him or her in a matter that may require court proceedings, those proceedings are not always undertaken immediately. The lawyers for the parties involved often attempt to negotiate a settlement of the dispute. When such attempts are unsuccessful, or when the limitation date by which a legal proceeding must be commenced is approaching, the legal proceeding is started.

Even after the legal proceeding is commenced, negotiations may continue. The various steps taken as the proceeding progresses make each party familiar with the position of the other and encourage settlement.

It is the goal of a lawyer acting for a client to resolve the problem without having to go to court. If that is impossible, an action or application is commenced, as discussed in subsequent chapters.

Terms and Concepts

court structure	Family Court
courts of first instance	Small Claims Court
appellate courts	Ontario Court of Justice
Supreme Court of Canada	court offices
Federal Court of Canada	court officials
Tax Court of Canada	judges
surrogate courts	registrar
family courts	master
Rules of Civil Procedure	sheriff
Court of Appeal for Ontario	action
Superior Court of Justice	application
Divisional Court	plaintiff

defendant

retainer

applicant

authorization

respondent

tickler slips

time calculation

record

litigation file set-up

settlement

Review Questions

1. For each of the following, indicate which court in your province would hear a legal proceeding for
   a. a dispute involving the sum of $9,000.00
   b. a dispute involving the sum of 66,000.00

2. What is meant when there is a reference to "the rules"?

3. If a legal proceeding is commenced in the court on behalf of a new client, what subfiles might you expect to establish in the main file? What is the purpose of having such subfiles?

4. Why might the lawyer ask the client to sign a retainer and an authorization?

5. Assume that today is November 1, in the current year. In preparing tickler slips, what date would you use to remind the lawyer of the approach of
   a. a limitation date of August 31, next year? _____
   b. a due date of November 17, this year? _____

6. Assume that today is Friday, the 1st of the month, and that next Monday is a holiday. A number of documents were served by your law firm today. For each of the following, indicate the day and date on which the next event must take place.
   a. a document that requires 3 days' notice _____
   b. a document that requires 10 days' notice _____
   c. a document that requires 2 days' notice _____

7. **Internet Research:**
   a. What is the name of the act that governs the courts in your province?
   b. What are the "rules of court" referred to as in your province, and where may they be accessed on the Internet?

CHAPTER 9

Preparing Court Documents

OBJECTIVES:

- Demonstrate an understanding of the preparation of court documents applying the *Rules of Civil Procedure*
- Identify and describe the various parts of court documents
- Use legal precedents to prepare affidavits and exhibits

All documents prepared for use in legal proceedings are used in either an action or an application. The *Rules of Civil Procedure* prescribe the requirements and basic formats for court documents and illustrate over 200 specimen forms, which are available at http://www.ontariocourtforms.on.ca. Many of these documents are prepared using the basic document format discussed in this chapter, with the wording of the body varying to fit the particular purpose of the document.

COURT DOCUMENTS

Many of the court forms are available in printed form from legal stationers or may be fully keyed. Alternatively, the shell of the forms may have been recorded in the computer; these forms require that the necessary information be manually inserted in the appropriate blanks. There are also a variety of commercial litigation software packages that may be used in preparing court documents. For example, Automated Civil Litigation (ACL) document assembly software by Korbitec Inc. allows the court and party information to be saved and assembled automatically into selected forms where required. ACL has been used to generate the majority of the civil litigation forms shown in this text. No matter which method is used, the following formatting guidelines should be noted:

1. Print, type, write, or reproduce legibly on one or both sides of good-quality letter-size white paper. Most court documents are prepared on one side of a page.
2. Use characters of at least 12-point or 10-point size.
3. Leave a left margin of approximately 40 mm (one and a half inches). This spacing is specified by the rules to allow for court documents to be bound. The rules do not specify the size of the right, top, or bottom margin; leave margins of one half or one inch, depending on the preference of your law firm.
4. Show the court file number on the first line, flush with the right margin on the first page.
5. Show the name of the court on page one, one or two lines after the court file number in all capital letters centred between the margins.
6. Single space the names of the parties to an action or application in capital letters, following the colon after **BETWEEN**; indicate the capacity of each party one double space after the name, in initial capitals, ending flush with the right margin.
7. Include the statutory authority for an application, that is, the rule or act, a double space after the listing of the parties.
8. Show the name of the document in all capital letters without underscoring.
9. Double space between lines.
10. Indent paragraphs one or two tabs. The rules do not specify the required indentation; patterns in the rules show 5 spaces, but many law offices prefer a 10-space (2 tabs) indentation.
11. Number each paragraph or capitalize the first word or group of words.
12. Leave a bottom margin of no more than 25 mm (or 1 inch).

13. Include at least two lines of the body of the document on the page with the date and information on the solicitors.
14. Number each page after the first page; page numbers appear centred across the top of the page. Backsheets are not numbered.
15. Use only figures for amounts referred to in court documents; it is not necessary to show references to dollar amounts or percentages, for example, in both words and figures.
16. Omit initial capitals on such words as plaintiff, defendant, affidavit, statement of claim, order, judgment, notice of discontinuance, etc., when they appear in the body of a legal document (or in correspondence). This is the practice followed in the rules. However, many lawyers still prefer initial capitals on such words; follow the practice preferred by the law firm when it varies from that followed in the rules.
17. Use boldface for the name of the court, the names of the parties, the title of the document, and initial words commencing unnumbered paragraphs in boldface if this is the preference of your law firm.

Precedent 9.1 illustrates a basic format for the first page of a court document; Precedent 9.2 illustrates a basic format for the last page of a court document. As various court documents are discussed in subsequent chapters, any variations in format are noted.

GENERAL HEADING

The heading of a court document is known as the **general heading** and contains the following information:

1. The court file number
2. The name of the court
3. The **title of proceeding** (formerly and still often referred to as the *style of cause*). This is the name of all parties and the capacity in which they are parties, such as plaintiff and defendant.
4. In an application, the statutory provision or rule under which there is authority to make the application

Once the general heading is established in the document that originates the proceeding, information in that heading cannot be changed without the permission of the court. For example, if a name of a party is misspelled, the correction cannot be made until the court authorizes the change.

The title of the document is not part of the general heading but is the first line of the body or text of the document.

Figure 9.1 illustrates a form of general heading for a document originating an action in the Ontario Superior Court of Justice; Figure 9.2 illustrates a form of general heading for a document originating an application in the Ontario Superior Court of Justice.

Figure 9.1 General Heading in an Action

Court File No. 0000000

ONTARIO
SUPERIOR COURT OF JUSTICE

B E T W E E N :

RICHARD PERCIVAL GOLDSTONE,
a minor, by his litigation guardian,
KENNETH PERCIVAL GOLDSTONE

Plaintiff

- and -

HENRY ALBERT BELL,
HERMAN ALGERNON BELL,
and MARY JANE WILLIAMSON

Defendants

Figure 9.2 General Heading in an Application

Court File No. 0000000

ONTARIO
SUPERIOR COURT OF JUSTICE

B E T W E E N :

AARON J. BELVEDERE

Applicant

- and -

DARRYL B. ROUTENBERG and
CHRISTINE E. SZYMANSKI

Respondents

APPLICATION UNDER s. 60 of the *Evidence Act*, R.S.O. 1990, c. E.23

Regardless of the length of the body of the document, the general heading appears at the top portion of the page. When a document is slightly too long to fit on one page, the name of the law firm on which it is to be served may appear on a separate page; alternatively, the spacing before and after the "and" in the title of proceeding may be increased to ensure that two lines of the body of the document will carry over to another page.

Short Title of Proceeding

The rules provide that where there are more than two parties to the proceeding, a short title of proceeding may be used on all court documents, *except* documents that originate a proceeding, pleadings, records, orders, and reports. Instead of using the full names and capacities of the parties, simply show a shortened version of a company name or the last name of the first party on each side, followed by the words "and others." Follow the preference of your lawyer or firm on using the full or short title of proceeding.

Correspondence and Citations

When referring to the title of proceeding of an action or application in correspondence and citations, use only the last name of the parties or a shortened version of the company name.

For an action, separate the names by a *v.* (versus), indicating that the first-named party is suing the second-named party. If there are a great many plaintiffs or defendants, show the name of the first party and then the words *and others* (used in place of *et al.*, which was formerly used to indicate more than one party) to indicate that other parties are involved. For example:

> *Goldstone and others v. Bell and others*

For an application, separate the names by an *and* (since the first party is not suing the other party) when referring to the parties in the subject line of correspondence; preface the names by a *Re* when referring to the parties in a citation (as discussed in Chapter 6). For example:

> In correspondence: *Wyndhard and Wyers*
> In a citation: *Re Wyndhard and Wyers*

BODY OF A COURT DOCUMENT

The body of a court document contains

1. The title of the document
2. The text of the document
3. Its date
4. When the document is filed and *not* issued by the registrar or is an originating process, the name, address, and telephone and fax numbers of the solicitor(s) filing the document, or where a party acts in person, his or her name, address, and telephone number

5. When the document *is* issued by a registrar, the address of the court office in which the proceeding was commenced
6. When the document is filed and not issued by the registrar and is served on solicitors for the other party, the name, address, and fax number (if known) of those solicitors

In listing the names of solicitors in the ending of the court document, many law firms also include the words *Barristers and Solicitors* on the next line; others omit these words. The name of the specific lawyer handling the file is also usually shown. Some law firms include this name above the name of the law firm; others include it following the name and address of the law firm.

The line *Solicitors for...* is also usually included. If the solicitors act for the only defendant or respondent or all of the defendants or respondents, use only the capacity in completing the Solicitors for... line. For example:

Acting for the only defendant:
Solicitors for the defendant

Acting for all of the respondents:
Solicitors for the respondents

If the solicitors act for one or more but not all of the defendants or respondents, use not only the capacity but also the names of those for whom the solicitors act. For example:

Acting for one but not all of the defendants:
Solicitors for the defendant Mary Jane Brown

Acting for two or more but not all of the respondents:
Solicitors for the respondents Henry John Black and Gertrude Maude Black

Follow the preference of your law firm or lawyer with regard to any of the optional procedures discussed above.

BACKSHEETS

Most court documents also require a backsheet setting out the following information:

1. The short title of proceeding, that is, the names of the parties
2. The name of the court and the court file number
3. The location of the court office in which the proceeding was commenced
4. The title of the document
5. The name, address, telephone and facsimile numbers, and law society registration number of the solicitor serving or filing the document. Custom also includes the name of the law firm (if applicable) and a line *Solicitors for... .*
6. The fax number, if known, of the lawyer being served with the document

Backsheets are prepared by showing the required information across the length of the paper, as illustrated in Precedent 9.4.

Practice varies on the wording used in the PROCEEDING COMMENCED line on the backsheet. Some court offices have indicated that they prefer the following:

PROCEEDING COMMENCED at (name of city or town)

Backsheets illustrated in this text follow this style.

Other court offices have indicated a preference for one of the following styles:

PROCEEDING COMMENCED at the (City or Town) of (name), in the (name of judicial region) or PROCEEDING COMMENCED at the (City or Town) of (name), in the (upper tier municipality) of (name) or PROCEEDING COMMENCED at (City or Town) of (name)

There may be other minor variations in style for the preparation of backsheets. Follow the preference of your court office or law firm.

When assembling the completed document, the backsheet is affixed so that the information appearing on it may be read. The edge of the backsheet showing the title of proceeding is on the side of the assembled document on which the staple or paper clip is placed.

AFFIDAVITS

The general heading of an affidavit is taken from the originating or some other document previously prepared in the legal proceeding. If there is more than one plaintiff and defendant or applicant and respondent, the short title of proceeding may be used:

The document is titled AFFIDAVIT of (name)

The first paragraph in the affidavit is unnumbered and identifies the deponent (the person swearing it) by full name and general address. If the deponent is a party or solicitor, officer, director, member, or employee of a party to the proceeding, that fact is included in the first unnumbered paragraph. The words MAKE OATH AND SAY end the first unnumbered paragraph; those words usually appear in solid capitals. Numbered paragraphs follow, setting out the facts to which the deponent swears. The jurat states where, when, and before whom the affidavit was sworn. An affidavit used for court purposes is similar to that used in affidavits where there are no court proceedings, as discussed in Chapter 7, except that instead of ending with "A Commissioner, etc.," the wording "Commissioner for Taking Affidavits" is used. Precedent 9.4 illustrates a precedent for a court affidavit.

A backsheet is required for all affidavits except affidavits of service (which are discussed in Chapter 11). In addition to identifying the document as an affidavit, include the name of the deponent. For example:

AFFIDAVIT
OF

PETER T. GRANT
SWORN (date) *or*
AFFIRMED (date)

Swearing an Affidavit

An affidavit may be sworn or affirmed before a solicitor in your office other than the solicitor who instructed that it be prepared. Only the original of the affidavit is sworn or affirmed and signed by the deponent. Photocopy the required number of copies of the affidavit after it has been sworn.

Exhibits to an Affidavit

Frequently, the person swearing or affirming the affidavit produces material in support of the facts set out in the affidavit. Such material is known as an exhibit.

Marking Exhibits

The exhibits referred to in an affidavit are usually identified by letters of the alphabet, commencing with A, but may also be identified by number. Each exhibit is stamped with an exhibit stamp, which is illustrated below:

> This is Exhibit .... referred to in the
> affidavit of ....….............
> sworn before me, this .....….............
> day of ....…......................20......

A COMMISSIONER, ETC.

The stamping is placed on the exhibit so that it does not obliterate any of the exhibit material. If at all possible, place it on the right-hand side of the page so that it is easy to find. If the exhibit is a large folded document, put the exhibit stamping on a small piece of paper and attach that paper to the outside of the upper right-hand corner of the folded exhibit. The exhibit stamping may be completed in ink or on a typewriter. Include the appropriate exhibit letter, the name of the deponent, and as much of the dated portion as possible. Omit the exact date unless it is known with certainty when the affidavit will be sworn. The commissioner who takes the affidavit will sign the exhibit stamping after completing the jurat and will also insert the date in the stamping.

Large-Size Exhibits

When exhibits are larger than a letter-size sheet of paper, either reduce them on the photocopier to letter size or fold them to letter size and insert them in a letter-size envelope marked with the appropriate exhibit letter or number.

Attaching Exhibits

There are two ways of referring to exhibits in an affidavit. If the affidavit says *attached (or annexed) hereto and marked Exhibit "A"...*, the exhibit is attached to and filed with the affidavit. The exhibits come after the typed affidavit pages but before the back-sheet. These exhibits are not returned when the legal proceeding has been completed.

If the affidavit says *Now produced and shown to me and marked Exhibit "A"...*, the exhibit is not attached to the affidavit or filed with it. It is left with the registrar of the court for the use of the court and is returned after the disposition of the proceeding.

Alterations in an Affidavit

Any ink insertion, erasure, or other alteration in an affidavit must be initialled by the person taking the affidavit; unless so initialled, the affidavit may not be used without court permission.

Number and Disposition of Copies

The number of copies required of an affidavit varies from two to four copies, depending on the purpose and nature of the affidavit and whether it is served and filed or only served. Most affidavits are first served on all interested parties, and the original is then filed with the court office with proof of service. With most court documents, you will need a minimum of three copies, plus one copy for each additional party to the proceeding.

Terms and Concepts

court document formatting guidelines
general heading
title of proceeding
style of cause
short title of proceeding
versus (v.)

and others (et al.)
backsheets
affidavit
deponent
jurat
exhibits

Review Questions

1. What information appears in the general heading of a court document?
2. When may you use the short title of proceeding in court documents?
3. What do the *Rules of Civil Procedure* specify in regard to margins, spacing, etc. for court documents?
4. How will the amount of $100,000.00 be shown in court documents?
5. What information appears on a backsheet for a court document?
6. There are two methods by which exhibits may form part of an affidavit. How do you know which method to use?
7. **Internet Research:** Search online to learn about the various litigation software packages that are currently available for the production of court documents. What are some of the advantages of using such software?

PRECEDENTS

Precedent 9.1 Court Document, Basic Format, First Page

GENERAL HEADING

including

Title of Proceeding (Style of Cause)

Court File No. 0000000

NAME OF COURT

B E T W E E N:

NAME(S) OF PARTY(IES)

Capacity

- and -

NAME(S) OF PARTY(IES)

Capacity

TITLE OF DOCUMENT

1.   The body of a court document is prepared in consecutively numbered paragraphs that are indented either 5 or 10 spaces. The body of the document is usually double-spaced.

2.   xxxxxxxxxxxxxxxxxxxxxxxxxxxxxxxxxxxxxxxxxxxxxxxxxxxxxxxxx xxxxxxxxxxxxxxxxxxxxxxxxxxxxxxxxxxxxxxxxxxxxxxx:

(a)   xxxxxxxxxxxxxxxxxxxxxxxxxxxxxxxxxxxxxxxxxxxxxxxxxxxxx

xxxxxxxxxxxxxxxxxxxxxxxxxxxxxxxxxxxxx

BODY

(b)   xxxxxxxxxxxxxxxxxxxxxxxxxxxxxxxxxxxxxxxxxxxxxxxxxxxxx

xxxxxxxxxxxxxxxxxxxxxxxxxxxxxxxxxxxxxxxxxxxxx

OR

THE BODY of the document is prepared in unnumbered paragraphs that are indented either 5 or 10 spaces. A double space is left between the paragraphs. The first words of the paragraphs are usually typed in solid capitals and may be in boldface if that is the preference of your law office.

Note: 1.5″ left margin on all court documents

Source: Korbitec Inc.

- 2 -

NOTE THAT at least two lines of the body of the document must be

carried over onto the last page with the date and the particulars of the court address

or law firm.

Month Day, Year

> *Most documents are dated
> the day of preparation.
> Notable exceptions are
> affidavits and originating
> documents.*

NAME OF LAW FIRM
Street Address
City, Province Postal Code

Name of individual lawyer
Telephone: Telephone Number
Facsimile: Fax Number

Solicitors for the *(capacity of party
OR capacity and name(s) if law firm
not acting for all parties of the
same capacity)*

TO: **NAME OF LAW FIRM**
Street Address
City, Province Postal Code

Name of individual lawyer
Telephone: Telephone Number
Facsimile: Fax Number

Solicitors for the *(capacity of party
or parties OR capacity and name(s)
if law firm is not acting for all the
parties of the same capacity)*

AND TO: *(if required)*

Source: Korbitec Inc.

AARON J. BELVEDERE

Plaintiff

-and-

DARRYL B. ROUTENBERG and others

Defendants

Court File No. 466980

ONTARIO
SUPERIOR COURT OF JUSTICE
PROCEEDING COMMENCED AT
BARRIE

JURY NOTICE

HILL, JOHNSTON & GRANT
Barristers & Solicitors
17 Princess Street South
Toronto ON M8Y 3N5

Lynda C. Ritchie (42212R)
Tel: 416-354-9900
Fax: 416-354-9909

Solicitors for the Plaintiff

Source: Korbitec Inc.

Court File No.

NAME OF COURT

TITLE OF PROCEEDING

AFFIDAVIT
OF (NAME OF DEPONENT)

I, *(full name of deponent)*, of *(City, Town, etc.)* of *(name)*, in the *(County, Regional Municipality, etc.)*, of *(name)*,[1] MAKE OATH AND SAY *(or AFFIRM)*:

1.   xxxxxxxxxxxxxxxxxxxxxxxxxxxxxxxxxxxxxxxxxxxxxxxxxxxxxxxxxxxx

xxxxxxxxxxxxxxxxxxxxxxxxxxxxxxxxxxxxxxxxxxxxxxx..

2.   xxxxxxxxxxxxxxxxxxxxxxxxxxxxxxxxxxxxxxxxxxxxxxxxxxxxxxxxxxxx

xxxxxxxxxxxxxxxxxxxxxxxxxxxxxxxxxxxxxxxxxxxxxxxxxxxxxxxxxxx-.

3.   xxxxxxxxxxxxxxxxxxxxxxxxxxxxxxxxxxxxxxxxxxxxxxxxxxxxxxxxxxxx

xxxxxxxxxxxxxxxxxxxxxxxxxxxxx-.

(The facts being sworn to are set out in consecutively numbered paragraphs. Each paragraph deals as far as possible with one particular statement of fact.)

SWORN before me at the   )
(or AFFIRMED)   )
(City, Town, etc.) of *(name)*   )
)
in the *(County, Regional*   )
)
Municipality, etc.) of *(name)*   )   _____
)
this   day of   , 20__)
)   Requires a back
)
Commissioner for Taking Affidavits)

[1] *Where the deponent is a party, or the solicitor, officer, director, member, or employee of a party, set out his or her capacity, for example: solicitor for the plaintiff, OR one of the plaintiffs, OR the above-named applicant.*

Source: Korbitec Inc.

CHAPTER 10

The Originating Process

OBJECTIVES:

- Define and describe the various steps in originating a civil proceeding

- Demonstrate an understanding of the purpose and originating steps in an action

- Demonstrate an understanding of mandatory mediation, case management, and simplified procedure as it applies to an action

- Use legal precedents to prepare originating documents, such as notice of action, statement of claim, and information for court use

When the lawyer acts for a client who has a claim against another party, it may be necessary to commence proceedings in the court. The issuance of the required document to commence a legal proceeding is known as the originating process, as illustrated in Figure 10.1.

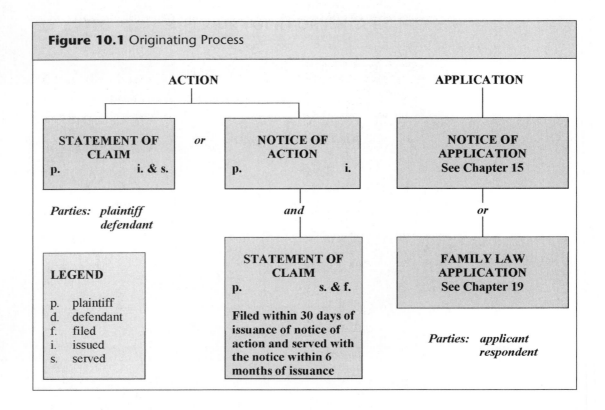

Figure 10.1 Originating Process

ACTION APPLICATION

STATEMENT OF CLAIM
p. i. & s.

or

NOTICE OF ACTION
p. i.

NOTICE OF APPLICATION
See Chapter 15

Parties: plaintiff defendant

and

or

STATEMENT OF CLAIM
p. s. & f.

Filed within 30 days of issuance of notice of action and served with the notice within 6 months of issuance

FAMILY LAW APPLICATION
See Chapter 19

Parties: applicant respondent

LEGEND

p. plaintiff
d. defendant
f. filed
i. issued
s. served

All originating processes are by way of an action unless a statute or a rule provides that it be commenced by way of an application, which is discussed in Chapter 15.

An action may be brought either in the Ontario Superior Court of Justice or in the Small Claims Court (a branch of the Superior Court of Justice), depending on the amount of damages being claimed. In this chapter, we consider actions brought in the Superior Court of Justice itself.

ORIGINATING AN ACTION

Originating Documents

Actions are commenced by either

1. issuing one of the following statements of claim:
   a. statement of claim (general) or (money only)
   b. statement of claim (mortgage action)
   c. statement of claim (action commenced by notice of action)

2. issuing a notice of action

A notice of action is usually prepared if there is insufficient time to prepare a statement of claim, for example, if a limitation period is expiring. Following the issuance of the notice of action, a statement of claim must be filed with the court within 30 days.

The parties to an action commenced by the issuance of a statement of claim or a notice of action are the **plaintiff(s)** and the **defendant(s)**. The document by which divorce proceedings are commenced is discussed in Chapter 19. In this and subsequent chapters, the term *pleading* may be used to refer to documents that set forth the cause and claim of the plaintiff or the defence of the defendant in a legal proceeding.

STATEMENT OF CLAIM TO ORIGINATE AN ACTION

A statement of claim is the pleading usually issued to originate an action at the request of the plaintiff, and it is addressed to the defendant. The document advises the defendant of a claim against him or her, outlines the steps to be taken if the proceeding is to be defended, indicates the possibility of legal aid if the defendant is unable to pay legal fees, and details the consequences if the proceeding is not defended. It sets out in numbered paragraphs the relief sought by the plaintiff and the facts on which the plaintiff's claim is based. The final paragraph of the claim specifies the place where the plaintiff wishes the action to be heard.

Statement of Claim (General)

A statement of claim (general) is most frequently used (Precedent 10.1). It originates most actions in the courts when the amount in dispute is uncertain or where the claim does not involve monetary damages. Damages that must be determined by the court are known as **unliquidated damages**.

Statement of Claim (Money Only)

A statement of claim (money only) is used when the amount of the relief is clear and certain, as in a claim for payment of an invoice for goods or under a promissory note (Precedent 10.2). Damages that are certain or can be determined to the penny are known as **liquidated damages**.

The only difference between a statement of claim (general) and a statement of claim (money only) is that the latter contains an additional paragraph in the instructions to the defendant on the steps to be taken to have the claim dismissed. This includes paying the claim and an amount for **costs**—money to which a party may be entitled as partial compensation for the expense of being a party in a legal proceeding.

Statement of Claim (Mortgage Action)

A statement of claim (mortgage action) is used when the plaintiff's claim arises under a mortgage debt under which the defendant is usually in default. The basic format for a statement of claim (mortgage action) is Form 14B of the rules.

Statement of Claim (Action Commenced by Notice of Action)

This is used when the action was originated by a notice of action instead of a statement of claim and is discussed later in this chapter.

PREPARATION OF STATEMENT OF CLAIM TO COMMENCE AN ACTION

General Heading

Leave the court file number blank when preparing a statement of claim. The number is inserted by the local registrar when the document is issued. Note the following information when formatting the names of the parties:

Corporations

A company that is a party in a legal proceeding is identified by its full corporate name. You should never make any changes to a corporate name. For example, if the proper corporate name of a company is Hawick Holdings Ltd., you should never change the Ltd. to Limited or vice versa.

Individuals

For individuals, use at least one given name in full, together with a surname. It is quite acceptable to use all the given names or one given name and the initial or initials of other given names. For example:

RONALD ANDERSON
RONALD C. ANDERSON
RONALD CRAIG ANDERSON

Individual under a Disability

Where a party to a legal proceeding is under a disability, he or she commences or defends a legal proceeding through a **litigation guardian**, a person over 18 who meets certain requirements set out in the rules. Disability includes being a **minor** (that is, under the age of majority, which in Ontario is 18), or being mentally incompetent, for example. When a party commences or defends a legal proceeding through a litigation guardian, the party and litigation guardian may not act in person but must be represented by a solicitor.

The party commencing a legal proceeding identifies his or her litigation guardian in the originating process document; the party defending does so through a litigation guardian appointed by order of the court. When a plaintiff acts through a litigation guardian, include the name of the litigation guardian in the title of proceeding. For example:

MARY J. SMITH, a minor, by her
litigation guardian HOWARD SMITH
Plaintiff

A defendant under disability is usually described in the originating document by his or her name only since a litigation guardian may not be appointed until after the action is originated. When the appointment is made by the court, the title of proceeding is amended to include the name of the litigation guardian.

Individual Carrying on Business

When a party to a legal proceeding is an individual carrying on business under a name other than his or her own name and the proceeding involves the business, the title of proceeding shows the name of the individual and the name of the business. For example:

JAMES BROWN, carrying on business under the
firm name and style of BROWN COMPUTER SALES
or
JANET GREEN, c.o.b. under the
trade name and style of GREENSENSE

Individual Identified by More than One Name

When a party to a legal proceeding is an individual known by more than one name, he or she is shown in the title of proceeding by both names. For example:

CARMEN MARTINCOLA also known as CARMEN MARTIN
or
LIHUA WANG aka LISA WANG

Partnership

When a partnership is a party to a legal proceeding, the title of proceeding shows the full partnership name. For example:

HILL, JOHNSTON & GRANT

Estate Trustees of an Estate

When the estate trustees (formerly referred to as *executors* or *administrators*) of an estate are parties to a legal proceeding, the title of proceedings shows the names of the estate trustees and identifies the estate for which they are acting. For example:

MATTHEW BLAKE and JENNIFER BLAKE,
Estate Trustees of the Last Will and
Testament of JANE BLAKE, deceased

Body of Statement of Claim Originating an Action

The body of the statement of claim consists of two parts:

1. The notice to the defendant indicating that an action has been commenced, the steps to be taken if the proceeding is to be defended, and the consequences if the proceeding is not defended.

   If the statement of claim is for money only, an additional paragraph advises the defendant of the amount claimed for costs and how the claim may be dismissed.

   The date of issuance of the statement of claim and the address of the court office where the proceeding is to be commenced are shown. When preparing the document, leave the date information blank or include only the month and year in the date section; leave five spaces for the registrar to insert the actual date of issuance, for example, *March   , 20__.*

   The statement of claim then indicates the name and address for service of each defendant.

2. The claim of the plaintiff against the defendant, also known as the relief sought. Paragraph 1 of this section indicates the specific relief sought by the plaintiff. When the damages are for money, they are referred to as general and special damages.

   General damages would be an amount of money to compensate the plaintiff for pain and suffering and are always a round sum of dollars.

   Special damages would be the amount required to reimburse the plaintiff for expenses incurred as a result of the defendant's conduct, such as loss of wages, medical expenses, and repairs to a vehicle. The amount of special damages set out in the statement of claim is that as of the date of issuance of the claim; an updated statement of such damages is filed before the trial of the action.

   Each allegation of fact (a statement or assertion) relied on to substantiate (to support) the claim is set out in consecutively numbered paragraphs, commencing with 2. A claim for prejudgment and postjudgment interest (discussed below) is usually included, as well as a claim for the costs of the action.

   A final unnumbered paragraph indicates the proposed place of trial. If this statement must be inserted, use the normal paragraph indentation and show the statement either a double or triple space following the last consecutively numbered paragraph.

   The date of issuance of the statement of claim appears after the paragraph dealing with the details of the claim. When preparing the claim, leave the date information blank or include the month and year, leaving sufficient space for the actual day of the month to be inserted by the local registrar when the statement of claim is issued. This date will be the same date that will be inserted on the first page of the claim.

   Opposite the date of issuance, set out the name, address, and telephone and facsimile numbers of the solicitors for the plaintiff, together with the name of the specific lawyer, his or her law society registration number, and a line "Solicitors for the plaintiff (or plaintiffs)."

Request for Interest on Damages Claimed

When the statement of claim is prepared, the plaintiff's claim in paragraph 1 usually includes a claim for interest on the amount the court is asked to award. Where a claim is made for damages, the request is for **prejudgment interest** from the date the cause of action arose to the date of the order or judgment and **postjudgment interest** from and after the date of the order or judgment until payment of the damages. The claim requests the appropriate interest and cites the section of the *Courts of Justice Act* that provides for such interest. Both prejudgment and postjudgment interest rates may be obtained at the Ministry of the Attorney General website (http://www.attorneygeneral.jus.gov.on.ca/english/courts/interestrates.asp). The quarters of a year shown on this website mean the three-month periods ending with the 31st day of March, 30th day of June, 30th day of September, and 31st day of December each year.

Backsheet

Each copy of the statement of claim except those prepared for inclusion in the trial record requires a backsheet. The short title of proceeding may be used; the court file number is left blank for completion by the local registrar when the document is issued. The place where the proceeding is commenced is set out below the name of the court, and the usual information is provided about the solicitors for the plaintiff (Precedent 10.1A).

Number and Disposition of Copies

Prepare a minimum of three copies, plus one for each defendant. The copies are used as follows:

1. One copy is kept in the file. Two copies are taken to the court office in the county where the proceeding is to be commenced. Upon payment of the required fee, the local registrar will **issue** the document; that is, he or she signs it, inserts the exact date of issuance, seals it with the court seal, and assigns and inserts the **court file number**. The issued copy of the document is returned to the law firm.
2. Make a minimum of three copies of the issued statement of claim plus one for each defendant. One is filed with the court; one is kept in the file as a "working copy," and one is for the Record subfile. The original issued statement of claim is placed in the Document subfile for safekeeping.
3. A copy of the issued statement of claim is served on each defendant. This must be done within six months of the date of issue. It is possible for the statement of claim to be issued and held, that is, not immediately served on the defendant. Usually, however, the statement of claim is personally served on the defendant immediately after it is issued. Personal service is discussed in Chapter 11. If the statement of claim is not served on the defendant within six months of the date of issue, the defendant may move to have the action dismissed for delay.

NOTICE OF ACTION TO ORIGINATE AN ACTION

There are two types of a notice of action: one for money only and one for use in all other actions (Precedent 10.3). This document contains only the information that would be found in the first part and in paragraph 1 of a statement of claim used to originate an action. Once a notice of action has been issued, an additional 30 days are allowed to file a statement of claim, which may repeat or amend the claim, and sets out the facts relied on by the plaintiff to support the claim made in the notice of action.

The notice of action *and* the statement of claim are served together on the defendants within six months from the date of issuance of the notice of action.

Preparation of a Notice of Action

A notice of action is prepared the same way as a statement of claim but omits the allegations of fact to support the relief sought and the place of trial. The claim portion of the notice may generally outline the relief or may set out precisely what is claimed. The backsheet of the notice of claim is completed in the same manner as that of the statement of claim.

Number and Disposition of Copies

Prepare a minimum of three copies plus one for each defendant. The copies are used as follows:

1. One copy is kept in the file. Two copies are taken to the court office in the county where the proceeding is to be commenced. Upon payment of the required fee, the local registrar issues the document (as discussed above). The issued copy of the document is returned to the law firm.
2. Make a minimum of three copies of the issued notice of action plus one for each defendant. One copy is filed with the court, one is kept in the file, and one is for the Record subfile. The original issued notice of action is placed in the Document subfile for safekeeping along with the additional copies for the defendants. Note that these copies are retained in the Document subfile until the statement of claim is prepared. At that time, one copy is served on each defendant, *together* with the statement of claim.

STATEMENT OF CLAIM (ACTION COMMENCED BY NOTICE OF ACTION)

When an action is originated by issuing a notice of action, the required statement of claim follows the pattern for a general court document (Precedent 10.4). The general heading of the statement of claim is copied from the notice of action, and the document is identified as *Statement of Claim*. One double space beneath the title of the document indicate the date the notice of action was issued. For example:

STATEMENT OF CLAIM
Notice of action issued on February 14, 20__

The statement of claim prepared for use with a notice of action contains the claim portion of the statement of claim form; the instructions to the defendant on how to defend the action, etc., are set out in the notice of action. The relief sought is set out in the first numbered paragraph, and other consecutively numbered paragraphs set out the allegations of fact relied on by the plaintiff to support the claim. The last unnumbered paragraph states the proposed place of trial.

The date in the ending of this form of statement of claim is the date of preparation. The usual information on the name, address, and telephone number of the law firm is included, but the document is not addressed to anyone. The persons upon whom it is to be served are shown in the notice of action. A backsheet similar to that prepared for a statement of claim is required.

Number and Disposition of Copies

Prepare a minimum of three copies plus one for each defendant. These are used as follows:

1. A copy is filed in the court within 30 days from the date of issue of the notice of action. One copy is kept in the file, and one is for the Record subfile. The original is placed in the Document subfile.
2. Make as many additional copies of the statement of claim as there are defendants. A copy of the notice of action *and* the statement of claim are personally served together within six months from the date of issue of the notice of action on each defendant.

INFORMATION FOR COURT USE FORM

An information for court use form must be completed and filed with the court when any originating document is issued (Precedent 10.5). The general heading from the originating document is to be copied into the form, and then a series of questions on the form are completed depending on the particulars of the action. Put the month and year for the date; the lawyer will insert the date when he or she signs the form. Make three copies of this form; one is for the file, and two copies are taken to the court when filing the originating document.

SOLICITORS OF RECORD

When a legal proceeding is commenced, the solicitors acting for the plaintiff and whose name appears on the originating documents are known as the solicitors of record. In other words, the name of that law firm appears in the court file as solicitors for one of the parties.

SIMPLIFIED PROCEDURE

As in other provinces, Ontario has a simplified procedure system, which was introduced to eliminate some of the procedures, time, and expenses for smaller claims. This procedure is mandatory (except for certain exclusions listed in the rules) for claims for $50,000 or less (real and/or personal property) exclusive of interest and costs. This procedure may also be used where the plaintiff chooses and there is no objection from the defendant(s).

If an action is being originated under the simplified procedure, the statement of claim or notice of action must indicate before the claim portion of the document that the action is being brought under the simplified procedure (Precedent 10.2). The originating document is usually served on the defendant immediately as the case may be dismissed by the registrar if no defence is filed within 180 days of the date of issue of the originating process.

The most significant differences in actions brought under simplified procedure are as follows:

1. Examinations for discovery, cross-examinations on affidavits, and examinations of witnesses on a motion are prohibited, and all potential witnesses must be listed in the affidavit of documents (discussed in Chapter 14).
2. A settlement conference must be held within 60 days after the statement of defence or notice of intent to defend is filed.
3. A **summary trial** is held. This type of hearing proceeds on the basis of affidavit evidence, with limited time for cross-examination, reexamination, and oral arguments, thus expediting the process.

CASE MANAGEMENT

Ontario, like some of the other provinces, has introduced a case management system in selected jurisdictions. The goal of this system is to ensure the efficient processing of a case from commencement to final disposition with or without a hearing, which should eliminate delays and reduce the cost to the parties involved. It should be noted that there are certain types of proceedings that are exempt under the rules. Currently in Ontario, case management applies to proceedings in the Regional Municipality of Ottawa-Carleton and the County of Essex and selected proceedings in Toronto.

The plaintiff's solicitor selects a "track," either fast or standard, on the Court Information Form, which determines the time limit within which required procedural steps must be taken. The time limits for completion of cases are different for each track and are set out in the *Rules of Civil Procedure*. Figure 10.2 sets out the current requirements for case management proceedings, which are *in addition* to the usual procedural requirements in action.

Figure 10.2 Requirements for Case Management Proceedings

Requirement	Time Period	Who Responsible
Issue Statement of Claim or Notice of Action *and* choose either fast or standard track	Within any statutory limitation period	Plaintiff and Court Registrar
Move to change track (optional)	Before close of pleadings	Plaintiff or Defendant
Action dismissed as abandoned	180 days after date of issue of originating process	Court Registrar
Assign case to case management judge	When statement of defence or notice of intent to defend filed	Court Registrar
Convene case conference	If any party fails to meet with any time requirement or for any other matter	Court Registrar (Judge or Master)
Schedule settlement conference	Within 150 days (fast track) or 240 days (standard track) after defence document filed	Registrar
Complete discoveries and/or any related motions	Before settlement conference	Plaintiff and Defendant
Deliver Settlement Conference Brief	Not later than 10 days before the settlement conference	Plaintiff
Deliver Settlement Conference Brief	Not later than 5 days before settlement conference	Defendant
Assign Trial Date	Done at settlement conference	Judge/Master
Serve and File Trial Record	At least 7 days before the trial	Plaintiff or Defendant
Conduct trial management conference	After trial date set	Parties and Judge/Master
Submit Trial Management conference form	Not later than the earlier of 14 days before trial or 4 days before trial management conference	Plaintiff and Defendant

MEDIATION

Mediation is a way for people to settle lawsuits outside of court by having a neutral third party (the mediator) help the disputing parties look for a solution without going to the time and expense of court. Mediators do not decide cases or impose settlements; rather, they facilitate communication and negotiation between the parties. All parties and their lawyers attend at the mediation session, which is an informal process. The mediator structures the discussion, during which all parties have an opportunity to present their side of the story, explain what is important to them, and ask questions. The mediator will then try and assist the parties in exploring settlement options. Mediation is mandatory for proceedings under the simplified rule and for case management proceedings. Figure 10.3 (p. 174) sets out the mandatory mediation steps, which are in addition to the ordinary steps in an action.

Figure 10.3 Mandatory Mediation Steps

Requirement	Time Period	Who Responsible
Selection of Mediator	Within 30 days after filing of first defence document	Plaintiff and Defendant
Notice of Name of Mediator to be filed with Mediation Coordinator	Within 30 days after filing of first defence document	Plaintiff
Assignment of Mediator	If mediation coordinator does not receive any of • Notice of Name of Mediator • An order that mediation has been postponed by court order • A consent to postpone mediation up to 60 days • Notice that action has been settled	Mediation Coordinator
Mandatory Mediation Session	Within 90 days after filing of first defence document	Plaintiff and Defendant
Statement of Issues	To be served on all other parties and the mediator at least 7 days before mediation session	Plaintiff and Defendant
Attendance at Mediation Session	At date set for mediation session	Plaintiff and Defendant
Mediator's Report	Within 10 days after mediation is concluded	Mediator

It should be noted that if a settlement is reached, a notice advising the court of the settlement must be filed within 10 days of the agreement being signed. If the action is not settled at the mediation session, the action will continue through the court process as usual.

COURT FEES

Whenever a document is issued or filed with the court, or if a service is requested of the court, a fee is charged. The *Schedules of Fees* is published in the *Rules of Civil Procedure* each year or may be accessed at the Ontario e-law website (http://www .e-laws.gov.on.ca/index.html). This court fee is charged to the client as a disbursement when the account is rendered.

TICKLER REMINDERS

If a notice of action is issued, a tickler slip should be prepared to remind the solicitor of the date by which the statement of claim must be filed with the court.

If the issued statement of claim is not to be served immediately, prepare a tickler slip to remind the solicitor of the six-month limitation period within which it must be served. Use a tickler date about a week before the limitation date.

If the originating documents are served immediately, prepare a tickler slip once the document has been served to remind the solicitor of the date by which the defendant must respond to the claim. If the statement of claim is for money only, the solicitor may very well wish to commence proceedings to have judgment signed by default should the defendant fail to defend the action. The number of days a defendant has to indicate an intent to defend is set out in the first part of the statement of claim or notice of action and depends on where the defendant is served. Default judgment proceedings are discussed in Chapter 17.

If a case management system operates in the court office in which the proceeding was originated, or if the simplified rule applies, ticklers should be prepared to remind the lawyers of the dates by which various steps in the case must be completed.

In subsequent chapters of this text dealing with civil litigation, the dates and time periods reflect those set out in the *Rules of Civil Procedure* for a general action with references to some of the different procedural steps for simplified and case managed proceedings.

Terms and Concepts

originating process	minor
action	format of names of parties
statement of claim (general, money only,	general damages
mortgage action, action commenced by	special damages
statement of claim)	prejudgment interest
notice of action	postjudgment interest
plaintiff	issue
defendant	court file number
unliquidated damages	solicitors of record
liquidated damages	simplified procedure
costs	case management
general heading	mandatory mediation
format of names of parties	ticklers
litigation guardian	

Review Questions

1. An action in Ontario may be brought in one of two courts. What are those courts, and what factor determines in which court the action is commenced?

2. What documents may be used to originate an action, and how do you determine which one to use?

3. What happens to the statement of claim when it is taken to the court office to be issued?

4. Explain the process of issuing and serving a statement of claim, action commenced by notice of action.

5. If the plaintiff is claiming both general and special damages, which one will appear as, for example, $100,000.00? How will the other be expressed?

6. What is meant by the term *solicitors of record*?

7. When may an action be commenced under simplified procedure? How is the originating document different from the regular originating document?

8. What is the purpose of case management?

9. Why is the preparation of tickler slips such an important part of the originating process procedures?

10. **Internet Research:** If the client is claiming prejudgment interest from August of this year, what rate of interest would he or she be entitled to if his or her claim is successful?

Automated Civil Litigation – Korbitec Inc.

Court File No.

ONTARIO
SUPERIOR COURT OF JUSTICE

B E T W E E N:

JOHN JOSEPH WILLIAMSON

Plaintiff

(Court Seal)

and

HENRY ARMAND DELOS-RAYES

Defendant

STATEMENT OF CLAIM

TO THE DEFENDANT(S)

A LEGAL PROCEEDING HAS BEEN COMMENCED AGAINST YOU by the plaintiff. The claim made against you is set out in the following pages.

IF YOU WISH TO DEFEND THIS PROCEEDING, you or an Ontario lawyer acting for you must prepare a statement of defence in Form 18A prescribed by the *Rules of Civil Procedure*, serve it on the plaintiff's lawyer or, where the plaintiff does not have a lawyer, serve it on the plaintiff, and file it, with proof of service, in this court office, WITHIN TWENTY DAYS after this statement of claim is served on you, if you are served in Ontario.

If you are served in another province or territory of Canada or in the United States of America, the period for serving and filing your statement of defence is forty days. If you are served outside Canada and the United States of America, the period is sixty days.

Instead of serving and filing a statement of defence, you may serve and file a notice of intent to defend in Form 18B prescribed by the *Rules of Civil Procedure*. This will entitle you to ten more days within which to serve and file your statement of defence.

IF YOU FAIL TO DEFEND THIS PROCEEDING, JUDGMENT MAY BE GIVEN AGAINST YOU IN YOUR ABSENCE AND WITHOUT FURTHER NOTICE TO YOU. IF YOU WISH TO DEFEND THIS PROCEEDING BUT ARE UNABLE TO PAY LEGAL FEES, LEGAL AID MAY BE AVAILABLE TO YOU BY CONTACTING A LOCAL LEGAL AID OFFICE.

Date _____   Issued by _____

Local Registrar

Address of
court office: 114 Worsley Street
Barrie ON L4M 1M1

TO: HENRY ARMAND DELOS-RAYES
R.R. #1
Honey Harbour ON L4N 3K9

Source: Korbitec Inc.

- 2 -

CLAIM

1. The plaintiff claims:

    (a) special damages in the amount of $27,771.76;

    (b) general damages in the amount of $500,000.00;

    (c) his costs of this action;

    (d) interest in accordance with sections 138 and 139 of the *Courts of Justice Act*, R.S.O. 1990; and

    (e) such further and other relief as to this honourable court may seem just.

2. The plaintiff is a truck driver who resides in the Town of Whitby, in the Province of Ontario.

3. The defendant is a farmer who resides at R.R. #1, Honey Harbour, in the Province of Ontario, and on the 17th day of February, 20__, was the owner of a Hereford heifer cow, which he kept on the said premises.

4. On the 17th day of February, 20__, the plaintiff was driving a motor vehicle in an easterly direction on No. 78 Highway and had reached a point approximately .5 km west of the junction of No. 80 Highway when suddenly and without warning the cow referred to in paragraph 3 hereof appeared on the highway in front of his said vehicle and an accident resulted.

5. The accident aforesaid was caused solely by the negligence of the defendant in permitting the said cow to be on the highway, particulars of such negligence being as follows:

    (a) he failed to properly enclose the cow on his premises when he knew or should have known that it would be a danger to traffic on the highway if it escaped from his said premises;

    (b) he failed to keep his fence in such repair so as to prevent the escape of the said cow from his premises; and

    (c) he failed to take sufficient steps to keep the said cow in the barn when he knew or should have known that if it escaped from the barn on to the

Source: Korbitec Inc.

- 3 -

adjacent fields, there was nothing to restrain it from wandering on to the highway.

6. As a result of colliding with the cow as aforesaid, the plaintiff sustained severe injuries, in particular a compound depressed fracture of the skull, damages to the optic nerve, multiple lacerations to the face and body, dislocation of the right elbow, compound fracture of the right wrist, and a fracture of the head of the radius.

7. As a result of these injuries, the plaintiff underwent severe operative procedures, his right arm was amputated from four inches below the elbow, he has lost the sight of his right eye, he has diminished sensation of taste and smell, and brain damage has impaired his ability to do productive work.

8. The plaintiff has thereby sustained severe pain and discomfort and will be permanently partially disabled.

9. Prior to the 17th day of February, 20___, the plaintiff was a truck driver and earned an average of $783.61 a week. Since the date of the accident, the plaintiff has been unable to return to his employment or any other employment and has thereby suffered a wage loss of $24,291.91; he will sustain a further loss in this respect for an undetermined time. The plaintiff has incurred medical expenses to date in the amount of $3,479.85 and may incur further such expenses.

The plaintiff proposes that this action be tried at Barrie.

Date of issue:

HARE, ROSS & WILKINSON
Barristers & Solicitors
94 Wimbleton Crescent
Barrie ON L4V 5X2

Patricia M. Cochrane (46992C)

Tel: 705-975-4891
Fax: 705-987-2468

Solicitors for the Plaintiff

Source: Korbitec Inc.

JOHN JOSEPH WILLIAMSON

Plaintiff

-and-

HENRY ARMAND DELOS-RAYES

Defendant

Court File No.

ONTARIO
SUPERIOR COURT OF JUSTICE

PROCEEDING COMMENCED AT
BARRIE

STATEMENT OF CLAIM

HARE, ROSS & WILKINSON
Barristers & Solicitors
94 Wimbleton Crescent
Barrie ON L4V 5X2

Patricia M. Cochrane (46692C)
Tel: 705-975-4891
Fax: 705-987-2468

Solicitors for the Plaintiff

Source: Korbitec Inc.

Automated Civil Litigation – Korbitec Inc.   Court File No.

ONTARIO
SUPERIOR COURT OF JUSTICE

B E T W E E N :

EAST HARDWARE LIMITED

Plaintiff

(Court Seal)   and

NORMAN G. MASTERWOOD

Defendant

STATEMENT OF CLAIM

TO THE DEFENDANT(S)

A LEGAL PROCEEDING HAS BEEN COMMENCED AGAINST YOU by the plaintiff. The claim made against you is set out in the following pages.

IF YOU WISH TO DEFEND THIS PROCEEDING, you or an Ontario lawyer acting for you must prepare a statement of defence in Form 18A prescribed by the *Rules of Civil Procedure*, serve it on the plaintiff's lawyer or, where the plaintiff does not have a lawyer, serve it on the plaintiff, and file it, with proof of service, in this court office, WITHIN TWENTY DAYS after this statement of claim is served on you, if you are served in Ontario.

If you are served in another province or territory of Canada or in the United States of America, the period for serving and filing your statement of defence is forty days. If you are served outside Canada and the United States of America, the period is sixty days.

Instead of serving and filing a statement of defence, you may serve and file a notice of intent to defend in Form 18B prescribed by the *Rules of Civil Procedure*. This will entitle you to ten more days within which to serve and file your statement of defence.

IF YOU FAIL TO DEFEND THIS PROCEEDING, JUDGMENT MAY BE GIVEN AGAINST YOU IN YOUR ABSENCE AND WITHOUT FURTHER NOTICE TO YOU. IF YOU WISH TO DEFEND THIS PROCEEDING BUT ARE UNABLE TO PAY LEGAL FEES, LEGAL AID MAY BE AVAILABLE TO YOU BY CONTACTING A LOCAL LEGAL AID OFFICE.

IF YOU PAY THE PLAINTIFF'S CLAIM, and $750.00 for costs, within the time for serving and filing your statement of defence, you may move to have this proceeding dismissed by the court. If you believe the amount claimed for costs is excessive, you may pay the plaintiff's claim and $400.00 for costs and have the costs assessed by the court.

Date _____   Issued by _____

                                               Local Registrar
                            Address of   393 University Avenue, 10th Floor
                            court office: Toronto ON M5G 1E6

TO: **NORMAN G. MASTERWOOD**
     970 Prince Henry Drive
     Toronto ON M4H 1T9

Source: Korbitec Inc.

- 2 -

THIS ACTION IS BROUGHT AGAINST YOU UNDER THE SIMPLIFIED
PROCEDURE PROVIDED IN RULE 76 OF THE *RULES OF CIVIL PROCEDURE.*

CLAIM

1.   The plaintiff claims:

   (a) the sum of $18,300.00 being the amount of an unpaid cheque tendered in
      payment of Invoice No. 4568 issued to the defendant by the plaintiff;

   (b) prejudgment interest thereon in accordance with the Courts of Justice Act
      from August 16, 20___, to the date of judgment or other final disposition
      of this action;

   (c) postjudgment interest in accordance with the Courts of Justice Act;

   (d) costs on a solicitor and client basis; and

   (e) such further and other relief as to this honourable court may seem just.

2.   A cheque for $18,300.00 dated August 18, 20___, drawn by the defendant
upon the Royal Bank of Canada, Grenview and Bloor Street Branch, Toronto,
payable to the plaintiff, was received by the plaintiff on August 16, 20___. The
cheque was duly presented on August 16, 20___, but was dishonoured.

3.   The amount owing by the defendant to the plaintiff is $18,300.00, particulars
of which are as follows:

   August 16, 20___   Dishonour of cheque $18,300.00
                             dated August 20___

4.   A written demand by the plaintiff for payment by certified cheque was made
on August 18, 20___, in a letter sent registered mail. To date the plaintiff has not
received any cheque from the defendant.

   The plaintiff proposes that this action be tried at Toronto.

Date of issue: October   , 20___   HILL, JOHNSTON & GRANT
                                                  17 Princess Street South
                                                  Suite 2501
                                                  Toronto ON M8Y 3N5

   Requires a back   Lynda C. Ritchie (42212R)
                                                  Phone: (416) 354-9900
                                                  Fax: (416) 354-9909

                                                  Solicitors for the plaintiff

Source: Korbitec Inc.

Automated Civil Litigation – Korbitec Inc.   Court File No.

ONTARIO
SUPERIOR COURT OF JUSTICE

B E T W E E N:

EAST HARDWARE LIMITED
and PATRICK THOMAS STONE

Plaintiffs

(Court Seal)   and

HUMBER MANUFACTURING LTD.

Defendant

NOTICE OF ACTION

TO THE DEFENDANT

    A LEGAL PROCEEDING HAS BEEN COMMENCED AGAINST YOU by the plaintiff. The claim made against you is set out in the statement of claim served with this notice of action.

    IF YOU WISH TO DEFEND THIS PROCEEDING, you or an Ontario lawyer acting for you must prepare a statement of defence in Form 18A prescribed by the *Rules of Civil Procedure*, serve it on the plaintiff's lawyer or, where the plaintiff does not have a lawyer, serve it on the plaintiff, and file it, with proof of service, in this court office, WITHIN TWENTY DAYS after this notice of action is served on you, if you are served in Ontario.

    If you are served in another province or territory of Canada or in the United States of America, the period for serving and filing your statement of defence is forty days. If you are served outside Canada and the United States of America, the period is sixty days.

    Instead of serving and filing a statement of defence, you may serve and file a notice of intent to defend in Form 18B prescribed by the *Rules of Civil Procedure*. This will entitle you to ten more days within which to serve and file your statement of defence.

    IF YOU FAIL TO DEFEND THIS PROCEEDING, JUDGMENT MAY BE GIVEN AGAINST YOU IN YOUR ABSENCE AND WITHOUT FURTHER NOTICE TO YOU. IF YOU WISH TO DEFEND THIS PROCEEDING BUT ARE UNABLE TO PAY LEGAL FEES, LEGAL AID MAY BE AVAILABLE TO YOU BY CONTACTING A LOCAL LEGAL AID OFFICE.

Date _____   Issued by _____
                                                    Local Registrar
                            Address of   393 University Avenue, 10th Floor
                            court office: Toronto ON M5G 1E6

TO: **HUMBER MANUFACTURING LTD.**
      9672 Park Lawn Road
      Etobicoke ON M8X 6G2

Source: Korbitec Inc.

2

CLAIM

The plaintiff's claim is for:

(a) a declaration that the Distributorship Agreement dated January 1, 2005, between the plaintiffs and the defendant has been terminated by the defendants wrongfully and in bad faith;

(b) an interlocutory injunction to restrain the defendants, their servants, employees or agents from attempting to seize the plaintiffs' inventories or the plaintiffs' accounts receivable or otherwise interfering with the conduct of the plaintiff's business pending the trial or other final disposition of the action;

(c) an interlocutory order permitting the plaintiffs to pay into court amounts owing from the plaintiffs to the defendant under the said Distributorship Agreement and permitting such amounts paid into court to be set off against any amount awarded to the plaintiffs as damages for the wrongful termination of the said Distributorship Agreement;

(d) damages and exemplary damages for the wrongful termination of the said Distributorship Agreement;

(e) interest in accordance with the *Courts of Justice Act*, R.S.O. 1990; and

(f) its costs of this action.

Date of issue:

HILL, JOHNSTON & GRANT
Barristers & Solicitors
17 Princess Street South, Suite 2501
Toronto ON M8Y 3N5

Peter T. Grant (12345G)

Tel: 416-354-9900
Fax: 416-354-9909

Requires a back

Solicitors for the plaintiffs

Source: Korbitec Inc.

Court File No.

ONTARIO
SUPERIOR COURT OF JUSTICE

TITLE OF PROCEEDING

STATEMENT OF CLAIM

Notice of Action issued on month day, year.

1.   The plaintiff claims:

  (a) ---

       --;

  (b) ---

       ----------------------------------;

  (c) ---

       ---;

  (d) --------------------------------------.

2.   ---

---.

3.   ---

---.

The plaintiff proposes that this action be tried at -----------------------------.

Month day, year

NAME OF LAW FIRM
Street address
City, Province Postal code

Name of individual lawyer
Telephone number
Fax number

Requires a back

Source: Korbitec Inc.

Automated Civil Litigation – Korbitec Inc.

Court File No.

ONTARIO
SUPERIOR COURT OF JUSTICE

B E T W E E N :

**EAST HARDWARE LIMITED
and PATRICK THOMAS STONE**

Plaintiffs

and

HUMBER MANUFACTURING LTD.

Defendant

INFORMATION FOR COURT USE

This proceeding is an: [X] action [ ] application

Has it been commenced under the *Class Proceedings Act*, 1992? [ ] yes [X] no

(If the proceeding is an action, answer all of the following:)

Rule 76 (Simplified Procedure) applies: [ ] yes [X] no

NOTE: Subject to the exceptions found in subrule 76.01(1), it is MANDATORY to proceed under Rule 76 for all cases in which the money amount claimed or the value of real or personal property claimed is $50,000 or less.

Rule 77 (Civil Case Management) applies: [ ] yes [X] no
If Rule 77 applies, choice of track is: [ ] fast [ ] standard
Rule 78 (Toronto Civil Case Management Pilot Project) applies: [ ] yes [X] no

The claim in this proceeding (action or application) is in respect of:
(Select the one item that best describes the nature of the main claim in the proceeding.)

Bankruptcy or insolvency law	[ ]	Motor vehicle accident	[ ]
Collection of liquidated debt	[ ]	Municipal law	[ ]
Constitutional law	[ ]	Partnership law	[ ]
Construction law *(other than construction lien)*	[ ]	Personal property security	[ ]
Construction lien	[ ]	Product liability	[ ]
Contract law	[X]	Professional malpractice *(other than medical)*	[ ]
Corporate law	[ ]	Real property *(including leases; excluding mortgage or charge)*	[ ]
Defamation	[ ]	Tort: economic injury *(other than from medical or professional malpractice)*	[ ]
Employment or labour law	[ ]	Tort: personal injury *(other than from motor vehicle accident)*	[ ]
Intellectual property law	[ ]	Trusts, fiduciary duty	[ ]
Judicial review	[ ]	Wills, estates	[ ]
Medical malpractice	[ ]		
Mortgage or charge	[ ]		

CERTIFICATION

I certify that the above information is correct, to the best of my knowledge.

Date: _____   _____

Peter T. Grant
(if no lawyer, party must sign)

Requires a back

Source: Korbitec Inc.

CHAPTER 11

Serving and Filing Court Documents

OBJECTIVES:

- Define and describe the process known as serving and filing of court documents

- Demonstrate an understanding of the methods of personal service alternatives to personal service, and ordinary service

- Use legal precedents to prepare various affidavits of service

SERVICE OF COURT DOCUMENTS

When court documents have been prepared, they may be issued and served; more frequently, they are served and filed.

Serving a court document means giving a copy of the document to all other parties in the proceeding.

Filing a court document means providing the original or a copy of the court document to the appropriate court office, usually with some proof that the document was served. Frequently, this requirement for proof is abbreviated *wpos*, meaning *with proof of service.*

If the document is an originating document, that is, a document that originates or starts a legal proceeding such as a statement of claim, it must first be taken to the courthouse to be **issued** and then is served on all other parties to the action. However, the majority of documents produced during litigation are those that follow the originating document, and these must be served on all other parties to the action and *then* filed at the court with proof that the document was served on all the parties to the action (Figure 11.1).

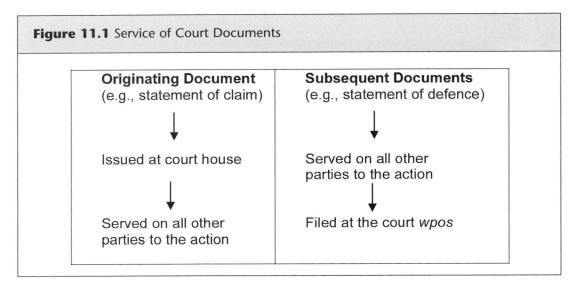

Figure 11.1 Service of Court Documents

Originating Document (e.g., statement of claim)	**Subsequent Documents** (e.g., statement of defence)
↓	↓
Issued at court house	Served on all other parties to the action
↓	↓
Served on all other parties to the action	Filed at the court *wpos*

Proof of Service

The most common method of proving personal service or service on solicitors is by having an **affidavit of service** sworn by the party who effected service. There are several affidavit forms that indicate the circumstances surrounding the service. Commercial software packages may be used; the template of the affidavit may already be recorded in the computer for completion, or the affidavit may be fully keyed. The affidavit may also be printed on the backsheet or by a rubber stamp affixed to the backsheet of the document served and then completed with the necessary information.

Note the following points:

1. Prepare one or two copies of an affidavit of service, depending on the preference of your law firm.

2. The contents identify the person swearing as to the service, the date of such service, the name of the person or law firm served, the title of the document(s) served, and how service was effected.

3. In some affidavits, it is necessary to also indicate the manner in which the identity of the person served was confirmed.

4. No backsheet is usually required for an affidavit of service as the affidavit is attached to the front of the copy of the serviced document that will be filed.

5. When the affidavit has been sworn, it is usually attached to the front of the document to be filed, and the assembled document is then filed with the court. If two copies of the affidavit are prepared, the second copy is kept in the office file. An affidavit of service is not, of course, served on the other side.

PERSONAL SERVICE

The rules specify that originating documents must be served personally or by one of the alternatives to personal service discussed below. **Personal service** of a document means leaving a copy of the document with the individual to be served, that is, putting a copy of the document into his or her hands. The *Rules of Civil Procedure* set out the form of personal service when serving a wide variety of parties, such as a municipality, a corporation, a minor, a partnership, and so on. Those responsible for service refer to the rules to verify the form of service if the party to be served falls within a special category.

Proof of service is made by having the person who made the service swear an affidavit of service. Precedent 11.1 illustrates the form of such an affidavit when service is made by a staff member of the law firm. If the personal service was made by a sheriff or a process server, a certificate of service is provided when the account for service is sent to the law firm.

Alternatives to Personal Service

There are a number of methods by which personal service is deemed to have been made that do not involve putting a copy of the document into the hands of the party being served. These are as follows:

1. **Acceptance of service:** having the solicitors for the party being served accept service on behalf of the party. This is accomplished by leaving a copy of the document with the solicitors for the party and having a statement similar to that shown in Figure 11.2 dated and signed on behalf of those solicitors:
This statement appears on the left side of the backsheet beneath the title of proceeding section of the original copy of the document that originates the legal proceeding. It may be put on the backsheet by using an acceptance of service stamp, or it may be keyed in when preparing the backsheet. A completed acceptance of service statement or stamp is considered proof of service.
Accepting service implies that the solicitors act for the parties being served; that is, they will be the solicitors of record. Since the proceeding is not finally commenced until the defendant or respondent is served with the originating

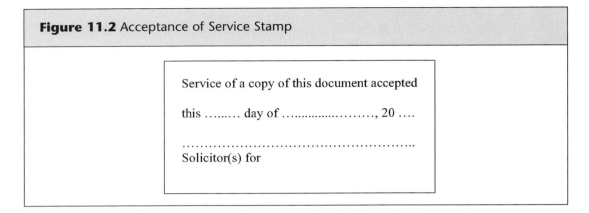

Figure 11.2 Acceptance of Service Stamp

Service of a copy of this document accepted

this .... day of ...., 20 ....

....
Solicitor(s) for

process, acceptance of service by a solicitor is an acknowledgement that the defendant or respondent is aware of the legal proceeding and intends to take the steps open to him, her, or them.

Never accept service of an originating process document unless specifically instructed by the solicitor to do so.

2. **Service by mail:** mailing a copy of the document to the last known address of the person to be served, together with an acknowledgement card (Precedents 11.2A and 11.2B). Service is said to be made only if the acknowledgement of receipt card or a post office receipt bearing a signature that appears to be that of the person to be served is received by the law office. The date of service is the date on which the signed receipt is received by the law office.

    Proof of service is provided by completing an affidavit (Precedent 11.3) to which is attached the acknowledgement of receipt card or a post office receipt form.

3. **Serving at place of residence:** leaving a copy of the document in a sealed envelope addressed to the person to be served with an adult member of the household and mailing a second copy of the document on the same or the next day to the person being served at the place of residence. This form of personal service is used only after an attempt has been made to serve the party personally at his or her place of residence.

    Proof of service is provided by having an affidavit of service completed by the person who carried out these procedures (Precedent 11.4). The date of service is the fifth day after the document was mailed.

Substitutional Service

When it appears to the court that prompt personal service of an originating process is impractical, an order may be made to dispense with service or for substitutional service.

Substitutional service usually means placing a notice in the legal column of the newspaper serving the area where the person to be served is last known to have resided. The notice advises him or her of the legal proceeding and sets out the steps necessary to be involved in the proceeding. The court order specifies when service of the document may be considered made so that time limits can be computed.

ORDINARY SERVICE

Documents that do not originate a legal proceeding may be served on the solicitors of record by any of the following methods, which are often referred to as **ordinary** or **regular service:**

1. **Mail:** mailing a copy to the solicitor's office by prepaid first-class, registered, or certified mail. Service of the document is deemed to have been made on the fifth day after mailing. The document is enclosed with a letter that informs the other solicitors that the document is being served on them in accordance with the rules.

   Proof of service is obtained by having the person who mailed the envelope containing the document complete an affidavit of service by mail on the solicitor or using an affidavit of service by mail stamp. The legal assistant who typed the letter, inserted the material in the envelope after signature, and placed the letter and document in the law firm's outgoing mail tray for processing is deemed to be the person who mailed it (Precedent 11.5). Service is effective on the fifth day after the document is mailed.

2. **Service on solicitor:** by leaving a copy of the document with a solicitor or employee in the solicitor's law office.

   Proof of service is obtained by having an **admission of service** statement similar to that in Figure 11.3 dated and signed on behalf of those solicitors.

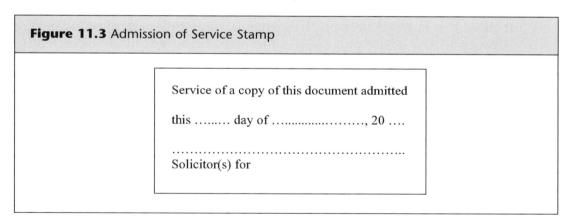

Figure 11.3 Admission of Service Stamp

> Service of a copy of this document admitted
>
> this .... day of ...., 20 ....
>
> ....
> Solicitor(s) for

This statement appears on the left side of the backsheet beneath the title of proceeding section of the copy of the document that is being served. It may be put on the backsheet by using an acceptance of service stamp, or it may be keyed in when preparing the backsheet. A completed admission of service stamp is considered proof of service.

If no one at the solicitor's office will admit service of the document, a copy of it may be left with an employee of that office. Proof of service is then obtained by having the individual who left the copy of the document with the employee complete an affidavit similar to that illustrated in Precedent 11.6. Service is effective as of the date the copy of the document was left with the employee of the solicitor being served.

3. **Depositing in document exchange:** depositing a true copy at a document exchange (where available) of which the solicitor or law firm is a subscriber. Service is effective only if the original document (or a copy of it) and the copy deposited are date stamped by the document exchange official in the presence of the person depositing the copy.

Proof of service is provided by the date stamp on the document. Service is deemed to be made on the day following the day on which the document was deposited and date stamped. If that day is a holiday, service is deemed to be made on the next day that is not a holiday.

4. **Courier:** having a copy delivered by courier to the solicitor's office. Service is effective on the second day following the date on which the courier is given the document.

Proof of service is obtained by having the person who prepared the courier slip complete an affidavit of service (Precedent 11.6). In some firms, the duplicate courier slip is attached as an exhibit to the affidavit. Follow the practice of your firm.

5. **Facsimile:** transmitting by facsimile a copy of the document to the solicitor's office. A document served by this method must include a cover page, as discussed in Chapter 2, showing the sender's name, address, and fax number; the name of the solicitor(s) to be served; the date and time of transmission; the total number of pages sent, including the cover page; the fax number from which the document is being sent; and the name and telephone number of a person to contact in the event that there are transmission problems.

It should be noted that faxes of 16 pages or more in length may be faxed only between 4 p.m. and 8 a.m., unless the party being served gives consent, and that records and authorities may not be served by fax at any time without the permission of the party being served.

Proof of service is obtained by having the individual who faxed the document complete an affidavit of service (Precedent 11.7) or an affidavit of service stamp imprinted on the backsheet of the served document. In some firms, the confirmation page printed out by the facsimile machine is attached as an exhibit to the keyed affidavit of service. Follow the practice of your firm.

6. **E-mail:** attaching the document to be served to an e-mail message to the solicitor of record. The e-mail message must include the sender's name, address, telephone number, fax number, e-mail address, the date and time of transmission, and the name and telephone number of the person to contact in case of transmission problems. Service is effective only if and when an acceptance of service by e-mail is received from the solicitor of record stating their acceptance and specifying the date of acceptance. If the acceptance is received between 4 p.m. and midnight, service shall be deemed to have been made on the next business day.

Proof of service is obtained by having the sender of the e-mail swear an affidavit of service or completing a certificate of service (Precedent 11.8), which may be stamped or keyed on the backsheet of the document to which it applies. The affidavit or certificate should state that he or she e-mailed the message in accordance with subrule (4) of the *Rules of Civil Procedure* and that he or she received by e-mail an acceptance of service, including the date and time of acceptance.

Figure 11.4 provides a quick reference chart for the service of documents under the *Rules of Civil Procedure.*

Figure 11.4 Reference Chart for Service of Documents

SERVICE OF DOCUMENTS
Rule 16 of the Rules of Civil Procedure

TYPE OF DOCUMENT	METHOD	EFFECTIVE DATE	PROOF OF SERVICE
ORIGINATING DOCUMENTS IN A PROCEEDING	personal service	same day	affidavit of service
	OR by an alternative to personal service		
	service at place of residence & mail another copy	5 days after mailing	affidavit of service
	acceptance by solicitor	same day	signed & dated acceptance
	mail, with acknowledgement card	day signed card received back	affidavit of service
SUBSEQUENT DOCUMENTS IN A PROCEEDING	Ordinary or regular service on solicitor of record by:		
	mail	5 days after mailing	affidavit of service
	admission of service	same day, if before 4 p.m.; otherwise next business day	signed & dated admission
	fax (with cover sheet)	same day, if before 4 p.m.; otherwise next business day	affidavit of service
	document exchange	next business day	date stamp from document exchange
	courier	2 days after given to courier—unless holiday then next business day	affidavit of service
	e-mail	date e-mail acceptance received, if before 4 p.m.; otherwise next business day	affidavit of service *or* certificate of service

TIME FOR SERVICE

Service other than by mail of a document that does not originate a legal proceeding should be made before 4:00 p.m. to be effective as of the day of service. Service made after 4:00 p.m. or on a holiday is deemed to be made on the next day that is not a holiday.

SERVICE ON YOUR LAW OFFICE OF A COURT DOCUMENT

Once the legal proceeding is commenced, if someone from another law office attends at your office to serve a copy of a document upon your law firm while your firm is acting as solicitors for the other side, the legal assistant in the office may admit service on behalf of your firm. This is done by completing the date portion of the admission of service stamp, signing in ink the name of your law firm, and indicating for which party the firm acts in the proceeding, as illustrated in Figure 11.5.

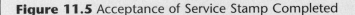

Figure 11.5 Acceptance of Service Stamp Completed

> Service of a copy of this document accepted
>
> this __*21st*__ day of __*March, 20xx*__
>
> __*Hill, Johnston & Grant*__
> Solicitor(s) for __*the plaintiffs*__

FILING A COURT DOCUMENT

Filing is delivering the original or a copy of a court document in person or by mail to the court office in which the legal proceeding was commenced. Proof of service of the document is usually required before the document will be accepted for filing. A document and the required proof of service are deemed to have been filed on the day of presentation if filed personally. A document and the required proof of service filed by mail are deemed to have been filed on the date stamped by the court.

A fee is payable when court documents are filed; the amount varies with the nature of the document. The amounts payable are set out in schedules to the rules. Such fees are paid by the law firm and are charged to the client when the account is rendered.

Terms and Concepts

serving
filing, with proof of service (wpos) issued
delivered
affidavit of service
personal service
alternatives to personal service
acceptance of service
service by mail
acknowledgement card

service at place of residence
substitutional service
ordinary or regular service
mail
admission of service
document exchange
facsimile transmission
time considerations for service
filing in court

Review Questions

1. There are a number of acceptable alternatives to personal service of an originating process document. Name three of those alternatives and indicate for each how proof of service is provided to the court.

2. When a legal proceeding has been originated, how may other documents prepared for use in that proceeding be served? List at least three methods and indicate for each on what date service is deemed to have been made.

3. Once a legal proceeding has been originated, why are most documents first served and then filed?

4. Under what circumstances may court documents be served by fax only with the permission of the receiving party?

5. Assume that today is Friday, October 7, 20__, and that Monday, October 10, is Thanksgiving Day. As of what date would service be effective for documents served on your office at
   a. 3:30 p.m.?
   b. 4:05 p.m.?
   c. 5:10 p.m.?

6. **Internet Research:** Use the Internet to research some of the local process servers in your area and learn what services they offer to the legal profession beside the service of legal documents.

Court File No. 0000-001

ONTARIO
SUPERIOR COURT OF JUSTICE

BETWEEN:

JOHN JOSEPH WILLIAMSON

PLAINTIFF

and

HENRY ARMAND DELOS-RAYES

DEFENDANT

AFFIDAVIT OF SERVICE

I, **JEREMY PAUL MATTHEWS**, of the City of Barrie, in the County of Simcoe, **MAKE OATH AND SAY**:

1. On November 5, 20__, at 3:27 p.m., I served the defendant Henry Armand Delos-Rayes with the statement of claim by leaving a copy with him at his residence on Delawana Road, Honey Harbour, Ontario.

2. I was able to identify the person by means of a photograph provided to me by the plaintiff.

Sworn before me at the	)
	)
City of Barrie	)
	)
in the County of Simcoe	) _____
	) *Jeremy Paul Matthews*
on November , 20__	)
	)
	)
	)
Commissioner for Taking Affidavits	)

Court File No. 000-0001

ONTARIO
SUPERIOR COURT OF JUSTICE

BETWEEN:

JOHN JOSEPH WILLIAMSON

Plaintiff

and

HENRY ARMAND DELOS-RAYES

Defendant

ACKNOWLEDGEMENT OF RECEIPT CARD

TO   HENRY ARMAND DELOS-RAYES

You are served by mail with the documents enclosed with this card in accordance with the *Rules of Civil Procedure.*

You are requested to sign the acknowledgement below and mail this card immediately after you receive it. If you fail to do so, the documents may be served on you in another manner and you may have to pay the costs of service.

ACKNOWLEDGEMENT OF RECEIPT

I ACKNOWLEDGE that I have received a copy of the following documents:

Statement of Claim

_____

Signature of person served

(The reverse side of this card must bear the name and address of the sender and the required postage.)

POST CARD

AFFIX
REQUIRED
POSTAGE

Lynda C. Ritchie
Hill, Johnston & Grant
Barristers & Solicitors
17 Princess Street South
Toronto, ON M8Y 3N5

{PRIVATE}Court File No. 0000-001

ONTARIO
SUPERIOR COURT OF JUSTICE

BETWEEN:

JOHN JOSEPH WILLIAMSON

PLAINTIFF

and

HENRY ARMAND DELOS-RAYES

DEFENDANT

AFFIDAVIT OF SERVICE

I, **JEREMY PAUL MATTHEWS**, of the City of Barrie, in the County of

Simcoe, MAKE OATH AND SAY:

1.   On November 4, 20__, I sent to the defendant Henry Armand Delos-Rayes by

prepaid registered mail a copy of the statement of claim dated October 30, 20__.

2.   On November 6, 20__, I received the attached acknowledgement of receipt card

bearing a signature that purports to be the signature of Henry Armand Delos-Rayes.

Sworn before me at the	)
	)
City of Barrie	)
	)
in the County of Simcoe	)_____
	) *Jeremy Paul Matthews*
on November , 20__	)
	)
Commissioner for Taking Affidavits	)

{PRIVATE}Court File No. 0000-001

ONTARIO
SUPERIOR COURT OF JUSTICE

BETWEEN:

JOHN JOSEPH WILLIAMSON

PLAINTIFF

and

HENRY ARMAND DELOS-RAYES

DEFENDANT

AFFIDAVIT OF SERVICE

I, **JEREMY PAUL MATTHEWS**, of the City of Barrie, in the County of Simcoe, MAKE OATH AND SAY:

1.   I served the defendant HENRY ARMAND DELOS-RAYES with the statement of claim by leaving a copy on November 5, 20__, at 11:15 a.m., with Mary Grace Henderson, who appeared to be an adult member of the same household in which Henry Armand Delos-Rayes is residing, at Delawana Road, Honey Harbour, Ontario, and by sending a copy by registered mail on November 5, 20__, to Henry Armand Delos-Rayes at the same address.

2.   I ascertained that the person was an adult member of the same household by means of personal observation and inquiring whether she resided at that address, to which she replied in the affirmative.

3.   Before serving the documents in this way, I made an unsuccessful attempt to serve the defendant personally at the same address on November 4, 20__.

Sworn before me at the	)
	)
City of Barrie, in the County of Simcoe	)
	) _____
on November , 20__	) *Jeremy Paul Matthews*
	)
Commissioner for Taking Affidavits	)

Court File No. 0000-0000

ONTARIO
SUPERIOR COURT OF JUSTICE

BETWEEN:

RICHARD PERCIVAL GOLDSTONE,
a minor, by his litigation guardian,
KENNETH PERCIVAL GOLDSTONE

PLAINTIFF

and

HENRY ALBERT BELL,
HERMAN ALGERNON BELL, and
MARY MARGARET WILLIAMSON

DEFENDANTS

AFFIDAVIT OF SERVICE

I, **JENNIFER ANNE WONG**, of the City of Toronto, MAKE OATH AND

SAY:

1.   I served the defendants with the jury notice by sending a copy by registered

mail on February 7, 20__, to Smith, Fraser, Hamid & Lee, the solicitors for the

defendants, at 75 Victoria Street, Suite 503, Toronto, Ontario, M5C 2B1.

Sworn before me at the	)
	)
City of Toronto,	)
	)
Province of Ontario	)_____
	) *Jennifer Anne Wong*
on , 20__	)
	)
	)
	)
Commissioner for Taking Affidavits	)

Court File No. 0000-0000

ONTARIO
SUPERIOR COURT OF JUSTICE

BETWEEN:

RICHARD PERCIVAL GOLDSTONE,
a minor, by his litigation guardian,
KENNETH PERCIVAL GOLDSTONE

PLAINTIFF

and

HENRY ALBERT BELL,
HERMAN ALGERNON BELL, and
MARY MARGARET WILLIAMSON

DEFENDANTS

AFFIDAVIT OF SERVICE

I, **JENNIFER ANNE WONG**, of the City of Toronto, MAKE OATH AND

SAY:

1.   I served the defendants with the jury notice by sending a copy by Federal

Express, a courier, to Smith, Fraser, Hamid & Lee, the solicitors for the

defendants, at 75 Victoria Street, Suite 503, Toronto, Ontario, M5C 2B1.

2.   The copy was given to the courier on February 7, 20___.

Sworn before me at the	)
	)
City of Toronto,	)
	)
Province of Ontario	)
	)_____
on , 20___	) *Jennifer Anne Wong*
	)
	)
	)
Commissioner for Taking Affidavits	)

Court File No. 0000-0000

ONTARIO
SUPERIOR COURT OF JUSTICE

BETWEEN:

RICHARD PERCIVAL GOLDSTONE,
a minor, by his litigation guardian,
KENNETH PERCIVAL GOLDSTONE

PLAINTIFF

and

HENRY ALBERT BELL,
HERMAN ALGERNON BELL, and
MARY MARGARET WILLIAMSON

DEFENDANTS

AFFIDAVIT OF SERVICE

I, JENNIFER ANNE WONG, of the City of Toronto, MAKE OATH AND

SAY:

1.   I served the defendants with the jury notice by sending a copy by fax to

416-233-9980 on November 7, 20___, to Smith, Fraser, Hamid & Lee, the

solicitors for the defendants.

Sworn before me at the	)
	)
City of Toronto,	)
	)
Province of Ontario	) _____
	) *Jennifer Anne Wong*
on _____, 20___	)
	)
	)
	)
Commissioner for Taking Affidavits	)

Court File No. 000-000-000

ONTARIO
SUPERIOR COURT OF JUSTICE

BETWEEN:

EAST HARDWARE LIMITED

PLAINTIFF

and

NORMAN G. MASTERWOOD

DEFENDANT

AFFIDAVIT OF SERVICE

I, JASON FISHER, of the City of Toronto, MAKE OATH AND SAY:

1. I served the defendant with the jury notice by e-mailing a copy in accordance with subrule 16.05(4) to Fox, Wolfe & Lyons, the solicitors for the defendant, on November 7, 20__ and received an acceptance of service on November 8, 20___ at 10:50 a.m.

Sworn before me at the City of   )
)
Toronto, in the Province of Ontario)
)   _____
on   , 20__   )
)

Commissioner for Taking Affidavits

OR

The following may be stamped or keyed on the backsheet of the document:

CERTIFICATE OF SERVICE

I, JASON FISHER, of the City of Toronto, MAKE OATH AND SAY:

1. I served the defendant with the jury notice by e-mailing a copy in accordance with subrule 16.05(4) to Fox, Wolfe & Lyons, the solicitors for the defendant, on November 7, 20__ and received an acceptance of service on November 8, 20___ at 10:50 a.m.

Sworn before me at the City of   )
)
Toronto, in the Province of Ontario)
)   _____
on   , 20__   )   *Jason Fisher*
)

Commissioner for Taking Affidavits

CHAPTER

Responses to the Originating Process

OBJECTIVES:

- Define and describe the responses to the originating process in a general action, including alternative pleadings

- Use legal precedents to prepare response documents such as a notice of intent to defend, a statement of defence, and a reply

Once an originating process document is served on the party to whom it is addressed, that party is required to take certain steps if he or she wishes to defend or take part in the proceeding. This chapter is concerned with the responses to a statement of claim or to a statement of claim and notice of action commencing a general action (Figure 12.1).

Figure 12.1 Responses to the Originating Process, General Action

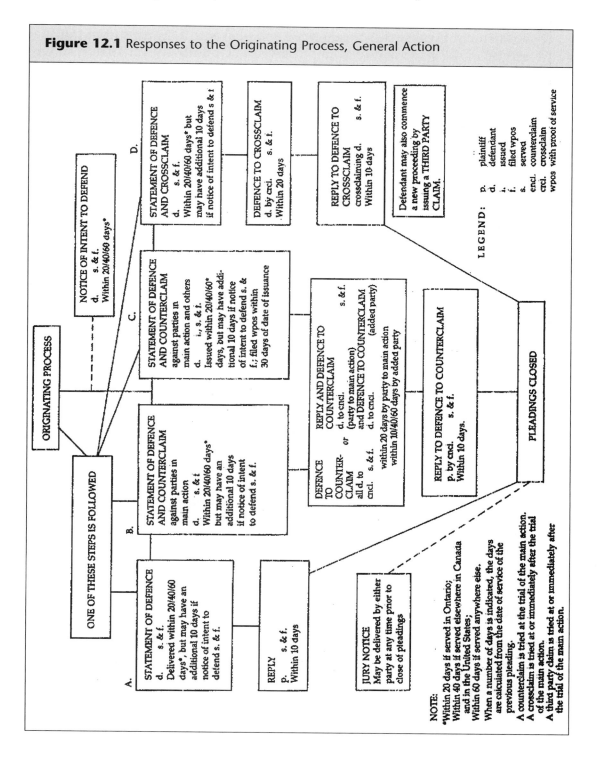

RESPONSES TO A STATEMENT OF CLAIM OR NOTICE OF ACTION AND STATEMENT OF CLAIM

The statement of claim (or notice of action and statement of claim) served on the defendant indicates that these steps should be taken to defend the legal proceeding:

1. a statement of defence is to be served and filed within 20 days from the date of service of the statement of claim, if served in Ontario; within 40 days, if served in another province or territory of Canada or in the United States; or within 60 days, if served outside Canada and the United States or
2. a notice of intent to defend may be served and filed within the time allowed for the statement of defence, in which case, the defendant is entitled to a further 10 days in addition to the 20/40/60 days in which to deliver a statement of defence.

Notice of Intent to Defend

A notice of intent to defend indicates that the defendants intend to defend the action (Precedent 12.1). The general heading is copied from the originating process. It is good practice to name the defendants, although this is unnecessary if the law firm is acting for all defendants.

If there are a number of defendants and the same law firm is not acting for all of them, the *Solicitors for...* line appears as

Solicitors for the defendants
(names of those for whom law firm acts)

If the law firm is acting for all the defendants, this line reads

Solicitors for the defendants

Statement of Defence

A statement of defence is the pleading filed and served by the defendant in which the defendant must admit, deny, or claim no knowledge of the allegations of fact set out in the statement of claim. It also sets out his or her version of the facts. A printed or recorded form of statement of defence may be used or the document may be fully keyed (Precedent 12.2).

Number and Disposition of Copies

Prepare at least four copies of a notice of intent to defend or a statement of defence. These copies are disposed of as follows:

1. One copy is served on the solicitors for the plaintiff.
2. One copy is filed with the court with proof of service within the time prescribed for filing the statement of defence.

3. One copy is for the file.
4. The original is retained in the Document subfile in the main client file.

Usually, no copies are prepared for the trial record because the record is usually prepared by solicitors for the plaintiff.

REPLY

Within 10 days of receipt of the statement of defence, the solicitors for the plaintiff may serve and file a reply. A reply is delivered to

1. set out a version of the facts different from that pleaded in the opposite party's defence and not already pleaded in his or her claim;
2. respond to a defence on any matter that might, if not brought out, take the opposite party by surprise; or
3. raise an issue that has not been raised by a previous pleading.

Number and Disposition of Copies

Prepare a minimum of four copies of the reply, plus one additional copy for each defendant who must be served. If the same law firm acts for all the defendants, only one additional copy is required. These copies are disposed of as follows:

1. One copy is served on the defendant's solicitors.
2. One copy is filed with the court with proof of service.
3. One copy is for the file.
4. One copy is for the Record subfile.
5. The original is retained in the Document subfile.

SIMPLIFIED PROCEDURE/CASE MANAGEMENT

If the action is under the requirements of simplified procedure or case management, additional procedural steps, including mandatory mediation, must be taken. Refer to Figures 10.2 and 10.3 to review the procedures and documentation that may be required.

ALTERNATIVE PLEADINGS

Only a statement of claim and a statement of defence must be served and filed in an action; other pleadings are used only if the facts of the case require that they be prepared. Such pleadings are a **counterclaim**, a **crossclaim**, and a **third party claim**. If the original proceeding was by way of simplified procedure and any counterclaim, crossclaim, or third party claim is for $50,000 or less, then the action can continue under the simplified procedure. If the claim exceeds $50,000, then the action will continue under the standard procedure.

Counterclaim

A counterclaim is a claim by the defendant in the main action (that is, the action originated by the statement of claim or notice of action and statement of claim) against the original plaintiff or against the plaintiff and another party.

Counterclaim Against Plaintiff Only

A counterclaim against the plaintiff in the main action only is set out as part of the defendant's statement of defence (Precedent 12.3), and the document is titled Statement of Defence and Counterclaim. The counterclaim follows immediately after the last numbered paragraph of the statement of defence and is titled Counterclaim. The paragraphs in the counterclaim are numbered in sequence, commencing with the number following the last paragraph number of the statement of defence.

The parties are then known as plaintiff(s) by counterclaim and defendant(s) to the counterclaim.

Number and Disposition of Copies

Prepare the same number of copies of a statement of defence and counterclaim that you would for a statement of defence. The copies are disposed of in the same way as the copies of that document.

Counterclaim Against Plaintiff and Another or Other Parties

A defendant may counterclaim against the plaintiff and a person or persons not a party to the main action. A statement of defence and counterclaim is issued to originate a new legal proceeding. A second title of proceedings is established to indicate who is the plaintiff by counterclaim and who are the defendants to the counterclaim (Figure 12.2).

A statement of defence and counterclaim originating a new proceeding is prepared that states what steps may be taken to defend the claim.

Number and Disposition of Copies

Prepare a minimum of five copies of a counterclaim against the plaintiff and another party. These copies are disposed of as follows:

1. The original is issued by the court and returned to the law firm. It is retained in the Document subfile in the main client file.
2. One copy of the issued document is filed with the court.
3. One copy is served on each defendant to the counterclaim. Any new party to the proceeding must be served by personal service or an alternative to personal service.
4. One copy is for the file.
5. One copy is for the Record subfile.

Figure 12.2 General Heading in Counterclaim Involving Other Parties

Court File No. 111-1111

ONTARIO
SUPERIOR COURT OF JUSTICE

B E T W E E N :

CHRISTOPHER BAXTER

Plaintiff

- and -

**MARY HOLMESTEAD
and JACOB HOLMESTEAD**

Defendants

A N D   B E T W E E N :

**MARY HOLMESTEAD
and JACOB HOLMESTEAD**

Plaintiffs
by counterclaim

- and -

**CHRISTOPHER BAXTER
and PATRICIA JANE SMITH**

Defendants
to the counterclaim

Other Pleadings When There Is a Counterclaim

When there is a counterclaim in an action, the original plaintiff and any other defendant to the counterclaim may serve and file a Defence to Counterclaim; alternatively, the original plaintiff (defendant by counterclaim) may serve and file a reply and defence to counterclaim. The defendant (the plaintiff by counterclaim) may serve and file a reply to defence to counterclaim. The basic formats for these documents are found in Forms 27C and 27D of the rules.

Crossclaim

A defendant in the main action may claim against another defendant in that action by including a crossclaim in the statement of defence. The document is then titled Statement of Defence and Crossclaim. The general heading of this document is taken from the statement of claim (Precedent 12.4). The crossclaim follows immediately after the last paragraph of the statement of defence and is titled Crossclaim. Paragraphs of the crossclaim are numbered in sequence, commencing with the number following the last paragraph number of the statement of defence.

The parties to a crossclaim are known as the crossclaiming defendant (the defendant who makes the crossclaim) and the defendant to crossclaim (the defendant against whom the claim is made). Those terms are used in the "Solicitors for..." line in the ending of the document. In the body of the crossclaim and in documents in response to the crossclaim, each defendant is described as the "defendant (name)...."

Number and Disposition of Copies

Prepare a minimum of six copies of the statement of defence and crossclaim because the crossclaim must be served on the defendant by crossclaim as well as on the plaintiff. These copies are disposed of as follows:

1. One copy is filed with the court with proof of service.
2. One copy is served on the plaintiff.
3. One copy is served on the defendant to crossclaim.
4. One copy is for the file.
5. The original copy is retained in the Document subfile.
6. One copy is the Record subfile.

Other Pleadings When There Is a Crossclaim

When there is a crossclaim in the action, the defendant to the crossclaim delivers a Defence to Crossclaim, and the crossclaiming defendant may deliver a Reply to Defence to Crossclaim. These documents follow the format of general court documents discussed in Chapter 11; basic formats for these pleadings are illustrated in Forms 28B and 28C of the rules.

Third Party Claim

The rules provide that under specified circumstances, such as when a party not already a party to the main action is or may be liable to the defendant for all or part of the plaintiff's claim, a defendant may issue a third party claim against that party, in which case, a new legal proceeding is originated. This document sets up a new title of proceeding that adds the name of the third party following those of the plaintiff and defendant and identifies the party as "Third Party" (Figure 12.3).

Figure 12.3 General Heading in a Third Party Claim

Court File No. 42001

ONTARIO
SUPERIOR COURT OF JUSTICE

B E T W E E N :

MARY MAUDE COCHRANE

Plaintiff

- and -

LADY HELEN'S DRESS SHOP LIMITED

Defendant

- and -

THE CORPORATION OF THE CITY OF BRAMPTON

Third Party

The court usually assigns a court file number to this proceeding by giving it the same file number as the main action followed by an A; for example, if the main action court file number were 9876192, the third party claim court file number would be 9876192A. The party named as third party in the defendant's third party claim may also claim against another party; this is a fourth party claim, and the court file number assigned would be 9876192B. The basic format for a third party claim is illustrated in Form 29A of the rules.

Number and Disposition of Copies

Prepare a minimum of six copies of a third party claim. These copies are disposed of as follows:

1. The original is issued by the court registrar, returned to the law firm, and retained in the Document subfile of the main client file.
2. A copy is retained by the court.
3. One copy is served on all parties in the action, that is, on the plaintiff and defendant.
4. One copy is served on the third party personally or by an alternative to personal service within 30 days of the issuance of the claim. The third party is also served with a copy of all previous pleadings in the proceeding.
5. One copy is for the file.
6. One copy is the Record subfile.

Other Pleadings When There Is a Third Party Claim

When there is a third party claim, the pleadings consist of the third party claim, the third party defence, and the reply to the third party defence, if any. The basic formats for these pleadings are illustrated in Forms 29A, 29B, and 29C of the rules.

DEMAND FOR PARTICULARS ALLEGED IN A PLEADING

Either party in a legal proceeding may demand particulars of an allegation in the pleading of an opposite party. If the opposite party fails to provide such particulars within seven days, the court may order that they be delivered within a specified time.

The rules do not specify the format for a demand for particulars; Precedent 12.5 illustrates the basic format for this document. The opposite party may provide the required particulars in a similar document or by way of affidavit. Prepare a minimum of three copies of documents relating to a demand for particulars. The original is served on the opposite party, one copy is for the use of the solicitor, and the third is for the office file. Copies of these documents are also required for the trial record.

CLOSE OF PLEADINGS

Pleadings in an action are said to be closed when the plaintiff has delivered a reply to every defence in the action (or the time for delivery of a reply has expired) and when every defendant who has not delivered a statement of defence in the action has been noted in default.

AMENDMENTS TO PLEADINGS

A party to an action who has delivered pleadings may amend the pleading without the permission of the court before the close of pleadings provided that the amendment does not involve the title of proceeding, or with the consent of all parties, or with the permission of the court after the close of pleading.

Amendments to a pleading are made on the copy filed in the court office, underlined to distinguish the amended wording from the original. The registrar notes on the amended pleading the date of the amendment and the authority under which it was authorized. If amendments are extensive, a fresh copy of the original pleading as amended, bearing the date of the original pleading and the title of the pleading preceded by the word "AMENDED," is filed in the court office.

A pleading may be amended more than once; each subsequent amendment is underlined with an additional line. For example, in a pleading being amended for the third time, the new changes would be underlined three times.

Service of Amended Pleading

An amended pleading is served forthwith on every person who at the time of service is a party to the action, unless the court orders otherwise. Proof of service of the amended pleading (other than an originating process) is filed in the court office after it is served.

Where the amended pleading is the originating process, it need not be personally served on the party who was served with and responded to the original pleading. It must be served personally or by an alternative to personal service on an opposite party who has not responded to the original pleading, whether or not that party has been noted in default.

Response to Amended Pleading

A party served with an amended pleading must respond within the time remaining for responding to the original pleading or within 10 days after service of the amended pleading, whichever period is longer, unless the court orders otherwise. If a party served with an amended pleading has already responded, that party is deemed to rely on his or her original pleading in answer to the amended pleading, unless he or she responds to it within 10 days after service of the amended pleading.

Terms and Concepts

notice of intent to defend	crossclaim
statement of defence	third party claim
reply	demand for particulars
notice of defence	close of pleadings
counterclaim	amendment to pleadings

Review Questions

1. Once a defendant has been served with the statement of claim, what steps are open to him or her to indicate that the proceeding will be defended? What are the time limits that must be adhered to?

2. What document would be prepared for a defendant who
   a. wished to claim against the original plaintiff in the proceeding?
   b. wished to claim against another defendant in the proceeding?
   c. wished to claim against a party not already a party to the proceeding?

3. Which, if any, of the documents you listed in item 2 originate a new proceeding?

4. The same solicitors act for all plaintiffs in an action. Do all defendants have to act through the same solicitors?

5. When are pleadings said to be "closed"?

6. When the originating process document was issued, there was an error in the spelling of the name of the defendant. How may that error be corrected?

7. You have been given copies of a pleading that contains an amendment and have been asked to do what is necessary to complete the preparation of the amended pleading. What exactly would you do?

Court File No. 000-001

ONTARIO
SUPERIOR COURT OF JUSTICE

B E T W E E N:

JOHN JOSEPH WILLIAMSON

Plaintiff

and

HENRY ARMAND DELOS-RAYES

Defendant

NOTICE OF INTENT TO DEFEND

The defendant, HENRY ARMAND DELOS-RAYES, intends to defend

this action.

November 18, 20___

HILL, JOHNSTON & GRANT
Barristers & Solicitors
17 Princess Street South, Suite 2501
Toronto, Ontario
M8Y 3N5

Peter T. Grant (12345G)

Tel: 416-354-9900
Fax: 416-354-9909

Solicitors for the defendant

TO: **HARE, ROSS & WILKINSON**
Barristers & Solicitors
94 Wimbleton Crescent
Barrie ON L4V 5K3

Patricia M. Cochrane (46992C)

Tel: 705-975-4801
Fax: 705-075-4802

Solicitors for the plaintiff

Requires a back

Court File No.

ONTARIO
SUPERIOR COURT OF JUSTICE

TITLE OF PROCEEDING

STATEMENT OF DEFENCE
or
STATEMENT OF DEFENCE
of the defendant (name)

1.   The defendant *(or* the defendant *(name) if not acting for all the defendants)* admits the allegations contained in paragraph *(insert numbers)* of the statement of claim.

2.   The defendant *(or* the defendant *(name))* denies the allegations contained in paragraphs *(insert numbers)* of the statement of claim.

3.   The defendant *(or* the defendant *(name))* has no knowledge in respect of the allegations contained in paragraphs *(insert numbers)* of the statement of claim.

4.   *(Each allegation of fact relied on by way of defence is set out in separate, consecutively numbered paragraphs.)*

Month day, year

NAME OF LAW FIRM
Street Address
City, Province Postal Code

Name of Specific Lawyer

Telephone Number
Fax Number

Solicitors for the defendant
(or the defendant *(name))*

TO: **NAME OF LAW FIRM**
Street Address
City, Province Postal Code

Name of Specific Lawyer

Telephone Number
Fax Number

Solicitors for the plaintiff(s)

Requires a back

Court File No.

ONTARIO
SUPERIOR COURT OF JUSTICE

TITLE OF PROCEEDING

STATEMENT OF DEFENCE AND COUNTERCLAIM

1. The defendant admits the allegations contained in paragraphs . . . . of the statement of claim.

2. The defendant denies the allegations contained in paragraphs . . . . of the statement of claim.

3. --
---.

COUNTERCLAIM

4. The defendant claims:

    (a) ---
    ------------------------------;

    (b) ---
    --------------------------------------;

5. --
--.

Month day, year   **NAME OF LAW FIRM**
                                        etc.

                                        Solicitors for the plaintiff
                                        by counterclaim

TO: **NAME OF LAW FIRM**
        etc.

        Solicitors for the defendant
        to the counterclaim

        Requires a back identified as a
        Statement of Defence and Counterclaim

Court File No.

ONTARIO
SUPERIOR COURT OF JUSTICE

TITLE OF PROCEEDING

STATEMENT OF DEFENCE AND CROSSCLAIM

1.   The defendant admits the allegations contained in paragraphs . . . . of the statement of claim.

2.   xxxxxxxxxxxxxxxxxxxxxxxxxxxxxxxxxxxxxxxxxxxxxxxxxxxxxxxxxxx xxxxxxxxxxxxxxxxxxxxxxxxxxxxxxxxx.

3.   xxxxxxxxxxxxxxxxxxxxxxxxxxxxxxxxxxxxxxxxxxxxxxxxxxxxxxxxxxx xxxxxxxxxxxxxxxxxxxxx.

CROSSCLAIM

4.   The defendant *(name)* claims against the defendant *(name)*:

(State the precise relief claimed.)

5.   xxxxxxxxxxxxxxxxxxxxxxxxxxxxxxxxxxxxxxxxxxxxxxxxxxxxxxxxxxx xxxxxxxxxxxxxxxxxxxxxxxxxxxxxxx.

6.   xxxxxxxxxxxxxxxxxxxxxxxxxxxxxxxxxxxxxxxxxxxxxxxxxxxxxxxxxxx xxxxxxxxxxxxxxxxxxxx..

Month day, year   **NAME OF LAW FIRM**
                                                   etc.

                                                   Solicitors for the crossclaiming
                                                   defendant

TO: **NAME OF LAW FIRM**
         etc.

         Solicitors for the defendant
         to crossclaim

> *Requires a back identified as*
> *Statement of Defence and Crossclaim*

Court File No.

ONTARIO
SUPERIOR COURT OF JUSTICE

TITLE OF PROCEEDING

DEMAND FOR PARTICULARS

The *(party making the demand of an opposite party in the proceeding)*
demands *(or demand)* particulars of the following allegations in the *(title of pleading)*, pursuant to rule 25.10 of the *Rules of Civil Procedure*.

1. Particulars of the --

    --------------------.

2. Particulars of the --

    --------------------.

(Continue with additional numbered paragraphs if required.)

Month day, year   **NAME OF LAW FIRM**
(Dated day prepared)   Street Address
                                     City, Province Postal Code

                                     Name of Specific Lawyer

                                     Telephone Number
                                     Fax Number

                                     Solicitors for the *(capacity of party)*

TO: **NAME OF LAW FIRM**
        Street Address
        City, Province Postal Code

        Name of Specific Lawyer

        Telephone Number
        Fax Number

        Solicitors for the *(capacity of the party)*

Requires a back

CHAPTER 13

Notices, Notices of Motion, Consents, and Requisitions

OBJECTIVES:

- Define and describe the various steps that may be taken after close of pleadings and prior to trial

- Demonstrate an understanding of preparations for motion court

- Use legal precedents to prepare a notice, notice of motion, motion record, confirmation of motion, consent, and requisition

Once a legal proceeding is commenced but before a trial or hearing, one of the parties may

1. advise the court and the other parties to the proceeding of some step or change in circumstances relating to the proceeding. For example, one party changes solicitors and advises the court of the name of the new solicitors, one party wishes the legal proceeding tried by a jury, or the plaintiff decides to discontinue the proceeding. A **notice** is the document prepared to accomplish this.
2. ask the court for an order requiring that something be done or not done. For example, one party requests an order permitting an amendment to the title of proceeding set out in the originating document or requests an order that the place of trial be changed from the place named in the originating document. A **notice of motion** is the document prepared to accomplish this.
3. ask the local registrar of the court to carry out a duty set out in the rules. For example, the local registrar may be asked to transfer a court file from one court office to another court office or to note the defendant in default for failing to take the steps open to him or her to defend the action. A **requisition** is the document prepared to accomplish this.
4. agree with the other party that something be done. For example, the solicitors for the parties may agree that a legal proceeding be dismissed without costs. A **consent** is the document prepared to accomplish this.

NOTICES

Once the legal proceeding is originated, either party in the proceeding may serve and file a notice to formally inform the court and the other parties of some step or change relating to the proceeding. A notice of motion is a special form of a notice and is discussed later in this chapter.

Form of Notice

A notice follows the basic format for court documents; that is, it contains the general heading of the proceeding, the title of the document, the body, the date of preparation, and the name, address, and telephone number of the law firm in whose office it is prepared. It is addressed to the law firm acting for the other parties (Precedent 13.1). The title of the document identifies the notice by its nature (for example, Notice of Payment into Court, Jury Notice, or Notice of Discontinuance).

Paragraphs

Although a notice may contain several paragraphs, most contain one short, unnumbered paragraph, similar to that found in a Notice of Intent to Defend, which is discussed in Chapter 12. The initial words of the paragraph of a notice are frequently in solid capitals. The precedents for notices set out in the rules show variations in this style. Follow the preference of your law office.

Ending

The notice is dated the date of preparation. The name, address, and telephone number of the law firm preparing it are set out. The notice is addressed to the solicitors for all interested parties in the proceeding, in the order in which they appear in the title of proceeding.

For example, if the notice is being prepared by the solicitors for the plaintiffs and there are two defendants, each of whom is represented by a different law firm, the notice is addressed first to the solicitors for the first-named defendant in the title of proceeding and then addressed to the solicitors for the second-named defendant.

Backsheet

A backsheet is required for each copy of the notice, identifying it by its nature (for example, Jury Notice).

Number and Disposition of Copies

Prepare a minimum of three copies of a notice informing the court and all other interested parties of the step or change. An additional copy is required for each additional party to whom the notice is addressed or for use in a record.

Most notices are first served on the party to whom it is addressed; the original, with proof of service, is then filed in the court office. Some notices, such as a notice of examination (discussed in Chapter 14), need only be served. The lawyer will indicate what happens to each notice until you know which must be served and filed and which need only be served.

NOTICE OF MOTION

Once a legal proceeding is commenced but before a trial or hearing, either of the parties in the proceeding may apply to the court for an order requiring that something be done or not done. The document prepared is a special form of a notice, a **notice of motion**, which is more commonly referred to simply as a motion. A motion may be made in either an action or an application by any party.

Motions are often referred to as **interlocutory proceedings**, meaning that they are made during the course of legal proceedings but do not finally determine the outcome of the proceedings. The party making the motion is known as the **moving party**; the other party is known as the **responding party**. These terms, however, are not used in the document itself, and the title of proceeding uses the terms "plaintiff" and "defendant," or "applicant" and "respondent." When the responding party opposes the relief requested by the moving party, the motion is contested. However, many motions are made with the approval of both parties and are then said to be made on consent.

Under certain circumstances, a notice of motion may not be addressed to anyone. The motion is then said to be made **without notice** (formerly known as an *ex parte* motion). For example, one party may wish the court to make an order permitting service of a statement of claim on the defendant by some method other than the traditional methods of service.

Who Hears Motions

A judge has the jurisdiction to hear any motion in a proceeding; a master has jurisdiction to hear any motion in a proceeding with exceptions set out in the rules. The lawyer will indicate whether the motion is to be made to the court to be heard by a master or whether it is to be made to a judge.

On a contested motion, the motion may be heard by a conference telephone call where there is consent from all counsel and the judge or officer before whom the motion is to be heard.

If a motion is on consent, unopposed, or without notice, it may be done in writing; that is, the judge or master will review the notice and supporting documents of the moving party and the documents of the responding party and make his or her decision. The lawyers do not have to attend at court in this situation.

Place of Hearing Motion

The lawyer requesting that a notice of motion be prepared will indicate where the motion is to be heard and the method of hearing, but a legal assistant should be aware of the general provisions of the rules.

Motions Made on Notice to the Responding Party

Subject to special provisions, the general rule is that a motion made on notice is brought in the county where the solicitor of record for any responding party practises law or where a responding party who acts in person resides. If no responding party resides in Ontario or is represented by an Ontario solicitor, the motion is brought in the county where the proceeding was commenced or where the solicitor of record for any party to the motion practises law.

Motions Made without Notice

A motion that is made without notice to any other party may be made in the county in which

1. the proceeding was commenced;
2. any party resides; or
3. the solicitor of record for any party practises law.

Hearing Date for the Motion

In most counties, the lawyer selects a date that appears suitable, and when the motion is filed with the court, it is included on the list of motions to be heard on that date. For all motions that it is estimated will require more than two hours to be heard, a hearing date must be obtained from the registrar before the notice of motion can be served.

For jurisdictions with a high volume of civil litigation cases, such as Toronto, there are additional requirements to obtain a date and time for a motion hearing. Such information may be obtained by consulting any practice directions in the *Rules of Civil Procedures* or looking on the government website for your judicial region.

Form of Notice of Motion

A notice of motion is prepared using the basic format for the general form of document of the other notices discussed earlier in this chapter. The general heading is the same as in the originating process documents. The body of the document, however, must state the precise relief sought and the grounds to be argued, including reference to any statutory provision or rule, and list the documentary evidence to be used at the motion hearing (Precedent 13.2).

Ending

Notices are dated the date of preparation and are usually addressed to the solicitors for the responding party, unless it is a motion made without notice.

Material Required with a Notice of Motion

The notice of motion requires a listing of the documentary evidence that is to be used on the hearing of the motion. The rules provide that such evidence may be in the form of an affidavit, unless a statute or rule provides otherwise. Affidavits are discussed in Chapter 9.

Number and Disposition of Copies

Where a motion is made on notice, prepare a minimum of six copies of the notice of motion. They are disposed of as follows:

1. One copy of the notice of motion and any accompanying affidavit are served on all interested parties at least four days before the date on which the motion is to be heard.
2. The original notice of motion and supporting affidavit are filed with proof of service at least four days before the hearing date in the court office where the motion is to be heard. Where a motion record is required, the documents may be filed as part of that record rather than separately.
3. One copy is retained in your office file.
4. Three copies are required for the motion record.

   Additional copies are required for each additional party to whom the notice of motion is addressed: one copy for service and one copy for the motion record that is served on all interested parties.

   When a motion is made without notice to any other party, it is, of course, not served on anyone. It may be filed with the court at or before the hearing.

MOTION RECORD

When a motion is made on notice, the moving party is required to serve and file a **motion record**, unless the court orders otherwise. The motion record must be served on every other party to the motion and is then filed, with proof of service, in the court office where the motion is to be heard at least three days before the hearing.

Contents of the Motion Record

The motion record contains, in consecutively numbered pages, the following material in the order shown:

1. A table of contents describing each document (including each exhibit) by its nature and date and, in the case of an exhibit, by exhibit number or letter
2. A copy of the notice of motion
3. A copy of all affidavits and other materials served by any party for use on the motion
4. Where applicable, a list of all relevant transcripts of evidence in chronological order, but not necessarily the transcripts themselves
5. A copy of any material in the court file that is necessary for the hearing of the motion

Preparing the Motion Record

To prepare the motion record:

1. Photocopy a minimum of three copies of each document required to be included in the record (omit backsheets) and assemble the pages in the appropriate order.
2. Consecutively number each page in the upper right-hand corner in ink or with a numbering machine.
3. Place a tabbed divider page in front of each document to be included in the record. These divider pages may be tabbed 1, 2, 3, 4, etc., or A, B, C, D, etc., depending on the preference of your law firm. The divider pages are not part of the consecutively numbered pages of the record.
4. Prepare:
   a. a front or face page identifying the material as a motion record and setting out the name, address, and telephone number of the solicitors for both the moving and responding parties. The name of the solicitors for the party preparing the record is listed first. Include the name of the particular solicitor in charge of the legal proceeding for each party.
   b. a table of contents page listing each document by
   i.the divider page tab number or letter;
   ii. the name and date of preparation or other relevant date information; and
   iii. the page number at which the document may be found.
   Alternatively, a combined face and table of contents page may be prepared (Precedent 13.3).

5. Prepare a back on light blue cover stock paper identifying the document as a motion record.
6. Assemble the material with the front page first, followed by the table of contents page (or the combined front and table of contents page), the documents (each with a tabbed divider page) in numbered order, and the backsheet.
7. Bind the assembled material down the left-hand side to form a booklet.

Number of Copies

Prepare a minimum of three copies of the motion record:

1. One copy is served on the other party to the motion.
2. One copy is retained for your office file.
3. One copy is filed with proof of service in the court office where the motion is to be heard no later than three days before the motion hearing. It is acceptable to file the notice of motion and other material served by a moving party for use on a motion as part of the motion record, but not separately.

Responding Party's Motion Record

When a motion record is served, the responding party (that is, the party to whom the notice is addressed) may serve on every other party and file a responding party's motion record. It must be filed, with proof of service, in the court office where the motion is to be heard not later than two days before the hearing. The motion record consists of consecutively numbered pages arranged in the following order:

1. The table of contents describing each document, including each exhibit, by its nature and date and, in the case of an exhibit, by exhibit number or letter
2. A copy of any material to be used by the responding party on the motion and not included in the motion record

TRANSCRIPT OF EVIDENCE

If a transcript of evidence is to be referred to on the hearing of a motion, a copy of the transcript for the use of the court is filed in the court office where the motion is to be heard no later than two days before the hearing. Such transcripts require a light grey backsheet.

FACTUM

A factum is a concise, written statement, without argument, of the facts and law relied on by the party. A factum is optional on many motions but is required on certain motions, such as on a motion to strike out pleadings as showing no cause of action or on motions for leave to appeal an interlocutory order of a judge.

The moving party's factum must be served no later than four days before the date of the hearing; the responding party's factum must be served no later than two days before the date of the hearing. Each party's factum must be filed, with proof of service, no later than two days before the date of the hearing.

Form of the Factum

Precedent 13.4 illustrates the basic format for a factum. The factum of the party making the motion is identified as follows:

> FACTUM OF THE MOVING PARTY
> (name of moving party)

The factum of the party to whom the motion is addressed is identified as follows:

> FACTUM OF RESPONDING PARTY
> (name of responding party)

The body of a factum contains consecutively numbered paragraphs, divided into parts that are numbered and titled. The ending of the factum shows the date of preparation of the document and that it is submitted by counsel for the party on whose behalf it has been prepared. Each copy of the factum served or filed is personally signed by the lawyer for the party or by someone he or she has authorized.

Cover

The factum of the moving party should be bound front and back in white cover stock pages, whereas the factum of any responding party should be bound front and back in green cover stock pages.

Number of Copies

Prepare a minimum of four copies of a factum. These copies are disposed of as follows:

1. One copy is served on the other party.
2. One copy is retained for your office file.
3. One copy is for the Document subfile.
4. The original is filed with the court, with proof of service, not later than 2 days before the date of the hearing.

CONFIRMATION OF MOTION

For any motion made on notice, the moving party must contact the other party and confirm their attendance at the scheduled motion hearing and then prepare a confirmation of notice (Precedent 13.5). This notice must be delivered, faxed, or e-mailed (where available) to the court office not later than 2:00 p.m. two days before the hearing date or the motion will not be heard.

Prepare a minimum of two copies of the confirmation of motion for use as follows:

1. One copy is retained in your office file.
2. The second copy may be delivered to the courthouse if it is not faxed or e-mailed.
3. A copy of the confirmation of motion must also be faxed or e-mailed to the other party.

DECISIONS ON MOTIONS

When a motion is heard, the decision of the judge or master is usually recorded in an order of the court; in specific circumstances, it may be set out in a judgment. A draft order is often prepared ahead to be taken to the motion hearing or sent with the motion record if the motion is to be in writing only. The lawyer will indicate what document is to be prepared. The preparation of orders and judgments is discussed in Chapter 16.

It is now the usual practice for masters or judges in Motions Court who hear motions to fix the costs at the conclusion of the hearing of the motion. Those appearing on the motion are expected to be prepared to speak to the matter of costs.

The legal assistant may be requested to have up-to-date information on the docket entries so that the lawyer is aware of who has spent how much time preparing for the motion. A computer printout of the disbursement ledger should also be available for the solicitor's use in speaking to the matter of costs. Bills of cost are discussed in detail in Chapter 16.

CONSENT

A consent (Precedent 13.6) formally puts into words an agreement reached by the solicitors affecting an action or application. The general heading in a consent follows that of the proceeding to which it relates. The title of the document is Consent, followed by an unnumbered paragraph beginning "The parties by their solicitors hereby consent to...." Following a DATED at...."" line in which the date is left blank for completion when the consent is signed, sufficient lines for the signatures of the parties are shown at the right-hand side of the page. The capacity of the person who is to sign the consent is indicated beneath each line.

Number and Disposition of Copies

Enough copies are prepared to provide the original signed copy for filing with the court, one signed copy for each firm of solicitors, and a copy for the office file.

REQUISITION

Where a party to a legal proceeding can require the registrar of a court to carry out a duty under the rules, a requisition (Precedent 13.7) is prepared.

General Heading and Body

The general heading of a requisition follows that established for the legal proceeding to which it relates. After the title of the document, the requisition is addressed to the local registrar of the appropriate court office (which may be the place of commencement or the place where a proceeding was or is to be tried, if different from the place of commencement).

The body of the document sets out the request that is being made of the registrar. Precedent 13.7 shows a standard template and some examples of different kinds of requisitions. When what is required is authorized by a court order, reference is made in the requisition to the order and a copy is attached to it. Where an affidavit or other document must be filed with the requisition, reference is made to it and a copy is attached.

Ending

A requisition is dated the date of preparation and shows the name, address, and telephone number of the solicitors filing it.

Backsheet

There is no backsheet for a single-page requisition. Other requisitions, such as one prepared for a default judgment (discussed in Chapter 17), do require a backsheet.

Number and Disposition of Copies

Prepare a minimum of one copy of the requisition for filing with the court. An additional copy may be prepared and retained in the office file.

Terms and Concepts

notice	securing motion date
notice of motion	without notice (*ex parte*)
requisition	motion record
consent	transcript
interlocutory proceedings	factum
moving party	confirmation of motion
responding party	

Review Questions

1. In your own words, what is the purpose of each of the following documents?
   a. consent:
   b. factum:
   c. notice:
   d. notice of motion:
   e. confirmation of motion:
   f. requisition:

2. Provide the term for each of the following:
   a. the party on whose behalf a motion is made: _____
   b. the term used to describe motions brought during the course of a legal proceeding: _____
   c. a motion in which the other party opposes the relief sought is this type of motion: _____
   d. a motion that is not served on the other party is this type of motion:

   _____

3. How many days' notice must be given to the other party in a motion?

4. What document is frequently used in support of a notice of motion?

5. If you are asked to prepare a notice for which you do not have a precedent, where could you usually locate a precedent for the document?

6. How many copies are prepared of a motion record, and what disposition is made of those copies?

Court File No. 000-001

ONTARIO
SUPERIOR COURT OF JUSTICE

B E T W E E N:

JOHN JOSEPH WILLIAMSON

Plaintiff

and

HENRY ARMAND DELOS-RAYES

Defendant

JURY NOTICE

THE DEFENDANT requires that this action be tried by a jury.

Date: November 25, 20___

HILL, JOHNSTON & GRANT
Barristers & Solicitors
17 Princess Street South, Suite 2501
Toronto, Ontario
M8Y 3N5

Peter T. Grant (12345G)

Tel: 416-354-9900
Fax: 416-354-9909

Solicitors for the plaintiff

TO: **HARE, ROSS & WILKINSON**
Barristers & Solicitors
94 Wimbleton Crescent
Barrie ON L4V 5K3

Patricia M. Cochrane (46992C)

Tel: 416-233-9985
Fax: 416-233-9980

Requires a back

Solicitors for the defendant

GENERAL HEADING

NOTICE OF MOTION

THE *(identify moving party)* will make a motion to the court *(or a judge)* on *(day)*, *(date)*, at *(time)*, or as soon after that time as the motion can be heard, at *(address of courthouse)*.

PROPOSED METHOD OF HEARING: The motion is to be heard *(choose appropriate option)*

[ ]　　in writing under subrule 37.12.1(1) because it

　　　　is *(insert one of* on consent, unopposed *or*

　　　　made without notice)*;

[ ]　　in writing as an opposed motion under subrule 37.12.1(4);

[ ]　　orally;

THE MOTION IS FOR *(state here the precise relief sought)*.

THE GROUNDS FOR THE MOTION ARE: *(specify the grounds to be argued, including a reference to any statutory provisions or rule to be relied on)*.

THE FOLLOWING DOCUMENTARY EVIDENCE will be used at the hearing of the motion:

(List the affidavits or other documentary evidence to be relied on. List each item separately, in consecutively numbered paragraphs. Identify each document by title and date.)

(Dated day of preparation)　　　　　*(Name, address, telephone and fax numbers of moving party's solicitor or moving party)*

　　　　　　　　　　　　　　　　　(Name of specific lawyer)

　　　　　　　　　　　　　　　　　Solicitors for *(moving party)*

TO: *(Name, address, telephone and fax numbers of responding party's solicitors or responding party)*

　　　(Name of specific lawyer)

　　　Solicitors for *(responding party)*

Requires a back

Court File No. 0000-000-000

ONTARIO
SUPERIOR COURT OF JUSTICE

B E T W E E N:

MARTHA COCHRANE and
JOHN MATTHEW COCHRANE

Plaintiffs

and

WALLACE HERMAN GENNEL

Defendant

MOTION RECORD

TABLE OF CONTENTS

Page

HILL, JOHNSTON & GRANT
17 Princess Street South, Suite 2501
Toronto ON M8Y 3N5

Peter T. Grant
Phone: (416) 354-9900
Fax: (416) 354-9909

Solicitors for the defendants

SMITH, FRASER, HAMID & LEE LLP
74 Victoria Street, Suite 503
Toronto ON M5C 2B1

L. A. Blackwell
Phone: (416) 233-9985
Fax: (416) 233-9980

Solicitors for the plaintiffs

Note: A separate front page and table of contents page may be prepared. See Precedents 14.5 and 14.6 for trial record example.

Requires a back prepared on heavy, light blue paper

Court File No. 0000-000-000

ONTARIO
SUPERIOR COURT OF JUSTICE

B E T W E E N:

MATTHEW JACOB LAMOUREAUX

Plaintiff
(Responding Party)

and

JOSEPH STEPHANO GENUA

Defendant
(Moving Party)

**FACTUM OF THE MOVING PARTY
JOSEPH STEPHANO GENUA**

PART I – THE FACTS

1. ---
---.

PART II – THE LAW

2. ---
---.

All of which is respectfully submitted.

*(Name, address, telephone and fax
numbers of responding party's solicitor)*

(Name of specific lawyer)

Solicitors for the defendant

TO: *(Name, address, telephone
and fax numbers of moving
party's solicitors)*

(Name of specific lawyer)

Solicitors for the plaintiff

*Requires front and back covers
Moving Party – white
Responding Party – green*

Court File No.

ONTARIO
SUPERIOR COURT OF JUSTICE

TITLE OF PROCEEDING

CONFIRMATION OF MOTION

I, *(name of lawyer),* with the law firm of *(name of law firm),* counsel for the moving party, confirm that the moving party has conferred or attempted to confer with the other party and that the motion to be heard on *(date of motion)* will proceed on the following basis:

[ ]   for an adjournment on consent to ....*(date).*

[ ]   for a contested adjournment to ....*(date),* for the following reason: *(specify who is requesting the adjournment and why, and who is opposing it and why)*

[ ]   for a consent order

[X]   for hearing of all the issues

[ ]   for hearing of the following issues only *(specify)*

Counsel will refer the presiding judge to the following materials:

1. *(List all documents that will be referred to at the motion hearing.)*

I estimate that the time required for the motion, including costs submissions, will be *(state number of minutes)* for the moving party and *(state number of minutes)* for the responding party for a total of *(state total number of minutes).*

Dated day of preparation

NAME OF LAW FIRM
etc.
(for moving party)

Solicitors for the *(moving party)*

TO: **NAME OF COURT**
       (Address of court)
       FAX: *(number of court)*

TO: **NAME OF LAW FIRM**
       etc.
       (for responding party)

Solicitors for the *(responding party)*

Court File No. 0000-000-000

ONTARIO
SUPERIOR COURT OF JUSTICE

B E T W E E N:

MATTHEW JACOB LAMOUREAUX

Plaintiff

and

JOSEPH STEPHANO GENUA

Defendant

C O N S E N T

The parties by their solicitors hereby consent to *(whatever parties are consenting to).*

DATED at *(place), (month day, year)*

NAME OF LAW FIRM
Street Address
City, Province Postal Code

Name of Specific Lawyer

Telephone Number
Fax Number

Solicitors for the *(capacity of party)*

> *If there is more than one firm of solicitors acting for the defendants or for the respondents, add as many additional signing sections as are required.*

NAME OF LAW FIRM
Street Address
City, Province Postal Code

Name of Specific Lawyer

Telephone Number
Fax Number

Solicitors for the *(capacity of party)*

> *Requires a back*

Court File No.

ONTARIO
SUPERIOR COURT OF JUSTICE

TITLE OF PROCEEDING

REQUISITION

TO THE LOCAL REGISTRAR at *(place)*

I REQUIRE *(Set out a concise statement of what is sought and include all particulars necessary for the registrar to act. Where what is sought is authorized by an order, refer to the order in the requisition and attach a copy of the entered order. Where an affidavit or other document must be filed with the requisition, refer to it in the requisition and attach it.)*

Date: *Date of Preparation*   **NAME OF LAW FIRM**
                                                Barristers and Solicitors
                                                Street Address
                                                City, Province Postal Code

                                                Name of Specific Lawyer
                                                Phone Number
                                                Fax Number

                                                Solicitors for the *(capacity of party)*

(The following are examples of different kinds of requisition.)

(Simple requisition)

I REQUIRE a certified copy of the *(identify document by nature and date)*.

(Order attached)
I REQUIRE, in accordance with the order dated *(date)*, a copy of which is attached, a commission authorizing the taking of evidence before the commissioner named in the order and a letter of request.

I REQUIRE, in accordance with the order dated *(date)*, a copy of which is attached, a certificate of pending litigation in respect of the land described in the statement of claim.

(Affidavit attached)

I REQUIRE an order to continue this action with *(name)* as plaintiff and *(name)* as defendants. An affidavit stating that the defendant *(name)* has reached the age of majority is attached.

CHAPTER 14

Proceeding to Trial: General Actions

OBJECTIVES:

- Demonstrate an understanding of the basic steps in an undefended and a defended action

- Demonstrate an understanding of the procedures to set up examinations for discovery

- Use legal precedents to prepare court documents such as an affidavit of documents, a notice of examination, and a trial record

Once an action is originated and the pleadings are closed, the rules require that other steps be taken to proceed to trial of the action. Figure 14.1 illustrates the basic steps on an action following the close of pleadings. Many things may happen during the course of proceeding to trial, but in this chapter, we consider only the basic steps required in all actions under the *Rules of Civil Procedure*.

AFFIDAVIT OF DOCUMENTS

Within 10 days after the close of pleadings, each party serves on every other party an **affidavit of documents**, disclosing all the documents relating to any matter and issue in the action in his or her possession, control, or power. Under the rules, a document includes a sound recording, videotape, film, photograph, chart, graph, map, plan, survey, book of account, and information recorded or stored by means of any device, including the date and information, in electronic form. A document is deemed to be in a party's power if that party is entitled to obtain the original document or copy, and the party seeking it is not so entitled.

There are two types of affidavits prescribed: one for an individual (Precedent 14.1) and one for a corporation or partnership (Precedent 14.2). The affidavit follows the general heading of the action for which it is prepared, requires the name and general address of the person swearing it, and sets out the facts that are being sworn.

Certificate of Solicitor

The solicitor for the plaintiff or defendant, depending on whom the law firm represents, is required to sign a certificate in the affidavit certifying that the deponent was advised of the necessity of making full disclosure of all relevant documents.

Listing Material in the Affidavit

Material that is being listed in the affidavit of documents is set out in chronological order, commencing with the earliest date. Undated material is placed into logical groupings, following the list of dated material. The list of material is set out in four schedules:

1. Schedule A lists all documents in the possession, control, or power of the person swearing the affidavit that the party does not object to producing for inspection. In the list, each document is numbered consecutively and is identified by the date and nature of the document, together with any other necessary information, to fully identify it.
2. Schedule B lists all documents that were or are in the possession, control, or power of the party that the party objects to produce on the grounds of privilege; that is, the documents are protected from disclosure under the laws relating to evidence. A document written without prejudice, for example, is a privileged document. In the list, each document is numbered consecutively and identified by the date and nature of the document, together with any other necessary information to fully identify it, as well as the grounds for claiming privilege for each document.

Figure 14.1 Basic Steps on a Defended Action Following Close of Pleadings

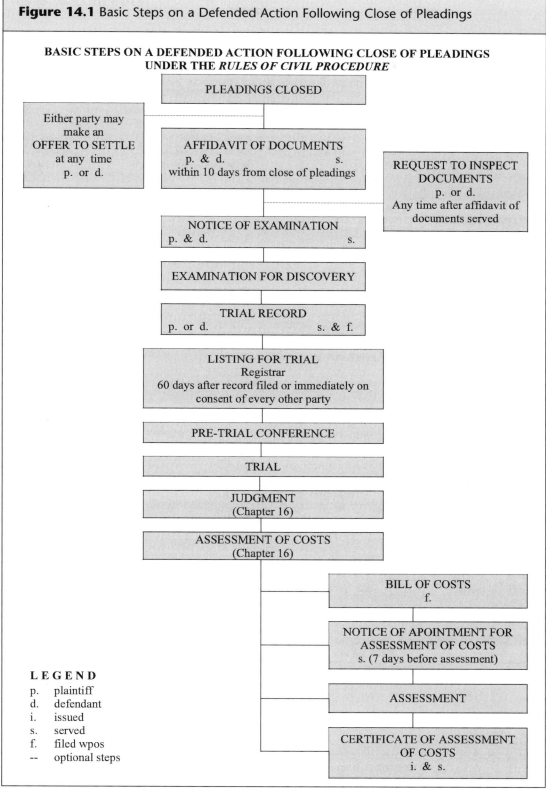

BASIC STEPS ON A DEFENDED ACTION FOLLOWING CLOSE OF PLEADINGS
UNDER THE *RULES OF CIVIL PROCEDURE*

PLEADINGS CLOSED

Either party may
make an
OFFER TO SETTLE
at any time
p. or d.

AFFIDAVIT OF DOCUMENTS
p. & d.   s.
within 10 days from close of pleadings

REQUEST TO INSPECT
DOCUMENTS
p. or d.
Any time after affidavit of
documents served

NOTICE OF EXAMINATION
p. & d.   s.

EXAMINATION FOR DISCOVERY

TRIAL RECORD
p. or d.   s. & f.

LISTING FOR TRIAL
Registrar
60 days after record filed or immediately on
consent of every other party

PRE-TRIAL CONFERENCE

TRIAL

JUDGMENT
(Chapter 16)

ASSESSMENT OF COSTS
(Chapter 16)

BILL OF COSTS
f.

NOTICE OF APOINTMENT FOR
ASSESSMENT OF COSTS
s. (7 days before assessment)

ASSESSMENT

CERTIFICATE OF ASSESSMENT
OF COSTS
i. & s.

LEGEND
p.   plaintiff
d.   defendant
i.   issued
s.   served
f.   filed wpos
--   optional steps

3. Schedule C lists all documents that were but are no longer in the possession, control, or power of the party; indicates when and how possession or control of or power over each such document was lost; and gives the current location of each document. In the list, each document is numbered consecutively and is identified by the date and nature of the document, together with any other necessary information to fully identify it. Each item must include information on when and how possession or control of or power over each document was lost and give the current location of each document.

4. Schedule D is completed only for an action under the simplified procedure. A list of the names and addresses of persons who might reasonably be expected to have knowledge of the transactions or occurrences in issue of the action is keyed in.

Number and Disposition of Copies

Prepare a minimum of three copies of the affidavit of documents. These copies are disposed of as follows:

1. The original sworn affidavit is served on the solicitors for the other party.
2. One copy is for the use of the lawyer.
3. One copy is for the file.

Note that this affidavit is not filed with the court.

Inspection of Documents

A party served with an affidavit of documents may arrange to inspect documents that are either not privileged or are referred to in an originating process or affidavit but are in another party's possession. A request to inspect documents is served on the other party. That party must immediately arrange a time between 9:30 a.m. and 4:30 p.m. within five days of service of the request for the inspection, either at the solicitor's office or another convenient location.

The party inspecting the documents is entitled to have a copy of any document at his or her own expense.

Supplementary Affidavit of Documents

Where additional material comes into the possession, control, or power of the party who swore the affidavit of documents, or where the original affidavit was inaccurate or incomplete, a supplementary affidavit is served listing the additional documents or indicating the extent to which the affidavit requires modification. It is a fully keyed document, titled "Supplementary Affidavit of Documents," and lists the additional documents or provides information on the inaccuracy.

Prepare a minimum of three copies of any supplementary affidavit of documents. The original is served on the other party, one copy is for your lawyer, and one copy is for the office file.

EXAMINATIONS FOR DISCOVERY

When the exchange of pleadings is completed and the affidavits of documents is filed, the next step is to hold examinations for discovery. The parties to the examination are examined under oath before trial; they answer questions touching upon the matters in dispute. The examination provides each party with a great deal of information about the case to be presented by the other party. When the party to be examined is an Ontario resident, the examination takes place in the office of a reporter. This may be at the office of an **official examiner**—a title that was conferred on certain court reporters, who still exist; however, the majority of court reporters do not hold this designation and are no longer required to do so in order to conduct examinations.

If the party to be examined is not an Ontario resident, special steps are required to arrange the examination; your lawyer will instruct you in this matter.

An examination for discovery may be an oral examination or, at the option of the examining party, may be by written questions and answers, but not both.

Arranging an Appointment for an Oral Examination for Discovery

When a suitable date for discovery has been determined by the solicitors or their legal assistants, the legal assistant may be required to arrange the appointment with the official examiner selected. The following information is given to the official examiner by telephone:

1. The date for the examination and whether in the morning or afternoon. Indicate the anticipated duration of the examination.
2. The name of the parties, that is, the title of proceeding.
3. The name of the firm of solicitors involved and the name of the individual lawyer who will be attending the discovery.
4. The number of people to be examined: the plaintiff, the defendant, or both.
5. The type of examination to be held since examinations may be held in other proceedings connected with a trial or a subsequent judgment, such as
   a. examination for discovery in an action,
   b. cross-examination of a party on an affidavit filed in support of a legal proceeding, or
   c. examination of a judgment debtor.

After the arrangements have been made, a minimum of two copies of a notice of examination of a party to the proceeding are prepared (Precedent 14.3) and served on the solicitors for the party to be examined at least two days before the date of the examination; the other copy remains in the document file in the main file.

Every other party in a proceeding other than the party to be examined is given not less than two days' notice of the time and place of the examination. This may be done by a letter addressed to the solicitors for the party or parties.

If the party being examined is not a party to the proceeding and resides in Ontario, he or she is served with a summons to witness for examination out of court. The precedent is found in Form 34B of the *Rules of Civil Procedure*. In addition, **attendance money**, similar to that paid to a witness who gives evidence at a trial, must be paid. Attendance money is provided to a witness to defray his or her expenses in attending to give evidence. The amounts to be paid are discussed later in this chapter, when a summons to witness to give evidence at the trial of the proceeding is considered.

Unless the lawyer indicates that very specific material is to be included in the wording of a notice of examination, it is not necessary to indicate the precise material or things to be brought to an examination. Such information must, however, be included in a summons to witness for examination out of court.

What Happens on an Oral Examination for Discovery

On an oral examination for discovery; the party being examined is asked questions that deal with the matters in dispute by the solicitor for the other side. The solicitor for the party being examined is also present. Frequently, questions are asked that the party being examined cannot immediately answer; an undertaking (promise) is given to provide the required information by letter.

The entire examination is recorded and then typed up to form a transcript of the examination, and a copy is sent to each solicitor, together with an account. Questions and answers appearing in a transcript may be used as evidence at the trial.

What Happens on a Written Examination for Discovery

An examination for discovery that is conducted by written questions and answers does not require an appointment with an official examiner.

The list of questions to be answered is set out in a document titled "Questions on Written Examination for Discovery," the format of which follows that of general court documents. Following an introductory paragraph that identifies both the examining party and the party to be examined and indicates the time and method of answering the questions, the questions are set out in numbered paragraphs. If the list of questions is a second list rather than the initial list, the numbering of the questions commences with the next number following the last-numbered question in the previous list.

The list of questions is answered in a document titled "Answers on Written Examination for Discovery," which follows the format of an affidavit. The answers are numbered to correspond to the question number. If the deponent objects to answering a question, the affidavit indicates that fact and sets out the grounds for the objection.

Number and Disposition of Copies

Prepare a minimum of three copies of each of these documents, which are disposed of as follows:

1. The original is served on the party to be examined.
2. One copy is for the use of the lawyer.
3. One copy is retained in the client file.

An additional copy is required for service on all other parties in the proceeding. For example, if there are two defendants in an action, the list of questions is served on both. The basic format for the question-and-answer documents on written examinations is found in Forms 35A and 35B of the rules.

SETTING AN ACTION DOWN FOR TRIAL

After the close of pleadings, the action may be set down for trial.

Undefended Action

When the court orders the trial of an undefended action, a party who wishes to set it down for trial files a trial record. Your lawyer will advise you of the necessary procedures when the action to be set down is a defended third party claim or an undefended third party claim.

Defended Action

A party who wishes to set a defended action down for trial serves a trial record on every party to the action or to a counterclaim or crossclaim in the action, as well as on any third or subsequent party. A copy of the trial record is then filed with proof of service.

Trial Record

The trial record is a booklet of documents relevant to the action. It provides the judge presiding at the trial with the documents setting out the positions of the plaintiff and defendant, as well as information on any court orders relating to the action made during the course of preparing for trial. The trial record contains, in the following order,

1. a table of contents that describes each document by its nature and date;
2. a copy of any jury notice;
3. a copy of all the pleadings, including those relating to any counterclaim or crossclaim; these appear in the record in chronological order, with the earliest pleading, that is, the statement of claim, first;
4. a copy of any demand or order for particulars of a pleading and the particulars delivered in response;
5. a copy of any notice of amounts and particulars of special damages delivered subsequent to the delivery of the statement of claim;
6. a copy of any order respecting the trial; and
7. a certificate signed by the solicitor setting the action down for trial (Precedent 14.4).

Only the first, third, and seventh items need be included in every trial record; the other material is included only if prepared for use in the action.

Number of Copies

Prepare a minimum of two copies of a trial record, plus one additional copy for each law firm acting for a defendant.

Preparing the Trial Record

To prepare the trial record, follow these steps:

1. Photocopy the required number of copies of each document to be included, omitting the backsheets, and assemble them in the proper order.
2. Consecutively number each page in the upper right-hand corner in ink or with a numbering machine. It should be noted that the rules do not state that a trial record must have consecutively numbered pages. However, when outlining the requirements for records for use on motions, applications, and appeals, the rules do stipulate that the record pages shall be consecutively numbered. As a result, most legal assistants also consecutively number the pages of a trial record.
3. Place a tabbed divider page in front of each document to be included in the record. These divider pages may be tabbed 1, 2, 3, 4, etc., or A, B, C, D, etc., depending on the preference of your law firm. The divider pages are not part of the consecutively numbered pages of the record.
4. Prepare the following:
   a. front or face page (Precedent 14.5) identifying the material as a trial record and setting out the name, address, and telephone number of the solicitors for all parties
   b. a table of contents page (Precedent 14.6) listing each document by
      i. the divider page tab number or letter,
      ii. the name and date of preparation or other relevant date information, and
      iii. the page number at which the document may be found
5. Prepare a back on heavy, light blue paper, identifying the document as a trial record.
6. Assemble the material with the front page first, followed by the table of contents page, the documents (each with a tabbed divider page) in numbered order, and the backsheet.
7. Bind the assembled material down the left-hand side to form a booklet.

Serving and Filing Record

The record is served on the solicitors acting for parties on the other side in the action and then filed with the court with proof of service. In the court office, the record is checked carefully against the documents previously filed to ensure that the material in the record is identical to that filed. If the material is complete, the court is said to pass the record, and upon payment of the prescribed court fees, the action is set down for trial.

Once an action has been set down for trial, the party who carried out this step may not commence or continue any motion or form of discovery without the consent of the court.

Subsequent Record Material

The party filing the trial record is responsible for seeing that copies of documents such as the following are placed with the record before trial:

1. A notice of amounts and particulars of special damages delivered after the filing of the record (Precedent 14.7)
2. Any order respecting the trial made after the trial record was filed
3. Any memorandum signed by counsel or any order made by the court, following a pre-trial conference
4. Any affidavit to be used in evidence in an undefended action
5. Any financial statement delivered after the filing of the trial record
6. Any report of the Official Guardian and supporting affidavit, and any dispute of or waiver of the right to dispute the report or affidavit

Placing Action on Trial List

Undefended Action

When an action is undefended (for example, when the defendant fails to take the steps open to defend an action), and the court orders that a trial be held, the action is placed on the trial list when the record is filed with the court.

Defended Action

When an action is defended, the action is placed on the appropriate trial list by the registrar 60 days after the action is set down for trial. If the written consent of every party other than the party who set the action down for trial is filed before the expiry of the 60 days, the action is placed on the appropriate trial list on the date the consent is filed.

Trial at Another Place

When the action is to be tried at a place other than where it was commenced, the party filing the trial record by requisition will require that the court file, including the trial record, be sent to the court office at the place of trial.

A defended action is not placed on a trial list for a sitting outside Toronto later than 10 days before the commencement of the sitting, except where a judge orders otherwise.

If an action is settled, the solicitors should notify the registrar of the settlement in writing. This is required whether or not the action has been placed on the trial list.

STATUS NOTICE

The registrar will send by mail to all solicitors of record, a **status notice**, when

1. a statement of defence has been filed and
2. the action has not been placed on a trial list or terminated by any means within two years of the filing of the statement of defence.

This notice advises that the plaintiff's solicitors must attend a hearing on the status of the action and that the action will be dismissed for delay unless it is set down for trial or terminated within 90 days after service of the notice.

The solicitor receiving the notice is required to provide a copy of the notice to his or her client. It is therefore very important to ensure that all due dates are properly met. Be sure to prepare tickler slips to remind the lawyer of such dates. For example, after the statement of defence has been delivered, prepare a tickler slip for a date one or two weeks before the expiry of the two-year period.

OFFER TO SETTLE

A party to a legal proceeding may serve an offer to settle (Precedent 14.8) any of the claims at any time. The terms are set out in the offer. The offer may be withdrawn at any time before it is accepted by serving a written notice of withdrawal on the party to whom the offer was made. This notice follows the format of a general court document, is identified as a notice of withdrawal, and may use wording similar to the following:

> The (identify party by capacity or capacity and name) withdraws the offer to settle dated (date of offer).

An offer to settle may be accepted at any time before it is withdrawn by serving an acceptance of offer. This document also follows the basic format for court documents, using the following wording:

> The (identify party) accepts your offer to settle dated (date of offer).

If the offer to settle specifies a time for acceptance, it is deemed to be withdrawn if not accepted by that time. Unless it is formally withdrawn, an offer to settle remains effective even if it is originally rejected or results in a counteroffer that is not accepted.

The rules have established the form of formal offers to settle. Some solicitors set out offers to settle in a letter written without prejudice, indicating the date by which it must be accepted or it will be withdrawn.

PRE-TRIAL CONFERENCE

A judge may direct that a pre-trial conference be held in certain circumstances. In Toronto, when a proceeding is placed on the list of cases for trial, a judge or pre-trial conference must be requested or waived within 12 months of the action being listed for trial. If this is not done, the action is struck from the list, unless all parties file a consent to dispose with such a conference.

Such a conference is a hearing before a judge before the trial to consider matters that might help to dispose of, shorten, or simplify the proceeding to encourage its just, most expeditious, and least expensive disposition. Each solicitor must provide a memorandum for the use of the judge, setting out concise information on the pertinent facts in the proceeding. Precedent 14.9 illustrates the first page of a recorded shell of such a pre-trial conference memorandum.

Each region has its own practice directions with regard to scheduling pre-trial conferences, which are listed in the *Rules of Civil Procedure*, as well as the time limits for filing the pre-trial memorandum. All other parties must file a pre-trial memorandum as well within the required time. Usually, solicitors for the parties agree on a tentative date. No formal notice is required; the other side can be advised by letter or telephone.

Medical reports and other experts' reports should be concisely summarized in half- to three- or four-page statements, setting out in chronological form the case of the plaintiff or defendant, and included in the pre-trial memorandum, which is filed for use of the pre-trial conference judge.

The rules do not set out any required method of presenting the memorandum. It may be stapled to a covering letter but more frequently is bound in covers of any colour and indexed to assist in locating particular material.

At the conclusion of the conference, counsel may sign a memorandum setting out the results of the conference, or the judge may make an order relating to the conduct of the proceeding. This material must be filed with the court to be placed with the trial record.

SIMPLIFIED PROCEDURE/CASE MANAGEMENT

If the action is under the requirements of simplified procedure or case management, alternative and additional procedural steps, including additional conferences, must be taken. Refer to Figures 10.2 and 10.3 to review the procedures and documentation that may be required.

BRIEFS

Although not required under the rules, both of the following briefs are usually requested by the lawyer. Note that in briefs, unlike records, the pages are not usually numbered, and depending on the size of the brief, they may be cerloxed or placed in binders.

Trial Brief

The exact content and arrangement of the trial brief differ with each lawyer, but it usually contains copies of the originating process, all pleadings, a copy of each affidavit of documents and relevant productions, any memoranda of law prepared for use in the action, and copies of pertinent file memoranda. To assemble a trial brief, make a photocopy of each relevant document. Each item in the brief is inserted after a divider with a numbered tab, and the first page of the assembled brief is an index, showing by tab number the location of each piece of material.

Brief of Authorities

A **brief of authorities** (also referred to as a case book) is a booklet containing photocopies of any case law that are relevant to the proceeding. A copy of this brief is prepared for the lawyer, who usually also gives a copy to the judge for his or her reference during the trial. A sample cover page for a brief is illustrated in Precedent 14.10. To prepare the brief, note the following procedures:

1. Make a minimum of three copies of each authority (case).
2. Following the directions of the lawyer, clearly highlight the particular passages in the cases to which the reference will be made.
3. Assemble the cases in the order requested by the lawyer (this may or may not be alphabetical order) and insert a tabbed divider page before each authority.
4. Prepare an index of the cases in alphabetical order indicating at which tab the case is located and place this page first in the assembled book.

To assemble these briefs, each item (whether a document or case law) is usually photocopied and then inserted after a divider with a numbered tab. A table of contents is prepared for each brief that outlines by the appropriate tab number the location of each piece of material.

SUMMONS TO WITNESS

A **summons to witness** (Precedent 14.11) is a command requiring the person to whom it is addressed to be present at a specified place and time. It may also require the person to produce at the trial documents or other things in his or her possession, control, or power relating to the action. The documents or things are listed in the summons.

One summons may be addressed to more than one witness. Prepare one original; photocopy sufficient copies to provide one for each witness to whom it is addressed and one copy for the office file. The original and the necessary number of copies are given to the sheriff for personal service upon the witness or witnesses, together with a cheque for **attendance money** for each witness. This money is provided to a witness to defray his or her expenses in attending the trial to give evidence.

When you prepare the summons, also prepare a cheque requisition to secure a cheque payable to each witness for the amount of attendance money to which he or she is entitled. Item 21 of Part II of Tariff A in the *Rules of Civil Procedure* sets out the amounts payable:

1. For each day of necessary attendance, $50
2. For travel allowance, where the hearing or examination is held:
   a. in a city or town in which the witness resides, $3 for each day of necessary attendance;
   b. within 300 kilometres of where the witness resides, 24 cents a kilometre each way between his or her residence and the place of hearing or examination; or

    c. more than 300 kilometres from where the witness resides, the minimum return air fare plus 24 cents a kilometre each way from his or her place of residence to the airport and from the airport to the place of hearing or examination

3. For overnight accommodation and meal allowances where the witness resides elsewhere than the place of hearing or examination and is required to remain overnight, $75 for each overnight stay

These amounts were correct as of December 31, 2007.

TRIAL

When the date for the trial is reached, the solicitor attends in court with the solicitor for the other party. Witnesses may be called by each side to present evidence, and exhibits in support of that evidence may be filed with the court. When all the evidence has been given, each solicitor presents his or her argument, that is, final presentation to the court.

    Judgment may be given at once, but it is usually reserved until the judge has had an opportunity to consider all the evidence presented at the trial. The solicitors for the parties are notified by the court office when the judge has handed down judgment, and the reasons for judgment may be secured from the court office. After judgment has been handed down, the solicitor for the successful party prepares and issues the formal judgment, following the procedures discussed in Chapter 16. The judgment may include a provision that the unsuccessful party on the trial is to pay costs to the successful party, which are also discussed in Chapter 16.

Terms and Concepts

affidavit of documents	status notice
solicitor–client privilege	offer to settle
examinations for discovery (oral/written)	pre-trial conference
official examiner	trial brief
set down for trial	brief of authorities (case book)
trial record	summons to witness
trial list	attendance money

Review Questions

1. What is the guideline for listing productions in Schedule A of an affidavit of documents?

2. What is meant by the term "examination for discovery"? Why do you feel such an examination is part of the procedure in an action?

3. What is the purpose of having a pre-trial conference?

4. What material must be included in a trial record?

5. Although your lawyer will have a copy of the trial record, why would he or she ask you to prepare a brief for his or her use at the trial of a legal proceeding?

6. Once the trial record has been filed, when is the action placed on the list for trial?

7. If a witness is to be summoned to give evidence for one day, and he lives in the city in which the trial will be held, what amount of attendance money would he receive?

8. You have prepared an offer to settle. What disposition will be made of the copies of that document?

9. What additional steps are required before an action is set down for trial if the proceeding is under the rules of
   a. simplified procedure?
   b. case management?

Automated Civil Litigation – Korbitec Inc.

Court File No. 0000-000

ONTARIO
SUPERIOR COURT OF JUSTICE

BETWEEN:

RICHARD PERCIVAL GOLDSTONE,
a minor, by his litigation guardian,
KENNETH PERCIVAL GOLDSTONE

Plaintiff

and

HENRY ALBERT BELL, HERMANN ALGERNON
BELL, and MARY MARGARET WILLIAMSON

Defendants

AFFIDAVIT OF DOCUMENTS

I, **RICHARD PERCIVAL GOLDSTONE,** of the City of Oshawa, in the Regional Municipality of Durham, litigation guardian for the plaintiff, MAKE OATH AND SAY:

1. I have conducted a diligent search of my records and have made appropriate enquiries of others to inform myself in order to make this affidavit. This affidavit discloses, to the full extent of my knowledge, information and belief, all documents relating to any matter in issue in this action that are or have been in my possession, control or power.

2. I have listed in Schedule A those documents that are in my possession, control or power and that I do not object to producing for inspection.

3. I have listed in Schedule B those documents that are or were in my possession, control or power and that I object to producing because I claim they are privileged, and I have stated in Schedule B the grounds for each such claim.

4. I have listed in Schedule C those documents that were formerly in my possession, control or power but are no longer in my possession, control or power, and I have stated in Schedule C when and how I lost possession or control of or power over them and their present location.

5. I have never had in my possession, control or power any document relating to any matter in issue in this action other than those listed in Schedules A, B and C.

SWORN BEFORE ME at the
City of Toronto, in the Province of Ontario

this .... day of March, 20__

}

_____
Commissioner for Taking Affidavits

RICHARD PERCIVAL GOLDSTONE

LAWYER'S CERTIFICATE

I CERTIFY that I have explained to the deponent,
(a)   the necessity of making full disclosure of all documents relating to any matter in issue in the action;
(b)   what kinds of documents are likely to be relevant to the allegations made in the pleadings; and
(c)   if the action is brought under the simplified procedure, the necessity of providing the list required under rule 76.03.

March   , 20__

_____
Peter T. Grant

Source: Korbitec Inc.

- 2 -

SCHEDULE A

Documents in my possession, control or power that I do not object to producing for inspection.

(Number each document consecutively. Set out the nature and date of the document and other particulars sufficient to identify it.)

Replace asterisk with list of Schedule A documents.

1. Letter from Henry Albert Bell to Richard Percival Goldstone, dated June 18, 20__.

2. Letter from Mary Margaret Williamson to Richard Percival Goldstone, dated July 29, 20__.

3. Copy of letter from Richard Percival Goldstone to Henry Albert Bell, dated September 6, 20__.

OR

Number	Date	Description
1.	June 18, 20__	Letter from Henry Albert Bell to Richard Percival Goldstone
2.	July 29, 20__	Letter from Mary Margaret Williamson to Richard Percival Goldstone
3.	September 6, 20__	Copy of letter from Richard Percival Goldstone to Henry Albert Bell

(Further productions are continued with the next consecutive number.)

Source: Korbitec Inc.

- 3 -

SCHEDULE B

Documents that are or were in my possession, control or power that I object to producing on the grounds of privilege.

(Number each document consecutively. Set out the nature and date of the document and other particulars sufficient to identify it. State the grounds for claiming privilege for each document.)

Replace asterisk with list of Schedule B documents.

1. Correspondence between the plaintiff and his solicitor asking for and receiving advice in anticipation of this litigation.

2. Correspondence concerning without prejudice settlement discussions between the plaintiff and the defendants.

SCHEDULE C

Documents that were formerly in my possession, control or power but are no longer in my possession, control or power.

(Number each document consecutively. Set out the nature and date of the document and other particulars sufficient to identify it. State when and how possession or control of or power over each document was lost and give the present location of each document.)

Replace asterisk with list of Schedule C documents.

1. Original of letter from Richard Percival Goldstone to Henry Albert Bell, dated September 6, 20__, which was mailed to the said Henry Albert Bell and should be in his possession.

Requires a back

Source: Korbitec Inc.

Automated Civil Litigation – Korbitec Inc.   Court File No. 0000-000-000

ONTARIO
SUPERIOR COURT OF JUSTICE

B E T W E E N:

EAST HARDWARE LIMITED

and   Plaintiff

HUMBER MANUFACTURING LTD.

Defendant

AFFIDAVIT OF DOCUMENTS

     I, **HOWARD WILLIAM EAST**, of the City of Toronto, in the Province of Ontario, MAKE OATH AND SAY:

1.   I am the President of EAST HARDWARE LIMITED, the plaintiff, which is a corporation.

2.   I have conducted a diligent search of the corporation's records and have made appropriate enquiries of others to inform myself in order to make this affidavit. This affidavit discloses, to the full extent of my knowledge, information and belief, all documents relating to any matter in issue in this action that are or have been in the possession, control or power of the corporation.

3.   I have listed in Schedule A those documents that are in the possession, control or power of the corporation and that it does not object to producing for inspection.

4.   I have listed in Schedule B those documents that are or were in the possession, control or power of the corporation and that it objects to producing because it claims they are privileged, and I have stated in Schedule B the grounds for each such claim.

5.   I have listed in Schedule C those documents that were formerly in the possession, control or power of the corporation but are no longer in its possession, control or power, and I have stated in Schedule C when and how it lost possession or control of or power over them and their present location.

6.   The corporation has never had in its possession, control or power any document relating to any matter in issue in this action other than those listed in Schedules A, B and C.

7.   I have listed in Schedule D the names and addresses of persons who might reasonably be expected to have knowledge of transactions or occurrences in issue.

SWORN BEFORE ME at the
City of Toronto, in the Province of Ontario

this .... day of ...., 20__

_____   }   _____
   Commissioner for Taking Affidavits   **HOWARD WILLIAM EAST**

LAWYER'S CERTIFICATE

I CERTIFY that I have explained to the deponent,
(a)   the necessity of making full disclosure of all documents relating to any matter in issue in the action;
(b)   what kinds of documents are likely to be relevant to the allegations made in the pleadings; and
(c)   if the action is brought under the simplified procedure, the necessity of providing the list required under rule 76.03.

    December   , 20__

                                 _____
                                     Peter T. Grant

Source: Korbitec Inc.

- 3 -

SCHEDULE B

Documents in the corporation's possession, control or power that it does not object to producing for inspection.

(Number each document consecutively. Set out the nature and date of the document and other particulars sufficient to identify it. State the grounds for claiming privilege for each document.)

Replace asterisk list of Schedule B documents

1. Correspondence between the plaintiff and its solicitor asking for and receiving advice in anticipation of this litigation.

2. Correspondence concerning without prejudice settlement discussions between the plaintiff and the defendant.

SCHEDULE C

Documents that were formerly in the corporation's possession, control or power but are no longer in its possession, control or power.

(Number each document consecutively. Set out the nature and date of the document and other particulars sufficient to identify it. State when and how possession or control of or power over each document was lost and give the present location of each document.)

1. Original of letter from the plaintiff to the defendant dated October 10, 2007, which was mailed to the defendants and should be in their possession.

SCHEDULE D

(To be filled in only if the action is being brought under the simplified procedure.)

Names and addresses of persons who might reasonably be expected to have knowledge of transactions or occurrences in issue.

Cheryl Anne Davich   4500 Yonge Street, Apt. 602
                            Thornhill ON L2K 4C9

John Bruce MacPherson   459 Botany Crescent
                            Newmarket ON M5K 1D4

Requires a back

Source: Korbitec Inc.

Automated Civil Litigation – Korbitec Inc.

Court File No. 0000-000-000

ONTARIO
SUPERIOR COURT OF JUSTICE

B E T W E E N:

EAST HARDWARE LIMITED
and PATRICK THOMAS STONE

Plaintiffs

and

HUMBER MANUFACTURING LTD.

Defendant

NOTICE OF EXAMINATION

TO: **EMILY ROBERTS**

YOU ARE REQUIRED TO ATTEND, on Friday, January 12, 20__, at 2:00 p.m. at the office of Toronto Court Reporters, 65 Queen Street West, Suite 1410, P.O. Box 69, Toronto, ON, M5H 2M5 (Phone Number: 416-364-2065), for *(choose one of the following)*:

[ ] Cross-examination on your affidavit dated

[X] Examination for discovery

[ ] Examination for discovery on behalf of or in place of *(identify party)*

[ ] Examination in aid of execution

[ ] Examination in aid of execution on behalf of or in place of *(identify party)*

YOU ARE REQUIRED TO BRING WITH YOU and produce at the examination the documents mentioned in subrule 30.04(4) of the *Rules of Civil Procedure*, and the following documents and things:

(Set out the nature and date of each document and give particulars sufficient to identify each document and thing.)

1. All original documents including any sound recording, videotape, film, photograph, chart, graph, map, plan, survey, book of account and information recorded or stored by means on any device in your possession, control or power which are relevant to any matters in issue in this proceeding and a list of all documents over which you claim privilege.

January 5, 20__

HILL, JOHNSTON & GRANT
17 Princess Street South, Suite 2501
Toronto ON M8Y 3N5
Peter T. Grant (12345G)

Tel: 416-354-9900
Fax: 416-354-9909

Solicitors for the Plaintiffs

TO: **SMITH, FRASER, HAMID & LEE LLP**
74 Victoria Street, Suite 503
Toronto ON M5C 2B1

Shelley A. Colangelo (42266C)

Tel: 416-233-9985
Fax: 416-233-9980

Solicitors for the Defendant

Requires a back

Source: Korbitec Inc.

Court File No. 0000-000-000

ONTARIO
SUPERIOR COURT OF JUSTICE

BETWEEN:

EAST HARDWARE LIMITED
and PATRICK THOMAS STONE

Plaintiffs

and

HUMBER MANUFACTURING LTD.

Defendant

SOLICITOR'S CERTIFICATE OF TRIAL RECORD

I, PETER T. GRANT, solicitor for the plaintiffs, certify that the trial record contains

the documents indicated below in the following order as required by clauses 48.03(l)(h):

[x] a table of contents, describing each document by its nature and date;

[x] a copy of any jury notice;

[x] a copy of the pleadings, including those relating to any counterclaim or crossclaim;

[ ] a copy of any demand or order for particulars of a pleading and the particulars

     delivered in response;

[ ] a copy of any notice of amounts and particulars of special damages delivered under

     clause 25.06(9)(b);

[x] a copy of any order respecting the trial; and

I ALSO CERTIFY:

[x] that the time for delivery of pleadings has expired

[ ] that the   failed to deliver   and has been noted in default;

[ ] that the action against the defendant whose name is

     has been [ ] discontinued   [ ] dismissed

Dated at Toronto

_____
Signature of solicitor

on January 29, 20__

HILL, JOHNSTON & GRANT
Barristers and Solicitors
17 Princess Street South, Suite 2501
Toronto ON M8Y 3N5

Peter T. Grant (12345G)

Tel: 416-354-9900
Fax: 416-354-9909

Solicitors for the Plaintiffs

Court File No. 0000-000

ONTARIO
SUPERIOR COURT OF JUSTICE

BETWEEN:

RICHARD PERCIVAL GOLDSTONE,
a minor, by his litigation guardian,
KENNETH PERCIVAL GOLDSTONE

Plaintiff

and

HENRY ALBERT BELL,
HERMANN ALGERNON BELL,
and MARY MARGARET WILLIAMSON

Defendants

TRIAL RECORD

HILL, JOHNSTON & GRANT
17 Princess Street South, Suite 2501
Toronto ON M8Y 3N5

Peter T. Grant (12345G)
Phone: (416) 354-9900
Fax: (416) 354-9909

Solicitors for the Plaintiff

ARMSTRONG, WARD & SIEGEL
16 Montreal Street West
Whitby ON L4R 3C2

Katherine R. Siegel (24331S)
Phone: (905) 687-4682
Fax: (905) 687-4690

Solicitors for the defendants
Henry Albert Bell and Hermann Algernon Bell

SMITH, FRASER, HAMID & LEE
74 Victoria Street, Suite 503
Toronto ON M5C 2B1

L. A. Blackwell (33412B)
Phone: (416) 233-9985
Fax: (416) 233-9980

Solicitors for the defendant
Mary Margaret Williamson

*Requires a back
prepared on heavy,
light blue paper*

Court File No. 0000-000-000

ONTARIO
SUPERIOR COURT OF JUSTICE

BETWEEN:

RICHARD PERCIVAL GOLDSTONE,
a minor, by his litigation guardian,
KENNETH PERCIVAL GOLDSTONE

Plaintiff

and

HENRY ALBERT BELL,
HERMANN ALGERNON BELL,
and MARY MARGARET WILLIAMSON

Defendants

TABLE OF CONTENTS

Page

Court File No. 0000-000-000

ONTARIO
SUPERIOR COURT OF JUSTICE

BETWEEN:

MAXINE JOSEPHINE PODOBA

Plaintiff

and

VINCENT JOSEPH MICHAELSON

Defendants

LIST OF SPECIAL DAMAGES

LOSS OF INCOME:

October 15, 1998, to July 1, 1999, 31 weeks at $578.08 per week	$17,920.48	
July 1, 1999, to July 1, 2000, 52 weeks at $624.33 per week (reflects an 8% increase)	<u>32,465.16</u>	
	$50,385.64	

LESS:

Amount received from Centennial Consulting Ltd. at $578.09 for 4 weeks	$ 2,312.32	
Amount received from Sun Life, $458.25 per week for 26 weeks	<u>11,914.50</u>	<u>14,226.82</u>

TOTAL INCOME LOST: <u>$36,158.82</u>

July 1, 20___

Court File No.

ONTARIO
SUPERIOR COURT OF JUSTICE

TITLE OF PROCEEDING

OFFER TO SETTLE

The *(identify party)* offers to settle this proceeding *(or the following claims in this proceeding)* on the following terms:

1. --

----------.

2. --

---.

3. --

---.

Month Day, Year   **NAME OF LAW FIRM**
(Date of Preparation)   Street Address
                                                    City, Province Postal Code

                                                    Name of Specific Lawyer

                                                    Telephone Number
                                                    Fax Number

                                                    Solicitors for the *(capacity of party)*

TO: **NAME OF LAW FIRM**
         (to whom offer is made)
         Street Address
         City, Province Postal Code

         Name of Specific Lawyer

         Telephone Number
         Fax Number
                                                    Requires a back

         Solicitors for the *(capacity of party)*

Court File No. 0000-000-000

ONTARIO
SUPERIOR COURT OF JUSTICE

PRE-TRIAL CONFERENCE MEMORANDUM

SHORT TITLE OF PROCEEDING: *

PRE-TRIAL DATE: *

LIST NO: *

SUBMITTED BY: *

THEORY OF THE PLAINTIFF'S CASE INCLUDING FACTUAL CONTENTIONS:

*

THEORY OF THE DEFENDANT'S CASE INCLUDING FACTUAL CONTENTIONS:

*

LEGAL ISSUES RAISED IN THE PLEADINGS AND TO BE DETERMINED AT TRIAL:

*

PLEADINGS AND RELEVANT MATTERS:

*

MOTIONS:

Will there be any motions at trial?   *

If so, what are they?   *

ADMISSIONS:

*

REPORTS:

*

BUSINESS RECORDS:

1. Will any be tendered under the Evidence Act and has the appropriate notice been given?

Court File No. 0000-000-000

ONTARIO
SUPERIOR COURT OF JUSTICE

BETWEEN:

**EAST HARDWARE LIMITED
and PATRICK THOMAS STONE**

Plaintiffs

and

HUMBER MANUFACTURING LTD.

Defendants

BRIEF OF AUTHORITIES

Description   Tab

1. <u>King v. Low</u>, [1985] 1 S.C.R. 87..1

2. <u>Martin v. Duffell</u> (1988), 65 O.R. (2d) 154, 27 C.P.C. (2d) 93,
   6 M.V.R. (2d) 191 (H.C.J.)...3

1. <u>Re Moores and Feldstein</u> (1973), 12 R.F.L. 273 5

2. <u>R. v. Price</u>, [1993] 3 S.C.R. 633 6

2. <u>Young v. Young</u> (1998), 162 D.L.R. (4th) 414, 111 O.A.C. 91,
   39 B.L.R. (2d) 66, 37 C.C.E.L. (2d) 1, C.L.L.C.................................10

(Continue in alphabetical order with as many cases as may be required.)

HILL, JOHNSTON & GRANT
17 Princess Street South, Suite 2501
Toronto ON M8Y 3N5

Peter T. Grant
Phone: (416) 354-9900
Fax: (416) 354-9909

Solicitors for the plaintiff

Automated Civil Litigation – Korbitec Inc.   Court File No. 0000-000-000

ONTARIO
SUPERIOR COURT OF JUSTICE

B E T W E E N:

EAST HARDWARE LIMITED
and PATRICK THOMAS STONE

Plaintiffs

(Court Seal)   and

HUMBER MANUFACTURING LTD.

Defendant

SUMMONS TO WITNESS

TO: **NORMAN GORDON MacLEOD**

YOU ARE REQUIRED TO ATTEND TO GIVE EVIDENCE IN

COURT at the hearing of this proceeding on May 12, 20__, at 10:00 a.m. at the

Court House, 393 University Avenue, 10th Floor, Toronto, Ontario, M5G 1E6,

and to remain until your attendance is no longer required.

YOU ARE REQUIRED TO BRING WITH YOU and produce at the

hearing the following documents and things:

All books, contract, letters, statements, records, bills, notes, securities,
vouchers, and copies of the same in your possession or under your
control, in any way relating to the matters which are within the scope of
this proceeding or have any reference thereto, and particularly all
documents relating to this action.

Source: Korbitec Inc.

- 2 -

ATTENDANCE MONEY for one (1) day of attendance is served with this summons, calculated in accordance with Tariff A of the *Rules of Civil Procedure*, as follows:

Attendance allowance of $50.00 daily	$50.00
Travel allowance	3.00
Overnight accommodation and meal allowance	0.00
TOTAL:	$53.00

If further attendance is required, you will be entitled to additional attendance money.

IF YOU FAIL TO ATTEND OR REMAIN IN ATTENDANCE AS REQUIRED BY THIS SUMMONS, A WARRANT MAY BE ISSUED FOR YOUR ARREST.

Date _____   Issued by   _____
                                                       Local Registrar

                         Address of
                         court office: 393 University Avenue
                                          10th Floor
                                          Toronto ON M5G 1E6

This summons was issued at the request of, and inquiries may be directed to:

HILL, JOHNSTON & GRANT
Barristers & Solicitors
17 Princess Street South, Suite 2501
Toronto ON M8Y 3N5

Peter T. Grant (12345G)

Tel: 416-354-9900
Fax: 416-354-9909

Requires a back

Solicitors for the plaintiffs

Source: Korbitec Inc.

CHAPTER 15

Application Proceedings

OBJECTIVES:

- Define and describe the various steps in an application in the Superior Court of Justice
- Use legal precedents to prepare documents for an application in the Superior Court of Justice
- Demonstrate an understanding of the purpose and content of a factum

Although an action is the most common form of legal proceeding, there are other proceedings heard that do not involve one party suing another. When the direction and advice of the court are sought on a legal question, or the court is asked to review the decision of an administrative tribunal such as the Ontario Municipal Board, the civil proceeding is known as an **application**.

For example, an application may be made to the Superior Court of Justice for advice on the interpretation of a will, for the division of family assets, for custody of children, or for support of a spouse. Application may also be made to the Divisional Court branch of the Superior Court of Justice.

Figure 15.1 outlines the steps that may be taken in an application in the Superior Court of Justice, which is more common, and these are the procedures discussed in this chapter.

COMMENCEMENT OF AN APPLICATION IN THE SUPERIOR COURT OF JUSTICE

An application in the Superior Court of Justice is originated by issuing and serving a **notice of application** (Precedent 15.1). This is a prescribed form. The party who makes the application is the **applicant**; any opposite party in the proceeding is the **respondent**.

NOTICE OF APPLICATION

General Heading

The title of proceeding of a notice of application shows the name of the party commencing the application, the name of any opposite party, and the statutory provision or rule, if any, under which the application is made.

Body

The first page of the application shows the date, time, and place of the hearing; instructions to the respondent outline the steps to be taken if he or she wishes to oppose the application. The application is dated as discussed below and is addressed to the respondent; the address of the court office is included beneath the line on which the local registrar signs. The court file number is inserted when the notice is issued.

Subsequent pages set out the nature of the application, the grounds on which it is brought, and a list of the documentary evidence to be used at the hearing of the application, which usually includes a supporting affidavit. The application is dated as discussed below, and the name, address, and telephone number of the law firm making the application (or similar information for the applicant, if no law firm is involved) appear at the end of the body.

Figure 15.1 Steps on an Application, Superior Court of Justice

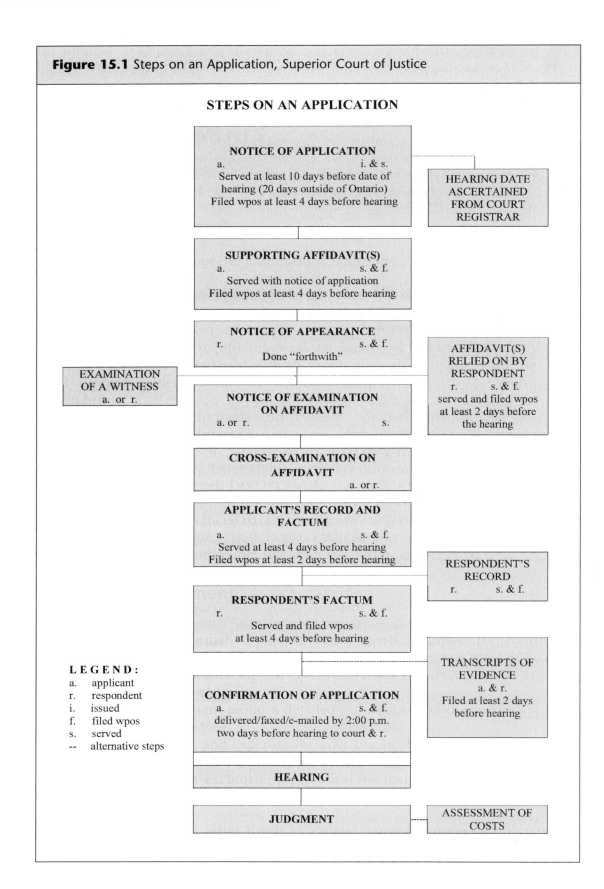

STEPS ON AN APPLICATION

NOTICE OF APPLICATION
a.   i. & s.
Served at least 10 days before date of
hearing (20 days outside of Ontario)
Filed wpos at least 4 days before hearing

HEARING DATE ASCERTAINED FROM COURT REGISTRAR

SUPPORTING AFFIDAVIT(S)
a.   s. & f.
Served with notice of application
Filed wpos at least 4 days before hearing

NOTICE OF APPEARANCE
r.   s. & f.
Done "forthwith"

EXAMINATION OF A WITNESS
a. or r.

AFFIDAVIT(S) RELIED ON BY RESPONDENT
r.   s. & f.
served and filed wpos
at least 2 days before
the hearing

NOTICE OF EXAMINATION ON AFFIDAVIT
a. or r.   s.

CROSS-EXAMINATION ON AFFIDAVIT
                 a. or r.

APPLICANT'S RECORD AND FACTUM
a.   s. & f.
Served at least 4 days before hearing
Filed wpos at least 2 days before hearing

RESPONDENT'S RECORD
r.   s. & f.

RESPONDENT'S FACTUM
r.   s. & f.
Served and filed wpos
at least 4 days before hearing

LEGEND:
a.   applicant
r.   respondent
i.   issued
f.   filed wpos
s.   served
--   alternative steps

TRANSCRIPTS OF EVIDENCE
a. & r.
Filed at least 2 days
before hearing

CONFIRMATION OF APPLICATION
a.   s. & f.
delivered/faxed/e-mailed by 2:00 p.m.
two days before hearing to court & r.

HEARING

JUDGMENT

ASSESSMENT OF COSTS

Date of Hearing

The notice must be served at least 10 days before the date of the hearing, and this fact is taken into consideration in selecting the date. If it is estimated that the hearing will take more than two hours, a hearing date is obtained from the registrar before the notice of application is issued.

The date must be inserted in two places in the application: once in the second paragraph and once at the end of the body. These dates will be inserted by the registrar when the application is issued. Either leave the date information blank or show only the month and the year, leaving sufficient space for the actual day of the month to be inserted by the local registrar when the application is issued.

Backsheet

Each copy of the notice of application requires a backsheet. A short title of proceeding may be used; the names of the parties are separated by an *and* whether or not their capacity is shown (that is, applicant and respondent).

Number of Copies

Prepare a minimum of six copies of a notice of application, plus extra copies for any additional respondents. These are disposed of as follows:

1. Original issued by the court and returned to the law firm and kept in the Document subfile
2. One copy retained by the court
3. One copy served on each respondent
4. One copy filed with the court with proof of service (at least 10 days before the hearing date)
5. One copy for the file
6. One copy for the Record subfile

EVIDENCE ON APPLICATION

Evidence to be presented on an application is given by affidavit, unless a statute or the rules provide otherwise. A witness may, however, give evidence in person at a hearing with the consent of the presiding judge or officer. Such a witness is summoned in the same manner as a witness to a trial.

Prepare at least four copies of each supporting affidavit for use as follows:

1. One copy served on each respondent
2. Original copy filed with the court with proof of service
3. One copy for the file
4. One copy for the Record subfile

Any supporting affidavit is served on the respondents with the notice of application and is filed with proof of service in the court office where the application is to be heard at least two days before the date of the hearing.

Any material served by a party for use on an application may be filed with proof of service as part of the party's application record and need not be filed separately if the record is filed within the time prescribed by the rules, as discussed later. This provision reduces the minimum number of required copies by one.

RESPONSES TO A NOTICE OF APPLICATION

A party served with a notice of application who wishes to be informed of future steps or who opposes the application serves and files a **notice of appearance** (Precedent 15.2).

Any respondent who does not deliver a notice of appearance is not entitled to file material, examine a witness, cross-examine on an affidavit filed for use on the application, or be heard at the hearing, except with the permission of the presiding judge.

Prepare three copies of the notice of appearance. The original is filed with the court with proof of service, one copy is served on the solicitors for the applicant, and the third copy is for the file.

CROSS-EXAMINATION ON AFFIDAVIT OR EXAMINATION OF A WITNESS

When a party to an application has served every other party with an affidavit to be used in the proceeding, he or she may cross-examine the deponent of any affidavit served by a party adverse in interest. The applicant and the respondent then hold a cross-examination of the deponent of any affidavit filed in support of the other party. The date for the hearing is adjourned with the consent of the court to permit such cross-examination.

Although the evidence in most applications is furnished by affidavits, the evidence of a witness may be taken by having him or her examined before the hearing; a transcript of that evidence is then available for use at the hearing. A witness whose evidence is provided through such an examination may be cross-examined by the examining party and any other party.

A cross-examination of a witness or the deponent of an affidavit is similar to an examination for discovery in an action. Follow the procedures outlined in Chapter 14 to arrange for the appointment for an oral cross-examination and serve a Notice of Examination on any witness who is a party to the proceeding and a summons to witness (examination out of court) if the witness is not a party to the proceeding. Written cross-examinations also follow the procedures outlined in Chapter 14.

Transcript of Evidence

If the evidence of a witness on the application is provided through a transcript of his or her examination, a copy of the transcript is filed in the court office where the application is to be heard not later than two days before the date of the hearing. A transcript need be filed only if it will be referred to at the hearing.

If the transcript of proceedings before the tribunal whose decision is being reviewed, of a cross-examination, or of an examination of a witness is to be filed with the court, a list of such transcripts is set out in the table of contents of the application record. The actual transcripts do not usually form part of the record; they are filed separately with the court.

The transcript of evidence for use on an application has a backsheet of heavy, light grey paper.

MATERIAL REQUIRED FOR APPLICATION HEARINGS

Applicant's Application Record

The applicant is required to serve every other party in the application with an application record and factum not later than four days before the hearing. It is filed with proof of service, in the court office where the application is to be heard, not later than two days before the date of the hearing.

Preparing Application Record

The record contains material in consecutively numbered pages, arranged in the following order:

1. A table of contents describing each document (including each exhibit) by its nature and date and, in the case of an exhibit, by exhibit number or letter
2. A copy of the notice of application
3. A copy of all affidavits and other materials served by any party for use on the application
4. A list of all relevant transcripts of evidence in chronological order, but not necessarily the transcripts themselves
5. A copy of any other material in the court file that is necessary for the hearing

To Assemble Application Record

To prepare the application record:

1. Photocopy a minimum of three copies of each document to be included in the record, omitting the backsheets, and assemble them in the proper order.
2. Consecutively number each page in the upper right-hand corner in ink or with a numbering machine.
3. Place a tabbed divider page in front of each document to be included in the record. The divider pages are not part of the consecutively numbered pages of the record.
4. Prepare the following:
   a. a front or face page identifying the material as an applicant's application record and setting out the name, address, and telephone number of the solicitors for the applicant. Include the name of the particular solicitor in charge of the application and

    b. a table of contents page listing each document by
       i. the divider page tab number or letter,
       ii. the name and date of preparation or other relevant date information, and
       iii. the page number at which the document may be found or a combined face and table of contents page.
5. Prepare a back on heavy, light blue paper identifying the document as an applicant's application record.
6. Assemble the material with the front page first, followed by the table of contents page (or the combined front and table of contents page), the documents (each with a tabbed divider page) in numbered order, and the backsheet.
7. Bind the assembled material down the left-hand side to form a booklet.

See the precedents for a trial record in Chapter 14 (Precedents 14.5 and 14.6), which are very similar.

Preparing a Factum

The applicant is also required to file a factum with the record, which consists of a concise statement, without argument, of the facts and law relied on by the applicant and usually includes a list and photocopy of any case law relied on. This is similar to a brief of authorities prepared in an action. Refer to Chapter 14 on how to prepare authorities.

Form of a Factum

Precedent 15.3 illustrates the basic format for a factum in an application. The document prepared by the solicitors for the applicant is titled "Applicant's Factum." The body of the factum is made up of consecutively numbered paragraphs, divided into parts that are also numbered and titled. The applicant's factum does not have a backsheet but is bound front and back in white cover stock pages.

Number and Disposition of Copies

Prepare a minimum of four copies of the record and the factum. One copy is served on the other party, one copy is for the use of the lawyer, and one copy is filed with proof of service in the court office where the application is to be heard, not later than four days before the date of the hearing.

Respondent's Application Record and Factum

If the respondent believes that the application record is not complete, a respondent's record may be served on every other party and filed not later than two days before the hearing.

Any respondent who has entered an appearance to an application is required to serve on every other party a respondent's factum and to file it with proof of service in the court office where the application is to be heard not later than four days before the date of the hearing. Follow the same format as used for the applicant's factum as discussed above but note that the respondent's factum is bound front and back in green cover stock pages.

Contents of the Respondent's Application Record

The respondent's application record contains consecutively numbered pages arranged in the following order:

1. a table of contents describing each document (including each exhibit) by its nature and date and, in the case of an exhibit, by exhibit number or letter and
2. a copy of any material to be used by the respondent on the application and not included in the application record.

Dispensing with the Record and Factum

Before or at the hearing of the application, a judge may stipulate that it is not necessary for either party to an application to serve and file an application record or a factum.

CONFIRMATION OF APPLICATION

The applicant must contact the other party and confirm their attendance at the scheduled application hearing and then prepare a confirmation of application (Precedent 15.4). This notice must be delivered, faxed, or e-mailed (where available) to the court office not later than 2:00 p.m. two days before the hearing date or the application will not be heard.

Prepare a minimum of two copies of the confirmation of application for use as follows:

1. One copy is retained in your office file.
2. The second copy may be delivered to the courthouse if it is not faxed or e-mailed.
3. A copy of the confirmation of application must also be faxed or e-mailed to the other party.

HEARING OF AN APPLICATION

When the application is to be heard, the solicitors for the parties attend in court. Evidence is by affidavit, unless a statute or the rules provide otherwise. The evidence of witnesses may also be given during the hearing by reading extracts from the transcripts of their examination or cross-examination. The decision of the court is contained in its judgment.

Judgment may be given at once but is usually reserved until the judge has had an opportunity to consider all the evidence presented at the hearing. In due course, the solicitors for the parties are notified by the court office that the judge has handed down judgment; any reasons for judgment may be secured from the court office.

After judgment has been handed down, the solicitors for the successful party usually prepare and issue the formal judgment, following the procedures discussed in Chapter 16. The judgment may include a provision that the unsuccessful party is to pay costs to the successful party. A bill of costs is then prepared, following the procedure for assessing costs, which are also discussed in Chapter 16.

Terms and Concepts

application
notice of application
applicant
respondent
hearing date
evidence on application

notice of appearance
examinations
application records
factum
list of authorities
confirmation of application

Review Questions

1. What is the usual purpose of an application?
2. How does the title of proceeding in an application differ from that in an action?
3. How is the date for hearing an application determined?
4. How may evidence on application be presented?
5. What is a "factum"?
6. What material is included in the applicant's application record?
7. What is the filing time for the record of the
   a. applicant?
   b. respondent?

Automated Civil Litigation – Korbitec Inc.   Court File No.

ONTARIO
SUPERIOR COURT OF JUSTICE

B E T W E E N :

WILLIAM McCLELLAND

Applicant

(Court Seal)   and

PUBLIC GUARDIAN AND TRUSTEE
and SHIRLEY ARLENE HOLMAN

Respondents

APPLICATION UNDER the *Crown Administration of Estates Act*, R.S.O. 1990, c. C.47

NOTICE OF APPLICATION

TO THE RESPONDENT(S)

A LEGAL PROCEEDING HAS BEEN COMMENCED by the applicant. The claim made by the applicant appears on the following page.

THIS APPLICATION will come on for a hearing on Thursday, November 15, 2007, at 10:00 a.m., at 393 University Avenue, 10th Floor, Toronto, Ontario, M5G 1E6.

IF YOU WISH TO OPPOSE THIS APPLICATION, to receive notice of any step in the application or to be served with any documents in the application you or an Ontario lawyer acting for you must forthwith prepare a notice of appearance in Form 38A prescribed by the *Rules of Civil Procedure*, serve it on the applicant's lawyer or, where the applicant does not have a lawyer, serve it on the applicant, and file it, with proof of service, in this court office, and you or your lawyer must appear at the hearing.

IF YOU WISH TO PRESENT AFFIDAVIT OR OTHER DOCUMENTARY EVIDENCE TO THE COURT OR TO EXAMINE OR CROSS-EXAMINE WITNESSES ON THE APPLICATION, you or your lawyer must, in addition to serving your notice of appearance, serve a copy of the evidence on the applicant's lawyer or, where the applicant does not have a lawyer, serve it on the applicant, and file it, with proof of service, in the court office where the application is to be heard as soon as possible, but at least two days before the hearing.

IF YOU FAIL TO APPEAR AT THE HEARING, JUDGMENT MAY BE GIVEN IN YOUR ABSENCE AND WITHOUT FURTHER NOTICE TO YOU. IF YOU WISH TO OPPOSE THIS APPLICATION BUT ARE UNABLE TO PAY LEGAL FEES, LEGAL AID MAY BE AVAILABLE TO YOU BY CONTACTING A LOCAL LEGAL AID OFFICE.

Date _____   Issued by _____

Local Registrar

Address of   393 University Avenue
court office: 10th Floor
                  Toronto ON M5G 1E6

TO: **PUBLIC GUARDIAN AND TRUSTEE**
             595 Bay Street, Suite 800
             Toronto ON M5G 2M6

AND TO: **SHIRLEY ARLENE HOLMAN**
             75 Parkdale Gardens Road
             Hamilton ON L2J 4K9

Source: Korbitec Inc.

2.

APPLICATION

1. The applicant makes application for:

    (a) an order declaring his rights as next of kin in respect to the estate of

    Francis McClelland, deceased, late of the City of Toronto; and

    (b) an order directing such inquires as may be necessary to determine

    the same.

2. The grounds for the application are:

    (a) the applicant is a first cousin of the deceased, Francis McClelland

    (b) the said deceased died intestate, and under the *Succession Law*

    Reform Act, R.S.O. 1990, c. C.27, s. 47(4), the applicant is entitled to

    share in the distribution of his estate

3. The following documentary evidence will be used at the hearing of the

    application:

    (a) affidavit of William McClelland, sworn November 2, 20__;

    (b) grant of certificate of appointment of estate trustee without a will,

    dated October 18, 20__; and

    (c) such further and other evidence as counsel may advise and this

    Honourable Court may permit.

(Date of issue)   **HILL, JOHNSTON & GRANT**
                           Barristers & Solicitors
                           17 Princess Street South, Suite 2501
                           Toronto ON M8Y 3N5

                           Peter T. Grant (12345G)

                           Tel: 416-354-9900
                           Fax: 416-354-9909

          Requires a back

                           Solicitors for the Applicant

Source: Korbitec Inc.

Automated Civil Litigation – Korbitec Inc.

Court File No. 66427

ONTARIO
SUPERIOR COURT OF JUSTICE

B E T W E E N:

WILLIAM McCLELLAND

Applicant

and

PUBLIC GUARDIAN AND TRUSTEE
and SHIRLEY ARLENE HOLMAN

Respondents

APPLICATION UNDER the *Crown Administration of Estates Act*, R.S.O. 1990, c. C.47

NOTICE OF APPEARANCE

The respondent SHIRLEY ARLENE HOLMAN intends to respond to this application.

November 4, 20__

GRAHAM & PARKER
Barristers & Solicitors
24160 Pickering Place, Suite 666
Hamilton ON L3N 4G3

Michel Cochrane (42713C)

Tel: 905-415-9000

Fax: 905-415-9001

Solicitors for the respondent,
Shirley Arlene Holman

TO: **HILL, JOHNSTON & GRANT**
Barristers & Solicitors
17 Princess Street South, Suite 2501
Toronto ON M8Y 3N5

Peter T. Grant (12345G)

Tel: 416-354-9900
Fax: 416-354-9909

Solicitors for the respondent
Shirley Arlene Holman

Requires a back

Source: Korbitec Inc.

Court File No.

ONTARIO
SUPERIOR COURT OF JUSTICE

TITLE OF PROCEEDING

APPLICANT'S FACTUM

F A C T S

1. *(Statement of what is requested)* ---
---.

2. *(Identification of the parties involved)* ---
--.

3. *(Facts and background. All authorities for factual assertions are set out,*
and their locations in the record noted.)

     Affidavit of (name), Record, p. 6

L A W

4. ---
--.

     Re Horton and others and Kenney and others (1985), 51 O.R.
     (2d) 181 at p. 183

5. ---
---------------------.

     Landlord and Tenant Act, R.S.O. 1990, c. L.7, s. 99

ORDER SOUGHT

6. ---
--.

Month day, year   NAME OF LAW FIRM
                                     (Address, telephone and fax
                                     numbers of applicant's law firm)

TO: NAME OF LAW FIRM
     (Address, telephone and
     fax numbers of respondent's
     law firm)

> *Requires front and back covers*
> *Applicant – white*
> *Respondent – green*

Automated Civil Litigation – Korbitec Inc.

Court File No. 66427

ONTARIO
SUPERIOR COURT OF JUSTICE

B E T W E E N:

WILLIAM McCLELLAND

Applicant

and

**PUBLIC GUARDIAN AND TRUSTEE
and SHIRLEY ARLENE HOLMAN**

Respondents

APPLICATION UNDER the *Crown Administration of Estates Act*, R.S.O. 1990, c. C.47

CONFIRMATION OF APPLICATION

I, **PETER T. GRANT**, with the law firm of Hill, Johnston & Grant, counsel for the applicant, confirm that the application to be heard on November 15, 20__, will proceed on the following basis:

[ ]   for an adjournment on consent to ....*(date)*.

[ ]   for a contested adjournment to ....*(date)*, for the following reason: *(specify who is requesting the adjournment and why, and who is opposing it and why)*

[ ]   for a consent order

[X]   for hearing of all the issues

[ ]   for hearing of the following issues only *(specify)*

I estimate that the time required for the application will be: **30 minutes** for the applicant and **20 minutes** for the respondent, for a total of **50 minutes.**

November 13, 20__

HILL, JOHNSTON & GRANT
17 Princess Street South, Suite 2501
Toronto ON M8Y 3N5

TO: **SUPERIOR COURT OF JUSTICE**

      393 University Avenue, 10th Floor
      Toronto, ON M5G 1E6

      Fax:

Peter T. Grant (12345G)

Tel: 416-354-9900
Fax: 416-354-9909

Solicitors for the applicant

AND TO: **PUBLIC GUARDIAN AND TRUSTEE**
      595 Bay Street, Suite 800
      Toronto ON M5G 2M6

      Tel: 416-314-2800
      Fax: 416-314-2695

AND TO: **GRAHAM & PARKER**
      24160 Pickering Place, Suite 660
      Hamilton ON L3N 4G3

      Michael Cochrane (42713C)
      Tel: 905-415-9000
      Fax: 905-415-9001

      Solicitors for the respondent Shirley Arlene Holman

Source: Korbitec Inc.

CHAPTER 16

Orders, Judgments, and Costs

OBJECTIVES:

- Identify and describe the difference between an order and a judgment and the disposition of each

- Demonstrate an understanding of the procedures for assessment of costs

- Use legal precedents to prepare orders, judgments, and bills of costs

When a legal proceeding has been heard, a formal document recording the decision of the judge or master is prepared, usually by the solicitors for the successful party. Such documents are known as judgments and orders.

A **judgment** is a decision of a judge of the court that finally disposes of an action or application on its merits. An **order** includes a judgment and also refers to a decision of a judge or master that is made during the course of an action or application but does not finally dispose of the proceeding.

FORM OF ORDERS AND JUDGMENTS

The format of documents recording the decision of a court differs from the format of general court documents. The basic format for a judgment following the trial of an action is illustrated in Precedent 16.1. The basic format for a judgment following the hearing of an application is illustrated in Precedent 16.2. The basic format for an order following the hearing of a notice of motion is illustrated in Precedent 16.3.

Heading

Below the reference to the court on the face of the document, every judgment (with the exception of a default judgment, discussed in Chapter 17) shows the name of the judge, judges, or master who handed down the judgment or made the order, as well as the day of the week, month, date, and year in which it was given or made (Figure 16.1). Actions and applications (other than for judicial review in the Divisional Court) are heard by a single judge. Appeals to the Court of Appeal and most proceedings in the Divisional Court are heard by three judges, whose names appear in the heading in order of seniority, which is the order of their appointment to the bench.

Body

Following the title of the document, both an order and a judgment begin with an unnumbered paragraph or paragraphs reciting a brief history of the action or application to which the document relates. The date of trial or hearing, the parties who were present or represented by counsel and those who were not, and any undertaking made by a party as a condition of the order or judgment are included. The judgment or order is then set out in numbered paragraphs, the first words of which are

1. THIS COURT ORDERS that....
2. THIS COURT ORDERS that....

In a judgment, the word "ORDERS" may be changed to "DECLARES" if the circumstances require; the words "AND ADJUDGES" or "CERTIFIES" may also be shown. The lawyer will indicate when the alternative wording is to be used.

If the order or judgment includes a court ruling on the payment of postjudgment interest, an unnumbered paragraph after the last numbered paragraph specifies the rate of interest applicable and the date from which such interest is payable. Determine the appropriate rate from the current interest table, as discussed in Chapter 10.

Figure 16.1 Judgment and Orders, Headings

ONTARIO
SUPERIOR COURT OF JUSTICE

THE HONOURABLE MR. JUSTICE	)	WEDNESDAY, JANUARY 22,
	)	20__
MacKEANCHIE	)	

ONTARIO
SUPERIOR COURT OF JUSTICE

MASTER ULRICH	)	THURSDAY, JANUARY 22, 20__
	)	
	)	

ONTARIO
SUPERIOR COURT OF JUSTICE
DIVISIONAL COURT

THE HONOURABLE MR. JUSTICE STAINTON	)	FRIDAY, MAY 21, 20__
	)	
THE HONOURABLE MADAM JUSTICE DAY	)	
	)	
THE HONOURABLE MR. JUSTICE LATIMER	)	

Ending

A signature line is included four or five lines after the last line of the document for the signature of the judge/master or court registrar. Do not key in any name beneath the signature line.

Backsheet

A backsheet is required for all copies of the order or judgment. The name of the judge and the date of the order or judgment are not shown on the backsheet.

Number and Disposition of Copies

The solicitors for either party in the proceeding may prepare a draft of the formal order or judgment; usually, however, this is done by the solicitors for the successful party. A minimum of four copies of the document are required. These are disposed of as follows:

1. One copy of the order or judgment is for the file.
2. A copy of the order is forwarded to all other interested parties for approval with regard to form and content, which approval is noted on the copy. The approved copy is returned to the solicitors who prepared the order or judgment. The order may then be signed and entered.
3. Two copies of the order or judgment are taken to the court office where the proceeding was commenced (along with the copy or copies showing the approval of other interested parties). The order may be signed by the judge or master who heard the proceeding but is usually signed by the registrar after he or she reviews the documents. The registrar will then enter the judgment or order. Entering an order in the court records means to insert a copy of the document into an entry book kept for that purpose. A notation of the appropriate entry book number is endorsed at the foot of the original order, together with the date of insertion, and one copy is returned with this information.
4. The original copy of the signed and entered order or judgment is kept in the Document subfile, and a copy is forwarded to all interested parties.

COSTS

In Ontario, like many other provinces, the successful party is often awarded costs. This means that the unsuccessful party is required to pay damages to cover the legal costs and disbursements of the successful party. However, cost awards are usually for only approximately 40 to 50 percent of a party's legal fees, although most disbursement expenses are allowed. The client is, of course, responsible for paying any portion of the legal account that is not covered by an award for costs.

There are two categories of costs:

1. **Partial indemnity.** Formerly known as "party and party costs," this is the type of cost calculation most widely applied. It provides costs awards at a lower hourly rate than most lawyers' actual time charges. In assessing costs, the complexity of the proceeding, any offers to settle, the conduct of the parties involved, the experience of the lawyers, and the ability of the unsuccessful party to pay damages are all considered. The following chart outlines the maximum legal hourly rates that may be applied, as suggested by the Costs Subcommittee of the Civil Rules Committee:

Law clerks	Maximum of $80.00 per hour
Student-at-law	Maximum of $60.00 per hour
Lawyer (less than 10 years)	Maximum of $225.00 per hour
Lawyer (10 years or more but less than 20 years)	Maximum of $300.00 per hour
Lawyer (20 years and over)	Maximum of $350.00 per hour

2. **Substantial indemnity**. Formerly known as "solicitor and client costs," this type of cost calculation is applied only in exceptional circumstances and is calculated at 1.5 times the partial indemnity costs.

When a motion is heard; when an action, application, appeal, or divorce proceeding has been completed; or when judgment is secured against the defendant by default, the order or judgment made usually contains some provision concerning the payment of costs. The lawyer must therefore be prepared to provide documentation about costs in these circumstances. If costs are not set at the hearing, or only an order indicating that costs are to be assessed on a partial indemnity or substantial indemnity scale is given, an assessment hearing may be ordered. The documents required to carry out these procedures are a bill of costs and a costs outline.

BILL OF COSTS

A bill of costs is a document stating the allowable fees and disbursements that may be considered in a judgment or an assessment officer's award of costs to the successful party in a proceeding. This will not necessarily include all time charges or disbursements on a client's docket.

Form of Bill of Costs

The general heading of a bill of costs follows that of the legal proceeding to which the bill relates and then details the allowed legal fees and disbursements followed by a statement of experience of the individuals who worked on the file. Note the following points in preparing the document:

1. The legal fees allowed are those set out in Part 1, Tariff A of the *Rules of Civil Procedure*. These are legal services directly related to the steps that lead to a hearing, such as drafting court documents, researching the law, examinations, or counsel fees (which refers to attendance time at the hearing itself). It does not usually include time charges for any meetings with clients, correspondence, or telephone calls. Time charges for law clerks and students-at-law (articling students) may also be included.
2. Each task performed is itemized, including who performed the task, the amount of time, the hourly rate, and the dollar amount.
3. The disbursements and the amounts allowed for them are listed in Part II of Tariff A of the *Rules of Civil Procedure*, and, again, these are disbursements directly related to the steps in a legal proceeding, such as payment of court fees, travelling or accommodation fees, medical or experts' reports, interpreters, research fees, transcripts, photocopies for the purpose of court documents, factums, case books, etc., including the GST on these amounts.
4. A listing of all lawyers (including years of experience) as well as law clerks and articling students who worked on the file must be shown at the end.

5. A printout of the client's docket as well as photocopies of any applicable invoices for disbursements will need to be attached to the bill of costs. Commercial legal accounting systems often allow the creation of prebilling reports, which may be customized to show only the legal fees and disbursements applicable for a bill of costs.

Precedent 16.4 illustrates a partial indemnity bill of costs.

Number of Copies and Disposition

A minimum of four copies of a bill of costs are prepared:

1. One copy is filed in the court office.
2. One copy is served on every other party interested in the assessment.
3. One copy is for the file.
4. One copy is for the Document subfile.

COSTS OUTLINE

If an assessment hearing is necessary, then a costs outline (Precedent 16.5) will need to be prepared. This document contains the information contained in the bill of costs plus information on the rationale for the fees charged, which would be provided by the lawyer. Additionally, the legal fees must be broken down into the partial indemnity rate, which would be a percentage of the normal rate charged to the client, which is also shown. The *Rules of Civil Procedure* state that the costs outline may not exceed three pages. A minimum of four copies will be required. One copy is for the file, one copy must be given to every other party before the assessment hearing, and at least two copies will be required for the assessment hearing itself.

ASSESSMENT OF COSTS

To secure an appointment for the assessment, the completed bill of costs and a copy of the judgment or order to which it pertains are filed in the place where the proceeding was commenced or heard or in a county agreed on by the parties. An **assessment officer** (a court official appointed to review costs) will then provide a Notice of Appointment for Assessment of Costs indicating the day and time set to assess the costs.

A copy of the appointment form and a copy of the bill of costs are served upon every party interested in the assessment at least seven days before the date fixed for the assessment. It is not necessary to serve a copy of the order or judgment; a copy of that document will have been provided when the order or judgment was signed.

On the day of assessment, the lawyer appears before the assessment officer with the original of the appointment, together with proof of service, along with copies of the bill of costs and the costs outline. Solicitors for the other party are normally present; they have the right to dispute items on the bill of costs. If they fail to appear, the assessment officer proceeds to assess the costs in their absence.

SETTLEMENT

When an offer of settlement is made during the course of a legal proceeding, there are cost consequences for failure to accept the offer; these consequences affect who is entitled to costs and what category of costs will be awarded. For example, suppose that the defendant in an action offers to pay $40,000 to settle an action. If the offer to settle is made

1. at least seven days before the commencement of the trial,
2. is not withdrawn and does not expire before the commencement of the trial, and
3. is not accepted by the plaintiff,

and the plaintiff obtains a judgment for $40,000 (or less than $40,000), there are cost consequences. The plaintiff is entitled to partial indemnity costs to the date the offer was served; however, the defendant is entitled to partial indemnity costs from that date, unless the court orders otherwise.

PAYMENT OF COSTS

Fixed by the Court

When costs are fixed by the court, the amount of costs payable will be set out in the order or judgment relating to the legal proceeding for which the costs are allowed. A cheque in payment of these costs will be sent to the law firm acting for the party to whom they are payable and will be deposited in its trust account to the credit of the client until the account is rendered to the client. The amount received for costs will then be applied against the firm's account to the client.

After Assessment

After the assessment, the assessment officer completes a certificate indicating the date of the assessment and the amount of costs allowed. When the certificate is received, a copy is made for each party. In due course, your office receives a cheque in payment of assessed costs. This cheque is deposited in the trust account to the credit of the client, to be accounted for when the account is rendered to the client.

If payment is not received, the steps outlined to enforce a judgment (discussed in Chapter 17) may be followed.

Terms and Concepts

judgment

order

form of orders and judgments

signed and entered

costs

partial indemnity costs

substantial indemnity costs

bill of costs

tariff of fees

costs outline

assessment of costs

assessment officer

notice of appointment for assessment of costs

settlement considerations

payment of costs

Review Questions

1. In your own words, what is meant by the term "order" and the term "judgment"?

2. What information appears on the face page of an order or judgment that does not appear on other court documents?

3. Which solicitors in a legal proceeding prepare the order or judgment? Why is the draft order sent to the other party's solicitor?

4. What is meant by the term "entering an order"? Why must this be done where the proceeding was commenced?

5. The general rule for court documents is that paragraphs are either numbered or show the first words in solid capitals. What is the practice for orders and judgments?

6. What is meant by costs? Describe in your own words the two categories of costs.

7. When costs are allowed following a proceeding, what procedures are followed by solicitors for the successful party?

8. You need to check for the appropriate amount for an item included in a bill of costs. Where can you find this information?

9. **Internet Research:** If a judgment dated January 17, (this year), contains a statement relating to the payment of postjudgment interest, what rate of interest would be shown?

Court File No.

NAME OF COURT

THE HONOURABLE *(name of judge)*)   DAY AND DATE OF JUDGMENT
)
)

TITLE OF PROCEEDING

JUDGMENT

THIS ACTION was heard this day *(or heard on (date) without (or with) a jury at (place)* in the presence of counsel for all parties *(where applicable, add (identify party)* appearing in person, *or* no one appearing for *(identify party)*, although properly served as appears from *(indicate proof of service))*,

ON READING THE PLEADINGS AND HEARING THE EVIDENCE and the submissions of counsel for the parties,

1.   THIS COURT ORDERS *(or DECLARES, if applicable) (where applicable, add: AND ADJUDGES)* that . . .

2.   THIS COURT ORDERS *(or as may be)* that . . .

(In a judgment for the payment of money on which postjudgment interest is payable, add:)

THIS JUDGMENT BEARS INTEREST at the rate of . . . . percent per year commencing on *(date)*.

Requires a back	_____
	(Signature of judge, officer or registrar)

Court File No.

NAME OF COURT

THE HONOURABLE *(name of judge)*   )   DAY AND DATE OF JUDGMENT
)
)

TITLE OF PROCEEDING

JUDGMENT

THIS ACTION was heard this day *(or* heard on *(date)* without *(or* with*)* a jury at *(place)* in the presence of counsel for all parties *(where applicable, add (identify party)* appearing in person, *or* no one appearing for *(identify party)* although properly served as appears from *(indicate proof of service))*,

ON READING THE NOTICE OF APPLICATION AND THE EVIDENCE FILED BY THE PARTIES, *(where applicable, add* on hearing the oral evidence presented by the parties,*)* and the submissions of counsel for the parties,

1.   THIS COURT ORDERS *(or* DECLARES, *if applicable) (where applicable, add:* AND ADJUDGES*)* that . . .

2.   THIS COURT ORDERS *(or as may be)* that . . .

     (In a judgment for the payment of money on which postjudgment interest is payable, add:)

     THIS JUDGMENT BEARS INTEREST at the rate of . . . . percent per year commencing on *(date)*.

Requires a back	_____
	(Signature of judge, officer or registrar)

Court File No.

NAME OF COURT

NAME OF JUDGE OR OFFICER) DAY AND DATE OF ORDER
)
)

TITLE OF PROCEEDING

O R D E R

THIS MOTION, made by *(identify moving party)* for *(state the relief sought in the notice of motion, except to the extent that it appears in the operative part of the order)*, *(where applicable add* made without notice,*)* was heard this day *(or* heard on *(date))*, at *(place)*, *(recite any particulars necessary to understand the order)*.

ON READING the *(give particulars of the material filed on the motion)* and on hearing the submissions of counsel for *(identify parties)*, *(where applicable, add (identify party)* appearing in person *or* no one appearing for *(identify party)*, although properly served as appears from *(indicate proof of service))*.

1. THIS COURT ORDERS that . . .

2. THIS COURT ORDERS that . . .

   (In a judgment for the payment of money on which postjudgment interest is payable, add:)

   THIS ORDER BEARS INTEREST at the rate of . . . . percent per year

commencing on *(date)*.

Requires a back	_____
	(Signature of judge, officer or registrar)

Court File No. 111-222-333

ONTARIO
SUPERIOR COURT OF JUSTICE

B E T W E E N:

DURHAM TECHNOLOGY INC.

Plaintiff

and

HAWICK HOLDINGS LTD.

Defendant

BILL OF COSTS

Partial Indemnity Costs	Fees	Disbursements
1. Pleadings		
Reviewing statement of claim; considering motion to strike pleadings; reviewing rules regarding motion to strike; researching and reviewing case law; preparing statement of defence		
Peter T. Grant – 16 hours		
Mitra J. Bonilla – 15 hours	$ 4,300.00	
Paid to file Statement of Defence		$ 144.00
Photocopies		15.00*
2. Discovery of Documents		
Reviewing documents and preparing affidavit of documents		
Peter T. Grant – 12 hours	2,100.00	
Photocopies		55.00*
3. Examination		
Including preparing for and attending examination of Conor Blackstone		
Peter T. Grant – 20 hours	3,500.00	
Paid to Official Examiner		325.00*

- 2 -

5. Motion for Summary Judgment

Preparing notice of motion, affidavit, factum,
book of authorities and drafting order,
researching and reviewing case law, preparing
for and attending motion

Peter T. Grant – 40 hours
Mitra J. Bonilla – 24 hours
Howard Podoba – 11 hours $ 9,950.00

Paid to file Notice of Motion
    for Summary Judgment $ 127.00
Photocopies   60.00*

Total Fees $19,850.00
GST on Fees   1,191.00

Total Disbursements   726.00
*GST on Disbursements   27.30

TOTAL PARTIAL INDEMNITY COSTS   **$21,794.30**

Statement of Experience	Rate
Peter T. Grant, Year of Call 1990	$175.00
Mitra J. Bonilla, Year of Call 2003	$100.00
Howard Podoba, Student, Year of Call 20__	$ 50.00

Automated Civil Litigation – Korbitec Inc.

Court File No.

ONTARIO
SUPERIOR COURT OF JUSTICE

TITLE OF PROCEEDING

COSTS OUTLINE

The *(name of party)* provides the following outline of the submissions to be made at the hearing in support of the costs the party will seek if successful:

Fees (as detailed below)	$	0.00
Estimated counsel fee for appearance	$	0.00
Disbursements (as detailed in the attached appendix)	$	0.00
Total	$	0.00

The following points are made in support of the costs sought with reference to the factors set out in subrule 57.01(1):

- the amount claimed and the amount recovered in the proceeding

- the complexity of the proceeding

- the importance of the issues

- the conduct of any party that tended to shorten or to lengthen unnecessarily the duration of the proceeding

- whether any step in the proceeding was improper, vexatious or unnecessary or taken through negligence, mistake or excessive caution

Source: Korbitec Inc.

- 2-

- a party's denial of or refusal to admit anything that should have been admitted

- the experience of the party's lawyer

- the hours spent, the rates sought for costs and the rate actually charged by the party's lawyer

FEE ITEM (e.g., pleadings, affidavits, cross-examinations, preparation, hearing, etc.)	PERSONS (identify the lawyers, students, and law clerks who provided services in connection with each item together with their year of call, if applicable)	HOURS (specify the hours claimed for each person identified in column 2)	PARTIAL INDEMNITY RATE (specify the rate being sought for each person identified in column 2)	ACTUAL RATE*

Specify the rate being charged to the client for each person identified in column 2. If there is a contingency fee arrangement, state the rate that would have been charged absent such arrangement.

- any other matter relevant to the question of costs

LAWYER'S CERTIFICATE

I CERTIFY that the hours claimed have been spent, that the rates shown are correct and that each disbursement has been incurred as claimed.

Date: _____   _____

Peter T. Grant

Date of Preparation   **NAME OF LAW FIRM**
Etc.

Source: Korbitec Inc.

CHAPTER 17

Disposition of Actions without Trial

OBJECTIVES:

- Describe the five ways in which an action may be disposed of without going to trial

- Demonstrate an understanding of the procedures in obtaining a default judgment

- Use legal precedents to prepare default judgment documents

Many actions are disposed of without completing all the formal procedural steps required to proceed to trial. There are a number of ways in which this is accomplished.

DISCONTINUANCE

A plaintiff may discontinue all or part of an action against a defendant

1. before the close of pleadings, by serving a notice of discontinuance on all parties who were served with the statement of claim. The discontinuance may be against all or some defendants for all or part of the action.

   Prepare a minimum of three copies of the notice. One copy is served on the solicitors for the defendant(s), the original is filed with proof of service, and one copy is for the file.
2. after the close of pleadings, with the permission of the court. Prepare three copies of a notice of motion and supporting affidavit. When the motion has been heard, prepare the resulting order.
3. at any time, by filing a consent in writing of all parties to the action. Prepare a minimum of three copies of the consent, all of which will be signed by the solicitors for the parties to the action. File the original signed consent with the court, provide one signed copy for the solicitors for the other party, and retain the third copy in the office file.

Unless the court orders otherwise, a defendant is entitled to costs when a plaintiff discontinues the action.

WITHDRAWAL BY DEFENDANT

A defendant who has not crossclaimed or made a third party claim may withdraw all or part of his or her statement of defence with respect to any plaintiff at any time. A notice of withdrawal of defence (Precedent 17.1) is delivered to all parties. This step may be taken only with the permission of the court where the defendant has crossclaimed or made a third party claim.

A defendant who withdraws the entire statement of defence is treated as if no defence at all has been entered; the provisions of default judgment, as discussed later in this chapter, then apply.

DISMISSAL

For Payment of Claim by the Defendant

If the plaintiff's claim is for money only, the defendant may pay the amount of the claim and any amount claimed for costs within the time prescribed for delivery of the statement of defence or before he or she is noted in default and bring a motion to have the court dismiss the action. If the defendant considers the amount claimed for costs to be too high, he or she may pay only $400 for costs and make a motion to the court to dismiss the action. The court will make an order indicating whether the defendant should pay the amount of costs claimed by the plaintiff or whether the costs should be assessed as discussed in Chapter 16.

For Delay by the Plaintiff

If a plaintiff delays in taking the required procedural steps (such as failing to serve the statement of claim on all defendants within the required time), a defendant who is not in default may bring a motion for an order dismissing the action. The court hearing the motion determines whether such an order should be issued. The procedures relating to notices of motion are discussed in Chapter 13.

SETTLEMENT

An action may be settled through informal settlement negotiations at any time before the trial commences. The required procedural steps leading to trial progress as the negotiations are conducted; if a settlement is arrived at, the solicitors sign a consent to the discontinuance of the proceeding or move for an order on the terms of the settlement. More formal methods of endeavouring to settle a proceeding involve the offer to settle discussed in Chapter 16. If an offer to settle is accepted before the trial commences, the local registrar should be advised immediately.

DEFAULT JUDGMENT

When a defendant fails to deliver a statement of defence within the prescribed time, or the statement of defence has been struck out, a plaintiff may ask the registrar to note the defendant in default.

If the claim is for a debt or liquidated demand, the recovery of possession of land, the recovery of personal property, or the foreclosure, sale, or redemption of a mortgage, the registrar is asked to sign a judgment against the defendant.

If the claim is for unliquidated damages that are to be determined by the court, a plaintiff must request a motion hearing (discussed in Chapter 13). The evidence is by affidavit, and if satisfied, the judge will grant judgment. If the judge is not satisfied that the judgment may be made based on the evidence presented, the plaintiff must follow the steps to trial.

A defendant noted in default is deemed to admit the facts in the statement of claim and may take no further steps in the action, other than bring a motion to set aside the noting of default or any judgment obtained, unless the plaintiff or the court consents.

To have the registrar sign a default judgment under a claim for liquidated damages and register the judgment with the sheriff of the appropriate county, prepare a requisition for default judgment.

Requisition for Default Judgment

The requisition for default judgment is a more detailed document than the usual requisition (Precedent 17.2). It is addressed to the local registrar where the proceeding was commenced. Identify the defendant by name as well as by capacity and indicate the grounds for judgment, which is usually failure to deliver a statement of defence. Place an X in the box that indicates the basis of the claim for default judgment; the most common basis is a claim for a debt or liquidated demand in money. Place an X in the box relating to the payment or non-payment on account of the claim since the statement of claim was issued. Whether one or the other of these two boxes is ticked determines whether Part A or Part B of the requisition is completed, together with Part C.

Part A

Part A is completed if payments have been received by the plaintiff. If no payments have been received, the page on which Part A appears is omitted when completing the requisition. Section 1 of Part A requires information on the principal amount of the claim, the amount of the payment(s), and the balance of the principal sum still outstanding.

Section 2 of Part A requires information on prejudgment interest and a calculation of the amount to which the plaintiff is entitled under the default judgment. The calculation of prejudgment interest covers the period from the starting date of the cause of action to the date of payment. A final calculation of interest is required for the period from the date of the last payment to the date judgment is to be signed.

To calculate the amount of prejudgment interest, follow these steps:

1. Count the number of days between the applicable start and end dates.
2. Multiply the number of days by the applicable rate of interest, which is either
   a. the rate fixed by the contract or document on which the claim is based, such as on an unpaid account or promissory note, or
   b. the appropriate quarterly rate set out in the table of interest rates published as discussed in Chapter 10.
3. Multiply the result of step 2 by the principal amount.
4. Divide the result of step 3 by 365 (or 366 in a leap year).

The formula for the above steps is: $\dfrac{\text{no. of days} \times \text{rate of interest} \times \text{principal}}{365}$

The total of the balance still outstanding for principal, plus the total amount due for prejudgment interest, is shown as the amount for which default judgment is to be signed.

Part B

Part B of the requisition is completed if no payments have been received by the plaintiff. If payments have been received and Part A is completed, the page on which Part B appears is omitted when completing the requisition.

Part B requires information on the principal sum claimed and a calculation of prejudgment interest. Complete the calculations in the same manner as you would for Part A. Note, however, that the end date for the interest calculation period is the date on which the default judgment is to be signed.

Part C

Part C is always completed when preparing a requisition for default judgment. It requires the basis on which postjudgment interest is claimed, together with the rate of interest. The rate is either the fixed rate applicable to the contract or document or the appropriate quarterly rate set out in the current table of interest rates as discussed in Chapter 10.

In addition, the plaintiff indicates whether the costs are to be fixed by the local registrar or assessed by a court assessment officer. The usual procedure is to have the costs fixed by the registrar. A bill of costs (as discussed in Chapter 16) will need to be filed with the requisition so that a determination of costs may be made.

The requisition is dated the date of preparation and must be signed by the plaintiff's solicitor. The original is filed with the court, and the other copy is retained in the office file. An affidavit proving service of the statement of claim and the original statement of claim are filed with the requisition.

Default Judgment

Prepare four copies of the default judgment (Precedent 17.3). This form of judgment does not include the name of a judge or other court officer after the court name since the judgment is not given following a trial.

There are other forms of default judgment as well as the one illustrated in Precedent 17.3. For example, there are default judgments for recovery of chattels, recovery of possession of land, foreclosure, sale, etc. The basic format for each of these alternative forms of default judgments is found in the Forms section of the Rules of Civil Procedure. This chapter discusses only the default judgment for a debt or liquidated demand in money.

Three copies of the default judgment are submitted to the court when the requisition is filed; the signed copy is returned to the law firm, and two copies are kept by the court. The other copy is retained in the office file. The signed copy of the default judgment is filed with the sheriff in the county in which the defendant resides or in the county in which he or she owns real property.

When the default judgment has been signed, the plaintiff is known as the judgment creditor, and the defendant is known as the judgment debtor.

WRIT OF SEIZURE AND SALE

When the default judgment is signed, many lawyers take additional steps to enforce it, such as having a writ of seizure and sale issued. To do this, prepare a requisition (discussed in Chapter 13) to the local registrar in which the proceeding was commenced. The requisition sets out the date and amount of any payment received since the order was made, the amount owing, and the rate of postjudgment interest.

The requisition, along with a copy of the court order and a writ of seizure and sale (Precedents 17.4A and 17.4B), which requires essentially the same information as the requisition, is filed in duplicate with the court office. The writ authorizes the sheriff to seize and sell the real and personal property of the judgment debtor and to realize the sum of money necessary to satisfy the judgment with interest, plus costs and the sheriff's fees and expenses.

Filing the default judgment and writ of seizure and sale with the sheriff results in an execution, which is searched for against the judgment debtor when he or she is the vendor in a real estate transaction. The judgment must be cleared (that is, paid) before the purchaser of the property will complete the transaction. The writ remains in force for six years and may be renewed for additional periods of six years. The sheriff will not enforce the writ of seizure and sale unless directed to do so by a writ of direction, which is issued by the registrar upon filing a requisition.

There are a number of types of writs that direct the sheriff to seize the property of a judgment debtor. The basic formats for these are found in Forms 60B, 60C, 60D, and 60F of the rules. The lawyer will indicate which form is to be used.

SUMMARY JUDGMENT

After the statement of defence has been delivered, either party may bring a motion asking the court to hand down judgment without holding a trial. This is known as a summary judgment. This is a judgment that may be granted when the pleadings and any affidavits show that there is no genuine issue of material fact and that a decision on all or part of the claim may be made as a matter of law.

A notice of motion and a supporting affidavit are served and filed, together with a factum. A plaintiff asks for judgment on all or part of the claim in the statement of claim; a defendant asks for judgment dismissing all or part of the claim in the statement of claim. The procedures discussed in Chapter 13 relating to notices of motion are followed when asking for summary judgment.

Terms and Concepts

discontinuance	preparation and disposition of requisition
withdrawal by defendant	for default judgment
dismissal	writ of seizure and sale
settlement	summary judgment
default judgment	

Review Questions

1. How may a plaintiff discontinue an action against a defendant?

2. What procedures must a defendant take to withdraw her or his statement of defence if
   a. the defendant has not made a crossclaim or a third party claim?
   b. the defendant has made a crossclaim or a third party claim?

3. Under what circumstances may an action be dismissed?

4. What documents are prepared when an action is settled?

5. If prejudgment interest is awarded, from what date will it be applicable and how is it calculated?

6. How is the sheriff involved in enforcing a default judgment?

7. What is meant by the term "summary judgment"?

Court File No.

ONTARIO
SUPERIOR COURT OF JUSTICE

TITLE OF PROCEEDING

NOTICE OF WITHDRAWAL OF DEFENCE

The defendant withdraws the statement of defence in this action.

OR The defendant withdraws paragraphs . . . of the statement of defence

in this action.

Month day, year

NAME OF LAW FIRM
Street Address
City, Province Postal Code

Name of Specific Lawyer

Telephone Number
Fax Number

Solicitors for the defendant

TO: NAME OF LAW FIRM
Street Address
City, Province Postal Code

Name of Specific Lawyer

Telephone Number
Fax Number

Solicitors for the plaintiff

Requires a back

Court File No. 0000-000-000

ONTARIO
SUPERIOR COURT OF JUSTICE

BETWEEN:

EAST HARDWARE LIMITED

PLAINTIFF

and

NORMAN GORDON MASTERWOOD

DEFENDANT

REQUISITION FOR DEFAULT JUDGMENT

TO THE LOCAL REGISTRAR AT TORONTO

I REQUIRE you to note the defendant Norman Gordon Masterwood in default in this action on the ground that no statement of defence has been delivered

I REQUIRE default judgment to be signed against the defendant Norman Gordon Masterwood.

Default judgment may be properly signed in this action because the claim is for:

[x]   a debt or liquidated demand in money

[ ]   recovery of possession of land

[ ]   recovery of possession of personal property

[ ]   foreclosure, sale or redemption of a mortgage

(Debt or liquidated demand)

[x] There has been no payment on account of the claim since the statement of claim was issued. — *Complete Parts B & C*

OR

[ ] The following payments have been made on account of the claim since the statement of claim was issued. — *Complete Parts A & C*

- 2 -

PART A – PAYMENT(S) RECEIVED BY PLAINTIFF

(Complete this Part only where part payment of the claim has been received. Where no payment has been received on account of the claim, omit this Part and complete Part B.)

1. Principal

Principal sum claimed in the statement of claim (without interest) $

Date of Payment	Amount of Payment	Payment Amount Principal	Applied to Interest	Principal Sum Owing
TOTAL $	$	$	A $	

2. Prejudgment interest
(Under section 128 of the **Courts of Justice Act**, *judgment may be obtained for prejudgment interest from the date the cause of action arose, if claimed in the statement of claim.)*

Date on which statement of claim was issued:

Date from which prejudgment interest is claimed:

The plaintiff is entitled to prejudgment interest on the claim, calculated as follows:
(Calculate simple interest only unless an agreement relied on in the statement of claim specifies otherwise. Calculate interest on the principal sum owing from the date of the last payment. To calculate the interest amount, count the number of days since the last payment, multiply that number by the annual rate of interest, multiply the result by the principal sum owing, and divide by 365.)

Principal Sum Owing	Start Date	End Date (Date of Payment)	Number of Days	Rate	Interest Amount

(The last End Date should be the date judgment is signed.)

TOTAL B	$
Principal Sum Owing (Total A above)	$
Total Interest Amount (Total B above)	$
SIGN JUDGMENT FOR	$

- 3 -

PART B – NO PAYMENT RECEIVED BY PLAINTIFF

(Complete this Part only where no payment has been received on account of the claim.)

1. Principal

Principal sum claimed in the statement of claim (without interest)   A $8,300.00

2. Prejudgment interest
(Under section 128 of the Courts of Justice Act, *judgment may be obtained for prejudgment interest from the date the cause of action arose, if claimed in the statement of claim.)*

Date on which statement of claim was issued: November 1, 20__

Date from which prejudgment interest is claimed: August 15, 20__

The plaintiff(s) is/are entitled to prejudgment interest on the claim, calculated as follows:
(Calculate simple interest only unless an agreement relied on in the statement of claim specifies otherwise. To calculate the interest amount, count the number of days and multiply that number by the annual rate of interest, multiply the result by the principal sum owing and divide by 365.)

Principal Sum Owing	Start Date	End Date (Date of Judgment)	Number of Days	Rate	Interest Amount
$8,300.00	Aug. 15, 20__	Nov. 22, 20__	102	11%	$ 255.14

(The last End Date should be the date judgment is signed.)

TOTAL B	$ 255.14
Principal Sum Owing (Total A above)	$8,300.00
Total Interest Amount (Total B above)	$ 255.14
SIGN JUDGMENT FOR	$8,555.14

- 4 -

PART C – POSTJUDGMENT INTEREST AND COSTS

1. Postjudgment interest

   The plaintiff is entitled to postjudgment interest at the rate of 11 percent per year.

[x] under the *Courts of Justice Act*, as claimed in the statement of claim.

OR

[ ] in accordance with the claim made in the statement of claim.

2. Costs

The plaintiff wishes costs to be

[x] fixed by the local registrar

OR

[ ] assessed by an assessment officer

Date: November   , 20__   _____
                                          (Signature of plaintiff's solicitor or plaintiff)

HILL, JOHNSTON & GRANT
Barristers and Solicitors
17 Princess Street South
Suite 2501
Toronto ON M8Y 3N5

Attention: Lynda C. Ritchie (42212R)

Phone: (416) 354-9900
Fax: (416) 354-9909

Solicitors for the plaintiff

Requires a back

ACL   Court File No.

ONTARIO
SUPERIOR COURT OF JUSTICE

B E T W E E N:

(Court Seal)

TITLE OF PROCEEDING

JUDGMENT

On reading the statement of claim in this action and the proof of service of the statement of claim on the defendant filed, and the defendant having been noted in default,

1.   **IT IS ORDERED AND ADJUDGED** that the defendant pay to the plaintiff the sum of $ ^{1} and the sum of $ ^{2} for the costs of this action.

This judgment bears interest at the rate of ^{3} percent per year from its date.

Date   Month   , 20__   Signed by _____

                                                        Local Registrar

	Address
Requires a back	of court office:

_____

1.   *Insert the figure from the *SIGN JUDGMENT FOR* line from either Part A or Part B of the requisition.*

2.   *No figure is inserted here when the judgment is prepared.*

3.   *Use the appropriate rate for postjudgment interest.*

Automated Civil Litigation – Korbitec Inc.

Court File No. 000-000-000

ONTARIO
SUPERIOR COURT OF JUSTICE

B E T W E E N:

EAST HARDWARE LIMITED

Plaintiff

And

NORMAN GORDON MASTERWOOD

Defendant

WRIT OF SEIZURE AND SALE

TO the Sheriff of the Territorial District of Sudbury

Under a judgment of this court made on November 22, 2007, in favour of EAST HARDWARE LIMITED, YOU ARE DIRECTED to seize and sell the real and personal property within your county or district of

Surname of individual or name of corporation/firm, etc.

First given name (individual only)	*Second given name (individual only) (if applicable)*	*Third given name (individual only) (if applicable)*
NORMAN	**GORDON**	**MASTERWOOD**

and to realize from the seizure and sale the following sums:

(a) $8,555.14 and interest at 11.00 percent per year commencing on November 22, 20__;

(b) $_____ and interest at _____ percent per year on the payments in default commencing on the date of default;

(c) $397.10 for costs together with interest at 11.00 percent per year commencing on November 22, 20__; and

(d) your fees and expenses in enforcing this writ.

YOU ARE DIRECTED to pay out the proceeds according to law and to report on the execution of this writ if required by the party or solicitor who filed it.

Dated at _____   Issued by _____
                                                                                            Registrar

on _____   Address of court office
                                                          393 University Avenue, 10th Floor
                                                          Toronto ON M5G 1E6

Source: Korbitec Inc.

EAST HARDWARE LIMITED

Plaintiff

and

NORMAN GORDON MASTERWOOD

Defendant

Court File No. 0000-000-000

ONTARIO
SUPERIOR COURT OF JUSTICE
PROCEEDING COMMENCED AT TORONTO

WRIT OF SEIZURE AND SALE

Creditor's Name: EAST HARDWARE LIMTIED
Creditor's Address: 300 King Street North
                      Toronto ON M8Y 3N5

Lawyer's Name: Peter T. Grant (12345G)

HILL, JOHNSTON & GRANT
Barristers & Solicitors
17 Princess Street South, Suite 2501
Toronto ON M8Y 3N5

Tel: 416-354-9900
Fax: 416-354-9909

FEES

Fee	Item	Officer
$55.00	Paid for this Writ	
$50.00	Lawyer's fee for issuing Writ	
	First Renewal	
	Second Renewal	
	Third Renewal	

RENEWAL

Date	Officer		

Source: Korbitec Inc.

CHAPTER 18

Introduction to Family Law

OBJECTIVES:

- Demonstrate an understanding of the different areas of family law, the legislative sources, and applicable courts

- Define and describe the various domestic contracts and terminology in family law

- Demonstrate an understanding of the purpose and contents of financial statements, net family property statements, and support deduction forms

- Use legal precedents to prepare family law documentation

When the legal proceedings dealt with by a lawyer or law firm relate to matters such as

1. divorce;
2. separation, marriage, and cohabitation agreements;
3. custody of children;
4. support for a spouse and/or children;
5. division of family property;
6. enforcement of maintenance support orders; and
7. adoption,

the lawyer or law firm is said to practise family law. The legal assistant will then be concerned with preparing the documents discussed in earlier chapters, as well as domestic contracts, financial statements, and court documentation.

LEGISLATIVE SOURCES

The law relating to family law matters is contained in both federal and provincial statutes.

On June 1, 1986, the *Divorce Act*, 1985, became effective. This federal statute outlines the law regarding divorces in Canada. The provincial rules of practice establish the procedures to be followed to carry out the provisions of this Act.

Most provinces have passed legislation covering family law matters. In Ontario, the applicable statutes are the *Family Law Act*, the *Children's Law Reform Act*, the *Family Responsibility and Support Arrears Enforcement Act*, the *Change of Name Act*, and the *Child and Family Services Act*.

As with civil litigation, many of the documents, terms, and procedures are similar across Canada for family law; however, the specific statutes and rules of court for the province and the court in which any family law matter is to proceed must be followed. For Ontario, these are the *Family Law Rules*, O. Reg. 441/99, as amended, which are used in explaining the documentation and procedures of family law for this text. The *Family Law Rules* may be accessed at http://www.elaws.gov.on.ca/index.html, and the family court forms are available at http://www.ontariocourtforms.on.ca.

DOMESTIC CONTRACTS

For many years, married persons or persons living together rarely entered into a formal contract, although married persons have always been in a certain contractual relationship in the eyes of the law. However, **domestic contracts** are becoming common. There are four types of such contracts:

Marriage Contract	A contract between two people who are married to each other or who intend to marry.
Separation Agreement	A contract between two people who cohabited (lived together) and who eventually separate and live apart. This agreement most commonly exists between a man and a woman who are married to each other.
Cohabitation Agreement	A contract between two people who are cohabiting or intend to cohabit and who are not married to each other. If these people should marry at a later date, the cohabitation agreement would become a marriage contract.
Paternity Agreement	A contract between two people who are not married to each other when there is a child or children of the relationship.

These contracts outline the rights and obligations of the parties, including ownership or division of property, support obligations, and the right to direct the education and moral training of their children and provide for any other matter in the settlement of their affairs.

Only in a separation agreement may one spouse relinquish his or her right to an interest in the matrimonial home. This point is relevant in family law proceedings and is also of great importance when the one spouse wishes to dispose of his or her interest in the matrimonial home, as is discussed in the chapters dealing with real estate procedures.

Each party to a domestic contract should receive independent legal advice to ensure that he or she fully understands the nature and effect of the provisions of the contract.

Preparing Domestic Contracts

Domestic contracts are usually made in duplicate, with additional copies for the solicitor for each party. The contract is prepared following the procedures discussed in Chapter 7. These contracts often use less traditional wording; however, they have the traditional attestation clause as the contract must be signed by the parties and witnessed to be valid, as illustrated in Precedents 18.1 and 18.2.

Certificate of Independent Legal Advice

Domestic contracts usually have attached to them a special form of affidavit and certificate completed by the solicitor for each signing party stating that the party received independent legal advice and that the terms of the agreement have been explained to him or her, as shown in Precedent 18.3. Alternatively, if a party to a domestic contract does not obtain independent legal advice, the lawyer will have such a party sign a waiver or acknowledgement stating that he or she was advised to seek independent legal advice but chose not to do so. Domestic contracts may also include a schedule setting out the assets, debts, and liabilities of each party as of the date of the contract.

DIVORCE

The contractual relationship between married persons can, in certain circumstances, be terminated by an order of the court, known as a **divorce**. The law for divorces is set out in the federal *Divorce Act*, which provides a standard divorce law for all Canadians. Under that act, divorces are heard by specified courts in each province.

Divorce proceedings are a form of legal proceeding, and parties in a divorce action are frequently represented by solicitors, but such parties may also act personally. In this text, we have assumed that the parties act through solicitors.

CENTRAL DIVORCE REGISTRY

Under the *Divorce Act*, it is possible for each spouse to start divorce proceedings against the other in two different provinces. The first of such originating documents filed takes precedence.

To avoid the possibility of duplicate actions, the **Central Divorce Registry** was established in Ottawa. Upon commencing a divorce proceeding, a fee is paid at the court office and Part 1 of the form is completed and sent to the Central Divorce Registry to obtain a clearance that divorce proceedings have not already been commenced or completed elsewhere. Once a divorce is finalized, court officials complete Part 2 of the form, which is then filed with the central registry in Ottawa to update the registry.

GROUNDS FOR DIVORCE

To have the right to originate a divorce action in a province in Canada, either spouse must have ordinarily been a resident in that province for at least one year immediately before the action is commenced.

In addition to meeting the residency requirement, there must be grounds on which the divorce can be granted. Under the *Divorce Act*, there is now a single ground for divorce: breakdown of the marriage. This ground may be established by proving a separation of one year, adultery, or cruelty.

The period of separation of one year need not be complete before the divorce action is originated. It is necessary only that the date of trial of the divorce be more than one year after the separation took place.

ONTARIO FAMILY LAW COURTS

There are three courts in Ontario that hear family law cases (as proceedings are referred to under the *Family Law Rules*):

Superior Court of Justice Family Court Branch	This court has comprehensive jurisdiction over all legal matters related to family law (divorce, property, custody, support, exclusive possession of family home, trust and unjust enrichment claims, adoption, and child protection). However, it currently operates only in certain areas of Ontario, as listed on the Ministry of the Attorney General website (http://www.attorneygeneral.jus.gov.on.ca/english/family/famcrtaddress.asp).

In those areas of Ontario where a Superior Court of Justice Family Court Branch does not currently exist, the jurisdiction over family law cases is divided between the Superior Court of Justice and the Ontario Court of Justice.

Superior Court of Justice	This court may hear all family law cases except for adoption and child protection cases, which must be commenced in the Ontario Court of Justice.
Ontario Court of Justice	This court may hear all family law cases except for cases involving divorce, the division of family property, or exclusive possession of the family home, which must be heard in the Superior Court of Justice.

The *Family Law Rules* apply to all family law cases in all three courts.

FINANCIAL INFORMATION IN FAMILY LAW PROCEEDINGS

Most family law matters require information that is not required in general civil litigation matters—information on the financial situation of each party and a valuation of all of his or her property. The legal assistant is thus required to prepare financial statements and net family property statements. To be able to do this, you should become familiar with the following terms and concepts as defined by the *Family Law Act*:

Valuation Date (referred to as *v-date*) is the earliest of
- the date the spouses separate and there is no reasonable prospect that they will resume cohabitation
- the date a divorce is granted
- the date the marriage is declared a nullity
- the date one of the spouses commences an application based on improvident depletion that is subsequently granted
- the day before the death of a spouse

Property
- real property (such as land) or personal property (cars, stocks, pensions, RRSPs, money owed to a person [such as an income tax refund], shares, jewellery, furniture, art, electronics, interest in an unincorporated business, etc.)
- may be present or future property (the right to purchase shares or future royalties)
- may be held alone or with another person (who is not the spouse)

Net Family Property (referred to as NFP)
The value of all property, except excluded property (defined below), that a spouse owns on the valuation date after deducting
- the spouse's debts and other liabilities and
- the value of property, other than a matrimonial home, that the spouse owned on the date of the marriage, after deducting the spouse's debts and other liabilities, calculated as of the date of the marriage

Excluded Property
Property that a spouse owns on the v-date that does not form part of the spouse's net family property, which may be
- property, other than the matrimonial home, that was a gift or inheritance received after the date of marriage
- any income from such property, if the person giving the property expressly stated that it was to be excluded from the spouse's net family property
- damages or settlement amounts received for personal injuries
- proceeds of a life insurance policy that are payable on the death of the life insured
- property, other than the matrimonial home, in which any of the property referred to above can be traced
- any property that the spouses have agreed by way of a domestic contract will not be included in the spouse's NFP

Matrimonial Home
- A property that a person has an interest in and that was, at the time of the separation, divorce, sale, or death, usually lived in by the person and his or her spouse as the family residence.
- When completing the financial documents, note the following:
  - If the ownership of the matrimonial home is in both spouses' names, then the value of the home is usually split evenly between the spouses when entering it as an asset.
  - If the ownership of the matrimonial home is only in one spouse's name, then the entire value of the home is entered as an asset for that spouse only.

FORMAT OF FAMILY COURT DOCUMENTS

Under the *Family Law Rules*, the court forms are structured as tables. All cases are by way of application; therefore, the parties are referred to as applicant(s) and respondent(s). The general heading requires the name and address of the court, the court file number (if known), and the name, address, telephone and fax numbers, and e-mail (if known) of all parties and their solicitors (Precedents 18.4 and 18.5). There are no backsheets for family law forms.

FINANCIAL STATEMENTS

When in a family law case either the applicant or the respondent makes a claim under the *Family Law Act* for

1. support (child or spousal),
2. property, or
3. exclusive possession of the matrimonial home and its contents,

a financial statement will be required to be served and filed. However, the requirement may be waived under certain circumstances, for example, if the case contains a claim for spousal support, or change in support, and both parties serve and file a consent agreeing not to require financial statements, or if it contains only a claim for child support in accordance with the applicable child support guidelines. The child support guidelines may be viewed at http://www.justice.gc.ca/en/ps/sup/grl/glp.html.

Usually, a law clerk in the law office will work closely with the client to collect the information for the financial statement. Accountants and professional evaluators may also assist in the preparation of financial statements to ensure accurate valuation of certain property. Once all the necessary information has been ascertained, the form will be completed. DIVORCEmate software, which is widely used across Canada and in the creation of the forms for this text, facilitates the entry and calculation of client and financial data. This software also calculates child and spousal support according to the Child Support Guidelines and the Spousal Support Guidelines and creates comprehensive draft separation agreements.

Body of the Statement

Financial statements are large affidavits in which the deponent is swearing to the truth of the financial information provided about herself or himself. The information inserted must be complete, up-to-date, and accurate. There are two types of financial statements: Form 13 is used for support claims and Form 13.1 (Precedent 18.4) is used for support and property claims.

The financial statement requires detailed information on the spouse's

1. income, deductions, and expenses in order to calculate, using the formula on page 3, each spouse's monthly surplus/deficit;
2. assets (including any excluded property and the matrimonial home);
3. debts and other liabilities on the date of marriage, the v-date, and the date of the statement;
4. property, debts, and other liabilities on the date of marriage (excluding any matrimonial home);

5. excluded property owned on the v-date; and
6. the value of all property that was disposed of during the two years immediately preceding the making of the statement or during the marriage, whichever is the shorter period.

Part 6 of either form is completed only if there is a claim for spousal support. The last page of the financial statement provides the formula for calculating the net family property of the spouse. A statement about whether there are any expected changes in the spouse's financial situation must also be completed, as well as the jurat.

Supporting Documents for Financial Statement

The following must be attached to any financial statement when it is filed in the court office:

- a copy of proof of income tax information as stated on the form or a direction to the Canada Revenue Agency to provide for disclosure of income tax information to the court
- a direction to the Canada Revenue Agency releasing income tax information to the other side (Precedent 18.5)
- a copy of proof of income as stated on the form

The local registrar will not accept any financial statement without these documents attached.

Other Party's Financial Statement

When a party is served with a financial statement in a family law proceeding, he or she must also file a financial statement and the necessary attachments, whether or not he or she wishes to defend the proceeding or answer a motion.

Updating Financial Statements

Before any case conference, motion, settlement conference, or trial, any financial statement that is more than 30 days old must be updated by serving and filing a new financial statement or serving and filing an affidavit stating that the information has not changed and is still true.

NET FAMILY PROPERTY

The *Family Law Act* views marriage as an economic contract and provides that upon the breakdown of a marriage, the value of any property built up during the marriage is to be shared equally between the spouses. Thus, in any family law case in which a claim is made for a division of property, each spouse is required to serve and file a net family property statement so that an **equalization of net family property** may be calculated. Each spouse is intended to receive an equal division of all family property, and the spouse with the smaller NFP is entitled to receive cash or property equal to half of the difference between his or her NFP and the NFP of the other spouse. This is often referred to as an **equalization payment**. The following provides an explanation and an example of how to calculate this:

Calculation Method	Husband	Wife
Add up value of spouse's assets at v-date		
(*including matrimonial home and excluded property*)	$150,000	$120,000
Subtract debts at v-date	60,000	65,000
Subtract excluded property	10,000	15,000
= v-date net worth	$80,000	$40,000
Add up the value of spouse's assets at date of marriage	$25,000	$15,000
Subtract debts at date of marriage	5,000	5,000
= date of marriage net worth	$20,000	$10,000
Subtract date of marriage net worth		
from v-date net worth = **NFP**	$60,000	$30,000

In the above example, the husband has a NFP of $60,000 and the wife has a NFP of $30,000. The wife will be entitled to receive $15,000 from the husband so that each will have an NFP of $45,000. A judge will approve an unequal division of the property only when it appears that to do otherwise would be "unconscionable."

NET FAMILY PROPERTY STATEMENT

If there is a claim for any division of family property, then a net family property statement must be prepared. In the net family property statement, the value of the net family property for each spouse may be determined by completing the form as follows:

Table 1: List and calculate the total value of all the spouse's property as of the v-date (including any matrimonial home and excluded property) in the same order as these items are listed in the financial statement.

Table 2: List and then calculate the total debts and liabilities of the spouse on the v-date.

Table 3: List and then calculate the total value of property (other than matrimonial home) on the date of marriage.
List and calculate the total debts on date of marriage.
Subtract the total debts from the total property items to obtain the net total.

Table 4: List and value all excluded property.

Total 5: This is the sum of Total 2, Total 3, and Total 4.

NFP: This is Total 1 minus Total 5.

See Precedent 18.6, where the NFP of the husband is $56,200.00 and the NFP of the wife is $58,500.00; thus, the husband is entitled to receive $1,150.00 from the wife as an equalization payment so that their NFP is equal.

Updating the Net Family Property Statement

Each party must deliver a new net family property statement or an affidavit stating that the information has not changed and is still true at least seven days before any conference. A new Net Family Property Statement must also be delivered not more than 30 days and not less than 7 days before a trial.

Number of Copies of Financial and Net Family Property Statements

Prepare a minimum of four copies of any financial statement and of any net family property statement. One copy is filed with the court, one is served on the other party in the proceeding, one is for the office file, and one is the Document subfile.

SUPPORT DEDUCTION ORDERS

Under the provisions of the *Family Responsibility and Support Arrears Enforcement Act*, each time the court makes an order for periodic support payments, the court will also make a **support deduction order** that provides for the automatic deduction of support from the payor's income. Therefore, in any case in which support or variation of support is claimed, the party making the claim must file two copies of a support deduction order information form (Precedent 18.7) and two copies of the support deduction order (Precedent 18.8).

Parts A and B are completed by the legal assistant from information provided by the client. Parts C, D, E, and F are completed by the court to provide specific information on the amount and frequency of payments, possible cost of living adjustments, payment of arrears, and whether a previous support order is to be terminated by the new one.

The support deduction order will be completed and signed by the court at the time the order that contains the provision for payment of support is made and will be entered in the court records immediately after it is signed. The clerk or registrar of the court will then file the support deduction order together with a copy of the completed support deduction information form with the director of the Family Responsibility Office, who will send a copy of the order to each income source from whom payment is sought. Those income sources will deduct the required amount—just as income tax, CPP, etc., are deducted from the spouse's paycheque—and will forward payments to the Family Responsibility Office, which will then pay the amounts collected under the order to the person to whom they are owed.

The *Family Responsibility and Support Arrears Enforcement Act* contains provisions whereby the court may also make an order to suspend the operation of a support deduction order. For example, this might occur when the parties agree that they do not want support payments collected through such an order and complete the necessary documentation.

Terms and Concepts

family law
Divorce Act
Family Law Act
Children's Law Reform Act
Family Responsibility and Support Arrears Enforcement Act
Family Law Rules
domestic contract
marriage contract
separation agreement
cohabitation agreement
paternity agreement
independent legal advice
divorce

Central Divorce Registry
grounds for divorce
Ontario family law courts
valuation date (v-date)
property
net family property (NFP)
excluded property
matrimonial home
financial statements
net family property statement
equalization of net family property
equalization payment
support deduction order
information form

Review Questions

1. What types of domestic contracts may you encounter? Briefly indicate the purpose of each.

2. What are the grounds for divorce?

3. What courts hear family law proceedings in your province?

4. In your own words, briefly explain what is meant by the following terms under the *Family Law Rules:*
   a. valuation date
   b. property
   c. net family property
   d. excluded property
   e. matrimonial home

5. When is a financial statement required in a family law case, and which party must file that document?

6. What is a "net family property statement," and when is it required?

7. What is the purpose of the support deduction information form and order?

8. Bob and Carly are getting divorced. When they married, they each brought $2,000 into the marriage. They have a matrimonial home (jointly owned) valued at $170,000 with a $90,000 mortgage, $10,000 in a joint savings account, and $3,000 in a joint chequing account and jointly own the contents of the family home, valued at $15,000. During the marriage, Bob received $50,000 in settlement from a work injury and $20,000 from life insurance proceeds when his mother died. During the marriage, Carly inherited art and antiques from her grandmother valued at $25,000. She also has $15,000 in RRSPs. Calculate the net family property for both Bob and Carly and what the equalization payment would be.

9. **Internet Research:** Using the child support guidelines available on the Internet, calculate the monthly child support payments for residents of your province in the following circumstances:

a. Mario has an annual income of $40,000 and will be paying child support for 2 children, aged 10 and 6 years.

b. Anita has an annual income of $65,000 and will be paying child support for 1 child, aged 17 years.

THIS IS A SEPARATION AGREEMENT made this 28th day of February, 20__.

B E T W E E N:

CRAIG CLELLAND MANDERLEY

herein called the "husband"

- and -

SARAH JESSICA MANDERLEY

herein called the "wife"

WHEREAS the husband and the wife married at Kingston, Ontario, on August 26, 1999;

AND WHEREAS the parties have two children, namely, Robert Crawford Manderley, born March 26, 2000; and Kimberly Sarah Manderley, born June 14, 2004. They are referred to herein collectively as the "children";

AND WHEREAS the parties have agreed to live separate and apart and have in fact lived separate and apart continuously since October 28, 2007.

NOW THEREFORE the parties agree as follows:

1.0   **DEFINITIONS**

1.1   In this agreement:

(a)   "income tax" and "income taxes" include tax, interest and penalties owing under the provisions of the Income Tax Act and any tax owing under similar federal or provincial legislation. It includes tax on both income and on capital gains;

(b)   "property" means real or personal property or any interest in such property;

5

18.0   GOVERNING LAW

18.1   The contract will be governed by and construed under the laws of the Province

of Ontario.

19.0   INDEPENDENT LEGAL ADVICE

19.1   Each party acknowledges that he or she:

(a)   has received independent legal advice;

(b)   understands his or her respective rights and obligations under this

contract, the nature of this agreement and the consequences of this

agreement;

(c)   has made full and complete disclosure of his or her financial

circumstances to the other, including but not limited to his or her

income, assets, debts or other liabilities (see Schedule "A") hereto; and

(d)   is signing this contract voluntarily.

TO EVIDENCE THEIR AGREEMENT, each of the parties has signed this

contract under seal before a witness.

SIGNED, SEALED AND DELIVERED)
)
)
_____)   _____
Witness as to the signature of:)   Craig Clelland Manderly
)
)
)
_____)   _____
Witness as to the signature of:)   Sarah Jessica Manderley

CERTIFICATE AND AFFIDAVIT OF SOLICITOR

I, PETER THOMAS GRANT, of the City of Toronto, Province of Ontario,

MAKE OATH AND SAY:

1.   I am the solicitor for SARAH JESSICA MANDERLEY, and a subscribing witness to this separation agreement, and I was present and saw it executed at the City of Toronto by the said SARAH JESSICA MANDERLEY.

2.   I believe that the person whose signature I witnessed is the party of the same name referred to in the said separation agreement.

3.   I have advised the said SARAH JESSICA MANDERLEY with respect to the attached separation agreement, and I believe that she is fully aware of the nature and consequences of the agreement in light of her present and future circumstances and is signing it voluntarily.

4.   I have given this advice to SARAH JESSICA MANDERLEY as her solicitor and in her interests only and without consideration or with regard to the interests of any other party. I am not acting as solicitor on behalf of any other persons in connection with this matter.

SWORN before me at the   )
)
City of Toronto,   )
)   _____
Province of Ontario   )   Peter T. Grant
)
on February   , 20__   )

Commissioner for taking affidavits

ONTARIO

Superior Court of Justice Family Court Branch
(Name of Court)

		Court File Number
		123456

at **50 Eagle Street West, Newmarket ON L3Y 6B1**
(Court office address)

Form 13.1: Financial Statement (Property and Support Claims) Sworn/Affirmed

Applicant(s)

Full legal name & address for service - street & number, municipality, postal code, telephone & fax numbers and e-mail address (if any).	Lawyer's name & address - street & number, municipality, postal code, telephone & fax numbers and e-mail address (if any).
JOHN CARL MATISKO **4100 Yonge Street, Apt 302** **Toronto ON M2P 1C5** **Tel: 416-332-4398**	**Peter T. Grant** **HILL, JOHNSTON & GRANT** **17 Princess Street South, Suite 2501** **Toronto ON M8Y 3N5** **Tel: 416-354-9900** **Fax: 416-354-9901** **ptgrant@hilljohngrant.com**

Respondent(s)

Full legal name & address for service - street & number, municipality, postal code, telephone & fax numbers and e-mail address (if any).	Lawyer's name & address - street & number, municipality, postal code, telephone & fax numbers and e-mail address (if any).
CHERYL ANNE MATISKO **42 Spring Gardens Avenue** **Aurora ON L2N 4J9** **Tel: 905-869-4335**	**Katherine R. Siegel** **ARMSTRONG, WARD & SIEGEL** **16 Montreal Street West** **Whitby ON L4R 8C2** **Tel: 905-687-4682** **Fax: 905-687-4690** **krsiegel@armstrong.ca**

INSTRUCTIONS

1. USE THIS FORM IF:
    - you are making or responding to a claim for property or exclusive possession of the matrimonial home and its contents; or
    - you are making or responding to a claim for property or exclusive possession of the matrimonial home and its contents together with other claims for relief.

2. DO NOT USE THIS FORM AND INSTEAD USE FORM 13 IF:
    - you are making or responding to a claim for support but NOT making or responding to a claim for property or exclusive possession of the matrimonial home and its contents.

1. **My name is** *(full legal name)* JOHN CARL MATISKO

    I live in *(municipality & province)* Toronto, Province of Ontario

    and I swear/affirm that the following is true:

    My financial statement set out on the following *(specify number)* **7** pages is accurate to the best of my knowledge and belief and sets out the financial situation as of *(give date for which information is accurate)* June 15, 20___ for

    Check one or more boxes, as circumstances require.   [X] me

    [ ] the following person(s): *(Give name(s) and relationship to you.)*

Source: DIVORCEmate Software Inc.

Form 13.1: Financial Statement (Page 2) | Court file number | 123456

NOTE: When you show monthly income and expenses, give the current actual amount if you know it or can find out. To get a monthly figure you must multiply any weekly income by 4.33 or divide any yearly income by 12.

PART 1: INCOME

for the 12 months from (*date*) June 15, 20___ to (*date*) June 15, 20___

Include all income and other money that you get from all sources, whether taxable or not. Show the gross amount here and show your deductions in Part 3.

CATEGORY	Monthly		
1. Pay, wages, salary, including overtime *(before deductions)*	$5,000.00	10. Canada Child Tax Benefit	
2. Bonuses, fees, commissions		11. Support payments actually received	
3. Social assistance		12. Income received by children	
4. Employment insurance		13. G.S.T. refund	
5. Workers' compensation		14. Payments from trust funds	
6. Pensions		15. Gifts received	
7. Dividends		16. Other *(Specify.)*	
8. Interest			
9. Rent, board received		17. **INCOME FROM ALL SOURCES**	$5,000.00

PART 2: OTHER BENEFITS

Show your non-cash benefits—such as the use of a company car, a club membership or room and board that your employer or someone else provides for you or benefits that are charged through or written off by your business.

ITEM	DETAILS	Monthly Market Value
	18. TOTAL	$0.00

19. **GROSS MONTHLY INCOME AND BENEFITS** (Add **[17]** plus **[18]**.) | $5,000.00

PART 3: AUTOMATIC DEDUCTIONS FROM INCOME

for the 12 months from (*date*) June 15, 20___ to (*date*) June 15, 20___

TYPE OF EXPENSE	Monthly		
20. Income tax deducted from pay	$1,200.00	25. Group insurance	$60.00
21. Canada Pension Plan	$250.00	26. Other *(Specify.)*	
22. Other pension plans			
23. Employment insurance		27. **TOTAL AUTOMATIC DEDUCTIONS**	$1,510.00
24. Union or association dues			

28. **NET MONTHLY INCOME** (Do the subtraction: **[19]** minus **[27]**.) | $3,490.00

Source: DIVORCEmate Software Inc.

Form 13.1: Financial Statement (Page 3)   Court file number   123456

PART 4: TOTAL EXPENSES

for the 12 months from (*date*)   June 15, 20___   to (*date*)   June 15, 20___.

Note: This part must be completed in all cases. You must set out your TOTAL living expenses, including those expenses involving any children now living in your home. This part may also be used for a proposed budget. To prepare a proposed budget, photocopy Part 4, complete as necessary, change the title to "Proposed Budget" and attach it to this form.

TYPE OF EXPENSE	Monthly
Housing	
29. Rent/Mortgage	$900.00
30. Property taxes & municipal levies	
31. Condominium fees & common expenses	
32. Water	
33. Electricity & heating fuel	$100.00
34. Telephone	$50.00
35. Cable television & pay television	$75.00
36. Home insurance	$50.00
37. Home repairs, maintenance, gardening	
Sub-total of items [29] to [37]	**$1,175.00**
Food, Clothing and Transportation	
38. Groceries	$350.00
39. Meals outside home	$250.00
40. General household supplies	$100.00
41. Hairdresser, barber & toiletries	$50.00
42. Laundry & dry cleaning	$75.00
43. Clothing	$75.00
44. Public transit	
45. Taxis	
46. Car insurance	$75.00
47. Licence	$15.00
48. Car loan payments	$350.00
49. Car maintenance and repairs	$100.00
50. Gasoline & oil	$150.00
51. Parking	
Sub-total of items [38] to [51]	**$1,590.00**
Health & Medical (*do not include child(ren)'s expenses*)	
52. Regular dental care	
53. Orthodontics/special dental care	
54. Medicine & drugs	
55. Eye glasses or contact lenses	
56. Life or term insurance premiums	
Sub-total of items [52] to [56]	**$0.00**

Child(ren)	
57. School activities (*field trips, etc.*)	
58. School lunches	
59. School fees, books, tuition, etc. (*for children*)	
60. Summer camp	
61. Activities (*music lessons, clubs, sports*)	
62. Allowances	
63. Baby sitting	
64. Daycare	
65. Regular dental care	
66. Orthodontics/special dental care	
67. Medicine & drugs	
68. Eye glasses or contact lenses	
Sub-total of items [57] to [68]	**$0.00**
Miscellaneous and Other	
69. Books for home use, newspapers, magazines, videos, compact discs	$60.00
70. Gifts	$100.00
71. Charities	
72. Alcohol & tobacco	$50.00
73. Pet expenses	
74. School fees, books, tuition, etc.	
75. Entertainment & recreation	$100.00
76. Vacation	$150.00
77. Credit cards (*but not for expenses mentioned elsewhere in the statement*)	
78. R.R.S.P. or other savings plans	
79. Support actually being paid in any other case	
80. Income tax and *Canada Pension Plan* (not deducted from pay)	
81. Other (*Specify.*)	
Sub-total of items [69] to [81]	**$460.00**
82. **Total of items [29] to [81]**	**$3,225.00**

SUMMARY OF INCOME AND EXPENSES

Net monthly income (item **[28]** above)	=	$3,490.00
Subtract actual monthly expenses (item **[82]** above)	−	$3,225.00
ACTUAL MONTHLY SURPLUS/(DEFICIT)	=	$265.00

Source: DIVORCEmate Software Inc.

Form 13.1: Financial Statement (Page 4)   Court file number   123456

PART 5: OTHER INCOME INFORMATION

1. I am [x] employed by *(name and address of employer)*
   Centennial Consulting Inc., 4000 Birchmount Avenue, Suite 500, Toronto ON M3C 4K9

   [ ] self-employed, carrying on business under the name of *(name and address of business)*

   [ ] unemployed since *(date when last employed)*

2. I attach the following required information *(if you are filing this statement to update or correct an earlier statement, then you do not need to attach income tax returns that have already been filed with the court)*:

   [x] a copy of my income tax returns that were filed with the Canada Revenue Agency for the past 3 taxation years, together with a copy of all material filed with the returns and a copy of any notices of assessment or re-assessment that I have received from the Canada Revenue Agency for those years; or

   [ ] a statement from the Canada Revenue Agency that I have not filed any income tax returns for the past 3 years; or

   [x] a direction in Form 13A signed by me to the Taxation Branch of the Canada Revenue Agency for the disclosure of my tax returns and assessments to the other party for the past 3 years.

   I attach proof of my current income, including my most recent

   [x] pay cheque stub.   [ ] employment insurance stub.   [ ] workers' compensation stub.
   [ ] pension stub.   [ ] Other *(Specify.)*

3. [ ] *(check if applicable)* I am an Indian within the meaning of the *Indian Act* (Canada) and all my income is tax exempt and I am not required to file an income tax return. I have therefore not attached an income tax return for the past three years.

PART 6: OTHER INCOME EARNERS IN THE HOME

Complete this part only if you are making or responding to a claim for undue hardship or spousal support. Indicate at paragraph 1 or 2, whether you are living with another person (for example, spouse, roommate or tenant). If you complete paragraph 2, also complete paragraphs 3 to 6.

1. [ ] I live alone

2. I am living with *(full legal name of person)*

3. This person has *(give number)* _____ child(ren) living in the home.

4. This person [ ] works at *(place of work or business)*

   [ ] does not work outside the home.

5. This person [ ] earns *(give amount)* $_____ per _____.
   [ ] does not earn anything.

6. This person [ ] contributes about $_____ per _____ towards the household expenses.
   [ ] contributes no money to the household expenses.

Source: DIVORCEmate Software Inc.

Form 13.1: Financial Statement (Page 5)   Court file number   123456

PART 7: ASSETS IN AND OUT OF ONTARIO

If any sections of Parts 7 to 12 do not apply, do not leave blank, print "NONE" in the section.

The date of marriage is: *(give date)* July 15, 2000

The valuation date is: *(give date)* June 15, 20___

The date of commencement of cohabitation is *(if different from date of marriage)*: *(give date)*

PART 7(a): LAND

*Include any interest in land **owned** on the dates in each of the columns below, including leasehold interests and mortgages. Show estimated market value of your interest, but do not deduct encumbrances or costs of disposition; these encumbrances and costs should be shown under Part 8 "Debts and Other Liabilities".*

Nature & Type of Ownership *(Give your percentage interest where relevant.)*	Address of Property	Estimated Market Value of YOUR Interest		
		on date of marriage	on valuation date	today
Matrimonial Home Joint – 50%	42 Spring Gardens Avenue Aurora ON L2N 4J9		$140,000.00	$140,000.00
83. TOTAL VALUE OF LAND		$0.00	**$140,000.00**	$140,000.00

PART 7(b): GENERAL HOUSEHOLD ITEMS AND VEHICLES

Show estimated market value, not the cost of replacement for these items owned on the dates in each of the columns below. Do not deduct encumbrances or costs of disposition; these encumbrances and costs should be shown under Part 8, "Debts and Other Liabilities."

Item	Description	Indicate if NOT in your possession	Estimated Market Value of YOUR Interest		
			on date of marriage	on valuation date	today
Household goods & furniture	50% of contents	X	$3,000.00	$5,000.00	$5,000.00
Cars, boats, vehicles	20___ Toyota Camry			$20,000.00	$19,000.00
Jewellery, art, electronics, tools, sports & hobby equipment	Electronics	X	$1,000.00	$2,000.00	$2,000.00
Other special items					
84. TOTAL VALUE OF GENERAL HOUSEHOLD ITEMS AND VEHICLES			$4,000.00	**$27,000.00**	$26,000.00

PART 7(c): BANK ACCOUNTS, SAVINGS, SECURITIES AND PENSIONS

Show the items owned on the dates in each of the columns below by category, for example, cash, accounts in financial institutions, pensions, registered retirement or other savings plans, deposit receipts, any other savings, bonds, warrants, options, notes, and other securities. Give your best estimate of the market value of the securities if the items were to be sold on the open market.

Category	Institution *(including location)*/ Description *(including issuer and date)*	Account Number	Amount/Estimated Market Value		
			on date of marriage	on valuation date	today
Joint Savings	Royal Bank of Canada 3500 Yonge Street, Toronto	993320	$10,000.00	$6,000.00	$6,000.00
Joint Chequing	Royal Bank of Canada 3500 Yonge Street, Toronto	423809	$2,000.00	$1,000.00	$1,000.00
100 Shares	Microsoft Corporation			$28,000.00	$32,000.00
85. TOTAL VALUE OF ACCOUNTS, SAVINGS, SECURITIES AND PENSIONS			$12,000.00	**$35,000.00**	$39,000.00

Source: DIVORCEmate Software Inc.

Form 13.1: Financial Statement (Page 6) Court file number 123456

PART 7(d): LIFE & DISABILITY INSURANCE

List all policies in existence on the dates in each of the columns below.

Company, Type & Policy Number	Owner	Beneficiary	Face Amount	Cash Surrender Value		
				on date of marriage	on valuation date	today
Sun Life – Whole Life – Policy No. 429Y3	Husband	Wife	$50,000.00		$10,000.00	$10,100.00
86. TOTAL CASH SURRENDER VALUE OF INSURANCE POLICIES				$0.00	**$10,000.00**	$10,100.00

PART 7(e): BUSINESS INTERESTS

Show any interest in an unincorporated business owned on the dates in each of the columns below. An interest in an incorporated business may be shown here or under "BANK ACCOUNTS, SAVINGS, SECURITIES AND PENSIONS" in Part 7(c). Give your best estimate of market value of your interest.

Name of Firm or Company	Interest	Estimated Market Value of YOUR Interest		
		on date of marriage	on valuation date	today
87. TOTAL VALUE OF BUSINESS INTERESTS		$0.00	**$0.00**	$0.00

PART 7(f): MONEY OWED TO YOU

Give details of all money that other persons owe to you on the dates in each of the columns below, whether because of business or from personal dealings. Include any court judgments in your favour and any estate money and any income tax refunds owed to you.

Details	Amount Owed to You		
	on date of marriage	on valuation date	today
88. TOTAL OF MONEY OWED TO YOU	$0.00	**$0.00**	$0.00

PART 7(g): OTHER PROPERTY

Show other property or assets owned on the dates in each of the columns below. Include property of any kind not listed above. Give your best estimate of market value.

Category	Details	Estimated Market Value of YOUR Interest		
		on date of marriage	on valuation date	today
89. TOTAL OF OTHER PROPERTY		$0.00	**$0.00**	$0.00

90. VALUE OF ALL PROPERTY OWNED ON THE VALUATION DATE (Add items **[83]** to **[89]**.)	$16,000.00	**$212,000.00**	$215,100.00

PART 8: DEBTS AND OTHER LIABILITIES

Show your debts and other liabilities on the dates in each of the columns below. List them by category such as mortgages, charges, liens, notes, credit cards, and accounts payable. Don't forget to include:
- any money owed to the Canada Revenue Agency;
- contingent liabilities such as guarantees or warranties given by you (but indicate that they are contingent); and
- any unpaid legal or professional bills as a result of this case.

Category	Details	Amount Owing		
		on date of marriage	on valuation date	today
Mortgage – Matrimonial Home	Royal Bank of Canada		$100,000.00	$98,000.00
Credit Card Debt	American Express		$1,800.00	$1,500.00
Car Loan	Royal Bank of Canada		$15,000.00	$13,000.00
91. TOTAL OF DEBTS AND OTHER LIABILITIES		$0.00	**$116,800.00**	$112,500.00

Source: DIVORCEmate Software Inc.

Form 13.1: Financial Statement (Page 7) | Court file number | 123456

PART 9: PROPERTY, DEBTS AND OTHER LIABILITIES ON DATE OF MARRIAGE

Show by category the value of your property and your debts and other liabilities **as of the date of your marriage**. *DO NOT INCLUDE THE VALUE OF A MATRIMONIAL HOME THAT YOU OWNED ON THE DATE OF MARRIAGE IF THIS PROPERTY IS STILL A MATRIMONIAL HOME ON THE VALUATION DATE.*

Category and Details	Value on Date of Marriage	
	Assets	Liabilities
Land *(exclude matrimonial home owned on date of marriage, unless sold before date of separation)*	$0.00	
General household items & vehicles	$4,000.00	
Bank accounts, savings, securities, pensions	$12,000.00	
Life & disability insurance	$0.00	
Business interests	$0.00	
Money owed to you	$0.00	
Other property *(Specify.)*	$0.00	
Debts and other liabilities *(Specify.)*		$0.00
Student Loan		$5,000.00
TOTALS	**$16,000.00**	**$5,000.00**
92. NET VALUE OF PROPERTY OWNED ON DATE OF MARRIAGE *(From the total of the "Assets" column, subtract the total of the "Liabilities" column.)*	**$11,000.00**	
93. VALUE OF ALL DEDUCTIONS *(Add items [91] and [92].)*	**$127,800.00**	

PART 10: EXCLUDED PROPERTY

Show by category the value of property owned on the valuation date that is excluded from the definition of "net family property" (such as gifts or inheritances received after marriage).

Category	Details	Value on Valuation Date
Gift or inheritance from third person	100 Microsoft Corporation shares inherited from father	$28,000.00
Income from property expressly excluded by donor/testator		
Damages and settlements for personal injuries, etc.		
Life insurance proceeds		
Traced property		
Excluded property by spousal agreement		
Other excluded property		
94. TOTAL VALUE OF EXCLUDED PROPERTY		**$28,000.00**

PART 11: DISPOSED-OF PROPERTY

Show by category the value of all property that you disposed of during the two years immediately preceding the making of this statement, or during the marriage, whichever period is shorter.

Category	Details	Value
95. TOTAL VALUE OF DISPOSED-OF PROPERTY		**$0.00**

Source: DIVORCEmate Software Inc.

Form 13.1: Financial Statement (Page 8)   Court file number   123456

PART 12: CALCULATION OF NET FAMILY PROPERTY

	Deductions	BALANCE
Value of all property owned on valuation date *(from item **[90]** above)*		$212,000.00
Subtract value of all deductions *(from item **[93]** above)*	$127,800.00	$84,200.00
Subtract total value of all excluded property *(from item **[94]** above)*	$28,000.00	$56,200.00
96. NET FAMILY PROPERTY		$56,200.00

[X]   I do not expect changes in my financial situation.

[ ]   I do expect changes in my financial situation as follows:

[ ]   I attach a proposed budget in the format of Part 4 of this form.

NOTE: *As soon as you find out that the information in this financial statement is incorrect or incomplete, or there is a material change in your circumstances that affects or will affect the information in this financial statement, you MUST serve on every other party to this case and file with the court:*
- *a new financial statement with updated information, or*
- *if changes are minor, an affidavit in Form 14A setting out the details of these changes.*

Sworn/Affirmed before me at:

City of Toronto

(municipality)

in   Province of Ontario

(province, state or country)

on   June   , 20__

(date)

Commissioner for taking affidavits
(Type or print below if signature is illegible.)

Signature
(This form to be signed in front of a lawyer, justice of the peace, notary public or commissioner for taking affidavits.)

Source: DIVORCEmate Software Inc.

ONTARIO

Superior Court of Justice Family Court Branch
(Name of Court)

at **50 Eagle Street West, Newmarket ON L3Y 6B1**
(Court office address)

Court File Number
123456

**Form 13A: Direction to
Canada Revenue
Agency**

Applicant(s)

Full legal name & address for service - street & number, municipality, postal code, telephone & fax numbers and e-mail address (if any).	Lawyer's name & address - street & number, municipality, postal code, telephone & fax numbers and e-mail address (if any).
JOHN CARL MATISKO **4100 Yonge Street, Apt 302** **Toronto ON M2P 1C5** **Tel: 416-332-4398**	**Peter T. Grant** **HILL, JOHNSTON & GRANT** **17 Princess Street South, Suite 2501** **Toronto ON M8Y 3N5** **Tel: 416-354-9900** **Fax: 416-354-9901** **ptgrant@hilljohngrant.com**

Respondent(s)

Full legal name & address for service - street & number, municipality, postal code, telephone & fax numbers and e-mail address (if any).	Lawyer's name & address - street & number, municipality, postal code, telephone & fax numbers and e-mail address (if any).
CHERYL ANNE MATISKO **42 Spring Gardens Avenue** **Aurora ON L2N 4J9** **Tel: 905-869-4335**	**Katherine R. Siegel** **ARMSTRONG, WARD & SIEGEL** **16 Montreal Street West** **Whitby ON L4R 8C2** **Tel: 905-687-4682** **Fax: 905-687-4690** **krsiegel@armstrong.ca**

TO THE CANADA REVENUE AGENCY:

My name is *(full legal name):*   JOHN CARL MATISKO

My latest address shown on tax record is:

4100 Yonge Street, Apt 302, Toronto ON M2P 1C5

My social insurance number is: 123456789

I authorize the Canada Revenue Agency to release to *(name and address of other party or other party's lawyer)*

Katherine R. Siegel, ARMSTRONG, WARD & SIEGEL, 16 Montreal Street West, Whitby ON L4R 8C2

copies of income and deduction printouts showing my income as assessed or re-assessed by the Canada Revenue Agency for the following years:

(Insert previous three years from date of filing application.)

> Ontario's *Family Law Rules* require the release of this information which will be used in this case only for:
> - a claim for support, property or exclusive possession of the matrimonial home and its contents; or
> - any other purpose ordered by the court.
>
> I understand that this information will become part of the court file, which is a public record.

_____ *Date of signature*	_____ *Signature of taxpayer*

Source: DIVORCEmate Software Inc.

ONTARIO

	Court File Number
Superior Court of Justice Family Court Branch	123456
(Name of Court)	

at **50 Eagle Street West, Newmarket ON L3Y 6B1**

(Court office address)

Form 13B: Net Family Property Statement

Applicant(s)

Full legal name & address for service - street & number, municipality, postal code, telephone & fax numbers and e-mail address (if any).	Lawyer's name & address - street & number, municipality, postal code, telephone & fax numbers and e-mail address (if any).
JOHN CARL MATISKO **4100 Yonge Street, Apt 302** **Toronto ON M2P 1C5** **Tel: 416-332-4398**	**Peter T. Grant** **HILL, JOHNSTON & GRANT** **17 Princess Street South, Suite 2501** **Toronto ON M8Y 3N5** **Tel: 416-354-9900** **Fax: 416-354-9901** **ptgrant@hilljohngrant.com**

Respondent(s)

Full legal name & address for service - street & number, municipality, postal code, telephone & fax numbers and e-mail address (if any).	Lawyer's name & address - street & number, municipality, postal code, telephone & fax numbers and e-mail address (if any).
CHERYL ANNE MATISKO **42 Spring Gardens Avenue** **Aurora ON L2N 4J9** **Tel: 905-869-4335**	**Katherine R. Siegel** **ARMSTRONG, WARD & SIEGEL** **16 Montreal Street West** **Whitby ON L4R 8C2** **Tel: 905-687-4682** **Fax: 905-687-4690** **krsiegel@armstrong.ca**

My name is *(full legal name)* JOHN CARL MATISKO

The valuation date for the following material is *(date)* January 1, 2007

The date of marriage is *(date)* July 15, 2000

(Complete the tables by filling in the columns for both parties, showing your assets, debts, etc. and those of your spouse)

Table 1: Value of Assets Owned on Valuation Date (*List in the order of the categories in the financial statement*)

PART 7(a): LAND

Nature & Type of Ownership *(State percentage interest)*	Address of Property	APPLICANT	RESPONDENT
Matrimonial Home – Joint – 50%	42 Spring Gardens Avenue, Aurora ON L2N 4J9	$140,000.00	$140,000.00
	172. Totals: Value of Land	**$140,000.00**	**$140,000.00**

PART 7(b): GENERAL HOUSEHOLD ITEMS AND VEHICLES

Item	Description	APPLICANT	RESPONDENT
Household goods & furniture	Contents of matrimonial home	$5,000.00	$5,000.00
Cars, boats,	20__ Toyota Camry	$20,000.00	
vehicles	20__ Ford Escape		$12,000.00
Jewellery, art, electronics, tools, sports & hobby equipment	Electronics	$2,000.00	$2,000.00
173. Totals: Value of General Household Items and Vehicles		**$27,000.00**	**$19,000.00**

Source: DIVORCEmate Software Inc.

Precedent 18.6 Continued

Form 13B: Net Family Property Statement (page 2)   Court File Number   123456

PART 7(c): BANK ACCOUNTS AND SAVINGS, SECURITIES AND PENSIONS

Category (Savings, Chequing, GIC, RRSP, Pensions, etc.)	Institution	Account Number	APPLICANT	RESPONDENT
Joint Savings	Royal Bank of Canada	993320	$6,000.00	$6,000.00
Joint Chequing	Royal Bank of Canada	423809	$1,000.00	$1,000.00
100 Shares	Microsoft Corporation		$28,000.00	
174. Totals: Value of Accounts and Savings			$35,000.00	$7,000.00

PART 7(d): LIFE AND DISABILITY INSURANCE

Company, Type & Policy No.	Owner	Beneficiary	Face Amount ($)	APPLICANT	RESPONDENT
Sun Life – Whole Life – Policy No. 429Y3	Husband	Wife	50,000	$10,000.00	
176. Totals: Cash Surrender Value of Insurance Policies				$10,000.00	$0.00

PART 7(e): BUSINESS INTERESTS

Name of Firm or Company	Interests	APPLICANT	RESPONDENT
177. Totals: Value of Business Interests		$0.00	$0.00

PART 7(f): MONEY OWED TO YOU

Details	APPLICANT	RESPONDENT
178. Totals: Money Owed to You	$0.00	$0.00

PART 7(g): OTHER PROPERTY

Category	Details	APPLICANT	RESPONDENT
179. Totals: Value of Other Property		$0.00	$0.00

180. VALUE OF PROPERTY OWNED ON THE VALUATION DATE, (TOTAL 1) (Add: item 172 to item 179 inclusive)	$212,000.00	$166,000.00

Table 2: Value of Debts and Liabilities on Valuation Date
PART 8: DEBTS AND OTHER LIABILITIES

Category	Details	APPLICANT	RESPONDENT
Mortgage on Matrimonial Home	Royal Bank of Canada	$100,000.00	$98,000.00
Credit Card Debt	American Express	$1,800.00	
Credit Card Debt	Visa		$2,500.00
Car Loan	Royal Bank of Canada	$15,000.00	
181. Totals: Debts and Other Liabilities, (TOTAL 2)		$116,800.00	$100,500.00

Source: DIVORCEmate Software Inc.

Form 13B: Net Family Property Statement (page 3)   Court File Number   123456

Table 3: Net Value of Property (Other Than a Matrimonial Home) and Debts on Date of Marriage		
PART 9: PROPERTY, DEBTS AND OTHER LIABILITIES ON DATE OF MARRIAGE		
Category and Details	**APPLICANT**	**RESPONDENT**
Land *(Exclude matrimonial home owned on the date of marriage, unless sold before date of separation).*		
General household items and vehicles	$4,000.00	$2,000.00
Bank accounts and savings	$12,000.00	$5,000.00
Life and disability insurance		
Business interests		
Money owed to you		
Other property		
3(a) TOTAL OF PROPERTY ITEMS	**$16,000.00**	**$7,000.00**
Debts and other liabilities *(Specify)* Student Loan	$5,000.00	
3(b) TOTAL OF DEBTS ITEMS	**$5,000.00**	**$0.00**
182. NET VALUE OF PROPERTY OWNED ON DATE OF MARRIAGE, (NET TOTAL 3)	**$11,000.00**	**$7,000.00**

Table 4: PART 10: VALUE OF PROPERTY EXCLUDED UNDER SUBS. 4(2) OF "FAMILY LAW ACT"		
Item	**APPLICANT**	**RESPONDENT**
Gift or inheritance from third person – 100 Microsoft Corporation shares from father	$28,000.00	
Income from property expressly excluded by donor/testator		
Damages and settlements for personal injuries, etc.		
Life insurance proceeds		
Traced property		
Excluded property by spousal agreement		
Other Excluded Property		
184. TOTALS: VALUE OF EXCLUDED PROPERTY, (TOTAL 4)	**$28,000.00**	**$0.00**

TOTAL 2: Debts and Other Liabilities *(item 181)*	$116,800.00	$100,500.00
TOTAL 3: Value of Property Owned on the Date of Marriage *(item 182)*	$11,000.00	$7,000.00
TOTAL 4: Value of Excluded Property *(item 184)*	$28,000.00	$0.00
TOTAL 5: (TOTAL 2 + TOTAL 3 + TOTAL 4)	**$155,800.00**	**$107,500.00**

	APPLICANT	**RESPONDENT**
TOTAL 1: Value of Property Owned on Valuation Date *(item 180)*	$212,000.00	$166,000.00
TOTAL 5: *(from above)*	$155,800.00	$107,500.00
TOTAL 6: NET FAMILY PROPERTY (Subtract: TOTAL 1 minus TOTAL 5)	**$56,200.00**	**$58,500.00**

EQUALIZATION PAYMENTS	**Applicant Pays Respondent**	**Respondent Pays Applicant**
	$0.00	**$1,150.00**

_____   _____
            Signature   *Date of signature*

Source: DIVORCEmate Software Inc.

Ontario

SUPPORT DEDUCTION ORDER
Family Responsibility and Support Arrears Enforcement Act, 1996

Form 1

Court File No.
123456

Superior Court of Justice Family Court Branch
Name of Court

50 Eagle Street West, Newmarket ON L3Y 6B1
Location

Judge

Date

Between

JOHN CARL MATISKO

Applicant/Petitioner/Plaintiff

and

CHERYL ANNE MATISKO

Respondent/Defendant

SUPPORT DEDUCTION ORDER

Upon making an order this day which provides for the payment of support and on making the necessary inquiries required by section 11 of the *Family Responsibility and Support Arrears Enforcement Act, 1996:*

1. **THIS COURT ORDERS THAT**

JOHN CARL MATISKO
(Name of Payor)

    pay support as set out in the attached information form.

2. **THIS COURT ORDERS THAT** any income source that receives notice of this support deduction order make payments to the Director of the Family Responsibility Office in respect of the payor out of money owed to or paid by the income source to the payor.

Signature of Judge, Registrar or Clerk of the Court

Source: DIVORCEmate Software Inc.

Ontario

SUPPORT DEDUCTION ORDER INFORMATION FORM

Family Responsibility and Support Arrears Enforcement Act, 1996

Form 2

	Court File No.
	123456

Name of Court **Superior Court of Justice Family Court Branch**

Location **50 Eagle Street West, Newmarket ON L3Y 6B1**

NOTE: Please Print. Complete Parts A and B ONLY. Leave Parts C, D, E and F blank to be completed by court.

A.   INFORMATION FOR THE FAMILY RESPONSIBILITY OFFICE

INFORMATION ON PARTIES   Family Responsibility Office Case Number *(if known)*

Payor

Payor Name	Birthdate (dd/mm/yyyy)	Sex
JOHN CARL MATISKO	01 01 1975	[x] M [ ] F

Street Number	Unit/Suite/Apt.	Street Name
4100	Apt. 302	Yonge Street

City/Town	Province	Postal Code
Toronto	Ontario	M2P 1C5

Social Insurance Number	Mother's Maiden Name	Language Preference
123 456 789	Snider	English

Home Telephone Number	Work/Business Telephone Number	Cell Phone Number
416-332-4398	416-289-4000	

Recipient

Recipient Name	Birthdate (dd/mm/yyyy)	Sex
CHERYL ANNE MATISKO	15 04 1977	[ ] M [x] F

Street Number	Unit/Suite/Apt.	Street Name
42		Spring Gardens Avenue

City/Town	Province	Postal Code
Aurora	Ontario	L2N 4J9

Social Insurance Number	Mother's Maiden Name	Language Preference
987 654 321	Bolger	English

Home Telephone Number	Work/Business Telephone Number	Cell Phone Number
905-687-4682	905-225-6891	

PAYOR'S EMPLOYMENT

Employer/Income Source Name

Centennial Consulting Inc.

Payroll Office Address

Street Number	Unit/Suite/Apt.	Street Name
4000	Suite 500	Birchmount Avenue

City/Town	Province	Postal Code
Toronto	ON	M3C 4K9

[ ]   Self employed *(provide legal name of business and address)*

[ ]   Unemployed

[ ]   Receiving welfare, family benefits or other form of social assistance

[ ]   Receiving employment insurance benefits

[ ]   Other *(i.e., workers' compensation, pension, etc.)*

[ ]   Recipient does not know

SUPPORT ORDER INFORMATION

Is the support order a variation of a previous support order?   [ ] Yes [X] No   If "Yes", date of previous order

Source: DIVORCEmate Software Inc.

Form 2: Support Deduction Order Information Form (page 2)   Court File Number   123456

C, D, E and F to be COMPLETED BY COURT

B. The attached support deduction order relates to a support order which says that:

C.

TYPE OF SUPPORT ORDER
☐ Temporary   ☐ Final

John Carl Matisko   is required to pay support
Payor Name

for the following persons:

Name	Birthdate (dd/mm/yyyy)	Amount Payable	Frequency	Start Date (dd/mm/yyyy)	End Date (if any) (dd/mm/yyyy)
Spouse:					
a.		$			
Other Dependants					
b. Jesse Brian Matisko	20 03 2002	$			
c.		$			
d.		$			
e.		$			
f.		$			

D.   SPECIAL EXPENSES

Name of Child / Children	Birthdate (dd/mm/yyyy)	Amount	Frequency	Start Date (dd/mm/yyyy)	End Date (if any) (dd/mm/yyyy)
		$			
		$			
		$			
		$			
		$			
		$			

E.   COST OF LIVING ADJUSTMENTS (DOES NOT APPLY TO CHILD SUPPORT)

Support is indexed in accordance with s. 34(5) of the *Family Law Act*   ☐ Yes   ☐ No

If other indexing, explain method of calculation:

F.   ARREARS – If the order is retroactive, if the order is a variation order or if the order provides for an arrears payment schedule, are arrears owing as of the date of the order? ☐ No   ☐ Yes If "Yes" the amount of arrears = $

and the arrears are to be paid as follows (if applicable)

PARTS A AND B COMPLETED BY: (please print)

Name	Title (if solicitor for a party, identify which party)	Telephone Number
Peter T. Grant	Solicitor for Applicant	416-354-9900

Source: DIVORCEmate Software Inc.

CHAPTER 19

Family Law Proceedings

OBJECTIVES:

- Describe the procedures and documentation requirements for a family law case
- Use legal precedents to prepare documentation for family law cases

In some provinces, family law proceedings are by way of action, with a Petition for Divorce as the originating document, and the process is similar to action proceedings as discussed in previous chapters. However, in Ontario, as mentioned in Chapter 18, all family law proceedings are by way of application under the Family Law Rules, which are used in explaining the documentation and procedures for matrimonial proceedings in this chapter. The Family Law Rules provide for more user-friendly documents and proceedings that encourage settlement and timely resolution of cases. The following is a description of some of the common procedural steps and documentation.

CONTINUING RECORD

A **continuing record** is a booklet or booklets that contain a copy of all the written documents in an organized and chronological order for a case. This provides a convenient and complete record for the court for motions and the mandatory conferences. It does not, however, eliminate the need for a trial record.

The continuing record is started by the originating party to the case, served on the other side with the originating document, and is then maintained by all parties to the case. The *Family Law Rules* are very specific on how the record is to be formatted and maintained as follows:

1. Except in certain types of cases (discussed below), the continuing record should consist of
   a. an endorsements volume containing a cumulative table of contents, an endorsements section (with a minimum of three blank sheets of paper for the judge's notations), and an orders section; each section is to be identified by an index tab. This volume requires a yellow cover showing the general heading and the title "Endorsements" in bold, font size 20.
   b. a documents volume containing all documents filed in the case, including applications, answers, replies, affidavits of service, financial statements, motion, affidavits, and trial management conference briefs. Each document is placed behind a separate numbered index tab. When a document is filed, it is inserted into the record under the supervision of the court clerk. The most recent document is inserted at the back, and if an affidavit of service is used as proof of service, it is placed behind the document to which it relates. This volume requires a red cover showing the general heading of the case and the title "Continuing Record" in bold, font size 20 (Precedent 19.1).
2. One cumulative table of contents (in the endorsements volume) is used to list all documents in all volumes (Precedent 19.2). The documents are filed chronologically, with the most recently filed document at the back. The table of contents should list the documents in the order in which they are filed and indicate the volume number and the tab number at which the document is located. The table of contents must be updated every time a document is filed. Thus, whenever a document is served on any other party, an updated table of contents must also be served, and then the document and updated table of contents are filed with the court. Most law firms maintain a "duplicate" continuing record in their office to facilitate this.

3. All documents to be inserted are to be three-hole punched. The court clerk will determine if a volume is full and advise the next party filing a document to create a new volume, which is numbered sequentially (Volume 1, Volume 2, etc.).
4. Additional records may be required if
   a. a support order is filed with the Director of the Family Responsibility Office; then the party doing so (usually the applicant) shall prepare a separate continuing record entitled "Support Enforcement Continuing Record"; the court may also order a separate record for the payor as well entitled "Payor's Enforcement Record." Both such record covers are to be green.
   b. the court orders a separate continuing record for the applicant and the respondent, in which case, the applicant's record cover is to be red and the respondent's record cover is to be blue.
      Any existing endorsements volume in connection with the same case may be used; otherwise, a separate endorsements volume will need to be created.
5. A separate endorsements volume is not required for cases of uncontested or joint application for divorce. Instead, an index tab labelled "Endorsements," with a single blank sheet for the judge's notations on the disposition of the case, should be inserted in the Continuing Record for the case.

MARRIAGE CERTIFICATE

To obtain a divorce, the marriage certificate or a registration of the marriage must be filed with the divorce application. If the client does not have the certificate, information and the necessary forms may be accessed at the Ministry of Government Services website (http://www.cbs.gov.on.ca/MCBS/english/4ULUQT.htm).

COMMENCING THE CASE

All family law cases start by way of application. If the case involves access or custody of children, then it should be started in the municipality in which the children live; otherwise, it may be started in the municipality where a party lives. There are a variety of application form documents appropriate to various circumstances; however, for our purposes, we discuss the usual method of originating a case using Form 8 (Application) or Form 8A (Divorce), which is discussed later in this chapter.

Form 8 (Application) is the most frequently used document to commence a case in family law and is used

1. if a divorce will or may be contested or
2. for any other relief or any claims that may be contested (for example, support, custody, property, etc.).

Precedent 19.3 illustrates Form 8. The court file number is left blank, to be inserted by the court clerk. Most cases proceed on the standard track, which must be selected on the first page. This document is in the form of an affidavit requiring that a series of questions be answered with information that will be obtained from the client. The application must be signed by *both* the client and the lawyer. On this form and many others under the *Family Law Rules*, on the signatory page any empty space must have a black line drawn diagonally through it.

Disposition of Documents

1. The following material is submitted to the local registrar, along with the appropriate filing fee, to originate the family law case:
   - original and one copy of the application
   - Central Divorce Registry form (completed at the courthouse when filing the application)
   - marriage certificate—or explain why it has not been filed in the application
   - financial statement—Form 13 if there is a claim for support or Form 13.1 if there is a claim for support and property, or exclusive possession of the matrimonial home, including the attachments as discussed in Chapter 18
   - Net Family Property Statement (Form 13B) if there is a claim for division of property
2. The court clerk will seal the application and assign a court file number to commence the case. Depending on the type of case and the judicial district, a first court date may be set by the court clerk; however, a mandatory information session or conference is usually required before a court date is set.
3. A copy of the sealed application must be immediately served on the other party by special service (as discussed below) with a copy of any financial statement and a copy of the continuing record.
4. Once served, a copy of all of these documents must be filed along with proof of service (added to the continuing record) with the court. If there is any claim for support, a support deduction information form and order (as discussed in Chapter 18) must also be filed with the court.
5. The original sealed application is placed in the Document subfile; copies are made for the file and the law firm's copy of the continuing record. Additional copies will be required if a trial record is required.

SERVICE OF DOCUMENTS

Under the *Family Law Rules*, court documents may be served in one of two ways: special service (similar to personal service, discussed in Chapter 11) or regular service (referred to as ordinary service in Chapter 11). A standard affidavit of service form (Precedent 19.4) is used for all methods of service.

Special Service

1. *Personal service.* Hand-delivering a copy of the document to the other party. Service would be effective the same day, unless it is delivered after 4 p.m.; then service would be effective on the next day that is not a holiday. An affidavit of service is completed by the person who hand-delivered the document.

2. *Service on solicitor.* Leaving a copy with the person's lawyer (provided that they accept service). Service would be effective the same day, unless it is delivered after 4 p.m.; then service would be effective on the next day that is not a holiday. A completed admission of service stamp on a copy of the document is the proof of service.
3. *Regular mail, with acknowledgement of service card (Form 6).* Service would be effective on the date the person acknowledges service, as shown on the bottom of the card. An affidavit of service and the completed card would be the proof of service.
4. *Serving at place of residence.* Leaving a copy of the document at the party's place of residence with an adult person and subsequently mailing another copy. Service is effective five days after mailing the document. An affidavit of service is completed by the person who delivered the document.

Regular Service

1. *Regular mail.* Service would be effective five days after mailing, and an affidavit of service would be completed by the person mailing the document.
2. *Courier.* Service would be effective the day after the courier picks it up, and an affidavit of service would be completed by the person arranging for the courier.
3. *Document exchange.* Service would be effective the day *after* the document is date stamped by the document exchange. The date stamp on the document would be the proof of service.
4. *Fax.* Service would be effective the same day as long it is before 4 p.m.; otherwise, it would be the next day that is not a holiday. An affidavit of service would be completed by the person faxing the document. The requirements regarding a fax cover page and the maximum number of pages that may be faxed are essentially the same as for documents served under the *Rules of Civil Procedure*, as explained in Chapter 11. The only significant difference is that documents must be faxed on days that the courthouse is open and before 4 p.m.
5. *Special Service.* Any of the special service methods mentioned above may also be used for regular service. The effective dates and proof of service would be as required by each of those methods.

Any originating document (the application), *some* notices of motion as specified in the *Family Law Rules*, and a summons to witness *must* be served by special service; all other documents may be served by regular service.

ANSWER AND REPLY

Any answer to an application must be delivered within 30 days of service of the application if served within Canada or the United States and within 60 days if served outside Canada or the United States. The answer document is similar to a statement of defence in an action in which the respondent may set out his or her version of the facts. The applicant may, if he or she wishes, also file a reply within

10 days of being served with the answer. A minimum of four copies of the answer or reply should be prepared. One copy would be served on the other side, one copy would be filed with the proof of service, one copy is for the office file, and one copy is for the continuing record maintained by the law firm.

CONFERENCES

In any case in which an answer is filed, at least one case conference must be held, and a judge may also hold a settlement conference and a trial management conference. The purpose of these conferences is to try and focus issues, ensure disclosure of relevant evidence, encourage settlement on some or all of the issues, and set the date for the next step in the case.

Before each conference, the following steps must be taken:

1. The party requesting the conference, usually the applicant, must serve on the other party and then file with proof of service at least seven days before the date of any conference
   a. a case conference notice (Precedent 19.5) setting out the date and time of the conference and briefly stating the issues of the case and
   b. a brief (Precedent 19.6), which requires that a series of questions be answered by the party to focus the conference on the unresolved issues.
2. Any responding party must serve and file their brief not later than four days before the date of any conference.
3. A confirmation form (Precedent 19.7) must also be filed with the court by all parties to the case not later than 2 p.m. two days before the date scheduled for the conference.

The case conference is held first, and if the case cannot be resolved at this conference, then a settlement conference and a trial management conference will be scheduled. The Family Law Rules allow that there may a "blending" of any of these conferences, and if the conferences are not successful in settling the case, then a trial date will be scheduled. Only the trial management conference brief is filed in the continuing record, unless ordered otherwise by the court.

MOTIONS

As discussed in Chapter 13, motions are interlocutory proceedings that ask the court or a judge to make a decision during the course of the case. Motion hearings for temporary orders are frequently held in family law cases because of the need for immediate decisions with regard to child custody or support issues. For example, one spouse may require an interim order setting out who has custody of any children of the marriage until the date of any conference or hearing. Motions may be conducted in writing, in court with the parties and/or their lawyers in attendance, or by videoconference or telephone conference with the consent of the parties. As with civil motions, evidence is presented by affidavit; oral testimony is allowed only with the permission of the court. Motions are not allowed before the case conference, except in hardship or urgent circumstances.

The following outlines the procedures and documents required for a motion made with notice in a family law case:

1. Obtain a date for the motion hearing from the court office.
2. Prepare a notice of motion (Precedent 19.8) setting out the date of the hearing, check off the box stating that an affidavit is served in support, list any documents that are contained in the continuing record that will be relied on, and state what order or orders are to be requested at the motion hearing.
3. Prepare an affidavit in support setting each fact as a separate numbered paragraph.
4. Serve the notice of motion, the affidavit, an updated financial statement (if applicable), and an updated cumulative continuing record table of contents on the other party at least four days before the hearing date of the motion.
5. File with proof of service the motion documents (listed in 4) as soon as possible after service but not later than two days before the hearing date of the motion.
6. Prepare a confirmation form confirming that the other side has or has not been contacted and file it with the court no later than 2 p.m. two days before the hearing date of the motion.

SUMMONS TO WITNESS

Unlike in a civil proceeding, the summons is prepared, served, and filed by the lawyer or the party. The court is not involved in issuing summonses for Family Court witnesses. The legal assistant would be required to prepare three copies of the summons, requisition the necessary cheque for payment of witness fees, and then provide whoever is serving the summons with two copies of the summons and the necessary cheque. Precedent 19.9 illustrates a completed summons to witness.

The witness fees under the Family Law Rules are slightly different from the tariff in the Rules of Civil Procedure and are as follows:

1. $50 for each day in court
2. travel money in the amount of
   a. $5 if the person lives in the city or town where they will give evidence;
   b. 30 cents per kilometre each way if the person lives within 300 kilometres of the court;
   c. the least expensive airfare available plus $10 a day for airport parking and 30 cents per kilometre each way from the person's home to the airport and from the airport to the court if the person lives more than 300 kilometres away from the court; and
3. $100 per night for meals and overnight accommodation if the person does not live in the city or town where the court is located.

These amounts were correct as of December 31, 2007.

TRIAL RECORD

All cases, if not already settled or withdrawn, must be set down for trial within 365 days of commencing the case. A notice will be sent by the court clerk to all parties shortly before the expiration of the 365-day period stating that the case will be dismissed if not set down within 60 days of receipt of the notice.

The trial record must be delivered by the applicant at least 14 days before the trial date containing a table of contents and the following documents. These documents may be photocopies as the originals will have been included in the continuing record:

1. The application, answer, and reply, if any
2. Any agreed statement of fact
3. Financial statements and net family property statements, if relevant to an issue at trial; these statements must be current to not more than 30 days before the record is served
4. Any assessment report
5. Any temporary order relating to a matter still in dispute
6. An order relating to the trial
7. Any relevant parts of any transcript on which the party intends to rely at trial
8. Any expert report on which the party intends to rely at trial

The respondent may make additions to the record up to seven days before the trial. It should be noted that the continuing record is not provided to the trial judge.

ORDERS

Under the *Family Law Rules*, all decisions of the court are called orders; there are no judgments. Orders are prepared by the successful party using the format illustrated in Precedent 19.10. The draft order must be served on all other parties for approval as to form and content, and then two copies of the order are taken to the court to be sealed and signed. A copy of the signed order must then be served (by regular service) on the other party. A support deduction order does not have to be served.

All orders made during the course of a case are filed with proof of service in the endorsement section of the continuing record.

SIMPLE DIVORCE

Quite often in family law cases, by the time people apply for a divorce, they have previously resolved issues such as custody, child or spousal support, and the division of family property. Thus, the divorce may be uncontested or undefended by the respondent or be a joint application by both spouses.

In such circumstances, Form 8A (Divorce) is therefore used for

1. joint or uncontested divorces or
2. joint divorces with additional claims as long as those claims are uncontested.

There are no motion hearings or trials for a simple divorce, and a separate endorsements volume of the continuing record is not required, as discussed earlier in this chapter. The application and supporting documents are submitted to the court office, reviewed by a judge, and, if satisfactory, a divorce will be granted.

Uncontested/Undefended Divorce

The original and one copy of the application (Precedent 19.11), along with the completed Central Divorce Registry form, the marriage certificate, and financial statements (if required), are prepared and taken to the court office to start the case. A copy of the sealed application is served by special service on the respondent. If the respondent does not file an answer within the required time, or if the answer is struck out, the applicant files the following documents with the court to obtain a divorce order:

1. an affidavit for divorce (Precedent 19.12) confirming that the information in the application is correct and provides information about any arrangements for support of any children of the marriage; any applicable income and financial information required by the child support guidelines of the *Family Law Act* should be attached as exhibits to the affidavit;
2. three copies of a draft divorce order (Precedent 19.13);
3. a stamped envelope addressed to each party; and
4. if the divorce order contains a support order,
   a. an extra copy of the draft divorce order for the clerk to file with the Director of the Family Responsibility Office and
   b. two copies of the draft support deduction order.

Once the 30-day waiting period has expired, either party may request the court clerk to mail the divorce certificate to the parties.

Joint Application for Divorce

For a joint divorce, in which there are no claims or any claim that is made will be uncontested, the parties may proceed by way of joint application for divorce. Both spouses will be applicants in the general heading. The husband, wife, and each of their lawyers (if applicable) are all required to sign on page 4 (Precedent 19.11).

The original and one copy of the application, along with the completed Central Divorce Registry form and the marriage certificate, are taken to the court office to commence the case. The application obviously does not need to be served on any other party in a joint application. The documents discussed in items 1 through 4 for uncontested divorce will need to be provided to the court; then, once the 30-day waiting period has expired, either party may request the court clerk to mail the divorce certificate to the parties.

Terms and Concepts

continuing record	case conference
endorsements volume	settlement conference
documents volume	trial management conference
marriage certificate	case conference notice
application	brief
Central Divorce Registry form	confirmation
financial statement	summons
Net Family Property Statement	witness fees
special service	trial record
regular service	orders
answer	simple divorce
reply	uncontested and joint divorce applications

Review Questions

1. Briefly describe the preparation and maintenance of a continuing record.

2. Under what circumstances would you prepare a
   a. application (general)?
   b. application (divorce)?

3. What other documents may be required to be filed with the court when an application is filed?

4. List and briefly describe the methods of
   a. special service
   b. regular service

5. What conferences are required to be held during the course of a family law case, and what is the purpose of these conferences?

6. Mario lives 250 kilometres from the courthouse where he is required as a witness for 2 days of a divorce trial. What will you need to do to summon this witness?

7. Is a motion hearing required for an uncontested or joint application for a divorce under the *Family Law Rules*? Explain.

Superior Court of Justice Family Court Branch
(Name of Court)

Court File Number
442103

at   **33 King Street West, Oshawa ON L1H 1A1**
(Court office address)

Volume: **1**

Applicant(s)

Full legal name & address for service - street & number, municipality, postal code, telephone & fax numbers and e-mail address (if any).	*Lawyer's name & address - street & number, municipality, postal code, telephone & fax numbers and e-mail address (if any).*
LAUREN MICHELLE COHEN **450 Martindale Road, Unit 113** **Oshawa ON L2D 3A8** **Tel: 905-488-9887**	**Peter T. Grant** **HILL, JOHNSTON & GRANT** **17 Princess Street South, Suite 2501** **Toronto ON M8Y 3N5** **Tel: 416-354-9900** **Fax: 416-354-9901** **ptgrant@hilljohngrant.com**

Respondent(s)

Full legal name & address for service - street & number, municipality, postal code, telephone & fax numbers and e-mail address (if any).	*Lawyer's name & address - street & number, municipality, postal code, telephone & fax numbers and e-mail address (if any).*
MATTHEW RICHARD COHEN **350 Walkerton Road, Apt. 303** **Whitby ON L6Q 6B2** **Tel: 905-422-9876**	**Katherine R. Siegel** **ARMSTRONG, WARD & SIEGEL** **16 Montreal Street West** **Whitby ON L4R 8C2** **Tel: 905-687-4682** **Fax: 905-687-4690** **krsiegel@armstrong.ca**

Children's Lawyer

Name & address of Children's Lawyer's agent for service (street & number, municipality, postal code, telephone & fax numbers, and e-mail address (if any)), and name of person represented.

Continuing Record

Source: DIVORCEmate Software Inc.

ONTARIO

Superior Court of Justice Family Court Branch	**Court File Number**
(Name of Court)	442103

at **33 King Street West, Oshawa ON L1H 1A1**

(Court office address)

Cumulative Table of Contents
Continuing Record

Applicant(s)

Full legal name & address for service - street & number, municipality, postal code, telephone & fax numbers and e-mail address (if any).	*Lawyer's name & address - street & number, municipality, postal code, telephone & fax numbers and e-mail address (if any).*
LAUREN MICHELLE COHEN **450 Martindale Road, Unit 113** **Oshawa ON L2D 3A8** **Tel: 905-488-9887**	**Peter T. Grant** **HILL, JOHNSTON & GRANT** **17 Princess Street South, Suite 2501** **Toronto ON M8Y 3N5** **Tel: 416-354-9900** **Fax: 416-354-9901** **ptgrant@hilljohngrant.com**

Respondent(s)

Full legal name & address for service - street & number, municipality, postal code, telephone & fax numbers and e-mail address (if any).	*Lawyer's name & address - street & number, municipality, postal code, telephone & fax numbers and e-mail address (if any).*
MATTHEW RICHARD COHEN **350 Walkerton Road, Apt. 303** **Whitby ON L6Q 6B2** **Tel: 905-422-9876**	**Katherine R. Siegel** **ARMSTRONG, WARD & SIEGEL** **16 Montreal Street West** **Whitby ON L4R 8C2** **Tel: 905-687-4682** **Fax: 905-687-4690** **krsiegel@armstrong.ca**

Document *(For an affidavit or transcript of evidence, include the name of the person who gave the affidavit or the evidence.)*	**Filed by** *(A = applicant or R = respondent)*	**Date of Document** *(d, m, y)*	**Date of Filing** *(d, m, y)*	**Volume/Tab**
Application	A	07/08/20__	10/08/20__	Volume 1, Tab 1
Affidavit of Service of Application on Respondent	A	09/08/20__	10/08/20__	Volume 1, Tab 1
Financial Statement	A	07/08/20__	10/08/20__	Volume 1, Tab 2
Answer	R	25/08/20__	28/08/20__	Volume 1, Tab 3
Affidavit of Service of Answer on Applicant	R	26/08/20__	28/08/20__	Volume 1, Tab 3
Notice of Motion	A	27/08/20__	28/08/20__	Volume 1, Tab 4

☒ *Continued on next sheet*

Source: DIVORCEmate Software Inc.

ONTARIO

Superior Court of Justice Family Court Branch

(Name of Court)

SEAL

at **33 King Street West, Oshawa ON L1H 1A1**

(Court office address)

Court File Number

**Form 8: Application
(General)**

Applicant(s)

Full legal name & address for service - street & number, municipality, postal code, telephone & fax numbers and e-mail address (if any).	*Lawyer's name & address - street & number, municipality, postal code, telephone & fax numbers and e-mail address (if any).*
LAUREN MICHELLE COHEN **450 Martindale Road, Unit 113** **Oshawa ON L2D 3A8** **Tel: 905-488-9887**	**Peter T. Grant** **HILL, JOHNSTON & GRANT** **17 Princess Street South, Suite 2501** **Toronto ON M8Y 3N5** **Tel: 416-354-9900** **Fax: 416-354-9901** **ptgrant@hilljohngrant.com**

Respondent(s)

Full legal name & address for service - street & number, municipality, postal code, telephone & fax numbers and e-mail address (if any).	*Lawyer's name & address - street & number, municipality, postal code, telephone & fax numbers and e-mail address (if any).*
MATTHEW RICHARD COHEN **350 Walkerton Road, Apt. 303** **Whitby ON L6Q 6B2** **Tel: 905-422-9876**	**Katherine R. Siegel** **ARMSTRONG, WARD & SIEGEL** **16 Montreal Street West** **Whitby ON L4R 8C2** **Tel: 905-687-4682** **Fax: 905-687-4690** **krsiegel@armstrong.ca**

TO THE RESPONDENT(S):

A COURT CASE HAS BEEN STARTED AGAINST YOU IN THIS COURT. THE DETAILS ARE SET OUT ON THE ATTACHED PAGES.

☐ **THE FIRST COURT DATE IS** *(date)* _____ **AT** _____ ☐ **a.m.** ☐ **p.m.** or as soon as possible after that time, at: *(address)*

NOTE: If this is a divorce case, no date will be set unless an Answer is filed. If you have also been served with a notice of motion, there may be an earlier court date and you or your lawyer should come to court for the motion.

☐ **THIS CASE IS ON THE FAST TRACK OF THE CASE MANAGEMENT SYSTEM.** A case management judge will be assigned by the time this case first comes before a judge.

☒ **THIS CASE IS ON THE STANDARD TRACK OF THE CASE MANAGEMENT SYSTEM. No court date has been set for this case** but, if you have been served with a notice of motion, it has a court date and you or your lawyer should come to court for the motion. A case management judge will not be assigned until one of the parties asks the clerk of the court to schedule a case conference or until a motion is scheduled, whichever comes first.

IF, AFTER 365 DAYS, THE CASE HAS NOT BEEN SCHEDULED FOR TRIAL, the clerk of the court will send out a warning that the case will be dismissed within 60 days unless the parties file proof that the case has been settled or one of the parties asks for a case or a settlement conference.

IF YOU WANT TO OPPOSE ANY CLAIM IN THIS CASE, you or your lawyer must prepare an Answer (Form 10 - a blank copy should be attached), serve a copy on the applicant(s) and file a copy in the court office with an Affidavit of Service (Form 6B). **YOU HAVE ONLY 30 DAYS AFTER THIS APPLICATION IS SERVED ON YOU (60 DAYS IF THIS APPLICATION IS SERVED ON YOU OUTSIDE CANADA OR THE UNITED STATES) TO SERVE AND FILE AN ANSWER. IF YOU DO NOT, THE CASE WILL GO AHEAD WITHOUT YOU AND THE COURT MAY MAKE AN ORDER AND ENFORCE IT AGAINST YOU.**

Source: DIVORCEmate Software Inc.

Form 8: Application (General) (page 2)   Court File Number ▢

Check the box of the paragraph that applies to your case

▢ This case includes a claim for support. It does not include a claim for property or exclusive possession of the matrimonial home and its contents. You **MUST** fill out a Financial Statement (Form 13 - a blank copy is attached), serve a copy on the applicant(s) and file a copy in the court office with an *Affidavit of Service* even if you do not answer this case.

☒ This case includes a claim for property or exclusive possession of the matrimonial home and its contents. You **MUST** fill out a Financial Statement (Form 13.1 - a blank copy attached), serve a copy on the applicant(s) and file a copy in the court office with an *Affidavit of Service* even if you do not answer this case.

IF YOU WANT TO MAKE A CLAIM OF YOUR OWN, you or your lawyer must fill out the claim portion in the Answer, serve a copy on the applicant(s) and file a copy in the court office with an *Affidavit of Service*.

- If you want to make a claim for support but do not want to make a claim for property or exclusive possession of the matrimonial home and its contents, you **MUST** fill out a Financial Statement (Form 13), serve a copy on the applicant(s) and file a copy in the court office.
- However, if your only claim for support is for child support in the table amount specified under the Child Support Guidelines, you do not need to fill out, serve or file a Financial Statement.
- If you want to make a claim for property or exclusive possession of the matrimonial home and its contents, whether or not it includes a claim for support, you **MUST** fill out a Financial Statement (Form 13.1, not Form 13), serve a copy on the applicant(s), and file a copy in the court office.

YOU SHOULD GET LEGAL ADVICE ABOUT THIS CASE RIGHT AWAY. If you cannot afford a lawyer, you may be able to get help from your local Legal Aid Ontario office. (*See your telephone directory under LEGAL AID.*)

_____   _____
Date of issue   *Clerk of the court*

Source: DIVORCEmate Software Inc.

Form 8: Application (General) (page 3)   Court File Number

FAMILY HISTORY

APPLICANT: Age: 32   Birthdate: *(d, m, y)*   10 July 1975

Resident in *(municipality & province)*   Oshawa, Ontario

since *(date)*   01 July 2000

Surname at birth: Newman

Surname just before marriage: Newman

Divorced before?   [X] No   [ ] Yes *(Place and date of previous divorce)*

RESPONDENT: Age: 37   Birthdate: *(d, m, y)*   08 September 1970

Resident in *(municipality & province)*   Whitby, Ontario

since *(date)*   15 June 2006

Surname at birth: Cohen

Surname just before marriage: Cohen

Divorced before?   [X] No   [ ] Yes *(Place and date of previous divorce)*

RELATIONSHIP DATES:

[x] Married on *(date)*   01 July 2000   [ ] Started living together on *(date)*

[x] Separated on *(date)*   15 June 20___   [ ] Never lived together   [ ] Still living together

---

THE CHILD(REN): *List all children involved in this case, even if no claim is made for these children.*

Full legal name	Age	Birthdate *(d, m, y)*	Resident in *(municipality & province)*	Now Living with *(name of person and relationship to child)*
Sarah Jessica Cohen	5	04 June 2002	Oshawa, Ontario	Lauren Michelle Cohen - Mother

PREVIOUS CASES OR AGREEMENTS

Have the parties or the children been in a court case before?

[X] No   [ ] Yes

Have the parties made a written agreement dealing with any matter involved in this case?

[X] No   [ ] Yes *(Give date of agreement. Indicate which of its items are in dispute.)*

Source: DIVORCEmate Software Inc.

Form 8: Application (General) (page 4) Court File Number [   ]

CLAIM BY APPLICANT

I ASK THE COURT FOR THE FOLLOWING: *(Claims below include claims for temporary orders.)*

Claims under the *Divorce Act* *(Check boxes in this column only if you are asking for a divorce and your case is in the Superior Court of Justice or Family Court of the Superior Court of Justice.)*	Claims under the *Family Law Act* or *Children's Law Reform Act*	Claims relating to property *(Check boxes in this column only if your case is in the Superior Court of Justice or Family Court of the Superior Court of Justice.)*
00 ☐ a divorce	10 ☐ support for me	20 ☒ equalization of net family properties
01 ☐ support for me	11 ☒ support for child(ren) – table amount	21 ☐ exclusive possession of matrimonial home
02 ☒ support for child(ren) – table amount	12 ☐ support for child(ren) – other than table amount	22 ☐ exclusive possession of contents of matrimonial home
03 ☐ support for child(ren) – other than table amount	13 ☒ custody of child(ren)	23 ☐ freezing assets
04 ☒ custody of child(ren)	14 ☐ access to child(ren)	24 ☐ sale of family property
05 ☐ access to child(ren)	15 ☐ restraining/non-harassment order	
	16 ☐ indexing spousal support	
	17 ☐ declaration of parentage	
	18 ☐ guardianship over child's property	

Other claims

30 ☒ costs

31 ☐ annulment of marriage

32 ☐ prejudgment interest

50 ☐ Other *(Specify.)* [   ]

Give details of the order that you want the court to make. *(Include any amounts of support (if known) and the names of the children for whom support, custody or access is claimed.)*

1. Custody of the child Sarah Jessica Cohen born 04 June 2002.

2. Support for the child Sarah Jessica Cohen in accordance with Child Support Guidelines in the amount of $557.00 per month.

3. Equalization of the net family property of the marriage.

4. Costs.

IMPORTANT FACTS SUPPORTING MY CLAIM FOR DIVORCE

☒ **Separation:** The spouses have lived separate and apart since *(date)* 15 June 20 [   ] and

☒ have not lived together again since that date in an unsuccessful attempt to reconcile.

☐ have lived together again during the following period(s) in an unsuccessful attempt to reconcile:
(Give dates.) [   ]

☐ **Adultery:** The respondent has committed adultery. *(Give details. It is not necessary to name any other person involved but, if you do name the other person, then you must serve this application on the other person.)* [   ]

Source: DIVORCEmate Software Inc.

Form 8: Application (General) (page 5)　　　　　Court File Number

☐ **Cruelty:** The respondent has treated the applicant with physical or mental cruelty of such a kind as to make continued cohabitation intolerable. *(Give details.)*

IMPORTANT FACTS SUPPORTING MY OTHER CLAIM(S)

(Set out below the facts that form the legal basis for your other claim(s).)

1. The child Sarah Jessica Cohen has always lived with me and I have always been primary caregiver.

2. The child Sarah Jessica Cohen is settled in her home, in her community, and at her school, which provides after-school daycare while I am at work.

3. The respondent is employed as a paramedic and earns an annual salary of $60,000.00.

4. The applicant and respondent separated abruptly and not amicably, and there has been no financial disclosure or discussion of the equalization of the family assets.

Put a line through any blank space left on this page.

_____　　　　　_____
Date of signature　　　　　　　　　　　Signature of applicant

LAWYER'S CERTIFICATE

For divorce cases only

My name is:　Peter T. Grant

and I am the applicant's lawyer in this divorce case. I certify that I have complied with the requirements of section 9 of the *Divorce Act*.

_____　　　　　_____
Date　　　　　　　　　　　　　　　　　Signature of Lawyer

ONTARIO

Superior Court of Justice Family Court Branch
(Name of Court)

at **33 King Street West, Oshawa ON L1H 1A1**
(Court office address)

Court File Number
442103

Form 6B: Affidavit of Service
Sworn/Affirmed

| August | , 20__ |

Applicant(s)

Full legal name & address for service - street & number, municipality, postal code, telephone & fax numbers and e-mail address (if any).	Lawyer's name & address - street & number, municipality, postal code, telephone & fax numbers and e-mail address (if any).
LAUREN MICHELLE COHEN **450 Martindale Road, Unit 113** **Oshawa ON L2D 3A8** **Tel: 905-488-9887**	**Peter T. Grant** **HILL, JOHNSTON & GRANT** **17 Princess Street South, Suite 2501** **Toronto ON M8Y 3N5** **Tel: 416-354-9900** **Fax: 416-354-9901** **ptgrant@hilljohngrant.com**

Respondent(s)

Full legal name & address for service - street & number, municipality, postal code, telephone & fax numbers and e-mail address (if any).	Lawyer's name & address - street & number, municipality, postal code, telephone & fax numbers and e-mail address (if any).
MATTHEW RICHARD COHEN **350 Walkerton Road, Apt. 303** **Whitby ON L6Q 6B2** **Tel: 905-422-9876**	**Katherine R. Siegel** **ARMSTRONG, WARD & SIEGEL** **16 Montreal Street West** **Whitby ON L4R 8C2** **Tel: 905-687-4682** **Fax: 905-687-4690** **krsiegel@armstrong.ca**

My name is
(full legal name)   **JENNIFER MONIQUE STAUFFER**

I live in
(municipality and province)   **the City of Toronto, Province of Ontario**

And I swear/affirm that the following is true:

1. On *(date)* **09 August 20__** , I served *(name of person to be served)*
Matthew Richard Cohen

with the following document(s) in this case: *(List the documents served.)*

Name of document	Author (if applicable)	Date when document signed, issued, sworn, etc.
Application	Applicant	07/08/20__
Financial Statement	Applicant	07/08/20__

NOTE: *You can leave out any part of this form that is not applicable.*

2. I served the document(s) mentioned in paragraph 1 by:

Check one box only and go to indicated paragraph.

[X] special service. *(Go to paragraph 3 below if you used special service.)*

[ ] mail. *(Go to paragraph 4 if you used mailed service.)*

[ ] courier. *(Go to paragraph 5 if you used courier.)*

[ ] deposit at a document exchange. *(Go to paragraph 6 if you used a document exchange.)*

[ ] fax. *(Go to paragraph 7 if you used fax..)*

[ ] substituted service or advertisement. *(Go to paragraph 8 if you used substituted service or advertisement.)*

Source: DIVORCEmate Software Inc.

Precedent 19.4 Continued

Form 6B: Affidavit of Service (page 2)   Court File Number   442103

dated August   , 20__

3. I carried out special service of the document(s) on the person named in paragraph 1 at *(place or address)*
    350 Walkerton Road, Apt. 303, Whitby ON L6Q 6B2
    by:

    [X] leaving a copy with the person.

    [ ] leaving a copy with *(name)*. _____

*Check one box only.
Strike out
paragraphs 4 to 8
and go to paragraph
9.*

    [ ] who is a lawyer who accepted service in writing on a copy of the document.

    [ ] who is the person's lawyer of record.

    [ ] who is the *(office or position)*. _____
         of the corporation named in paragraph 1.

    [ ] mailing a copy to the person together with a prepaid return postcard in Form 6 in an envelope
         bearing the sender's return address. This postcard, in which receipt of the document(s) is
         acknowledged, was returned and is attached to this affidavit.

    [ ] leaving a copy in a sealed envelope addressed to the person at the person's place of residence
         with *(name)* _____
         who provided me with identification to show that he/she was an adult person residing at the same
         address and by mailing another copy of the same document(s) on the same or following day to the
         person named in paragraph 1 at that place of residence.

    [ ] other *(Specify. See rule 6 for details.)*
         _____

4. I mailed the document(s) to be served by addressing the covering envelope to the person named in paragraph 1
    at: *(set out address.)* _____

    which is the address

    [ ] of the person's place of business.

    [ ] of a lawyer who accepted service on the person's behalf.

*Check appropriate paragraph and
strike out paragraphs 3, 5, 6, 7, 8
and 9.*

    [ ] of the person's lawyer of record.

    [ ] of the person's home.

    [ ] on the document most recently filed in court by the person.

    [ ] other *(Specify.)*
         _____

5. The document(s) to be served was/were placed in an envelope that was picked up at *(time)* _____
    on *(date)* _____ by *(courier service)* _____
    a private courier service, a copy of whose receipt is attached to this affidavit.
    The envelope was addressed to the person named in paragraph 1 at *(Set out address.)*
    _____

    which is the address

    [ ] of the person's place of business.

    [ ] of a lawyer who accepted service on the person's behalf.

*Check appropriate paragraph and
strike out paragraphs 3, 4, 6, 7, 8
and 9.*

    [ ] of the person's lawyer of record.

    [ ] of the person's home.

    [ ] on the document most recently filed in court by the person.

    [ ] other *(Specify.)*
         _____

PRECEDENT 19.4   2

Source: DIVORCEmate Software Inc.

Form 6B: Affidavit of Service (page 3)   **Court File Number**   442103

dated August   , 20__

6.   The document(s) was/were deposited at a document exchange. The exchange's date stamp on the attached copy shows the date of the deposit. *(Strike out paragraphs 3, 4, 5, 7, 8 and 9.)*

7.   The document(s) to be served was/were faxed. The fax confirmation is attached to this affidavit. *(Strike out paragraphs 3, 4, 5, 6, 8 and 9.)*

8.   An order of this court made on *(date)*   allowed

☐   substituted service.

☐   service by advertisement. *(Attach advertisement.)*

The order was carried out as follows: *(Give details. Then go to paragraph 9 if you had to travel to serve substitutionally or by advertisement.)*

9.   To serve the document(s), I had to travel   20   kilometres. My fee for service of the document(s) is

$ 25.00   , including travel.

Sworn/Affirmed before me at:

City of Toronto

                              (municipality)

in   Province of Ontario

                              (province, state or country)

on   August   , 20__

          (date)

                    Commissioner for taking affidavits
     (Type or print name below if signature is illegible.)

          Signature
(This form is to be signed in front of a lawyer,
justice of the peace, notary public or
commissioner for taking affidavits.)

NEL

ONTARIO

Court File Number
442103

Superior Court of Justice Family Court Branch
(Name of Court)

**Form 17:
Conference
Notice**

at **33 King Street West, Oshawa ON L1H 1A1**
(Court office address)

Applicant(s)

Full legal name & address for service - street & number, municipality, postal code, telephone & fax numbers and e-mail address (if any).	Lawyer's name & address - street & number, municipality, postal code, telephone & fax numbers and e-mail address (if any).
LAUREN MICHELLE COHEN **450 Martindale Road, Unit 113** **Oshawa ON L2D 3A8** **Tel: 905-488-9887**	**Peter T. Grant** **HILL, JOHNSTON & GRANT** **17 Princess Street South, Suite 2501** **Toronto ON M8Y 3N5** **Tel: 416-354-9900** **Fax: 416-354-9901** **ptgrant@hilljohngrant.com**

Respondent(s)

Full legal name & address for service - street & number, municipality, postal code, telephone & fax numbers and e-mail address (if any).	Lawyer's name & address - street & number, municipality, postal code, telephone & fax numbers and e-mail address (if any).
MATTHEW RICHARD COHEN **350 Walkerton Road, Apt. 303** **Whitby ON L6Q 6B2** **Tel: 905-422-9876**	**Katherine R. Siegel** **ARMSTRONG, WARD & SIEGEL** **16 Montreal Street West** **Whitby ON L4R 8C2** **Tel: 905-687-4682** **Fax: 905-687-4690** **krsiegel@armstrong.ca**

Name & address of Children's Lawyer's agent (street & number, municipality, postal code, telephone & fax numbers and e-mail address (if any)) and name of person represented.

TO: *(name of party or parties or lawyer(s))* Matthew Richard Cohen

A [X] CASE CONFERENCE [ ] SETTLEMENT CONFERENCE [ ] TRIAL MANAGEMENT CONFERENCE

WILL BE HELD AT *(place of conference)*
33 King Street West, Oshawa ON L1H 1A1

at *(time)* 10:00 a.m. **on** *(date)* 20 September 20___

The conference has been arranged at the request of [X] the applicant [ ] the respondent

[ ] the case management judge [ ] *(Other; specify.)* _____

to deal with the following issues:
1.   Custody of the child Sarah Jessica Cohen born 04 June 2002
2.   Equalization of the net family property

You must participate at that time and date by [X] coming to court at the address set out above.

[ ] video-conference or telephone at *(location of video terminal or telephone)*

as agreed under arrangements already made by *(name of person)*

for video/telephone conferencing

IF YOU DO NOT PARTICIPATE AS SET OUT ABOVE, THE CASE MAY GO ON WITHOUT YOU OR THE COURT MAY DISMISS THE CASE.

_____   _____
Date of signature   *Signature of clerk of the court*

NOTE: *The party requesting the conference (or, if the conference is not requested by a party, the applicant) must serve and file a Case Conference Brief (Form 17A or 17B), Settlement Conference Brief (Form 17C or 17D), or Trial Management Conference Brief (Form 17E) not later than 7 days before the date scheduled for the conference. The other party must serve and file a brief not later than four days before the conference date. Each party must also file a Confirmation (Form 14C) not later than 2 p.m. two days before the conference.*

Source: DIVORCEmate Software Inc.

ONTARIO

Superior Court of Justice Family Court Branch
(Name of Court)

at **33 King Street West, Oshawa ON L1H 1A1**
(Court office address)

Court File Number
442103

Form 17A:
Case Conference Brief -
General

Name of party filing this brief	Date of case conference
LAUREN MICHELLE COHEN	**20 September 20__**

Applicant(s)

Full legal name & address for service - street & number, municipality, postal code, telephone & fax numbers and e-mail address (if any).	Lawyer's name & address - street & number, municipality, postal code, telephone & fax numbers and e-mail address (if any).
LAUREN MICHELLE COHEN **450 Martindale Road, Unit 113** **Oshawa ON L2D 3A8** **Tel: 905-488-9887**	**Peter T. Grant** **HILL, JOHNSTON & GRANT** **17 Princess Street South, Suite 2501** **Toronto ON M8Y 3N5** **Tel: 416-354-9900** **Fax: 416-354-9901** **ptgrant@hilljohngrant.com**

Respondent(s)

Full legal name & address for service - street & number, municipality, postal code, telephone & fax numbers and e-mail address (if any).	Lawyer's name & address - street & number, municipality, postal code, telephone & fax numbers and e-mail address (if any).
MATTHEW RICHARD COHEN **350 Walkerton Road, Apt. 303** **Whitby ON L6Q 6B2** **Tel: 905-422-9876**	**Katherine R. Siegel** **ARMSTRONG, WARD & SIEGEL** **16 Montreal Street West** **Whitby ON L4R 8C2** **Tel: 905-687-4682** **Fax: 905-687-4690** **krsiegel@armstrong.ca**

Name & address of Children's Lawyer's agent (street & number, municipality, postal code, telephone & fax numbers and e-mail address (if any)) and name of person represented.

PART 1: FAMILY FACTS

1. **APPLICANT:** Age: 32 Birthdate: *(d, m, y)* 10 July 1975
2. **RESPONDENT:** Age: 36 Birthdate: *(d, m, y)* 08 September 1970
3. **RELATIONSHIP DATES:**
   - [x] Married on *(date)* 01 July 2000
   - [x] Separated on *(date)* 15 June 2006
   - [ ] Other (Explain.)
   - [ ] Started living together on *(date)*
   - [ ] Never lived together.

4. The basic information about the child(ren) is as follows:

Child's full Legal name	Age	Birthdate (day, month, year)	Grade/Year and School	Now Living With (name of person and relationship to child)
Sarah Jessica Cohen	5	04 June 2002		Lauren Michelle Cohen - Mother

Source: DIVORCEmate Software Inc.

Form 17A: Case Conference Brief (General) (page 2)   Court File Number   442103

PART 2: THE ISSUES

5. What are the issues in this case that **HAVE** been settled:

    [ ] child custody   [ ] spousal support   [ ] possession of home
    [ ] access   [X] child support   [ ] equalization of net family property
    [ ] restraining order   [ ] ownership of property
    [ ] other *(Specify.)*

6. What are the issues in this case that have **NOT** yet been settled:

    [X] child custody   [ ] spousal support   [ ] possession of home
    [X] access   [ ] child support   [X] equalization of net family property
    [ ] restraining order   [ ] ownership of property   *(Attach Net Family Property Statement, Form 13B)*
    [ ] other *(Specify.)*

7. If child or spousal support is an issue, give the income of the parties:

    Applicant: _____   per year for the year 20____
    Respondent: _____   per year for the year 20____

8. Have you explored any ways to settle the issues that are still in dispute in this case?

    [X] No.   [ ] Yes. *(Give details.)*

9. Have any of the issues that have been settled turned into a court order or a written agreement?

    [X] No.
    [ ] Yes.   [ ] an order dated _____
                [ ] a written agreement that is attached.

10. Have the parents attended a family law or parenting education session?

    [X] No. *(Should they attend one?.....)*

    [ ] Yes. *(Give details.)*

PART 3: ISSUES FOR THIS CASE CONFERENCE

11. What are the issues for this case conference? What are the important facts for this case conference?

    1. The applicant has applied for sole custody of the child Sarah Jessica Cohen.
    2. The respondent has requested joint custody of the child Sarah Jessica Cohen.
    3. An assessment and equalization of the net family property including disclosure regarding a joint venture business the respondent has entered into.

12. What is your proposal to resolve these issues?

    1. An order of the court in favour of the applicant on the issues.

13. Do you want the court to make a temporary or final order at the case conference about any of these issues?

    [X] No.   [ ] Yes. *(Give details.)*

Source: DIVORCEmate Software Inc.

Form 17A: Case Conference Brief (General) (page 3)   Court File Number   442103

PART 4: FINANCIAL INFORMATION

NOTE: *If a claim for support has been made in this case, you must serve and file a new Financial Statement (Form 13 or 13.1), if it is different from the one filed in the continuing record or if the one in the continuing record is more than 30 days old. If there are minor changes but no major changes in your financial statement, you can serve and file an affidavit with details of the changes instead of a new financial statement. If you have not yet filed a financial statement in the continuing record, you must do it now. The page/tab number of the financial statement in the continuing record is*

14. If a claim is being made for child support and a claim is made for special expenses under the child support guidelines, give details of those expenses or attach additional information.

15. If a claim is made for child support and you claim that the child support guideline table amount should not be ordered, briefly outline the reasons here or attach an additional page.

PART 5: PROCEDURAL ISSUES

16. If custody or access issues are not yet settled:

    (a) Is a custody or access assessment needed?

        [X] No.   [ ] Yes. *(Give names of possible assessors.)*

    (b) Does a child or a parent under 18 years of age need legal representation from the Office of the Children's Lawyer?

        [X] No.   [ ] Yes. *(Give details and reasons.)*

17. Does any party need an order for the disclosure of documents, the questioning of witnesses, a property valuation or any other matter in this case?

    [X] No.   [ ] Yes. *(Give details.)*

18. Are any other procedural orders needed?

    [X] No.   [ ] Yes. *(Give details.)*

19. Have all the persons who should be parties in this case been added as parties?

    [X] Yes.   [ ] No. *(Who needs to be added?)*

20. Are there any other issues that should be reviewed at the case conference?

    [X] No.   [ ] Yes. *(Give details.)*

_____   _____
Date of party's signature   *Signature of party*

_____   _____
Date of lawyer's signature   *Signature of party's lawyer*

Source: DIVORCEmate Software Inc.

ONTARIO

Superior Court of Justice Family Court Branch

Court File Number

442103

(Name of Court)

at   **33 King Street West, Oshawa ON L1H 1A1**

Form 14C: Confirmation

(Court office address)

Applicant(s)

Full legal name & address for service - street & number, municipality, postal code, telephone & fax numbers and e-mail address (if any).	*Lawyer's name & address - street & number, municipality, postal code, telephone & fax numbers and e-mail address (if any).*
LAUREN MICHELLE COHEN **450 Martindale Road, Unit 113** **Oshawa ON L2D 3A8** **Tel: 905-488-9887**	**Peter T. Grant** **HILL, JOHNSTON & GRANT** **17 Princess Street South, Suite 2501** **Toronto ON M8Y 3N5** **Tel: 416-354-9900** **Fax: 416-354-9901** **ptgrant@hilljohngrant.com**

Respondent(s)

Full legal name & address for service - street & number, municipality, postal code, telephone & fax numbers and e-mail address (if any).	*Lawyer's name & address - street & number, municipality, postal code, telephone & fax numbers and e-mail address (if any).*
MATTHEW RICHARD COHEN **350 Walkerton Road, Apt. 303** **Whitby ON L6Q 6B2** **Tel: 905-422-9876**	**Katherine R. Siegel** **ARMSTRONG, WARD & SIEGEL** **16 Montreal Street West** **Whitby ON L4R 8C2** **Tel: 905-687-4682** **Fax: 905-687-4690** **krsiegel@armstrong.ca**

Name & address of Children's Lawyer's agent (street & number, municipality, postal code, telephone & fax numbers and e-mail address (if any)) and name of person represented.

1.   My name is *(full legal name)* Peter T. Grant

and I am   [X]   the lawyer for *(name)* LAUREN MICHELLE COHEN

[ ]   *(Other; Specify.)*

2.   I have   [ ]   not been able to contact the opposing lawyer or party in this case to confirm the matters set out in paragraphs 3 to 7 below because: *(Give reason for inability to contact other side.)*

[X]   contacted the opposing lawyer or party and confirmed the matters set out in paragraphs 3 to 7 below.

3.   The scheduled date and time for this   [ ] motion   [X] case conference   [ ] settlement conference

[ ]   trial management conference, is *(date)* **20 September 20___**   at *(time)*   **10:00 a.m.**

Complete only if motion is being confirmed.   [ ] A case conference was held on the issues in this motion before Justice.

[ ] A case conference has not been held on the issues in this motion.

4.   This matter is going ahead   [ ]   on all the issues.   [X]   on only the following issues: *(Specify.)*

   1.   Custody of the child Sarah Jessica Cohen
   2.   Assessment and equalization of the net family property

[ ]   for a consent order regarding: *(Specify.)*

[ ]   for an adjournment on consent to *(date)*   because *(Give reason for adjournment.)*

[ ]   for a contested adjournment to *(date)*   asked for by

because *(Give reason.)*

5.   The judge should read pages/tabs 2 and 4   of the continuing record.

6.   Total time estimate: applicant   15   minutes;   respondent   15   minutes;   for a total of   30   minutes.

7.   The case management judge for this case is *(Justice)*   Hamilton

_____   _____
Date of signature   *Lawyer's or party's signature*

Source: DIVORCEmate Software Inc.

ONTARIO

	Court File Number
Superior Court of Justice Family Court Branch	**442103**
(Name of Court)	

at __33 King Street West, Oshawa ON L1H 1A1__
(Court office address)

Form 14: Notice of Motion

Applicant(s)

Full legal name & address for service - street & number, municipality, postal code, telephone & fax numbers and e-mail address (if any).	*Lawyer's name & address - street & number, municipality, postal code, telephone & fax numbers and e-mail address (if any).*
LAUREN MICHELLE COHEN **450 Martindale Road, Unit 113** **Oshawa ON L2D 3A8** **Tel: 905-488-9887**	**Peter T. Grant** **HILL, JOHNSTON & GRANT** **17 Princess Street South, Suite 2501** **Toronto ON M8Y 3N5** **Tel: 416-354-9900** **Fax: 416-354-9901** **ptgrant@hilljohngrant.com**

Respondent(s)

Full legal name & address for service - street & number, municipality, postal code, telephone & fax numbers and e-mail address (if any).	*Lawyer's name & address - street & number, municipality, postal code, telephone & fax numbers and e-mail address (if any).*
MATTHEW RICHARD COHEN **350 Walkerton Road, Apt. 303** **Whitby ON L6Q 6B2** **Tel: 905-422-9876**	**Katherine R. Siegel** **ARMSTRONG, WARD & SIEGEL** **16 Montreal Street West** **Whitby ON L4R 8C2** **Tel: 905-687-4682** **Fax: 905-687-4690** **krsiegel@armstrong.ca**

The person making this motion or the person's lawyer must contact the clerk of the court by telephone or otherwise to choose a time and date when the court could hear this motion.

TO THE PARTIES:

THE COURT WILL HEAR A MOTION on *(date)* 10 October 20__

at *(time)* 10:00 a.m. **, or as soon as possible after that time at:** *(place of hearing)*

33 King Street West, Oshawa ON L1H 1A1

This motion will be made by *(name of person making motion)* LAUREN MICHELLE COHEN

who will be asking the court for an order for the item(s) listed on page 2 of this notice

☒ A copy of the affidavit(s) in support of this motion is served with this notice.

☐ A notice of a case conference is served with this notice to change an order.

If this material is missing, you should talk to the court office immediately.

The person making this motion is also relying on the following documents in the continuing record: *(List documents)*

1. Application dated 10 August 20__

2. Financial Statement of Lauren Michelle Cohen dated 1 October 20__

3. Financial Statement of Matthew Richard Cohen dated 30 September 20__

Source: DIVORCEmate Software Inc.

Form 14: Notice of Motion (page 2)   Court File Number   442103

If you want to oppose this motion or to give your own views, you should talk to your own lawyer and prepare your own affidavit, serve it on all other parties not later than 4 days before the date above and file it at the court office not later than 2 days before that date. Only written and affidavit evidence will be allowed at a motion unless the court gives permission for oral testimony. You may bring your lawyer to the motion.

IF YOU DO NOT COME TO THE MOTION, THE COURT MAY MAKE AN ORDER WITHOUT YOU AND ENFORCE IT AGAINST YOU.

_____
Date of signature

Signature of person making this motion or of person's lawyer

Peter T. Grant
HILL, JOHNSTON & GRANT
17 Princess Street South, Suite 2501
Toronto ON M8Y 3N5

Tel: 416-354-9900
Fax: 416-354-9901
ptgrant@hilljohngrant.com

Typed or printed name of person or of person's lawyer, address for service, telephone & fax number & e-mail address (if any)

NOTE TO PERSON MAKING THIS MOTION: *You MUST file a Confirmation (Form 14C) not later than 2:00 p.m. two days before the date set out above.*

If this is a motion to change past and future support payments under an order that has been assigned to a government agency, you must also serve this notice on that agency. If you do not, the agency can ask the court to set aside any order that you may get in this motion and can ask for court costs against you.

State the order or orders requested on this motion.

1. An order for temporary custody of the child Sarah Jessica Cohen born 04 June 2002 to the applicant Lauren Michelle Cohen.

2. An order for temporary child support for $577 per month in accordance with the Child Support Guidelines payable by the respondent Matthew Richard Cohen to the applicant Lauren Michelle Cohen.

ONTARIO	Court File Number
Superior Court of Justice Family Court Branch	442103

(Name of Court)

at 33 King Street West, Oshawa ON L1H 1A1

(Court office address)

Form 23: Summons to Witness

Applicant(s)

Full legal name & address for service - street & number, municipality, postal code, telephone & fax numbers and e-mail address (if any).	Lawyer's name & address - street & number, municipality, postal code, telephone & fax numbers and e-mail address (if any).
LAUREN MICHELLE COHEN 450 Martindale Road, Unit 113 Oshawa ON L2D 3A8 Tel: 905-488-9887	**Peter T. Grant** **HILL, JOHNSTON & GRANT** **17 Princess Street South, Suite 2501** **Toronto ON M8Y 3N5** Tel: 416-354-9900 Fax: 416-354-9901 ptgrant@hilljohngrant.com

Respondent(s)

Full legal name & address for service - street & number, municipality, postal code, telephone & fax numbers and e-mail address (if any).	Lawyer's name & address - street & number, municipality, postal code, telephone & fax numbers and e-mail address (if any).
MATTHEW RICHARD COHEN 350 Walkerton Road, Apt. 303 Whitby ON L6Q 6B2 Tel: 905-422-9876	**Katherine R. Siegel** **ARMSTRONG, WARD & SIEGEL** **16 Montreal Street West** **Whitby ON L4R 8C2** Tel: 905-687-4682 Fax: 905-687-4690 krsiegel@armstrong.ca

TO: (full legal name of witness) ANDRE COUSINEAU

of (address: – street & number, municipality, postal code)

625 Sheffield Road, Whitby ON L7T 4K2

YOU MUST:

(1) **come to** (address: – street & number, municipality, postal code)

33 King Street West, Oshawa ON L1H 1A1

on (date) December 15, 20___   at (time) 10:00 a.m. ;

(2) **give evidence in the case or examination before** (court or other person)

the court

(3) **bring with you the documents and things listed on page 2 of this summons; and**

(4) **remain there until this case or examination is finished or until the person conducting it says otherwise.**

With this summons, you should get a fee that is calculated for 1 day(s) of attendance as follows:

Appearance allowance of	($)	50.00	daily	$ 50.00
+ Travel allowance of	($)	2.50	each way	$ 5.00
+ Overnight hotel and meal allowance of	($)		daily	$ 0.00
			TOTAL	$ 55.00

If the case or examination takes up more of your time, you will be entitled to an additional fee.

Source: DIVORCEmate Software Inc.

Form 23: Summons to Witness (page 2)   Court File Number   442103

_____

Date of issue

IF YOU DO NOT COME AND REMAIN AS REQUIRED BY THIS SUMMONS, A WARRANT MAY BE ISSUED FOR YOUR ARREST.

(Give the date of every document that the witness must bring and give enough of a description to identify each document or thing that the witness must bring.)

1. Financial records pertaining to the joint venture between Matthew Richard Cohen and yourself.

Draw a line through any blank space left on this page.

Name, address, telephone & fax numbers and e-mail address of person or lawyer who prepared this summons.	Peter T. Grant HILL, JOHNSTON & GRANT 17 Princess Street South, Suite 2501 Toronto ON M8Y 3N5 Tel: 416-354-9900 Fax: 416-354-9901 ptgrant@hilljohngrant.com

Source: DIVORCEmate Software Inc.

	ONTARIO	Court File Number
SEAL	**Superior Court of Justice Family Court Branch**	442103
	(Name of Court)	
	at <u>33 King Street West, Oshawa ON L1H 1A1</u>	**Form 25: Order (General)**
	(Court office address)	[X] Temporary
		[ ] Final

Applicant(s)

(Full legal name & address for service: street, number, municipality, postal code telephone & fax numbers & e-mail address (if any).	*Lawyer's name & address: street, number, municipality, postal code, telephone & fax numbers & e-mail address (if any).*
LAUREN MICHELLE COHEN **450 Martindale Road, Unit 113** **Oshawa ON L2D 3A8** **Tel: 905-488-9887**	**Peter T. Grant** **HILL, JOHNSTON & GRANT** **17 Princess Street South, Suite 2501** **Toronto ON M8Y 3N5** **Tel: 416-354-9900** **Fax: 416-354-9901** **ptgrant@hilljohngrant.com**

The Honourable

<u>Justice Webber</u>

Judge (Print or type name)

<u>October 10, 20___</u>

Date of order

Respondent(s)

Full legal name & address for service: street, number, municipality, postal code telephone & fax numbers & e-mail address (if any).	*Lawyer's name & address: street, number, municipality, postal code, telephone & fax numbers & e-mail address (if any).*
MATTHEW RICHARD COHEN **350 Walkerton Road, Apt. 303** **Whitby ON L6Q 6B2** **Tel: 905-422-9876**	**Katherine R. Siegel** **ARMSTRONG, WARD & SIEGEL** **16 Montreal Street West** **Whitby ON L4R 8C2** **Tel: 905-687-4682** **Fax: 905-687-4690** **krsiegel@armstrong.ca**

The court heard an application/motion made by *(name of person or persons)*

Lauren Michelle Cohen

The following persons were in court *(names of parties and lawyers in court)*

Lauren Michelle Cohen represented by Peter T. Grant
Matthew Richard Cohen represented by Katherine R. Siegel

The court received evidence and heard submissions on behalf of *(name or names)*

Lauren Michelle Cohen and Matthew Richard Cohen

THE COURT ORDERS THAT:

1. The applicant Lauren Michelle Cohen shall have temporary custody of the child Sarah Jessica Cohen born 04 June 2002.

2. The respondent Matthew Richard Cohen shall have reasonable access to the child Sarah Jessica Cohen.

3. The respondent Matthew Richard Cohen shall pay temporary child support in the amount of $577 per month.

Put a line through any blank space left on this page.

_____   _____
Date of signature   *Signature of judge or clerk of the court*

Source: DIVORCEmate Software Inc.

	ONTARIO	Court File Number
SEAL	**Superior Court of Justice**	**Form 8A: Application**
	(Name of Court)	**(Divorce)**
	at **393 University Avenue, 10th Floor, Toronto ON M5G 1E6**	[X] Simple (divorce only)
	(Court office address)	[ ] Joint

Applicant(s)

Full legal name & address for service - street & number, municipality, postal code, telephone & fax numbers and e-mail address (if any).	Lawyer's name & address - street & number, municipality, postal code, telephone & fax numbers and e-mail address (if any).
HERMIONE GRACE DRAYAN **46 Fairisle Lane** **Toronto ON M4T 9G1** **Tel: 416-473-2243**	**Peter T. Grant** **HILL, JOHNSTON & GRANT** **17 Princess Street South, Suite 2501** **Toronto ON M8Y 3N5** **Tel: 416-354-9900** **Fax: 416-354-9901** **ptgrant@hilljohngrant.com**

Respondent(s)

Full legal name & address for service - street & number, municipality, postal code, telephone & fax numbers and e-mail address (if any).	Lawyer's name & address - street & number, municipality, postal code, telephone & fax numbers and e-mail address (if any).
HAROLD POTTER DRAYAN **26 Castle Parkway, Suite 1000** **Mississauga ON L1G 8P6** **Tel: 905-226-4709**	**Brianna T. Wolfe** **Fox, Wolfe & Lyons** **976 City Centre Crescent** **Mississauga ON L4V 8B2** **Tel: 905-552-0034** **Fax: 905-552-0034** **brianna.wolfe@foxwolfelyons.ca**

[X]   IN THIS CASE, THE APPLICANT IS CLAIMING DIVORCE ONLY.

TO THE RESPONDENT(S): A COURT CASE FOR DIVORCE HAS BEEN STARTED AGAINST YOU IN THIS COURT. THE DETAILS ARE SET OUT ON THE ATTACHED PAGES.

THIS CASE IS ON THE STANDARD TRACK OF THE CASE MANAGEMENT SYSTEM. No court date has been set for this case but, if you have been served with a notice of motion, it has a court date and you or your lawyer should come to court for the motion. A case management judge will not be assigned until one of the parties asks the clerk of the court to schedule a case conference or until a motion is scheduled, whichever comes first.

IF, AFTER 365 DAYS, THE CASE HAS NOT BEEN SCHEDULED FOR TRIAL, the clerk of the court will send out a warning that the case will be dismissed within 60 days unless the parties file proof that the case has been settled or one of the parties asks for a case or a settlement conference.

IF YOU WANT TO OPPOSE ANY CLAIM IN THIS CASE, you or your lawyer must prepare an *Answer* (Form 10 - a blank copy should be attached), serve a copy on the applicant and file a copy in the court office with an *Affidavit of Service* (Form 6B).
YOU HAVE ONLY 30 DAYS AFTER THIS APPLICATION IS SERVED ON YOU (60 DAYS IF THIS APPLICATION IS SERVED ON YOU OUTSIDE CANADA OR THE UNITED STATES) TO SERVE AND FILE AN ANSWER. IF YOU DO NOT, THE CASE WILL GO AHEAD WITHOUT YOU AND THE COURT MAY MAKE AN ORDER AND ENFORCE IT AGAINST YOU.

IF YOU WANT TO MAKE A CLAIM OF YOUR OWN, you or your lawyer must fill out the claim portion in the Answer, serve a copy on the applicant(s) and file a copy in the court office with an Affidavit of Service.
- If you want to make a claim for support but do not want to make a claim for property or exclusive possession of the matrimonial home and its contents, you **MUST** fill out a Financial Statement (Form 13), serve a copy on the applicant(s) and file a copy in the court office.
- However, if your only claim for support is for child support in the table amount specified under the Child Support Guidelines, you do not need to fill out, serve or file a Financial Statement.
- If you want to make a claim for property or exclusive possession of the matrimonial home and its contents, whether or not it includes a claim for support, you **MUST** fill out a Financial Statement (Form 13.1, not Form 13), serve a copy on the applicant(s), and file a copy in the court office.

YOU SHOULD GET LEGAL ADVICE ABOUT THIS CASE RIGHT AWAY. If you cannot afford a lawyer, you may be able to

Source: DIVORCEmate Software Inc.

Form 8A: Application (Divorce) (page 2)   Court File Number

get help from your local Legal Aid office. (*See your telephone directory under LEGAL AID.*)

☐ **THIS CASE IS A JOINT APPLICATION FOR DIVORCE. THE DETAILS ARE SET OUT ON THE ATTACHED PAGES.** The application and affidavits in support of the application will be presented to a judge when the materials have been checked for completeness.

If you are requesting anything other than a simple divorce, such as support or property or exclusive possession of the matrimonial home and its contents, then refer to page 1 for instructions regarding the Financial Statement you should file.

_____   _____
Date of issue   *Clerk of the court*

Source: DIVORCEmate Software Inc.

Form 8A: Application (Divorce) (page 3) Court File Number [   ]

FAMILY HISTORY

APPLICANT: Age: 42 Birthdate: *(d, m, y)* 07 July 1965

Resident in *(municipality & province)* Toronto, Ontario

since *(date)* 03 March 2005

Surname at birth: Walsh

Surname just before marriage: McCormack

Divorced before? ☐ No ☒ Yes *(Place and date of previous divorce)*
London, Ontario

RESPONDENT/JOINT APPLICANT:

Age: 43 Birthdate: *(d, m, y)* 10 October 1964

Resident in *(municipality & province)* Mississauga, Ontario

since *(date)* 10 October 1964

Surname at birth: Drayan

Surname just before marriage: Drayan

Divorced before? ☒ No ☐ Yes *(Place and date of previous divorce)*

RELATIONSHIP DATES

☒ Married on *(date)* 01 June 1990 ☐ Started living together on *(date)*

☒ Separated on *(date)* 03 March 2005 ☐ Never lived together

THE CHILD(REN)
List all children involved in this case, even if no claim is made for these children.

Full legal name	Age	Birthday *(d, m, y)*	Resident in *(municipality & province)*	Now Living with *(name of person and relationship to child)*

PREVIOUS CASES OR AGREEMENTS

Have the parties or the children been in a court case before?
☒ No ☐ Yes

Have the parties made a written agreement dealing with any matter involved in this case?
☐ No ☒ Yes *(Give date of agreement. Indicate which of its items are in dispute.)*
Separation Agreement dated December 1, 2005 in full force and effect.

Source: DIVORCEmate Software Inc.

Form 8A: Application (Divorce) (page 4)   Court File Number ▭

CLAIMS

| USE THIS FRAME ONLY IF THIS CASE IS A JOINT APPLICATION FOR DIVORCE. |

WE JOINTLY ASK THE COURT FOR THE FOLLOWING:

Claims under the *Divorce Act*

- 00 ☐ a divorce
- 01 ☐ spousal support
- 02 ☐ support for child(ren) – table amount
- 03 ☐ support for child(ren) – other than table amount
- 04 ☐ custody of child(ren)
- 05 ☐ access to child(ren)

Claims under the *Family Law Act* or *Children's Law Reform Act*

- 10 ☐ spousal support
- 11 ☐ support for child(ren) – table amount
- 12 ☐ support for child(ren) – other than table amount
- 13 ☐ custody of child(ren)
- 14 ☐ access to child(ren)
- 15 ☐ restraining/non-harassment Order
- 16 ☐ indexing spousal support
- 17 ☐ declaration of parentage
- 18 ☐ guardianship over child's property

Claims relating to property

- 20 ☐ equalization of net family properties
- 21 ☐ exclusive possession of matrimonial home
- 22 ☐ exclusive possession of contents of matrimonial home
- 23 ☐ freezing assets
- 24 ☐ sale of family property

Other Claims

- 30 ☐ costs
- 31 ☐ annulment of marriage
- 32 ☐ prejudgment interest
- 50 ☐ other *(Specify.)*

| USE THIS FRAME ONLY IF THE APPLICANT'S ONLY CLAIM IN THIS CASE IS FOR DIVORCE. |

I ASK THE COURT FOR:
(Check if applicable.)

00 ☒ a divorce   30 ☐ Costs

IMPORTANT FACTS SUPPORTING THE CLAIM FOR DIVORCE

☒ **Separation:** The spouses have lived separate and apart since *(date)* 03 March 2005 and

☒ have not lived together again since that date in an unsuccessful attempt to reconcile.

☐ have lived together again during the following period(s) in an unsuccessful attempt to reconcile:
(Give dates.) ▭

☐ **Adultery:** *(Name of spouse)* ▭
has committed adultery. *(Give details. It is not necessary to name any other person involved, but if you do name the other person, then you must serve this application on the other person.)*
▭

☐ **Cruelty:** *(Name of spouse)* ▭
has treated *(name of spouse)* ▭
with physical or mental cruelty of such a kind as to make continued cohabitation intolerable. *(Give details.)*
▭

Source: DIVORCEmate Software Inc.

Form 8A: Application (Divorce) (page 5) Court File Number [   ]

USE THIS FRAME ONLY IF THIS CASE IS A JOINT APPLICATION FOR DIVORCE.

The details of the other order(s) that we jointly ask the court to make are as follows: (*Include any amounts of support and the names of the children for whom support, custody or access is to be ordered.*)

IMPORTANT FACTS SUPPORTING OUR CLAIM(S)

(Set out the facts that form the legal basis for your claim(s)).

Put a line through any blank space left on this page.

Complete this section if your claim is for a divorce. Your lawyer, if you are represented, must complete the Lawyer's Certificate below.

Date of signature	Signature of applicant

Complete this section if you are making a joint application for divorce. Your lawyer, if you are represented, must complete the Lawyer's Certificate below.

Date of signature	Signature of joint applicant

Date of signature	Signature of joint applicant

LAWYER'S CERTIFICATE

My name is: Peter T. Grant

and I am the lawyer for *(name)* HERMIONE GRACE DRAYAN

in this divorce case. I certify that I have complied with the requirements of section 9 of the *Divorce Act*.

Date of signature	Signature of Lawyer

My name is: [   ]

and I am the lawyer for *(name)* [   ]

in this divorce case. I certify that I have complied with the requirements of section 9 of the *Divorce Act*.

Date of signature	Signature of Lawyer

Source: DIVORCEmate Software Inc.

ONTARIO

Superior Court of Justice

(Name of Court)

Court File Number
99674

at   **393 University Avenue, 10th Floor, Toronto ON M5G 1E6**

(Court office address)

Form 36: Affidavit for Divorce

Applicant(s)

Full legal name & address for service - street & number, municipality, postal code, telephone & fax numbers and e-mail address (if any).	Lawyer's name & address - street & number, municipality, postal code, telephone & fax numbers and e-mail address (if any).
HERMIONE GRACE DRAYAN **46 Fairisle Lane** **Toronto ON M4T 9G1** **Tel: 416-473-2243**	**Peter T. Grant** **HILL, JOHNSTON & GRANT** **17 Princess Street South, Suite 2501** **Toronto ON M8Y 3N5** **Tel: 416-354-9900** **Fax: 416-354-9901** **ptgrant@hilljohngrant.com**

Respondent(s)

Full legal name & address for service - street & number, municipality, postal code, telephone & fax numbers and e-mail address (if any).	Lawyer's name & address - street & number, municipality, postal code, telephone & fax numbers and e-mail address (if any).
HAROLD POTTER DRAYAN **26 Castle Parkway, Suite 1000** **Mississauga ON L1G 8P6** **Tel: 905-226-4709**	**Brianna T. Wolfe** **FOX, WOLFE & LYONS** **976 City Centre Crescent** **Mississauga ON L4V 8B2** **Tel: 905-552-0034** **Fax: 905-552-0034** **brianna.wolfe@foxwolfelyons.ca**

My name is *(full legal name)*   **HERMIONE GRACE DRAYAN**

I live in *(municipality & province)*   **Toronto, Province of Ontario**

And I swear/affirm that the following is true:

1.   I am the applicant in this divorce case.

2.   There is no chance of reconciliation between the respondent and me.

3.   All information in the application in this case is correct, except: *(State any corrections or changes to the information in the application. Write "NONE" if there are no corrections or changes.)*

      NONE

4.   ☒   The certificate or registration of my marriage to the respondent has been signed and sealed by the Registrar of Ontario and

            ☒   has been filed with the application.

            ☐   is attached to this affidavit.

      ☐   The certificate of my marriage to the respondent was issued outside Ontario. It is called *(title of certificate)*.

      It was issued at *(place of issue)*

      on *(date)*   by *(name and title of person who issued the certificate)*

      and the information in it about my marriage is correct.

Source: DIVORCEmate Software Inc.

Form 36: Affidavit for Divorce (page 2) Court File Number 99674

☐ I have not been able to get a certificate or registration of my marriage. I was married to the respondent

on *(date)*

at *(place of marriage)*

The marriage was performed by *(name and title)*

who had the authority to perform marriages in that place.

5. The legal basis for the divorce is:

☒ that the respondent and I have been separated for at least one year.
We separated on *(date)* 03 March 2005

☐ *(Other. Specify.)*

6. I do not know about and I am not involved in any arrangement to make up or to hide evidence or to deceive the court in this divorce case.

Strike out the following paragraphs if they do not apply.

7. I do not want to make a claim for a division of property in this divorce case, even though I know that it may be legally impossible to make such a claim after the divorce.

8. I want the divorce order to include the following paragraph numbers of the attached consent, settlement, separation agreement or previous court order: *(List the numbers of the paragraphs that you want included in the divorce order.)*

Separation Agreement dated December 1, 2005 to remain in full force and effect in its entirety.

9. There are *(number)* 0 children of the marriage. They are:

Full legal name of child	Birthdate *(d, m, y)*

10. The custody and access arrangements for the child(ren) are as follows: *(Give summary.)*

11. These are the arrangements that have been made for the support of the child(ren) of the marriage:

(a) The income of the party paying child support is ($) per year.

(b) The number of children for whom support is supposed to be paid is *(number)* .

(c) The amount of support that should be paid according to the applicable table in the child support guidelines is ($) per month.

(d) The amount of child support actually being paid is ($) per month.
 (***NOTE:*** - Where the dollar amounts in clauses [c] and [d] are different, you must fill out the frame on the next page. If the amounts in clauses [c] and [d] are the same, skip the frame and go directly to paragraph 12.)

Fill out the information in this frame only if amounts in 11(c) & 11(d) are different. If they are the same, go to paragraph 12.

(a) Child support is already covered by:

(i) ☐ a court order dated *(date)* that was made before the child support guidelines came into effect *(before May 1st, 1997)*. I attach a copy of the order.

(ii) ☐ a domestic contract order dated *(date)* that was made before the guidelines came into effect *(before May 1st, 1997)*. I attach a copy of the contract.

(iii) ☐ a court order or written agreement dated *(date)* made after the guidelines came into effect that has some direct or indirect benefits for the child(ren). I attach a copy.

Source: DIVORCEmate Software Inc.

Form 36: Affidavit for Divorce (page 3)   **Court File Number**   99674

(iv) ☐   a written consent between the parties dated *(date)* _____ agreeing to the payment of an amount different from that set out in the guidelines.

(b) The child support clauses of this order or agreement require payment of ($) _____ per month in child support.

(c) These child support clauses

☐   are not indexed for any automatic cost-of-living increases.

☐   are indexed according to *(Give indexing formula)*

_____

(d) These child support clauses

☐   have not been changed since the day the order or agreement was made.

☐   have been changed on *(Give dates and details of changes)*

Date(s)	Detail(s)

(e) *(If you ticked off box (i), you can go to paragraph 12. If you ticked off boxes (ii), (iii) or (iv) above, then fill out the information after box of the corresponding number below. For example, if you ticked off box (iii) above, you would fill out the information alongside box (iii) below.)*

(ii) ☐   The amount being paid under this agreement is a fair and reasonable arrangement for the support of the child(ren) because: *(Give reasons.)*

_____

(iii) ☐   The order or agreement directly or indirectly benefits the child(ren) because: *(Give details of benefits.)*

_____

(iv) ☐   The amount to which the parties have consented is reasonable for the support of the child(ren) because: *(Give reasons.)*

_____

12. I am claiming costs in this case. The details of this claim are as follows: *(Give details.)*

_____

13. The respondent's address last known to me is: *(Give address.)*

HAROLD POTTER DRAYAN, 26 Castle Parkway, Suite 1000, Mississauga ON L1G 8P6

Put a line through any blank space on this page.

Sworn/Affirmed before me at:

City of Toronto

(municipality)

in   Province of Ontario

(province, state or country)

on   _____

(date)

_____
Commissioner for taking affidavits
(Type or print name below if signature is illegible)

_____
Signature
(This form is to be signed in front of a lawyer, justice of the peace, notary public or commissioner for taking affidavits.)

Source: DIVORCEmate Software Inc.

ONTARIO

Superior Court of Justice

(Name of Court)

Court File Number	99674

SEAL

at 393 University Avenue, 10th Floor, Toronto ON M5G 1E6

(Court office address)

Form 25A: Divorce Order

Applicant(s)

Full legal name & address for service - street & number, municipality, postal code, telephone & fax numbers & e-mail address (if any).	Lawyer's name & address - street & number, municipality, postal code, telephone & fax numbers & e-mail address (if any).
HERMIONE GRACE DRAYAN **46 Fairisle Lane** **Toronto ON M4T 9G1** **Tel: 416-473-2243**	**Peter T. Grant** **HILL, JOHNSTON & GRANT** **17 Princess Street South, Suite 2501** **Toronto ON M8Y 3N5** **Tel: 416-354-9900** **Fax: 416-354-9901** ptgrant@hilljohngrant.com

The Honourable

Justice Webber

Judge (print or type name)

December 15, 20__

Date of order

Respondent(s)

Full legal name & address for service - street & number, municipality, postal code, telephone & fax numbers & e-mail address (if any).	Lawyer's name & address - street & number, municipality, postal code, telephone & fax numbers & e-mail address (if any).
HAROLD POTTER DRAYAN **26 Castle Parkway, Suite 1000** **Mississauga ON L1G 8P6** **Tel: 905-226-4709**	**Brianna T. Wolfe** **FOX, WOLFE & LYONS** **976 City Centre Crescent** **Mississauga ON L4V 8B2** **Tel: 905-552-0034** **Fax: 905-552-0034** brianna.wolfe@foxwolfelyons.ca

The court heard an application of (name) HERMIONE GRACE DRAYAN

on (date) December 15, 20__

~~The following persons were in court~~ (Give name of parties and lawyers in court. This paragraph may be struck out if the divorce is uncontested.)

This court received evidence and considered submissions on behalf of (name or names).

Hermione Grace Drayan and Harold Potter Drayan

THIS COURT ORDERS THAT:

1. *If the court decides that the divorce shall take effect earlier, replace "31" with the smaller number.*

   (full legal names of spouses) HERMIONE GRACE DRAYAN and HAROLD POTTER DRAYAN

   who were married at (place) Toronto

   on (date) 01 June 1990

   be divorced and that the divorce take effect   31   days after the date of this order.

(Add further paragraphs where the court orders other relief.)

2. Separation Agreement dated December 1, 2005 between HERMIONE GRACE DRAYAN and HAROLD POTTER DRAYAN to remain in full force and effect.

Date of signature	Signature of judge or clerk of the court

NOTE: Neither spouse is free to remarry until this order takes effect, at which time you can get a **Certificate of Divorce** from the court office.

PART 3

Real Estate

CHAPTER 20

Introduction to Real Estate

OBJECTIVES:

- Identify and describe the two types of land registration systems in Ontario

- Explain the impact of the *Land Registration Reform Act* on the practice of real estate, including POLARIS documentation and electronic registration

- Define the special terms associated with real estate work

- Describe real property in any one or combination of the prescribed three ways: municipal address, legal description, and/or property identifier

One of the most important areas of legal practice is the area of legal work dealing with real property. **Real property** is immovable property, such as lands, buildings, and things attached to land. **Personal property** is movable property, such as cars, furniture, appliances, or draperies referred to as **chattels**. In a residential real estate practice, the lawyer is generally concerned with the buying, selling, and financing (for example, a mortgage) of property that is for personal use as a residence. In a commercial real estate practice, the lawyer is generally concerned with the buying, selling, financing, leasing, and development of property such as office buildings or shopping centres. A commercial real estate practice usually involves the drafting and revisions of lengthy contracts, the general guidelines for the preparation of which are discussed in Chapter 7. Before considering what steps a lawyer takes in any of these areas, some other aspects of real estate practice should be noted.

SYSTEMS OF LAND REGISTRATION

All documents relating to real estate may be registered to record the interest of the document holder in the real property. In Canada, there are two systems of land registration: the registry system and the land titles system.

Both systems of land registration are still found in the Province of Ontario. However, under the provisions of the *Land Registration Reform Act*, as discussed later in this chapter, it is anticipated that in the near future all registrations in the registry system will have been converted to the land titles system and that all registration and title searches will occur electronically.

Registry System

The registry system is the older of the two systems. The Province of Ontario is divided into registry divisions that are identified by the name of the area each serves and by a number. For example:

The Land Registry Office for the Registry Division of Peel (No. 43)

Each land registry office is administered by a land registrar. When property is registered in this system, previously registered documents relating to a particular piece of property may be reviewed to establish that the vendor has the right to transfer title (to sell) to the purchaser. The responsibility to establish good title (ownership) is that of the purchaser's solicitor; for this reason, lawyers arrange to have titles searched when acting for a purchaser. Depending on the circumstances, the search to establish good title may extend back as far as 40 years or, in some cases, may go back to the root, which is the first grant from the Crown. The lawyer can then certify title to the purchaser.

Simply put, the registry system is a system of recording documents relating to land; the province is responsible for keeping the records but is not responsible for guaranteeing the title.

Land Titles System

In some provinces, including Ontario, the Torrens or land titles system of land registration is also used. Land title offices are identified by the name of the area each serves and by a number. Such offices are administered by a land registrar, and no instrument relating to real property registered in that office is accepted until the land registrar is satisfied that it does what it purports to do.

For example, before the land registrar will accept for registration a transfer of land from A to Z, he or she must first be satisfied that A is shown in the records as the registered owner. Then a check is made to ensure that the transfer is correctly executed by A and is a proper transfer. Having done all this, the land registrar registers Z as the new owner and, upon payment of a fee, issues Z with a certificate of title certifying Z to be the owner with an absolute title, subject to any qualifications and restrictions the land registrar may make. Under the land titles system, the title is guaranteed by the government.

Simply put, the land titles system is a system of recording documents relating to land; the province is responsible for maintaining the records and for guaranteeing the title and specific interests.

LAND REGISTRATION REFORM ACT

In the early 1980s, the Ontario government established POLARIS (Province of Ontario Land Registration and Information System) to standardize and modernize land registration systems in Ontario. As a result of this project, the Land Registration Reform Act was enacted and became effective on April 1, 1985.

When the act became effective, the registry and land titles systems were brought closer together. Search requirements in the registry system were amended to eliminate some searches, and common documents replaced the different documents formerly used by each system, as shown below:

Registry	Land Titles	POLARIS
deed	transfer	transfer/deed
mortgage	charge	charge/mortgage
discharge of mortgage	cessation of charge	discharge of charge/mortgage

No legal seals are required on any document, and there are no affidavits. Instead, there are statements, the truth of which is indicated by the execution of the document. Each document is a single page, although additional pages may be included as a schedule. The documents are designed to allow the information to be maintained easily in a computerized record system, permitting automated registration and searching functions.

The conversion of the manual index books and registers to a computerized registration and searching facility was commenced when the act became effective; the two systems of land registry offices were maintained. Once the conversion has been completed, the registry system will no longer function. Until all real property has been converted to computerized registration and title searching and the conversion to a single land registry system is completed throughout Ontario, manual registration and title searches will be required in some land registry offices. Thus knowledge of the procedures unique to each of the current two systems is necessary.

REAL ESTATE TERMINOLOGY

In real estate law, there are special terms that are encountered frequently.

Names of Parties and Instruments

The person selling real property is the **vendor**; the person buying is the **purchaser**. The legal document by which title is transferred in a real estate transaction is a **transfer/deed** (Form 1). The parties to a transfer/deed are the **transferor** and **transferee**.

The legal document used to formalize the loan when real property is used as collateral is a **charge/mortgage** (Form 2). The parties to a charge/mortgage are called the **chargor** and **chargee**; traditionally, they have been called the **mortgagor** and **mortgagee**, and those terms are still encountered.

The agreement by which the owner of real property allows another party to occupy and use the property is called a **lease**. The parties to a lease are the **lessor** and **lessee**.

Joint Tenants and Tenants in Common

More than one person may have an interest in the same real property. This is known as co-ownership, and the owners may hold it either as joint tenants or as tenants in common. As joint tenants, each tenant (that is, owner) holds the same interest as the other, and the surviving co-owner acquires the interest of the deceased. The right of survivorship is the reason joint tenancy is so popular among married people as a means of holding title to real property.

As tenants in common, each tenant may dispose of his or her interest independently of the other by transfer/deed or will. In this type of tenancy, there is no right of survivorship.

Condominium

A **condominium** is a type of corporation in which each member has exclusive ownership of a specific unit in a project, such as a high-rise building or a row of townhouses, but shares ownership as a tenant in common with all other members in the **common elements** of the project, such as the grounds, halls, elevators, swimming pool, and lobby.

For a condominium to be a registered condominium corporation, a declaration setting out the rights and obligations governing the use of the units and the common elements must be registered. The *Condominium Act* provides that if the project is situated in an area in which the land titles system functions, the condominium must be registered in that system.

The condominium corporation holds meetings in which the owners are entitled to vote on decisions concerning the management, upkeep, and operation of the condominium. Each owner contributes to the common expenses of maintaining and repairing the common elements and to the contingency fund that is established to meet unexpected expenses or to build up a reserve to meet major repairs or replacements in the future.

Title Insurance

Title insurance provides coverage to the owners of real property in the case of a defect in title, and lawyers are obligated to advise their clients about it. In Ontario, title insurance has become popular because when it is obtained (at the time of purchase of the real property), certain searches and/or a new survey may not be required, which reduces the disbursement costs for the client and provides title insurance as well.

Family Law Act

Under the provisions of the Family Law Act, marriage is recognized as a form of economic partnership, and all property accumulated by the spouses during the marriage is to be shared equally if the marriage ends. Assets brought into the marriage by each party do not form part of such property, unless it is the home in which the parties were living at the time the marriage broke up. Such a home is known as the matrimonial home and is also referred to as the family residence.

Matrimonial Home

A matrimonial home is a property in which a person has an interest and that is his or her usual family residence or, if the spouses have separated, was at the time of separation their usual family residence.

If title to the matrimonial home is in the name of one spouse, he or she cannot dispose of or encumber the property unless

1. the other spouse joins in the instrument or consents to the transaction;
2. the other spouse has released all rights under the Family Law Act by a separation agreement;
3. the transaction is authorized by court order or an order has been made releasing the property as a matrimonial home; or
4. the property is not designated by both spouses as a matrimonial home, and a designation by both spouses of another property as a matrimonial home has been registered and has not been cancelled.

DESCRIPTION OF REAL PROPERTY

There are several ways in which a particular property may be described:

1. By its municipal address
2. By the traditional legal description of lower and upper tier municipality, together with the lot and concession numbers, the lot and plan numbers, or the lot and reference plan numbers
3. By a property identifier

Municipal Address

Real property is generally described by its street address, such as 135 Stephen Drive, Toronto. This is usually called the mailing address; it is also used for some municipal property records. A municipal address, however, does not provide any means of determining the dimensions or boundaries of the property, which must be set out when the property is bought or sold.

Municipalities

Describing real property in legal documents requires a reference to the lower tier municipality in which it is located and to the upper tier municipality of which the lower tier municipality is a part. Some lawyers also include a reference to the province in which the lower and upper tier municipalities are located. For example:

> City of Kitchener Regional Municipality of Waterloo
> *or*
> Township of Worthington District of Rainy River Province of Ontario

By Township and Concession

This method is usually used in describing real property in rural areas. Land in a county was originally surveyed by a qualified surveyor on behalf of the Crown. It was divided into townships that were, in turn, divided into smaller units called concessions, each of which was then divided into lots. A concession lot usually contains 200 acres. The concession lots could, in turn, be divided into smaller lots. For example, a description using township and concession might read as follows:

> Part of Lot 9, Concession IV
> Township of Hope, County of Northumberland

By Lot and Plan of Subdivision

This method is usually used in describing real property in urban areas, such as cities, villages, and towns. Township lots in a concession have usually been divided into smaller building lots on registered plans of subdivision. A parcel of land is then described by reference to a lot number on a certain plan of subdivision as it was registered and approved by the land registrar in the appropriate land registry office. For example:

> Lot 12, Plan 399
> City of Toronto

Metes and Bounds

When land has been identified by township and concession or by lot and plan number, it may also be necessary to describe the parcel with some particularity, especially if any of the boundaries are irregular. The property is more particularly described by indicating a determinable point of commencement and outlining its perimeter by setting out direction and distances. This is known as a description by metes and bounds and may be described in two ways: by feets and inches or metres and decimals of metres (referred to as a **distance**) or by compass bearings of degrees, minutes, and seconds (referred to as a **course**).

By Unit and Condominium Plan

This method is used when the real property is a unit in a property such as a row of townhouses or an apartment in a high-rise building. The property is registered as a condominium corporation in a land registry office and is assigned a condominium plan number that begins with the name of the upper tier municipality in which the condominium is located. An individual unit is then described by the unit number (and level number, if appropriate, to indicate on which floor the unit is located) and the condominium plan number. For example:

Unit 12, Level 10
Peel Condominium Plan 10000
City of Mississauga Regional Municipality of Peel

By Reference Plan

This method is usually used in legal descriptions of parts or blocks of certain lots referred to on a registered plan of subdivision or on a portion of a registered parcel. A survey of the portion of block, lot, or parcel of land showing the land as described by a metes and bounds description is known as a reference plan (or an R plan) when it is filed in the land titles or registry office. This distinguishes it from other types of plans, including a plan of subdivision. Filed reference plans are numbered consecutively, with each number prefixed by the number of the land registry office and the letter R.

For example, if the owner of a large lot on a plan of subdivision wished to divide it into three lots, a detailed survey of the portions of the lot to be sold would be prepared and filed in the appropriate land registry office. When describing those lots in the necessary documents, it would not be necessary to include a metes and bounds description of the property. The description would refer to the reference plan.

For example, a description by reference to an R plan might read as follows:

Part of Lot 51, Plan 4969 designated as Parts 1 and 2,
Plan 20R-3119 Town of Oakville, Regional Municipality of Halton

Section and Parcel

In the land titles system, property is identified not only by one of the methods discussed above but also by a parcel and section number. In many land titles offices, the parcel and section numbers are those of the lot and plan, with one exception. For example, Lot 25, Plan M-22340 is shown as Parcel 25-1, Section M-22340; the designation 25-1 indicates that this is the first section number allocated to Lot 25. If the owner of Lot 25 were to transfer title to part of it, the section number for the part transferred would be Parcel 25-2.

In some land titles offices, parcel and section numbers follow a consecutive numbering system. The parcel is assigned a number, and the section is given a number that indicates the municipality: for example, Parcel 135-1, Section M-589, Toronto.

Property Identifier Number

A property identifier number (known as PIN) will eventually be assigned to all property in the province as part of the POLARIS project.

The land in the province will be divided into blocks, and the blocks will be divided into properties. A block will be an area containing at least one property and bounded by such limits as land titles or registry division boundaries, roads, railway lines, major utility corridors, water, boundaries, and property limits. A property will be the land held by a single ownership, such as a lot on a plan of subdivision or several abutting (touching) lots held by one owner.

Property maps will be created for the land in a land registry system and will show the blocks and properties. Each property will be assigned a property identifier consisting of four digits; each block will be assigned a number consisting of five digits. The property identifier assigned to a property will be its block number followed by its property number.

Property will continue to be described by the traditional legal description of lot, plan, and municipalities in paper-based registrations, but the property identifier will be used as the index or file number to permit access to computerized title records when searching title or doing electronic registrations.

FORMS OF REAL ESTATE DOCUMENTS

Since April 1, 1985, only five documents have been accepted for registration in the land titles and registry systems:

FORM 1: Transfer/Deed of Land (replaces all former deed and transfer forms)

FORM 2: Charge/Mortgage of Land (replaces all former mortgage and charge forms)

FORM 3: Discharge of Charge/Mortgage (replaces all former discharge of mortgage and cessation of charge forms)

FORM 4: Document General (used for all documents that cannot be accommodated on Form 1, 2, or 3)

FORM 5: Schedule (used for additional information for which there is inadequate space on Form 1, 2, 3, or 4)

Each of these forms is a single page; additional pages (in the form of schedules or attachments) may be included in Forms 1, 2, 3, and 4 and are counted in determining the total number of pages in the document.

If there is insufficient space in any of the boxes on Forms 1, 2, 3, or 4, a schedule (Form 5) is used to continue the information. Form 5 is a blank page, titled "Schedule"; the number and title of the box to which the additional information relates are included above the typed material. The schedule is given the next consecutive page number, which is shown in the upper right-hand corner. Legal-size paper may also be used for a schedule. Head it *Schedule* and number it in the upper righthand corner with the next consecutive page number.

Document Preparation

Documents prepared for registration in land registry offices are microfilmed, and any document not suited to this process will be rejected. Note the following points in preparing documents for registration:

1. Prepare all documents in a black font of uniform quality and density.
2. Place all inserted material within the boxes on the form. Anything appearing to the left or right of a box, or above or below a box, may result in the document being rejected.
3. Do not insert material over words or characters already on the forms, unless you are deleting parts of statements that are inapplicable.
4. Use only photocopies that are legible and suitable for microfilming.
5. If there is insufficient room in a box on a form, use a schedule (Form 5) or plain paper of legal size. Use the title of the box to identify the information.
6. Attachments that are not a schedule should be on legal size paper.

Commercial software packages such as The Conveyancer, widely used in law offices and in the precedents for this text, facilitate the preparation of the forms and supporting documents as well as the management of real estate files. Using The Conveyancer, the client data is entered only once, and the data may also be exported to Teraview, the electronic registration software discussed below.

Electronic Registration

Electronic registration (commonly called e-reg) is the final stage of the *Land Registration Reform Act* to be implemented. This initiative is a joint effort of the Ontario government and Teranet Inc. (a private corporation) to provide a fully electronic registration system for all real estate transactions in Ontario *once* all real property has been converted to the land titles systems.

Teranet is the name of the corporation that is doing the conversions creating the necessary software and will support remote access by law firms for electronic searches and registration. The software itself is called Teraview.

Once a registry office has been completely converted to the land titles system and designated as an electronic registration area under Part III of the *Land Registration Reform Act*, users may conduct searches and enter documents electronically, either at self-serve stations at the registry office or online from the law firm via the Internet.

The "document template" is accessed by the legal assistant from a computer in the law firm, and any existing information about the property (for example, legal description and current owners names) is inserted (or prepopulated, as Teranet refers to this process) by retrieving the data from the POLARIS system. The additional required "fields" or boxes are completed much in the way that the traditional paper forms are completed, although most of the standard statements may be selected from a list of preprogrammed statements. Once drafted, it would be reviewed, and then it is sent to the other party's solicitor for approval before being digitally "signed" by the lawyer and electronically filed at the appropriate registry office on the closing date.

E-reg was implemented in the London registry office in 1999 and will shortly extend across the province; in the interim, the paper POLARIS documents discussed in this text will continue to be used. In either situation, a similar understanding of real estate terminology and procedures is required to prepare a paper or an electronic form. For these reasons, and because an understanding of the hard-copy documents facilitates a fundamental understanding of real estate transactions, this text provides an overview of the preparation of the hard copies as well as the electronic registration procedures for Forms 1, 2, and 3. Form 4 (Document General) is not covered as this form was essentially a catch-all document for any registration not covered by Form 1, 2, or 3 under the Registry or Land Titles System. For example, Form 4 was used for a change in the name of the owner. Under the e-reg system, a separate electronic document has been created for each separate circumstance that might previously have required a document general to be created. See Figure 20.1 for a list of the electronic document formats available in the e-reg system. Reference is made to these electronic documents as necessary in discussing residential real estate transactions in the following chapters.

The traditional paper-based system for searches and registration is generally referred to as the "manual system," and searches and registration carried out using the Teraview software are referred to as "e-reg." These are the terms that are used in this text as the procedures for both systems are discussed.

Getting Started in Teraview

For the law firm to access the Teraview system, the necessary software, a registration account number, an encrypted disk called a "Personal Security Diskette," and a unique passphrase are required. Documents that pass through the system are encrypted to provide security. There are two types of users: lawyers and non-lawyers. Only lawyers may "digitally" sign documents that contain compliance with law statements, such as the *Planning Act* statement, in a transfer/deed. Non-lawyers (laws clerks and legal administrative assistants) are able to conduct title and writ of execution searches and prepare draft electronic documents for review and signature by the lawyers. Documents require a digital signature before they will be accepted for electronic registration.

Although not precedents in the traditional form, the Teraview instructions that are provided in this and the following chapters are identified as precedents and located at the end of the chapter for ease of reference. Before beginning to use Teraview and the instructions provided, note the following:

- The words **document** and **instrument** have the same meaning in the context of real estate practice and are used interchangeably in Teraview and in the instructions provided in this text.

Figure 20.1 Electronic Documents

TERAVIEW: Electronic Documents

Transfer
Transfer by Partnership
Transfer by Personal Representative
Transfer by Religious Organization
Transfer by Trustee in Bankruptcy
Transfer Easement
Transfer, Release, and Abandonment
Transfer Power of Sale

Charge
Charge by Partnership
Charge by Religious Organization
Charge/Mortgage
Notice of Charge of Lease

Discharge of Charge or Other Interest
Application Delete Housing Dev. Lien
Discharge of an Interest
Discharge of Charge
Discharge of Common Element Interest
Discharge of Condominium Lien
Discharge of Construction Lien

Application (General)
Application Consolidate Parcel
Application Delete Execution
Application Vesting Order
Application Foreclosure Order
Application to Register a Court Order
Application to Amend Based on Court Order
Application to Register Court Order

By-laws and Government Order
Application By-law Deeming Plan Not a Plan
Application By-law to Establish Public Highways
Application to Register By-law
Application to Register Government Order
Condominium By-law (Condominium Act 1998)

Cautions
Caution – Charge
Caution – Land (Estates Administration Act)
Renew – Caution
Withdrawal of Caution
Caution – Land
Caution of Agreement of Purchase and Sale
Caution – Land

Certificate
Change of Name Application
Application to Change Name – Instrument
Application to Change Name – Owners

Compliance Subdivision Agreement
Compliance of Subdivision Agreement
Partial Compliance of Subdivision Agreement

Death of Owner Application
Survivorship Application – Charge
Survivorship Application – Land
Transmission by Personal Representative – Charge
Transmission by Personal Representative – Land
Transmission by Devisee/Heir at Law – Land

Inhibiting Orders
Application for Inhibiting Order – Charge
Application for Inhibiting Order – Transfer
Application to Delete Inhibiting Order

Lease or Interest in a Lease Document
Application for Leasehold Parcel
Notice of Assessment of Lessee's Interest in Lease
Notice of Assignment of Lessor's Interest in Lease
Notice of Determination/Surrender of Lease
Notice of Lease
Notice of Oil and Gas Lease
Notice of Sublease
Power of Sale for Notice of Charge of Lease

Liens
Certificate Lien – Housing Development Act
Condominium Lien (Condominium Act 1998)
Construction Lien
Lien

Notice of Change of Address for Service
Notice Change of Address for Service – Condominium
Notice Change of Address for Service – Instrument
Notice Change of Address – Owner

Notice of Option to Purchase

Notice
Notice of Assignment of Rents – General
Notice of Assignment of Rents – Specific
Notice of Security Interest
Notice of Subdivision Agreement
Notice of Vendor's Lien
Notice Under S. 71 of Land Titles Act

Plan Document

Postponement of Interest

Power of Attorney
Revocation of Power of Attorney

Restrictive Covenants
Annex Restrictive Covenants – S.118 – Charge
Application to Annex Restrictive Covenants S.118
Application to Annex Restrictive Covenants S.119
Application to Delete Restrictions

Title Application Documents
Application for Absolute Title
Notice of Application for Absolute Title

Transfer of Charge

Trustee in Bankruptcy Application
Application Trustee in Bankruptcy – Instrument
Application Trustee in Bankruptcy – Owner
Caution – Charge (Bankruptcy & Insolvency Act)
Caution – Land (Bankruptcy & Insolvency Act)

Source: Teranet Inc.

- In Teraview, as in other Windows products, there is more than one way to accomplish a task; however, for the sake of brevity, only one method is discussed.
- Teraview will generally save any work in progress provided that you exit the software correctly, but it is recommended that you use the Save button on the toolbar on a regular basis when you are working in Teraview.
- These instructions are provided as an overview of the most common functions and electronic documents prepared in residential real estate transactions. Further information on Teranet Inc. and Teraview may be found at http://www.teranet.ca.
- Figure 20.2 provides of a list of the instructional precedents provided for Teraview in this text.

Figure 20.2 List of Teraview Instructional Precedents

TERAVIEW E-REG INSTRUCTIONAL PRECEDENTS

Precedent 20.1	Logging On Opening and Changing Dockets Changing Land Registry Office Logging Off
Precedent 21.3	Creating an Electronic Transfer Document
Precedent 22.4	Creating an Electronic Charge Document
Precedent 23.2	Creating an Electronic Discharge of Charge
Precedent 24.6	Opening an Instrument in Progress Printing an Instrument in Progress Creating an Acknowledgement and Direction Report
Precedent 25.1	Sending and Receiving a Message
Precedent 25.4	Signing a Document Registering a Document
Precedent 25.5	Searching for Writs of Execution Clearing by Writs Statement
Precedent 26.4	To Search Title by PIN

Source: Teranet Inc.

To begin working in Teraview, a new docket must first be created. It is recommended that you create a separate docket for each document that you create. The client file number is generally used as law firms maintain an e-reg account with Teranet for each client. This allows the law firm to easily maintain a record of registration fees and Land Transfer Tax, which are transferred from the client's e-reg account to Teranet upon authorization from the law firm.

Because a docket must always be open before you can do anything in Teraview, it is also recommended that you create a docket named "Admin" to use when you are not yet sure which client file will be used for the docket entry.

Precedent 20.1 outlines the steps for accessing Teraview, creating and opening a docket, selecting a Land Registry Office (LRO), and logging off the system.

Terms and Concepts

conveyancing	common elements
real property	declaration
personal property	common expenses
chattels	contingency fund
registry system	title insurance
land titles	matrimonial home
Land Registration Reform Act	municipal address
transfer/deed	lower and upper tier municipalities
charge/mortgage	township and concession
discharge of charge/mortgage	lot and plan of subdivision
vendor	metes and bounds
purchaser	distance
transferor	course
transferee	unit and condominium plan
chargor/mortgagor	reference plan
chargee/mortgagee	section and parcel
lease	property identifier number (PIN)
lessor	electronic registration (e-reg)
lessee	Teranet Inc.
joint tenants	Teraview
tenants in common	manual system
right of survivorship	Teraview procedures
condominium	document/instrument

Review Questions

1. Identify and briefly describe the two land registry systems in Ontario.

2. What is the significance when parties hold title to real property as "joint tenants"?

3. A friend of your family has indicated that she is going to buy a condominium. What exactly is she buying?

4. What is meant by the term "matrimonial home"?

5. What are the various ways in which real property may be legally described?

6. What is meant by the term "e-reg"? What is necessary to be done before property in a registry division can switch to e-reg?

7. Newlyweds Vince and Silvana are purchasing their first home, a condominium, from John and Mary Chan. Vince and Silvana will be borrowing the money from Algonquin Permanent Trust Company to purchase the house.
   a. How should Vince and Silvana hold title if they want right of survivorship?
   b. Who would be the transferors on the transfer/deed document?
   c. Who would be the transferees on the transfer/deed document?
   d. Who would be the mortgagors on the charge/mortgage document?
   e. Who would be the mortgagees on the charge/mortgage document?

PRECEDENTS

Precedent 20.1 Teraview: Logging On, Dockets, LRO Selection, and Logging Off

---

To Log on to Teraview

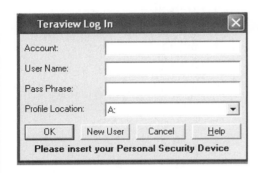

- ► Teraview icon and the Terraview Log In dialog box will open as shown here
- ► Key in your account name and user name (which will be on the diskette)
- ► Key in pass phrase (which will be provided to you by Teraview)
- ► Enter your profile location (usually A:)
- ► Insert your disk and press OK
- ► Wait for the system to log you on

To Create a New Docket

Menu Bar	► Administration
	► Create Docket
Dialog box will open	► key in docket ID number (file number of client)
	► key in docket name (surname of client or company name)
	► OK

To Open an Existing Docket

Menu Bar	► Administration
	► Create Docket
Dialog box will open	►key in docket ID Number (or Docket Name)
	►Find
	►OK

Always check the title bar (at the top of the screen) for which docket you are in.

To Change Land Registry Office (LRO)

Menu Bar	► Administration
	► Change LRO
Dialog box will open	►select LRO
	►OK

Always check the status bar (at the bottom of the screen) for the LRO you are in.

To Exit Teraview

Menu Bar	►Products
	►Exit Teraview
	►Yes
	►Yes

Each time you exit Teraview, you must log out properly and wait for the system to exit completely (the green light will go out) or you may corrupt or lose your data.

Source: Teranet Inc.

CHAPTER 21

Transfer/Deed

OBJECTIVES:

- Identify and describe the legal document by which title is transferred
- Demonstrate an understanding of the completion of the various components of a transfer/deed in paper and electronic formats
- Define the specialized terminology used in a transfer/deed

The legal document by which title is transferred in a real estate transaction is known as a transfer/deed (Form 1).

Before April 1, 1985, each land registry system had a different document by which title to real property was conveyed. A deed was used in the registry system; a transfer was used in the land titles system. Both of these documents will still be encountered for many years as property is sold by the present owners. These documents were multipaged and identified the parties by name, general address, occupation, and a general term specifying their role in the transaction: grantor and grantee in a deed, transferor and transferee in a transfer.

The transfer/deed of land is a much simpler, one-page document to which schedules may be attached. There is only one form of the document, which can be adapted to meet many needs. Although the formal name of the document is Transfer/Deed of Land, the term "transfer" is used in government regulations. To avoid confusion with the old form of transfer, this chapter uses the term "transfer/deed" to refer to the document.

PARTIES TO A TRANSFER/DEED

The parties to a transfer/deed are the transferor(s), the person or persons transferring title to the real estate, and the transferee(s), the person or persons receiving title to the real estate. The transferor is the vendor, and the transferee is the purchaser in the transaction. The transferor is the party who received title under the last registered title document, which may be a transfer/deed, transfer, or deed.

PREPARING THE TRANSFER/DEED OF LAND

In some jurisdictions, the transfer/deed is prepared by the solicitors for the transferee (the purchaser); the more common practice is to have the document prepared by solicitors for the transferor (the vendor). The latter is the practice followed in this text.

The document contains 17 numbered boxes that must be completed by the solicitors for the party preparing it, either by inserting an X into the appropriate box within the main box or by providing the required information. The document also contains several boxes that are marked "For Office Use Only." Nothing is inserted in those boxes in the law office. Precedents 21.1 and 21.2 illustrate examples of a completed transfer/deed.

Box 1

Indicate for which land registry system the document is prepared in this box.

Box 2: Number of Pages

Box 2 indicates the total number of pages in the document as presented for registration. There are always at least two pages: the transfer/deed itself and an affidavit of residency and value of the consideration, which the transferee's solicitors attach to the transfer/deed after closing but before registration, or a schedule, stamped by the Ministry of Revenue, indicating that the required land transfer tax has already been paid (discussed further in Chapter 26). Count any schedules to the transfer/deed in the figure entered in Box 2, representing the total number of pages.

Box 3: Property Identifier(s)

If property identifiers (PIN) have been assigned to the property by the land registry office, a maximum of two such numbers are inserted in this box. If there are more than two, two are entered in the box, an X is inserted in the box marked Additional: See Schedule, and the remaining identifiers are listed on a schedule. If no property identifiers have been assigned, leave this box blank.

Box 4: Consideration

In Box 4 of the transfer/deed, enter the monetary value for the real property only, that is, the part of the total purchase price that is covering the purchase of the land. The total purchase price may include an amount for the purchase of chattels or the amount of applicable GST. Only the portion relating to the land is shown in the transfer/deed.

Where the purchase price is inclusive of GST, as is often the situation with new home purchases, it is necessary to determine what portion of that price represents the cost of the land and what represents the GST. To calculate this, divide the inclusive price by 105 and multiply the resulting answer by 100 to determine the actual purchase price. The difference between that price and the inclusive price represents the amount of GST. For example, if a purchase price that includes GST were $300,000.00, the actual purchase price for the land would be $285,714.28, and the GST would be $14,285.72. Box 4 in the transfer/deed would then show the consideration as $283,018.87.

If it is the practice of your lawyer to reduce the purchase price to reflect the purchase of chattels, you will be advised of the value to be put on such chattels. This amount is then deducted from the purchase price, and the resulting amount is the consideration shown in Box 4.

If the consideration or the purchase is nominal or non-monetary (as when a husband transfers title to property to a spouse, a son, or a daughter), a brief explanation is required (for example, $2.00—natural love and affection).

Box 4 is left blank when the land transfer tax levied on the sale of property will be paid directly to the Ministry of Revenue, and the document is stamped accordingly.

Box 5: Legal Description

Key in the lot and plan numbers (Precedent 21.1); parcel and section numbers; unit, level, and plan numbers for condominiums (Precedent 21.2); or the lot and concession numbers, as well as the lower and upper tier municipality. The name of the land registry office must be shown if the property being conveyed is a condominium; however, most lawyers include this information in all legal descriptions.

If the legal description contains a metes and bounds description, insert in Box 5 the words "See Schedule" and attach a schedule with the information.

Box 5 also contains two boxes that are completed only under certain circumstances.

Severances

If the property being transferred is only part of the property described in the previous deed or transfer (that is, one part of the property is being severed from the balance of the property), the real estate transaction is said to be dividing property, and an X is inserted in the box titled Property Division. The legal description of the property being severed is set out on a schedule. A party is usually not entitled to divide property without the consent of the Land Division Committee or Committee of Adjustments of the municipality; the consent of the committee is an attachment to the transfer/deed.

Consolidations

If the property being transferred is to be added to other abutting (touching) property owned by the purchaser, the real estate transaction is said to be consolidating property, and an X is inserted in the box titled Property Consolidation. The legal description of the consolidated property is set out on a schedule.

Box 6: This Document Contains

Box 6 is completed to indicate special points about the document. An X is placed in Box 6(a) if

1. the legal description in the transfer/deed differs from that set out in the previous title document,
2. a new right of way or easement has been created, or
3. a plan or sketch of the property is an attachment to the document.

An X is placed in the appropriate box within Box 6(b) if

1. a schedule containing a legal description is attached,
2. a schedule listing additional parties to the document is attached, or
3. a schedule for any other purpose is attached.

Any number of the three boxes in Box 6(b) may be marked. If you have inserted an X in a box in another place on the document, indicating that a schedule is attached, you still must note that fact in Box 6(b).

Box 7: Interest/Estate Transferred

Usually nothing is inserted in this box because most individuals hold title to real property in fee simple (Precedent 21.2). If title is qualified, however, or if title is not in fee simple, the way title is held must be shown. If appropriate, delete fee simple and enter the interest or estate transferred to the purchaser, such as life estate or leasehold or if the property is subject to an easement (Precedent 21.1).

Box 8: Transferor(s)

Box 8 shows the names of the transferors and, if individuals, their legal age and spousal status. The names inserted are those shown on the previous deed or transfer or transfer/deed as the grantee(s) or transferee(s).

A statement at the beginning of Box 8 says that the transferor transfers the land to the transferee and that the transferor is at least 18 years of age.

Spousal Status

Space is then provided for a statement to comply with the provisions of the *Family Law Act*. As discussed in Chapter 24, if a transferor is a spouse and the property being transferred is a matrimonial home, title cannot be transferred without the consent of the other spouse, unless certain circumstances make that consent unnecessary. As a result, the spousal status of the transferor is required and an additional statement may be required, as outlined in Figure 21.1 (p. 400).

The *Family Law Act* provides that a statement made by an attorney of the person making the disposition of the property, on the basis of the attorney's personal knowledge, is sufficient proof that the property is not the matrimonial home.

If the transferor is a corporation, there is no statement about spousal status (Precedent 21.2). The statement regarding age may be deleted, but this is not a mandatory requirement. Do not amend the statement in Box 8 to reflect plurals; terms are intended to reflect singular or plural, as appropriate.

If different statements apply to different transferors, attach a schedule where each transferor sets out the statements appropriate to his or her spousal situation. If the same statement applies to all transferors, but there is insufficient space to enter the names of all transferors, attach a schedule and repeat the contents of the statement on the schedule.

Names of Parties

The name of the transferor is shown with the last name first, in solid capitals, followed by given names, as shown in the previous document in which title was taken.

If the name of the transferor has changed since the last registered title document in the land titles system, a change of name application must be completed on a Document General (Form 4) and registered in a paper system or an application to change the name is completed for the e-reg system. The new name of the transferor is then used in the transfer/deed.

If the name of the transferor has changed since the last registered title document in the registry system, use the new name of the transferor. A schedule setting out the circumstances of the change of name may be attached to the transfer/deed.

Status of Parties

If more than one party is listed as a transferor, or if the party listed as transferor is not the party listed as owner in the last title document, indicate the capacity of the party or parties, for example, joint tenants, partners, administrators, executor, etc.

If the transfer/deed is executed under a power of attorney, the document must show the registration number and date of the power of attorney; it must also include a statement that, to the best of the attorney's knowledge and belief, the power of attorney is still in full force and effect and that the principal was at least 18 years old when it was executed. These statements may be set out in Box 8, if there is sufficient space, or may be set out on a schedule.

Figure 21.1 Family Law Statements

1. We are spouses of one another.
> This statement is included when the transferors are married to each other. No other statement is required.

2. The person consenting below is my spouse.
> This statement is included if title to the property is in the name of one spouse and the property is a matrimonial home. The other spouse executes the transfer/deed to indicate consent for the transaction. No other statement is required (Precedent 21.1).

3. I am not a spouse.
> No other statement is required.

4. I am a spouse.
> If this statement is used, an explanation is required as to why the other spouse is not a party to the document; *one* of these additional statements must also be included:

> (a) The property transferred is not ordinarily occupied by me and my spouse, who is not separated from me, as our family residence.

> (b) I am separated from my spouse and the property transferred was not ordinarily occupied by us at the time of our separation as our family residence.

> (c) The property is not designated under section 20 of the Family Law Act as a matrimonial home by me and my spouse, but there is such a designation of another property as our matrimonial home, which has been registered and which has not been cancelled.

> (d) My spouse has released all rights under Part 11 of the Family Law Act by a separation agreement.

> (e) This transaction is authorized by court order under section 23 of the Family Law Act registered as Instrument No. _____, which has not been stayed.

> (f) The property transferred is released from the application of Part 11 of the Family Law Act by court order registered as Instrument No. _____, which has not been stayed.

Corporate Transferor

If a corporation is the transferor, the transfer/deed is either executed under corporate seal (if the corporation has elected to have a seal) or executed without affixing the seal. If the document is to be executed under corporate seal, show the name of the corporation in capital letters and, beneath the line where the authorized party will sign, indicate his or her office if that is the preference of your law office. The office held is not mandatory information. If the document is to be executed without a corporate seal, include the statement "I or We have authority to bind the corporation" beneath the space where the document will be executed (Precedent 21.2).

In the Date of Signature boxes, the date is shown in figures. Leave the exact date blank, to be completed when the document is executed. Note that two digits are used to represent the month; for example, 06 represents June, 07 is July, and so on. Note also that the year is shown in full (for example, 1990).

Box 9: Spouse(s) of Transferor(s)

If the property is a matrimonial home and title is in the name of one spouse, either the other spouse is a party to consent to the transaction or one of the statements indicating why the consent is not required is included in Box 8. If the other spouse is a party to consent, his or her name is entered with the last name first, in solid capitals, followed by the first and middle name(s) in uppercase and lowercase (Precedent 21.1).

Box 10: Transferor's Address for Service

Box 10 shows the address at which the transferor(s) may be served. This may be the address to which he or she is moving following the sale of the property, or it may be the address of the solicitor. If it is the address of a solicitor, include not only the address but also the name of the solicitor. If more space is required to provide information for this box (for example, when there are several transferors, each of whom will have a different address), use a schedule.

Box 11: Transferee(s)

The name(s) of the transferee(s) is listed in this box. This information is provided by the purchaser's solicitors and confirmed on closing the transaction by an executed direction re-title (discussed further in Chapter 26).

Where possible, list each transferee on a separate line. Identify an individual by last name, in solid capitals, followed by the first and at least one other middle name and birth date. Although the *Land Registration Reform Act* requires the first name followed by a middle name, no evidence is necessary to prove that the transferee has no middle name, nor will the document be refused if only a first name is shown. Identify a corporation by its entire corporate name, in solid capital letters; no birth date, of course, is required.

If there is insufficient room in Box 11 to list all the transferees, place an X in Box 6(b), Additional Parties, and attach a schedule.

Box 12: Transferee's Address of Service

Box 12 shows the address at which the transferee(s) may be served. This may be the address of the property that he or she is purchasing, another address, or the address of a solicitor. If it is the address of a solicitor, include not only the address but also the name of the solicitor.

If more space is required to provide information for this box (for example, when there are several transferees, each of whom will have a different address), use a schedule.

Boxes 13 and 14: Planning Act

The statements in boxes 13 and 14 ensure that there is no contravention of the *Planning Act*. The act states that an owner cannot sell part of a property and retain another abutting part unless certain conditions exist. If there was any previous contravention of the act, completion of these boxes on the transfer/deed cures the problem. The completion of these boxes is optional, and the lawyer will advise you if these boxes are to be completed on the document.

Box 13 is completed by the transferor, after discussion with his or her solicitor, and by the individual solicitor for the transferor. Complete as much as possible of the date of signature section, leaving the exact day to be inserted when the document is executed (Precedents 21.1 and 21.2).

The solicitor for the transferee completes Box 14. That lawyer does not receive the executed copies of the transfer/deed until the day the real estate transaction closes. If he or she is attending on the closing, Box 14 may be completed following receipt of the transfer/deed but before registration. If, however, the solicitor is not attending, a separate Box 14 is completed on paper with adhesive backing and affixed to the document before registration.

Box 15: Assessment Roll Number of Property

The Province of Ontario sends homeowners a Provincial Assessment Notice. It contains an assessment roll number identifying the county or district, the lower tier municipality, and the map, subdivision, and parcel of the property. This assessment roll number is not the number that appears on the tax bill. It is a formula of five groups of numbers, each made up of a specified number of digits, for example, 19 08 018 505 13700 (Precedents 21.1 and 21.2). If the last number, the parcel number, does not contain five digits, add sufficient zeros to make it a five-digit number.

If the property does not as yet have an assessment roll number, indicate this by the words "Not Assigned" in the last block in the box. If there is more than one property on the transfer/deed, or if the property has more than one assessment roll number, enter the word "Multiple" in the last block in the box.

Box 16: Municipal Address of Property

Enter the full municipal address of the property in this box: street number, street name, unit type (apartment, suite, etc.), unit number, municipality, province, and postal code (Precedents 21.1 and 21.2). If the property being transferred has more than one municipal address, enter "Multiple." If the property has not been assigned a municipal address (for example, in rural areas), enter "Not Assigned."

Box 17: Document Prepared By

Enter the name of the individual solicitor, the name of the law firm, and the law firm's address and postal code in Box 17 (Precedents 21.1 and 21.2).

NUMBER OF COPIES AND DISPOSITION

A minimum of four copies are usually required. One copy of the draft transfer/deed is sent to the transferee's solicitors for approval as to form. When it is approved, two copies are executed by the transferors and then held in the file until the closing date. Note that when the transfer/deed is prepared, the face page and any schedules or attachments are assembled and held by a paper clip, not a staple, because a Land Transfer Tax affidavit is attached at the closing of the transaction. The fourth copy remains in the office file.

E-REG TRANSFER

Precedent 21.3 outlines the steps for creating an electronic transfer document in Teraview. Note that all parts of completion of the transfer are discussed. In practice, the majority of the document is completed by the solicitors for the vendor, with the exception of the steps for completing the information on the transferee(s), doing a writ search, and Land Transfer and School Tax statements, which are completed by the solicitors for the transferee when the draft electronic document is sent to them.

Precedent 21.4 illustrates a printout of an electronic transfer in progress.

Terms and Concepts

transfer/deed	consolidations
grantor	life estate
grantee	leasehold
transferor	easement
transferee	spousal status and the *Family Law Act*
property identifiers (PIN)	corporate signatories
consideration	*Planning Act*
GST	assessment roll number
legal descriptions	execution and registration of transfer/deed
severances	e-reg transfer/deed preparation

Review Questions

1. Presume that the purchase price is $200,000. Indicate under what circumstances that figure would not be shown as the amount of consideration in Box 4 of the new transfer/deed.

2. Why is it necessary to know the marital status of an individual who is the vendor?

3. What party is the purchaser in the new transfer/deed, and what information must be shown for him/her/them?

4. How many copies are required of a transfer/deed, and what disposition is made of those copies?

5. The old document from which you are taking the legal description contains a long metes and bounds description. How is this description included in the new transfer/deed?

6. If there is insufficient room in any box on the transfer/deed, what procedure is followed to record the required information?

7. What happens to the transfer/deed when it has been executed?

PRECEDENTS

Precedent 21.1 Transfer/Deed of Land, Registry

Province of Ontario

Transfer/Deed of Land
Form 1 — Land Registration Reform Act

A

(1) Registry [X] **Land Titles** ☐	**(2) Page 1** of **2** pages

(3) Property Identifier(s)   Block   Property   **42221-8732**   Additional: See Schedule ☐

(4) Consideration
TWO HUNDRED THIRTY FIVE THOUSAND------------------------------
Dollars $ **235,000.00**

(5) Description   This is a: Property Division ☐   Property Consolidation ☐

East Half of Lot 105, Plan 5948
City of Toronto

Registry Division of the Toronto Registry Office No. 64

FOR OFFICE USE ONLY

New Property Identifiers   Additional: See Schedule ☐

Executions   Additional: See Schedule ☐

(6) This Document Contains   (a) Redescription New Easement Plan/Sketch ☐   (b) Schedule for: Description ☐   Additional Parties ☐   Other ☐ | **(7) Interest/Estate Transferred** Fee Simple **Subject to easement**

(8) Transferor(s) The transferor hereby transfers the land to the transferee and certifies that the transferor is at least eighteen years old and that
I am a spouse. The person consenting below is my spouse

Name(s)	Signature(s)	Date of Signature Y / M / D
PETERSON, Ryan Andrew		**2008** / **02** /

(9) Spouse(s) of Transferor(s) I hereby consent to this transaction

Name(s)	Signature(s)	Date of Signature Y / M / D
PETERSON, Kristen Lynn		**2008** / **02** /

(10) Transferor(s) Address for Service   **42 Oaklea Blvd., Oakville, ON L3J 4V1**

(11) Transferee(s)

	Date of Birth Y / M / D
ANDERSON, Ronald Craig	**1970** / **08** / **28**
ANDERSON, Kelly Anne	**1973** / **01** / **15**
as joint tenants	

(12) Transferee(s) Address for Service   **984 Helena Avenue, Toronto, ON M9R 3G6**

Planning Act – OPTIONAL

(13) Transferor(s) The transferor verifies that to the best of the transferor's knowledge and belief, this transfer does not contravene section 50 of the Planning Act.
Ryan Andrew Peterson
Date of Signature Y / M / D   **2008** / **02** /
Signature ....
Date of Signature Y / M / D
Signature ....

Solicitor for Transferor(s) I have explained the effect of section 50 of the Planning Act to the transferor and I have made inquiries of the transferor to determine that this transfer does not contravene that section and based on the information supplied by the transferor, to the best of my knowledge and belief, this transfer does not contravene that section. I am an Ontario solicitor in good standing.
Name and Address of Solicitor **Peter T. Grant** **17 Princess Street South, Suite 2501** **Toronto ON M8Y 3N5**
Date of Signature Y / M / D   **2008** / **02** /
Signature...................

(14) Solicitor for Transferee(s) I have investigated the title to this land and to abutting land where relevant and I am satisfied that the title records reveal no contravention as set out in subclause 50 (22) (c) (ii) of the Planning Act and that to the best of my knowledge and belief this transfer does not contravene section 50 of the Planning Act. I act independently of the solicitor for the transferor(s) and I am an Ontario solicitor in good standing.
Affix Statement by Solicitor for Transferee(s) here if necessary
Name and Address of Solicitor **Drew C. Crawford** **53 Suffolk Street** **Guelph, ON N1H 7B4**
Date of Signature Y / M / D   **2008** / **02** /
Signature...................

(15) Assessment Roll Number of Property   Cty. **19** / Mun. **04** / Map **231** / Sub. **882** / Par. **00600**

(16) Municipal Address of Property
984 Helena Avenue
Toronto ON M9R 3G6

(17) Document Prepared by:
Peter T. Grant
HILL, JOHNSTON & GRANT
17 Princess Street South, Suite 2501
Toronto ON M8Y 3N5

FOR OFFICE USE ONLY

Fees and Tax

Registration Fee	
Land Transfer Tax	
Total	

Source: Do Process Software Ltd.

Transfer/Deed of Land
Form 1 — Land Registration Reform Act

File 2222

A

Province of Ontario

(1) Registry ☐   Land Titles [X]   (2) Page 1 of **2** pages

(3) Property Identifier(s)   Block   Property   **33451-2806**   Additional: See Schedule ☐

(4) Consideration

TWO HUNDRED THOUSAND------------ Dollars $ 200,000.00

(5) Description   This is a: Property Division ☐   Property Consolidation ☐

Unit 21, Level 20,
Peel Condominium Plan No. 266
and its appurtenant common interest
City of Mississauga
Regional Municipality of Peel
Land Titles Division of Peel (No. 43)

FOR OFFICE USE ONLY

New Property Identifiers   Additional: See Schedule ☐

Executions   Additional: See Schedule ☐

(6) This Document Contains   (a) Redescription New Easement Plan/Sketch ☐   (b) Schedule for: Description ☐   Additional Parties ☐   Other ☐

(7) Interest/Estate Transferred **Fee Simple**

(8) Transferor(s) The transferor hereby transfers the land to the transferee ~~and certifies that the transferor is at least eighteen years old and that~~ x

Name(s)	Signature(s)	Date of Signature Y M D
GEORGIAN FINANCIAL INC.	Per: **Name: Maria Griffiths** **Title: President**	**2007 10**
	I have authority to bind the Corporation	

(9) Spouse(s) of Transferor(s) I hereby consent to this transaction

Name(s)	Signature(s)	Date of Signature Y M D

(10) Transferor(s) Address for Service   **400 West Simcoe Street, Barrie, ON L4M 2J9**

(11) Transferee(s)

	Date of Birth Y M D
CHIOVITTI, Franco	**1965 04 20**
IGAV, Francesco	**1973 11 23**
each as to a 50% interest as tenants in common	

(12) Transferee(s) Address for Service   **500 Northern Avenue, Unit 2021, Mississauga, ON L6A 4E9**

(13) Transferor(s) The transferor verifies that to the best of the transferor's knowledge and belief, this transfer does not contravene section 50 of the Planning Act.

GEORGIAN FINANCIAL INC.   Date of Signature Y M D   **2007 10**   Date of Signature Y M D

Signature ....   Signature............

Solicitor for Transferor(s) I have explained the effect of section 50 of the Planning Act to the transferor and I have made inquiries of the transferor to determine that this transfer does not contravene that section and based on the information supplied by the transferor, to the best of my knowledge and belief, this transfer does not contravene that section. I am an Ontario solicitor in good standing.

Name and Address of Solicitor   **Peter T. Grant, Hill, Johnston & Grant** **17 Princess Street South, Suite 2501** **Toronto ON M8Y 3N5**   Date of Signature Y M D   **2007 10**

Signature............

Planning Act – OPTIONAL

Affix Statement by Solicitor for Transferee(s) here if necessary

(14) Solicitor for Transferee(s) I have investigated the title to this land and to abutting land where relevant and I am satisfied that the title records reveal no contravention as set out in subclause 50 (22) (c) (ii) of the Planning Act and that to the best of my knowledge and belief this transfer does not contravene section 50 of the Planning Act. I act independently of the solicitor for the transferor(s) and I am an Ontario solicitor in good standing.

Name and Address of Solicitor   Date of Signature Y M D

Signature............

(15) Assessment Roll Number of Property   Cty. **21**   Mun. **05**   Map   Sub.   Par.

(16) Municipal Address of Property
500 Northern Avenue, Unit 2021
Mississauga, ON L6A 4E9

(17) Document Prepared by:
Peter T. Grant
HILL, JOHNSTON & GRANT
17 Princess Street South, Suite 2501
Toronto ON M8Y 3N5

FOR OFFICE USE ONLY

Fees and Tax	
Registration Fee	
Land Transfer Tax	
Total	

Source: Do Process Software Ltd.

To Create an Electronic Transfer Document

Menu Bar ► Instrument
► Create New…

The Create New Form window will open displaying all document types available in a file directory tree
► Expand the Transfer branch by clicking on the plus sign
► Transfer
► OK

Work in Progress window opens as shown here:

Create the document by moving through each branch of the directory shown on the left-hand side.

Always expand the directory for each branch by clicking on the plus sign, then click on each subdirectory, and complete the data entry fields as required on the right-hand side, noting the guidelines below:

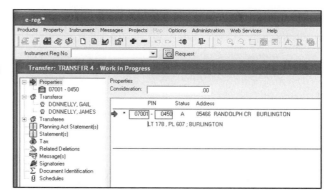

Properties:
► Insert consideration
► Insert PIN number, and the data fields will be prepopulated beginning with the legal description
► Click on PIN number (in the directory) and review Transferor information, changing if necessary

Transferor:
► Transferor's name(s) should already be prepopulated
► Click on the name of the Transferor (in the directory) and complete the screens for **each** of the tabs, noting the following:

Family Law Act and Age Statements – Not applicable for a company. For an individual, click on "I am at least 18 years old" and the appropriate spousal statement. If the spousal statement has a word in full caps (e.g., NAME), double click on the word to open a dialog box to insert the appropriate information.

Other Statements – Select statements as appropriate. Note: The statement "This document is not authorized under a Power of Attorney by this party." **must** be selected, unless it is under a power of attorney, and then the appropriate statement would be selected and information inserted. If the statement has a word in full caps (e.g., NAME), double click on the word to open a dialog box to insert the appropriate information.

Writs – The system will show beside "Status" whether any writs have been previously searched. In order to do a writs search:
Menu Bar ► Instruments
► Writs
► Retrieve Writs
The search will be done and "Status" will change to show "clear" or if there are any writs they will be displayed.

Address for Service – Insert the Transferor's address (after the closing date). If the address is the same for both Transferors, you only need to insert the address for the first Transferor.

Note: These steps must be completed for **each** Transferor.

Source: Teranet Inc.

Transferee:
► Click on New Party (in the directory) and complete the following:

Name: If an individual, key in last name first, followed by a comma (or Teraview thinks the client is a company), followed by the given name(s). If a company, key in the full corporate name.

Capacity: Select the appropriate statement from the drop-down menu. This is an optional field depending on the circumstances of the Transferee.

Share: Completed if there is more than one Transferee and each owns a percentage interest; may be entered as a percentage or decimal, but the total may not exceed 100 percent.

Birthdate: Key in year/month/day format—e.g., 1985/01/01.

Other Statements: Complete as appropriate or leave blank.

Address for Service Tab: This will default to the property address; change if necessary.

To add a second Transferee:
Menu Bar   ► Instrument
                 ► Add Transferee
                 ► NEW PARTY (and complete as above)

Planning Act Statement(s)
As in paper documents, completion of the Planning Act statements is optional. Complete as instructed.

Statements – If required, select the appropriate statement(s) from this screen.

Tax
Complete the screens for **each** of the tabs, as appropriate, noting the following guidelines:

Deponents: You may add the name(s) of all deponents by clicking on the All button or may click the ellipses button (beside the All button) and select from the pop-up dialog box the names to include; then select the appropriate statement for the individual(s) making the oath.

>$400,000: If the consideration is over $400,000, select the appropriate statements.

Consideration: Enter the appropriate amounts (see Figure 26.1 for further information).

Nominal/Explanations/Exemptions: Completed only if the consideration is for nominal consideration or exempt from Land Transfer Tax—select the appropriate statements.

School Tax: Select the appropriate statement.

Related Deletions – Sometimes as a result of the current transaction, some previous registrations on the property may be deleted. The lawyer will advise if you need to do this. If so, key in the instrument number.

Messages – Displays any messages you have sent or received—discussed further in Chapter 25

Signatories – Displays the signatory status of the document, i.e., whether it has been "digitally" signed.

Document Identification
Allows you to save work in progress and charge the disbursements to the client's account. The document name may be up to 40 characters. Key in the client's name and the type of document—e.g., Donnelly s/t Kelso Transfer. Once entered, the name is displayed in the Title Bar.

Schedules – Displays any attached schedules or statement information.

Note: See Precedent 24.6 for instructions on how to print an instrument in progress.

Source: Teranet Inc.

**** NOT VALID - TO BE USED FOR TRAINING PURPOSES ONLY ****

This document has not been submitted and may be incomplete.

LRO # 20   **Transfer**

yyyy mm dd   Page 1 of 1

In preparation on 2007 07 30   at 13:38

Properties

PIN	07001 - 0450 LT	Interest/Estate	Fee Simple
Description	LT 178 , PL 607 ; BURLINGTON		
Address	05466 RANDOLPH CR BURLINGTON		

Consideration

Consideration $ 250,000.00

Transferor(s)

The transferor(s) hereby transfers the land to the transferee(s).

Name	DONNELLY, GAIL Acting as an individual
Address for Service	420 MacKenzie Drive Waterloo ON L6J 4X9

I am at least 18 years of age.

James Donnelly and I are spouses of one another and are both parties to this document

This document is not authorized under Power of Attorney by this party.

Name	DONNELLY, JAMES Acting as an individual
Address for Service	

I am at least 18 years of age.

Gail Donnelly and I are spouses of one another and are both parties to this document

This document is not authorized under Power of Attorney by this party.

Transferee(s)

		Capacity	Share
Name	KELSO, JOHN Acting as an individual	Joint Tenants	
Date of Birth	1985 01 01		
Address for Service	05466 RANDOLPH CR BURLINGTON		
Name	KELSO, MARIAN Acting as an individual	Joint Tenants	
Date of Birth	1986 05 05		
Address for Service	05466 RANDOLPH CR BURLINGTON		

STATEMENT OF THE TRANSFEROR (S): The transferor(s) verifies that to the best of the transferor's knowledge and belief, this transfer does not contravene the Planning Act.

Calculated Taxes

Retail Sales Tax	$160.00
Land Transfer Tax	$3,695.00

Source: Teranet Inc.

CHAPTER 22

Charge/Mortgage of Land

OBJECTIVES:

- Identify and describe the legal document to formalize a loan in real estate transactions

- Demonstrate an understanding of the completion of the various components of a charge/mortgage in paper and electronic formats

- Distinguish between amortized and non-amortized mortgages and be able to accurately calculate the repayment clauses for each

- Define the specialized terminology used in a charge/mortgage

When a person borrows money using real property as collateral, the document completed to formalize the loan is known as a charge/mortgage of land. The act dealing with real estate uses the term "charge" to refer to this document; it is still usual, however, to refer to it as a mortgage.

Sometimes the purchaser may give the vendor a mortgage back, instead of actual cash, to satisfy part of the purchase price; alternatively, the purchaser may assume an existing mortgage on the property. No new charge/mortgage is prepared when a mortgage is assumed, but a new document is required when there is a mortgage back.

There may be more than one mortgage on real property; frequently, there are two. The mortgage that is registered first is known as the first mortgage, and the other is the second mortgage. If it is necessary to sell the property because the mortgagor fails to pay the debt, the mortgagee under the first mortgage is entitled to have that claim paid in full before the mortgagee under the second mortgage receives anything. When the mortgagee enforces his or her right to recover mortgaged property because of nonpayment, the mortgagor is said to be foreclosed.

PARTIES TO A CHARGE/MORTGAGE

The parties to the mortgage are referred to in the legislation and on the charge/mortgage forms as the chargor—the person who gives the mortgage—and the chargee—the person who receives the mortgage; however, these parties are still usually referred to as the mortgagor and mortgagee.

REPAYMENT OF MORTGAGES

There are a number of ways in which the monies covered by the mortgage may be repaid. To understand the repayment provisions of the mortgage, note the following terms:

1. The **principal** of the mortgage is the amount of the mortgage debt, upon payment of which (together with any accrued interest) the mortgage is paid in full and discharged.
2. The **terms** of the mortgage refer to the conditions of repayment, that is, how much is paid on each repayment, how frequently payments are to be made, the rate of interest to be charged per year, and the **term** of the mortgage (the number of years over which the mortgage will be repaid at a specified interest rate).
3. **Maturity** refers to the date on which all monies secured by the mortgage are due. A mortgage is said to run from the date on which it is given, which is the date of closing the real estate transaction or a date agreed upon when the mortgagor already owns the property that is to be the subject of the mortgage. A mortgage is said to mature a certain number of years from the date on which it was given at the end of the term of the mortgage. For example, a mortgage commencing on December 1, 2008, that has a term of three years matures on December 1, 2011.

Repayment of a mortgage is usually made in one of two ways:

1. A set amount is paid monthly, quarterly, or half-yearly, on account of principal, with interest on the balance still outstanding on the mortgage. The set amount payable is said to be paid on account of principal. This form of payment is no longer widely used.
2. A fixed, combined payment of principal and interest is made of the same amount every month during the term of the mortgage. This is called a **blended payment** because it includes both principal and interest. The blended payment is first applied to payment of interest owing on the balance of the principal outstanding, and the remainder of the payment, that is, what is not required to cover the interest, is applied to reduce the amount of principal. When the mortgage matures, the balance of principal and any accrued interest then outstanding are due.

In most mortgages that call for a blended payment, the payment is calculated to completely amortize or pay off the mortgage over a given number of years. Amortized payments are usually made monthly.

Amortized Mortgages

Amortized mortgages are very common because the amount of each mortgage payment remains the same during the term of the mortgage.

Many mortgages are based on amortization periods of 20 or 25 years; this represents the total number of years over which the mortgage payments will be made. Note carefully that the amortization period and the term of the mortgage are rarely the same period of time.

When an amortized mortgage is first arranged, the mortgagor and mortgagee first agree on the amortization period; then they agree on the number of years (or term) over which payments are to be made at a stipulated rate of interest. That term has often been for a period of 5 years, but in times of fluctuating interest rates, it may be shorter.

Usually, a mortgage contains a clause allowing it to be renewed on maturity for a further term but at the then-prevailing rate of interest. The amount of monthly payment is adjusted to reflect the revised rate of interest.

A mortgage that may be paid off at any time without giving notice or paying additional interest as a bonus is known as an "open mortgage."

The law firm will usually have a booklet indicating a schedule of amortized payments for various interest rates and for a various number of years (the amortization period) or use a commercial software program, such as *The Conveyancer*, which allows the printing out of amortization schedules when the basic details of the mortgage amount, interest rate, and amortization period are provided, as illustrated in Figure 22.1.

Figure 22.1 Amortization Schedule

AMORTIZATION SCHEDULE

Prepared for: **Peter T. Grant (CENTENNIAL & PARTNERS)**			*Principal:* **$100,000.00**	
Borrower: **WINDSTAR CONSULTANTS INC.**			*Interest rate:* **7.0% per annum**	*calculated:* **Semi**
Lender: **Data Bank of Canada**			*Payments:* **$706.78 Monthly**	**Annually**

Payment #	Date	Principal	Interest	Balance
1	Oct 1, 2008	$131.78	$575.00	$99,868.22
2	Nov 1, 2008	$132.53	$574.25	$99,735.69
3	Dec 1, 2008	$133.30	$573.48	$99,602.39
4	Jan 1, 2009	$134.06	$572.72	$99,468.33
5	Feb 1, 2009	$134.83	$571.95	$99,333.50
6	Mar 1, 2009	$135.61	$571.17	$99,197.89
7	Apr 1, 2009	$136.39	$570.39	$99,061.50
8	May 1, 2009	$137.17	$569.61	$98,924.33
9	Jun 1, 2009	$137.96	$568.82	$98,786.37
10	Jul 1, 2009	$138.75	$568.03	$98,647.62
11	Aug 1, 2009	$139.55	$567.23	$98,508.07
12	Sep 1, 2009	$140.35	$566.43	$98,367.72
13	Oct 1, 2009	$141.16	$565.62	$98,226.56
14	Nov 1, 2009	$141.97	$564.81	$98,084.59
15	Dec 1, 2009	$142.79	$563.99	$97,941.80
16	Jan 1, 2010	$143.61	$563.17	$97,798.19
17	Feb 1, 2010	$144.44	$562.34	$97,653.75
18	Mar 1, 2010	$145.27	$561.51	$97,508.48
19	Apr 1, 2010	$146.10	$560.68	$97,362.38
20	May 1, 2010	$146.94	$559.84	$97,215.44
21	Jun 1, 2010	$147.79	$558.99	$97,067.65
22	Jul 1, 2010	$148.64	$558.14	$96,919.01
23	Aug 1, 2010	$149.49	$557.29	$96,769.52
24	Sep 1, 2010	$150.35	$556.43	$96,619.17
25	Oct 1, 2010	$151.22	$555.56	$96,467.95
26	Nov 1, 2010	$152.09	$554.69	$96,315.86
27	Dec 1, 2010	$152.96	$553.82	$96,162.90
28	Jan 1, 2011	$153.84	$552.94	$96,009.06
29	Feb 1, 2011	$154.72	$552.06	$95,854.34
30	Mar 1, 2011	$155.61	$551.17	$95,698.73
31	Apr 1, 2011	$156.51	$550.27	$95,542.22
32	May 1, 2011	$157.41	$549.37	$95,384.81
33	Jun 1, 2011	$158.31	$548.47	$95,226.50
34	Jul 1, 2011	$159.22	$547.56	$95,067.28
35	Aug 1, 2011	$160.14	$546.64	$94,907.14
36	Sep 1, 2011	$161.06	$545.72	$94,746.08
		$5,253.92	$20,190.16	

These calculations have been prepared using conventional compound interest principles. No liability is undertaken in regard to the interpretation or use which may be made of these calculations. It is your responsibility to ensure that the terms on which this schedule is based correspond to those in your mortgage. E. & O. E.

Source: Do Process Software Ltd.

PREPARING THE CHARGE/MORTGAGE OF LAND

In most jurisdictions, a mortgage is prepared by the solicitors acting for the person giving it, the mortgagor (chargor). Precedents 22.1 and 22.2 illustrate examples of a completed charge/mortgage. The document contains several unnumbered boxes marked "For Office Use Only"; nothing is inserted in these boxes when the document is prepared in the law office. The document contains 18 numbered boxes to be completed by the solicitors for the party preparing it, either by inserting an X into the appropriate box within the main numbered box or by providing the required information.

Boxes 1, 3, 5, 6, 7, 16, 17, and 18

These boxes have the same completion requirements as in a transfer/deed, as discussed in Chapter 21.

Box 2: Number of Pages

Box 2 indicates the total number of pages in the document as presented for registration. There is always at least one page in the document. If there are any schedules or attachments to the charge/mortgage, each is included in the figure entered in Box 2 to represent the total number of pages in the document. If, however, a set of standard charge terms is referred to in Box 8 of the document, the pages of terms are not included in the Box 2 figure.

Box 4: Principal Amount

In Box 4, enter the total amount secured by the mortgage (the principal), first in words and then in numbers. The amount of any mortgage back is indicated in the agreement of purchase and sale originating the real estate transaction; the client will provide information on the amount of any mortgages secured from a financial institution.

Box 8: Standard Charge Terms

The old charges and mortgages contained two pages of special provisions that applied to the mortgage, relating to the payment of taxes on the property, insurance on the property, procedures on default of payment, covenants to keep the lands and buildings in good condition and repair, possession of the property during the term of the mortgage, changes in status of the parties to the mortgage, etc. These provisions are not included in the printed form of the new charge/mortgage.

Mortgagors still need to be aware of the provisions applicable to the mortgage. Thus, financial institutions register with the Director of Land Registration a standard set of charge terms to incorporate the terms and covenants formerly included in the mortgage document. When the standard set of charge terms is registered, a filing number is assigned and a copy of the terms is forwarded to every land registry office in the province for inclusion in a charge book.

Insert the filing number in the blank space on the first line of Box 8. All the filed terms are then automatically incorporated into the new charge/mortgage without being set out in a schedule. The chargor/mortgagor must be given a copy of the standard charge terms incorporated into the mortgage before the document is signed.

If any of the terms in the standard charge terms are to be varied for the specific document, the changes are set out in Box 10, Additional Provisions, or a schedule is attached (if a schedule is attached, be sure to mark the Other box in Box 6(b). Precedent 22.3 illustrates the first page of standard charge terms that have been registered by Northern Credit Union Limited.

If the mortgagee has not registered standard charge terms, the terms are set out on a schedule to the charge/mortgage.

Box 9: Payment Provisions

Blended and Amortized Payments

Box 9 states the payment provisions for amortized or other blended payments: the amount of the principal, the interest rate, the interest calculation period, the date of any interest adjustment (if money was advanced before the effective date of the mortgage), the payment dates, the date on which the first and last payments are to be made, the date the mortgage matures, the amount of each payment, and information on insurance coverage.

The agreement of purchase and sale may provide this information if it is a vendor take-back mortgage, but more often it is provided in the form of mortgage instructions from the financial institution from which the mortgagor is receiving the mortgage funds.

Figure 22.2 (p. 416) illustrates the basic format for completing Box 9 for blended and amortized payments. Precedents 22.1 and 22.2 illustrate a completed Box 9.

Non-amortized Payments

When non-amortized payments are to be made under the mortgage, the payment provisions cannot be conveniently entered in Box 9. Instead, a schedule is attached. Insert the words "See Schedule for All Payment Provisions" in one of the blanks in Box 9. Remember to mark the Other box in Box 6(b) with an X.

For example, if a three-year mortgage is to be given as of November 1, 2008, to be repayable quarterly, payments will be due on the first days of February; May, August, and November in each year, except the year in which the mortgage matures. Payments made on the first days of those months in each of the years 2008, 2009, and 2010 are on account.

In 2011 (the year in which the mortgage matures), the payment due on November 1, 2011 (the maturity date of the mortgage), is not on account but is the total balance still unpaid that is due on that date. Therefore, if payment is to be $500 quarterly on account of principal, the schedule would therefore state the following:

The amount of principal secured by the Charge/Mortgage is Twenty Thousand Dollars ($20,000.00) and the rate of interest chargeable thereon is seven (7) percent per annum calculated quarterly not in advance.

Figure 22.2 Charge/Mortgage, Box 9, Repayment Guide, Amortized Payments

(9) Payment Provisions 1 (a) Principal Amount $				(b) Interest 2 Rate	% per annum	(c) Calculation 3 Period		
(d) Interest Adjustment Date	Y 4	M	D	Payment 5 (e) Date and Period		First (f) Payment Date	Y 6	M : D
(g) Last Payment Date	7			Amount 8 (h) of Each Payment		Dollars $		
(i) Balance Due Date	9			(j) Insurance 10		Dollars $		

LEGEND:

1. Enter the principal amount of the mortgage in figures only.

2. Enter the rate of interest being charged in figures only.

3. Show the period of interest calculation (i.e., half-yearly) and indicate "not in advance" if applicable.

4. Enter the date up to which interest on any monies advanced prior to the effective date of the mortgage must be paid. This adjustment is frequently necessary when monies are advanced prior to the effective date of the mortgage.

5. Enter the date and period of each payment under the mortgage. For example: 15th of each month or 15th monthly.

6. Enter the first regular payment date. If the mortgage is being paid monthly and is effective the 1st day of February, 20__, payments will be made on the 1st day of each month. The first regular payment will be March 1, 20__, and will be shown as 20__/03/01.

7. Enter the last regular payment date. This is the date on which the mortgage matures.

8. Enter the amount of each payment first in words and then in figures.

9. Enter the date on which the balance due under the mortgage is payable; this is the maturity date of the mortgage.

10. Enter the amount of insurance coverage carried on the property, or the standard statement "Full Insurable Value," or enter "See Standard Charge Terms No...." (insert filing number) to refer to the special provisions set out relating to insurance coverage if required by the mortgagee.

Provided that this charge/mortgage to be void upon payment of Twenty Thousand Dollars ($20,000.00) of lawful money of Canada with interest at seven (7) percent per annum as follows:

The sum of FIVE HUNDRED ($500.00) DOLLARS on account of principal shall become due and payable quarterly on the first days of August and November in the year 2008, on the first days of February, May, August, and November in the years 2009 and 2010 and on the first days of February, May, and August in the year 2011.

The said principal sum of Twenty Thousand Dollars ($20,000.00) shall become due and payable on the 1st day of November, 2011 and interest at the said rate calculated as aforesaid as well as before maturity and both before and after default on such portion of the principal as remains from time to time unpaid on the 1st days of February, May, August, and November in each year until the principal is fully paid; the first payment of interest to be computed from the 1st day of November, 2008 upon the whole amount of principal hereby secured, to become due and payable on the 1st day of February, 2009.

Box 10: Additional Provisions

Mortgages frequently contain special provisions, for example, renewal privileges, the right to pay additional amounts on the mortgage without notice or bonus to the mortgagee, or the requirement that mortgage payments for a calendar year be provided by postdated cheques.

These provisions are either included in the agreement of purchase and sale originating a real estate transaction or negotiated by the solicitors for the parties when a mortgage is given on property the mortgagor already owns.

Any additional provisions are entered in Box 10, if there is room. If there is insufficient space for each additional provision, insert "See Schedule," enter an X in the Continued on Schedule box in the lower right-hand corner of the box, and set out the additional provisions on a schedule. Be sure also to enter an X in the Other box in Box 6(b).

Figure 22.3 illustrates specimen provisions often added to the standard charge terms. There are, of course, many other clauses that may be used; as these are encountered, add them to your precedents.

Box 11: Chargor(s)

Box 11 shows the name of the chargor/mortgagor and, if an individual, the legal age and spousal status. The chargor/mortgagor is always the same party or parties who took title under the most recent transfer/deed. If the mortgage is prepared for use in a real estate transaction, the transferee is the chargor/mortgagor in the mortgage.

A statement at the beginning of Box 11 says that the chargor charges the land to the chargee, which simply means that the chargee has a claim against the property. The statement further indicates that the chargor is at least 18 years of age. Although the singular form of the word chargor is used, the term is interpreted as meaning singular or plural, as appropriate.

Figure 22.3 Specimen Mortgage Clauses

PREPAYMENT CLAUSES

Start each clause with: Provided that the chargor(s) when not in default hereunder

1. shall have the privilege of prepaying any amount of principal hereby secured at any time without notice or bonus.

2. shall have the privilege of prepaying the whole or any part of the principal hereby secured at any time or times without notice upon payment of three months' interest as penalty for repayment calculated on the amount of principal prepaid from time to time.

3. shall have the privilege of paying on any anniversary date an additional amount of principal not in excess of ten (10) percent of the original amount of the mortgage, it being agreed that such privilege shall not be cumulative notwithstanding any such payment; the regular monthly payment of *(amount)* shall continue thereafter to be paid in the same amount until the maturity of this charge/mortgage or the monies hereby secured shall have been repaid in full, whichever shall first occur.

4. shall have the privilege of paying an additional \$_____ or any sum in multiples thereof on account of principal on any interest date without notice or bonus.

RENEWAL CLAUSES

Provided that the chargor(s) when not in default hereunder (*optional:* and upon providing the chargee(s) during the term of the within charge/mortgage, at least _____ (days'/months') notice in writing,) shall have the privilege of renewing the within charge/mortgage for a further period of _____ years upon the same terms and conditions and at the interest rate prevailing at the time of maturity, but with no right of further renewal.

SALE BY CHARGOR(S)

Provided that if the chargor(s) at any time shall sell or transfer the herein described lands without the prior written consent of the chargee(s), at the chargee(s)' option the herein described charge/mortgage, together with the principal sum secured hereunder and all accrued interest, shall immediately become due and payable in full.

POST-DATED CHEQUES

1. Provided that the chargor(s) shall provide the chargee(s) a series of post-dated cheques for the entire period of this charge/mortgage covering the monthly principal and interest payments.

Space is then provided for a statement to comply with the provisions of the *Family Law Act*. As discussed in Chapter 21, property that is a matrimonial home may not be transferred or encumbered without the spouse being a party either as an owner of the property or to consent to the transaction, unless certain circumstances make such consent unnecessary. As a result, the spousal status of the chargor is required, and one of the statements shown in Figure 21.1 in Chapter 21 is required.

If the chargor is a corporation, a statement about spousal status is not needed, nor is it necessary to cross out the statement concerning age.

If different statements apply to different chargors, attach a schedule where each chargor sets out the statement appropriate to his or her spousal status.

Name of Parties

The names of the chargors are shown with the last name first, in capital letters, followed by the first name and at least one middle name. Insert the year and month in the Date of Signature box; the actual date is inserted when the document is signed.

If the name of the chargor has changed from the name shown on the last title document in the registry system, enter the new name of the chargor. A schedule setting out the circumstances of the change of name may be attached to the charge. For example, a woman who held title to property before she married but now wishes to place a mortgage on the property in her married name would be shown in the charge by her new last name. The schedule would outline the circumstances of her marriage to explain the change in name.

Precedents 22.1 and 22.2 illustrate variations in completing Box 11.

Box 12: Spouse(s) of Chargors

If the property is a matrimonial home and title is in the name of one spouse, either the other spouse consents to the transaction or one of the statements indicating why such consent is not required is included in Box 11.

If the other spouse is a party to the document to consent, his or her name is entered, with the last name first in solid capitals, followed by the first and middle names in upper- and lowercase.

In the Date of Signature section of the box, include the year and month, leaving the exact date blank until the document is signed.

Box 13: Chargor's Address for Service

Box 13 indicates the address at which the chargor/mortgagor may be served. This may be the address of the property, another municipal address, or the address of a solicitor. If it is the address of a solicitor, include not only the address but also the name of the solicitor.

If more space is required to provide information for this box (for example, when there are several chargors, each having a different address), use a schedule.

Box 14: Chargee(s)

The name(s) of the chargee(s)/mortgagee(s) is listed in this box. This information is furnished by the chargee's solicitors.

Where possible, list each chargee on a separate line. Identify an individual by last name in solid capitals, followed by the first and at least one middle name. Identify a corporation by its full corporate name in solid capitals.

If two individuals are jointly acting as chargees, indicate the way in which they are taking the charge/mortgage. If they wish to hold it so that the share of one chargee will pass to the other chargee in the event of death, do not use the words "joint tenants"; use "on joint account with right of survivorship," as illustrated in Precedent 22.1.

Box 15: Chargee's Address for Service

Box 15 indicates the address at which the chargee/mortgagee may be served. This information is provided by the chargee's solicitors. If the address shown is that of the chargee's solicitors, the name of the solicitors, as well as their address, is shown.

If more space is required to provide information for this box (for example, when there are several chargees, each of whom will have a different address), use a schedule.

NUMBER OF COPIES AND DISPOSITION

A minimum of four copies are usually required. One copy of the charge/mortgage is sent to the mortgagee's solicitors for approval as to form. When it is approved, two copies are executed by the mortgagors and then held in the file until the closing date. The fourth copy remains in the office file.

E-REG MORTGAGE

Precedent 22.4 outlines the steps to create an electronic charge document in Teraview. Precedent 22.5 illustrates a printout of an electronic charge document in progress.

Terms and Concepts

charge/mortgage	principal
first mortgagee	terms
second mortgagee	term
foreclosed	maturity
chargor	blended payment
chargee	amortized
mortgagor	open mortgage
mortgagee	standard charge terms
assumed mortgage	*Family Law Act* implications

Review Questions

1. What is the purpose of a charge/mortgage?

2. Which party in the most recent transfer/deed is the chargor in the new charge/mortgage?

3. How do the provisions of the *Family Law Act* affect the completion of a mortgage?

4. The "term" of the mortgage is for 3 years, but the "amortization period" is for 15 years. In your own words, explain what this means.

5. If two chargees are to hold the charge/mortgage jointly, what wording is used to reflect that act?

6. What are "standard charge terms"?

7. Why are the birth dates of the parties to a charge/mortgage not required in that document?

8. How many copies are prepared of a charge/mortgage, and what disposition is made of those copies?

9. **Internet Research:** Vince and Silvana are purchasing a condominium for $150,000. They have a down payment of $25,000 and will be borrowing the rest from a financial institution. The mortgage will be amortized over 25 years; the term is for 5 years at 7.5% interest. Use the Internet to research what their monthly payments will be. What would the monthly payments be if the interest rate was 6.5%?

Charge/Mortgage of Land
Form 2 — Land Registration Reform Act

File 1111

B

Province of Ontario

FOR OFFICE USE ONLY

(1) Registry [X]   Land Titles [ ]   (2) Page 1 of **1** pages

(3) Property Identifier(s)   Block   Property   **42221-8732**   Additional: See Schedule [ ]

(4) Principal Amount

TWENTY FIVE THOUSAND------------- Dollars $ **25,000.00**

(5) Description

East Half of Lot 105, 5948
City of Toronto

Registry Division of the Toronto Registry Office No. 64

New Property Identifiers   Additional: See Schedule [ ]

Executions   Additional: See Schedule [ ]

(6) This Document Contains
(a) Redescription New Easement Plan/Sketch [ ]
(b) Schedule for: Description [ ] Additional Parties [ ] Other [ ]
(7) Interest/Estate Charged **Fee Simple**
Subject to easement

(8) Standard Charge Terms — The parties agree to be bound by the provisions in Standard Charge Terms filed as number _____ and the Chargor(s) hereby acknowledge(s) receipt of a copy of these terms.

(9) Payment Provisions

(a) Principal Amount $ **25,000.00**			(b) Interest Rate **8.00** % per annum	(c) Calculation Period **half-yearly not in advance**			

	Y	M	D			First (f) Payment Date	Y	M	D
(d) Interest Adjustment Date	**2008**	**02**	**28**	(e) Payment Date and Period **28th day of each month**			**2008**	**03**	**28**
(g) Last Payment Date	**2013**	**02**	**28**	(h) Amount of Each Payment **One Hundred Eighty Three**------------44/100 Dollars $ **183.44**					
(i) Balance Due Date	**2013**	**02**	**28**	(j) Insurance **Full insurable value**	Dollars $				

(10) Additional Provisions

Provided that the chargors, when not in default hereunder, shall have the privilege of paying the whole or any part of the principal sum hereby secured at any time to times without notice or bonus, provided any such prepayment is in accorandance with teh amortization schedule for this mortgage.

Continued on Schedule [ ]

(11) Chargor(s) The chargor hereby charges the land to the chargee and certifies that the chargor is at least eighteen years old and that

We are spouses of one another.

The chargor(s) acknowledge(s) receipt of a true copy of this charge.

Name(s)	Signature(s)	Date of Signature Y M D
ANDERSON, Ronald Craig		
ANDERSON, Kelly Anne		
as joint tenants		

(12) Spouse(s) of Chargor(s) I hereby consent to this transaction.

Name(s)	Signature(s)	Date of Signature Y M D

(13) Chargor(s) Address for Service   **984 Helena Avenue, Toronto ON M9R 3G6**

(14) Chargee(s)

PETERSON, Ryan Andrew

PETERSON, Kristen Lynn

on joint account with right of survivorship

(15) Chargee(s) Address for Service   **42 Oaklea Blvd., Oakville ON L3J 4V1**

(16) Assessment Roll Number of Property	Cty.	Mun.	Map	Sub.	Par.
	19	**04**	**231**	**882**	**00600**

FOR OFFICE USE ONLY

Fees

Registration Fee

Total

(17) Municipal Address of Property

984 Helena Avenue
Toronto ON M9R 3G6

(18) Document Prepared by:

Peter T. Grant
HILL, JOHNSTON & GRANT
17 Princess Street South, Suite 2501
Toronto ON M8Y 3N5

Source: Do Process Software Ltd.

Charge/Mortgage of Land   **B**

Province of Ontario   Form 2 — Land Registration Reform Act

FOR OFFICE USE ONLY

(1) Registry ☐   Land Titles ☒   (2) Page 1 of **1** pages

(3) Property Identifier(s)   Block   Property   **54328 4432**   Additional: See Schedule ☐

(4) Principal Amount

ONE HUNDRED THOUSAND----------- Dollars $ 100,000.00

(5) Description

New Property Identifiers

**Parcel 9-1, Section 3211
Lot 9, Plan 3211
being Part 1 on Plan 62R-3499
City of Hamilton
Hamilton Land Titles Office (No. 62)**

Additional: See Schedule ☐

Executions

Additional: See Schedule ☐

(6) This Document Contains   (a) Redescription New Easement Plan/Sketch ☐   (b) Schedule for: Description ☐   Additional Parties ☐   Other ☐

(7) Interest/Estate Charged
Fee Simple

(8) Standard Charge Terms — The parties agree to be bound by the provisions in Standard Charge Terms filed as number _____ and the Chargor(s) hereby acknowledge(s) receipt of a copy of these terms.

(9) Payment Provisions

(a) Principal Amount $ **100,000.00**		(b) Interest Rate **7.00** % per annum		(c) Calculation Period **half-yearly not in advance**			
(d) Interest Adjustment Date	Y **2008** M **09** D **01**	(e) Payment Date and Period **1st day of each month**			(f) First Payment Date	Y **2008** M **10** D **01**	
(g) Last Payment Date	Y **2011** M **09** D **01**	(h) Amount of Each Payment **Seven Hundred Six------------------------78/100** Dollars $ **706.78**					
(i) Balance Due Date	Y **2011** M **09** D **01**	(j) Insurance **Full insurable value**		Dollars $			

(10) Additional Provisions

Continued on Schedule ☐

(11) Chargor(s) The chargor hereby charges the land to the chargee and certifies that the chargor is at least eighteen years old and that XXXX

The chargor(s) acknowledge(s) receipt of a true copy of this charge.

Name(s)

WINDSTAR CONSULTANTS INC.

Signature(s)

**Per:
Name: Julie Mennard
Title: President
I have authority to bind the Corporation**

Date of Signature
Y **2007** M **10** D

(12) Spouse(s) of Chargor(s) I hereby consent to this transaction.

Name(s)   Signature(s)   Date of Signature Y M D

(13) Chargor(s) Address for Service

500 Wellington Street, Hamilton ON L8E 4G1

(14) Chargee(s)

DATA BANK OF CANADA

(15) Chargee(s) Address for Service

Suite 1000, 500 Fortune Ave., Toronto, Ontario M0N 1E1

(16) Assessment Roll Number of Property	Cty. **25**	Mun. **18**	Map **442**	Sub. **306**	Par. **00500**	

Fees

FOR OFFICE USE ONLY

Registration Fee

(17) Municipal Address of Property

**500 Wellington Street
Hamilton ON L8E 4G1**

(18) Document Prepared by:

**Peter T. Grant
HILL, JOHNSTON & GRANT
17 Princess Street South, Suite 2501
Toronto ON M8Y 3N5**

Total

Source: Do Process Software Ltd.

STANDARD CHARGE TERMS
Collateral Charge

FILED BY: NORTHERN CREDIT UNION LIMITED   FILING DATE: **January 6, 2004**

FILING NUMBER: **200401**

This set of standard charge terms shall be deemed to be included in every charge in which this set of charge terms is referred to by its filing number as provided in section 9 of the Land Registration Reform Act

CONTENTS

A   GENERAL PROVISIONS

1   Definitions

(1)   In the Charge and these charge terms,

(a)   "**Act**" means Ontario's Land Registration Reform Act;

(b)   "**Agreement**" means an accepted letter of offer, terms letter, commitment letter or offer to finance, lending agreement, loan agreement, credit agreement, security agreement, or guarantee between NCU and the Member in writing dealing with, or relating to, the Secured Indebtedness and Obligations, or any of them;

(c)   "**Basic Variable Mortgage Rate**" means the variable interest rate per annum declared by Northern Credit Union Limited from time to time as a reference rate of interest

(d)   "**Charge**" means the charge or mortgage of Property, as the case may be, made under the Act and granted by the Member to NCU, and in which a reference is made to these charge terms;

(e)   "**Costs**" includes all fees, Legal Costs, costs, charges and expenses of NCU incurred in connection with or otherwise incidental to,

(i)   the preparation, execution and registration of the Charge and any other instruments or security agreements collateral to the Charge or related to any transaction to which the Charge relates,

(ii)   the collection, enforcement and realization of the security on the Property provided for in the Charge and of any collateral security held with respect thereto, including the legal and other costs of foreclosure, power of sale or execution proceedings, whether commenced by NCU or by another person with respect to the Property secured by the Charge,

(iii)   the enforcement of payment of the Secured Indebtedness and Obligations, whether by way of court action, other legal process or otherwise,

(iv)   any inspection or appraisal of the Property and all Legal Costs relating to the examination of the title of the Property,

(v)   any repairs required to be made to the Property, or that in the reasonable opinion of NCU, are advisable, in connection with the realization of the security in the Property,

(vi)   NCU taking possession of the Property'

(vii)   NCU securing, completing or equipping any building, structure or thing on the Property,

(viii)   the renewal of any leasehold interest in the Property by NCU,

(ix)   all condominium Common Expenses paid by NCU on behalf of the Member,

(x)   any premium relating to any liability, fire or other insurance on the Property or any part of the Property,

(xi)   the defence of the interest of NCU in the Property against the claims of other persons, including any amount paid by NCU in compromise of any such claim or to pay any Taxes to which the Property is subject or to redeem or discharge any encumbrance on the Property, whether or not ranking in priority to the Charge;

Source: Northern Credit Union Limited

To Create an Electronic Charge Document

Menu Bar   ► Instrument
                      ► Create New…

The Create New Form window will open displaying all document types available in a file directory tree
► Expand the Charge branch by clicking on the plus sign
► Charge
► OK

Work in Progress window opens as shown here:

Create the document by moving through each branch of the directory shown on the left-hand side.

Always expand the directory for each branch by clicking on the plus sign, then click on each subdirectory, and complete the data entry fields as required on the right-hand side, noting the guidelines below:

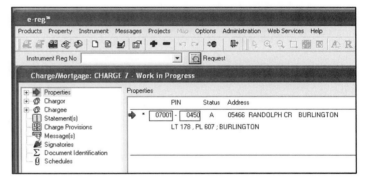

Properties:
► Insert PIN number, and the data fields will be prepopulated beginning with the legal description
► Click on PIN number (in the directory) and review title information, changing if appropriate

Chargor(s):
► Chargor's name(s) should already be prepopulated
► Click on the name of the Chargor (in the directory) and complete the screens for **each** of the tabs, noting the following:

> *Family Law Act and Age Statements* – Not applicable for a company. For an individual, click on "I am at least 18 years old" and the appropriate spousal statement. If the spousal statement has a word in full caps (e.g., NAME), double click on the word to open a dialog box to insert the appropriate information.

> *Other Statements* – Select statements as appropriate. Note: The statement "This document is not authorized under a Power of Attorney by this party." **must** be selected, unless it is under a power of attorney, and then the appropriate statement would be selected and information inserted. If the statement has a word in full caps (e.g., NAME), double click on the word to open a dialog box to insert the appropriate information.

> *Address for Service* – Insert the Chargor's address (after the closing date). If the address is the same for both Chargors, you only need to insert the address for the first Chargor.

> Note: These steps must be completed for **each** Chargor.

Source: Teranet Inc.

Chargee:
► Click on NEW PARTY (in the directory) and complete the following:

Name: If an individual, key in last name first, followed by a comma (or Teraview thinks the client is a company), followed by the given name(s). If a company, key in the full corporate name.

Capacity: Select the appropriate statement from the drop-down menu. This is an optional field depending on the circumstances of the Chargee.

Share: Completed if there is more than one chargee and each has a percentage interest; it may be entered as a percentage or decimal, but the total may not exceed 100 percent.

Other Statements: Complete as appropriate or leave blank.

Address for Service Tab: Key in address for service of the Chargee.

To add a second Chargee:
Menu Bar   ► Instrument
           ► Add Chargee
           ► NEW PARTY (and complete as above)

Statements – If required, select the appropriate statement(s) from this screen.

Charge Provisions

All fields, except Guarantor and Additional Provisions, must be completed. See example below:

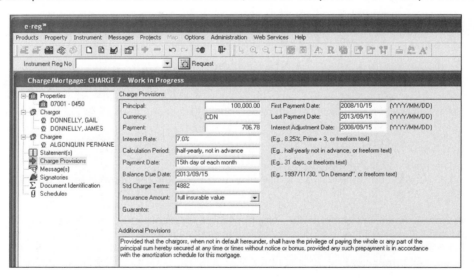

Messages – Displays any messages you have sent or received—discussed further in Chapter 25.

Signatories – Displays the signatory status of the document, i.e., whether it has been "digitally" signed.

Document Identification
Allows you to save work in progress and charge the disbursements to the client's account. The document name may be up to 40 characters. Key in the client's name and the type of document—e.g., Donnelly - Charge. Once entered, the name is displayed in the Title Bar.

Schedules – Displays any attached schedules or statement information.

Source: Teranet Inc.

**** NOT VALID - TO BE USED FOR TRAINING PURPOSES ONLY ****

This document has not been submitted and may be incomplete.

LRO # 20   **Charge/Mortgage**

yyyy mm dd   Page 1 of 2
In preparation on 2007 07 30   at 13:25

Properties

PIN	07001 - 0450 LT	Interest/Estate	Fee Simple
Description	LT 178 , PL 607 ; BURLINGTON		
Address	05466 RANDOLPH CR BURLINGTON		

Chargor(s)

The chargor(s) hereby charges the land to the chargee(s). The chargor(s) acknowledges the receipt of the charge and the standard charge terms, if any.

Name	DONNELLY, GAIL Acting as an individual
Address for Service	5466 Randolph Crescent Burlington ON

I am at least 18 years of age.

James Donnelly and I are spouses of one another and are both parties to this document

This document is not authorized under Power of Attorney by this party.

Name	DONNELLY, JAMES Acting as an individual
Address for Service	

I am at least 18 years of age.

Gail Donnelly and I are spouses of one another and are both parties to this document

This document is not authorized under Power of Attorney by this party.

Chargee(s)

		Capacity	Share
Name	WHITE, ROBERT ALLEN Acting as an individual		
Address for Service	500 Tower Road Newmarket ON L6R 9V2		

Provisions

Principal	$ 100,000.00	Currency	CDN
Calculation Period	half-yearly, not in advance		
Balance Due Date	2013/09/15		
Interest Rate	7.0%		
Payments	$ 706.78		
Interest Adjustment Date	2008 09 15		
Payment Date	15th day of each month		
First Payment Date	2008 10 15		
Last Payment Date	2013 09 15		
Standard Charge Terms	4882		
Insurance Amount	full insurable value		
Guarantor			

CHAPTER 23

Discharge of Charge

OBJECTIVES:

- Describe the steps that might be taken once the mortgage has been executed and registered but before all payments have been made

- Demonstrate an understanding of the completion of the various components of a discharge of charge/mortgage in paper and electronic formats

- Define the specialized terminology used in a discharge of charge/mortgage

Once executed and registered, but before all the mortgage payments have been made, a charge/mortgage may be

1. assumed (taken over) from the original mortgagor by another party;
2. assigned (sold) by the original mortgagee to another party; or
3. renewed (extended for a further period of time).

In addition to the above, the mortgagee may give the mortgagor a document stating that the claim under the mortgage has been satisfied and that the mortgage is therefore discharged. This simply means that part or all of the money owing under the mortgage has been paid and that the mortgagee is giving up his or her right to a claim against all or some of the property to which the mortgage relates.

The original charge/mortgage was registered to record the mortgagee's claim against the property in the event that the mortgage loan was not repaid. To record the payment of the claim, another document, called a discharge of charge/mortgage, is registered.

The discharge may record full payment of the mortgage loan, which is considered a full discharge for the property to which the mortgage relates. The discharge may record partial payment of the mortgage loan, considered a partial discharge for the property to which the mortgage relates. Although part of the property is no longer subject to the mortgage, the balance of the property is still subject to the mortgage.

For example, a builder may mortgage the property on which houses are to be built to secure funds. When a house is sold, the company will wish to discharge that part of the mortgage relating to the property on which that house is built so that the purchaser will receive an unencumbered title to the property being purchased. The company receives a partial discharge for that property only; the original mortgage still covers the balance of the property.

When a mortgage on property has been discharged in part by one or more partial discharges, the document by which the balance of the mortgage loan is acknowledged as having been paid is known as a final partial discharge.

WHO PREPARES THE DISCHARGE?

The discharge is usually prepared by the solicitors for the mortgagee holding the mortgage at the time of its payment, but the fee is paid by the mortgagor. Solicitors for the mortgagor may also prepare this document and forward it to the solicitors for the mortgagee for execution and return.

REQUIRED INFORMATION

The following information is required to complete a discharge of charge/mortgage:

1. The registration details of the original charge/mortgage
2. The registration details any assignments of the charge/mortgage
3. The registration details of any previous partial discharge

4. If the discharge is being registered in the manual system, duplicate copies of the above documents, as applicable, will be required or a statement will be required as to why they are not available.

PREPARING THE DISCHARGE

Precedent 23.1 is a discharge of charge/mortgage form. The document contains several boxes marked "For Office Use Only"; nothing is inserted in those boxes when the document is prepared in the law office.

The document contains 10 boxes that must be completed by the solicitors for the party preparing it. Insert an X into the appropriate box within the main numbered box or provide the required information.

Box 1

Indicate for which land registry system the document is prepared. If the document deals with land under both systems, mark both boxes and prepare either two separate original documents or an original and a copy certified by the land registrar in whose land registry office the first document was registered.

Box 2

Indicate the total number of pages that make up the document; there will always be at least one page. The document consists of all attached schedules and the form itself. Be sure that each page of the document is numbered consecutively in the upper righthand corner.

Box 3: Property Identifier(s)

If a property identifier has been assigned to the property, the number may appear in the charge/mortgage being discharged. That number should be included in Box 3. A maximum of two property identifiers may be inserted; any additional identifiers are listed on a schedule, and an X is inserted in the box marked "Additional: See Schedule." Leave the box blank if no property identifier has been assigned.

Box 4: Legal Description

If the discharge relates to the entire property described in the charge/mortgage, the full legal description need not be included in the discharge.

Land Titles System

Enter only the parcel and section, the name of the lower and upper tier municipality, and the name of the land registry office. If the description in the charge/mortgage contains a metes and bounds description, such a description need not be repeated in the discharge.

Registry System

Enter only the lot and plan (or lot and concession), the name of the lower and upper tier municipality, and the name of the land registry office. If the description in the charge/mortgage contains a metes and bounds description, such a description need not be repeated in the discharge. If there is insufficient space in Box 4 to complete the description, continue it in Box 7.

Part of Property

If the discharge relates to only part of the property described in the charge/mortgage, a legal description of the part being discharged is required and may, if it forms part of the original description, include a metes and bounds description.

Box 5: Charge to Be Discharged

In this box, enter the registration number of the charge/mortgage that is to be discharged and the date of registration. This information appears on the back of old forms and in the upper lefthand corner of the POLARIS charge/mortgage forms.

Box 6: This Is a...

This box indicates whether the discharge covers all the property described in the charge/mortgage, only part of the property, or the last part of the property, the other parts of which have been previously discharged.

When all the property is being discharged, put an X in the Complete Discharge box. When only part is being discharged and the balance is still covered by the charge/mortgage, put an X in the Partial Discharge box. When parts of the property have already been discharged and the remaining part is now being discharged, put an X in the Final Partial Discharge box.

Box 7: Description (cont'd), Recitals, Assignments

Box 7 is used to continue a legal description that cannot be fully set out in Box 4 and to list the details of documents registered subsequent to the registration of the mortgage that affect the mortgage (such as an assignment of the mortgage or previously registered partial discharges). The information for the registration number and date of registration for such documents appear on them. If Box 7 contains insufficient space, mark the Continued on Schedule box and attach a schedule. If the duplicate original of the charge/mortgage cannot be produced, a statement stating this fact is made in Box 7 (see Precedent 23.1).

Box 8: Chargee(s)

The party who holds the charge/mortgage at the time of discharge is shown as the chargee.

Individual Chargee

Enter the name with the last name first in solid capitals, followed by the other name or names of the party (in upper- and lowercase) as shown in the mortgage documents. Precedent 23.1 illustrates a completed Box 8 for an individual chargee. Use a schedule if there is insufficient space in the box to list all the chargees.

Corporate Chargee

If a corporation is the chargee, show the full corporate name in solid capitals, together with the name of the person who will sign on behalf of the corporation. The individual's name appears in upper- and lowercase. The following words appear beneath his or her name: "I have authority to bind the corporation."

Changed Names of Chargees

If the names of the chargees have changed since the registration of the most recent mortgage document, the lawyer will advise you of the additional steps to be taken.

Deceased Chargee

If the discharge is being given by someone on behalf of a deceased chargee, a schedule is completed and attached to the discharge. It identifies the individual as the executor or trustee of the estate of the deceased and details the authority granted to him or her by the Superior Court of Justice to deal with the estate.

Box 9: Chargee's Address for Service

The address at which the chargee (mortgagee) may be served is indicated in Box 9. The address may be that of the chargee's solicitors; in that case, show the name of the solicitors as well as their address.

Box 10: Document Prepared By

In Box 10, enter the name of the individual solicitor, the name of the law firm, and the law firm's address and postal code.

EXECUTION OF DISCHARGE OF CHARGE/MORTGAGE

The prepared discharge of charge/mortgage document is executed by the chargee. If the charge/mortgage was not assigned by the original chargee, that chargee executes the discharge. If the original chargee has assigned the charge/mortgage to another party, that party executes the discharge.

NUMBER AND DISPOSITION OF COPIES

Two copies of the discharge of charge/mortgage are usually prepared. One copy is signed by the mortgagee and then given to the mortgagor for registration. The second copy is for the file.

If the discharge is prepared by the solicitors for the mortgagor, three copies should be prepared. The solicitors for the mortgagee receive two copies; the third copy is retained in the file.

REGISTRATION OF DISCHARGE

The mortgagor/chargor registers the discharge in the appropriate land registry office with the mortgage to which the discharge refers. When the office has made the necessary entry or checks, the mortgagor may receive the duplicate copy of the mortgage.

RELEASE OF INTEREST IN INSURANCE

At the time the mortgagee gives the discharge, he or she must also release all interest in the policy of insurance that the mortgagor has been required to carry on the property. This release is given to the mortgagor, who, in turn, forwards it to the insurance company.

E-REG DISCHARGE

Unlike an electronic transfer or mortgage document, the electronic discharge searches for the property information by the registration number of the charge/mortgage instrument being discharged rather than by the PIN number of the property. If the instrument number of the charge/mortgage is not known, an electronic title search of the property will be required to obtain the instrument number, which is discussed in Chapter 26.

Precedent 23.2 outlines the steps to create an electronic discharge of charge in Teraview. Precedent 23.3 illustrates a printout of a discharge of charge in progress.

Terms and Concepts

discharge of charge/mortgage	full discharge
assumed	partial discharge
assigned	final partial discharge
renewed	release of insurance interest

Review Questions

1. Once a mortgage has been given and registered, what may happen to it?

2. Why does the mortgagor wish to receive a discharge of mortgage when the mortgage has been fully paid?

3. John Smith originally gave a mortgage to Henry Black. Henry assigned the mortgage to Peter Green. Who will give Mr. Smith the discharge of mortgage?

4. What material is required to assist the completion of the discharge of mortgage?

5. James Ray gave a mortgage to Jason Chow. Mr. Chow has recently died. Mr. Ray has now completely paid off the mortgage. How can Mr. Ray receive a discharge of the mortgage?

6. Why does the person giving the discharge of mortgage also sign a release of interest in the insurance on the property?

7. Who usually prepares the discharge of mortgage?

PRECEDENTS

Precedent 23.1 Discharge of Charge/Mortgage, Land Titles

Discharge of Charge/Mortgage
Form 3 — Land Registration Reform Act

Province of Ontario

C

(1) Registry ☐   Land Titles ☒   (2) Page 1 of **1** pages

(3) Property Identifier(s)   Block   Property   **46691 7804**   Additional: See Schedule ☐

FOR OFFICE USE ONLY

(4) Description

Parcel 16-1, Section M-3267
Lot 16, Plan 3267
City of Mississauga
Regional Muncipality of Peel

Land Titles Division of Peel (No. 43)

New Property Identifiers   Additional: See Schedule ☐

(5) Charge to be Discharged

Registration Number   Date of Registration   Y   M   D

438920   **1999 09 09**

(6) This is a

Complete Discharge ☒   Partial Discharge ☐   Final Partial Discharge ☐

(7) Description (cont'd.), Recitals, Assignments

| 569218 | Transfer of Charge/Mortgage | 2001/06/31 |
| 572189 | Agreement Extending Charge/Mortgage | 2004/09/09 |

The duplicate registered charge/mortgage and other registered documents have been lost or misplaced.

Continued on Schedule ☐

(8) Chargee(s) I am the person entitled by law to grant the discharge and this charge is hereby discharged as to the land described herein.

Name(s)	Signature(s)	Date of Signature Y M D
BAGDURIA, Rajit		**2008 09**

Additional: See Schedule ☐

(9) Chargee(s) Address for Service

420 Bovaird Drive, Unit 500
Brampton ON L3X 4P9

(10) Document Prepared by:

Peter T Grant
HILL, JOHNSTON & GRANT
17 Princess Street South, Suite 2501
Toronto ON M8Y 3N5

FOR OFFICE USE ONLY

Fees	
Registration Fee	
Total	

Source: Do Process Software Ltd.

To Create an Electronic Discharge of Charge Document

Menu Bar   ► Instrument
                  ► Create New…

Create New Form window will open displaying all document types available in a file directory tree.
► Expand the Discharge Charge or Other Interest branch by clicking on the plus sign
► Discharge of Charge
► OK

Work in progress screen opens as shown here:

Create the document by moving through each branch of the directory shown on the left-hand side.

Always expand the directory for each branch by clicking on the plus sign, then click on each subdirectory, and complete the data entry fields as required on the right-hand side, noting the guidelines below:

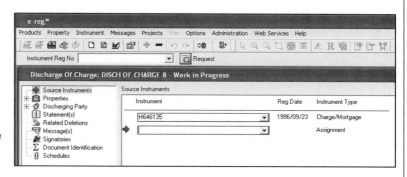

Source Instrument
Unlike a Transfer or Charge, this document searches by an Instrument No. rather than a PIN number; thus, the Instrument No. for the Charge being discharged must be keyed in, as well as the Instrument No. for any assignment(s) of the Charge.

Properties:
► Click on Properties (in the directory) and select either "Partial" or "All" as appropriate
► Click on PIN number (in the directory) and review title information, changing if appropriate

Discharging Party
► Discharging Party's name should already be prepopulated
► Click on name of the Discharging Party (in the directory) and complete the screens for **each** of the tabs, noting the following:

Family Law Act and Age Statements – Not applicable for a company. For an individual, click on "I am at least 18 years old" and the appropriate spousal statement. If the spousal statement has a word in full caps (e.g., NAME), double click on the word to open a dialog box to insert the appropriate information.

Other Statements – Select statements as appropriate. Note: The statements "This document is not authorized under a Power of Attorney by this party." **and** "I am the party entitled by law to grant the discharge as to the land described herein" **must** be selected, unless it is under a power of attorney, or there are other circumstances; then the appropriate statement(s) would be selected and information inserted.

Address for Service – Insert the Discharging Party's address (after the closing date). If the address is the same for both Discharging Parties, you only need to insert the address for the first Discharging Party.

Note: These steps must be completed for **each** Discharging Party.

For instructions regarding **Statements, Related Deletions, Messages, Signatories, Document Identification,** and **Schedules**, see Precedent 21.3.

Source: Teranet Inc.

**** NOT VALID - TO BE USED FOR TRAINING PURPOSES ONLY ****

This document has not been submitted and may be incomplete.

LRO # 20   **Discharge Of Charge**

yyyy mm dd   Page 1 of 1

In preparation on 2007 07 30   at 13:44

Properties

PIN	24924 - 0253 LT
Description	PCL 48-1, SEC 20M602 ; LT 48, PL 20M602 , S/T H592196 ; S/T H587231 OAKVILLE
Address	01112 SHELTERED OAK COURT OAKVILLE

Document to be Discharged

Registration No.	*Date*	*Type of Instrument*
H646135	1996 09 23	Charge/Mortgage

Discharging Party(s)

This discharge complies with the Planning Act. This discharge discharges the charge.

Name	ROYAL BANK OF CANADA Acting as a company
Address for Service	123 Main Street Toronto ON L3M 2J9

I, John Fox, have the authority to bind the corporation.

This document is not authorized under Power of Attorney by this party.

NEL

CHAPTER 24

Commencing the Real Estate Transaction

OBJECTIVES:

- Demonstrate an understanding of how the Goods and Services Act applies to real estate transactions

- Interpret accurately the information contained in an agreement of purchase and sale

- Describe the steps taken when opening a residential real estate file and the significance of dates and tickler slips

Before considering the procedures involved in commencing the real estate transaction, it is necessary to consider briefly how the Goods and Services Tax (GST) affects such transactions.

GST IN REAL ESTATE TRANSACTIONS

Under the provisions of the *Excise Tax Act*, GST is levied on sales and rentals of real property unless a specific exemption applies. Numerous points must be considered when dealing with the GST implications in a real estate transaction; these are the responsibility of the lawyer handling the file. A legal assistant should, however, have some basic understanding of the effect of the GST on a real estate transaction.

Exempt Real Estate Transactions

Included in the real estate transactions that are exempt from GST are sales of

1. Personal-use residential housing, including condominiums (that is, owner-occupied residential property). (The terms "used" and "resale" are generally used instead of "personal use." These terms are used in this text.)
2. Personal-use property such as cottages and hobby farms
3. Transfers of farm land between related parties
4. Longterm and specific short-term residential rents

Taxable Real Estate Transactions

Included in the real estate transactions to which GST applies are sales of new and substantially renovated residential housing. In this chapter and all subsequent chapters relating to real estate transactions, a reference to new residential property will include substantially renovated property.

Who Pays the GST?

GST may be payable to the vendor by the purchaser of new residential property when possession or ownership of the property is transferred to the purchaser, whichever comes first. If the new residential property is a condominium, GST is payable when ownership of the unit is transferred to the purchaser or 60 days after the complex is registered as a condominium, whichever comes first. (In some sales of new residential property, the purchase/sale price is quoted as "GST included." That means that the price includes not only the amount to be paid for the real property but also the amount of the applicable GST.) The vendor is responsible for remitting GST to Canada Revenue Agency.

GST New Housing Rebate

The purchaser of new residential property that costs less than $450,000 and is to be used as a primary place of residence may claim a GST new housing rebate. The amount of the rebate is graduated depending on the purchase price. There is no rebate for homes selling for $450,000 or more. For details on how this rebate affects the procedures followed in a real estate transaction, see Chapter 25.

AGREEMENT OF PURCHASE AND SALE

The first step in a real estate transaction is the execution of an offer to purchase. These forms are usually completed by a real estate agent for used property. When the property is new residential housing, the offer is usually prepared by a member of the builders' sales staff or by real estate agents acting for the builders.

If Mr. and Mrs. Anderson wish to purchase a house that the Petersons are offering for sale, the Andersons sign an **offer to purchase** and submit it to the Petersons for consideration. If the Petersons accept the offer, they sign their names, and the completed agreement is known as an **agreement of purchase and sale** and is then usually referred to as "the agreement."

The agreement is a five-page document that uses the terms "seller" and "buyer" rather than the traditional terms of "vendor" and "purchaser," which law firms still use. Precedent 24.1 illustrates an agreement for the purchase of used residential property. The agreement for the purchase of new residential housing may be a slightly different form and may contain many additional provisions relating, for example, to the construction, completion, and financing of the new residential property; it may also include several schedules relating to matters involved in new construction. The first page of the agreement sets out the particulars of the parties, the property, and the applicable dates; pages 2 and 3 set out standard text regarding the purchase and sale of the property; and page 4 contains the signature of the parties and the names and addresses of the solicitors for both the seller and buyer. Page 5, Schedule A, sets out the terms for the payment of the balance of the purchase price, including details of any mortgages taken back (discussed in Chapter 25) and instructions regarding the deposition of the deposit funds.

When the property being purchased is new residential property, the purchase price shown in the agreement of purchase and sale will be either

1. the price for the real property exclusive of GST (that is, GST is levied on the purchase price shown in the agreement) or
2. the price for the real property inclusive of GST (that is, the price includes not only the price of the real property but also the applicable GST).

A schedule to the agreement of purchase and sale for new residential property will indicate whether the purchase price is inclusive of the net amount of GST.

The agreement sets out the property involved and states the price, the terms of payment, the **closing date**, and other special terms and conditions. The agreement also indicates the amount of money paid as a deposit toward the total purchase price. The deposit is held by the real estate agent, if any, who negotiated the sale of the property. It is applied against the commission to which the agent is entitled when the transaction is completed.

In addition, the agreement of purchase and sale provides that the purchaser may search title and submit any **requisitions** (questions as to the validity of title to the property) within a stated number of days. The last day of this period is known as the **requisition date**. If there are claims or questions that the vendor cannot answer or satisfy, the agreement may be null and void and any deposit money returned to the purchaser.

If the agreement contains a provision that the deposit is to be held by the real estate agent in an interest-bearing account, the purchasers and/or the vendors indicate their social insurance numbers beneath their signatures. This information is required to assist in completing the T5 slips that must be furnished when the interest is paid.

STEPS UPON RECEIPT OF AGREEMENT OF PURCHASE AND SALE

Frequently, the first indication a lawyer has that a client is buying or selling real property is receipt of an agreement of purchase and sale. Upon receipt of this agreement, a file and docket are opened for the client, and the necessary tickler slips are prepared.

File and Docket

When preparing the file and docket opening forms, you must assign a name to the new matter. The name of the client of your law firm appears first, followed by the name of the other party. The file name also indicates whether the file relates to a sale or a purchase and sets out the municipal address of the property. For example, if the law office acts for the vendor in the real estate transaction commenced by Precedent 24.1, the file name is

PETERSON sale to (*or* s/t) ANDERSON
984 Helena Avenue, Toronto

If your law firm acts for the purchaser, the file name would be

ANDERSON purchase from (*or* p/f) PETERSON
984 Helena Avenue, Toronto

Some offices use a coloured file folder to identify all files concerned with real estate transactions; others use a buff-coloured folder and a checklist stapled onto the inside of the file folder cover. Precedents 24.2 and 24.3 illustrate specimen checklists for acting for the vendor and for the purchaser. As a step is completed, a note is made on the checklist so that anyone who works on the file can see at a glance what has been done and what remains to be completed. On all folders, staple or tape the agreement of purchase and sale to the right side of the inside of the file folder. Many legal assistants also print the closing date in large letters in the upper right-hand portion of the cover of the file folder.

When opening a new file, complete as much of the checklist as possible, including the name, address, and telephone number of your client and of the solicitors for the other party; the closing date of the transaction; the requisition date; the legal description and municipal address of the property; and the address of your client after closing. Commercial software packages such as *The Conveyancer* may also be used by the legal assistant to enter all the client information into a customized database, which then generates all the necessary forms, checklists, and documents, including the file opening sheet.

Many documents will be prepared during the course of acting for either the vendor or the purchaser in a real estate transaction. These are not executed immediately after preparation but are held in the main file in a special inner file, entitled *For Execution*, until shortly before the closing date. This allows all documents to be executed at the same time for use on closing.

Tickler Slips

Prepared by Solicitors for the Vendor

Prepare a tickler slip to remind the solicitor handling the file of the approach of the closing date. Use a date three or four days before the closing date as the tickler date. A tickler slip may also be prepared to remind the lawyer of the requisition date; alternatively, a note may be made in his or her diary. The requisition date is the last day on which the solicitors for the purchaser may bring questions on the validity of title to the attention of the vendor; nothing need actually be done in the office on that date.

Prepared by Solicitors for the Purchaser

Prepare two tickler slips: one to remind the solicitor of the closing date and the other to remind the solicitor of the requisition date. The tickler dates should be three or four days before both dates.

Following receipt of the agreement of purchase and sale, the opening of the client records, and the preparation of the necessary tickler slips, the handling of the transaction depends on whether the lawyer acts for the vendor or purchaser.

Chapter 25 considers the steps taken by solicitors for the vendor; Chapter 26 discusses the steps taken by solicitors for the purchaser.

E-REG

Electronic registration will mean that most real estate closing will happen in escrow rather than at the actual registry office. Thus, one party's lawyer will register the document(s) electronically on behalf of both parties, subject to any previous arrangements. This procedure requires preparing and completing a document registration agreement (Precedent 24.4) and an acknowledgement and direction using the Teraview system (Precedent 24.5). The document registration agreement may also be accessed through commercial software packages such as *The Conveyancer* or at the Law Society of Upper Canada website (http://mrc.lsuc.on.ca/jsp/eReg/index.jsp).

These documents are signed by each lawyer's clients indicating that the lawyer will be electronically signing on their behalf and directing that the closing will be done in escrow.

Precedent 24.6 outlines the steps to open an instrument (a document) in progress, how to print an instrument in progress, and how to create an acknowledgement and direction report in Teraview.

Terms and Concepts

Goods and Services Tax (GST)

exempt and taxable real estate

offer to purchase

agreement of purchase and sale

closing date

requisitions

requisition date

file opening procedures

sale and purchase checklists

tickler dates and slips

document registration agreement

acknowledgement and direction

Review Questions

1. What is the main form of real estate transaction that is exempt from GST?

2. When does an offer to purchase become an agreement of purchase and sale?

3. Who holds the deposit that is made when an offer is accepted?

4. What is meant by the "requisition date" in a real estate transaction?

5. What steps are taken when the lawyer receives an agreement of purchase and sale and agrees to act for one of the parties in the transaction?

6. What tickler slips would you prepare if your lawyer was acting for
   a. the vendors?
   b. the purchasers?

7. What is the advantage of showing the closing date of the transaction on the outside of the file?

8. Why would you hold documents to be signed by your clients until just prior to the closing date of the real estate transaction?

PRECEDENTS

Precedent 24.1 Agreement of Purchase and Sale, Ontario Real Estate Assocation

---

OREA Ontario Real Estate Association

Agreement of Purchase and Sale

Form 100
for use in the Province of Ontario

This Agreement of Purchase and Sale dated this ...... 10th ...... day of ...... January ...... 20 08 .

BUYER, ... RONALD CRAIG ANDERSON and KELLY ANNE ANDERSON ......, agrees to purchase from
(Full legal names of all Buyers)

SELLER, ... RYAN ANDREW PETERSON ......, the following
(Full legal names of all Sellers)

REAL PROPERTY:

Address ...... 984 Helena Avenue ...... fronting on the ...... South ...... side

of ... Helena Avenue ...... in the ...... City of Toronto

and having a frontage of ...... 40 feet ...... more or less by a depth of ...... 100 feet ...... more or less

and legally described as ... Easterly half of Lot 105, Plan 5948, Toronto ......

...... (the "property").
(Legal description of land including easements not described elsewhere)

PURCHASE PRICE: Dollars (CDN$) ...... $235,000.00 ......

...... TWO HUNDRED AND THIRTY-FIVE THOUSAND ...... Dollars

DEPOSIT: Buyer submits ...... herewith ......
(Herewith/Upon Acceptance/as otherwise described in this Agreement)

...... TWENTY THOUSAND ...... Dollars (CDN$) ...... $20,000.00 ......

by negotiable cheque payable to ...... H.R. SWARTZ REAL ESTATE LIMITED ...... "Deposit Holder"
to be held in trust pending completion or other termination of this Agreement and to be credited toward the Purchase Price on completion. For the purposes of this Agreement, "Upon Acceptance" shall mean that the Buyer is required to deliver the deposit to the Deposit Holder within 24 hours of the acceptance of this Agreement. The parties to this Agreement hereby acknowledge that, unless otherwise provided for in this Agreement, the Deposit Holder shall place the deposit in trust in the Deposit Holder's non-interest bearing Real Estate Trust Account and no interest shall be earned, received or paid on the deposit.

Buyer agrees to pay the balance as more particularly set out in Schedule A attached.

SCHEDULE(S) A ...... attached hereto form(s) part of this Agreement.

1. **IRREVOCABILITY:** This Offer shall be irrevocable by ...... Buyer ...... until ...... 6:00 p.m. ...... a.m./p.m. on
(Seller/Buyer)
the ...... 10th ...... day of ...... January ...... 20 08 ..., after which time, if not accepted, this Offer shall be null and void and the deposit shall be returned to the Buyer in full without interest.

2. **COMPLETION DATE:** This Agreement shall be completed by no later than 6:00 p.m. on the ...... 28th ...... day
of ...... February ...... 20 08 . Upon completion, vacant possession of the property shall be given to the Buyer unless otherwise provided for in this Agreement.

3. **NOTICES:** Seller hereby appoints the Listing Brokerage as Agent for the purpose of giving and receiving notices pursuant to this Agreement. **Only if the Co-operating Brokerage represents the interests of the Buyer in this transaction,** the Buyer hereby appoints the Co-operating Brokerage as Agent for the purpose of giving and receiving notices pursuant to this Agreement. Any notice relating hereto or provided for herein shall be in writing. This offer, any counter offer, notice of acceptance thereof, or any notice shall be deemed given and received, when hand delivered to the address for service provided in the Acknowledgement below, or where a facsimile number is provided herein, when transmitted electronically to that facsimile number.

FAX No. (416) 228-4480 ...... (For delivery of notices to Seller) FAX No. (416) 479-8933 ...... (For delivery of notices to Buyer)

INITIALS OF BUYER(S): ( ) **INITIALS OF SELLER(S):** ( )

Form 100 2008 **Page 1 of 5**

---

4. **CHATTELS INCLUDED:** All existing electric light fixtures, built-in dishwasher, broadloom in living room, dining room, halls, stairs, and master bedroom.

....

....

....

5. **FIXTURES EXCLUDED:** Dining room chandelier.

....

....

....

6. **RENTAL ITEMS:** The following equipment is rented and **not** included in the Purchase Price. The Buyer agrees to assume the rental contract(s), if assumable: Electric water heater.

....

7. **GST:** If this transaction is subject to Goods and Services Tax (G.S.T.), then such tax shall be ......N/A...... (included in/in addition to) the Purchase Price. If this transaction is not subject to G.S.T., Seller agrees to certify on or before closing, that the transaction is not subject to G.S.T.

8. **TITLE SEARCH:** Buyer shall be allowed until 6:00 p.m. on the ......31st...... day of ......January......, 20 08, (Requisition Date) to examine the title to the Property at Buyer's own expense and until the earlier of: (i) thirty days from the later of the Requisition Date or the date on which the conditions in this Agreement are fulfilled or otherwise waived or; (ii) five days prior to completion, to satisfy Buyer that there are no outstanding work orders or deficiency notices affecting the Property, and that its present use (......Residential......) may be lawfully continued and that the principal building may be insured against risk of fire. Seller hereby consents to the municipality or other governmental agencies releasing to Buyer details of all outstanding work orders affecting the property, and Seller agrees to execute and deliver such further authorizations in this regard as Buyer may reasonably require.

9. **FUTURE USE:** Seller and Buyer agree that there is no representation or warranty of any kind that the future intended use of the property by Buyer is or will be lawful except as may be specifically provided for in this Agreement.

10. **TITLE:** Provided that the title to the property is good and free from all registered restrictions, charges, liens, and encumbrances except as otherwise specifically provided in this Agreement and save and except for (a) any registered restrictions or covenants that run with the land providing that such are complied with; (b) any registered municipal agreements and registered agreements with publicly regulated utilities providing such have been complied with, or security has been posted to ensure compliance and completion, as evidenced by a letter from the relevant municipality or regulated utility; (c) any minor easements for the supply of domestic utility or telephone services to the property or adjacent properties; and (d) any easements for drainage, storm or sanitary sewers, public utility lines, telephone lines, cable television lines or other services which do not materially affect the use of the property. If within the specified times referred to in paragraph 8 any valid objection to title or to any outstanding work order or deficiency notice, or to the fact the said present use may not lawfully be continued, or that the principal building may not be insured against risk of fire is made in writing to Seller and which Seller is unable or unwilling to remove, remedy or satisfy or obtain insurance save and except against risk of fire in favour of the Buyer and any mortgagee, (with all related costs at the expense of the Seller), and which Buyer will not waive, this Agreement notwithstanding any intermediate acts or negotiations in respect of such objections, shall be at an end and all monies paid shall be returned without interest or deduction and Seller, Listing Brokerage and Co-operating Brokerage shall not be liable for any costs or damages. Save as to any valid objection so made by such day and except for any objection going to the root of the title, Buyer shall be conclusively deemed to have accepted Seller's title to the property.

11. **CLOSING ARRANGEMENTS:** Where each of the Seller and Buyer retain a lawyer to complete the Agreement of Purchase and Sale of the Property, and where the transaction will be completed by electronic registration pursuant to Part III of the Land Registration Reform Act, R.S.O. 1990, Chapter L4 and the Electronic Registration Act, S.O. 1991, Chapter 44, and any amendments thereto, the Seller and Buyer acknowledge and agree that the exchange of closing funds, non-registrable documents and other items (the "Requisite Deliveries") and the release thereof to the Seller and Buyer will (a) not occur at the same time as the registration of the transfer/deed (and any other documents intended to be registered in connection with the completion of this transaction) and (b) be subject to conditions whereby the lawyer(s) receiving any of the Requisite Deliveries will be required to hold same in trust and not release same except in accordance with the terms of a document registration agreement between the said lawyers. The Seller and Buyer irrevocably instruct the said lawyers to be bound by the document registration agreement which is recommended from time to time by the Law Society of Upper Canada. Unless otherwise agreed to by the lawyers, such exchange of the Requisite Deliveries will occur in the applicable Land Titles Office or such other location agreeable to both lawyers.

INITIALS OF BUYER(S): ( )   **INITIALS OF SELLER(S):** ( )

Form 100 2008 **Page 2 of 5**

 Ontario Real Estate Association

Schedule A
Agreement of Purchase and Sale

Form 100
for use in the Province of Ontario

This Schedule is attached to and forms part of the Agreement of Purchase and Sale between:

BUYER, RONALD CRAIG ANDERSON and KELLY ANNE ANDERSON , and

SELLER, RYAN ANDREW PETERSON

for the purchase and sale of 984 Helena Avenue, Toronto, Ontario

dated the 10th day of January , 20 08 .

Buyer agrees to pay the balance as follows:

1. BUYER agrees to pay an additional sum of ONE HUNDRED AND NINETY-EIGHT THOUSAND DOLLARS ($198,000.00) in cash by certified cheque to the Seller on closing, subject to the usual adjustments.

2. This OFFER is conditional upon the Buyer arranging, at the Buyer's own expense, a new first Charge/Mortgage for not less than ONE HUNDRED AND SEVENTY-FIVE THOUSAND DOLLARS ($175,000.00) bearing interest at a rate of not more than 8% per annum, calculated semi-annually, not in advance, repayable in blended monthly payments of about ONE THOUSAND AND FOUR HUNDRED DOLLARS ($1,400.00) including principal and interest and to run for a term of not less than five years from the date of completion of this transaction. Unless the Buyer gives notice in writing delivered to the Seller not later than 6:00 p.m. on the 15th day of January, 2008, that this condition is fulfilled, this Offer shall be null and void and the deposit shall be returned to Buyer in full without deduction. This condition is included for the benefit of the Buyer and may be waived at the Buyer's sole option by notice in writing to the Seller within the time period stated herein.

3. SELLER agrees to take back a Second Mortgage in the amount of TWENTY-FIVE THOUSAND DOLLARS ($25,000.00) bearing interest at the rate of 8% per annum, calculated semi-annually, not in advance, based on a 10 year amortization schedule and having a 5 year term. This mortgage shall contain a clause permitting the prepayment of all or part of the outstanding balance on any payment date or dates without notice or bonus provided that such partial prepayment shall be the sum of the next consecutive principal payments according to the amortization schedule.

4. THE BUYER AND THE SELLER hereby direct the real estate agent holding the deposit in this transaction to place same into an interest bearing account or term deposit with any accrued interest to be paid to the buyer as soon as possible after closing or other termination of this Agreement. In the event the closing is advanced or conditions not met, the Buyer agrees to accept the short-term rate allowed for deposits withdrawn before maturity. Prior to that payment the Buyer agrees to provide his Social Insurance Number for the required Revenue Canada T5 forms.

This form must be initialed by all parties to the Agreement of Purchase and Sale..

INITIALS OF BUYER(S): ( )   **INITIALS OF SELLER(S):** ( )

Form 100   2008   **Page 5 of 5**

SALE CHECKLIST

Client	_____	File No.	_____
Sale to	_____	Lot/Plan	_____
Address	_____	Section/Parcel	_____
	_____	PIN	_____
Tel (Home)	_____	Municipality	
Tel (Bus)	_____		
New	_____	Conditional Date	_____
Address	_____	Requisition Date	_____
	_____	**CLOSING DATE**	_____

Purchaser's Solicitor/Firm _____

Address	_____		
Telephone	_____	Fax	_____
E-mail	_____	Teraview User Name	_____

Letter to Purchaser's Solicitor

Title	_____
Survey	_____
Insurance	_____
Birth Date(s)	_____
Assess Roll #	_____
Last Inst. #	_____

Adjustments

	Req'd	Rec'd
Taxes	_____	_____
Water/Sewage	_____	_____
Fuel Oil	_____	_____
Rent	_____	_____
Common Expenses	_____	_____
Rental Contracts	_____	_____

Mortgages

	Req'd	Rec'd	
Mortgage Statements			**Closing Notes**
Assumed	_____	_____	_____
Discharge	_____	_____	_____
Mortgage Taken Back	_____	_____	_____
Draft	_____	_____	_____
Charge Terms	_____	_____	_____
Executions	_____	_____	_____
Amort. Schedule	_____	_____	

Documents & Closing Materials

	Prep'd	Fw'd	App'd
Statement of Adjustments	_____	_____	_____
Transfer	_____	_____	_____
Planning Act Statements		_____	
Client's Acknow.		_____	
Direction re funds		_____	
Direction re title		_____	
Decl. of possession		_____	
Decl. re chattels		_____	
Survey		_____	
Undertaking to re-adjust		_____	
Insurance	_____	_____	
Keys	Req'd _____	Rec'd _____	

After Closing

Tax & Assess. Letters	_____
Re-adjustments	_____
Advise Mtgee	_____
Pay Commission	_____
Condo Notice	_____
Mortgage Discharge	_____
Mtgee Ins. Release	_____
Insurance Canc.	_____
Preliminary Report	_____
Account	_____
Final Report	_____

PURCHASE CHECKLIST

Client	_____	File No.	_____
Sale to	_____	Lot/Plan	_____
Address	_____	Section/Parcel	_____
	_____	PIN	_____
Tel (Home)	_____	Municipality	_____
Tel (Bus)	_____		
Birth Date(s)	_____	Conditional Date	_____
	_____	Requisition Date	_____
	_____	**CLOSING DATE**	_____

Vendor's Solicitor/Firm	_____
Address	_____
Telephone	_____ Fax _____
E-mail	_____ Teraview User Name _____

Letter to Vendor's Solicitor

	Req'd	Rec'd
Survey	_____	_____
Stat. of Adj	_____	_____
Draft Trans.	_____	_____

Title Search	Req'd	Rec'd
Search	_____	_____
Executions	_____	_____
Corp. Status	_____	_____

PA Stmts.	_____
Last Inst. #	_____

	Pre'd	Fw'd
Requisition Let.	_____	_____

Searches

	Req'd	Rec'd
Tax	_____	_____
Improvements	_____	_____
Spec. Levies	_____	_____
Estoppel Cert.	_____	_____
Zoning Use	_____	_____
Zoning Set/Bk	_____	_____
Work Orders	_____	_____
Water	_____	_____
Hydro	_____	_____
Gas	_____	_____
Subdiv. Agmt.	_____	_____
Bankruptcy	_____	_____
HUDAC	_____	_____
Elevator	_____	_____
Health	_____	_____
Environ.	_____	_____
Fire	_____	_____
Insurance	_____	
Mtgee. Inter.	_____	

Documents & Closing Materials

	P'd	Fw'd	App'd
Mortgage Back	_____	_____	_____
Dec. of Possess.	_____	_____	_____
Vendor's Undertaking	_____	_____	_____
Direction re title	_____	_____	_____

Acknow. Re Charge Terms	_____
Statement of Funds	_____
s. 116 Statement	_____
LTT Affidavit	_____
HUDAC Warranty	_____
Tax Bills	_____
Keys	_____
Planning Act Sticker	_____
Corporate Documents	_____

Closing Memo	_____
	_____
	_____
	_____
	_____

Mortgages

Mtg. Statement	_____
Copy of Mtg. Assumed	_____
Standard Charge Terms	_____
1st Mtgee. Address	_____
2nd Mtgee. Address	_____
Amortization Schedule	_____

After Closing

Undertakings Fulfilled	_____
Readjustments	_____
Tax & Assess Letters	_____
Condo Notice	_____
Interest on Deposit	_____
Preliminary Report	_____
Account	_____
Final Report	_____

DOCUMENT REGISTRATION AGREEMENT

BETWEEN:

DREW C. CRAWFORD

(hereinafter referred to as the **"Purchaser's Solicitor"**)

AND:

PETER T. GRANT

(hereinafter referred to as the **"Vendor's Solicitor"**)

RE: Ronald Craig Anderson and Kelly Anne Anderson (the **"Purchaser"**) purchase from Ryan Andrew Peterson (the **"Vendor"**) of 984 Helena Avenue, North York (the **"Property"**) pursuant to an agreement of purchase and sale dated December 15, 2007, as amended from time to time (the **"Purchase Agreement"**), scheduled to be completed on February 28, 2008 (the **"Closing Date"**)

FOR GOOD AND VALUABLE CONSIDERATION (the receipt and sufficiency of which is hereby expressly acknowledged), the parties hereto hereby undertake and agree as follows:

Holding Deliveries in Escrow

1.   The Vendor's Solicitor and the Purchaser's Solicitor shall hold all funds, keys and closing documentation exchanged between them (the "Requisite Deliveries") in escrow, and *shall* not release or otherwise deal with same except in accordance with the terms of this Agreement. Both the Vendor's Solicitor and the Purchaser's Solicitor have been authorized by their respective clients to enter into this Agreement. Once the Requisite Deliveries can be released in accordance with the terms of this Agreement, any monies representing payout funds for mortgages to be discharged shall be forwarded promptly to the appropriate mortgage lender.[1]

Advising of Concerns with Deliveries

2.   Each of the parties hereto shall notify the other as soon as reasonably possible following their respective receipt of the Requisite Deliveries (as applicable) of any defect(s) with respect to same.

Selecting Solicitor Responsible for Registration

3.   The Purchaser's Solicitor shall be responsible for the registration of the Electronic Documents (as hereinafter defined) unless the box set out below indicating that the Vendor's Solicitor will be responsible for such registration has been checked. For the purposes of this Agreement, the solicitor responsible for such registration shall be referred to as the "Registering Solicitor" and the other solicitor shall be referred to as the "Non-Registering Solicitor":

Vendor's Solicitor will be registering the Electronic Documents

Responsibility of Non-Registering Solicitor

and

Release of Requisite Deliveries by Non-Registering Solicitor

4.   The Non-Registering Solicitor shall, upon his/her receipt and approval of the Requisite Deliveries (as applicable), electronically release for registration the Electronic Documents and shall thereafter be entitled to release the Requisite Deliveries from escrow forthwith following the earlier of:

a)   the registration of the Electronic Documents;

b)   the closing time specified in the Purchase Agreement unless a specific time has been inserted as follows 10:00 a.m.. on the Closing Date (the **"Release Deadline"**), and provided that notice under paragraph 7 below has not been received; or

c)   receipt of notification from the Registering Solicitor of the registration of the Electronic Documents.

If the Purchase Agreement does not specify a closing time and a Release Deadline has not been specifically inserted the Release Deadline shall be 6.00 p.m. on the Closing Date.

---

[1] Solicitors should continue to refer to the Law Society of Upper Canada practice guidelines relating to recommended procedures to follow for the discharge of mortgages.

Responsibility of Registering Solicitor	5. The Registering Solicitor shall, subject to paragraph 7 below, on the Closing Date, following his/her receipt and approval of the Requisite Deliveries (as applicable*)*, register the documents listed in Schedule "A" annexed hereto (referred to in this agreement as the "**Electronic Documents**") in the stated order of priority therein set out, as soon as reasonably possible once same have been released for registration by the Non-Registering Solicitor, and immediately thereafter notify the Non-Registering Solicitor of the registration particulars thereof by telephone or telefax (or other method as agreed between the parties).
Release of Requisite Deliveries by Registering Solicitor	6. Upon registration of the Electronic Documents and notification of the Non-Registering solicitor in accordance with paragraph 5 above, the Registering Solicitor shall be entitled to forthwith release the Requisite Deliveries from escrow.
Returning Deliveries where Non-registration	7. Any of the parties hereto may notify the other party that he/she does not wish to proceed with the registration[2] of the Electronic Documents, and provided that such notice is received by the other party before the release of the Requisite Deliveries pursuant to this Agreement and before the registration of the Electronic Documents, then each of the parties hereto shall forthwith return to the other party their respective Requisite Deliveries.
Counterparts & Gender	8. This Agreement may be signed in counterparts, and shall be read with all changes of gender and/or number as may be required by the context.
Purchase Agreement Prevails if Conflict or Inconsistency	9. Nothing contained in this Agreement shall be read or construed as altering the respective rights and obligations of the Purchaser and the Vendor as more particularly set out in the Purchase Agreement, and in the event of any conflict or inconsistency between the provisions of this Agreement and the Purchase Agreement, then the latter shall prevail.
Telefaxing Deliveries & Providing Originals if Requested	10. This Agreement (or any counterpart hereof), and any of the closing documents hereinbefore contemplated, may be exchanged by telefax or similar system reproducing the original, provided that all such documents have been properly executed by the appropriate parties. The party transmitting any such document(s) shall also provide the original executed version(s) of same to the recipient within 2 business days after the Closing Date, unless the recipient has indicated that he/she does not require such original copies.

Dated this _____ day of <u>February, 2008.</u>

Name/Firm Name of Vendor's Solicitor   Name/Firm Name of Purchaser's Solicitor

<u>Peter T. Grant</u>   <u>Drew C. Crawford</u>

<u>HILL, JOHNSTON & GRANT</u>   <u>SIMPSON, STAINTON & CRAWFORD</u>

Name of Person Signing   Name of Person Signing

(Signature)   (Signature)

Note: This version of the Document Registration Agreement was adopted by the Joint LSUC-CBAO Committee on Electronic Registration of Title Documents on <u>March 29, 2004</u> and posted to the web site on <u>April 8, 2004</u>.

SCHEDULE "A" TO THE DOCUMENT REGISTRATION AGREEMENT

Electronic Documents to be registered on closing (in order of priority)

Transfer/Deed of the Property from the Vendor in favour of the Purchaser.

First Charge/Mortgage against the Property from the Purchaser in favour of Algonquin Permanent Trust Company.

Second Charge/Mortgage against the Property from the Purchaser in favour of Ryan Andrew Peterson and Kristen Lynn Peterson.

---

[2] For the purpose of this Agreement, the term "registration" shall mean the issuance of registration number(s) in respect of the Electronic Documents by the appropriate Land Registry Office.

ACKNOWLEDGEMENT AND DIRECTION

TO: <u>John Smith</u>
(insert Lawyer's name)

AND TO: <u>Smith & Smith</u>
(insert Lawyer's name)

RE: _____ ("the transaction")
(insert brief description of transaction)

This will confirm that:

- I/we have reviewed the information set out this Acknowledgement and Direction and in the documents described below (the "Documents"), and that this information is accurate;

- You, your agent or employee are authorized and directed to sign, deliver, and/or register electronically, on my/our behalf the Documents in the form attached.

- You are hereby authorized and directed to enter into an escrow closing arrangement substantially in the form attached hereto being a copy of the version of the Document Registration Agreement, which appears on the website of the Law Society of Upper Canada as of the date of the Agreement of Purchase and sale therein. I/we acknowledge the said Agreement has been reviewed by me/us and that I/we shall be bound by its terms;

- The effect of the documents has been fully explained to me/us, and I/we understand that I/we are parties to and bound by the terms and provisions of the Documents to the same extent as if I/we had signed them; and

- I/we are in fact the parties named in the Documents and I/we have not misrepresented our identities to you.

- I, _____, am the spouse of _____, the (Transferor/Chargor), and hereby consent to the transaction described in the Acknowledgement and Direction. I authorize you to indicate my consent on all the Documents for which it is required.

DESCRIPTION OF ELECTRONIC DOCUMENTS

The Document(s) described in the Acknowledgement and Direction are the document(s) selected below which are attached hereto as "Document in Preparation" and are:

☐ A Transfer of the land described above.

☐ A Charge of the land described above.

☐ Other documents set out in Schedule "B" attached hereto.

Dated at _____ **, this** _____ **day of** _____ **, 20** _____ .

WITNESS
(As to all signatures, if required)

_____   _____

Properties

PIN   08567 – 0058 LT   *Interest/Estate*   Fee Simple
Description   LT 21, RCP 434; Newbury
Address   Newbury

Consideration

Consideration $132, 456.00

Transferor(s)

The transferor(s) hereby transfers the land to the transferee(s)

Name   CHARLES, WAYNE
                         Acting as an individual

Address for Service   123 Roadway Rd
                         Newbury

I am at least 18 years of age

This document is not authorized under Power of Attorney by this party

Transferee(s)   Capacity   Share

Name   URSINO, DAVID   Registered Owner
                         Acting as an individual

Date of Birth   1965 08 05

Address for Service   987 Roadway Rd
                         Newbury

Calculated Taxes

Retail Sales Tax $0.00

Land Transfer Tax $115.00

Precedent 24.6 Teraview: Open and Print an Instrument in Progress and Create and Print an Acknowledgement and Direction Report

To Open an Instrument in Progress

▶ Open Docket

Menu Bar   ▶ Instrument
                ▶ View in Progress…

Instruments in Progress window opens and displays all documents created for the current docket.

     ▶ Double click on the document you wish to open

If you wish to delete a document from the Instruments in Progress window:

     ▶ Right click on the document and select Delete Instrument

To Print an Instrument in Progress

▶ Open Docket
▶ Open Document related to the report you wish to create

Menu Bar   ▶ Instrument
                ▶ Reports…

     Instrument Report Selection dialog box will open:

     ▶ Select Document Preparation from drop-down menu
     ▶ Click Include Attachments or Land Transfer Tax Affidavit if applicable
     ▶ Click Print (to send to your printer)

To Create an Acknowledgement and Direction Report (ADR)

▶ Open Docket
▶ Open Document related to the ADR report you wish to create

Menu Bar   ▶ Instrument
                ▶ Reports…

Instrument Report Selection dialog box will open:

     ▶ Select Acknowledgement/Direction from drop-down menu
     ▶ Click on Include Attachments or Include Land Transfer Tax Statements Report if applicable
     ▶ Select party (client) name from the drop-down box
     ▶ Click Print (to send to your printer)

Note: The ADR must be completed prior to registering any document.

CHAPTER 25

Acting for the Vendor

OBJECTIVES:

■ Describe the procedure for opening and processing a real estate file when acting for the vendor

■ Demonstrate an understanding of the terms, documentation, and terminology used in this process

■ Use legal precedents to prepare the documentation required when acting for the vendor

In a real estate transaction, in most jurisdictions, the vendor's solicitors are responsible for ensuring that the vendor gives good title and receives in return the purchase price and all adjustments to which he or she is entitled.

The property being purchased by a vendor in a real estate transaction may be either new or used residential property. In this chapter, we mainly consider the procedures to be followed in the sale of used residential property. Many of these procedures, such as preparation of the required transfer/deed, replying to requisitions on title, and arranging discharges of mortgages on the property, are also followed in the sale of new residential property. The Goods and Services Tax (GST) applies to new residential property, and the procedures relating to that tax are considered briefly where appropriate.

Technology has had a great impact on how residential real estate transactions are conducted, especially in the area of communications between the law firms, their clients, and any financial institutions. Most communications are now by e-mail instead of letters, and any reference to a letter (and its accompanying precedent) should be considered to include e-mail communication as well.

Additionally, communication is done between the law firms using the e-reg system. The only way to send the electronic documents to the other party's solicitor for their review is by a *message*; this is how Teraview refers to their e-mail system. The message system in Teraview is much like regular e-mail software except that it may only be used to send and receive messages with other registered Teraview users and the only attachments available are the electronic documents. Reference will be made as to when the electronic documents are sent and received, but legal assistants who work in real estate and have active files should check their message box in Teraview every day.

Precedent 25.1 outlines the instructions for sending and receiving a message in Teraview.

Once the client records and necessary tickler or diary notations are in order, the steps outlined in this chapter are taken.

MATERIAL FROM THE VENDOR

Contact the vendor(s) and ask them to provide the law firm with the following (as applicable):

1. The copy of the transfer/deed for the property or registration details
2. A copy of any charge/mortgage on the property or registration details and the address of the mortgagee
3. A plan of survey of the property, if there is one
4. The tax bills for the current year and the previous year
5. The provincial assessment notice
6. Copies of leases (if any) and names of tenants
7. Water bills if the property is located in a municipality that bills for water twice a year on a flat rate
8. The last fuel bill and information on the size of the oil tank if the property is heated by oil
9. The vendor's address for service after the transaction closes

10. The reporting letter received at the time the property was purchased if your law firm did not act for the vendor in that transaction
11. Information on the vendor's use of the property being sold, such as for living quarters, rental income, or commercial activity, to determine whether or not the property is exempt from GST (most used residential property is exempt)

If the property being sold is a condominium, the vendor is also requested to provide all available information on the condominium, such as copies of the declaration; the condominium by-laws (the rules by which all owners are bound, indicating, for example, what owners may or may not do with their units, how common expenses are to be assessed and collected, and so on); the management agreement, which is the agreement with the company authorized to manage the condominium for the owners; and information on the contingency reserve and the monthly charge for common expenses.

LETTER TO THE PURCHASER'S SOLICITORS

Once the agreement of purchase and sale has been received, the solicitors for the vendor usually send a letter (Precedent 25.2) to the solicitors for the purchaser to

1. Provide information on the title: the legal description, PIN number, and any survey
2. Request information on how the purchaser wishes to take title to the property, his or her date of birth, and the address for service after the closing of the transaction

MORTGAGE

As mentioned previously, the *Land Registration Reform Act* and the electronic documents in Teraview use the word "charge"; however, the term "mortgage" is still used by most financial institutions and the general public and is the term used in this chapter to refer to a charge/mortgage.

See Chapter 22 for instructions on how to prepare an e-reg or hard copy of a mortgage.

To Be Discharged

Arrangements need to be made to discharge any existing mortgage on the property as mortgages are rarely assumed by the purchaser any longer. A letter (Precedent 25.3) is written to the mortgagee requesting a mortgage statement showing

1. the amount required to pay off the mortgage fully as of the closing date,
2. the per diem interest rate that must be paid if the transaction does not close when expected, and
3. the name of the solicitors acting for the mortgagee so that arrangements can be made with those solicitors to have the discharge registered on the closing date.

When an existing mortgage is to be discharged, the monies paid on closing may be payable to the vendor's solicitors so that they will have funds to discharge the mortgage. Alternatively, part of the monies paid on closing may be directed to be made payable to the mortgagee for the amount required to pay off the mortgage, with the balance payable to the vendor's solicitors.

A draft discharge of charge (manual or e-reg) is prepared and sent to the solicitors for the mortgagee for approval prior to the closing date. If in e-reg, and depending on the financial institution, the draft electronic document may be signed for release by the mortgagee and then held in escrow until the closing date when the solicitors for the mortgagor would electronically register the mortgage and forward the discharge funds to the financial institution.

See Chapter 23 for instructions on how to prepare an e-reg or hard copy of a discharge of mortgage.

Mortgage Back

If the vendor is taking back a mortgage as part of the purchase price, the purchaser's solicitors are requested to prepare and submit a draft mortgage for approval. If there is more than one vendor, the vendors must decide how to hold the mortgage; usually, a husband and wife hold a mortgage on joint account with right of survivorship, which offers the same rights as a joint tenancy in a deed. Information on how the vendor wishes to hold any mortgage back, as well as an address for service after the transaction has closed, is provided by letter or e-mail to the purchaser's solicitors.

In the e-reg system, a draft mortgage will be received through the Teraview system, and if satisfactory, the document will be electronically signed by the solicitor for the mortgagee (the vendor) and a message with the approved mortgage attached will be sent back to the solicitors for the mortgagor to hold until the closing date, when it will be registered electronically. Precedent 25.4 outlines the instructions for digitally signing and registering a document in Teraview.

If there is a vendor take-back mortgage, a writ of execution search will also need to be done against the names of the mortgagor(s), and if there are any executions (an unpaid judgment registered with the sheriff) against the mortgagor(s), they must be cleared before the closing date by the solicitors for the mortgagor(s). Precedent 25.5 outlines the instructions to conduct a writ search on a name in the Teraview WritSearch product.

In the manual system, a hard copy of the mortgage will be sent by the purchaser's solicitor for review, and if satisfactory, they are advised by letter or e-mail.

To Be Assumed

Mortgages are rarely assumed these days, but if there is an existing mortgage on the property that the purchaser is to assume, the vendor furnishes full particulars of this mortgage. A letter is written to the mortgagee requesting a mortgage statement for assumption purposes, showing the balance outstanding on the mortgage, plus interest, as of the date of closing. This information is required for the statement of adjustments.

RESPONSES TO REQUISITION ON TITLE

The agreement of purchase and sale allows the purchasers a certain number of days within which to bring any problems on title to the attention of the vendors. Such problems are often referred to as a cloud on title. The purchaser's solicitors write a letter, known as a letter of requisition, to the vendor's solicitors on or before the last day of the period of time allowed. The vendor's solicitors then respond in a letter that endeavours to answer each of the points made by the purchaser's solicitors.

For example, the letter of requisition may state that there is an existing mortgage registered on the title to the property or that there are unpaid realty taxes and require assurances from the vendor's solicitors that these items will be paid on or before closing.

There may also be executions that were found registered against an individual of the same or similar name as the vendor. The judgment must be satisfied (if it applies to the vendor), or a statutory declaration must be prepared and executed to prove that he or she is not the individual named in the execution. For executions under $50,000, the declaration may be executed by the vendor; for executions of $50,000 or more, the declaration must be executed by the solicitor for the vendor, who must satisfy himself or herself that the vendor is not the person named in the execution.

In the manual system, a hard copy of the declaration is attached to the transfer/deed when it is registered; in the e-reg system, the writ of execution is cleared by the solicitors for the vendor by selecting the appropriate statement in the Teraview system.

Precedent 25.5 outlines the instructions for searching and clearing writs of execution by statement in an e-reg document.

FIRE INSURANCE

Most vendors hold a homeowner's or comprehensive policy of insurance on their property. This policy includes fire insurance coverage. The vendor will cancel the policy of insurance on the property, effective as of the date of closing. The purchaser will arrange for his or her own insurance coverage from and after the date of closing.

If a property is subject to a vendor take-back mortgage, fire insurance coverage must be carried in an amount at least equal to the principal amount of the mortgage, with any loss payable to the mortgagees as their interests may be in the property, and proof of insurance must be provided to the vendor's solicitors.

TRANSFER/DEED

In the e-reg system, the majority of the draft transfer is completed by the solicitors for the vendor, with the exception of the steps for completing the information on the names and dates of birth of the transferee(s), conducting a writ of execution search, and Land Transfer and School Tax statements, which are completed by the solicitors for the transferee when the draft transfer is electronically messaged to them. The transferee's solicitor will review the document and, if satisfactory, input this information, electronically sign the document, and send a message back. The electronic document will then be held until the closing date, when the transferor's solicitor will digitally sign the document for release so that it may be registered.

In the manual system, a draft of the entire hard-copy document is prepared and sent to the purchaser's solicitors for approval. If approved, two copies are made and held for execution by the client.

See Chapter 21 for instructions on how to prepare an e-reg or hard copy of a transfer/deed.

STATUS CERTIFICATE

If the property being conveyed is a condominium, the vendor may be required to provide a status certificate (formerly referred to as an estoppel certificate) showing the vendor's status in regard to the payment of the common expenses; any anticipated increase in common expenses; the amount held in the reserve fund; whether there is any pending litigation; and the names and addresses of the directors of the condominium corporation. The condominium corporation is requested to provide this certificate, for which they charge a fee The certificate is given to the purchaser's solicitors on closing.

Frequently, the solicitors for the purchaser will request this status certificate directly from the condominium corporation, as discussed in Chapter 26.

DECLARATION OF POSSESSION

The vendor may complete a statutory declaration known as a declaration of possession. It sets out the time the vendor has been in possession of the property being conveyed; information on any existing charge/mortgage; the status of realty taxes; details of any encumbrances or liens that may affect title of the property; residency status as required under the *Income Tax Act*; and certification as to the vendor's use of the property as required for GST purposes.

The declaration is usually prepared by the purchaser's solicitors and sent to the vendor's solicitors for approval and completion by the vendor. The sworn declaration is then given to the purchaser's solicitors on closing.

STATEMENT OF ADJUSTMENTS

The solicitor for the vendor prepares and submits a detailed statement outlining the exact amount of money the purchaser must pay on closing. Included in this amount are adjustments that must be made because of realty taxes paid or unpaid on the property for a period before and after the closing date or, for example, for a full tank of oil left for the use of the purchaser.

These and other items are set out in the statement of adjustments. Information on adjustments required on closing is included in the agreement of purchase and sale. Other necessary information is set out in the mortgage statement (if the purchaser is assuming an existing mortgage) and in material provided by the vendor to his or her solicitor, such as realty tax bills and water, hydro, and fuel bills. If the property being sold is a condominium, information on the common expenses and the contingency fund will also be ascertained from material furnished by the vendor.

Preparation and Set-Up

A minimum of four copies of the statement of adjustments are prepared. Two copies are sent to the solicitors for the purchaser for approval; if a mortgage is being assumed, the mortgage statement is also sent with the statement of adjustments. One copy is sent to the vendor when the transaction has closed; the fourth copy is for the file.

The style of set-up of a statement of adjustments varies from office to office. Many law offices have prepared a basic template containing all possible adjustments; details are inserted for the applicable items and unnecessary wording is struck out. Commercial real estate software programs, such as *The Conveyancer*, will calculate and print the complete statement of adjustments when the variable information is keyed in and merged with the standard wording. Legal assistants should, however, have an understanding of how to format and calculate a statement of adjustments.

Heading

There are different ways of heading a statement of adjustments. Although the arrangement of information varies, the same information appears in all headings:

1. The name of the document, that is, Statement of Adjustments
2. The date as of which the adjustments are made (usually, the date on which the transaction is to close)
3. The names of the parties to the transaction
4. A brief description of the property that is the subject of the transaction

Body

The body of the statement sets out the amounts due to the vendor and the amounts the purchaser has already paid or will pay to close the transaction. A simple formula is as follows: prepaid or overpaid expenses are an allowance to the vendor; unpaid or underpaid expenses are an allowance to the purchaser.

Allowances to the vendor appear in the right-hand column of figures and allowances to the purchaser in the left-hand column. Sufficient detail is provided for all items to allow the computations to be checked by the purchaser's solicitor. The difference between the amounts due to the vendor and the amounts paid by or allowed to the purchaser is the balance due on closing.

Figure 25.1 is a guide to preparing the statement of adjustments.

Figure 25.1 Guide to Statement of Adjustments

ITEM	SOURCE OF INFORMATION	ALLOWANCE TO
Accrued interest	Mortgage statement	Purchaser
Common expenses	Condominium status certificate	Vendor
Contingency reserve	Condominium status certificate	No adjustment
Deposit	Agreement of purchase and sale	Purchaser
Fuel oil	Fuel bills	Vendor
Goods and Services Tax	Agreement of purchase and sale Solicitor	Vendor
Insurance, fire Placed by Condo. Corp.	Condominium estoppel certificate	No adjustment
Insurance	Solicitor	No adjustment
Mortgage, new	Client	No adjustment
Mortgage back	Agreement of purchase and sale	Purchaser
Mortgage assumed	Agreement of purchase and sale Mortgage statement	Purchaser
Rent, prepaid	Lease	Purchaser
Rent, unpaid	Lease	Vendor
Sale price	Agreement of purchase and sale	Vendor
Taxes, prepaid	Tax bills/mortgage statement	May be to either
Taxes, unpaid	Tax bills	Purchaser
Water, other than on meter	Water bills	Vendor

Balance Due

The difference between the amounts due to the vendor and the amounts paid by or allowed to the purchaser is the balance due on closing.

Ending

The abbreviation E. & O.E. (errors and omissions excepted) is typed in the lower left-hand portion of the statement.

Precedents 25.6 and 25.7 illustrate two styles of statement of adjustments.

HOW TO CALCULATE STATEMENTS OF ADJUSTMENTS

Adjustment Date

All adjustments are usually made as of the date of closing of the real estate transaction. Practice varies as to whether the purchaser or the vendor is responsible for the actual day of closing. Many agreements of purchase and sale specify that the day of closing itself is apportioned to the purchaser; this chapter proceeds on this basis.

The vendor is charged for realty taxes, accrued interest on any mortgage being assumed, etc., up to and preceding the date of closing. The purchaser is charged for realty taxes, water on a flat rate, and so on, from and after the date of closing.

Sale Price

This amount is credited to the vendor. Refer to the agreement of purchase and sale for the amount of the sale price.

Deposit(s)

Any deposit(s) is credited to the purchaser. Refer to the agreement of purchase and sale for the amount of any deposits made.

Goods and Services Tax

Tax-Exempt Property
GST is not usually levied on the sale of used residential property, and no reference to the tax appears on the statement of adjustments.

New or Substantially Renovated Property
GST is levied on the purchase price of new or substantially renovated residential housing. The statement of adjustments shows an allowance to the vendor for the full amount of the GST payable by the purchaser on the sale price.

When the purchase price is less than $450,000 and the property will be the purchaser's primary place of residence, the purchaser is entitled to a rebate of GST on a sliding-scale basis.

Any GST new housing rebate for which the purchaser may be eligible is either paid directly to the purchaser by the vendor or is shown as a credit to the purchaser on the statement of adjustments. The purchaser will, in turn, assign to the vendor the actual rebate to be received when the new housing rebate application has been filed and processed and complete a statutory declaration certifying that he or she is eligible to apply for the rebate. A Form Completion Guide and the application may be accessed at the Canada Revenue Agency website (http://www.cra-arc.gc.ca/E/pub/gp/rc4028/README.html).

GST Included in Purchase Price

The purchase price as set out in the agreement of purchase and sale is shown as an allowance to the vendor on the statement of adjustments. It is usual, however, to include information on how that price is apportioned to indicate the amount on which land transfer tax will be levied. For example:

Sale price		$169,000.00
(Sale price	$160,952.38	
+	8,047.62)	

Charges/Mortgages

In real estate transactions, a charge/mortgage is often used in lieu of money to finance part of the purchase price. The purchaser will arrange a mortgage with a financial institution or an individual, assume an existing mortgage, or give back to the vendor a mortgage on the property.

A statement of adjustments is concerned only with a mortgage back or a mortgage assumed.

Mortgage Back

If the vendor is taking back a mortgage, the amount of the mortgage back is shown as if the vendor had already received the money, that is, as a credit to the purchaser.

Mortgage Assumed

If the purchaser is to assume an existing mortgage, the vendor's solicitor writes to the mortgagee for a mortgage statement that indicates the amount of principal and accrued interest outstanding as of the closing date. The purchaser is credited for the total amount of the principal and accrued interest outstanding on closing because this is a liability the purchaser is assuming from the vendor; it is therefore deducted from the amount to be paid to the vendor.

To help the purchaser's solicitors verify items on the statement of adjustments relating to an assumed mortgage, the vendor's solicitors send a copy of the mortgage statement when forwarding the statement of adjustments.

Taxes

The tax bills furnished by the vendor and the mortgage statement assist in the calculation of the realty tax adjustment.

Realty taxes are paid yearly, covering the period from January 1 to December 31. Tax bills are issued in early spring on an interim basis; a second final bill is usually issued in June, when the exact tax assessment rate for the year has been established. Usually, taxpayers are given the option of paying the total assessed taxes in a number of instalments over the year, or the taxes may be fully paid by paying the full amount of the interim bill and the balance shown as owing on the final bill.

At the time the vendor sells the real property, all or part of the realty taxes for the current year may have been paid, or if the closing date of the sale is in January or February, none of the taxes for the current year may have been paid. When the vendor has an existing mortgage on the property with a financial institution, the monthly payments on the mortgage often include an amount equal to one-twelfth of the estimated yearly realty taxes; this amount stands to the credit of the vendor. Information on the balance of such a tax account appears on the mortgage statement.

Because the vendor is responsible for realty taxes for the period of the year in which he or she is the owner of the property, an adjustment for realty taxes is included on the statement of adjustments and shows an allowance to either the vendor or the purchaser.

Calculating the Tax Adjustment

To calculate the adjustment for realty taxes, follow these steps:

1. Determine the total amount of taxes for the year. This information is obtained from the client's copy of the municipal tax bill. If the total realty tax bill has not yet been determined, taxes are adjusted on the basis of the total taxes for the previous year plus a certain estimated increase (usually 5 to 10 percent). The solicitor for the vendor then undertakes to re-adjust the taxes when the actual amount of realty taxes is known.
2. Determine the vendor's share of the taxes for the year, based on the number of days for which he or she is responsible. The purchaser's share may also be calculated; the two totals should equal the full amount of the taxes.
3. Calculate the per diem (daily) rate by dividing the total taxes for the year by the number of days in the year (365 or 366). Then multiply this rate by the number of days for which the vendor is responsible to calculate the vendor's share. Many law firms round the per diem to two decimal places and show this calculation on the statement of adjustments, as illustrated in Precedent 25.6.
4. Determine the total amount already paid by the vendor for realty taxes. If the vendor has paid *all or more than* his or her share of the realty taxes for the year, show the difference between what has been paid and the amount for which the vendor is responsible as an allowance to the vendor on the statement of adjustments. If the vendor has paid *nothing or less* than his or her share of the realty taxes for the year, show the difference between the amount the vendor is responsible for and the any amount the vendor has paid as allowance to the purchaser on the statement of adjustments.

For example, assume that the real estate transaction is to close on September 28 in a year that is not a leap year and that the realty taxes for the year are $1,695.36:

Number of days vendor responsible for:	January 1 to September 27, or 270 days
Number of days purchaser responsible for:	September 28 to December 31, or 95 days

Vendor's share of the taxes: $\dfrac{\$1,695.36}{365}$ = $4.6448219 per diem × 270 days = $1,254.10

Purchaser's share: $\dfrac{\$1,695.36}{365}$ = $4.6448219 per diem × 95 days = $441.26

Vendor Has Paid Taxes in Full

If the vendor has paid the full amount of the realty taxes for the year, there is an adjustment to the vendor on the statement of adjustments for $441.26, arrived at as follows:

20__ taxes paid in full	$1,695.36
Vendor's share ($4.6448219 × 270 days)	1,254.10
Allow vendor	$ 441.26

Vendor Has Not Paid Any Taxes

If the vendor has paid no realty taxes at all, there is an adjustment to the purchaser on the statement of adjustments for $1,254.10, arrived at as follows:

20__ taxes not paid	$1,695.36
Purchaser's share ($4.6448219 × 95 days)	441.26
Allow purchaser	$1,254.10

Taxes Paid by Installment

If the vendor has paid two installments on the realty taxes in the total amount of $500.00, there is an allowance to the purchaser of $754.10, arrived at as follows:

20__ taxes $1,695.36	
Vendor's share for ($4.6448219 × 270 days)	$1,254.10
Vendor has paid	500.00
Allow purchaser	$ 754.10

In the above example, the vendor has paid less than his or her share of the taxes for the period of ownership of the real property. However, if the vendor has paid installments totalling $1,500.00, there is an allowance to the vendor of $245.90, calculated as follows:

20__ taxes	$1,695.36
Paid by vendor	1,500.00
Vendor's share ($4.6448219 × 270 days)	1,254.10
Allow vendor	$ 245.90

Taxes Paid with Monthly Amortized Mortgage Payment

If the vendor pays one-twelfth of the yearly realty taxes together with a monthly amortized mortgage payment, many law firms credit the vendor on the statement of adjustments with the full amount standing to his or her credit in the tax account with the mortgagee. Calculate the tax adjustment on the basis that the vendor has paid no realty taxes at all, which results in an allowance to the purchaser for the period in which the vendor was the owner of the property. This method simplifies the calculation of the adjustment for realty taxes and has no effect at all on the final figure for the balance due on closing.

Fuel Oil

If the real property being sold is heated by oil, the vendor is expected to leave the oil tank completely full on the date of closing. Most oil tanks hold 200 gallons (or 909 litres). The vendor is therefore given an allowance for a full tank of oil on closing. A quotation for the price of the fuel oil including the amount of the GST will need to be obtained from the fuel company. This amount is credited to the vendor on the statement of adjustments.

Water

Water provided to the real property being sold is charged to the vendor either following a meter reading to record the actual water used or on a flat rate, payable in advance, covering half of the year.

Meter

If the water is charged by a meter reading, the water department of the municipality in which the property is located is requested to attend on the day of closing for a reading so that the vendor is billed up to the day of closing. There is then no adjustment for water on the statement of adjustments.

Flat Rate

If the water is paid for in advance on a flat rate, there is an allowance to the vendor on the statement of adjustment for the period for which he or she has paid for water but for which the purchaser should be responsible. To calculate the allowance, determine the number of days in the six-month period and the number of days for which the vendor was responsible for the cost of water. Determine the vendor's share of the water bill; the difference between the amount paid and the vendor's share is allowed to the vendor.

Hydro, Telephone, and Gas

Usually, there is no provision in the statement of adjustments for these utility services. The vendor informs the municipal hydro commission, the telephone company, and the gas company (if the building is heated by gas) that he or she is selling and giving up possession on a particular day. The vendor requests them to attend on that day to read the appropriate meters or to disconnect the telephone so that the vendor is billed up to the day of closing.

Fire Insurance

Condominiums

If the property being sold is a condominium, there is no adjustment for prepaid fire insurance. The condominium corporation is responsible for the premium, which is paid for out of the common expenses contribution by each condominium owner.

Other Buildings

If the property being sold is a building on which the vendor carries a policy of fire insurance, the vendor cancels the policy and the purchasers place their own coverage on the property.

Although there is usually no adjustment to be made for insurance premiums, most statements include this item with a notation such as "Purchaser to place own coverage."

Rent

If any part of the property is rented, an adjustment for prepaid rent must be included in the statement of adjustments.

The vendor usually receives rent in advance and is entitled to it only up to the day preceding the date of closing. Any rent received for a period after that date is shown as a credit to the purchaser.

Common Expenses and Contingency Reserve

If the vendor is selling a condominium, an adjustment is required for the monthly contribution to the common expenses. The agreement of purchase and sale specifically stipulates that there is no adjustment for the vendor's contribution to the contingency reserve.

The vendor is entitled to credit for any prepaid contribution to the common expenses for the period following the date of closing. Refer to the material provided by the vendor to his or her solicitor and to the condominium status certificate when calculating this adjustment.

Other Adjustments

On statements of adjustments prepared on the sale of new residential property, there may also be adjustments for such items as grading, water installation, or driveway finishing. The statement shows an allowance to the vendor for the actual cost, plus an allowance for GST.

Balance Due

On closing, the purchaser pays the total of all amounts due to the vendor, less all amounts already paid by or allowed to the purchaser. The balance due on closing and to whom that amount is to be paid are shown on the statement of adjustments.

Usually, the balance due is payable to the vendor's solicitors in trust, but it may be payable to those solicitors and a named person or company other than the vendor; for example, this could be a mortgagee when a mortgage is being discharged or a municipality when there are unpaid realty taxes.

FORWARDING THE STATEMENT OF ADJUSTMENTS

When the statement of adjustments is prepared, two copies of it are sent to the solicitors for the purchaser.

If the real estate transaction involves the purchase of new residential property, and the GST new housing rebate is being assigned to the vendor, the solicitors for the vendor also forward the draft GST new housing rebate application form, the assignment of that rebate to the vendor, and the statutory declaration certifying that the purchaser is eligible to apply for the GST new housing rebate. These documents will be executed by the purchaser and given to the solicitors for the vendor on the closing of the transaction.

UNDERTAKING AND DIRECTION RE PROCEEDS

Two other documents are prepared and held in the office file until the vendor comes in just before closing to execute all required documents: an undertaking and a direction in respect of the proceeds.

Undertaking

Items to be Adjusted

Certain items on the statement of adjustments, such as realty taxes, may require re-adjustment at a later date. The commitment to do this is contained in an undertaking (Precedent 25.8) executed by the vendor and given to the purchaser's solicitors on closing. The undertaking is not usually limited to re-adjustment of items on the statement of adjustments but usually covers any commitments that are part of the real estate transaction.

Frequently, this undertaking is prepared by the solicitors for the purchaser and forwarded to the vendor's solicitors for completion by their client. Most law offices have a standard form of undertaking, which is adapted to the particular transaction as appropriate. For example, the undertaking to leave a full tank of fuel oil does not apply when the transaction is the sale of a condominium or if the property is heated by gas or electricity.

Number and Disposition of Copies

A minimum of three copies are required. The vendor executes two copies; one is produced to the purchaser's solicitors on closing, and one is retained in the office file. The third copy is for the vendor.

Direction re Proceeds

The statement of adjustments indicates to whom the balance due on closing is to be paid. A signed direction by the vendor authorizing payment of the proceeds in this manner is produced on closing.

Prepare two copies of a direction re proceeds (Precedent 25.9) to be executed by the vendor before closing. Most law firms have a standard form of direction requiring only insertion of the details of the particular real estate transaction. One executed copy is provided to the solicitors for the purchaser on closing; the other executed copy is retained in the office file.

If the balance due on closing is payable to the vendor's solicitors, the vendor may also execute a second direction (Precedent 25.10) authorizing the payment of the amount to discharge a mortgage, of any outstanding balance of real estate commission, and of the law firm's fees and disbursements, with the balance being payable to the vendor.

Prepare two copies of this direction; one executed copy is for the vendor's solicitors, and the other is for the vendor.

PREPARING TO CLOSE

Arrange an appointment with the client to attend at the law firm to execute all documents required for the closing. As a general rule, two copies of all documents are executed. These documents may include but are not limited to the following:

1. Acknowledgement and Direction and Document Registration Agreement if an e-reg transaction; alternatively, in the manual system, hard copies of the transfer/deed will be executed
2. Declaration of Possession
3. Undertaking to Re-adjust
4. Direction re Proceeds

A copy of the statement of adjustments is also provided to and reviewed with the client at this appointment. The procedures on closing and the steps that follow closing are discussed in Chapter 27.

Terms and Concepts

material to be received from vendor	deposit(s)
GST considerations	GST calculations
mortgage (discharged, back, assumed)	mortgage calculations
requisitions on title	tax adjustment calculations
fire insurance	fuel oil calculations
transfer/deed	water
condominium status certificate	utilities
declaration of possession	common expenses calculations
statement of adjustments	balance due
adjustment date	undertaking to re-adjust
sale price	direction re proceeds

Review Questions

1. Why do the solicitors for the vendors require such material as the old transfer/deed, tax bills, water bills, fuel bills, etc.?

2. Why is it necessary to establish how the property was "used"? How may this be accomplished in a real estate transaction?

3. What is meant by "assuming a mortgage"?

4. What is a "mortgage back"?

5. What is required when there is an existing mortgage on the property that the purchasers are not assuming?

6. What is the purpose of the condominium status certificate?

7. What information is found in a declaration of possession? Which solicitors usually prepare this declaration?

8. As of what date are adjustments apportioned on the statement of adjustments usually?

9. Name three items other than a deposit and a mortgage back for which there may be an adjustment on the statement of adjustments.

10. If you have prepared a statement of adjustments, what other document or documents would you also expect to prepare?

PRECEDENTS

Precedent 25.1 Teraview: Send and Receive a Message

To Send a Message

▶ Open Docket

Menu Bar ▶ Messages
         ▶ Compose…

Compose Message Dialog Box will open with two drop-down menus:

Account Name (key in the name of the account)
To (key in the name of the individual person)

If you do not know the Teraview user name of the account or the person, you may do a search by keying in the following after either Account Name *or* To:

%, followed by a space, then key the first few characters of the account or name, and click Find.

Wait for the system to search and then use the drop-down menu to select the correct name from the list provided.

▶ Use Re: Instrustment drop-down menu to select the document you wish to send
▶ Key in an appropriate message
▶ Click Send

To View/Accept Messages

▶ Open Docket – Use the generic docket "Admin" until you see the message and then decide which Docket ID (client) to assign the message to

Menu Bar ▶ Messages
         ▶ View New Messages

Received Messages window opens.
▶ Right click on any received messages
▶ Accept Access
A dialog box will open, requesting confirmation that you wish to accept access to this document.
▶ Yes
Docket List dialog box will open.
▶ Key in Docket ID (or click List All to view all Docket ID numbers and select the desired docket)
▶ OK

Note: You should check for messages on the Teraview system daily.

Source: Teranet Inc.

Hill, Johnston & Grant

Barristers & Solicitors

www.hilljohngrant.com

Suite 2501, 17 Princess Street South
City, Province Postal Code

Telephone: (000) 354-9900
Facsimile: (000) 354-9909

January 20, 20__

Drew C. Crawford
Simpson, Stainton & Crawford
Barristers and Solicitors
53 Suffolk Street
Guelph ON N1H 7B4

Dear Drew:

PETERSON sale to ANDERSON
984 Helena Avenue, Toronto
Closing Date: February 28, 2008
Our File No. 05022/0598

Please be advised that we act for the vendor in the above-noted transaction and understand that you act for the purchasers, Ronald and Kelly Anderson.

Please advise us of the manner in which your clients will be taking title, together with their birthdates and their address for service following the closing of this transaction.

For your information, attached is a copy of the legal description of the property and the survey.

Yours very truly,

HILL, JOHNSTON & GRANT

Peter T. Grant

PTG/ri
Enc.

Hill, Johnston & Grant

Barristers & Solicitors

www.hilljohngrant.com

Suite 2501, 17 Princess Street South
City, Province Postal Code

Telephone: (000) 354-9900
Facsimile: (000) 354-9909

January 20, 20___

Mrs. Christine Peterson
20 Georgian Road
Guelph ON N1H 3J8

Dear Mrs. Peterson:

PETERSON sale to ANDERSON
984 Helena Avenue, Toronto
Closing Date: February 28, 2008
Our File No. 05022/0598

Please be advised that we act for the vendor in the above-noted transaction and understand that you hold the first mortgage on the said premises.

For purposes of discharge, would you please forward to our office a mortgage statement advising of the principal balance outstanding and accrued interest thereon.

The closing date of the transaction is February 28, 20__, and the statement should be based on this date.

Yours very truly,

HILL, JOHNSTON & GRANT

Peter T. Grant

PTG/ri

To Sign a Document

► Open Docket
► Open Document you wish to sign

Select **Signatories** in the directory and check to see if the document has been signed already.

Menu Bar ► Instrument
           ► Sign...

   Signature dialog box will open.
       ► Key in your Pass Phrase. (Note: Only lawyers may sign documents that contain compliance with law statements such as the Planning Act statement in a transfer.)

   Under Type of Signature
       ► Click on Completeness and/or Release as appropriate

   Under On Behalf of
       ► Choose Party From (Transferor/Mortgagor), Party To (Transferee/Mortgagee), or Both
       ► Click Sign

Teraview will check the document to ensure that all necessary statements have been selected and then adds the electronic signature. The screen will update to show that the document has been electronically signed. Note: If any changes are made to the document (by any party), the signatures will be automatically removed. The document will then need to be reviewed and electronically signed again.

To Register

► Open Docket

Menu Bar ► Options
           ► Document Registration Report (make sure there is a check mark beside this so that the registration report will print once registration has been completed

Menu Bar ► Instrument
           ► Register...

   Register dialog box opens (shown at right):

   The left window will show Instruments in Progress. The right window will show Instruments for Registration.

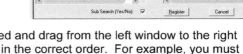

   ► Click on the instrument you wish to be registered and drag from the left window to the right window. Note: Make sure the instruments are in the correct order. For example, you must register the transfer first and then the mortgage on a new purchase.

   ► If you wish a sub search and writs search done before registration, click the Sub Search box

   ► Click Register

Registration Window will open (shown at right) indicating the registration was successful and displays the registration number (which you should record).

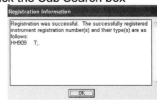

Source: Teranet Inc.

To Search for Writs of Execution & Clear by Statement

There are two methods of searching for writs of executions:
- Using the writs product *or*
- Using the e-reg product, which also allows you to clear writs by statement

To Search from the WritSearch Product:

► Open Docket

Menu Bar   ► Products
            ► WritSearch

Menu Bar   ► Writs
            ► Select whether you wish to seach by name or Writ #

    ► If searching by name: select whether a person or company
    ► Key in either the name or the Writ # in the dialog box.
         You may click on Add Name to search additionial parties
Print Writ Certificate Dialog Box opens.
    ► Key in your name and the reference (e.g., Client File Number)
    ► Click OK
Writ Certificate will print and Writs of Execution Search List window opens.
    ► Click on Detail for further information on the writ if desired, which may also be printed

To Search from the e-reg document:

► Open Docket
► Open Document (that contains the names of the parties you wish to search)
► Expand the second directory (e.g., Transferor) by clicking on the plus sign and highlight the first name
    (Note: e-reg will automatically search all names in that directory)

Menu Bar   ► Instrument
            ► Retrieve Writs

If there are no writs, nothing will appear to happen but the search has been conducted. You can select:
► Instruments
► Writ Certficate
To print out a certificate for the file.
You can also go to the Writs tab and beside Status: it will either state "Clear" or if there is a writ it will state "Subject To" and the particulars of any writ will be displayed in the screen below.

To clear a writ by statement:

From the Writs tab (within the e-reg document):
    ► Click on the drop-down arrow beside "This property is subject to a writ" and
    ► Select the appropriate statement

The status will now change to clear.

Source: Teranet Inc.

STATEMENT OF ADJUSTMENTS

VENDOR: Ryan Andrew Peterson

PURCHASER: Ronald Craig Anderson and
Kelly Anne Anderson

PROPERTY: 984 Helena Avenue, Toronto

**ADJUSTMENT
DATE:** February 28, 20__

Sale Price		$235,000.00
Deposit	$ 20,000.00	
Second mortgage back to Vendor	25,000.00	
Taxes		
Municipal taxes for 20__ $1,468.94		
Estimated increase of 10% 146.89		
$1,615.83		
Vendor has paid Nil		
Vendor's share (58 days x $4.43 per diem)		
Allow Purchaser	256.94	
Insurance		
Purchaser to place own insurance coverage		
Fuel Oil		
900 litres at $1.02 per litre		
Allow Vendor		918.00
Allow Vendor GST		55.08
Utilities		
Final readings on closing		
BALANCE DUE on closing by certified		
cheque payable to Simpson, Stainton		
& Crawford, in trust as per direction		
	190,716.14	
	$235,973.08	$235,973.08

E. & O. E.

STATEMENT OF ADJUSTMENTS

Vendor:	GEORGIAN FINANCIAL INC.
Purchaser:	Franco Chiovitti and Francesco Igav
Property:	500 Northern Avenue, Unit 2021, Mississauga
Adjusted as of:	October 23, 2007

		Credit Purchaser	Credit Vendor
SALE PRICE			$200,000.00
AUGUST 15, 2008		$15,000.00	
SEPTEMBER 15, 2008		15,000.00	
REALTY TAXES			
2007 total taxes:	2,040.00		
Vendor has paid:	2,040.00		
Vendor's share for 295 days:	1,648.77		
Credit Vendor:			391.23
COMMON EXPENSES			
Monthly Common Expenses:	125.00		
Paid by Vendor for			
month of October, 2007			
Vendor's share for 22 days:	88.71		
Credit Vendor:			36.29
BALANCE DUE ON CLOSING			
payable to			
CENTENNIAL & PARTNERS, in trust			
or as further directed		170,427.52	
		$200,427.52	**$200,427.52**

E.&O.E.

Source: Do Process Software Ltd.

UNDERTAKING

TO: Ronald Craig Anderson and
Kelly Anne Anderson

AND TO: Simpson, Stainton & Crawford
Their solicitors herein

RE: Sale of 984 Helena Avenue, Toronto

In consideration of the closing of the above transaction, I hereby undertake as follows:

1. To deliver vacant possession of the premises on closing and all keys to the premises.

2. To pay all hydro, water, and gas accounts, if any, up to the date of the closing.

3. To pay all arrears of taxes and penalties, including local improvement rates, and to re-adjust realty taxes and local improvement rates for the current year, upon written demand, if necessary.

4. To fill the fuel oil tank or to pay for same if not filled, in accordance with the statement of adjustment.

5. To register a discharge of mortgage number 328046 W.D. in favour of Christine Peterson.

6. To leave on the premises all chattels, fixtures, and additional items included in this transaction, as listed in the Agreement of Purchase and Sale herein, free from all encumbrances, liens, charges, or claims of any kind whatsoever.

7. To re-adjust any of the items shown on the statement of adjustments, if necessary.

DATED this   day of February, 20___.

                                       _____
                                       Ryan Andrew Peterson

DIRECTION

TO: Ronald Craig Anderson and   *(the purchasers)*
                      Kelly Anne Anderson

AND TO: Simpson, Stainton & Crawford
                      Their solicitors herein

RE: Sale of 984 Helena Avenue, Toronto

I, the undersigned, the vendor of the above lands by way of an Agreement of Purchase and Sale, do hereby authorize and direct you to make the proceeds of the above sale payable to my solicitors:

Hill, Johnston & Grant

or as they may direct, and this shall be your good and sufficient authority for so doing.

DATED this   day of February, 20__.

_____
Ryan Andrew Peterson

*Signed by the party or
parties who signed the
Agreement of Purchase
and Sale*

DIRECTION

TO: Hill, Johnston & Grant

RE: Sale of 984 Helena Avenue, Toronto

I, the vendor of the above lands by way of an Agreement of Purchase and Sale, do hereby authorize and direct you to pay the following amounts from the proceeds of the above-noted sale:

1. The amount required to pay in full the existing first mortgage in favour of Christine Peterson.

2. Your fees and disbursements in this transaction.

3. The balance to Ryan Andrew Peterson.

DATED this   day of February, 20__.

_____
Ryan Andrew Peterson

CHAPTER 26

Acting for the Purchaser

OBJECTIVES:

- Describe the procedure for opening and processing a real estate file when acting for the purchaser

- Demonstrate an understanding of the terms, documentation, and terminology used in this process

- Use legal precedents to prepare documentation required when acting for the purchaser

In a real estate transaction, the solicitors for the purchaser must protect their client's interest and ensure that the purchaser acquires good and valid title. Once the client records and necessary tickler slips are completed, take the steps outlined below.

DIRECTION RE TITLE

To verify the information on how title is to be taken, the purchasers sign a direction re title (Precedent 26.1) setting out how they wish to hold title, that is, in whose name, and if the title is to be taken jointly by the purchasers whether as joint tenants or as tenants in common. The birth date of each person taking title is also required, as well as an address for service following the close of the transaction. The same individuals who signed the agreement of purchase and sale as purchasers must sign the direction. For example, if the agreement was signed by John and Mary as purchasers, and title is to be taken in Mary's name alone, both John and Mary must sign the direction that sets out that fact; if only John signed the agreement of purchase and sale, and title is to be taken in the names of John and Mary, only John would sign the direction.

Prepare two copies of the direction re title and hold them for signature when the purchasers attend at the law office to execute all documents required to close the transaction.

The solicitors for the vendor are informed as to how the vendor wishes to take title. This information may be set out in a letter (Precedent 26.2), which will also indicate that a signed direction will be produced on closing. The letter also requests a draft deed (manual or e-reg), a statement of adjustments, and a copy of a survey of the property being sold. The survey is important because the purchaser's solicitors must ensure that the property being purchased is exactly as described.

SEARCHES

Of all the steps taken by the solicitor for the purchaser, searches are perhaps the most important. The solicitor must ensure that the purchaser gets valid title to the real property. To do this, a number of steps must be taken.

Title

The solicitor for the purchaser checks on the state of title to the property to ensure that the vendor has the right to convey title to another party, free and clear of any claims or clouds. To accomplish this, a title search is undertaken.

To undertake a search of title, the purchaser's solicitors must know the legal description or PIN of the property and have any available survey of the property. The vendor's solicitors provide this information either in a letter or an e-mail. If the vendor cannot provide a survey, the solicitors for the purchasers either request instructions from the purchasers to order a survey or ask the purchasers to sign a direction that no survey be secured and releasing the solicitors from any responsibility as a result of the lack of a survey (Precedent 26.3).

The automated system of title searching that is part of Teraview allows properties to be searched electronically. A legal assistant may be required to retrieve the title information from e-reg, and this information would be reviewed by the solicitor to confirm that the purchaser will obtain good and valid title to the property. Precedent 26.4 outlines the instructions for conducting a search by PIN in Teraview so that the information from the **Parcel Register** for the property may be obtained. A Parcel Register (Precedent 26.5) shows the property description and the abstract of title information, that is, a chronological history of all instruments and events that affect title to the real property.

Until the automated system is fully functioning, however, the traditional methods of title searching will still be followed in some areas.

For properties still registered under the registry system, the abstract of title is prepared by searching the record books at the Land Registry Office. It commences with the present owner, lists all instruments registered in connection with title to the property, and shows all registered sales and mortgages. This search goes back for a period of 40 years. (If the property is under the land titles system, the government guarantees title, and only the most recent entries must be searched.)

The offices dealing with land registration records charge a fee for searching a title (whether e-reg or manual) and for any printouts of documents or registers. These fees are a disbursement charged to the client when the account is rendered following the close of the transaction.

A writ of execution search is also conducted against the names of the vendor to ensure that there are no unpaid judgments registered against the owner of the property. See Precedent 25.5 in Chapter 25 on how to do a writ of execution search in e-reg.

Condominium Search

If the property being purchased is a condominium, the purchaser's solicitors also search the condominium declaration and the by-laws registered on title; the solicitors then request from the vendor's solicitors a condominium corporation status certificate, certifying information such as the amount of the contingency fund, the common expenses, whether the condominium corporation is a party to any litigation, and any other points on which the purchaser wishes confirmation.

Although it is the responsibility of the vendor to arrange for this certificate, frequently, the purchaser's solicitors obtain the certificate directly from the condominium corporation, which will charge a fee for this service.

Letter Inquiry Searches

The solicitors for the purchaser make a number of inquiries by letter on various items relating to the property. These inquiry letters are often called "clearances" because they ensure that there are no claims or liens against the title to the property and ensure compliance with all governmental regulations governing the use of the property.

Preparing for Letter Searches

A directory of the current addresses of municipal departments and authorities to which letter inquiries are regularly sent should be maintained and kept current. This directory should include the name, address, and telephone number of municipal departments such as tax, assessment, and water, as well as the local hydro commission. It should also include information on the amount of any fee payable to receive a response to an inquiry. Commercial real estate software packages such as The Conveyancer have this information in their database.

Cheques for fees payable to a municipal department are payable to the treasurer of the municipality; cheques for authorities such as the local hydro commission are payable to that body.

Realty Tax Certificates

The tax department of the municipality in which the property is located is requested by letter to provide the certificate showing the amount of paid and unpaid realty taxes on the property outstanding as of the closing date of the transaction (Precedent 26.6). There is usually a fee payable to the municipality for this certificate.

It is important to know the status of the realty taxes because this is one area in which an adjustment is made on closing.

Building Restrictions

Zoning

The building department of the municipality in which the property is located is requested to indicate what zoning restrictions might affect the property; for example, size and type of construction, distance from street and side lot lines, and minimum floor and lot areas. This request is made by letter (Precedent 26.7). Forward a copy of the survey of the property with the letter to help the department determine whether the survey shows any transgressions of existing or proposed municipal by-laws.

By-Laws

Copies of the by-laws affecting the property may be checked against any existing use or uses the purchaser intends to make of the property. The by-laws will also reveal any limitations or prohibitions on additions or improvements the purchaser may intend to make to the property.

Other Searches

The purchaser's solicitors will write other inquiry letters or do other searches to verify the state of charges for local improvement charges, water, gas, or rental of hydro equipment (such as a heater); to verify that there are no unregistered Ontario Hydro easements affecting the property; to check on the status of a corporation whose name appears on the chain of title to the property; or to ensure that there are no outstanding chattel mortgages, conditional sales, or Workers' Compensation Board liens that affect title to the property.

Other inquiries are made as required by the circumstances of the particular real estate transaction. For example, such inquiries may include ensuring that the property is not designated under the *Ontario Heritage Act* because of its historical or architectural importance, that any septic tank is functioning properly, or that when the property is rented it complies with the *Residential Rent Regulation Act*. There are, of course, many other similar inquiries that may be required as determined by the lawyer handling the file.

TITLE INSURANCE

Title insurance protects the purchaser against possible defects in title. The lawyer is required to advise the client about the availability of title insurance, although the client is under no obligation to purchase it. Many clients, however, do purchase it because it provides added protection *and* reduces some of the disbursement costs associated with purchasing the property. An acknowledgement and direction from the purchaser (Precedent 26.8) is prepared when the client arranges for title insurance through the law firm. When title insurance is purchased, certain letter and execution searches, as well as a new survey, may not be required. The title insurance companies will specify which searches are required. Often verbal confirmation (by telephone) is required in lieu of letter searches from the various municipal departments. The lawyer is then required to provide a report to the title insurance company regarding the validity of the title after the closing of the transaction.

Several private companies are available from which to purchase title insurance. Usually, a law firm will deal with one insurance company, and often the necessary procedures and forms are done in connection with specialized software. The law firm issues the insurance policy and bills the client as a disbursement in the account. The law firm will then on a regular basis forward the information regarding policies sold and the fees collected to the title insurance company.

DRAFT TRANSFER/DEED

E-Reg

The draft electronic transfer will be received as a message through Teraview. The names and dates of birth of the transferee(s), how title is to be held if more than one transferee, and the Land Transfer and School Tax information (discussed later in this chapter) are inserted into the document. A writ of execution search against the vendors will also be conducted. See Precedent 25.5 on how to do a writ search in e-reg.

Once this has been done, the solicitor will review the document and, if satisfactory, will digitally sign it for completion. The vendor's solicitors are advised (by a message in Teraview) of the approval or of any required corrections or amendments.

Manual

The hard copy of the draft deed is reviewed and the vendor's solicitors are advised (usually by e-mail) of the approval or of any required corrections or amendments.

LETTER OF REQUISITION

When the search reveals an encumbrance or cloud on title, for example, an undischarged mortgage, an execution, or a lien for unpaid corporation taxes, a letter of requisition (Precedent 26.9) is written to the vendor's solicitors requesting that the encumbrance be removed before closing. In the event it is not removed, the purchaser does not have to complete the transaction. The letter will also set out other points on which the purchaser's solicitors require assurance, such as confirming the GST status of the property being purchased.

The letter of requisition must be received by the requisition date, that is, by the last day of the period allowed in the agreement of purchase and sale to search the state of title. If it is not, the vendor is under no obligation to rectify any encumbrances relating to title to the property, and the real estate transaction proceeds to closing.

MORTGAGES

In most real estate transactions, part of the purchase price is covered by a mortgage. This mortgage is usually a new mortgage arranged with a financial institution, although sometimes a mortgage is taken back by the vendor or an existing mortgage on the property is assumed by the purchaser. See Chapter 22 for information on how to prepare a charge/mortgage.

Mortgage with Financial Institution

The purchaser will usually arrange to secure the funds to close the real estate transaction by a mortgage with a financial institution. The purchaser or more likely the financial institution will provide your firm with **mortgage instructions**. These are the specific requirements and documentation that the financial institution requires to advance the funds. Although similar, each financial institution has its own requirements that must be reviewed and then met. For example, some financial institutions now require personal identification verification of the client through a driver's licence or other photo identification (to avoid identity theft). Additionally, the instructions will also set out the reporting requirements after the close of the transaction.

The purchaser's solicitors usually prepare the draft mortgage (e-reg or hard copy) and send it to the mortgagee for approval. Some financial institutions have their solicitors prepare the mortgage documents, which would be sent to your firm for approval.

Arrangements are then made for the funds to be available on the closing date. This may be done electronically or by a cheque, which, in either case, is deposited into your firm's trust account. The mortgagee may ask that the purchaser sign a direction authorizing the mortgage proceeds to be payable to the law firm. This direction is similar to the direction in respect of proceeds executed by the vendor, as discussed in Chapter 25.

Mortgage Back

If the vendor takes back part of the purchase price by way of a mortgage, the purchaser is giving the vendor a mortgage on the property. In most jurisdictions, the solicitors for the purchaser draft the document, as discussed in Chapter 25, and forward an electronic or hard copy (as appropriate) to the vendor's solicitors for approval.

Mortgage Assumed

If the purchaser is assuming a mortgage already on the property, a mortgage statement should be obtained from the mortgagee that certifies the exact amount owing on the mortgage on the day of closing. A copy of the mortgage is either sent by the vendor's solicitors or obtained from the land registry office. The lawyer ensures that the mortgage does not contain any special clauses that adversely affect the purchaser.

INSURANCE

If the property is subject to a mortgage or mortgages, the purchaser will arrange for fire insurance coverage either for the full insurable value of the property or for an amount at least equal to the principal of the mortgage or mortgages, with any loss payable to the mortgagees as their interests may be in the property. Proof of coverage is produced on closing.

UNDERTAKING

The vendor usually executes an undertaking relating to various details of the real estate transaction, such as the need to re-adjust the statement of adjustments or to discharge an existing mortgage. Frequently, this document is prepared by the solicitors for the purchaser and forwarded to the vendor's solicitors for completion by the vendor before closing. Undertakings are discussed and illustrated in Chapter 25.

DECLARATION OF POSSESSION

Two copies of a declaration of possession are usually prepared and forwarded to the vendor's solicitors for completion by the vendor; a third copy is retained in the office file. There are two kinds of this form: one for a single vendor (Precedent 26.10) and one for joint tenants. The declaration is a type of statutory declaration.

The heading requires a brief description of the property that is the subject matter of the real estate transaction and the names of the parties. The body of the declaration sets out information on any mortgage on the property; how long the vendors have been in possession; the status of realty taxes; details about encumbrances, liens, or claims; residency status as required under the *Income Tax Act*; and the GST status of the property that may affect the title of the property.

LAND TRANSFER TAX AFFIDAVIT

There is a tax on the transfer of real property, called a land transfer tax, which must be paid by the purchaser before the transfer can be registered on closing. The amount of tax is calculated based on the information in a Land Transfer Tax Affidavit, which is completed by the purchaser and included as part of the e-reg transfer document or attached to the hard copy of transfer/deed in the manual system before it is registered.

Completion of Affidavit

The requirements and format are essentially the same for e-reg and manual; just the preparation method is slightly different. Precedent 26.11 illustrates a manual system Land Transfer Tax Affidavit, Precedent 26.12 illustrates a printout of an e-reg Land Transfer Tax Affidavit, and Precedent 26.13 provides instructions for completing the e-reg Land Transfer Tax Affidavit as part of the transfer document.

Note the following when completing this affidavit:

In the manual system, the affidavit requires a brief description of the property, similar to that appearing in the transfer/deed but with the name of the land registry office omitted, along with the names of the transferors and transferees. This information is not required in the e-reg system as it is already prepopulated.

Item 1 (manual) Deponent Tab (e-reg) Insert the name of the deponent(s). The affidavit may be sworn by both transferees (if more than one), by one spouse on behalf of both spouses, by an agent authorized in writing, or by the purchaser's solicitor; one of the boxes in item 1 must be also be marked with an X as appropriate.

Item 2 (manual); Consideration Tab (e-reg) Details about the total consideration for the property and how the amount is allocated are set out. See Figure 26.1 for guidelines on completing this section of the affidavit:

Figure 26.1 Guidelines for Inserting Consideration Amounts in the Land Transfer Tax Affidavit

Item	Guideline
Monies to be paid in cash	This is the total amount to be paid, *less* any amounts entered for an assumed mortgage, vendor take-back mortgage, any other valuable consideration (e.g., property transferred in exchange), and the value of all chattels. Note: this is *not* the amount shown as the balance due on the statement of adjustments.
Assumed mortgage	Obtain amount from the assumption statement but note that round figures are generally used
Mortgage back to vendor	Obtain amount from agreement of purchase and sale
Other valuable consideration, land exchange, liens, etc.	Rarely completed, but do so if appropriate as advised by solicitor
Value of all chattels	Enter the amount (in round figures) that has been determined for the value of the chattels
Other consideration	Again, rarely completed, but do so if advised by solicitor
Total consideration (manual – not applicable for e-reg)	This is the total of the items above and should be the same as the amount shown on the agreement of purchase and sale for the purchase price of the property

Item 3 (manual); >$400,000 Tab (e-reg) This is completed only if the value of the consideration is in excess of $400,000 to provide information on how many residences are contained in the property. A single-family residence is defined as a unit or proposed unit under the Condominium Act or a structure or part of a structure that is designed for occupation as the residence of one family, including dependants or domestic employees of a member of the family. Complete as appropriate.

Items 4 and 5 (manual); Nominal, Explanations, Exemptions Tabs (e-reg) These items/tabs are completed only if applicable, for example, if property is being transferred from the names of two spouses into the name of one spouse as a result of a separation agreement.

Jurat (manual only) Complete where it will be sworn and the month and year; leave the actual date blank to be completed when the client attends at the office to execute the document.

Property Information Record (Manual); Assessment Nos. (e-reg) Insert the required information.

School Support (manual); School Tax (e-reg) If the transferees are Roman Catholics or have French language education rights, this voluntary election may be completed to assign school tax support accordingly.

Number and Disposition of Copies (Manual)

Prepare a minimum of four copies of the affidavit for execution by the purchaser when he or she attends at the law office a few days before the closing. One executed copy is required for each executed copy of the transfer/deed that will be received on closing; it is attached to the back of the transfer/deed before registration. (The solicitors for the vendor will have included this page in the number of pages said to be in the transfer/deed at the time the document was prepared.) The land registrar requires another executed copy of the affidavit when the document is registered; the fourth copy is for the office file.

Calculating Land Transfer Tax

When a document is registered transferring title to real property, the purchaser is required to pay a tax of

1. 0.5 percent or $5 on every $1,000 of consideration up to $55,000;
2. 1 percent or $10 on every $1,000 of consideration in excess of $55,000 up to $250,000; and
3. 1.5 percent or $15 on every $1,000 of consideration in excess of $250,000,

unless the consideration is more than $400,000 *and* the property being transferred contains at least one but not more than two single-family residences, as defined by the act. In that event, the tax on consideration up to $250,000 is as set out above, but the tax on that part of the consideration in excess of $250,000 is

1. 1.5 percent or $15 on every $1,000 of consideration in excess of $250,000 up to $400,000 and
2. 2 percent or $20 on every $1,000 on that part of the consideration over $400,000.

To calculate the amount of land transfer tax payable, determine the value of the land using the consideration figure in the transfer/deed or the value of the land set out in the affidavit of residence and value of the consideration. The amounts set out must be identical, so either document may be used.

The easiest way to calculate tax on property valued at less than $250,000 is to multiply the value of the land by 1 percent and from the result deduct $275, which represents the excess tax calculated on the first $55,000. (Remember, the amount of tax on the first $55,000 is at the rate of 0.5 percent, not 1 percent.) For example:

Value of the property: $210,000
Tax of $10 (1%) on $210,000 $2,100
Less: 275
Amount of land transfer tax $1,825

or

Tax of $5 (0.5%) on every $1,000 up to $55,000 $ 275
Tax of $10 (1%) on every $1,000 in excess of
         $55,000, i.e., on $155,000   1,550
                                                                 $1,825

Note that the land transfer tax payable on the first $250,000 of consideration is always $2,225 and that the tax payable on the first $400,000 of consideration is always $4,475. These figures will be very useful when tax is being calculated on considerations over $250,000 or when consideration is more than $400,000 and the special tax provisions relating to single family residences are applicable.

To calculate the amount of land transfer tax payable when the property is at least one but not more than two single-family residences under the act and the purchase price is more than $400,000, multiply the amount in excess of $400,000 by 2 percent and add $4,475 (representing the amount of land transfer tax payable on $400,000). For example:

Value of the property: $475,000
Tax on $400,000 $4,475
Tax of $20 (2%) on every $1,000 consideration in
         excess of $400,000, i.e., $75,000   1,500
                                                                 $5,975

City of Toronto Land Transfer Tax

Effective February 1, 2008, a separate land transfer tax is applied to all property purchased in the City of Toronto and is paid by the purchaser at the time of closing. This tax is in addition to the provincial land transfer tax discussed above. The City of Toronto land transfer tax is calculated as follows for residential properties:

1. 0.5 percent or $5 on every $1,000 of consideration up to and including $55,000
2. 1.0 percent or $10 on every $1,000 of consideration in excess of $55,000 up to and including $400,000
3. 2.0 percent or $20 on every $1,000 of consideration in excess of $400,000 for properties that contain one and/or two single-family residences

Use a similar method of calculation to that used in calculating the provincial sales tax to determine the amount of the municipal land transfer tax. Note that the land transfer tax payable on the first $250,000 of consideration is always $2,225 (which is the same as the provincial land transfer tax rate) and that the tax payable on the first $400,000 of consideration is always $3,725 (which is different from the provincial land transfer tax rate). For example, if the consideration on a property in the City of Toronto is $240,000, then the provincial land transfer tax would be $2,125 and the municipal land transfer tax would be $2,125, for a total tax payable of $4,250. If the consideration is $425,000, then the provincial land transfer tax would be $4,975 and the municipal land transfer tax would be $4,225, for a total tax payable of $9,200.

A rebate of up to $3,725 is available to first-time purchasers of both new and existing housing in the City of Toronto. This means that for residential properties where the consideration is $400,000 or less, the full amount of the municipal land transfer tax would be rebated to the purchaser.

It should be noted that commercial properties (including multi-residential units) purchased in the City of Toronto are assessed at a different rate, which is 1.5 percent of the value of the consideration exceeding $400,000 up to 40 million and 1 percent of the value of the consideration that exceeds $40 million.

Calculating Retail Sales Tax

To calculate the amount of retail sales tax, multiply the value of the chattels by 0.08 ($8 on each $100). For example, the amount of retail sales tax is $80 on chattels valued at $1,000.

STATEMENT OF ADJUSTMENTS

When the statement of adjustments is received, the solicitors for the purchaser carefully check it for accuracy. The purchasers are then asked to provide the solicitors with funds to complete the real estate transaction.

If the property is new residential property, the application for a GST new housing rebate is usually forwarded with the statement of adjustments. The application should be checked and then placed in the file containing all documents to be executed by the purchaser before closing.

If the purchaser is assigning the rebate to the vendor, the solicitors for the vendor also forward the necessary assignment and statutory declaration for execution by the purchaser. This document should also be checked and then placed in the file containing the documents to be executed by the purchaser before closing.

PREPARING TO CLOSE

Arrange an appointment with the client to attend at the law firm to provide the necessary funds for closing and to execute all documents.

Closing Funds

Before the client attends, the total amount of funds required to close is calculated, and this includes

1. the amount to pay the land transfer tax,
2. the amount to pay retail sales tax on the chattels, and
3. the amount due on closing, as set out in the statement of adjustments.

Frequently, the law firm also asks the client to provide an additional amount sufficient to pay the account for fees and disbursements. If this is the practice of your firm, requisition or prepare a prebilling report for both fees and disbursements.

These funds, as well as any mortgage monies received from a financial institution, are deposited in the firm's trust account. The law firm then has the necessary closing funds to complete the transaction.

For an e-reg closing, the fees for registration and Land Transfer Tax are deducted by Teranet Inc. directly from the law firm's e-reg account for the client. An Authorization of Withdrawal by Teranet (Precedent 26.13) is prepared for execution by the client to allow this transfer.

For a manual closing, requisition a certified cheque to deliver to the vendor's solicitors on closing, payable as instructed in the statement of adjustments, and a cheque payable to the Minister of Finance to pay the land transfer, any retail sales taxes, and the registration fees for the transfer/deed. All cheques are written on the trust account. The amount remaining in the trust account is transferred to the firm account when the transaction is completed, in payment of the law firm's account for services rendered. Requisition all cheques at least the day before the closing to allow adequate time to have the cheques for the vendor certified.

Execution of Documents

As a general rule, two copies of all documents are executed (except where noted otherwise). These documents may include but are not limited to

1. Acknowledgement and Direction and Document Registration Agreement if an e-reg transaction; alternatively, in the manual system, hard copies of any mortgage(s) and three copies of the Land Transfer Tax Affidavit will be executed
2. Direction re title
3. Acknowledgement and Direction from Purchaser re title insurance (if applicable)
4. Authorization of Withdrawal by Teranet (if an e-reg transaction)
5. Direction re survey (if applicable)
6. An undertaking to provide a copy of the fire insurance policy if there is a mortgage back and the policy of insurance is not yet available
7. Three copies of the GST new housing rebate application form received from the solicitors for the vendor if the property being purchased is new residential property, as well as three copies of the assignment of the GST new housing rebate to the vendor, if applicable, and the statutory declaration certifying that the purchaser is eligible to claim the GST new housing rebate

Closing the Transaction

The solicitors for the purchaser and vendor arrange an exact time to close the transaction on the day specified by the agreement of purchase and sale. The procedures on closing and the steps that follow closing are discussed in Chapter 27.

Terms and Concepts

direction re title	letter of requisition
title search	mortgage
Parcel Register	mortgage instructions
condominium search	mortgage back
status certificate	mortgage assumed
letter searches	insurance
building restrictions	undertaking to re-adjust
zoning	declaration of possession
by-laws	Land Transfer Tax Affidavit
title insurance	calculating land transfer tax
reviewing draft transfer/deed and	closing funds
statement of adjustments	execution of documents

Review Questions

1. How are the purchasers described in the new transfer/deed?

2. What is meant by the term "requisition date"?

3. Why do the solicitors for a purchaser check on the status of realty taxes, work orders, etc.?

4. List three ways in which a mortgage may be involved in the purchase of real property.

5. What is the purpose of a declaration of possession?

6. Calculate the amount of land transfer tax payable by the purchaser for the following properties:
   a. Single-family residence in London Ontario, purchase price $210,000
   b. Single-family residence in Kingston, Ontario, purchase price $325,000
   c. Single-family residence in Toronto, Ontario, purchase price $450,000

7. How would you determine the amount of funds that the purchasers will be asked to provide to their solicitors on closing?

DIRECTION

TO: Ryan Andrew Peterson

AND TO: Hill, Johnston & Grant
      His solicitors herein

RE: Purchase of 984 Helena Avenue, Toronto

    WE, the undersigned purchasers of the above lands by way of an

Agreement of Purchase and Sale, hereby authorize and direct you to make the deed in the

above transaction as hereinafter set out, and this shall be your good and sufficient

authority for so doing:

      Ronald Craig Anderson   Born August 28, 1970

      Kelly Anne Anderson   Born January 15, 1973

      as joint tenants and not as tenants in common

      DATED this   day of February, 20__

            _____
            Ronald Craig Anderson

            _____
            Kelly Anne Anderson

Simpson, Stainton & Crawford

Barristers & Solicitors

53 Suffolk Street, Guelph, Ontario N1H 7B4
Tel: 519-424-6744   Fax: 519-524-6745

January 5, 20__

Hill, Johnston & Grant
Barristers & Solicitors
17 Princess Street South
Suite 2501
Toronto ON M8Y 3N5

Dear Sirs/Mesdames:

Re: ANDERSON purchaser from PETERSON
**   984 Helena Avenue, Toronto**
**   East Half Lot 105, Plan 5948**
**   Closing Date: February 28, 20__**
**   Our File No.: 1111/4808**

We act for the purchasers, Ronald Craig Anderson and Kelly Anne Anderson, and understand that you act for the vendor, Ryan Andrew Peterson.

Our clients wish to take title to the above property in the following manner:

      Ronald Craig Anderson   Born August 28, 1970
      Lucille Caroline Anderson   Born January 15, 1973

      as joint tenants and not as tenants in common

A signed direction will be produced on closing. Their address for service following the closing of this transaction will be 984 Helena Avenue, Toronto ON M9R 3G6.

Please forward your draft deed, sketch of survey, and statement of adjustments. Our draft mortgage back will be forwarded to you shortly.

Yours very truly,

SIMPSON, STAINTON & CRAWFORD

Drew C. Crawford

DCC/ri

DIRECTION

TO: Hill, Johnston & Grant

RE: Drohan and Wyers
            Purchase of 5843 19th Concession, Uxbridge

Notwithstanding that you have advised us that there is no up-to-date survey available with respect to the above-noted premises, and that without such survey you cannot give an opinion as to the building and zoning by-laws, regulations and requirements regarding the said property, WE HEREBY AUTHORIZE AND DIRECT YOU to close the said transaction.

DATED at Toronto, this   day of May, 20___

_____
Richard Wayne Drohan

_____
Lauren Natalie Drohan

To Search Title by PIN – Page 1

► Open Docket

Menu Bar ► Property
      ► Search by PIN

Search by PIN dialog box opens.
► Key in PIN of the property you wish to search

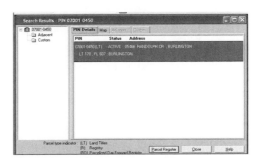

Search Results dialog box opens (shown at right).
From this screen, you may do the following:

1. **View Parcel Register**
  ► Click Parcel Register button
   Parcel Register Opens dialog box opens
  ► Select All Active Instruments and
   Include Deleted Instruments (as appropriate)

 Parcel Register opens as shown at right:

 You can click on the various tabs to view the
 information and print out copies for the lawyer's
 review as follows:

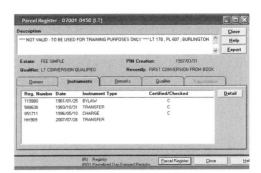

2. **Print the Parcel Register:**
  Menu Bar ► Print Parcel Register
       ► Click Yes, to confirm

3. **View and print an instrument**
  ► Click on Instruments tab in Parcel Register window

 All instruments will be displayed.

  ► RIGHT CLICK on the instrument to view it
  ► Click on the Request Instrument pop-up box
   (as shown at right)

 Instrument Options window opens.

  ► Scroll through the list of instruments to seach
   for the instrument you require
  ► Select the instrument(s) you wish to view
  ► Click View Button

 Instrument will be displayed.

  ► Click on printer icon button if you wish a paper copy

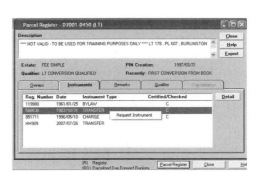

Note: Instruments with "0" pages are not available as an image and must be ordered
using the e-mail or courier option tabs shown below the instrument numbers.

Source: Teranet Inc.

To Search Title by PIN – Page 2

4.   **View property map**
      ► Click on Map Tab
      ► Click Yes to confirm when prompted

A map of the property will appear as shown below.

► RIGHT CLICK to select viewing options (zoom in/out, etc.)

To view adjacent properties (from property map screen)
► Double click the Adjacent branch folder in the directory
► Click Yes to confirm when prompted

Search Results window open displaying adjacent properties (shown highlighted on the map) and the PINs will be displayed in the directory.

► Click Adjacent Tab and search results for adjacent properties are shown
► Double Click (or highlight and Click Parcel Register button) to access the Parcel Register for any adjacent property you wish to view and follow the steps in No. 1 above

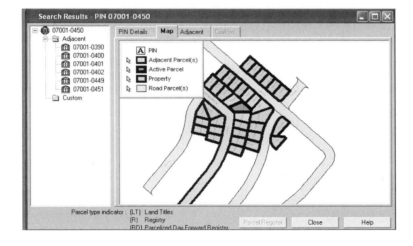

Source: Teranet Inc.

Precedent 26.5 Parcel Register

PARCEL REGISTER (ABBREVIATED) FOR PROPERTY IDENTIFIER

TRAINING	

**** NOT VALID – TO BE USED FOR TRAINING PURPOSES ONLY **** LT 178 , PL 607 ; BURLINGTON
* CERTIFIED BY LAND REGISTRAR IN ACCORDANCE WITH LAND TITLES ACT * SUBJECT TO RESERVATIONS IN CROWN GRANT *

Ministry of Government Services

LAND REGISTRY OFFICE #20

PAGE 1 OF 1
PREPARED FOR BBCENTENNIAL
ON 2007/07/30 AT 13:49:53

07001-0450 (LT)

PROPERTY DESCRIPTION:

PROPERTY REMARKS:

ESTATE/QUALIFIER:
FEE SIMPLE
LT CONVERSION QUALIFIED

RECENTLY:
FIRST CONVERSION FROM BOOK

PIN CREATION DATE:
1997/03/31

OWNERS' NAMES
DONNELLY, JAMES
DONNELLY, GAIL

CAPACITY   SHARE
JTEN
JTEN

REG. NUM.	DATE	INSTRUMENT TYPE	AMOUNT	PARTIES FROM	PARTIES TO	CERT/CHKD
				EFFECTIVE 2000/07/29 THE NOTATION OF THE "BLOCK IMPLEMENTATION DATE" OF 1997/03/31 ON THIS PIN		
				WAS REPLACED WITH THE "PIN CREATION DATE" OF 1997/03/31		
				** PRINTOUT INCLUDES ALL DOCUMENT TYPES AND DELETED INSTRUMENTS SINCE: 1997/03/27 **		
				**SUBJECT, ON FIRST REGISTRATION UNDER THE LAND TITLES ACT, TO:		
				** SUBSECTION 44(1) OF THE LAND TITLES ACT, EXCEPT PARAGRAPH 11, PARAGRAPH 14, PROVINCIAL SUCCESSION DUTIES *		
				** AND ESCHEATS OR FORFEITURE TO THE CROWN.		
				** THE RIGHTS OF ANY PERSON WHO WOULD, BUT FOR THE LAND TITLES ACT, BE ENTITLED TO THE LAND OR ANY PART OF		
				** IT THROUGH LENGTH OF ADVERSE POSSESSION, PRESCRIPTION, MISDESCRIPTION OR BOUNDARIES SETTLED BY		
				** CONVENTION.		
				** ANY LEASE TO WHICH THE SUBSECTION 70(2) OF THE REGISTRY ACT APPLIES.		
				**DATE OF CONVERSION TO LAND TITLES: 1997/04/01 **		
119980	1961/01/25	BYLAW				
588638	1983/10/31	TRANSFER	$1		DONNELLY, JAMES DONNELLY, GAIL	C
851711	1996/05/10	CHARGE	$30,000		CANADA TRUSTCO MORTGAGE COMPANY	C
HH909	2007/07/26	TRANSFER	$250,000	DONNELLY, GAIL DONNELLY, JAMES	KELSO, JOHN KELSO, MARIAN	C

NOTE: ADJOINING PROPERTIES SHOULD BE INVESTIGATED TO ASCERTAIN DESCRIPTIVE INCONSISTENCIES, IF ANY, WITH DESCRIPTION REPRESENTED FOR THIS PROPERTY.
NOTE: ENSURE THAT YOUR PRINTOUT STATES THE TOTAL NUMBER OF PAGES AND THAT YOU HAVE PICKED THEM ALL UP.

Source: © Queen's Printer for Ontario, 2007. Reproduced with permission.

Simpson, Stainton & Crawford

Barristers & Solicitors

53 Suffolk Street, Guelph, Ontario N1H 7B4
Tel: 519-424-6744   Fax: 519-524-6745

January 5, 20___

Tax Department
City of Toronto
Revenue Services
Etobicoke Civic Centre
399 The West Mall
Etobicoke ON M9C 2Y2

Dear Sir or Madam:

Re: **ANDERSON purchaser from PETERSON**
  984 Helena Avenue, Toronto
  East Half Lot 105, Plan 5948
  Roll No.: 19 04 231 882 00600
  Closing Date: February 28, 20___
  Our File No.: 1111/4808

We are the solicitors for the vendor in the above transaction, which is scheduled to be completed on February 28, 20___.

Please provide our office with a tax certificate indicating whether there are any arrears of taxes affecting the property and also setting out the amount of the current tax bill and the portion, if any, which has been paid to date.

In this regard, we are enclosing herewith our firm cheque in the amount of $65.00 payable to Treasurer, City of Toronto on account of your fee herein. Thank you for your co-operation.

Yours truly,

SIMPSON, STAINTON & CRAWFORD

Drew C. Crawford

DCC/ri
Enc.

Simpson, Stainton & Crawford

Barristers & Solicitors

53 Suffolk Street, Guelph, Ontario N1H 7B4
Tel: 519-424-6744   Fax: 519-524-6745

January 5, 20___

Urban Planning & Development Dept.
City of Toronto
17th Floor, East Tower, New City Hall
100 Queen Street West
Toronto, Ontario M5H 2N2

Dear Sir or Madam:

Re: ANDERSON purchaser from PETERSON
**   984 Helena Avenue, Toronto**
**   East Half Lot 105, Plan 5948**
**   Closing Date: February 28, 20___**
**   Our File No.: 1111/4808**

We are the solicitors for the vendor in the above transaction, which is scheduled to be completed on February 28, 2008. Please advise as to the following:

1. What is the zoning for the subject property?
2. Are there any work orders or notices of violation outstanding pursuant to the applicable building or zoning by-laws or any other matters within your jurisdiction?
3. Are the buildings or dwelling houses, as shown on the enclosed survey, in conformity with your zoning regulations for the subject property?
4. Are there final inspections outstanding with respect to plumbing, heating, drainage, sewage, or building permits?
5. Are there any local improvements which have taken place or which are in process or planned in the near future?

In this regard, we are enclosing herewith our firm cheque in the amount of $100.00 payable to Treasurer, City of Toronto on account of your fee herein. Thank you for your co-operation.

Yours very truly,

SIMPSON, STAINTON & CRAWFORD

Drew C. Crawford

DCC/ri
Enc.

ACKNOWLEDGEMENT AND DIRECTION FROM PURCHASER

TO: Drew C. Crawford
SIMPSON, STAINTON & CRAWFORD
Barristers & Solicitors

RE: ANDERSON purchaser from PETERSON
984 Helena Avenue, Toronto
ANDERSON, first mortgage to ROYAL BANK OF CANADA

This will confirm that you, as my lawyer, have reviewed and explained to the undersigned the various options available to protect my ownership interests arising from the purchase of the above property, and that, in particular, you have explained the advantages and disadvantages of protecting my interests through the purchase of title insurance as compared to a lawyer's opinion on title.

I hereby instruct you to proceed by way of the purchase of title insurance from First Canadian Title.

DATED at Guelph, this   day of February, 20__.

_____
Ronald Craig Anderson

_____
Kelly Anne Anderson

Simpson, Stainton & Crawford
Barristers & Solicitors

53 Suffolk Street, Guelph, Ontario N1H 7B4
Tel: 519-424-6744   Fax: 519-524-6745

January 5, 20__

Hill, Johnston & Grant
Barristers & Solicitors
17 Princess Street South
Suite 2501
Toronto ON M8Y 3N5

Dear Sirs/Mesdames:

Re: **ANDERSON purchaser from PETERSON**
        984 Helena Avenue, Toronto, East Half Lot 105, Plan 5948
        Closing Date: February 28, 20__
        Our File No.: 1111/4808

Without prejudice to the rights of our client under the Agreement of Purchase and Sale, and reserving the right to submit such further and other requisitions as may be deemed necessary from time to time as well as the right to waive any or all of them, we wish to raise the following requisitions:

1. Instrument No. 399987 is a mortgage dated September 1, 20__, and registered September 2, 19__, from Ryan Peterson to Christine Peterson.

    REQUIRED: On or before closing production and registration of a statutory discharge of the said mortgage.

2. **REQUIRED:** The enclosed general undertaking to be signed by your client and to be turned over on closing.

4. **REQUIRED:** The enclosed declaration of possession to be signed by your client and turned over on closing.

5.   **REQUIRED:** On or before closing evidence from the vendor that the property is a "used residential complex" within the meaning of the Goods and Services Act, and is an exempt supply within the provisions of Schedule V to the said Act.

Yours very truly,

SIMPSON, STAINTON & CRAWFORD

Drew C. Crawford

DCC/ri
Enc.

<table>
<tr><td>

CANADA

PROVINCE OF ONTARIO

</td><td>

IN THE MATTER OF THE TITLE
to   984 Helena Avenue, Toronto
being   East Half Lot 10, Plan 5948
("the Lands")

AND THE SALE THEREOF
from   Ryan Andrew Peterson
to   Ronald Craig Anderson
        Kelly Anne Anderson

</td></tr>
</table>

I, RYAN ANDREW PETERSON, of the City of Toronto, Province of Ontario,

SOLEMNLY DECLARE that:

1. Subject to a charge/mortgage in favour of Christine Peterson on which there is due for principal $26,598.17, and interest from the 2nd day of February, 20___, I am the absolute owner of the Lands and either personally or by my tenants have been in the actual, peaceable, continuous, exclusive, open, undisturbed and undisputed possession and occupation of the Lands and the houses and other buildings used in connection therewith since on or about the 2nd day of June 1990, when I obtained a conveyance thereof.
2. Except for the above-mentioned charge/mortgage and any taxes and local improvements rates charged thereon, there is no encumbrance or easement affecting the Lands except as the records of the Land Registry Office disclose.
3. I have no knowledge of any claim or interest by any person or corporation in the Lands which is adverse to or inconsistent with my title and I am positive that none exists.
4. My possession and occupation of the Lands has been undisturbed throughout by any legal proceedings of any nature or adverse possession or otherwise. During my ownership I have not made any payment or acknowledgement of title to any person or corporation in respect of any right, title, interest or claim upon the Lands and I do not have any knowledge of any other person or corporation having made any such payment or acknowledgement.
5. The deeds, evidences of title and other papers which have been produced by me are all the documents relating to the title to the Lands that are in my possession or power and to the best of my knowledge and belief, these documents, together with this declaration and the records of the Land Registry Office, fully and fairly disclose all facts material to the title claimed by me and all contracts and dealings which affect my title to the Lands.
6. To the best of my knowledge and belief the houses and other buildings used in connection with the Lands are situate wholly within the limits of the Lands and there is no dispute as to the boundaries of the Lands. I have no knowledge of any claim of easement for light, drainage, right of way or otherwise affecting the Lands except as the records of the Land Registry Office disclose.
7. There are no construction liens registered against the Lands nor any claim for which such liens could be registered as all such claims have been paid in full.
8. That Kristen Lynn Peterson who has executed the conveyance together with myself is my spouse and we are each of the full age of eighteen years.
9. There are no executions in the Sheriff's hands affecting the Lands to my knowledge.
10. All taxes on the Lands have been paid up to the 31st day of December, 20___.
11. To the best of my knowledge and belief, during the period of time that I have been the owner of the Lands, there have been no structural changes to the houses and other buildings on the Lands nor any changes in the location of fences, houses, and other buildings from those shown on a survey of the Lands prepared by Lawrence Matthews OLS dated March 18, 1980, a copy of which is attached.
12. When I agreed to sell the Lands to the purchaser(s) I was and at the time of closing shall not be a "non-resident person" within the meaning and for the purposes of Section 116 of the *Income Tax Act* of Canada.
13. The property is a "used residential complex" within the meaning of the *Excise Tax Act* of Canada and is an exempt supply within the provisions of Schedule 5 of the said Act.

AND I make this solemn declaration conscientiously believing it to be true and knowing that it is of the same force and effect as if made under oath.

DECLARED before me at the

City of Toronto

Province of Ontario

this   day of February, 20___

_____
Ryan Andrew Peterson

Page 2

Ontario

Ministry of Finance
Motor Fuels and
Tobacco Tax Branch
PO Box 625
33 King St West
Oshawa ON L1H 8H9

Refer to instructions on reverse side.

Property Identifier(s) No.

Land Transfer Tax Affidavit
Land Transfer Tax Act

In the Matter of the Conveyance of *(insert brief description of land)* **East half of Lot 105, Plan 5948, City of Toronto**

BY *(print names of all transferors in full)* **Ryan Andrew Peterson**

TO *(print names of all transferees in full)* **Ronald Craig Anderson and Kelly Anne Anderson**

I Ronald Craig Anderson

have personal knowledge of the facts herein deposed to and Make Oath and Say that:

1. I am *(place a clear mark within the square opposite the following paragraph(s) that describe(s) the capacity of the deponents):*
   - ☐ (a) the transferee named in the above-described conveyance;
   - ☐ (b) the authorized agent or solicitor acting in this transaction for the transferee(s);
   - ☐ (c) the President, Vice-President, Secretary, Treasurer, Director or Manager authorized to act for _____
     (the transferee(s));
   - ☒ (d) a transferee and am making this affidavit on my own behalf and on behalf of *(insert name of spouse or same-sex partner)* _____
     Kelly Anne Anderson who is my spouse or same-sex partner.
   - ☐ (e) the transferor or an officer authorized to act on behalf of the transferor company and ☐ I am tendering this document for registration and ☐ no tax is payable on registration of this document.

2. **THE TOTAL CONSIDERATION FOR THIS TRANSACTION IS ALLOCATED AS FOLLOWS:**

(a) Monies paid or to be paid in cash	$	209,000.00
(b) Mortgages (i) Assumed *(principal and interest)*	$	Nil
(ii) Given back to vendor	$	25,000.00
(c) Property transferred in exchange *(detail below in para. 5)*	$	Nil
(d) Other consideration subject to tax *(detail below)*	$	Nil
(e) Fair market value of the lands *(see Instruction 2)*	$	Nil
(f) Value of land, building, fixtures and goodwill subject to Land Transfer Tax *(Total of (a) to (e))*	$ 234,000.00 $	234,000.00
(g) Value of all chattels - items of tangible personal property which are taxable under the provisions of the *Retail Sales Tax Act*	$	1,000.00
(h) Other consideration for transaction not included in (f) or (g) above	$	Nil
(i) Total Consideration	$	235,000.00

   All blanks must be filled in. Insert "Nil" where applicable.

3. To be completed where the value of the consideration for the conveyance exceeds $400,000.00.
   I have read and considered the definition of "single family residence" set out in subsection 1(1) of the Act. The land conveyed in the above-described conveyance:
   - ☐ does not contain a single family residence or contains more than two single family residences;
   - ☐ contains at least one and not more than two single family residences; or
   - ☐ contains at least one and not more than two single family residences and the lands are used for other than just residential purposes. The transferee has accordingly apportioned the value of consideration on the basis that the consideration for the single family residence is $ _____ and the remainder of the lands are used for _____ purposes.

   Note: Subsection 2(1)(b) imposes an additional tax at the rate of one-half of one per cent upon the value of the consideration in excess of $400,000.00 where the conveyance contains at least one and not more than two single family residences and 2(2) allows an apportionment of the consideration where the lands are used for other than just residential purposes.

4. If consideration is nominal, is the land subject to any encumbrance? ☐ Yes ☐ No

5. Other remarks and explanations, if necessary. **N/A**

Sworn/affirmed before me in the **City of Toronto**
Province of Ontario

this _____ day of _____ **February** _____, 20 ___

Ronald Craig Anderson Signature(s)

_____
A Commissioner for taking Affidavits, etc.

Property Information Record

A. Describe nature of instrument: **Transfer**

B. (i) Address of property being conveyed *(if available)* **984 Helena Avenue, Toronto M9R 3G6**

   (ii) Assessment Roll No. *(if available)* **1906 231 852 00600**

C. Mailing address(es) for future Notices of Assessment under the *Assessment Act* for property being conveyed
   984 Helena Avenue, Toronto ON M9R 3G6

D. (i) Registration number for last conveyance of property being conveyed *(if available)* **R46992**
   (ii) Legal description of property conveyed: Same as in D(i) above. ☒ Yes ☐ No ☐ Not known

E. Name(s) and address(es) of each transferee's solicitor: **Drew C. Crawford, SIMPSON, STAINTON & CRAWFORD**
   53 Suffolk Street, Guelph ON N1H 7B4

For Land Registry Office Use Only
Registration No.

Registration Date *(Year/Month/Day)*

Land Registry Office No.

School Support (Voluntary Election) (See reverse for explanation)

	Yes	No
(a) Are all individual transferees Roman Catholic?	☐	☒
(b) If Yes, do all individual transferees wish to be Roman Catholic Separate School Supporters?	☐	☐
(c) Do all individual transferees have French Language Education Rights?	☐	☒
(d) If Yes, do all individual transferees wish to support the French Language School Board (where established)?	☐	☐

Note: As to (c) and (d) the land being transferred will receive French Public School Board Election unless otherwise directed in (a) and (b).

0449K (2004-04)

Source: Teranet Inc.

**** NOT VALID - TO BE USED FOR TRAINING PURPOSES ONLY ****

LAND TRANSFER TAX STATEMENTS

In the matter of the conveyance of: 07001 - 0450   LT 178 , PL 607 ; BURLINGTON

BY:	DONNELLY, GAIL		
	DONNELLY, JAMES		
TO:	KELSO, JOHN	Joint Tenants	%(all PINs)
	KELSO, MARIAN	Joint Tenants	%(all PINs)

1. KELSO, JOHN AND KELSO, MARIAN

    I am

    ☐ (a) A person in trust for whom the land conveyed in the above-described conveyance is being conveyed;

    ☐ (b) A trustee named in the above-described conveyance to whom the land is being conveyed;

    ☑ (c) A transferee named in the above-described conveyance;

    ☐ (d) The authorized agent or solicitor acting in this transaction for _____ described in paragraph(s) (_) above.

    ☐ (e) The President, Vice-President, Manager, Secretary, Director, or Treasurer authorized to act for _____ described in paragraph(s) (_) above.

    ☐ (f) A transferee described in paragraph ( ) and am making these statements on my own behalf and on behalf of _____ who is my spouse described in paragraph (_) and as such, I have personal knowledge of the facts herein deposed to.

3. **The total consideration for this transaction is allocated as follows:**

(a) Monies paid or to be paid in cash	348,000.00
(b) Mortgages (i) assumed (show principal and interest to be credited against purchase price)	0.00
(ii) Given Back to Vendor	0.00
(c) Property transferred in exchange (detail below)	0.00
(d) Fair market value of the land(s)	0.00
(e) Liens, legacies, annuities and maintenance charges to which transfer is subject	0.00
(f) Other valuable consideration subject to land transfer tax (detail below)	0.00
(g) Value of land, building, fixtures and goodwill subject to land transfer tax (total of (a) to (f))	348,000.00
(h) VALUE OF ALL CHATTELS - items of tangible personal property	2,000.00
(i) Other considerations for transaction not included in (g) or (h) above	0.00
(j) Total consideration	350,000.00

PROPERTY Information Record

A. Nature of Instrument: Transfer

LRO   20   Registration No.   Date:

B. Property(s):   PIN 07001 - 0450   Address 05466 RANDOLPH CR   Assessment Roll No   2402080 - 82209300
BURLINGTON

C. Address for Service: 05466 RANDOLPH CR
BURLINGTON

D. (i) Last Conveyance(s):   PIN 07001 - 0450   Registration No.

(ii) Legal Description for Property Conveyed : Same as in last conveyance? Yes ☑ No ☐ Not known ☐

School Tax Support (Voluntary Election)
   1. All individual transferees are Roman Catholic.

Source: Teranet Inc.

FORM 19B
Authorization of Withdrawal by Teranet

RE: **ANDERSON purchase from PETERSON**
984 Helena Avenue, Toronto
Closing Date: February 28, 20__

Authorization *(Number)*   4889920

Amount of funds to be withdrawn: $2,295.00
(Specify amount)

Re:

(Specify name of client)   RONALD CRAIG ANDERSON

                                            KELLY ANNE ANDERSON

(Specify file reference number)   4444/4808

Reason for withdrawal: *(Give reason for*   Payment of Land Transfer Tax
withdrawal, e.g., payment of land transfer tax,   and document registration fees
document registration fees)

Trust Account to be debited:

Name of financial institution: *(Specify*   Data Bank of Canada
name)

Account number: *(Specify number)*   4480-332902

Person authorizing withdrawal: *(Print the* Peter T. Grant
person's name)

DATED this   day of February, 20__

_____
                                            Peter T. Grant

Source: Teranet Inc.

CHAPTER 27

Closing the Real Estate Transaction

OBJECTIVES:

- Demonstrate an understanding of the procedures followed in closing a real estate transaction
- Use precedents to prepare closing documents, correspondence, and accounts

The closing date, and sometimes the time for the closing, will be set out in the agreement of purchase and sale; alternatively, a time will be agreed upon by the solicitors for the vendor and the purchaser. The procedures for closing will depend on whether it is a manual or an e-reg closing.

DAY OF CLOSING PROCEDURES

Manual System

At the agreed time on the date scheduled to close the real estate transaction, representatives for the solicitors for both the vendor and the purchaser meet at the appropriate land registry office. Although the representative may be the solicitor who handled the file, more frequently, it is a trained real estate law clerk, often called a conveyancer.

Immediately before the closing, the representative for the purchaser checks with the sheriff's office for executions against the property and brings the title search up-to-date to ensure that no additional documents have been registered against the property since the date of the original search. This search on closing is called a subsearch.

The representative for the purchaser delivers to the vendor's representative any mortgage back, executed in duplicate, and a certified cheque for the balance due on closing, payable as set out in the statement of adjustments and verified by the executed direction regarding payment of proceeds that the vendor's representative presents at closing.

The vendor's representative delivers to the purchaser's representative the duly executed transfer/deed in duplicate, the keys to the property, any declaration of possession, and any undertaking. A copy of the insurance policy is given to the vendor's representative if there is a mortgage back.

The representative for the vendor will pay the required fee and register any discharge of charge/mortgage on the property first. The representative for the purchaser will then attach the Land Transfer Tax affidavit to the transfer, pay the required tax and registration fees, and register the transfer/deed, followed by any first charge/mortgage, second charge/mortgage, etc., as they must be registered in priority order. The land registry office officials will stamp both copies of the transfer/deed and any charge/mortgage with the date and time of registration, along with the document registration number in the upper left-hand box at the top of the document. One copy of the document is retained in the land registry office, and the second copy is returned to the party registering it. In the registry system, the duplicate copy is usually returned at the time of registration or later that day; in the land titles system, the duplicate will be returned days later, when the document has been checked and recorded.

E-Reg System

On the closing date, the solicitors for each side will digitally sign to release the e-reg instruments, and once the necessary funds and documents (declaration of possession, directions, undertakings, etc., as discussed above) have been received by both sides, then, at the agreed time, the instruments will be registered electronically. The sub-search box on the register instrument window is checked so that a final up-to-date search of the property may be conducted just prior to registration, and as noted previously, any discharge of charge is registered first, followed by the transfer, any 1st charge, 2nd charge, etc. A document registration report (Precedent 27.1) is printed out for the law firm's records. See Precedent 25.4 for instructions on how to register and print out the document registration report in Teraview.

The Land Transfer Tax, Retail Sales Tax, and registration fees are electronically deducted from the law firm's e-reg account by Teranet. The cheques, documents, and keys for the property are usually delivered by staff messenger or courier between the two law firms.

ACTING FOR THE PURCHASER AFTER CLOSING

Taxes

Although the land registrar forwards the third executed copy of the affidavit of residence and value of the consideration to the municipal assessment department, many municipalities request that they also be advised by the solicitors when ownership of property changes, to ensure that all subsequent tax bills are sent to the new owners. This notification may be set out in a letter or by inserting information in a section for this purpose included in many realty tax certificates received when checking the status of the realty taxes.

Insurance

Fire Insurance

The purchasers will have placed their own fire insurance on the property, to be effective as of the closing date. If the transaction provided for a mortgage back to the vendor and a copy of the policy of insurance was not available on closing, a copy is mailed to the vendor's solicitors as soon as it is received from the insurance company.

Title Insurance

If title insurance was secured by the purchasers, the policy will either be issued by the law firm or will need to be obtained directly from the title insurance company.

GST New Housing Rebate Application

If the property being purchased is new residential housing, the purchaser may be entitled to a GST new housing rebate. If any applicable rebate was not paid directly to the purchaser by the vendor or credited to the purchaser on the statement of adjustments, the purchaser has four years from the day ownership of the property was transferred to claim the rebate directly from Canada Revenue Agency.

Real Estate Agent

If the agreement of purchase and sale contains a provision (as does the agreement illustrated as Precedent 24.1) that the deposit should be placed in an interest-bearing account or term deposit with any accrued interest to be paid to the purchaser after closing or other termination of the agreement, the real estate agent is asked to forward a cheque for the appropriate amount to the purchaser.

Reporting Letter and Account

When the details of the transaction are completed, a reporting letter is sent to the purchaser about the transaction, along with the law firm's account.

The reporting letter to the purchaser is much more detailed than that sent to the vendor. The purchaser's solicitors give their client details of the sale; most importantly, they certify that the purchaser has a good, marketable title to the property purchased. The purchaser is sent copies of the important documents relating to the purchase, including:

1. The duplicate executed copy of the registered transfer/deed (manual) or the document registration report (e-reg)
2. A copy of any assumed mortgage
3. A copy of any mortgage back to the vendor along with registration details
4. Title insurance policy, if any
5. Certificates of realty and other taxes
6. A copy of the statement of adjustments
7. A copy of the sheriff's certificate of executions

Precedent 27.2 illustrates a purchaser's reporting letter; Precedent 27.3 illustrates a trust ledger statement showing the monies received and paid out, which is referred to in the letter.

The account for services performed is enclosed with the reporting letter. If monies were received in advance to pay the account, the account is marked "Paid in Full."

ACTING FOR THE VENDOR AFTER CLOSING

Realty Tax Office

The appropriate assessment department may be notified of the change in ownership. Follow the practice of your law firm.

Fire Insurance

The policy of fire insurance held by the vendor on the property will have been cancelled effective the date of closing, and the purchaser will have arranged his or her own insurance coverage on the property. When the transaction has closed, the vendor should immediately notify the insurance company by telephone that closing has taken place.

If the transaction involved a mortgage back, a copy of the purchaser's insurance policy must be provided to the vendor (the mortgagee). If the copy of the policy was not available at the time of closing, the purchaser's solicitors will send it to the vendor's solicitors as soon as the policy is received from the insurance company.

Real Estate Agent

The real estate agent who negotiated the sale and received and retained the deposit is notified of the closing. The agent is entitled to receive commission on the completed sale at the rate set out in the agreement, plus the applicable GST on the total commission.

The agent may be asked to forward to the vendor a cheque for any deposit monies not required to satisfy the real estate commission and applicable GST; alternatively, the agent may receive a cheque from the vendor's solicitors to satisfy the amount of commission and GST to which the agent is entitled.

Reporting Letter and Account

A reporting letter to the vendor is not as detailed as that to the purchaser. The vendor is given details of the sale, and the following documents are returned:

1. A copy of the statement of adjustments
2. The duplicate registered copy of any mortgage (manual) or the document registration report (e-reg) the vendor may have taken back
3. Any other material the vendor may have furnished that was not forwarded to the purchaser's solicitors

You will recall that, on closing, the vendor usually signs a direction indicating how the proceeds are to be made payable. Usually, the proceeds are made payable to the vendor's solicitors so that their fees and disbursements are paid, and the balance is then paid over to the vendor. Normally, the vendor has received these monies before the reporting letter is forwarded. If not, a cheque for the appropriate amount is enclosed with the letter.

Precedent 27.4 illustrates a reporting letter to the vendor; Precedent 27.5 illustrates a trust ledger statement showing the monies received and paid out on behalf of the vendor.

The client is sent the firm's account for services rendered. If the account has been paid from the amount received on closing, the account enclosed with the reporting letter is marked "Paid in Full."

CLOSING THE FILE

When the account is paid and any undertakings given on closing have been satisfied, the file is closed. If undertakings were given on closing, the file should be kept open until all the undertakings have been carried out. A tickler slip is usually prepared to remind the lawyer to fulfill the undertakings.

In most law firms, files relating to the purchase and sale of real property are retained indefinitely in the closedfile storage facility.

Terms and Concepts

closing procedures for manual and e-reg
tax and insurance documentation
GST new housing rebate application

real estate commission
reporting letter and account

Review Questions

1. What material does the solicitor for the purchaser provide on closing?

2. What material does the solicitor for the vendor provide on closing?

3. Who registers any mortgages involved in the real estate transaction?

4. Who registers the transfer/deed? What must be done before that document can be registered?

5. What material is forwarded to the purchaser with his or her reporting letter?

6. After closing, what does the real estate agent
   a. receive?
   b. provide?

**** NOT VALID - TO BE USED FOR TRAINING PURPOSES ONLY ****

The applicant(s) hereby applies to the Land Registrar.	yyyy mm dd Page 1 of 2
LRO # 20 **Transfer**	Receipted as HH909 on 2007 07 26 at 12:54

Properties

PIN	07001 - 0450 LT	*Interest/Estate*	Fee Simple
Description	LT 178 , PL 607 ; BURLINGTON		
Address	05466 RANDOLPH CR BURLINGTON		

Consideration

Consideration $ 250,000.00

Transferor(s)

The transferor(s) hereby transfers the land to the transferee(s).

Name   DONNELLY, GAIL

Address for Service

I am at least 18 years of age.

James Donnelly and I are spouses of one another and are both parties to this document

This document is not authorized under Power of Attorney by this party.

Name   DONNELLY, JAMES

Address for Service

I am at least 18 years of age.

Gail Donnelly and I are spouses of one another and are both parties to this document

This document is not authorized under Power of Attorney by this party.

Transferee(s)

		Capacity	Share
Name	KELSO, JOHN	Joint Tenants	
Date of Birth	1985 01 01		
Address for Service	05466 RANDOLPH CR BURLINGTON		
Name	KELSO, MARIAN	Joint Tenants	
Date of Birth	1988 12 15		
Address for Service	05466 RANDOLPH CR BURLINGTON		

Simpson, Stainton & Crawford
Barristers & Solicitors

53 Suffolk Street, Guelph, Ontario N1H 7B4
Tel: 519-424-6744   Fax: 519-524-6745

March 20, 20__

Mr. and Mrs. Ronald C. Anderson
984 Helena Avenue
Toronto ON M9R 3G6

Dear Mr. and Mrs. Anderson:

Re: ANDERSON purchase from PETERSON
**   984 Helena Avenue, Toronto**
**   East Half Lot 105, Plan 5948**
**   Closing Date: February 28, 20__**
**   Our File No.: 1111/4808**

The above transaction of purchase and sale having now been completed, we are pleased to enclose herewith the following documents for your records:

1.   Duplicate copy of transfer/deed (*or* Transfer Document Registration Report).

2.   Copy of first charge/mortgage (*or* First Charge Document Registration Report).

3.   Amortization schedule for the first mortgage payments.

4.   Copy of charge/mortgage back (*or* Second Charge Document Registration Report).

5.   Amortization schedule for the second mortgage payments.

6.   Survey of the property.

7.   Tax bill from the City of Toronto for 20__.

8.   Statement of adjustments.

9.   Trust Ledger Statement.

10. Our receipted account herein.

Mr. and Mrs. Ronald C. Anderson
Page 2
March 20, 20__

TRANSFER/DEED

The transfer/deed gives you ownership as joint tenants to the easterly half of Lot No. 105, Plan 5948, registered in the Land Registry Office for Toronto (No. 64) on February 28, 20__, at 11:47 a.m., as Instrument No. 468057. The law of survivorship applies to joint tenants; therefore, if either of you should die, the survivor is automatic owner of the whole.

STATEMENT OF ADJUSTMENTS

Adjustments were made as of February 28, 20__, the date of closing the transaction. Amounts in the right-hand column are the credits of the vendor; amounts in the left-hand column are your credits.

The vendor has undertaken to re-adjust items on the statement of adjustment if necessary.

FIRST MORTGAGE

Prior to closing, you agreed to provide the Royal Bank of Canada with a first mortgage on the property on the terms set out in your mortgage application dated January 18, 200x. On closing, we registered a mortgage from you to the Royal Bank of Canada, particulars of which are as follows:

Principal outstanding:	$175,000.00
Rate of interest:	7.5%
Mortgage payments:	$1,223.63
Payments made:	28th day of each month – deducted automatically from your account at the Royal Bank of Canada branch at: 5100 Yonge Street Toronto ON M5J 1J1
Mortgage number:	01-01234-8975023
Last payment:	February 28, 20__
Mortgage matures:	February 28, 20__

Mr. and Mrs. Ronald C. Anderson
Page 2
March 10, 20___

SECOND MORTGAGE BACK

The agreement of purchase and sale provided that the vendor would take back a second mortgage, particulars of which are as follows:

Principal:	$25,000.00
Rate of interest:	8%
Mortgage payment:	$183.44
Payments made:	28th day of each month
First payment:	March 28, 20___
Last payment:	February 28, 20___
Mortgage matures:	February 28, 20___
Payments to:	Mr. Ryan Peterson 42 Oaklea Blvd. Oakville ON L3J 4V1

We are enclosing herewith an amortization schedule with respect to the second mortgage, in order to allow you to see the pro rata share of principal and interest for each payment.

DISCHARGE OF EXISTING FIRST MORTGAGE

Our search of title indicated the existence of a mortgage registered against the property given by the vendor to Christine Peterson securing the original principal amount of $40,000.00. On closing we received the personal undertaking of the vendor's solicitors to obtain and register the discharge of this mortgage.

We will follow up on this matter to ensure that the necessary discharge is registered.

REALTY TAXES

Taxes on the property for last year have been paid in full. Taxes for 20___ were estimated at $1,615.83, based on the 20___ taxes of $1,468.94 plus an estimated 10% increase. The vendor's responsibility for 200x taxes is 58 days.

Mr. and Mrs. Ronald C. Anderson
Page 2
March 10, 20__

You were therefore allowed a credit of $256.94 on the statement of adjustments for
unpaid taxes for 20__. All payments of realty taxes subsequent to the date of closing are
your responsibility. The Assessment Department and the City of Toronto have been
advised that you are the new registered owners of the property. They will forward all
future assessment and tax bills to you.

INSURANCE

You were responsible for arranging for your own fire insurance on the property, and prior
to closing we confirmed particulars with Guardian Insurance Company of Canada. Please
ensure that a copy of the policy is sent to each mortgagee as soon as you receive it.

ACCRUED INTEREST ON DEPOSIT

We have advised the real estate agent that this transaction has closed and asked that their
cheque for the accrued interest earned on the deposit of $20,000.00 be forwarded to you
as soon as possible.

TITLE

We have investigated the title to the land and premises described in the transfer/deed of
land, and in our opinion you have a good and marketable title, in fee simple, as joint
tenants, to the said lands and premises, subject to the interest of the Royal Bank of Canada
as first mortgagee, and Ryan Peterson as second mortgagee.

We are enclosing a copy of our trust ledger statement together with our receipted account.

Thank you for permitting us to act on your behalf in connection with this transaction.
Please contact me if you have any questions.

Yours very truly,

SIMPSON, STAINTON & CRAWFORD

Drew C. Crawford

DCC:ri
Enclosures

Hill, Johnston & Grant

Barristers & Solicitors
Suite 2501, 17 Princess Street South
City, Province M8Y 3N5
Canada

www.hilljohngrant.com
Telephone: (416) 354-9900
Facsimile: (416) 354-9909

Peter T Grant
Direct Line: (000) 354-9898
e-mail: ptgrant@hilljohngrant.com

Our Reference No. 05099/0076

March 15, 20___

Mr. Ryan Peterson
42 Oaklea Blvd.
Oakville ON L3J 4V1

Dear Mr. Peterson:

Peterson sale to Anderson
984 Helena Avenue, Toronto

We are pleased to advise that the above transaction closed on February 28, 20___, and we now submit the following report.

1.   Statement of Adjustments

We enclose a copy of the statement of adjustments showing how the balance payable on closing was arrived at. We received on closing the sum of $190,716.14 on your behalf. This is shown as a credit on our account.

2.   Discharge of Mortgage

In accordance with the provisions of the agreement of purchase and sale, you were responsible for discharging the existing mortgage to Christine Peterson.

You directed that the balance due on closing be payable to this law firm, and from that sum we paid to Christine Peterson the sum of $26,794.92 to pay off this mortgage. We enclose a copy of the discharge of charge/mortgage registered in Toronto on February 28, 20___ as No. 468057.

Mr. Ryan Peterson   2   March 15, 20__

3.   Mortgage Back

As part of the consideration for the sale, you agreed to take back a second mortgage for $25,000.00. This mortgage bears interest at the rate of 8 percent per annum, calculated half-yearly. The mortgage is repayable in monthly amortized payments of $183.44 on the 28th day of each month. The mortgage payments are based on a 10-year amortization period, but the mortgage itself has a term of 5 years. The first payment is due on the 28th day of March. The mortgage contains a clause permitting the prepayment of all or part of the principal sum outstanding on any payment date or dates without notice or bonus, provided that partial prepayment is in accordance with the amortization schedule for the mortgage.

We enclose your duplicate registered copy of the mortgage (*or* Document Registration Agreement), which was filed in Toronto as instrument number 468058.

4.   Taxes

Taxes for last year had been paid in full. Taxes for the 20__ were estimated at $1,615.83, based on the last year's taxes of $1,468.94 plus an estimated 10% increase. You are responsible for taxes for 58 days of the current year, and the purchaser was therefore allowed a credit of 256.94 for unpaid taxes.

5.   Undertaking

On closing we delivered to the solicitors for the purchasers your undertaking to re-adjust items on the statement of adjustments if necessary, to pay all utility charges up the date of closing, and to register a discharge of your mortgage in favour of Christine Peterson. A copy of that undertaking is enclosed.

6.   Fuel Oil

On closing you arranged to have the oil tank filled, and you were credited on the statement of adjustments with $918.00, representing 900 litres of fuel oil at $1.02 per litre plus $55.08 for the GST. Any account outstanding to the date of closing is your responsibility in accordance with your undertaking.

7.   Real Estate Commission

Real estate commission fees of $9,400.00 plus GST of $564.00 were payable in this transaction. The purchasers paid $20,000.00 as a deposit, which was held in trust by the realtor. We understand that H. R. Schwartz Real Estate Limited has forwarded directly to you a cheque for $1,003.36 being the balance owing to you from the deposit monies.

Mr. Ryan Peterson   2   March 15, 20__

8.   Utilities

All meters were to be read on closing and any amounts outstanding as of closing are your responsibility to pay in accordance with your undertaking.

9.   Insurance

You arranged to cancel your existing policy of fire insurance, and the purchasers have arranged to place their own insurance coverage on the property. A certified copy of that policy will be forwarded to you as soon as it is received, showing your interest as second mortgagee.

10.   Statement of Account

We are enclosing a copy of our statement of account, stamped paid in full, together with our trust ledger statement.

You attended in our office on February 28, 20__, to pick up our trust cheque for $162,000.00, and we now enclose herewith our trust cheque for $884.95, representing the balance due to you from the proceeds of the transaction.

It has been a pleasure acting on your behalf in this transaction.

Yours very truly

HILL, JOHNSTON & GRANT

Peter T. Grant

PTG/ri

Enclosures

Simpson, Stainton & Crawford
Barristers & Solicitors

TRUST LEDGER STATEMENT

Re: ANDERSON purchase from PETERSON

Received from 1st Mortgagee – Royal Bank of Canada		$175,000.00
Received from you		19,307.92
Paid vendor as per Statement of Adjustments	$190,716.14	
Paid Ontario Land Transfer Tax	2,075.00	
Paid legal fees and disbursements	1,516.78	
	$194,307.92	$194,307.92

March 20, 20__
E. & O.E.

Hill, Johnston & Grant
Barristers & Solicitors

TRUST LEDGER STATEMENT

Re: PETERSON sale to ANDERSON

Received from purchaser as per Statement of Adjustments		$190,716.14
Paid to Christine Peterson to discharge previous 1st Mortgage	$26,794.92	
Paid legal fees and disbursements	$1,036.27	
Paid to you, February 28, 20__	162,000.00	
Paid to you, March 15, 20__	884.95	
	$190,716.19	$199,716.14

March 15, 20__
E. & O.E.

PART 4

Corporate Law

Introduction to Corporate Practice

OBJECTIVES:

- Describe the different types of business organizations and how they may be created

- Identify two types of corporations in Ontario and their governing statutes

- Define and explain basic corporate terms

Corporate practice provides legal services to individuals carrying on business either as a sole proprietor, a partnership, or as a corporation (often referred to as a company). The largest area of corporate work involves services to a corporation: organizing a new corporation; maintaining the records required to conduct the affairs of an existing corporation; drafting contracts and agreements; or handling real estate transactions and court proceedings in which the corporation is a party.

The individuals concerned in sole proprietorships or partnerships jointly own all the assets of the business entity, share in the profits, and have full liability for any obligations of the business to the extent of their personal assets.

A corporation is a legal entity and is considered a person. Its members share in any profits but have limited liability for the obligations of the business.

The purpose of incorporating is to create a legal entity that can legally conduct business transactions while limiting the personal financial responsibility of the incorporators. There are many types of corporations, created by federal or provincial law. For example, the Arthritis Society is a charitable, non-profit corporation; Canada Post is a Crown corporation; The Royal Bank of Canada and National Trust Limited are financial corporations; The United Church of Canada is a religious, non-profit corporation; and the Canadian Tire Corporation is a business corporation.

The most common type of corporation is a limited-liability business corporation with share capital. Such a corporation is an association of individuals, called shareholders, each of whom subscribes money (or the equivalent of money) to a common fund, called capital, to be used for a common purpose. Each individual's proportionate contribution to such capital is his or her share in the corporation. The shareholders share in any profits earned by the corporation in proportion to their contribution, but their personal financial liability for the obligations of the corporation is limited to the amount of the full subscription price of their shares. The record of a contribution to the capital is contained in the share certificate provided to each shareholder.

HOW CORPORATIONS ARE CREATED

A corporation may be incorporated under federal jurisdiction to conduct business throughout Canada or under provincial jurisdiction to conduct business mainly in the province of incorporation. A provincial corporation may operate in another province by obtaining a licence from that province; the corporation is then known as an extra-provincial corporation. A corporation incorporated under the laws of another country is known as a non-resident corporation.

Some types of corporations, such as insurance and trust companies and banks, follow special procedures when applying for incorporation. Others are incorporated in one of the ways outlined in this section.

Royal Charter

This method, whereby the Crown grants a charter, is extremely rare today. However, The Hudson's Bay Company, incorporated by royal charter in 1670, is still in existence.

Special Act of Parliament or Provincial Legislature

This method is not common. However, a number of corporations, such as Air Canada and Canadian National Railways, have been incorporated by special acts of the federal Parliament. Several Crown corporations have been set up in Ontario by acts of the provincial legislature.

Memorandum of Association

In several provinces, a memorandum setting out the name and purpose of the proposed corporation, the amount of its capital, and any other necessary information is registered with the Registrar of Companies of the appropriate province. If the memorandum is approved, a certificate of registration is received in due course.

Letters Patent

This method is followed in several provinces. It was used in Ontario for the incorporation of all companies until December 31, 1970. Since that date, the letters patent system of incorporation has been used in Ontario only for the incorporation of organizations without share capital, such as social or charitable associations.

Articles of Incorporation

This method of creating a corporation is used in most provinces as well as federally. If a company is going to operate in several or all provinces and territories, it will usually be incorporated under the federal Canada *Business Corporations Act*. Most corporations, however, are incorporated under the province in which they will substantially operate and where their registered office will be located. Each province has an act or acts and a ministry concerned with the incorporation and operation of companies in the province. Note that the name of the province, such as "Ontario" or "Alberta," does not appear in the name of the provincial business corporations acts, only in the federal Canada Business Corporations Act. To avoid any confusion, many legal documents that cite the provincial statute include the name of the applicable province either before or in brackets after the name of the act, but it is not part of the proper name of the statute and is not italicized, for example, *Business Corporations Act* (Ontario) or Alberta *Business Corporations Act*.

Although the terminology, documentation, and procedures are similar across Canada, the specific acts and rules for the jurisdiction under which a corporation is or will be incorporated and will operate must be followed. In Ontario, there are several Ontario acts that govern corporations. The two most frequently encountered in a legal assistant's corporate work are

1. the Ontario *Corporations Act*, which governs corporations without share capital, corporations that are of a social nature, and insurers, and
2. the *Business Corporations Act* (Ontario), which governs corporations with share capital except those governed under the *Corporations Act* or other corporate acts. The term "company" is not used in the Act; the term used is "corporation."

This chapter primarily concerns corporations to which the provisions of the *Business Corporations Act* (Ontario) apply, and this act is used to explain the documentation and procedures of corporate practice in this text.

TERMINOLOGY

A number of terms relevant to incorporation in Ontario should be understood before considering the procedure.

Types of Corporations

There are two types of limited-liability corporations in Ontario: a corporation that offers its shares for sale to the public, formerly called a *public* company and now known as an *offering* corporation, and a corporation that does not offer its shares for sale to the public, formerly called a *private* company and now known as a *non-offering* or closely held corporation.

Professional Corporations

Most provinces and territories now allow members of certain professions, which traditionally were only allowed to enter into partnerships, to incorporate as a form of non-offering limited liability corporation. In Ontario, chartered accountants, lawyers, health professionals, social workers, and veterinarians currently have this option, provided that they satisfy the following conditions:

1. The name of the corporation cannot be a number name, and the name of the corporation must include the words "Professional Corporation" or "Société Professionnelle."
2. All the officers and directors of a professional corporation must also be shareholders of the corporation.
3. The articles of incorporation of a professional corporation must state that the corporation may not carry on a business other than the practice of the specific profession of the members.
4. All the issued and outstanding shares of a professional corporation shall be owned, directly or indirectly, by one or more members of the same profession except in the case of health physicians and dentists. Shares of such professional corporations may be owned, directly or indirectly, by a member of the College of Physicians and Surgeons of Ontario or the Royal College of Dental Surgeons of Ontario, as applicable, *or* by a family member (spouse, child, or parent), *or* by one or more individuals as trustees in trust for the child or children of a member of the profession.

An example of a professional corporation name would be Ward & Melini Professional Corporation or Dr. Joseph Colangelo Professional Corporation. Note that an individual may incorporate as a professional corporation.

Shareholders

Shareholders "own" the corporation and have a voice in its management. They elect a board of directors, who manage or supervise the operation of the corporation.

At shareholders' meetings, the directors report on the activities of the corporation and submit reports and recommendations for approval by the shareholders.

Directors

The operation of a corporation is supervised or managed by directors elected by the shareholders of the corporation. The articles of incorporation specify the number of directors or, alternatively, the minimum and maximum number that may be elected. The board of directors has at least one director for a non-offering corporation and at least three directors for an offering corporation. Unless the articles provide otherwise, a director need not hold shares in the corporation, but at least 25 percent of the directors must be resident Canadians (except when the corporation is a non-resident corporation).

The directors named in the articles of incorporation are known as *first* directors and hold office from the date the certificate of incorporation is endorsed by the Ministry until the first meeting of shareholders. No director named in the articles may resign that office unless, at the time the resignation is to become effective, a successor is elected or appointed.

Officers

The directors designate the offices of the corporation, appoint the individuals to hold each office, and specify the duties and delegate the powers to manage the affairs of the corporation. A director may be appointed to any office of the corporation; two or more offices of the corporation may be held by the same person.

It is usual for a corporation to have at least two officers: a president and a secretary. Officers of the corporation need not be directors or shareholders, although the president of a corporation is usually a director. Large corporations have other officers, such as a managing director, vice-president, treasurer, or comptroller.

In small corporations, it is not unusual for the shareholders to be also the directors and the officers. In large corporations, shareholders are not usually directors or officers.

Shares of a Corporation

An incorporated business corporation issues shares to those who invest in it, the shareholders; the amount received for such shares is referred to as the capital of the corporation. The shares must be in registered form and without nominal or par value, that is, they do not have any stipulated dollar value. The value of a share is an interest in the worth of a business.

A corporation may have only one class of shares or may have different classes. There may be a specified *or* an unlimited number of any or each class.

If a corporation has only one class of shares, the shares of that class are frequently identified as common shares; they could also be called ordinary or Class A shares.

When there is only one class of shares, the rights of the holders of that class are equal in all respects and include the right to vote at all shareholders' meetings and to receive the remaining property of the corporation upon dissolution.

If a corporation has more than one class of shares, the articles of incorporation set out the rights, privileges, restrictions, and conditions attaching to each class. The right to vote at shareholders' meetings and to receive the remaining property of the corporation upon dissolution must be attached to at least one class of shares, but all the rights need not be attached to the same class.

When there are two classes of shares, the shares of one class are often called common and the second preferred. Preferred shares confer on the holder some preferences over the shareholders of another class and usually restrict the right to vote at shareholders' meetings.

HOW A CORPORATION ACTS

Resolutions and By-Laws

Corporations act through their directors and shareholders, whose decisions are set out in resolutions and by-laws.

By-laws are the rules and regulations governing the internal affairs and operations of the corporation. They deal, for example, with the powers, qualifications, election, and term of office of the directors; the duties of the officers of the corporation; the method of giving notice of meetings; the fiscal year of the corporation; and who may sign documents on behalf of the corporation. By-laws are first passed by the directors and then submitted to the next meeting of shareholders for confirmation, rejection, amendment, or repeal.

Resolutions are formal expressions of opinion or intention and may be passed by either directors or shareholders. A special resolution is one submitted to a special meeting of shareholders called for the purpose of considering the resolution. It must be passed with or without amendment by two-thirds of the votes cast at the meeting or by the unanimous consent in writing of all shareholders.

Meetings

The directors or shareholders of a corporation may act at meetings at which they are personally present and pass or confirm resolutions or by-laws through formal motions duly moved, seconded, and carried.

Once a corporation is organized, the directors meet as frequently as necessary; shareholders are required by the *Business Corporations Act* (Ontario) to meet "annually." The first annual meeting of shareholders must be held not later than 18 months after the incorporation of the corporation and subsequently at least every 15 months. At other times, special meetings of shareholders may be held to deal with specific business.

Unless the article or by-laws of the corporation state otherwise, any meeting of shareholders or directors may be held by telephone or electronic means and any shareholder who votes or director who participates is considered to be in attendance at the meeting.

At all such meetings, a **quorum** (that is, the minimum number of directors or shareholders required to hold a valid meeting, as set out in the by-laws) must be present. The act states that the holders of a majority of the shares entitled to vote at a meeting of shareholders, whether present in person or by **proxy**, constitute a quorum, unless the by-laws provide otherwise. A proxy is a written authorization to someone else to act in the place of the shareholder and is discussed further in Chapter 30.

The act states that, subject to the articles of by-laws, a majority of the number of directors constitutes a quorum but that in no case shall a quorum be less than two-fifths of the number of directors or minimum number of directors, as the case may be. If a corporation has fewer than three directors, all directors must be present at any meeting of directors to constitute a quorum.

Acting Without Meetings

The directors or shareholders of a corporation may act without holding meetings. Any resolution or by-law consented to at any time during the life of a corporation by the signatures of *all* the directors or of *all* the shareholders is as valid and effective as if it had been passed at a meeting. This form of corporate action is known as *consent in writing*. Many small corporations conduct the business of the corporation in this way.

The effective date of matters consented to in writing is the date on which the last director or shareholder signs the resolution or by-law.

BOOKS OF RECORD

The provincial or federal act under which a corporation is incorporated prescribes that certain books be maintained to record details of the corporation's activities.

Records Required

The records that are maintained at a corporation's registered office or at such other place in Ontario as designated by the directors are

1. the articles and the by-laws and all amendments thereto and a copy of any unanimous shareholder agreement known to the directors;
2. minutes of meetings and resolutions of shareholders;
3. minutes of meetings and resolutions of the directors and any committee thereof;
4. a directors' register;
5. a securities' register in which the securities issued by the corporation are recorded; and
6. adequate account records.

Form of Records

The records that a corporation is required to maintain may be kept in a bound or loose-leaf book or may be entered into or recorded in an computerized information storage system.

Many law offices prepare and maintain corporate records on a computer system but also maintain paper copies in traditional record books.

Corporations that offer their shares to the public and large non-offering corporations usually maintain their books of record in their registered office (formerly called the head office). Small corporations that do not offer their shares to the public often use the office of their solicitors as their registered office. Most of the records of small non-offering corporations are maintained in the minute book, which is divided into sections relating to the different subject matters to be recorded.

If the books of record are kept at a registered office location other than the office of the solicitors acting for the corporation, it is not unusual for a duplicate set of records to be kept in the solicitors' office. When books of record are kept in the law office, a legal assistant usually keeps the records up-to-date and performs other duties on behalf of the corporation, as discussed in Chapter 31.

Minute Book

The most common book of record is the minute book, in which the decisions or acts of the directors and shareholders as recorded in minutes or resolutions are kept. This book also usually contains a copy of the certificate of incorporation, a copy of the articles of incorporation, and the by-laws of the corporation. Many small corporations maintain in the minute book the names and addresses of past and present directors and shareholders and the number and classes of shares held by the shareholders; larger corporations maintain this information in separate books of record.

Before the use of electronic equipment to prepare corporate material, many minute books required the use of paper slightly wider and longer than traditional 8.5-by-11-inch paper. Some minute books were bound on the left; one other type was bound at the top.

With the introduction of computer technology and the electronic preparation of much corporate material, the size of minute books has changed to allow material to be inserted in the book to be prepared on 8.5-by-11-inch paper.

You may secure a minute book for a new corporation from a legal stationer; many law firms stock a supply of minute books for use by new corporations. The minute book and other corporate books of record may be lettered in gold with the corporation's name on the cover or spine. This makes identification of a particular minute book easier when it is one of many similar books kept for corporations for which the law firm maintains corporate records.

Special heavy-duty corporation record boxes are available from many legal stationers and will hold the minute book, the securities' registers, and the corporate seal. A nameplate holder on one edge of the box permits easy identification of the contents. These boxes may be labelled either with the name of the corporation or numerically, in which case, an alphabetical crossreference index is maintained.

PREPARATION OF CORPORATE DOCUMENTS

Documents for Minute Books

Material prepared for inclusion in the minute book is prepared on paper that fits the minute book. This is now usually letter size but may be paper slightly wider or longer than normal letter-size paper, depending on the size of the minute book. Most law offices use only one size of minute book for new corporations so that only one size of minute-book paper is required. However, in law offices that maintain the corporate records for a considerable number of corporations, you may still encounter minute books that are larger than letter size. Follow the practice of your law office with regard to the size of paper used for documents to be inserted in such a book.

When preparing material for inclusion in a minute book that binds pages at the left, allow a margin of 1.5 inches (40 mm) on the left of the page and 1 inch (25 mm) on the right. It is essential to have the wider margin on the left because this is the edge that is inserted into the minute book.

Documents Forwarded to the Companies and Personal Property Security Branch

The *Business Corporations Act* (Ontario) states that all documents are to be submitted to the director, that is, the person appointed by the government to accept corporate filings. In actual practice, the documents are filed in person, by mail or electronically, to the Companies and Personal Property Security Branch of the Ministry of Government Services. This government office was formerly and is still often referred to as the *Companies Branch*; however, the government uses the acronym CPPSB, and this is the term used in this text to refer to this government office.

Documents submitted to the CPPSB should be printed, typewritten, or reproduced legibly so as to be suitable for photographing on microfilm and should be capable of being signed without smudging. Use good quality white paper that is 8.5 by 11 inches. A document that consists of two or more pages requires no back or binding and is stapled in the upper left-hand corner; each page is numbered consecutively.

Articles, applications, and statements filed with the CPPSB that require the signature of one or more persons must be signed manually by each person and not by an attorney. Note, however, that documents filed electronically do not have to be signed.

Any document that does not conform to this standard will not be accepted for filing. It is permissible to forward a photocopy of a notice or document that is required to be sent to the CPPSB. This provision does not apply to articles, applications, or documents filed relating to the name of the corporation.

Electronic Filing and Services

As with many other areas of legal practice, the *Business Corporations Act* (Ontario) now allows for searching of records or filing of documentation electronically via the Internet through commercial companies under contract with the Ministry of Government Services. These are referred to as private sector service providers or PSPs. Only certain searches and document filings are currently available. Because these services are offered through private third-party companies, a fee will be charged for their services, in addition to the filing fee for the government service. The private service fees are subject to GST; the government's filing fees are not. All filing and private service fees are charged to the client as disbursements. Complete information on these services and fees is available at the ministry website, accessed at http://www.mgs.gov.on.ca by clicking on "Service for Business."

Execution of Documents

The *Business Corporations Act* (Ontario) has an interesting provision relating to the execution of documents. Usually, the same copy of a document is executed by all parties who must do so. However, the act provides that any article, notice, resolution, requisition, statement, or other document required or permitted to be executed by more than one person for the purpose of the act may be executed by having each person execute a separate document, each of which must be identical, and that such documents, when duly executed by all persons required or permitted to do so, will be considered one document for the purposes of the act.

CORPORATE AGREEMENTS

A large amount of the documentation prepared in the area of corporate practice is in the creation and amendment of corporate agreements. There are many types and forms of agreements, for example:

Shareholders' agreements, which set out the rights and responsibilities of the shareholders of the corporation.

Joint venture agreements, which are prepared when the corporation enters into an agreement with another entity (a corporation, a partnership, or individuals) to together produce or do something. For example, car manufacturing companies often enter into agreements with parts manufacturing companies to together produce a specific component of cars, such as the seats.

Franchise agreements, whereby a corporation enters into an agreement with another entity for the use of specified brand names, products, and/or processes for a predetermined fee. The person giving the rights is the franchisor; the person receiving the rights is the franchisee. An example of this would be the McDonald's Restaurants franchises.

Security agreements, which are prepared when the corporation obtains financing (borrows money) using the assets of the corporation, such as inventory, equipment, or accounts receivables, as collateral for repayment of the loan. Most provinces have enacted a Personal Property Security Act, under the regulations of which a document referred to as a financing statement may be electronically filed so that the lender may register notice of their security interest in the corporation that borrowed the funds. This database of registered debtors may then be searched electronically using the name of the corporate entity to reveal any security interests registered against it.

Development or Leasing agreements, which are prepared when the corporation enters into a development or a long-term leasing agreement that might involve the purchase, construction, or renovation of lands or buildings to develop manufacturing, retail, or office complexes. This area of law is often referred to as corporate commercial practice.

These agreements may be only 2 or 3 pages in length or may extend to 50 pages or more depending on the circumstances. Refer to Chapter 7 for guidelines and precedents on the preparation of agreements.

CAPITALIZATION IN CORPORATE MATERIAL

In corporate material prepared in many law offices, you will find initial capitals used on terms such as directors, shareholders, corporation, by-laws, president, or chairman. The *Business Corporations Act* (Ontario), however, does not use initial capitals on these terms.

Section 1 of the act uses both the terms *Director* and *director*, with two distinct meanings. The *Director* is defined as someone appointed under section 276 of the act to receive articles of incorporation and endorse them to incorporate a corporation, as well as to perform other duties set out in the act. A *director* is defined as a person occupying the position of director of a corporation.

Follow whatever capitalization practice is preferred by your law firm. If, however, you are given no direction, it is suggested that initial capitals be avoided.

Terms and Concepts

corporation
sole proprietor
partnership
charitable
non-profit corporation
Crown corporation
limited-liability business corporation
royal charter
memorandum of association
letters patent
articles of incorporation
Corporations Act
Business Corporations Act (Ontario)
public or offering corporation
private or non-offering corporation
professional corporations
shareholders
directors
Canadian residency requirement
first directors
officers
shares

capital
common and preferred shares
by-laws
resolutions
meetings
quorum
proxy
books of record
directors' register
securities' register
minute book
preparation and execution of corporate
   documents
Companies and Personal Property
   Securities Branch (CPPSB)
private sector service providers (PSPs)
corporate agreements
shareholders' agreement
joint venture agreement
franchise agreement
security agreement
financing statement

Review Questions

1. Samantha Sabatino operates a printing business. Why would she consider incorporating that business?

2. Samantha Sabatino decides to incorporate an "offering corporation." What does this mean?

3. If Ms. Sabatino incorporates an offering corporation, how many directors must it have?

4. What is meant by the term "first" directors?

5. Ms. Sabatino wants her new corporation to have two classes of shares. How would they be identified?

6. What is the difference between a by-law and a resolution?

7. How can a corporation approve resolutions without holding an actual meeting?

8. If the last annual meeting of a corporation was held on March 17, (this year), the next annual meeting must be held before what date?

9. If Ms. Sabatino's new corporation has seven directors, how many should be present at a meeting to establish a quorum?

10. What records must be maintained by Ms. Sabatino's new corporation?

11. **Internet Research:** Use the Internet to research the advantages and disadvantages of incorporating under a provincial or the federal business corporations statute.

CHAPTER 29

Incorporating an Ontario Corporation

OBJECTIVES:

- Describe the guidelines and procedures when selecting a corporate name
- Use legal precedents accurately to prepare articles of incorporation
- Demonstrate an understanding of the initial steps in organizing a new corporation

Corporate practice involves incorporating both large and small business corporations with share capital, under federal or provincial jurisdiction. This text discusses only the incorporation of a small, provincial corporation that does not offer its shares to the public. It is this type of corporation with which the legal assistant is usually most involved. Figure 29.1 illustrates the steps in incorporating an Ontario corporation.

SELECTING A CORPORATE NAME

Every corporation must have either a word name or a number name.

Word Name

If a word name is desired, a name not exceeding 120 characters and using the alphabet of the English language or Arabic numerals, or a combination thereof with punctuation marks and spaces, is chosen. The name must end in *Limited*, *Limitée*, *Incorporated*, *Incorporée*, or *Corporation* (or the corresponding abbreviations *Ltd.*, *Ltée*, *Inc.*, *or Corp.*). The name may be in an English form, a French form, an English and French form, or a combined English and French form. There are, of course, legal principles involved in choosing a name, but these are not the subject of this text. For example, under certain conditions, other languages may be used.

Checking the Word Name

Once a proposed corporate name is chosen, it is checked against existing corporate names, trademarks, trade names, or names of unincorporated business enterprises for similarity. To do this, a search must be conducted using the NUANS (New Upgraded Automated Name Search) system to check the proposed name against the name database operated by Industry Canada. The search may be done directly with NUANS for federal incorporations only. For provincial incorporations, a company that is registered to provide these services must be used. A list of private sector service providers (PSPs) across Canada who are registered members with NUANS is available at the NUANS website (http://www.nuans.com). A fee is charged for each name searched.

The requesting law firm or lawyer receives a computer-printed search report, listing names in a descending order of similarity. This original search report, dated not more than 90 days before the date of submitting the articles of incorporation, accompanies the articles when a word name is chosen. No such name-search report is required when the corporation chooses a number name, which is assigned by the Ministry. Note that if a bilingual French-English name is chosen, both the French and English versions must be searched with NUANS.

Number Name

A number name consists of the corporation number assigned by the director on incorporation. At the time of publication, the Ministry was assigning corporate numbers of eight digits (for example, 83456782 Ontario Limited).

Figure 29.1 Steps for Incorporating an Ontario Corporation

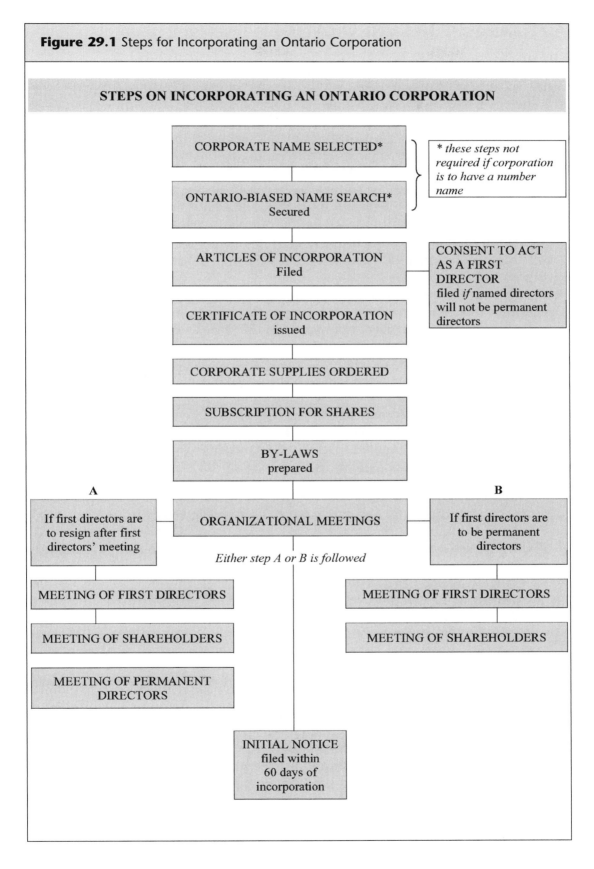

ARTICLES OF INCORPORATION

To apply for incorporation of a company with share capital, articles of incorporation must be prepared and filed with the Companies and Personal Property Security Branch of the Ministry of Consumer and Business Services and an incorporation fee must be paid. The fee will depend on the method of filing, discussed later in this chapter. Precedent 29.1 illustrates completed articles of incorporation.

The articles are prepared strictly according to the instruction sheets accompanying the printed forms, which may be secured from the Ministry of Government Services website; commercial software companies, such as Fast Company, which was used to create the corporate forms in this text; or a PSP. The PSP enables you to complete and file the articles of incorporation online for an additional fee.

Three or more persons of legal age must apply for the incorporation of an offering corporation, but only one person need apply to incorporate a non-offering corporation.

The pages in a set of articles of incorporation are numbered 1 to 6 and must remain in that order. If any article is inapplicable, state "nil" or "not applicable"; if additional pages are required, number them the same as the original but add letters of the alphabet to indicate sequence. For example, supplementary pages for page 4 would be numbered 4A, 4B, etc.

Prepare a minimum of three copies; the original and a copy are submitted to the Ministry of Government Services, Companies and Personal Property Securities Branch (CPPSB), and the third copy is kept in the office file. Many legal assistants make a file copy by photocopying the executed articles before they are submitted to the CPPSB.

The following information that must be provided in the articles of incorporation:

1. **Name** Set out the name of the corporation in block capital letters, including any punctuation, in the spaces provided on the form, commencing in the first space of the first line. The name must correspond exactly with the name set out in the computer-printed name-search report from the NUANS system. Where a number name is desired, the first nine spaces on the form are left blank, followed by *ONTARIO* and either *LIMITED, LTD., INCORPORATED, INC., CORPORATION, CORP.*, or the French equivalent.
2. **Address of Registered Office** Set out the address of the registered office (formerly called the head office) of the corporation in full, including the postal code. If the office is in a multiple-office building, include the room or suite number as well. The name of the municipality where the registered office is situated is also set out.

   When a small corporation is incorporated, the problem of what address to use often arises because no office premises have been rented. The Business Corporations Act (Ontario) states that certain books of records and accounts are to be maintained at the registered office; use the address in Ontario, therefore, where the books of records are maintained. Frequently, the address is that of the law firm.
3. **Number of Directors** Set out the exact number of directors or the minimum and maximum number of directors that may compose the board of directors of the corporation. The number of directors may be the same or greater than the number of directors for whom information is required, as discussed in item 5.

4. **Information on First Directors** Provide this information for each named director in the articles: surname; first or other given name by which he or she is commonly known; address for service (not necessarily the person's home address); and an indication as to whether he or she is a resident Canadian. (At least 25 percent of the directors on the board of every corporation, other than a non-resident corporation, must be resident Canadians.) When a corporation has less than four directors, then at least one must be a resident Canadian. The directors must be individuals, not corporations.

   The first directors named in the articles meet after incorporation to organize the new corporation. To facilitate these organizational proceedings, members of the lawyer's office staff are often named the first or office directors of a corporation. When the new corporation is organized by the directors, the first or office directors resign, and permanent directors are elected or appointed at the first meeting of shareholders following incorporation. Thereafter, directors are normally elected at the regular annual meeting of shareholders.

5. **Business of Corporation** It is not necessary to state the exact business to be carried on by the proposed corporation (unless it is a professional corporation). A corporation is deemed to have the capacity, rights, privileges, and powers of a natural person and, with certain exceptions set out in the act, may conduct any business a natural person is entitled to conduct. Any restrictions, however, on the business the corporation may carry on or on the powers the corporation may exercise are stated. If there are no such restrictions, state this fact.

6. **Classes of Share** Identify the classes and any maximum number of shares the corporation is authorized to issue.

   The articles of incorporation may or may not limit the number of shares that may be issued. When the number is limited, the amount of consideration that could be received for such shares is frequently called the authorized capital. Issued capital refers to the amount realized by the issuance of shares from the authorized capital.

   The articles may authorize the issue of any class of shares in one or more series. They may also authorize the directors to fix the number of shares in and determine the designation, rights, privileges, restrictions, and conditions attaching to the shares of each series, subject to the articles. The most common form of designating a series of a class of shares is Series A, Series B, or Series 1, Series 2, etc.

7. **Special Provisions Attaching to Shares** Set out any rights, privileges, restrictions, and conditions attaching to each class of shares, as well as the directors' authority with respect to any class of shares issued in series, if appropriate.

8. **Restrictions Re Transfer of Shares** Include any restrictions on the issue, transfer, or ownership of any class of shares, if appropriate.

9. **Other Provisions** Describe any other provisions; if there are none, state "nil" or "N/A."

10. **Incorporators** The following information is provided for each incorporator:
    a. first or other given name by which he or she is commonly known,
    b. first letter of other given names,
    c. surname, and
    d. address for service.

When all the directors of a new corporation are office directors, they are also the incorporators. Once the corporation is organized, the first directors resign and transfer their shares to the individuals who are to be permanent shareholders of the corporation.

Execution of Articles of Incorporation

The articles of incorporation are signed in duplicate by each of the incorporators if the articles are to be mailed or delivered in person to the Ministry. The signature on both copies of the articles must be original signatures, not photocopies. Articles that are to be filed electronically do not have to be signed.

Consent to Act as a First Director

A director of a corporation need not be a shareholder as well. When a person, therefore, who is not an incorporator is named in the articles of incorporation as a first director, his or her consent to act as a first director forms part of the articles submitted to the Ministry (Precedent 29.2).

Issuance of Certificate of Incorporation

The completed articles of incorporation (in duplicate); the computer-printed NUANS name-search report; a covering letter giving a contact name, return address, and telephone number; and any supporting documents may be mailed to the CPPSB in Toronto. Under normal circumstances, articles forwarded by mail are processed within five to six weeks of receipt. A special processing service is provided for fast incorporation; this requires personal attendance at the CPPSB. In January 2008, the fee payable to incorporate a corporation in Ontario is $360 if the articles are submitted in person or mailed to the CPPSB in Toronto or submitted in person at the following land registry offices: Barrie, Hamilton, Kingston, Kitchener, London, Oshawa, Ottawa, Peterborough, Sarnia, Sault Ste. Marie, Sudbury, Thunder Bay, Welland, and Windsor. The fee is payable by cheque or money order, made out to the Minister of Finance. Where a cheque is tendered in payment, show the name of the corporation on the face of the cheque.

The fee for electronic filing of articles of incorporation, which provides prompt processing of the articles, is currently $300; however, electronic filing is available only through the PSPs, which charge approximately $100 for their services.

When the fully and correctly completed articles of incorporation and the prescribed fee are received by the CPPSB, the top section of the first page on both copies is endorsed with the day, month, and year of endorsement and the corporation number. The endorsed articles then become the certificate of incorporation, with the corporation coming into legal existence on the endorsement date. One endorsed copy of the articles remains in the CPPSB; the second endorsed copy is returned to the incorporators or their solicitors.

The corporation number on the certificate of incorporation must be used when filing additional material with the CPPSB. If no word name was chosen for the new corporation, the corporation number becomes the number name.

The certificate of incorporation is inserted into the minute book. Copies may be made for the duplicate minute book and for the auditors. A number of notarial copies are usually made as well, as illustrated in Precedent 29.3.

Corporate Supplies

When the articles of incorporation are ready for filing, arrange to secure the following corporate supplies:

1. Share certificates for the classes of shares of the corporation. Many law firms use blank certificates prepared in the office; the blank form may be on paper or recorded in the computer for completion with the necessary personalized information.
2. A minute book, if paper records are to be maintained. Many law firms have a supply of minute books in their corporate stationery inventory, in which case, one can be requisitioned. The cost is then charged to the client as a disbursement.
3. Other registers to record security holders, directors, and officers if paper records are to be maintained and not kept in the minute book.
4. A corporate seal if it is decided that the corporation is to have one. The act does not require a corporation to have a seal, but one is often obtained. Many organizations are accustomed to having documents executed by a corporation under seal.

Any corporate supplies that are not available in the law office may be secured from a legal stationer.

ORGANIZING THE NEW CORPORATION

Subscription for Shares

The shareholders of the new corporation formally subscribe for their shares by executing a subscription for shares (one acceptable form of which is illustrated in Precedent 29.4) and paying the purchase price assessed by the directors in full.

Resignation of Directors

If any of the first directors are to resign, prepare a resignation (Precedent 29.5) for presentation at the first meeting of the shareholders. A consent (Precedent 29.6) is also prepared so that it may be executed by the individual who is to be elected or appointed a permanent director.

By-Laws

Prepare the first general by-laws of the corporation, as well as any special banking and borrowing by-laws that are necessary. These are discussed in Chapter 30.

Share Certificates

Prepare share certificates for each shareholder, together with corporate registers. These are discussed in Chapter 31.

Organizational Meetings

When the certificate of incorporation has been received, the corporation is then a legal entity but has no means to conduct business. The corporation must be organized. The first directors and the shareholders hold organizational meetings, as discussed in Chapter 30.

Initial Return/Notice of Change

An initial return/notice of change form accompanies the certificate of incorporation (Precedent 29.7). It must be completed and filed with the CPPSB, within 60 days of the date of incorporation. The form requires the registered office address and names and addresses for service of directors and officers of the corporation. The information given is kept up to date. Any subsequent changes in the registered office address or officers or directors must be furnished within 15 days of the change; the form is then completed as a notice of change.

Prepare a minimum of two copies of the form; the original may be mailed or delivered to the CPPSB and will be processed in approximately 25 days or may be electronically filed through a PSP and will be processed immediately. There is no fee charged if the notice is mailed or delivered to the CPPSB; however, processing fees are payable to any PSP for electronic filing. The duplicate copy is maintained at the registered office of the corporation.

This information about the corporation is entered into the Ontario Business Information System (ONBIS), which is Ontario's public database of corporate information maintained since June 27, 1992, which may be searched electronically through the services of PSPs.

Terms and Concepts

corporate word or number name
NUANS
preparation and filing of articles of
    incorporation
registered office
first directors
address for service
incorporator
consent to act as a first director

corporate supplies including share
    certificate
minute book
register
corporate seal
share subscription
directors' resignation
general and borrowing by-laws
initial return/notice of change

Review Questions

1. Why must the information on the director for the new corporation indicate whether he or she is a resident Canadian?

2. You are going to be a "first" director of a new corporation. What does this mean?

3. What corporate supplies will be required for a new corporation?

4. What is meant by reference to the "registered" office of a corporation?

5. How do you know what class or classes of shares a new corporation will have?

6. What is meant by a reference to the "authorized capital" of a corporation?

7. Why does the Ministry require a new corporation to file an initial return?

8. Who determines what price will be assessed for the shares of a new corporation?

9. What is received from the Ministry to indicate that the corporation has, in fact, been incorporated? What happens to that document when it is received?

10. You are told you must quote the "corporation number" in certain documents. What is meant by "corporation number," and where can it most easily be found?

PRECEDENTS

Precedent 29.1 Articles of Incorporation

For Ministry Use Only *À l'usage exclusif du ministère*	Ontario Corporation Number *Numéro de la société en Ontario*

Form 1
Business
Corporations
Act

*Formule 1
Loi sur les
sociétés par
actions*

ARTICLES OF INCORPORATION
STATUTS CONSTITUTIFS

1. The name of the corporation is: (Set out in BLOCK CAPITAL LETTERS)
Dénomination sociale de la société: (Écrire en LETTRES MAJUSCULES SEULEMENT)

E	A	S	T		H	A	R	D	W	A	R	E		L	I	M	I	T	E	D				

2. The address of the registered office is:
Adresse du siège social:

17 Princess Street South, Suite 2501
(Street & Number or R.R. Number & if Multi-Office Building give Room No.)
(Rue et numéro ou numéro de la R.R. et, s'il s'agit d'un édifice à bureaux, numéro du bureau)

Toronto   ONTARIO   **M 8 Y 3 N 5**
(Name of Municipality or Post Office)   (Postal Code)
(Nom de la municipalité ou du bureau de poste)   *(Code postal)*

3. Number (or minimum and maximum number) of directors is/are:
Nombre (ou nombres minimal et maximal) d'administrateurs:

       minimum/*minimal*   maximum/*maximal*
       one (1)   **ten (10)**

4. The first director(s) is/are:
Premier(s) administrateur(s):

First name, middle names and surname *Prénom, autres Prénoms et nom de famille*	Address for service, giving Street & No. or R.R. No., Municipality, Province, Country and Postal Code *Domicile élu, y compris la rue et le numéro, le numéro de la R.R. ou le nom de la municipalité, la province, le pays et le code postal*	Resident Canadian? Yes or No *Résident canadien?* *Oui/Non*
Christopher W. East	**950 Merton Street** **Toronto, Ontario M4S 2D9**	Yes
Hoaln W. East	**76 Prince Albert Road** **Toronto, Ontario M4R 6N2**	Yes
Lauren M. East	**76 Prince Albert Road** **Toronto, Ontario M4R 6N2**	Yes
Peter T. Grant	**17 Princess Street South** **Toronto, Ontario M8Y 3N5**	Yes

07116 (01/2002)

Source: Do Process Software Ltd.

2

5. Restrictions, if any, on business the corporation may carry on or on powers the corporation may exercise.
   Limites, s'il y a lieu, imposées aux activités commerciales ou aux pouvoirs de la société.

There are no such restrictions on the business the Corporation may carry on or on the powers the Corporation may exercise.

6. The classes and any maximum number of shares that the corporation is authorized to issue:
   Catégories et nombre maximal, s'il y a lieu, d'actions que la société est autorisée à émettre:

1.   An unlimited number of Common shares.

07116 (01/2002)

Source: Do Process Software Ltd.

3

7. Rights, privileges, restrictions and conditions (if any) attaching to each class of shares and directors authority with respect to any class of shares which may be issued in series:
Droits, privilèges, restrictions et conditions, s'il y a lieu, rattachés à chaque catégorie d'actions et pouvoirs des administrateurs relatifs à chaque catégorie d'actions qui peut être émise en série:

Not Applicable

07116 (01/2002)

Source: Do Process Software Ltd.

4

8. The issue, transfer or ownership of shares is / is not restricted and the restrictions (if any) are as follows:
L'émission, le transfert ou la propriété d'actions est / n'est pas restreint. Les restrictions, s'il y a lieu, sont les suivantes:

No shares shall be transferred without the consent of the board of directors evidenced by a resolution or by their consent in writing.

07116 (01/2002)

Source: Do Process Software Ltd.

5

9. Other provisions if any:
    Autres dispositions, s'il y a lieu:

(a)   That the board of directors may from time to time, in such amounts and on such terms as it deems expedient:

(i)   borrow money on the credit of the Corporation;

(ii)   issue, reissue, sell or pledge debt obligations (including bonds, debentures, notes or other evidences of indebtedness or guarantee, secured or unsecured) of the Corporation;

(iii)   to the extent permitted by the Business Corporations Act (as from time to time amended) give directly or indirectly financial assistance to any person by means of a loan, a guarantee or otherwise on behalf of the Corporation to secure performance of any present or future indebtedness, liability or obligation of any person; and

(iv)   charge, mortgage, hypothecate, pledge or otherwise create a security interest in all or any of the currently owned or subsequently acquired real or personal, movable or immovable property of the Corporation, franchises and undertaking, to secure any debt obligations or any money borrowed, or other debt or liability of the Corporation.

(b)   To the extent permitted by the Business Corporations Act (as from time to time amended), that the board of directors may from time to time delegate to such one or more of the directors and officers of the Corporation as may be designated by the board all or any of the powers conferred on the board above to such extent and in such manner as the board shall determine at the time of each such delegation.

(c)   That the outstanding securities of the Corporation are beneficially owned, directly or indirectly, by not more than thirty-five persons or companies, exclusive of:

(i)   persons or companies that are, or at the time they last acquired securities of the Corporation were, accredited investors (as defined under applicable Ontario securities laws, as may be amended from time to time); and

(ii)   current or former directors, officers or employees of the Corporation or a corporation, company, syndicate, partnership, trust or unincorporated organization (each, an "Entity") affiliated (as defined under applicable Ontario securities laws, as may be amended from time to time) with the Corporation, or current or former consultants (as defined under applicable Ontario securities laws, as may be amended from time to time), who in each case beneficially own only securities of the Corporation that were issued as compensation by, or under an incentive plan of, the Corporation or an Entity affiliated with the Corporation;

provided that:

(A)   two or more persons who are the joint registered holders of one or more securities of the Corporation shall be counted as one beneficial owner of those securities; and

(B)   an Entity shall be counted as one beneficial owner of the securities of the Corporation unless such Entity has been created or is being used primarily for the purpose of acquiring or holding securities of the Corporation, in which event each

07116 (01/2002)

Source: Do Process Software Ltd.

5A.

9. continued

beneficial owner of an equity interest in the Entity or each beneficiary of the Entity, as the case may be, shall be counted as a separate beneficial owner of those securities of the Corporation.

(d)   That subject to the provisions of the Business Corporations Act, the Corporation shall have a lien on the shares registered in the name of a shareholder who is indebted to the Corporation to the extent of such debt.

(e)   That subject to the provisions of the Business Corporations Act, the Corporation may purchase any of its issued shares.

07116 (01/2002)

Source: Do Process Software Ltd.

6

10. The names and addresses of the incorporators are:
   Noms et adresses des fondateurs:

First name, middle names and surname or corporate name *Prénom, autres prénoms et nom de famille ou dénomination sociale*	Full address for service or address of registered office or of principal place of business giving street & No. or R.R. No., municipality and postal code *Domicile élu au complet, adresse du siège social ou adresse de l'établissement principal, y compris la rue et le numéro ou le numéro de la R.R., le nom de la municipalité et le code postal*
Christopher W. East	**950 Merton Street** **Toronto, Ontario M4S 2D9**
Hoaln W. East	**76 Prince Albert Road** **Toronto, Ontario M4R 6N2**
Peter T. Grant	**17 Princess Street South** **Toronto, Ontario M8Y 3N5**

These articles are signed in duplicate.
Les présents statuts sont signés en double exemplaire.

Signatures of incorporator(s)/ *Signatures des fondateurs*

Christopher W. East   **Hoaln W. East**

Peter T. Grant

07116 (01/2002)

Source: Do Process Software Ltd.

Form 2
Business
Corporations
Act

*Formule 2
Loi sur les
sociétés par
actions*

CONSENT TO ACT AS A FIRST DIRECTOR
CONSENTEMENT DU PREMIER ADMINISTRATEUR

I,/Je soussigné(e), **LAUREN M. EAST**

(First name, middle names and surname)
(Prénom, autres Prénoms et nom de famille)

address for service
domicile élu

76 PRINCE ALBERT ROAD TORONTO, ONTARIO M4R 6N2

(Street & No. or R.R. No., Municipality, Province, Country & Postal Code)
(Rue et numéro, ou numéro de la R.R., nom de la municipalité, province, pays et code postal)

hereby consent to act as a first director of
accepte par la présente de devenir premier administrateur de

EAST HARDWARE LIMITED

(Name of Corporation)
(Dénomination sociale de la société)

(Signature of the Consenting Person)
(Signature de l'acceptant)

07117 (06/01)

Source: Do Process Software Ltd.

C A N A D A   )

)   **TO ALL WHOM THESE PRESENTS**

PROVINCE OF ONTARIO)

)   **MAY COME, BE SEEN OR KNOWN**

        To Wit   )

      I, PETER THOMAS GRANT, a Notary Public, in and for the Province of

Ontario, by Royal Authority duly appointed, residing at the City of Toronto, in the said

Province, **DO CERTIFY AND ATTEST** that the paper-writing hereto annexed is a true

copy of a document produced and shown to me from the custody of Hill, Johnston &

Grant and purporting to be a certificate of incorporation granted to East Hardware Limited

dated the 1st day of August, 20__x, the said copy having been compared by me with the

said original document, an act whereof being requested I have granted under my notarial

form and seal of office to serve and avail as occasion shall or may require.

      IN TESTIMONY WHEREOF I have hereto subscribed my name and affixed

my notarial seal of office at the City of Toronto, this   day of August, 20__

_____

A Notary Public
in and for the Province of Ontario

SUBSCRIPTION FOR SHARES

TO: NAME OF CORPORATION

The undersigned hereby subscribes for *(number of shares–in figures only)* shares of the above Corporation at a price of $*(price to be paid per share– in figures only)* per share. Attached hereto is a cheque payable to the above Corporation in full payment of the purchase price therefor. The shares are to be registered in the name of the undersigned.

_____
Name of individual

RESIGNATION

TO: **NAME OF CORPORATION**

AND TO: the directors thereof
(if resignation of a first director during initial organization of the corporation then the resignation is addressed to and accepted by the shareholders)

I hereby tender my resignation as a director of the above Corporation to take effect upon acceptance by the board (*or* the shareholders *or* to take effect upon the adjournment of the meeting of directors to be held on the day of   , 20__).

DATED the   day of   , 20__

_____
Name of individual

<u>**CONSENT TO ACT AS DIRECTOR**</u>

TO: **EAST HARDWARE LIMITED**

AND TO: **the directors thereof**

       I, THE UNDERSIGNED, hereby:

(i)   consent to being elected and to acting as director of the above Corporation, such consent to take effect immediately and to continue in effect until I give written notice to the Corporation revoking such consent or until I otherwise cease to be a director of the Corporation;

(ii)   consent to the holding of meetings of directors or of committees of directors by means of such telephone, electronic or other communication facilities as permit all persons participating in the meetings to communicate with each other simultaneously and instantaneously; and

(iii)   certify that I am a resident Canadian within the meaning of the *Business Corporations Act* (Ontario) and that I shall notify the Corporation forthwith in the event of a change in such status.

       DATED the 1st day of August, 20__.

                         _____

                          CHRISTOPHER W. EAST

                               950 Merton Street

                              Toronto ON M4S 2D9

                   ****

"Resident Canadian" is defined under the *Business Corporations Act* (Ontario) as an individual who is:

(a)   a Canadian citizen ordinarily resident in Canada;

(b)   a Canadian citizen not ordinarily resident in Canada who is a member of a prescribed class of persons; or

(c)   a permanent resident within the meaning of the *Immigration Act* (Canada) and ordinarily resident in Canada.

Ontario

Ministry of Consumer and Business Services	Ministère des Services aux consommateurs et aux entreprises	Companies and Personal Property Security Branch 393 University Ave Suite 200 Toronto ON M5G 2M2	Direction des compagnies et des sûretés mobilières 393 av., University, bureau 200 Toronto ON M5G 2M2

For Ministry Use Only
À l'usage du ministère seulement
Page/Page **1** of/de _____

Form 1 – Ontario Corporation
Formule 1 – Personnes morales de l'Ontario

Initial Return/Notice of Change/
Rapport initial/Avis de modification
Corporation Information Act/*Loi sur les renseignements exigés des personnes morales*

1.

	Notice of Change
	Initial Return Rapport initial / Avis de modification
Business Corporation/ Société par actions	**X** ☐
Not-For-Profit Corporation/ Personne morale sans but lucratif	☐ ☐

Please type or print all information in block capital letters using black ink.
Prière de dactylographier les renseignements ou de les écrire en caractères d'imprimerie à l'encre noire.

2. Ontario Corporation Number
Numéro matricule de la personne morale en Ontario

3. Date of Incorporation or Amalgamation/
Date de constitution ou fusion

Year/Année	Month/Mois	Day/Jour

For Ministry Use Only
À l'usage du ministère seulement

4. Corporation Name Including Punctuation/Raison sociale de la personne morale, y compris la ponctuation

EAST HARDWARE LIMITED

5. Address of Registered or Head Office/Adresse du siège social
c/o / a/s

For Ministry Use Only
À l'usage du ministère seulement

Street No./N° civique	Street Name/Nom de la rue	Suite/Bureau
17	**PRINCESS STREET SOUTH**	**2501**

Street Name (cont'd)/Nom de la rue (suite)

City/Town/Ville
TORONTO   **ONTARIO, CANADA**

Postal Code/Code postal
M8Y 3N5

6. Mailing Address/Adresse postale

X Same as Registered or Head Office/
Même que siège social

Street No./N° civique

☐ Not Applicable/
Ne s'applique pas

Street Name/Nom de la rue   Suite/Bureau

Street Name (cont'd)/Nom de la rue (suite)

City/Town/Ville

Province, State/Province, État   Country/Pays   Postal Code/Code postal

7. Language of Preference/Langue préférée

English - Anglais **X**   French - Français ☐

8. Information on Directors/Officers must be completed on Schedule A as requested. If additional space is required, photocopy Schedule A./**Les renseignements sur les administrateurs ou les dirigeants doivent être fournis dans l'Annexe A, tel que demandé.** Si vous avez besoin de plus d'espace, vous pouvez photocopier l'Annexe A.

Number of Schedule A(s) submitted/Nombre d'Annexes A présentées   **3**   (At least one Schedule A must be submitted/Au moins une Annexe A doit être présentée)

9. (Print or type name in full of the person authorizing filing / Dactylographier ou inscrire le prénom et le nom en caractères d'imprimerie de la personne qui autorise l'enregistrement)

I/Je   **PETER T. GRANT**

Check appropriate box
Cocher la case pertinente

D) ☐ Director/Administrateur

certify that the information set out herein, is true and correct.
atteste que les renseignements précités sont véridiques et exacts.

O) ☐ Officer/Dirigeant

P) **X** Other individual having knowledge of the affairs of the Corporation/Autre personne ayant connaissance des activités de la personne morale

NOTE/REMARQUE: Sections 13 and 14 of the **Corporations Information Act** provide penalties for making false or misleading statements or omissions. Les articles 13 et 14 de la **Loi sur les renseignements exigés des personnes morales** prévoient des peines en cas de déclaration fausse ou trompeuse, ou d'omission.

Source: Do Process Software Ltd.

Form 1 – Ontario Corporation/Formule 1 – Personnes morales de l'Ontario
Schedule A/Annexe A

For Ministry Use Only
À l'usage du ministère seulement
Page/Page _____ of/de _____

Please type or print all information in block capital letters using black ink.
Prière de dactylographier les renseignements ou de les écrire en caractères d'imprimerie à l'encre noire.

Ontario Corporation Number
Numéro matricule de la personne morale en Ontario

Date of Incorporation or Amalgamation
Date de constitution ou fusion

Year/Année Month/Mois Day/Jour

DIRECTOR / OFFICER INFORMATION – RENSEIGNEMENTS RELATIFS AUX ADMINISTRATEURS/DIRIGEANTS
Full Name and Address for Service/Nom et domicile élu

Last Name/Nom de famille: **EAST**
First Name/Prénom: **CHRISTOPHER**
Middle Names/Autres prénoms: **W.**

Street Number/Numéro civique: **950**
Suite/Bureau:

Street Name/Nom de la rue: **MERTON STREET**

Street Name (cont'd)/Nom de la rue (suite):

City/Town/Ville: **TORONTO**

Province, State/Province, État: **ONTARIO**
Country/Pays: **CANADA**
Postal Code/Code postal: **M4S 2D9**

*OTHER TITLES (Please Specify)
*AUTRES TITRES (Veuillez préciser)

Chair / Président du conseil
Chair Person / Président du conseil
Chairman / Président du conseil
Chairwoman / Présidente du conseil
Vice-Chair / Vice-président du conseil
Vice-President / Vice-président
Assistant Secretary / Secrétaire adjoint
Assistant Treasurer / Trésorier adjoint
Chief Manager / Directeur exécutif
Executive Director / Directeur administratif
Managing Director / Administrateur délégué
Chief Executive Officer / Directeur général
Chief Financial Officer / Agent en chef des finances
Chief Information Officer / Directeur général de l'information
Chief Operating Officer / Administrateur en chef des opérations
Chief Administrative Officer / Directeur général de l'administration
Comptroller / Contrôleur
Authorized Signing Officer / Signataire autorisé
Other (Untitled) / Autre (sans titre)

Director Information/Renseignements relatifs aux administrateurs

Resident Canadian/Résident canadien: **X** YES/OUI ___ NO/NON
(Resident Canadian applies to directors of business corporations only.)/
(Résident canadien ne s'applique qu'aux administrateurs de sociétés par actions)

Date Elected/Date d'élection: Year/Année **2007** Month/Mois **08** Day/Jour **01**
Date Ceased/Date de cessation: Year/Année Month/Mois Day/Jour

Officer Information/Renseignements relatifs aux dirigeants

	PRESIDENT/PRÉSIDENT Year/Année Month/Mois Day/Jour	SECRETARY/SECRÉTAIRE Year/Année Month/Mois Day/Jour	TREASURER/TRÉSORIER Year/Année Month/Mois Day/Jour	GENERAL MANAGER/ DIRECTEUR GÉNÉRAL Year/Année Month/Mois Day/Jour	*OTHER/AUTRE Year/Année Month/Mois Day/Jour
Date Appointed/Date de nomination				2007 08 01	
Date Ceased/Date de cessation					

DIRECTOR / OFFICER INFORMATION – RENSEIGNEMENTS RELATIFS AUX ADMINISTRATEURS/DIRIGEANTS
Full Name and Address for Service/Nom et domicile élu

Last Name/Nom de famille: **EAST**
First Name/Prénom: **HOALN**
Middle Names/Autres prénoms: **W.**

Street Number/Numéro civique: **76**
Suite/Bureau:

Street Name/Nom de la rue: **PRINCE ALBERT ROAD**

Street Name (cont'd)/Nom de la rue (suite):

City/Town/Ville: **TORONTO**

Province, State/Province, État: **ONTARIO**
Country/Pays: **CANADA**
Postal Code/Code postal: **M4R 6N2**

*OTHER TITLES (Please Specify)
*AUTRES TITRES (Veuillez préciser)

Chair / Président du conseil
Chair Person / Président du conseil
Chairman / Président du conseil
Chairwoman / Présidente du conseil
Vice-Chair / Vice-président du conseil
Vice-President / Vice-président
Assistant Secretary / Secrétaire adjoint
Assistant Treasurer / Trésorier adjoint
Chief Manager / Directeur exécutif
Executive Director / Directeur administratif
Managing Director / Administrateur délégué
Chief Executive Officer / Directeur général
Chief Financial Officer / Agent en chef des finances
Chief Information Officer / Directeur général de l'information
Chief Operating Officer / Administrateur en chef des opérations
Chief Administrative Officer / Directeur général de l'administration
Comptroller / Contrôleur
Authorized Signing Officer / Signataire autorisé
Other (Untitled) / Autre (sans titre)

Director Information/Renseignements relatifs aux administrateurs

Resident Canadian/Résident canadien: **X** YES/OUI ___ NO/NON
(Resident Canadian applies to directors of business corporations only.)/
(Résident canadien ne s'applique qu'aux administrateurs de sociétés par actions)

Date Elected/Date d'élection: Year/Année **2007** Month/Mois **08** Day/Jour **01**
Date Ceased/Date de cessation: Year/Année Month/Mois Day/Jour

Officer Information/Renseignements relatifs aux dirigeants

	PRESIDENT/PRÉSIDENT Year/Année Month/Mois Day/Jour	SECRETARY/SECRÉTAIRE Year/Année Month/Mois Day/Jour	TREASURER/TRÉSORIER Year/Année Month/Mois Day/Jour	GENERAL MANAGER/ DIRECTEUR GÉNÉRAL Year/Année Month/Mois Day/Jour	*OTHER/AUTRE Year/Année Month/Mois Day/Jour
Date Appointed/Date de nomination	2007 08 01				
Date Ceased/Date de cessation					

07200 (03/2002)

Source: Do Process Software Ltd.

CHAPTER 30

Corporate By-Laws, Meetings, Minutes, and Resolutions

OBJECTIVES:

- Identify and demonstrate an understanding of the organizational by-laws of a corporation

- Describe the two methods by which directors and shareholders conduct corporate business

- Demonstrate an understanding of the procedures required for corporate meetings

- Use legal precedents to prepare corporate by-laws, minutes, and resolutions

As discussed in Chapter 28, an Ontario corporation acts through its directors and shareholders, according to the procedures set out in its by-laws, and conducts the business of the corporation by meetings or in writing by resolutions. The by-laws and the decisions of the directors and shareholders are formally recorded for inclusion in the minute book.

BY-LAWS

By-laws are the permanent rules or regulations that govern the internal affairs of a corporation. They set out, among other things, the corporation's fiscal year-end; the procedures to be followed in calling and holding meetings of directors and shareholders; the number, qualifications, election, and terms of office of directors; and the officers of the corporation, their duties, and their authority to sign on behalf of the corporation.

As each by-law is prepared, it is identified by number (for example, By-Law No. 1, By-Law No. 2, and so on). A by-law is made by the directors of a corporation and is effective until the next meeting of shareholders, when it must be confirmed, rejected, or amended to remain in effect.

Any by-law or other action of a corporation that has only one shareholder that is consented to at any time during the life of the corporation by the signature of such shareholder is as valid and effective as if it were passed at a meeting of shareholders.

By-Law No. 1 contains the general rules for governing the internal affairs of the corporation and is usually quite lengthy. Most law firms and their clients use a standard form of by-law and insert just the variable information as required. Precedents 30.1 A through E illustrate page 1 and the pages of by-law that require the variable information (which has been bolded for reference purposes only) and the signatory page of a by-law passed at meetings of the directors and shareholders; Precedent 30.2 illustrates the format for the signatory page of a by-law consented to in writing by all the directors and shareholders.

By-Law No. 2 is often referred to as the *borrowing by-law*. It is not required by statute because directors have the power to conduct the banking and borrowing transactions of a corporation. However, the bank with which the corporation deals may require either completion of a standard by-law, as illustrated in Precedent 30.2, or their own form of by-law, which deals with borrowing. Alternatively, a certificate executed by the secretary may state that the by-laws of the corporation contain no restrictions on borrowing.

Banking forms must be prepared and executed for the corporation to conduct business. These forms were traditionally prepared by the law firms; however, most banks now prepare these forms electronically and then provide a copy to the corporation to insert in the minute book. These forms usually include the following:

1. a banking resolution (which includes a certificate certifying that the by-laws of the corporation do not restrict the power of the corporation to borrow money or carry out other financial dealings, such as mortgaging, property, and so on), which may be used in lieu of By-Law No. 2

2. a list of officers and directors of the corporation
3. an operation and verification of account agreement
4. a signature card bearing the signature of the signing officers of the corporation

Note that the names of the offices (titles) that have authority to deal with the bank, rather than the names of those who hold the offices, are used in these documents. If the individuals who fill those offices change, only a new list of officers and directors and signature card are required instead of a new banking resolution.

PREPARING BY-LAWS

The general by-laws of a new corporation are prepared by any of the methods discussed in Chapter 2. Legal stationers have printed by-laws that can be completed with the personalized information for the new corporation. Frequently, law firms have prepared printed specimen by-laws that may be completed, but by-laws are more frequently created from commercial software (such as Fast Company) or recorded for recall and completion or modification as required; the necessary number of copies can be either printed or photocopied.

Paper

Because by-laws form part of the corporate records and are maintained in the minute book, the original is prepared on minute-book paper, which is usually of slightly heavier weight and higher quality than standard paper. Any additional copies that may be required may be photocopied on standard paper.

Heading

The form of heading of by-laws varies with the individual law office. The heading shows the by-law number and the name of the corporation.

Body

In many law offices, By-Law No. 1 begins with a definition of the terms used throughout the by-law. The individual items are usually divided into a number of sections, often referred to as articles. Each section is identified by a general heading and sometimes by an article number. It may be divided into a number of related subsections, each of which is numbered either consecutively (1, 2, 3, and so on, throughout the entire by-law) or by article number and consecutive paragraph number (5.01, 5.02, and so on).

Ending

When the by-laws are enacted at a meeting of directors and subsequently confirmed at a meeting of shareholders, the president and secretary of the corporation date and sign them (Precedent 30.2). If the by-laws are enacted by the directors and confirmed by the shareholders by consent in writing, end the by-laws as shown in Precedent 30.2.

Note these points when preparing by-laws:

1. Show the by-law number in capital letters and figures, centred and underscored.
2. Single space the body of the by-laws, unless the law firm prefers that they be double spaced.
3. Capitalize the first word or group of words of an unnumbered paragraph; bold-face type is often used for the introductory words.
4. Show article headings in capital letters and centred. Underscoring and bolding are optional.
5. Number each item in an article. Item numbers may run sequentially from 1 throughout the entire by-law, or each article may be identified by an article number and an item number, commencing at 1 in each instance.
6. Show each item heading on the same line as the item number, commencing at the normal paragraph indentation, either in all capital letters with no underscoring or in uppercase and lowercase and underscored.

CERTIFIED COPY OF A BY-LAW

Sometimes, the secretary of the corporation must provide a certified copy of a by-law. Photocopy the actual by-law and include the following paragraph at the bottom of the page:

> **CERTIFIED** to be a true copy of By-Law No. 2 of EAST HARDWARE LIMITED which was enacted by all of the directors of the Corporation on the 2nd day of August, 20__ and subsequently confirmed by all the shareholders of the Corporation on the 2nd day of August, 20__, as set forth in the minute book of the Corporation, which said by-law has not been amended and is now in full force and effect.
>
> **DATED** at Toronto on August 2, 20__.
>
> _____ (c/s)
> Secretary

If the corporation has one, affix the corporate seal over the signature of the secretary. Alternatively, the by-law may be prepared on plain paper and the above certification included at the end of the by-law.

MEETINGS

A fully organized and active corporation usually holds two types of meetings during the business year: directors' meetings and the annual meeting of shareholders. General meetings of shareholders may also be called for a specific purpose, such as amendment to the articles of incorporation, which requires the passing of a special resolution. (The term "special general meeting" is sometimes used to distinguish the meeting from an annual meeting of shareholders.)

Governing Procedure

The by-laws of the corporation set out the procedure followed at each meeting (for example, how notices of meetings are to be given, how the chair is to be elected, and what number of directors or shareholders must be present to constitute a quorum).

Place of Meeting

Shareholders' meetings are held in a room large enough to accommodate all the shareholders at such place in or outside Ontario as the directors determine. Large corporations frequently use meeting rooms in a hotel; smaller corporations usually use their registered office.

Directors' meetings are held at the registered office of the corporation (which may be the law firm's offices), unless the by-laws provide that meetings may be held elsewhere. In any financial year of the corporation, a majority of the meetings of directors must be held within Canada.

If the by-laws permit it and all directors consent, directors' meetings may be held by conference telephone or any other form of electronic communication that permits all participants to hear each other. If a majority of the directors participating are present in Canada, the meeting is deemed to be held in Canada.

First Meetings of a Corporation

Once the certificate of incorporation is received, the first directors and the shareholders must organize the corporation. They may hold meetings, or they may make organizational decisions by way of resolutions consented to in writing by all the directors and shareholders. A corporation is normally organized by holding

1. a meeting of first directors,
2. a meeting of shareholders, and
3. a meeting of permanent directors (if the first directors are office directors who attend the meeting of the first directors and then submit their resignations to the meeting of shareholders).

Meeting of First Directors
To organize a new corporation, the first directors pass resolutions to

1. enact a general by-law dealing with the general operation of the corporation (By-Law No. 1);
2. enact a by-law dealing specifically with borrowing (By-Law No. 2) if such a by-law is required by the bank with which the corporation will conduct its business affairs;
3. adopt forms of security certificates and corporate records; for most new corporations, the security will be share certificates;
4. authorize the issue of securities;
5. appoint officers;
6. appoint one or more auditors, if necessary, to hold office until the first annual or special meeting of shareholders;

7. make banking arrangements, which includes passing the banking resolution required by the bank with which the corporation will conduct its business affairs;
8. approve and adopt a form of corporate seal, if the corporation is to have such a seal; and
9. transact any other business.

The *Business Corporations Act* (Ontario) does not stipulate the order in which these resolutions are to be passed; the order varies from office to office.

First Meeting of Shareholders

At their first meeting, the shareholders pass resolutions to

1. confirm the general By-Law No. 1;
2. confirm the borrowing By-Law No. 2, if there is a borrowing by-law;
3. appoint an auditor, if necessary;
4. accept the resignation of the first directors, if they are not the permanent directors of the corporation;
5. appoint permanent directors if the first directors resign; and
6. approve any transfer of shares from first directors to other shareholders if the by-laws of the corporation give the shareholders this authority.

Meeting of Permanent Directors When First Directors Resign

If the first directors of a corporation resign and permanent directors are appointed, the permanent directors meet to pass resolutions to

1. appoint permanent officers;
2. approve any transfer of shares from first directors to other shareholders if the by-laws require the directors' approval; and
3. deal with any other matters.

If the shareholders have authorized the directors to determine the number of directors within a flexible number, the directors may pass such a resolution at a meeting held after the organizational meetings of the first directors and the shareholders.

Shareholders' Meetings

A corporation must hold an annual meeting of its shareholders not less than 18 months after its incorporation and thereafter at least every 15 months. Use the tickler system to remind the lawyer of the dates; a tickler date one month before the required annual meeting date is appropriate.

The agenda for an annual meeting of shareholders generally follows a pattern: the financial statements are approved; auditors or accountants are appointed to hold office until the next annual meeting of shareholders; directors are elected to hold office for the following year or until their successors are duly elected or appointed; and the by-laws, resolutions, contracts, acts, and proceedings taken by the board of directors since the last annual meeting of shareholders are approved and confirmed.

Special meetings of shareholders are called to deal either with special resolutions that must be passed by the shareholders or with other corporate business requiring immediate shareholder approval.

Notice of Meeting

The by-laws outline the number of days' notice a director or shareholder should receive of the time and place of a meeting and when notice may be waived. Directors and the auditor (if the corporation has appointed an auditor) receive notice of shareholders' meetings. The *Business Corporations Act* (Ontario) states that notice of a meeting of shareholders must be sent not less than 21 days before the meeting in the case of an offering corporation and not less than 10 days in the case of any other corporation. (In either case, it must not be sent more than 50 days before the meeting.) For shareholders, the notice is sent to shareholders of record, that is, shareholders registered on the corporate records on a date determined by the directors. This date is frequently the day preceding the date on which notice must be given of the meeting.

A notice of meeting of shareholders (Precedent 30.3) outlines not only the time and place of the meeting but also the nature of the business to be considered. A notice of a special meeting of shareholders indicates the nature of the special business in sufficient detail to allow the shareholder to form a reasoned judgment on the matter. The text of any special resolution or by-law to be considered at the meeting is included with the notice.

A notice of meeting may be delivered personally or sent by prepaid mail, addressed to the directors or shareholders at their latest addresses, as shown in the corporate records. A notice that is mailed is deemed to have been received on the fifth day after mailing.

Proxy

The by-laws usually provide that a shareholder who cannot attend a meeting may appoint someone as a proxy to exercise his or her voting rights. To appoint a proxy, the shareholder executes the proxy form enclosed with the notice of meeting. The by-laws specify the form of proxy. Precedent 30.4 illustrates a proxy for a non-offering corporation. (Note that the by-laws of some corporations may require a witness to the signature.)

MINUTES

The **minutes** are a summary of what was decided and how such decisions were made at a directors' or shareholders' meeting. Minutes usually include the following details: date, time, place, and nature of the meeting; the names of persons present (or the number present if the meeting was a very large one); the names of the chair and secretary; and the text of all resolutions passed at the meeting.

The shareholders or directors may meet and confirm and pass resolutions; their decisions are recorded in the form of minutes. However, the directors and shareholders may also consult each other by conference telephone or other acceptable means of electronic communication; their decisions are also recorded in the form of minutes. The directors and shareholders of a corporation may also make decisions by consenting in writing to resolutions or by-laws, and such consents are considered "minutes" for the purposes of recording the acts of the corporation.

Minutes are kept in the minute book under the appropriate section: directors' minutes or shareholders' minutes.

FORMAT OF MINUTES

If you are preparing minutes for a corporation that has been incorporated for some time, consult the minute book and follow the format used for minutes of earlier meetings. If, however, minutes are being prepared for a meeting of a new corporation, you may have the responsibility to establish the format to be followed or may be expected to follow the format adopted by the law firm for all minutes prepared in that office. Precedents 30.5 and 30.6 illustrate two formats for minutes.

Heading

The heading usually sets out the name of the corporation, the type of meeting, and the time and place of the meeting. It may commence flush with the left margin, may be indented on the first line, or may appear on the right side of the page, depending on the style of the minutes used. Use one of these formats for the minutes:

1. centred headings in capital letters (Precedent 30.5)
2. shoulder headings in either capital or regular type (Precedent 30.6)

Follow the preference of your law firm or lawyer.

Preparation Guide for Minutes

When preparing minutes, follow these practices:

1. Single or double space the minutes, depending on the preference of the law office or the individual lawyer.
2. Indent paragraphs when shoulder or centred headings are used.
3. Underscore or bold shoulder or centred headings.
4. Show the words **IT WAS RESOLVED** or **BE IT RESOLVED** in bold capital letters in the body of the minutes.

Ending

Meetings of a corporation end when all the business on the agenda has been dealt with. The term "adjourned" is used if a meeting is to be reconvened; if the meeting is concluded, it is said to be terminated.

The minutes are ended with the statement that the meeting was officially adjourned or terminated, followed by signature lines for the chair and secretary. The office of the person signing is shown beneath each line. If the directors or shareholders waived notice of the meeting, a statement appears beneath the signatures of the chair and secretary, as shown in Precedent 30.7. Include a signature line for each director or shareholder (as appropriate) with his or her name beneath the line. If possible, the paragraph dealing with the termination or adjournment of the meeting should not commence a new page in the minutes; the paragraph dealing with the waiver of notice may, if necessary, appear on a separate page bearing the next consecutive page number.

Numbering Pages

In addition to numbering the individual pages that make up each set of minutes of meetings of the shareholders or directors, it is common practice to number all pages of the minute book in a consecutive numbering pattern. This permits reference to other records and to the exact page of the minutes where some specific point is recorded.

For example, page 4 of the minutes of a shareholders' meeting may be the 67th page of the minutes in the shareholders' minute book. To number this page, *4* is shown at the top of the page and centred. In the upper right-hand corner, approximately one or two spaces from the top of the page and flush with the right-hand margin, show *67*. Use this last figure when the *Minute-Book Folio* or *M.B. Folio* number is required.

Signing and Approval

The secretary of the corporation usually signs the minutes as soon as they are prepared. This is not the secretary who prepares them but the officer in the corporation who holds the position of secretary.

The minutes of the meeting are presented at the next meeting for approval; when approved, they are signed by the chair to indicate that they correctly record the decisions made.

Where a meeting of directors has been held by conference telephone or another acceptable means of communication, the minutes are either signed by the chair and secretary or consented to by having all directors sign a notice at the end of the minutes.

Correction

Signed minutes cannot be altered—even to correct errors—unless the alterations are authorized at a subsequent meeting. The page is not removed from the minute book, nor is the error erased; instead, the errors are neatly struck out in ink, and the corrections are made in ink. The corrections are then initialled by the person who signed as chair when the original minutes were approved.

Number of Copies

The original is on minute-book paper and is inserted into the appropriate section of the minute book. Copies may also be made for any duplicate minute book or the auditor if required. The copies may also be on minute-book paper but more often are photocopied onto standard paper.

RESOLUTIONS

As discussed earlier in this chapter, if all the directors or shareholders of a corporation consent in writing to a resolution, the resolution is as effective as if it had been passed at a meeting. Precedents 30.8 and 30.9 illustrate acceptable formats for resolutions consented to in writing by either all directors or all shareholders. Resolutions passed by the consent in writing of the director(s) or shareholder(s) of a corporation are inserted into the appropriate minute section of the minute book.

Format

If you are preparing resolutions for a corporation that has been incorporated for some time, follow the format already used in the minute book. If the corporation is new, however, follow either the practice of the law office or the format illustrated in Precedents 30.8 and 30.9.

The heading usually names the corporation and states whether the resolutions are of directors or of shareholders. The resolutions being approved are then set out and are usually numbered consecutively when there are two or more.

Preparation Guide for Resolutions

When preparing resolutions, follow these practices:

1. Single space the resolutions, unless the law office prefers that they be double spaced.
2. Double or triple space between each numbered resolution, depending on the spacing required to complete them.
3. Underscore or bold the heading for each individual resolution if a heading is used.

Ending

Resolutions consented to in writing usually end with a paragraph indicating the approval of the directors or shareholders (Precedents 30.8 and 30.9) or may appear above the resolution(s), as shown in Precedent 30.10). Include appropriate signature lines; the name of each individual is shown beneath the line on which he or she will sign.

The date used when resolutions are consented to in writing is the date on which the last person required to consent signs the resolution.

Single Director or Shareholder

A corporation may be incorporated by a single shareholder or have a single director. He or she acts by way of resolution consented to in writing. Modify the format used when there are a number of directors or shareholders; references to *all of the directors* or *all of the shareholders* become *the sole director* or *the sole shareholder*, respectively. Only one signature line is required (Precedent 30.10).

Certified Copy of a Resolution

Sometimes, it is necessary for the secretary of the corporation to provide a certified copy of a resolution passed or consented to by the directors or shareholders. For a certified copy of a resolution consented to by all the directors and/or shareholders, photocopy or key the actual resolution and then insert the paragraph beneath:

<u>CERTIFICATE</u>

CERTIFIED to be a true copy of a resolution of EAST HARDWARE LIMITED consented to by the signatures of all of the directors (and/or shareholders) of the Corporation and dated the 2nd day of August, 20__, as set forth in the minute book of the Corporation, which said resolution has not been amended and is now in full force and effect.

DATED at Toronto on December 13, 20__.

_____ (c/s)
Secretary

Terms and Concepts

by-law	first meeting of directors and shareholders
By-Law No. 1	annual meeting of shareholders
By-Law No. 2	notice of meeting
borrowing by-law	proxy
banking forms	minute preparation
by-law preparation guidelines	M.B. Folio
certified copy	signing and correction of minutes
corporate meetings	preparation and signing of resolutions
place of meeting	certified copy of a resolution

Review Questions

1. What are the purpose of by-laws of the corporation, and how may they be enacted?
2. What are the two methods by which directors and shareholders conduct the business of a corporation?
3. What circumstances must exist to permit a meeting by conference telephone?
4. Where are meetings of shareholders and of directors held?
5. When is it necessary to hold annual meetings of shareholders?
6. Where could you find the corporation's requirements for the number of days' notice required to be given of a meeting of shareholders or of directors?
7. What is meant by a "proxy"?
8. What is meant by the term "M.B. Folio"?
9. If an error is found in minutes when they are presented for approval at the next meeting, how is such an error connected?
10. What is the effective date of a resolution consented to in writing?

BY-LAW NO. 1

A by-law relating generally to the conduct
of the business and affairs of

EAST HARDWARE LIMITED

CONTENTS

BE IT ENACTED as a by-law of EAST HARDWARE LIMITED as follows:

1. INTERPRETATION

1.1   <u>Definitions</u> - In this by-law and all other by-laws and resolutions of the Corporation, unless the context otherwise requires:

"Act" means the *Business Corporations Act* (Ontario), including the Regulations made pursuant thereto, and any statute or regulations substituted therefor, as amended from time to time;

"appoint" includes "elect", and *vice versa*

"articles" means the Articles of Incorporation and/or other constating documents of the Corporation as amended or restated from time to time;

"board" means the board of directors of the Corporation and *"director"* means a member of the board;

- 3 –

1.2 <u>Corporate Seal</u> - The Corporation may, but need not, have a corporate seal; if adopted, such seal shall be in the form approved from time to time by the board.

1.3 <u>Fiscal Year</u> - Unless and until another date has been effectively determined, the fiscal year or financial year of the Corporation shall end on **December 31st** in each year.

1.4 <u>Execution of Documents</u> - Deeds, transfers, assignments, contracts, obligations and other instruments in writing requiring execution by the Corporation may be signed by the President and the Secretary together*.
Notwithstanding the foregoing, the board may from time to time direct the manner in which and the person or persons by whom a particular document or class of documents shall be executed. Any person authorized to sign any document may affix the corporate seal thereto.

1.5 <u>Banking</u> - All matters pertaining to the banking of the Corporation shall be transacted with such banks, trust companies or other financial organizations as the board may designate or authorize from time to time. All such banking business shall be transacted on behalf of the Corporation pursuant to such agreements, instructions and delegations of powers as may, from time to time, be prescribed by the board.

2. DIRECTORS

2.1 <u>Powers</u> - Subject to the express provisions of a unanimous shareholder agreement, the directors shall manage or supervise the management of the business and affairs of the Corporation.

2.2 <u>Transaction of Business</u> - Business may be transacted by resolutions passed at meetings of directors or committees of directors at which a quorum is present or by resolution in writing, signed by all the directors entitled to vote on that resolution at a meeting of directors or a committee of directors. A copy of every such resolution in writing shall be kept with the minutes of the proceedings of the directors or committee of directors.

2.3 <u>Number</u> - Until changed in accordance with the Act, the board shall consist of that number of directors, being **a minimum of one (1) and a maximum of ten (10),** as determined from time to time by special resolution or, if the special resolution empowers the directors to determine the number, by resolution of the board.

2.4 <u>Resident Canadians</u> - If the board consists of only one director, that director shall be a resident Canadian. If the board consists of two directors, at least one of the two directors shall be a resident Canadian. Except as aforesaid, a majority of the directors of the Corporation shall be resident Canadians.

- 10 -

a)   the nature of that business in sufficient detail to permit the shareholder to form a reasoned judgment thereon; and

b)   the text of any special resolution or by-law to be submitted to the meeting.

In the event of the adjournment of a meeting, notice, if any is required, shall be given in accordance with the provisions of the Act.

2.5   Waiving Notice - A shareholder and any other person entitled to attend a meeting of shareholders may in any manner and at any time waive notice of a meeting of shareholders, and attendance of any such person at a meeting of shareholders is a waiver of notice of the meeting, except where such person attends a meeting for the express purpose of objecting to the transaction of any business on the grounds that the meeting is not lawfully called.

2.6   Persons Entitled to be Present - The only persons entitled to be present at a meeting of shareholders shall be those entitled to vote thereat, the directors and the auditor of the Corporation and such other persons who are entitled or required under any provision of the Act, articles or by-laws of the Corporation to be present at the meeting. Any other person may be admitted only on the invitation of the chairman of the meeting or with the consent of the meeting.

2.7   Quorum - **The holders of a majority of shares entitled to vote at a meeting of shareholders, whether present in person or represented by proxy, constitute a quorum** for the transaction of business at any meeting of shareholders. If a quorum is present at the opening of a meeting of shareholders, the shareholders present may proceed with the business of the meeting even if a quorum is not present throughout the meeting. If the Corporation has only one shareholder, or only one holder of any class or series of shares, the shareholder present in person or by proxy constitutes a meeting.

2.8   Right to Vote - Unless the articles otherwise provide, each share of the Corporation entitles the holder thereof to one vote at a meeting of shareholders.

2.9   Proxies - Every shareholder entitled to vote at a meeting of shareholders may by means of a proxy appoint a proxyholder or one or more alternate proxyholders who need not be shareholders, as the shareholder's nominee to attend and act at the meeting in the manner, to the extent and with the authority conferred by the proxy. A proxy shall be in writing, shall be executed by the shareholder or by his attorney authorized in writing and shall, in all other respects, be in a form which complies with the Act.

2.10   Time for Deposit of Proxies - The Corporation shall recognize a proxy only if it has been deposited with the Corporation and it shall be so deposited before any vote is taken under its authority, or at such earlier time as the board, in compliance with the Act, prescribes and which has been specified in the notice calling the meeting.

- 11 -

2.11   <u>Corporate Shareholders and Associations</u> - As an alternative to depositing a proxy, a body corporate or an association may deposit a certified copy of a resolution of its directors or governing body authorizing an individual to represent it at meetings of shareholders of the Corporation.

2.12   <u>Joint Shareholders</u> - Where two or more persons hold shares jointly, one of those holders present at a meeting of shareholders may in the absence of the others vote the shares, but if two or more of those persons are present, in person or by proxy, they shall vote as one on the shares jointly held by them.

2.13   <u>Votes to Govern</u> - Subject to the Act, the articles, the by-laws and any unanimous shareholder agreement, all questions proposed for the consideration of the shareholders shall be determined by a majority of the votes cast thereon and, in case of an equality of votes, the chairman of the meeting **shall (*or* shall not)** have a second or casting vote.

2.14   <u>Show of Hands</u> - Except where a ballot is demanded as hereafter set out, voting on any question proposed for consideration at a meeting of shareholders shall be by show of hands, and a declaration by the chairman as to whether or not the question or motion has been carried and an entry to that effect in the minutes of the meeting shall, in the absence of evidence to the contrary, be evidence of the fact without proof of the number or proportion of the votes recorded in favour of or against the motion.

2.15   <u>Ballots</u> - For any question proposed for consideration at a meeting of shareholders, either before or after a vote by show of hands has been taken, the chairman, or any shareholder or proxyholder may demand a ballot, in which case the ballot shall be taken in such manner as the chairman directs and the decision of the shareholders on the question shall be determined by the result of such ballot.

2.16   <u>Resolution in Lieu of Meeting</u> - Except where, pursuant to the Act, a written statement is submitted to the Corporation by a director or representations in writing are submitted to the Corporation by an auditor:

   a)   a resolution in writing signed by all the shareholders entitled to vote on that resolution at a meeting of shareholders is as valid as if it had been passed at a meeting of the shareholders; and

   b)   a resolution in writing dealing with all matters required by the Act to be dealt with at a meeting of shareholders, and signed by all the shareholders entitled to vote at that meeting, satisfies all the requirements of the Act relating to that meeting of shareholders.

- 15 -

2.17   Notice to Joint Shareholders - Notice required to be given to a shareholder where two or more persons are registered as joint holders of any share shall be sufficiently given to all of them if given to any one of them.

2.18   Notices Given to Predecessors - Every person who by transfer, death of a shareholder, operation of law or otherwise becomes entitled to shares, is bound by every notice in respect of such shares which was duly given to the registered holder of such shares from whom his title is derived prior to entry of his name and address in the records of the Corporation.

2.19   Waiver of Notice - Any shareholder, proxyholder, director, officer, member of a committee of the board or auditor may waive or abridge the time for any notice required to be given him, and such waiver or abridgement, whether given before or after the meeting or other event of which notice is required to be given shall cure any default in the giving or in the time of such notice, as the case may be. Any such waiver or abridgement shall be in writing except a waiver of notice of a meeting of shareholders or of the board or of a committee of the board, which may be given in any manner.

3.   **EFFECTIVE DATE**

3.1   Effective Date - Subject to its being confirmed by the shareholders, this by-law shall come into force when enacted by the board, subject to the provisions of the Act.

ENACTED by the board this   day of August, 20__

_____
President

_____
Secretary

c/s

CONFIRMED by the shareholders the   day of August, 20__.

_____
Secretary

BY-LAW NO. 2

A by-law respecting the borrowing of money,
the issuing of securities and the securing of liabilities by

EAST HARDWARE LIMITED
(herein called the "Corporation")

BE IT ENACTED as a by-law of the Corporation as follows:

1.   <u>Borrowing Powers</u> - Without limiting the borrowing powers of the Corporation as set forth in the Act, the board may, subject to the articles and any unanimous shareholder agreement, from time to time, on behalf of the Corporation, without the authorization of the shareholders:

   a)   borrow money on the credit of the Corporation;

   b)   issue, re-issue, sell or pledge debt obligations of the Corporation, whether secured or unsecured;

   c)   subject to the Act, give a guarantee on behalf of the Corporation to secure performance of an obligation of any person; and

   d)   mortgage, hypothecate, pledge or otherwise create a security interest in all or any property of the Corporation, owned or subsequently acquired, to secure any obligation of the Corporation.

2.   <u>Delegation of Powers</u> - Subject to the Act, the articles, the by-laws and any unanimous shareholder agreement, the board may, from time to time, delegate any or all of the powers hereinbefore specified, to a director, a committee of directors or one or more officers of the Corporation.

      The foregoing by-law is hereby enacted by the directors of the Corporation as evidenced by the respective signatures hereto of all of the directors of the Corporation in accordance with the provisions of section 129(1) of the *Business Corporations Act* (Ontario).

      DATED the   day of August, 20__.

_____
CHRISTOPHER W. EAST

_____
HOALN W. EAST

_____
LAUREN M. EAST

_____
PETER T. GRANT

- 2 -

In lieu of confirmation at a general meeting of the shareholders, the foregoing by-law is hereby confirmed by all the shareholders of the Corporation entitled to vote at a meeting of shareholders in accordance with the provisions of section 104(1) of the *Business Corporations Act* (Ontario), this 2nd day of August, 2007.

        DATED the   day of August, 20__.

_____
CHRISTOPHER W. EAST

_____
HOALN W. EAST

_____
LAUREN M. EAST

HUMBER PROPERTY SERVICES LIMITED

NOTICE OF ANNUAL MEETING OF SHAREHOLDERS

Notice is hereby given that the annual meeting of the shareholders of Humber Property Services Limited will be held at the registered office of the Corporation, Suite 908, 17 Edward Street, Toronto, Ontario, on Thursday, the 31st day of January, 20__, at the hour of ten o'clock in the forenoon, Toronto time, to:

(a) receive and consider the annual report, the financial statements and the report of the auditor[1];

(b) elect directors;

(c) appoint auditors[1] and authorize the directors to fix their remuneration;

(d) ratify all acts, by-laws and proceedings of the directors and officers since the last annual meeting of shareholders[2]; and

(e) transact such further business as may properly be brought before the meeting or any adjournment thereof.

Shareholders who are unable to attend the meeting in person are requested to date, sign and return in the envelope provided the enclosed form of proxy. To be effective, the completed proxy must be received by the Secretary of the Corporation not less than 48 hours before the time fixed for the meeting.

DATED at Toronto, this 30th day of December, 20__.

By order of the board of directors.

_____
Secretary

_____

[1] *If the Corporation is exempt from the provisions requiring the appointment of auditors, then accountants will report on the financial statements, and accountants will be appointed.*

[2] *This clause is included in the notice, if appropriate; the directors may not have met since the last annual meeting of shareholders.*

P R O X Y

The undersigned shareholder of Humber Property Services Limited hereby appoints

_____ *name of person being appointed* _____ .

proxy, with power of substitution, to attend and vote for and on behalf of the undersigned at the meeting of shareholders of the Corporation to be held on Thursday, the 31st day of January, 20__, and at any adjournment thereof, with full power to the said proxy to waive notice of such meeting on behalf of the undersigned.

DATED the   day of January, 20__.

_____

(Name of person giving proxy)

MINUTES of a meeting of the Board of Directors of **CENTENNIAL CONSULTANTS INC.** held at the registered office of the Corporation, on Monday, the 31st day of December, 20__, at three o'clock in the afternoon.

PRESENT: Sean Devlin   ⎫ *listed in order*
          Marilyn Goldman   ⎬ *of office held*
          Joseph Woleski   ⎬ *or*
          Jennifer Wong   ⎭ *alphabetically*

being all the directors of the Corporation.

CHAIRMAN AND SECRETARY

The President of the Corporation, Seal Devlin, took the chair, and, with the consent of the meeting, Joseph Woleski acted as secretary of the meeting.

NOTICE

The Chairman stated that as all of the directors of the corporation were present in person, no notice of the calling of the meeting was required under the provisions of the Corporation's by-laws and declared the meeting to be properly constituted for the transaction of business.

TRANSFER OF SHARES

ON MOTION duly made, seconded and unanimously carried, **IT WAS RESOLVED** that the following transfers of shares in the capital stock of the Corporation be and the same are hereby approved and consented to:

Transferor	Transferee	No. and Class of Shares
Sarah Adachi	Martin Williamson	5 Common
Stephanie Morsillo	Joseph Woleski	1 Common

MINUTES of a meeting of the Board of Directors of HUMBER PROPERTY SERVICES LIMITED held at Suite 490, 760 Elderwood Blvd. North, Toronto, Ontario, on Monday, the 31st day of December, 20__, at the hour of eleven o'clock in the forenoon.

PRESENT: RONALD CRAIG ANDERSON
                 KYLE MARVYN GATESTONE

being a quorum of the directors of the Corporation.

CHAIRMAN AND SECRETARY

On motion duly made, seconded and unanimously carried, Mr. Anderson acted as Chairman of the meeting, and Mr. Gatestone acted as Secretary of the meeting.

WAIVER OF NOTICE AND CONSENT

The Chairman presented a waiver of notice of the meeting signed by all of the directors of the Corporation which was directed to be annexed to the minutes of this meeting. A quorum being present and all of the directors having waived notice of the meeting, the Chairman declared the meeting regularly constituted for the transaction of business.

FINANCIAL STATEMENTS

The Chairman presented to the meeting the financial statements of the Corporation for the last completed financial year, together with the report thereon of the auditor of the Corporation. After discussion and on motion duly made, seconded and unanimously carried, the following resolution was passed:

BE IT RESOLVED:

That the said financial statements be, and they are hereby approved by the directors of the Corporation, and two directors of the Corporation be, and they are hereby authorized and directed to sign the balance sheet contained in the said financial statements in order to evidence such approval.

ANNUAL MEETING OF SHAREHOLDERS

On motion duly made, seconded and unanimously carried, the following resolution was passed:

That an annual meeting of shareholders of the Corporation be held on Tuesday, the 15th day of January, 20__, at the hour of ten o'clock in the

- 3 -

There being no further business to transact, on motion the meeting was terminated.

_____   _____
                Secretary   Chairman

WE, the undersigned, being all the shareholders of the corporation, do hereby waive notice of the calling of the meeting being held at the above time and place, and we do hereby ratify, approve, confirm and sanction the resolutions passed and business transacted as above set out.

_____   _____
            Mary A. Seinfeldt   Frank Bhaduria

_____
                Joseph Hockley

RESOLUTION OF THE DIRECTORS
OF
EAST HARDWARE LIMITED

R E S O L V E D:

1. <u>By-Laws</u>

   That By-law No. 1, being a general by-law, is hereby made as a by-law of the Corporation.

2. <u>Issue of Shares</u>

   That 300 common shares in the capital of the Corporation be allotted and issued to Hoaln W. East, Christopher W. East, and Lauren M. East pursuant to their subscription for such shares at $100.00 per share, and that the Corporation having received the sum of $30,000.00 in respect of such shares, that the said 300 common shares are hereby declared to be fully paid and non-assessable shares.

3. <u>Form of Share Certificate</u>

   That the form of share certificate for common shares in that capital of the Corporation initialled for identification by the president and attached hereto, is hereby approved.

4. <u>Corporate Seal</u>

   That the corporate seal of the Corporation shall be in the form impressed hereon, until changed by the board.

5. <u>Appointment of Officers</u>

   That the following are hereby appointed officers of the Corporation to hold office during the pleasure of the board, namely:

President	Hoaln W. East
Secretary	Lauren M. East
Treasurer	Christopher M. East

2.

6.   <u>Banking Resolution</u>

That the banking resolution, in the standard form of the Royal Bank of Canada attached hereto, is hereby passed.

7.   <u>Location of Records</u>

That the records of the Corporation required to be maintained by the *Business Corporations Act*, be kept at 17 Princess Street South, Suite 2501, Toronto, Ontario.

Each and every of the foregoing resolutions is hereby passed by the directors of the Corporation pursuant to the *Business Corporations Act* (Ontario), this   day of August, 20__.

_____   _____
       Hoaln W. East   Christopher W. East

_____
       Lauren M. East

**RESOLUTION OF THE SHAREHOLDERS
OF
EAST HARDWARE LIMITED**

R E S O L V E D:

1. By-Laws

    That By-law No. 1, being a general by-law, is hereby made as a by-law of
    the Corporation.

2. Appointment of Auditors

    That Walker Sheridan, Professional Corporation, is hereby appointed
    auditors of the Corporation to hold office until the first annual meeting of
    shareholders.

    Each of the foregoing resolutions is hereby passed by the shareholders of
    the Corporation pursuant to the *Business Corporations Act* (Ontario), this
    day of August, 20__.

_____   _____
        Hoaln W. East   Christopher W. East

                    _____
                            Lauren M. East

1002975 ONTARIO LIMITED

The undersigned, being the sole director of the above-named corporation, hereby consents to the following resolution pursuant to the *Business Corporations Act* (Ontario):

<u>Appointment of Officers</u>

BE IT RESOLVED

That the following persons be and they are hereby appointed officers of the Corporation to hold the office set forth opposite their respective names for the ensuing year:

President	Matthew William MacLeod
Secretary	Melissa Sheila Mercer
Treasurer	Jason Paul Kozak

Dated the   day of February, 20__

_____
Matthew William MacLeod

CHAPTER 31

Corporate Securities, Records, and Changes

OBJECTIVES:

- Demonstrate an understanding of the various types of share certificates and how they are issued and transferred

- Describe the contents and explain the procedures for completing the various corporate registers and records required by the *Business Corporations Act* (Ontario)

- Demonstrate an understanding of the requirements and procedures for corporate changes

- Use legal precedents to prepare share certificates, corporate registers, and articles of amendment

The *Business Corporations Act* (Ontario) refers to the "securities" issued by a corporation. A "security" is a medium for investment and may, for example, represent an investment in shares, participation or other interest in property, rights or an enterprise of the corporation, or an obligation of the corporation. Such securities may be shares, warrants, debentures, bonds, or other types of debt obligations.

Every security holder is entitled to a security certificate in respect of the security held by him or her or to a non-transferable written acknowledgement of the right to obtain a security certificate in respect of the securities of the corporation held by him or her.

Large corporations may have a number of different types of securities and issue a variety of security certificates.

Small corporations usually have only one type of security—shares—and issue share certificates.

In this chapter, we consider only shares and the related security certificate and records that the legal assistant will encounter.

SHARE CERTIFICATES

A large corporation usually employs a transfer agent, such as a trust company, to issue and transfer its shares. For a small corporation, the lawyer may act in this capacity, and the legal assistant is then advised to issue a share certificate for a definite number and class of shares to each shareholder.

When the corporation's application for articles of incorporation is approved, the legal assistant, on instructions from the lawyer, may arrange for a supply of blank share certificates for the class(es) of shares being issued; alternatively, they may be prepared using commercial software or a blank template of a share certificate recorded on a computer, and these can be used to prepare any certificates to be issued. Legal stationers also provide blank share certificates, usually in a bound book containing a number of blank shares and a portion separated by a perforated line and known as the stub. Printed share certificates may be a different colour for each type of share, and the printed certificate includes wording indicating the particular type (for example, "common share"). It is also possible to secure a printed share certificate that contains no wording as to its type; this form of certificate may then be used for any shares issued, and the wording identifying the type of share can be inserted when it is issued.

Original Issue

An original issue refers to a share that has never before been issued by the corporation. The certificate of incorporation authorizes the corporation to issue a stated number of shares, which need not all be issued immediately. As each share is issued, it is considered an original issue and is said to be from treasury.

Issuance of a Share Certificate

Follow these steps to issue a share certificate:

1. Obtain the appropriate blank for the class of share certificates being issued (either a hard-copy certificate or a software-generated form) or obtain a blank share certificate on which wording identifying the class of share can be inserted.

2. If the hard copy of the certificate is from a bound book, print the name of the person to whom the share is issued, the number of shares represented by the certificate, and the next consecutive certificate number on the stub. Separate the share certificate from the stub. Retain the stub either in the bound book of shares or in a special file for stubs of shares of the corporation. This step is not required for software-generated certificates. If the share being issued is the first share certificate, its number is 1; the next certificate issued is 2, and so on.

3. Show the name of the corporation in the large box at the top of the certificate.

4. Show the name of the person to whom the certificate is issued and the number of shares represented by the certificate. Insert the class of shares if the certificate being prepared does not include such identifying wording.

5. If the corporation has more than one class of shares, the rights, privileges, restrictions, and conditions must be stated on the certificate; alternatively, a statement must appear on the certificate that there are rights, privileges, restrictions, and conditions attaching to that class of share and that a full text is obtainable on request and without cost from the corporation.

6. Have the certificate signed. A share certificate is signed manually by at least one officer or director of the corporation or by or on behalf of a registrar, transfer agent, branch transfer agent, or other authenticating agent of the corporation. Any other signatures may be printed or mechanically reproduced; for example, a rubber stamp of a signature may be used.

7. If the corporation has a corporate seal, affix it in the space indicated in the lower left-hand corner of the certificate.

8. If the share certificate must be mailed, send it by registered mail.

Precedent 31.1 illustrates the front of a share certificate ready to be issued.

Transfer of Certificate

Subject to any restrictions on the transfer of shares, a shareholder who wishes to transfer his or her shares, or some of them, completes either the form on the back of the original certificate or an Instrument of Transfer document (Precedent 31.2). When shares are transferred, the corporation issues a new certificate to the new shareholder. The holder, for example, of 25 shares who has met the requirements to transfer shares might wish to transfer all 25 shares; then a new share certificate for 25 shares would be made out to the transferee (the new shareholder). If, however, the original shareholder wished to transfer only 10 shares and retain the other 15, two new certificates would be issued: one to the transferee for 10 shares and one to the original shareholder for 15 shares. When a certificate is transferred, follow the procedure outlined for the original issuance of a certificate. If a bound book of shares is used, then the stub of a certificate for transferred shares is completed to show from whom the shares are transferred, the original certificate number, and the name of the transferor.

When new certificates have been prepared, write in ink across the face of the old certificate the word "Cancelled." Date and initial the cancelled certificate and either retain it in a special file or paste it to the stub in the bound book of certificates, as near as possible to its original position.

REGISTERS AND RECORDS

The *Business Corporations Act* (Ontario) requires a corporation to maintain and retain certain records at its registered office, including

1. the articles and the by-laws, all amendments thereto, and a copy of any unanimous shareholders' agreement known to the directors;
2. minutes of meetings and resolutions of shareholders;
3. a register of directors, including their addresses and dates of starting and ceasing in office;
4. a securities' (usually referred to as a shareholders') register;
5. a register of security transfers;
6. adequate accounting records; and
7. minutes of meetings and resolutions of directors and any committee thereof.

In a large corporation where the number of shareholders may be in the thousands, and where there are many directors as well as changes in the ownership of shares, record keeping is very detailed and usually involves the use of computers and other electronic equipment. In a small corporation, however, where the number of shareholders is small and where records may be maintained in the minute book, the procedure is much simpler.

Three types of records must be maintained: a securities' register, a directors' register, and a transfer register. An officers' register may also be useful.

As share certificates are issued or transferred, or as directors are appointed or retire, the appropriate register is completed in order that the records of the corporation are at all times up to date.

These records may be maintained on paper or electronically. The records illustrated in this chapter are created electronically using Fast Company software.

These records are cross-indexed. They may also refer to the appropriate page or folio in the minute book or to the number of the register sheet on which the original entry concerning the sale or transfer is recorded.

Securities' or Shareholders' Register

The shareholders' register of a corporation shows

1. the names, alphabetically arranged, of persons who
   a. are or have been within six years registered as shareholders of the corporation, their complete address while a shareholder, and the number and class of shares registered in the name of such shareholder;
   b. are or have been within six years a registered holder of debt obligations of the corporation, their complete address while a holder, and the class or series and principal amount of the debt obligations registered in the name of such holder; or
   c. are or have been within six years registered as holders of warrants of the corporation, other than warrants exercisable within one year from the date of issue; their address while a registered holder; and the class or series and number of warrants registered in the name of such holder; and

2. the date and particulars of the issue of each security and warrant.

For small, non-offering corporations, only the information on persons who are or have been shareholders as outlined in 1a above is usually kept.

The individual shareholders are first listed in the shareholders' register (Precedent 31.3), which shows the date of acquisition of the shares, the name and address of the shareholder, and the class and number of shares held. Each sheet in this register is consecutively numbered.

A separate ledger (Precedent 31.4) is kept for each class of share. It contains, in alphabetical order, individual ledger sheets for each current shareholder and for past shareholders for the previous six years; these sheets record the number of shares held.

Directors' Register

A record (Precedent 31.5) is kept of past and present directors, indicating the page in the minutes of the appropriate meeting of shareholders at which the appointment or retirement of a director was ratified (that is, approved) by the shareholders. A register of directors should show the following information for each director:

1. the date of first election as a director,
2. the date of retirement as a director,
3. the residence address, and
4. occupation.

Officers' Register

A register of officers should indicate the following information for each officer:

1. the date elected to office,
2. the date of retirement from office,
3. the office(s) held, and
4. the residence address.

Precedent 31.6 illustrates an officers' register.

Transfer Register

When shares are transferred, the appropriate information is recorded (Precedent 31.7) to show the transfer number, the certificate covering the shares being transferred, the name of the present shareholder (that is, the transferor), the name of the new shareholder (that is, the transferee), and the number of shares covered by each new certificate issued.

CORPORATE CHANGES

Once a corporation is incorporated, it may make changes in its corporate structure. For example, the address of the registered office may change, the individuals serving as directors or officers of the corporation may change, or the corporation may wish to change its name or create a new class of shares. Some changes may require the passing of an appropriate resolution and the filing of a notice of change; other changes require that a special resolution be passed and that amended articles of incorporation be filed.

Changes in Directors and Officers

When the change involves the retirement and election of directors or appointment of officers of a corporation, take the following steps:

1. Bring the appropriate register up to date. Show the retirement date for any director or officer ceasing to act in that capacity and list the names of any new director or officer and the date of election or appointment. The dates in both instances should usually be the same. However, the dates would be different, for example, if a director has died and his replacement was elected; such a director would retire as of the date of death, and his or her replacement would be elected on the date the shareholders met and elected him or her.
2. Prepare a new information sheet to be filed with the bank (as discussed in Chapter 30).
3. Prepare a notice of change to record the change in the names and information on current directors or officers. Enter the date that any director or officer ceased to hold office under his or her name. List any new director or officer, the full residence address, and the date of election or appointment. The dates in both instances should usually be the same. This notice must be filed within 15 days of the change.

Change in Address of Registered Office

Within the Same Municipality

A corporation may, by resolution of the directors, change the location of the registered office within the municipality. A notice of change is then filed with the director within 15 days of the change.

To a New Municipality in Ontario

A corporation may by special resolution change the municipality or geographic township in which its registered office is located to another place in Ontario. A notice of change is also filed within 15 days of the change.

Other Changes in Corporate Structure

A corporation may make other changes to its corporate structure as set out in its articles of incorporation. Such changes, for example, may include changing a name; adding, changing, or removing any restrictions upon the business or businesses that the corporation may carry on; amending the maximum number of shares that the corporation is allowed to issue; or creating new classes of shares. Many other possible areas of change are allowed under the *Business Corporations Act* (Ontario).

To make such a change, either the directors or the shareholders (as the case may be under the act) pass a resolution to amend the articles; then the articles of amendment are filed.

Your lawyer will advise you whether the directors or shareholders must pass the resolution, whether a notice of change must be filed, and whether amended articles of amendment are required.

Changes by Resolution and Articles of Amendment

Many corporate changes require a resolution by the directors or a special share-holders' resolution, in which case, the following steps are taken:

1. The directors or shareholders pass the necessary resolution authorizing the change.
2. Articles of amendment are prepared.
3. The articles of amendment are submitted to the director in duplicate, together with the required filing fee, which as of December 31, 2007, was $150.00.
4. If the amendment involves a change in the name of the corporation, the arti-cles of amendment must be accompanied by a NUANS report, similar to that required when filing articles of incorporation.
5. A notice of change is prepared and filed within 10 days of the change if the change involves information contained in the notice. Note, however, that a notice of change is not required if only the name of the corporation is being changed.

For example, if a corporation incorporated with a number name wishes to amend its articles to change that name to a word name, the directors determine a word name and secure the NUANS report to ensure the availability of the desired name. The directors then pass a resolution (Precedent 31.8) to amend the articles and file amended articles of incorporation (Precedent 31.9). Because the change involves only a change in corporate name, no notice of change need be filed.

Articles of Amendment

Prepare a minimum of three copies of the articles of amendment to be signed in duplicate by an officer or director of the corporation. If the corporation has a cor-porate seal, it is affixed next to the signature.

The original and one copy are submitted to the director with the appropriate filing fee; the third copy remains in the office file. When the director has approved the articles of amendment, one duplicate endorsed copy will be returned, stating in the upper portion of the first page the date on which the fully and correctly com-pleted amendment was received by the director, as well as the corporation number (which remains unchanged).

Insert the endorsed articles of amendment, which become the certificate of amendment, into the minute book and make photocopies of it for any duplicate minute book and for the auditors.

Terms and Concepts

share certificate
original issue
fractional share
scrip certificates
procedures for issuing and
    transferring shares
registered office records
securities' register

directors' register
officers' register
transfer register
procedure for changes in officers and
    directors or registered office
preparation and filing of articles of
    amendment

Review Questions

1. What is meant by the following terms:
   a. security
   b. "class" of shares
   c. "original share"

2. If an individual has subscribed for 1,000 shares in a new corporation, what will he or she receive to acknowledge that holding?

3. How is the holder of a share certificate aware when there are restrictions on the transfer of the shares?

4. What records must be kept for individuals who have invested in the corporation?

5. What disposition is made of a share certificate that has been cancelled?

6. What information will you maintain on the directors of a corporation?

7. What records must a corporation maintain at its registered office?

8. List two examples of routine changes that a corporation might make in its corporate structure.

9. Under what circumstances would your directors' register show a date of retirement for one director and another date for the election of his or her replacement?

10. Why is new bank information required when there is a change in directors?

11. When is a corporation required to file a notice of change with the Ministry?

12. How can a corporation amend a provision set out in its articles of incorporation?

13. Give an example of when you might be asked to prepare articles of amendment for a corporation.

NO. 2

INCORPORATED UNDER THE LAWS OF THE PROVINCE OF ONTARIO

100 SHARES

EAST HARDWARE LIMITED

This is to Certify **LAUREN M. EAST**
is the registered holder of one hundred
Common shares in the capital of
EAST HARDWARE LIMITED

The class or series of shares represented by this Certificate has rights, privileges, restrictions or conditions attached thereto and the Corporation will furnish to a shareholder, on demand and without charge, a full copy of the text of:

(i) the rights, privileges, restrictions and conditions attached to the shares represented by this certificate and to each class authorized to be issued and to each series insofar as the same have been fixed by the directors; and

(ii) the authority of the directors to fix the rights, privileges, restrictions and conditions of subsequent series, if applicable.

The Corporation has a lien on the shares represented by this Certificate for the indebtedness of the shareholder to the Corporation.

The right of the shareholder to transfer the shares represented by this Certificate is subject to restrictions.

IN WITNESS WHEREOF the Corporation has caused this Certificate to be signed by its duly authorized officers.

DATED this 2nd day of August, 2007

President (Hoaln W. East)   Secretary (Lauren M. East)

INSTRUMENT OF TRANSFER

FOR VALUE RECEIVED, I hereby sell, assign and transfer unto CHRISTOPHER W. EAST the fifty (50) Common shares in the capital of EAST HARDWARE LIMITED registered in my name and represented by share certificate number 2, and I hereby irrevocably constitute and appoint Christopher W. East as attorney to transfer the said stock on the books of the Corporation with full power of substitution in the premises.

DATED the 3rd day of August, 20__.

LAUREN M. EAST

EAST HARDWARE LIMITED

SHAREHOLDERS' REGISTER

Date	Name	No. of Shares	Class Of Shares Held
Aug 2, 2007	Hoaln W. East	100	Common
Aug 2, 2007	Christopher W. East	100	Common
Aug 3, 2007	Christopher W. East	50	Common
Aug 3, 2007	Lauren M. East	50	Common

Effective date: Aug 03, 2007

Source: Do Process Software Ltd.

EAST HARDWARE LIMITED

SHAREHOLDER'S LEDGER

HOALN W. EAST

76 Prince Albert Road
Toronto, Ontario
M4R 6N2
Occupation: Retailer
Share Class: Common

Date	Certif. No.	Transfer No.	Transferred From/To	Sold	Bought	Balance
Aug 2, 2007	1	1	FROM: TREASURY		100	100

Effective date Aug 03, 2007

Source: Do Process Software Ltd.

EAST HARDWARE LIMITED
DIRECTORS' REGISTER

Name of Director	Date Elected	Date Resigned
CHRISTOPHER W. EAST 950 Merton Street Toronto, Ontario M4S 2D9 Occupation: Retailer	Aug 2, 2007	
HOALN W. EAST 76 Prince Albert Road Toronto, Ontario M4R 6N2 Occupation: Retailer	Aug 2, 2007	
LAUREN M. EAST 76 Prince Albert Road Toronto, Ontario M4R 6N2 Occupation: Retailer	Aug 2, 2007	
PETER T. GRANT	Aug 2, 2007	Aug 3, 2007

Effective date: Aug 03, 2007

Source: Do Process Software Ltd.

EAST HARDWARE LIMITED
OFFICERS' REGISTER

Name of Officer	Office Held	Date Elected	Date Resigned
HOALN W. EAST 76 Prince Albert Road Toronto, Ontario M4R 6N2 Occupation: Retailer	President	Aug 2, 2007	
LAUREN M. EAST 76 Prince Albert Road Toronto, Ontario M4R 6N2 Occupation: Retailer	Secretary	Aug 2, 2007	
CHRISTOPHER W. EAST 950 Merton Street Toronto, Ontario M4S 2D9 Occupation: Retailer	Treasurer	Aug 2, 2007	

Effective date: Aug 03, 2007

Source: Do Process Software Ltd.

EAST HARDWARE LIMITED
STOCK TRANSFER REGISTER

Trnsf. No.	Date	SURRENDERED			Transferred From	Transferred To	ISSUED		
		Share Class	Cert. No.	No. of Shares			Share Class	Cert. No.	No. of Shares
1	Aug 2, 2007				TREASURY	Hoaln W. East	Common	1	100
2	Aug 2, 2007				TREASURY	Lauren M. East	Common	2	100
3	Aug 2, 2007				TREASURY	Christopher W. East	Common	3	100
4	Aug 3, 2007	Common	2	50	Lauren M. East	Christopher W. East	Common	4	50
5	Aug 3, 2007	Common	2	50	Lauren M. East	Lauren M. East	Common	5	50

Effective date Aug 03, 2007

Source: Do Process Software Ltd.

SPECIAL RESOLUTION

OF

1001357 ONTARIO LIMITED

1.   CHANGE OF CORPORATE NAME

BE IT RESOLVED AS A SPECIAL RESOLUTION OF THE CORPORATION THAT:

the name of the Corporation be changed to:

BRETTER GRAPHICS INC.

and the director and proper officers of the Corporation be and they are hereby authorized to do all things and execute all instruments and documents necessary or desirable to carry out the foregoing.

THE FOREGOING SPECIAL RESOLUTION is hereby consented to by the sole director of the Corporation, as evidenced by his signature hereto in accordance with the provisions of the *Business Corporations Act* (Ontario), this 2nd day of October, 20__.

_____
MAXWELL J. BRETT

THE FOREGOING SPECIAL RESOLUTION is hereby consented to and passed by the sole shareholder of the Corporation entitled to vote thereon at a meeting of shareholders, as evidenced by his signature hereto in accordance with the provisions of the *Business Corporations Act* (Ontario), this 2nd day of October, 20__.

_____
MAXWELL J. BRETT

1.

For Ministry Use Only
À l'usage exclusif du ministère

Ontario Corporation Number
Numéro de la société en Ontario

1001357

Form 3
Business
Corporations
Act

*Formule 3
Loi sur les
sociétés par
actions*

ARTICLES OF AMENDMENT
STATUTS DE MODIFICATION

1. The name of the corporation is: (Set out in BLOCK CAPITAL LETTERS)
Dénomination sociale actuelle de la société (écrire en LETTRES MAJUSCULES SEULEMENT):

1	0	0	1	3	5	7		O	N	T	A	R	I	O		L	I	M	I	T	E	D						

2. The name of the corporation is changed to (if applicable):(Set out in BLOCK CAPITAL LETTERS)
Nouvelle dénomination sociale de la société (s'il y a lieu) (écrire en LETTRES MAJUSCULES SEULEMENT):

B	R	E	T	T	E	R		G	R	A	P	H	I	C	S		I	N	C	.							

3. Date of incorporation/amalgamation:
Date de la constitution ou de la fusion:

2006 - August - 02
(Year, Month, Day)
(année, mois, jour)

4. **Complete only if there is a change in the number of directors or the minimum / maximum number of directors.**
Il faut remplir cette partie seulement si le nombre d'administrateurs ou si le nombre minimal ou maximal d'administrateurs a changé.

Number of directors is/are: **or** <u>minimum and maximum</u> number of directors is/are:
Nombre d'administrateurs: **ou** *nombres <u>minimum et maximum</u> d'administrateurs:*

| Number | **or** | minimum | and | maximum |
| Nombre | **ou** | *minimum* | *et* | *maximum* |

5. The articles of the corporation are amended as follows:
Les statuts de la société sont modifiés de la façon suivante :

Source: Do Process Software Ltd.

2.

6. The amendment has been duly authorized as required by sections 168 and 170 (as applicable) of the *Business Corporations Act*.
   La modification a été dûment autorisée conformément aux articles 168 et 170 (selon le cas) de la Loi sur les sociétés par actions.

7. The resolution authorizing the amendment was approved by the shareholders/directors (as applicable) of the corporation on
   Les actionnaires ou les administrateurs (selon le cas) de la société ont approuvé la résolution autorisant la modification le

2007 - August - 02
(Year, Month, Day)
(année, mois, jour)

These articles are signed in duplicate.
Les présents statuts sont signés en double exemplaire.

1001357 ONTARIO LIMITED

(Name of Corporation) (If the name is to be changed by these articles set out current name)
(Dénomination sociale de la société) (Si l'on demande un changement de nom, indiquer ci-dessus la dénomination sociale actuelle).

By/
Par:

_____
(Signature)
(Signature)

_____
(Description of Office)
(Fonction)

Source: Do Process Software Ltd.

PART 5

Estates

CHAPTER 32

Wills and Powers of Attorney

OBJECTIVES:

- Demonstrate an understanding of the purpose and terminology of wills and codicils

- Use legal precedents to prepare wills, codicils, and affidavits of execution

- Describe the procedures for execution and disposition of wills or codicils

A **will** is an individual's written statement of how he intends his real and personal property, called the **estate**, to be distributed after death. The appropriate act in each province sets out certain requirements that must be followed to make a valid will; in Ontario, this is the *Succession Law Reform Act*. A will is more formally known as a *last will and testament*. Originally, a will disposed of real property and a testament of personal property. Today, the single word *will* covers the disposition of both real and personal property.

Many other terms used in connection with estates are derived from the word **testament: testate**, or having a will; **intestate**, or not having a will; **testator**, a man who has made a will; and **testatrix**, a woman who has made a will.

Wills may be fully keyed, prepared on a printed form with a handwritten or typed insertion, or completely handwritten. In most Canadian provinces, including Ontario, a completely handwritten will (called a **holograph will**) is valid if made on or after March 31, 1978. In his will, the testator designates and appoints the person or persons who will carry out the terms of his will after his death; he may name one or more individuals or a trust company. Traditionally, this person was known as the **executor(s)** if a male or a trust company or as **executrix(rices)** if female. However, over the past decade, the procedures and documentation for the administration of estates in Ontario have been changed substantially, and the terms **estate trustee** (*Rules of Civil Procedure*) and **personal representative** (*Estates Administration Act*) are now used to refer to such a person. The traditional terms referred to above will be encountered for many years for existing wills and are still used by some lawyers in the creation of new wills; thus, a legal assistant should be aware that an executor, executrix, estate trustee, and personal representative all refer to a person(s) or trust company appointed by the testator to manage the disposition of the testator's estate according to his or her wishes. Chapter 33 discusses in more detail the rules and terminology of estate administration.

In this text, the terms *testator, executor, estate trustee*, and *personal representative* should be understood to include both the masculine and feminine genders.

PARTS OF A WILL

Heading

The heading of a will states exactly what the document is and sets out the name of the testator and his general address, including the province. His occupation may also be shown, if that is the preference of the law office. Although the date of the will is traditionally part of the ending, some lawyers prefer to have the date appear in the heading.

Body

The body of a will contains clauses that outline how the testator wishes to dispose of his estate after his death. The first clause is the revocation clause, cancelling any previous will made by the testator. This is followed by clauses dealing with the appointment of one or more estate trustees; the payment of debts and taxes; specific gifts to individuals, known as **beneficiaries**; the disposition of the balance (residue) of the estate; and other clauses as required by the circumstances. For example, if a minor is beneficiary, special clauses are necessary to authorize payment to the parent or guardian before the minor reaches the age of 18.

Many of the clauses used in the body of a will are standard. When you are instructed to use such clauses, ensure that the necessary changes in gender and case are made.

Ending

The ending of a will contains a **testimonium** and **attestation** clause, as illustrated in Precedent 32.1. The ending varies depending on whether a man or woman executes the will. The initial wording of the testimonium clause is either *IN TESTIMONY WHEREOF...* or *IN WITNESS WHEREOF . . .* and may be followed by a reference to the number of pages in the will, exclusive of the backsheet.

Backsheet

Each copy of a will has a backsheet showing the date, the name of the document, and the name and address of the law firm. This information may be shown in a number of ways, two of which are illustrated in Precedents 32.2 and 32.3.

The paper for the back may be of quality, colour, and size similar to those used for the will itself or may be heavier and coloured (usually blue or grey) and may be printed with the name of the document.

Alternatively, some law firms insert the will into a special folder purchased from legal stationers with the above information keyed on the front.

PREPARING A WILL

Wills may be prepared in any of the ways discussed in Chapter 2. Many clauses are standard in all wills and are recorded for use as required with appropriate changes for case and gender. The lawyer selects from the index of stored material the specific clause(s) to be incorporated into the will being drafted and notes any changes or amendments to be made. The complete will can then be assembled by stringing together the standard common clauses, as amended, and adding customized clauses setting out the special personal wishes of the testator.

Types of Paper

Because the forms used in estate matters in the Superior Court of Justice are letter size, most wills are prepared on paper of that size. For many years, the paper was ruled in a variety of ways, the most common being with blue margin rulings on all four edges. However, with the increased use of word processors, most wills are now prepared on unruled paper. Precedent 32.4 illustrates a short will prepared on ruled paper. Precedent 32.5 illustrates a first page of a longer will prepared on unruled paper.

Date of Will

Wills are dated the day of execution. When preparing a will, leave the date of the month blank unless you know with certainty that it will be executed on a specific day. Traditionally, a will is dated in the ending; you may, however, also see the date in the heading, particularly if a printed will form is used.

Number of Copies

Most law offices follow the traditional practice of preparing three copies of a will and having the original executed. Other law offices, however, prepare additional copies of the will and have at least two copies of the will executed.

Guidelines for Preparing Wills

When preparing a will, note the following points:

1. If plain, unruled paper is used, the tradition has been to leave a margin of approximately 1.5 inches or 40 mm on the left and 1 inch or 25 mm on the right. If the will is to be inserted into a will folder, these margins should be used. If not, the default margins of the word processing software may be used.
2. If ruled margin paper is used, leave two spaces before and after the ruled lines, as shown in Precedent 32.4.
3. On unruled paper, commence the heading of the will approximately six lines (1 inch) from the top of the page.
4. Double space the heading and the body of the will. Double or triple space between paragraphs, depending on the preference of the law office.
5. All bold font is optional but if used should be done so in a consistent format.
6. Show the name of the testator in solid capitals wherever it appears in the will; show other names appearing in the body of the will in solid capitals or in upper- and lowercase, depending on the preference of the law office.
7. Number each paragraph in the body of the will and label subparagraphs with letters of the alphabet in brackets, for example, (*a*), (*b*), etc.
8. Show the initial directive words of each paragraph, such as *I HEREBY REVOKE*, *I APPOINT*, or *I GIVE*, in solid capitals. Also use solid capitals when directive words appear in the body of the will.
9. Number each page after the first, beginning with the Figure 2. If the will is prepared on four-sided, margin-ruled paper, the page number appears above the top ruling of the page.
10. Single space the attestation clauses, all of which should be on the same page.
11. Type in three lines for each witness, to allow for the signature, address, and occupation. If there is insufficient room on the left side of the page for both sets of lines, place one set on the right side, below the testimonium clause and the signature of the testator.
12. Show at least two lines of the body of the will on the page with the attestation and testimonium clauses. Cross out with a Z any unused space on the second last page. Some lawyers ask that each page end in the middle of a sentence so that no page except the first begins with a new sentence or paragraph.

EXECUTION OF A WILL

When the will is prepared, the testator reads it over carefully and, if he or she approves, executes it.

Corrections

When a testator considers a will for execution, the best practice is to never permit an alteration in the contents of the will by erasure or ink. If the will must be executed immediately, and there is no time to prepare a revised page, the testator and both witnesses should initial the correction. The initials should appear immediately *before* and immediately *after* the change so that there can be no doubt as to the extent of the alteration or that the change was made at the time the will was executed (see Precedent 32.6).

Signature of Testator

Many law offices have the testator initial the bottom corner of each page of the will except the first, as well as sign the will. If at all possible, have the testator initial and execute the will using a pen with black ink.

All provinces require wills other than holograph wills to be signed in the presence of two witnesses. Although the person signing the will is normally the person making it, in some provinces (including Ontario), someone else may sign on behalf of the person making the will, but only in that person's presence, on his direction, and in the presence of two witnesses.

Witness

Before March 31, 1978, a testator in Ontario was required to execute the will in the presence of two witnesses, who, in the presence of each other, signed in the space to the left of his signature, beneath the attestation clause. Since March 31,1978, only wills that are keyed (or partly keyed and partly handwritten) must still be executed this way; holograph wills do not require witnesses. If the testator initialled each page of the will or any alteration, each witness does as well.

Once the will is executed, show the name of each witness below his or her signature or make a note of the names on the records for the office's wills index.

Witnesses only witness the signature of the testator; they do not read the will itself, nor need they be aware of its contents. In Ontario and most of the other provinces and territories, no person who is to benefit under a will or who is married to a beneficiary named in the will should act as a witness. If such a person does, both spouses may be unable to benefit from the testator's estate.

Affidavit of Execution of Will

An affidavit of execution of will or codicil must be executed by at least one of the witnesses. The affidavit is a one-page document with no backsheet. One of the witnesses swears the affidavit, which states the date on which the witnesses saw the will executed, certifies that the testator was of legal age at the time of execution, and provides the name and general address of the other witness. The will is attached as Exhibit "A" to the affidavit. See Chapter 9 for how to mark exhibits to affidavits.

True Copies

When the will is executed, make true copies of all unsigned copies of the will or photocopy the executed will.

DISPOSITION OF A WILL

A signed will is a very valuable document. It must be treated with care and immediately put in safekeeping, in accordance with the testator's instructions. The signed will may be

1. kept in safekeeping by the law firm in whose office it was drawn (prepared);
2. deposited with a trust company named as estate trustee in the will;
3. deposited with the estate registrar of the estates section of the Superior Court of Justice in the upper tier municipality where the testator resides; or
4. taken by the testator to be kept by him.

If the signed will is not retained in your law office, note its location on your file copy.

Safekeeping of Wills

If the executed copy of the will is to be kept in safekeeping by the law firm, follow the procedures of your office as soon as possible after the will has been executed. Each law office has its own system of maintaining wills. Some firms place all wills in envelopes marked *Last Will and Testament of....* Others place wills in special covers similarly identified; some insert them in labelled file folders. These wills may then be deposited in locked drawers in an office vault or a "will vault" maintained at a financial institution.

An alphabetical index is usually maintained under the name of the testator, showing the date of the will and the names of witnesses and executor(s). This may be maintained manually or electronically.

Destruction of a Previous Will

When a new will is executed, it revokes any previous will. The signed, earlier will is then burned, torn, or otherwise destroyed by the testator or by some person in his presence and by his direction.

CODICIL

A testator may change the terms of an existing will by executing a document known as a codicil. It usually contains only a minor change to the will; if a major change is required, the lawyer usually recommends that the testator execute a new will.

A codicil is prepared, witnessed, and executed in the same way as a will. Each copy of the codicil may have a backsheet or cover identified as *Codicil to the Last Will and Testament of...*; alternatively, the backsheet or cover may be omitted if that is the preference of your law firm.

An affidavit of execution of will or codicil is executed following the same procedure as for a will. The executed affidavit and signed codicil are filed with the executed will to which it refers.

POWER OF ATTORNEY

A **power of attorney** is a legal document by which one person empowers another to represent her or him to act in her or his place. The person so empowered may be given certain specified powers or, alternatively, wide general powers. A power of attorney may be given by one or more people to one or more individuals at the same time.

The party who gives the power of attorney is the **grantor**, or principal. The party who gets the power is the **grantee**, or agent, also called an attorney. The term "attorney" does not refer to a lawyer in these circumstances.

In Ontario, under the *Substitute Decisions Act*, the Public Guardian and Trustee will act as attorney only for mentally incapable people who have no one who is willing or able to act as their attorney. Under this act, there are two forms of power of attorney to be used for individuals to appoint someone to act on their behalf. One is the **continuing power of attorney for property**. This document allows the grantee complete authority over the grantor's property except for any restrictions stipulated in the power of attorney. The second form is the **power of attorney for personal care**, which only allows the grantee the power to make decisions regarding the personal care of the grantor. Precedents 32.8 and 32.9 illustrate examples for these powers of attorney based on templates accessible at the Ontario Ministry of the Attorney General website (http://www.attorneygeneral.jus.gov .on.ca/english/family/pgt/poa.asp).

To complete the power of attorney, the names of the grantor and grantee(s) are inserted. The person appointed as attorney must be at least 18 years of age and, in the case of the power of attorney for personal care, must not be a caregiver unless such caregiver is also a relative.

The paragraph regarding joint and several is applicable only if more than one attorney is appointed. The phrase "jointly and severally" means that the appointed attorneys may act together or separately from each other in making decisions. If this phrase is not included, then they must act together at all times, which may not always be convenient or possible. Thus, most powers of attorney include this phrase. The name of any substitute attorney(s) is inserted if applicable, as well as any restrictions or conditions that may limit the attorney's authority; alternatively, the word "none" is inserted if there are no restrictions.

The continuing power of attorney for property has a standard paragraph regarding the compensation for attorneys in accordance with the rate stipulated by the *Substitute Decisions Act*, as amended. Alternatively, the amount of any agreed upon compensation may be set out in this paragraph. Any changes to the standard form would be based on discussions with the client and then drafted by the lawyer for inclusion in the document, who would ensure that it meets the requirements of the *Substitute Decisions Act.*

A power of attorney must be witnessed by two people who are both present at the same time when the grantor signs the document. The witnesses must be 18 years of age or older; may not be the grantor's child, spouse, or common-law spouse; and may not be the attorney's spouse, common-law spouse or partner, or anyone whose property is under guardianship.

The power of attorney is prepared in duplicate and dated the day of execution. The original may be held in safekeeping by the law firm on the client's behalf until it is required to be implemented. Alternatively, the executed copy may be given to the grantee if the appointment of the attorney is to begin immediately.

Terms and Concepts

will	testimonium
estate	attestation
testament	preparation and disposition of wills
testate	affidavit of execution of will or codicil
intestate	exhibits
testator	will destruction
testatrix	preparation and disposition of codicils
holograph will	power of attorney
executor(s)	grantor
executrix(rices)	grantee
estate trustee	continuing power of attorney for property
personal representative	power of attorney for personal care
beneficiaries	joint and several

Review Questions

1. What is the purpose of a will?
2. If it is necessary to make a change in a prepared will before it is signed, and there is no opportunity to prepare a revised page, what procedure should be followed when the will is, in fact, signed?
3. When is it possible for a testator to sign his will without witnesses being present?
4. An executed will should be kept in safekeeping. How may this be accomplished?
5. What are the guidelines to be followed when an old will is to be destroyed?
6. Who may witness a will?
7. How may an individual change the terms of an existing will without the necessity of having a completely new will?
8. What is the purpose of a power of attorney?
9. Who may not act as a power of attorney for personal care?
10. Who may not witness a power of attorney?

6.

whether before the due date or otherwise, any mortgage or mortgages

existing at the time of my death or afterwards created.

IN TESTIMONY WHEREOF I have to this to my last will and

testament, written upon this and five preceding pages of paper, subscribed my name

this   day of January, 20___.

SIGNED, PUBLISHED AND DECLARED)
by the said testator, **JACOB NATHANIEL**)
CAPWOOD, as and for his last will and)
testament, in the presence of us, both present)
at the same time, who at his request, in his)   _____
presence and in the presence of each other,)   Jacob Nathaniel Capwood
have hereunto subscribed our names as)
witnesses.)
)
)
_____)
)
_____)
)
_____)
)
)
_____)
)
_____)
)
_____)

DATED: February   , 20

LAST WILL AND TESTAMENT

OF

JACOB NATHANIAL CAPWOOD

KINGSLEY CAMP
Barrister & Solicitor
49 Queensway Street North
Ottawa ON K4F 9H3

DATED: February   , 20___

LAST WILL AND TESTAMENT

of

RONALD CRAIG ANDERSON

HILL, JOHNSTON & GRANT
17 Princess Street South, Suite 2501
Toronto ON M8Y 3N5

THIS IS THE LAST WILL AND TESTMENT of me, **EMILY KATHERINE DROHAN**, of the City of London, in the County of Middlesex, and Province of Ontario.

1.   **I HEREBY REVOKE** all wills and testamentary dispositions of every nature and kind whatsoever by me heretofore made.

2.   **I GIVE** all my property, including any property over which I may have a general power of appointment, to my husband, **THOMAS IAN DROHAN**, for his own use absolutely, and I appoint him sole Estate Trustee of this my will.

        IN TESTIMONY WHEREOF I have to this my last will and testament, written upon this single page of paper, subscribed my name this   day of February, 20___.

SIGNED, PUBLISHED AND DECLARED)
by the said testator, **BERYLE KATHERINE**)
DROHAN, as and for her last will and   )
testament, in the presence of us, both present)
at the same time, who at her request, in her   )
presence and in the presence of each other,   )
have hereunto subscribed our names as   )
witnesses.   )
)
)
_____   )
)
_____   )
)
_____   )
)
)
_____   )
)
_____   )
)
_____   )

THIS IS THE LAST WILL AND TESTAMENT of me, **JACOB NATHANIEL CAPWOOD**, of the City of Ottawa, in the Regional Municipality of Ottawa-Carlton, Province of Ontario..

1.   **I REVOKE** all former wills and testamentary dispositions made by me.

2.   **I APPOINT** my wife, Jennifer Norma Capwood, the Executrix and Trustee of this my will, but should she be unable or unwilling to act, or to continue to act as Executrix and Trustee, **I APPOINT** my brother Michael Keith Capwood to be my Executor and Trustee of this my will in her place. I refer to my Executor and Trustee whether original or substitute as "my Trustee".

3.   **I GIVE** all property, including any property over which I may have general power of appointment, to my Trustee upon the following trusts:

(a) to use her or his discretion in the realization of my estate, with power to my Trustee to sell any part of my estate at such time or times, in such manner and upon such terms, and either for cash or credit or for part cash and part credit, as my Trustee may in her or his discretion decide upon, or to postpone the sale of any part of my estate as long as she or he pleases.

(b) to pay my debts, funeral and testamentary expenses, and to pay or transfer the residue of my estate to my wife, if she survives

- 4 -

(b)   to pay or transfer one of such shares to my godson Harrison Kyle Laxton, if he shall then be living;

(c)   to pay or transfer one of such shares to my nephew Jeffrey Nicholas Stauffer, if he shall then be living;

(d)   to pay or transfer two of such shares to my nephew Harvey Harold Stauffer, if he shall then be living;

(e)   to pay or transfer two of such shares to my niece, Margaret ~~Ann~~ *Amy* Stauffer Patrick, if she shall then be living.

MAS
PRA
JCE

9.   If any person shall become entitled to a share, either of capital or of income in my estate before attaining the age of eighteen years, the share of such person shall be held and invested by my Trustees and the share or so much thereof and the income therefrom or so much thereof as my Trustees in their uncontrolled discretion consider necessary or advisable may be used for the benefit of such person until he or she attains the age of eighteen years. I authorize my Trustees to make any payment for any person under the age of eighteen years, or under other disability, to the parent, guardian or committee of such person or to anyone to whom my Trustees in their uncontrolled discretion deem it advisable to make such payment, whose receipt shall be a sufficient discharge to my Trustees.

10.   In addition to all other powers by this my will or any codicil hereto or by any statute or law conferred upon them, but subject to the other provisions of this my will, my Trustees shall have power:

MAS
JCE
PRA

AFFIDAVIT OF EXECUTION
OF WILL OR CODICIL
Form 74.8
Courts of Justice Act

Ontario
Superior Court of Justice

(insert name)

In the matter of the execution of a will or codicil of **Jacob Nathaniel Capwood**

**AFFIDAVIT OF EXECUTION
OF WILL OR CODICIL**

(insert name)

I, **SUSAN DEBORAH REID**,

(insert city or town and county or district, metropolitan or regional municipality of residence)

of **the Township of West Carleton in the Regional Municipality of Ottawa-Carleton**,

make oath and say / affirm:

(insert date)

(insert name)

1.   On **May 2, 2007**, I was present and saw the document marked as Exhibit "A" to this affidavit executed by **Jacob Nathaniel Capwood**.

(insert name)

2.   **Jacob Nathaniel Capwood** executed the document in the presence of myself and **Pierre Tremblay**,

(insert name of other witness and city or town, county or district, metropolitan or regional municipality of residence)

of **the Township of Cumberland in the Regional Municipality of Ottawa-Carleton**.

We were both present at the same time, and signed the document in the testator's presence as attesting witnesses.

SWORN / AFFIRMED BEFORE ME
at the **City**
of **Ottawa**
in the **Regional Municipality**
of **Ottawa-Carleton**
this   day of

_____
A Commissioner for Taking Affidavits
(or as may be)

SUSAN DEBORAH REID

NOTE : If the testator was blind or signed by making his or her mark, add the following paragraph:

3.   Before its execution, the document was read over to the testator, who (was blind) (signed by making his or her mark). The testator appeared to understand the contents.

WARNING : A beneficiary or the spouse of a beneficiary should not be a witness.

RCP-E 74.8 (November 1, 2005)

Source: © Queen's Printer for Ontario, 2007. Reproduced with permission.

CONTINUING POWER OF ATTORNEY
FOR PROPERTY

1. APPOINTMENT

I, _____ HAFIZ WALJI _____,
Name of Grantor
revoke any previous continuing power of attorney for property made by me and **APPOINT**:

_____ NASIR WALJI and AHMED WALJI _____
Name or names of person(s) granted power of attorney
to be my attorney(s) for property.

2. JOINT AND SEVERAL

If more than one attorney is appointed and if they are to have the authority to act separately, insert the words "jointly and severally" here: _____ jointly and severally _____

3. SUBSTITUTION

If the person(s) I have appointed, or any one of them, cannot or will not be my attorney because of refusal, resignation, death, mental incapacity, or removal by the court, **I SUBSTITUTE:** *(This may be left blank.)*

_____ SHADEEN WALJI _____
Name or names of any persons to be substitute attorney

to act as my attorney for property with the same authority as the person he or she is replacing.

4. AUTHORIZATION

I AUTHORIZE my attorney(s) for property to do on my behalf anything in respect of property that I could do if capable of managing property, except make a will, subject to the law and to any conditions or restrictions contained in this document. I confirm that he/she may do so even if I am mentally incapable.

5. CONDITIONS AND RESTRICTIONS

This power of attorney is subject to the following conditions and restrictions:
(Attach, sign, and date additional pages if required, or state "None".)

_____ None _____

_____

- 2 -

6. DATE OF EFFECTIVENESS

Unless otherwise stated in this document, this continuing power of attorney will come into effect on the date it is signed and witnessed.

7. COMPENSATION

Unless otherwise stated in this document, I authorize my attorney(s) to take annual compensation from my property in accordance with the fee scale prescribed by regulation for the compensation of attorneys for property made pursuant to Section 90 of the *Substitute Decisions Act, 1992*.

8. SIGNATURE

Executed at _____ on _____, 20_____
                              (Insert Place and Date of Execution)

_____)
Witness #1 - Signature   )
)
_____)
Print name and address of witness)
)
_____)
)
_____)
)
)   _____
)   Hafiz Walji
_____)
Witness #2 - Signature   )
)
_____)
Print name and address of witness)
)
_____)
)
_____)

[Note: The following people cannot be witnesses: the attorney or his or her spouse or partner; the spouse, partner, or child of the person making the document, or someone that the person treats as his or her child; a person whose property is under guardianship or who has a guardian of the person; a person under the age of 18.]

NEL

POWER OF ATTORNEY
FOR PERSONAL CARE

1. APPOINTMENT

I, _____JENNIFER ANNE MINOVSKI_____,
Name of Grantor
revoke any previous continuing power of attorney for personal care made by me and **APPOINT**:

_____WALTER JOHN MINOVSKI_____
Name or names of person(s) granted power of attorney

to be my attorney(s) for personal care in accordance with the *Substitute Decisions Act, 1992.*

[Note: A person who provides health care, residential, social, training or support services to the person giving this power of attorney for compensation may not act as his or her attorney unless that person is also his or her spouse, partner, or relative.]

2. JOINT AND SEVERAL

If more than one attorney is appointed and if they are to have the authority to act separately, insert the words "jointly and severally" here: _____.

3. SUBSTITUTION

If the person(s) I have appointed, or any one of them, cannot or will not be my attorney because of refusal, resignation, death, mental incapacity, or removal by the court,
I SUBSTITUTE: *(This may be left blank.)*

_____SHANNON ANNE MINOVSKI_____
Name or names of any persons to be substitute attorney

to act as my attorney for personal care in the same manner and subject to the same authority as the person he or she is replacing.

4. AUTHORIZATION

I give my attorney(s) the **AUTHORITY** to make any personal care decision for me that I am mentally incapable of making for myself, including the giving or refusing of consent to any matter to which the *Health Care Consent Act, 1996* applies, subject to the *Substitute Decisions Act, 1992,* and any instructions, conditions or restrictions contained in this form.

- 2 -

5. CONDITIONS AND RESTRICTIONS

This power of attorney is subject to the following conditions and restrictions:
(Attach, sign, and date additional pages if required or state "None".)

_____ None _____

_____

6. DATE OF EFFECTIVENESS

Unless otherwise stated in this document, this power of attorney for personal care will come into effect on the date it is signed and witnessed.

7. SIGNATURE

Executed at _____ on _____, 20_____
(Insert Place and Date of Execution)

```
                                          )
                                          )
_____         )
Witness #1 - Signature                    )
                                          )
                                          )
_____         )
Print name and address of witness         )
                                          )
_____         )
                                          )
_____         )
                                          )
                                          )         _____
                                          )              Jennifer Anne Minovski
                                          )
_____         )
Witness #2 - Signature                    )
                                          )
                                          )
_____         )
Print name and address of witness         )
                                          )
_____         )
                                          )
_____         )
```

[Note: The following people cannot be witnesses: the attorney or his or her spouse or partner; the spouse, partner, or child of the person making the document, or someone that the person treats as his or her child; a person whose property is under guardianship or who has a guardian of the person; a person under the age of 18.]

CHAPTER 33

Administration of Estates

OBJECTIVES:

- Define and explain the terminology associated with estates
- Describe the initial steps on the death of a client
- Demonstrate an understanding of the procedure for obtaining a certificate of appointment of estate trustee(s) with *and* without a will
- Use legal precedents to prepare estate documentation
- Calculate the court fees payable for obtaining a certificate of appointment

When an individual dies, the property he or she leaves is known as his or her **estate**. The laws of each province set out the conditions that must be fulfilled before distributing the estate. In Ontario, for example, the *Family Law Act* contains provisions relating to the share of the estate a surviving spouse may elect to receive regardless of the terms of the will.

In Ontario, estate matters are dealt with in the Superior Court of Justice and proceedings are conducted in accordance with Rules 74 and 75 of the *Rules of Civil Procedure*, which has prescribed forms and associated terminology for estate matters. Many terms used under the *Estates Act* reflect the previous terminology that were used in estates, and these terms are frequently still used in wills and estate correspondence; however, the new terms must be used in court documents. Figure 33.1 provides a list of the old and new terminology.

If the deceased died testate, his will usually names the personal representatives he wishes to carry out his intentions. This representative is known as the **estate trustee** for the purpose of the prescribed court documents; however, in the actual day-to-day administration of estates, the term *personal representative* is becoming more frequently used to refer to an executor or estate trustee. The chapters in this text on estates use both terms interchangeably.

If the deceased died intestate, the court, upon application, appoints a personal representative to carry out the administration of the estate according to the laws of the province.

Prescribed forms are used for almost all required estate documents; these may be secured from a legal stationer, may have been recorded in computer memory, or may be produced using commercial software package such as Estate-a-Base, which was used to create the forms in this text.

FIRST STEPS ON THE DEATH OF A CLIENT

When a solicitor first learns of the death of a client, he or she ascertains whether there is a signed will and, if there is, where it is located, such as

- the wills vault of your law firm or another firm that prepared the will
- the safety deposit box of the deceased or another family member
- the deceased's home or office
- the wills depository of the Superior Court of Justice

It may also be necessary to advertise for the will by placing an advertisement in the *Ontario Reports*, with wording similar to the following:

> Any having knowledge of a will of RANI D'SOUZA nee FARSHAM, formerly of 346 Wynham Road, Richmond Hill, Ontario, L4P 4K9, who died on or about January 1, 2000, is requested to contact Peter T. Grant of Hill, Johnston & Grant, 17 Princess Street South, Suite 2501, Toronto, Ontario M8Y 3N5. Telephone (416) 354-9900, Fax (416) 354-9909.

Figure 33.1 Estate Terminology

ESTATE TERMINOLOGY

Current Term	Previous Term(s)
application for a certificate of appointment of estate trustee with a will	application for probate application for administration with will annexed
application for a certificate of appointment of estate trustee without a will	application for administration
certificate of appointment of estate trustee with a will	letters probate letters of administration with will annexed
certificate of appointment of estate trustee without a will	letters of administration
estate trustee	executor/executrix administrator/administratrix
estate trustee with a will	executor/executrix or administrator/administratrix with will annexed
estate trustee without a will	administrator/administatrix
objection to issuing of certificate of appointment	caveat
orders for assistance	citation
succeeding estate trustee with a will	administrator *de bonis non administratis* with will annexed
succeeding estate trustee without a will	administrator *de bonis non administratis*

Once the will has been located, several notarial copies are made of it, and the original is put away for safekeeping. Any special instructions contained in the will are noted, and if necessary, the estate trustee is notified. Often the estate trustee is aware of the circumstances and is the individual who gets in touch with the law firm.

The trustee is not obliged to have the solicitors who drew the will act in the administration of the estate, but in practice, they usually do.

Information Required

To handle the estate of a deceased individual, the solicitors who will be handling the estate matters require certain basic information. The **next of kin** of a deceased person, or his or her personal representatives, are usually in a position to provide or ascertain this required information:

1. The full name, address, social insurance number, occupation, and marital status of the deceased and details of any common law relationships or divorce(s)
2. Whether the deceased died intestate or testate (and the dates of any will or codicils)
3. The place and date of birth of the deceased
4. The place and date of death of the deceased
5. The name(s), address(es), and telephone number(s) of estate trustee(s)
6. The name and address, birth date, and relationship to the deceased of each beneficiary named in the will
7. If an affidavit of execution of the will (and any codicils) is not attached to these documents, the name and address of each witness to the will (and any codicils) and their relationship, if any, to the deceased will be required to have at least one witness sign an affidavit of execution of will (or codicil).
8. The location and number of a safety deposit box and whether such box was held jointly with another person
9. The location, type, and number of bank accounts and whether such accounts were held jointly with another person
10. Details of all insurance policies
11. The location and manner of holding title to real estate, as well as the method of acquiring such property
12. Other details of assets: cash on hand, mortgages, pensions, group insurance, annuities, registered retirement savings plans, stock, bonds, car, or household goods
13. Details of debts, such as funeral or medical expenses
14. The income tax return for the preceding taxation year
15. Copies of the deceased's death certificate, usually furnished by the funeral home
16. When the deceased is married and is survived by his or her spouse, the information in items 8 through 13 is required to determine the value of the deceased spouse's net family property.

ADMINISTERING THE ESTATE

If the deceased died testate, an application will be made for a **certificate of appointment of estate trustee with a will**. This application is used when

1. the will names the estate trustee,
2. there is a will, but no estate trustee is appointed, or
3. the estate trustee named in the will is unable or unwilling to act.

If the deceased died intestate, an application will be made for a **certificate of appointment of estate trustee without a will**.

Usually, there is no controversy surrounding the will (for example, a question as to its validity), and the appropriate certificate is granted without any formal hearing following the filing of the appropriate documents. There are also other types of applications that may be applied for, such as the *certificate of appointment of foreign estate trustee's nominee as estate trustee without a will* or the *certificate of appointment of estate trustee during litigation*. The lawyer handling this type of estate matter will instruct you on the steps to follow in these special circumstances. In this chapter, we are concerned with the two most frequently encountered forms of estate applications.

FAMILY LAW ACT

As discussed in Chapter 18, the *Family Law Act* views marriage as an economic contract and, thus, upon the death of a spouse, allows the surviving spouse to choose to set aside the will of the deceased spouse or the laws of intestacy (as applicable) and to elect to receive what the spouse would be entitled to under the *Family Law Act* provisions regarding net family property if that would be to his or her financial benefit. In other words, the *Family Law Act* views the death as if it was a divorce and allows for an equalization of net family property. A complete financial review of all the assets of the deceased and surviving spouse and a review of the applicable provisions of the *Family Law Act* and *Succession Law Reform Act* would be done by the lawyer before advising the surviving spouse of whether or not to choose this election; the particulars of this are beyond the scope of this text. However, it is important for a legal assistant to be aware that the *Family Law Act* prohibits any distribution of the deceased spouse's estate for six months after the date of death, unless the surviving spouse has consented in writing to such distribution.

CERTIFICATE OF APPOINTMENT OF ESTATE TRUSTEE WITH A WILL

A will usually names the person or persons appointed by the deceased to be the estate trustees of his or her estate. The law firm acts on behalf of the estate trustee in his or her application to the court to confirm the validity of the will of the deceased and to confirm the appointment of the estate trustee with a will. The certificate of appointment of estate trustee is usually required to handle the deceased's estate and distribute it to the beneficiaries named in the will. Although obtaining the certificate is not mandatory, only in small estates, without real property or investments, is the certificate not applied for. If any estate trustee named in the will is unable or unwilling to act as estate trustee, then a **renunciation** (rejecting their right to be appointed estate trustee) is completed by such estate trustee. Additionally, a **consent** to the applicant's appointment as estate trustee must be prepared and signed by a majority of the persons entitled to share in the distribution of the estate.

Notice to Beneficiaries

Once the will and all necessary information have been obtained, but before applying to the court for the certificate, all beneficiaries (other than the estate trustee) named in the will must be served, by regular mail to the beneficiary's last known address, with a **notice of application for a certificate of appointment of estate trustee with a will** (Precedent 33.1). If the beneficiary is a minor, the notice is served on his or her parent or guardian *and* the Children's Lawyer. If the beneficiary is mentally incapable, the notice is served on his or her guardian, or an attorney under a power of attorney, or if there is no guardian appointed, then on the Public Guardian and Trustee. The rules do not specific a required amount of time for serving notice before applying for the certificate. Note the following points when completing this form:

1. The name of the deceased as it appears in the will (in all capitals) and the date of death are inserted.
2. A complete photocopy of the will must be attached to this notice, unless the beneficiary is to receive a specific item of property or stated amount of money, in which case, only a photocopy of that part of the will that pertains to the bequest needs to be attached.
3. The full names and addresses of all estate trustees are to be inserted.
4. Numbers 4 to 8 are completed only if applicable.
5. The names and addresses of all other beneficiaries named in the will are also inserted.
6. It may be dated the day of preparation.

Number and Disposition of Copies

A minimum of four copies of each notice should be prepared. One copy (along with a full or partial photocopy of the will) will need to be mailed to each beneficiary under the will. One copy is for the lawyer's use; another is for the file. Additional copies will be required for each estate trustee.

Affidavit of Service

An **affidavit of service of notice of an application for a certificate of appointment of estate trustee** should then be prepared for execution by the estate trustee. This is a standard form prescribed by the rules and is illustrated in Precedent 33.2. The name and municipal description of the estate trustee should be inserted. Note that it states in the second numbered paragraph that the estate trustee "sent or caused to be sent a notice...." This enables the law firm to mail the notices under the direction of the estate trustee. If any person cannot be served the notice, for example, if no recent address is available, add at the end of paragraph 4 "except for (*insert the name*), who cannot be served because (*give an explanation*)."

Number and Disposition of Copies

Prepare a minimum of three copies. The original will be submitted to the court. One copy is for the lawyer's use and one is for the file; additional copies may be required for the estate trustee(s).

Preparation of the Application

The application for a certificate of appointment of estate trustee with a will is completed by the estate trustee or jointly by all estate trustees, if more than one. Precedent 33.3 illustrates the form of application when individuals are the applicants. Precedent 33.4 illustrates the form of application when one applicant is a corporate estate trustee. Note the following points when completing this form:

1. The application is to the Superior Court of Justice at the county in which the deceased resided or in which he held property if he had no fixed abode in Ontario or resided out of Ontario. For example:
   - Superior Court of Justice at Toronto
   - Superior Court of Justice at Brampton
2. The top portion of the application requires the details of the deceased: legal name, fixed place of abode, last occupation, date and place of death, date of last will and codicil, age at date of will, marital status, relationship of witnesses to beneficiaries, and value of the estate.
3. If the deceased was commonly known by a name other than his legal name, include both names.
4. If the deceased was under 18 at the date of the will, details are set out of the circumstances that qualify the will for probate.
5. If the deceased had been married but was divorced after the date of the will, details of the divorce—including the court that granted it, the date of the divorce judgment, and the names and addresses of all parties, including issue— are set out in a schedule attached to the application.

   Unless the will expressly states otherwise, termination of marriage after the deceased made the will revokes a gift to a former spouse, as well as revoking any appointment of such spouse as executor or trustee. The will is construed as if the former spouse had predeceased (died before) the testator.
6. If the deceased married after the date of the will, the grounds on which application is requested are set out in a schedule attached to the application. In these circumstances, the will usually states that it was made in contemplation of marriage.
7. If any witness or their spouses are beneficiaries, attach a schedule giving details since witnesses or their spouses cannot receive gifts under a will.
8. The value of the estate is set out in the application. It is divided into personal property and real property. Personal property is all assets (cars, house contents, art work, etc.) that are not real property (land that the deceased own at the date

of death less the amount of any mortgages). Insurance payable to a named beneficiary, assets held on joint account and passing by survivorship (including land held as joint tenants), and real property situated outside Ontario are not included in the total value of the estate. The total of these two amounts is used to calculate the court fees discussed at the end of this chapter.

9. If an estate trustee named in the will is not an applicant, the reason must be set out. For example:

> The second estate trustee, Kathryn Jane Waymond, predeceased the deceased.

10. If the only beneficiaries are also the applicants, place an "X" beside "No." If there are any beneficiaries who are not applicants to the certificate, place an "X" beside "Yes."

11. If a person not named in the will as estate trustee is not an applicant, a reason why he or she is entitled to be estate trustee must be set out. For example:

> The applicant is the son of the deceased.

12. *Family Law Act* Election; see the explanation above.

13. The original executed will is Exhibit "A" to the application; the first codicil is Exhibit "B" to the application, the second codicil is Exhibit "C," and so on.

14. Each estate trustee swears the affidavit at the bottom of the form; if there are more than two estate trustees, an additional sheet with additional affidavits may be attached.

Number and Disposition of Copies

Prepare a minimum of three copies of the application. The original will be submitted to the court; one copy is for the lawyer's use and one is for the file. Additional copies may be required for the estate trustee(s).

Affidavit of Execution of Will and Codicil(s)

If affidavits of execution of the will and any codicil(s) were executed at the time the will and any codicil(s) were signed, make photocopies of the originals for the office file and then attach the originals to the appropriate will or codicil to be filed with the application.

If no affidavit of execution of will or codicil was sworn at the time of execution, such an affidavit must be prepared in duplicate, as discussed in Chapter 32.

Affidavit of Condition of Will or Codicil

Usually, the affidavit of a witness to the will as to its execution is all that is required. When in a will or codicil there are interlineations, alterations, erasures, or obliterations that were not initialled by the deceased and the witnesses, an affidavit of condition of will or codicil is usually required to provide that such changes existed in the will before its execution and were not made after the will was executed.

The affidavit, when required, is completed by one of the witnesses to the will or codicil; it outlines the details of any alterations, erasures, obliterations, or interlineations that were not initialled by the deceased and witnesses when the document was executed.

The affidavit concludes with a statement that the document is in the same condition as when it was executed. If this statement is not correct, the words "except that" are added, and details of the exception are set out.

Prepare three copies of the affidavit. The original copy is attached to the application; one copy is for the lawyer's use, and one copy remains in the office file.

Exhibits Filed

Regardless of the number of affidavits to which they are produced as exhibits, only the original signed copy of the will and any codicil(s) are filed with the estate registrar of the court.

The original signed copy of the will is produced as Exhibit A to the various affidavits, including the affidavit of execution of will. If the affidavit of execution of will was done at the time the testator signed the will, the Exhibit A stamp for that witness will have already been completed. An additional completed Exhibit A stamp will be required for each applicant. Stamping and the endorsement appear on the back of the last page of the will, that is, the reverse side of the page on which the testator executed the will, as illustrated in Figure 33.2 (p. 630).

Any original signed codicils are endorsed and stamped in the same manner. The first codicil is Exhibit B to the affidavit of the applicant and Exhibit A to the affidavit of the witness to the codicil. A second codicil would be Exhibit C to the affidavit of the applicant and Exhibit A to the affidavit of the witness to that codicil.

Certificate of Appointment of Estate Trustee with a Will

Precedent 33.5 illustrates this form, which requires only the insertion of the name, address, occupation, and date of death of the deceased. Three copies should be prepared: one for submission to the court, one for the lawyer's use, and one for the office file. Note that this is one of the few forms in estate proceedings that requires a back.

Obtaining Certificate

To have the certificate of appointment of estate trustee with a will issued, the following lists the most common documents that must delivered or sent by registered mail with a covering letter to the estate registrar of the Superior Court of Justice of the county in which the deceased resided:

1. Application for certificate of appointment of estate trustee with a will (either individual or corporate)
2. Renunciation and Consent, if the estate trustee(s) is not the person named in the will
3. Original will (and any codicils, if applicable)
4. Affidavit of execution of will (and of any codicils, if applicable)
5. Affidavit of service of notice of an application for a certificate of appointment of estate trustee with a will
6. Certificate of appointment of estate trustee with a will
7. Court fees payable to the Minister of Finance

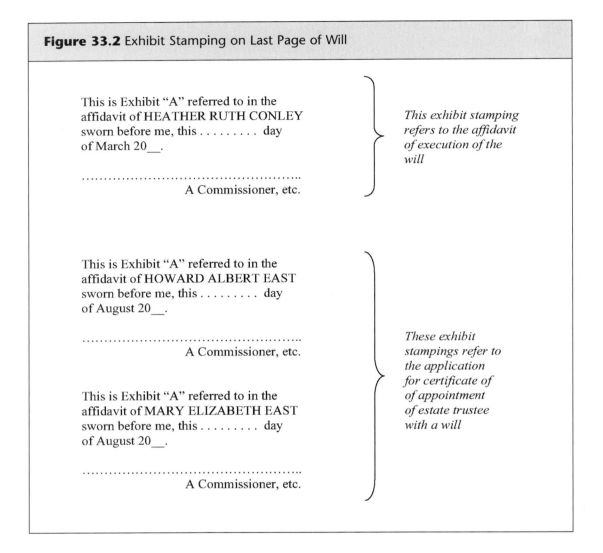

Figure 33.2 Exhibit Stamping on Last Page of Will

This is Exhibit "A" referred to in the affidavit of HEATHER RUTH CONLEY sworn before me, this . . . . day of March 20___.

....
A Commissioner, etc.

This exhibit stamping refers to the affidavit of execution of the will

This is Exhibit "A" referred to in the affidavit of HOWARD ALBERT EAST sworn before me, this . . . . day of August 20___.

....
A Commissioner, etc.

This is Exhibit "A" referred to in the affidavit of MARY ELIZABETH EAST sworn before me, this . . . . day of August 20___.

....
A Commissioner, etc.

These exhibit stampings refer to the application for certificate of of appointment of estate trustee with a will

Additional documents, such as an affidavit of condition of will, affidavit attesting to the handwriting, and signature of a holograph will or codicil, may be required in certain circumstances, for which the lawyer would provide instruction.

When all the original forms have been considered by the court, the original certificate of appointment of estate trustee with a will is obtained. The original signed will remains in the custody of the court; a photocopy of the will is attached to the certificate.

CERTIFICATE OF APPOINTMENT OF ESTATE TRUSTEE WITHOUT A WILL

When a person dies intestate, no one has been appointed to distribute his or her estate, and the court considers applications for appointment of estate trustee without a will. The *Succession Law Reform Act* sets outs who is entitled to share in the estate and how much they receive, whereas the *Estates Act* sets out who may apply for appointment as estate trustee. The spouse of the deceased has first priority and after that, children, grandchildren, great-grandchildren, parents, siblings, or other next of kin. Anyone who has a prior right to administration, such as a widow of the deceased who chooses not to be the estate trustee, must renounce her right before administration will be granted.

To distribute the estate, a certificate of appointment of estate trustee without a will needs to be obtained by preparing and submitting the following documents to the estate registrar of the Superior Court of Justice in which the deceased resided:

1. **Notice of application for a certificate of appointment of estate trustee without a will** on all persons entitled to share in the distribution of the estate, which is virtually the same as the notice and procedure as when there is a will, as discussed earlier in this chapter
2. **Affidavit of service of notice without a will** to be executed by the applicant(s)
3. **Application for a certificate of appointment of estate trustee without a will**. There is a form for an individual applicant illustrated in Precedent 33.6 and one for a corporate applicant. Note the following information that will need to be completed:
   a. the name, place, address, occupation, and date of death of the deceased;
   b. the marital status of deceased and details of the deceased's marital history;
   c. the name, address, relationship to the deceased, and age (if under 18) of those persons entitled to share in the estate;
   d. the value of the estate;
   e. why the applicant is entitled to apply to be appointed estate trustee; and
   f. the name, occupation, and full address of the applicant, which must be inserted into the affidavit portion of the form.
4. **Renunciation of prior right to a certificate of appointment of estate trustee without a will** needs to be prepared and then completed by every person who has a priority right to be named estate trustee, if necessary (Precedent 33.7)
5. **Consent to the applicant's appointment as estate trustee without a will** completed by those persons who together have a majority interest in the value of estate as of the deceased's date of death (Precedent 33.8). A consent will need to be prepared and then signed by each individual consenting to the applicant being appointed estate trustee.
6. **Administration Bond** as may be required by the *Estates Act*
7. Certificate of Appointment of Estate Trustee without a will, which is prepared in the same manner as a certificate of appointment of estate trustee with a will, as previously discussed
8. Court fees payable to the Minister of Finance

Number and Disposition of Copies

A minimum of three copies should be made of each of these documents. The original will must be submitted to the court. One copy is for the lawyer's use and one for the office file. Additional copies may be required for the individual parties who are signing the documents.

ADMINISTRATION BONDS

The *Estates Act* states that any applicant for a certificate of appointment of estate trustee without a will shall provide a bond payable to the Superior Court of Justice of the county in which the application is made to ensure faithful administration of the estate. A bond is also required when there is a will, but the applicant is not named in the will as the estate trustee, or when the applicant is named in the will but is not a resident of Ontario. The act provides that the amount of the bond shall be double the amount of the value of the estate, although, in practice, the amount is usually equal to the amount of the estate.

Such a bond is not required of a trust company whose charter provides that it may act as estate trustee or where the applicant is a spouse and the net value of the estate is below $200,000 and an affidavit of debts is filed with the application for administration.

The bond is usually given by a **surety**, that is, a person or company that promises to satisfy the obligation of another in the event of the other's default. No solicitor may be a surety to a bond, and a surety must be a resident of Ontario. Where the value of the deceased's property is $100,000 or less, only one surety is required; where the value exceeds $100,000, at least two sureties are required unless the judge directs otherwise.

It should be noted that a judge may, under special circumstances, reduce the amount of a bond or dispense with it entirely.

When the administration of the estate is complete, the following material is filed with the estate registrar to release the bond: a draft order cancelling the bond, an affidavit in support of the order that sets out the facts proving the completed administration of the estate, releases from the next of kin or beneficiaries, and an affidavit proving the publishing of an advertisement for creditors. If the material submitted is satisfactory, the order will be signed, and the order and the bond are returned to the solicitors acting for the estate trustee.

COURT FEES

In Ontario, the Superior Court of Justice levies a fee for granting certificates of appointment of estate trustee with or without a will (formerly and still often referred to probate fees) depending on the value of the estate being administered. As of January 1, 2008, the fees were as follows:

1. on the first $50,000 of the value of the estate,
   per thousand, or part thereof $ 5.00
2. on any portion above $50,000, per thousand,
   or part thereof $15.00

Thus, if the value of an estate being administered has a value of $500,000 (real and personal property), the fees would be calculated as follows:

Amount payable on first $50,000 ($5 × $50,000) =	$ 250
Amount payable on balance ($15 × $450,000) =	$6,750
Total fees payable	$7,000

Terms and Concepts

estate

estate trustee

locating will

obtaining information on deceased

next of kin

certificate of appointment of estate trustee
with a will

certificate of appointment of estate trustee
without a will

renunciation

consent

notice of application for a certificate of
appointment of estate trustee with a will

affidavit of service of notice of an
application for a certificate of
appointment of estate trustee

affidavit of execution of will and codicil

affidavit of condition of will or codicil

marking exhibits

notice of application for a certificate of
appointment of estate trustee without
a will

affidavit of service of notice without a will

renunciation of prior right to a certificate of
appointment of estate trustee without
a will

consent to the applicant's appointment as
estate trustee without a will

Administration Bond

surety

releasing the bond

calculating court fees for estates

Review Questions

1. What steps may be taken to locate a will?

2. What information does a law firm require to act for the personal representatives
of an estate?

3. Why might the law firm wait six months before distributing any of the assets of
an estate?

4. What must be submitted to the estate registrar to obtain a certificate of appointment of estate trustee with a will?

5. How can one original will be an exhibit to both the application and the affidavit
of execution of a will?

6. What must be submitted to the estate trustee to obtain a certificate of appointment of estate trustee without a will?

7. Under what circumstances is an administration bond required?

8. Bronwyn's estate is composed of the following: a $200,000 home held jointly with
her husband; a $3,000 vehicle; $25,000 in GICs held jointly with her husband;
$2,000 in her chequing account; and a $100,000 cottage property in her name
with a $25,000 mortgage. Complete the following and calculate the court fees:

Table		
Personal Property	**Real Estate, Net of Encumbrances**	**Total**
$	$	$

9. **Internet Research:** Research the amount of probate fees for the provinces and
territories of Canada. Which province/territory has the highest fees? Which
province/territory has the lowest fees?

PRECEDENTS

Precedent 33.1 Notice of Application for a Certificate of Appointment of Estate Trustee with a Will

NOTICE OF AN APPLICATION
FOR A CERTIFICATE OF APPOINTMENT
OF ESTATE TRUSTEE WITH A WILL
Form 74.7
Courts of Justice Act

Ontario
Superior Court of Justice

(Page 1)

(insert name) IN THE ESTATE OF **HENRY JAMES EAST**, deceased.

NOTICE OF AN APPLICATION FOR A
CERTIFICATE OF APPOINTMENT OF ESTATE
TRUSTEE WITH A WILL

(insert date) 1.   The deceased died on **January 31, 2007**.

2.   Attached to this notice are:

(A)   If the notice is sent to or in respect of a person entitled only to a specified item of property or stated amount of money, an extract of the part or parts of the will or codicil relating to the gift, or a copy of the will (and codicil(s), if any).

(B)   If the notice is sent to or in respect of any other beneficiary, a copy of the will (and codicil(s), if any).

(C)   If the notice is sent to the Children's Lawyer or the Public Guardian and Trustee, a copy of the will (and codicil(s), if any), and if it is not included in the notice, a statement of the estimated value of the interest of the person represented.

3.   The applicant named in this notice is applying for a certificate of appointment of estate trustee with a will.

APPLICANT

Name	Address
Howard Albert East	**19 King Street** **Brampton, Ontario, L5S 3C8**
Mary Elizabeth East	**145 William Street** **Toronto, Ontario, M9C 4S8**

4.   The following persons who are less than 18 years of age are entitled, whether their interest is contingent or vested, to share in the distribution of the estate:

Name	Date of Birth *(day, month, year)*	Name and Address of Parent or Guardian	Estimated Value of Interest in Estate*
Not Applicable			

* Note: *The Estimated Value of Interest in Estate may be omitted in the form if it is included in a separate schedule attached to the notice sent to the Children's Lawyer.*

RCP-E 74.7 (November 1, 2005)

NOTICE OF AN APPLICATION
FOR A CERTIFICATE OF APPOINTMENT
OF ESTATE TRUSTEE WITH A WILL
Form 74.7
Courts of Justice Act

(Page 2)

(insert name) IN THE ESTATE OF **HENRY JAMES EAST**, deceased.

5.   The following persons who are mentally incapable within the meaning of section 6 of the *Substitute Decisions Act, 1992* in respect of an issue in the proceeding, and who have guardians or attorneys acting under powers of attorney with authority to act in the proceeding, are entitled, whether their interest is contingent or vested, to share in the distribution of the estate:

Name and Address of Person   **Name and Address of Guardian or Attorney***

Not Applicable

*Specify whether guardian or attorney

6.   The following persons who are mentally incapable within the meaning of section 6 of the *Substitute Decisions Act, 1992* in respect of an issue in the proceeding, and who do not have guardians or attorneys acting under powers of attorney with authority to act in the proceeding, are entitled, whether their interest is contingent or vested, to share in the distribution of the estate:

Name and Address of Person   **Estimated Value of Interest in Estate***

Not Applicable

* Note: The Estimated Value of Interest in Estate may be omitted in the form if it is included in a separate schedule attached to the notice sent to the Public Guardian and Trustee.

(Delete if not applicable) 7.   ~~Unborn or unascertained persons may be entitled to share in the distribution of the estate.~~

8.   All other persons and charities entitled, whether their interest is contingent or vested, to share in the distribution of the estate are as follows:

Name	Address
Kyle Andrew East	**145 William Street** **Toronto, Ontario, M9C 4S8**
Mary Allison East	**350 Greystone Road** **Mississauga, Ontario, L1B 6M9**

9.   This notice is being sent, by regular lettermail, to all adult persons and charities named above in this notice (except to an applicant who is entitled to share in the distribution of the estate), to the Public Guardian and Trustee if paragraph 6 applies, to a parent or guardian of the minor and to the Children's Lawyer if paragraph 4 applies, to the guardian or attorney if paragraph 5 applies, and to the Children's Lawyer if paragraph 7 applies.

RCP-E 74.7 (November 1, 2005)

Source: © Queen's Printer for Ontario, 2005. Reproduced with permission.

NOTICE OF AN APPLICATION
FOR A CERTIFICATE OF APPOINTMENT
OF ESTATE TRUSTEE WITH A WILL
Form 74.7
Courts of Justice Act

(Page 3)

(insert name) IN THE ESTATE OF **HENRY JAMES EAST**, deceased.

If paragraph 10 does not apply insert "Not Applicable."

10.   The following persons named in the Will or being a member of a class of beneficiaries under the Will may be entitled to be served but have not been served for the reasons shown below:

Name of person (as it appears in will, if applicable)   Reason not served

Not Applicable

DATE: **August   , 20__**

RCP-E 74.7 (November 1. 2005)

AFFIDAVIT OF SERVICE OF NOTICE
Form 74.6
Courts of Justice Act

Ontario
Superior Court of Justice

(Page 1)

(insert name) IN THE ESTATE OF **HENRY JAMES EAST**, deceased.

AFFIDAVIT OF SERVICE OF NOTICE

(insert name) I, **Howard Albert East**,

(insert city or town and country or district of residence) **of the City of Brampton in the Regional Municipality of Peel**,

make oath and say/affirm:

1. I am **an applicant** for a certificate of appointment of estate trustee with a will in the estate.

2. I have sent or caused to be sent a notice in Form 74.7, a copy of which is marked as Exhibit "A" to this affidavit, to all adult persons and charities named in the notice (except to an applicant who is entitled to share in the distribution of the estate), to the Public Guardian and Trustee if paragraph 6 of the notice applies, to a parent or guardian of the minor and to the Children's Lawyer if paragraph 4 applies, to the guardian or attorney if paragraph 5 applies, and to the Children's Lawyer if paragraph 7 applies, all by regular lettermail sent to the person's last known address.

3. I have attached or caused to be attached to each notice the following:

    (A) In the case of a notice sent to or in respect of a person entitled only to a specified item of property or stated amount of money, an extract of the part or parts of the will or codicil relating to the gift, or a copy of the will (and codicil(s), if any).

    (B) In the case of a notice sent to or in respect of any other beneficiary, a copy of the will (and codicil(s), if any).

    (C) In the case of a notice sent to the Children's Lawyer or the Public Guardian and Trustee, a copy of the will (and codicil(s), if any) and a statement of the estimated value of the interest of the person represented.

If paragraph 4 does not apply insert "Not Applicable." 4. The following persons and charities specifically named in the Will are not entitled to be served for the reasons shown:

Name of person (as it appears in will, if applicable) Reason not served

Not Applicable

If paragraph 5 does not apply insert "Not Applicable." 5. The following persons named in the Will or being a member of a class of beneficiaries under the Will may be entitled to be served but have not been served for the reasons shown below:

Name of person (as it appears in will, if applicable) Reason not served

Not Applicable

RCP-E 74.6 (November 1, 2005)

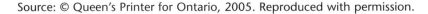

Source: © Queen's Printer for Ontario, 2005. Reproduced with permission.

AFFIDAVIT OF SERVICE OF NOTICE
Form 74.6
Courts of Justice Act

(Page 2)

(insert name) IN THE ESTATE OF **HENRY JAMES EAST**, deceased.

6. To the best of my knowledge and belief, subject to paragraph 5 (if applicable), the persons named in the notice are all the persons who are entitled to share in the distribution of the estate.

Sworn/Affirmed before me at the **City**

of **Toronto**

in the **Province**

of **Ontario**

this .... day of .... **August** ...., 20 ....

_____
Signature of applicant
Howard Albert East

_____
A Commissioner for taking Affidavits *(or as may be)*

RCP-E 74.6 (November 1, 2005)

ONTARIO

SUPERIOR COURT OF JUSTICE

APPLICATION FOR CERTIFICATE OF APPOINTMENT OF ESTATE TRUSTEE WITH A WILL (INDIVIDUAL APPLICANT)
(Form 74.4 Under the Rules (Page 1 of 3))
Courts of Justice Act

at **Toronto**

This application is filed by *(insert name and address)*
Peter T. Grant, HILL, JOHNSTON & GRANT
17 Princess Street South, Suite 2501
Toronto ON M8Y 3N5   Tel: (416) 354-9000   Fax: (416) 354-9909

DETAILS ABOUT THE DECEASED PERSON

Complete in full as applicable

First given name	Second given name	Third given name	Surname
HENRY	JAMES		EAST

And if the deceased was known by any other name(s), state below the full name(s) used including surname.

First given name	Second given name	Third given name	Surname

Address of fixed place of abode *(street or postal address) (city or town)*
145 William Street
Toronto, Ontario, M9C 4S8

(county or district)
City of Toronto

If the deceased person had no fixed place of abode in Ontario, did he or she have property in Ontario?   **N/A** ☐ No   ☐ Yes

Last occupation of deceased person
Retired Dentist

Place of death *(city or town; county or district)*

City of Toronto in the Province of Ontario

Date of death
(day, month, year)

31 Jan 2007

Date of last will
(marked as Exhibit "A")
(day, month, year)

07 Nov 1993

Was the deceased person 18 years of age or older at the date of the will (or 21 years of age or older if the will is dated earlier than September 1, 1971)?   ☐ No   ☒ Yes
If not, explain why certificate is being sought. Give details in an attached schedule.

Date of codicil (marked as Exhibit "B")
(day, month, year)

19 Apr 1995

Date of codicil (marked as Exhibit "C")
(day, month, year)

N/A

Marital Status ☐ Unmarried   ☒ Married   ☐ Widowed   ☐ Divorced

Did the deceased person marry after the date of the will?   ☒ No   ☐ Yes
If yes, explain why certificate is being sought. Give details in an attached schedule.

Was a marriage of the deceased person terminated by a judgment absolute of divorce, or declared a nullity, after the date of the will?   ☒ No   ☐ Yes
If yes, give details in an attached schedule.

Is any person who signed the will or a codicil as witness or for the testator, or the spouse of such person, a beneficiary under the will?   ☒ No   ☐ Yes
If yes, give details in an attached schedule.

RCP-E 74.4 (November 1, 2005)

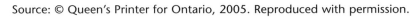

Source: © Queen's Printer for Ontario, 2005. Reproduced with permission.

VALUE OF ASSETS OF ESTATE

Do not include in the total amount: insurance payable to a named beneficiary or assigned for value, property held jointly and passing by survivorship, or real estate outside Ontario.

Personal Property	Real estate, net of encumbrances	Total
$ 165,829.00	$ 160,000.00	$ 325,829.00

Is there any person entitled to an interest in the estate who is not an applicant? ☐ No ☒ Yes

If a person named in the will or a codicil as estate trustee is not an applicant, explain.

N/A

If a person not named in the will or a codicil as estate trustee is an applicant, explain why that person is entitled to apply.

N/A

If the spouse of the deceased is an applicant, has the spouse elected to receive the entitlement under section 5 of the *Family Law Act?*
If yes, explain why the spouse is entitled to apply.   ☒ No ☐ Yes

AFFIDAVIT(S) OF APPLICANT(S)

(Attach a separate sheet for additional affidavits, if necessary)

I, an applicant named in this application, make oath and say/affirm:

1. I am 18 years of age or older.
2. The exhibit(s) referred to in this application are the last will and each codicil (where applicable) of the deceased person and I do not know of any later will or codicil.
3. I will faithfully administer the deceased person's property according to law and render a complete and true account of my administration when lawfully required.
4. If I am not named as estate trustee in the will or codicil, consents of persons who together have a majority interest in the value of the assets of the estate at the date of death are attached.
5. The information contained in this application and in any attached schedules is true, to the best of my knowledge and belief.

Name *(surname and forename(s))*	Occupation
East, Howard Albert	**Dentist**

Address *(street or postal address)*	*(city or town)*	*(province)*	*(postal code)*
19 King Street	**Brampton**	**Ontario**	**L5S 3C8**

Sworn/Affirmed before me at the City ....

of Toronto ....

in the Province ....

of Ontario ....

this .... day of .... August ...., 20 ....

Signature of applicant
Howard Albert East

A Commissioner for taking Affidavits *(or as may be)*

RCP-E 74.4 (November 1, 2005)

AFFIDAVIT(S) OF APPLICANT(S)

(Attach a separate sheet for additional affidavits, if necessary)

I, an applicant named in this application, make oath and say/affirm:

1. I am 18 years of age or older.
2. The exhibit(s) referred to in this application are the last will and each codicil (where applicable) of the deceased person and I do not know of any later will or codicil.
3. I will faithfully administer the deceased person's property according to law and render a complete and true account of my administration when lawfully required.

4. If I am not named as estate trustee in the will or codicil, consents of persons who together have a majority interest in the value of the assets of the estate at the date of death are attached.
5. The information contained in this application and in any attached schedules is true, to the best of my knowledge and belief.

Name *(surname and forename(s))*	**Occupation**
East, Mary Elizabeth	Retired Nurse

Address *(street or postal address)*	*(city or town)*	*(province)*	*(postal code)*
145 William Street	Toronto	Ontario	M9C 4S8

Sworn/Affirmed before me at the City ....

of Toronto ....

in the Province ....

of Ontario ....

this .... day of ...., 20 ....

Signature of applicant
Mary Elizabeth East

_____
A Commissioner for taking Affidavits *(or as may be)*

RCP-E 74.4 (November 1, 2005)

Precedent 33.4 Application for a Certificate of Appointment of Estate Trustee with a Will (Corporate Applicant)

ONTARIO

SUPERIOR COURT OF JUSTICE

APPLICATION FOR CERTIFICATE OF APPOINTMENT OF ESTATE TRUSTEE WITH A WILL (CORPORATE APPLICANT)
(Form 74.5 Under the Rules (Page 1 of 2))
Courts of Justice Act

at **Whitby**

This application is filed by *(insert name and address)*
Peter T. Grant, HILL, JOHNSTON & GRANT
17 Princess Street South, Suite 2501
Toronto ON M8Y 3N5   Tel: (416) 354-9000   Fax: (416) 354-9909

DETAILS ABOUT THE DECEASED PERSON

Complete in full as applicable

First given name	Second given name	Third given name	Surname
NORMAN	HAROLD		SPRING

And if the deceased was known by any other name(s), state below the full name(s) used including surname.

First given name	Second given name	Third given name	Surname

Address of fixed place of abode *(street or postal address) (city or town)*	*(county or district)*
4800 Walker's Line Pickering, Ontario, L8C 4V6	**Regional Municipality of Durham**

If the deceased person had no fixed place of abode in Ontario, did he or she have property in Ontario? N/A ☐ No ☐ Yes	**Last occupation of deceased person** Mechanic

Place of death *(city or town; county or district)*	**Date of death** *(day, month, year)*	**Date of last will** (marked as Exhibit "A") *(day, month, year)*
Town of Pickering in the Regional Municipality of Durham	**28 Jun 2007**	**28 Jun 1989**

Was the deceased person 18 years of age or older at the date of the will (or 21 years of age or older if the will is dated earlier than September 1, 1971)?   ☐ No   ☒ Yes
If not, explain why certificate is being sought. Give details in an attached schedule.

Date of codicil (marked as Exhibit "B") *(day, month, year)*	**Date of codicil** (marked as Exhibit "C") *(day, month, year)*
N/A	**N/A**

Marital Status ☐ Unmarried   ☐ Married   ☒ Widowed   ☐ Divorced

Did the deceased person marry after the date of the will?   ☒ No   ☐ Yes
If yes, explain why certificate is being sought. Give details in an attached schedule.

Was a marriage of the deceased person terminated by a judgment absolute of divorce, or declared a nullity, after the date of the will?   ☒ No   ☐ Yes
If yes, give details in an attached schedule.

Is any person who signed the will or a codicil as witness or for the testator, or the spouse of such person, a beneficiary under the will?   ☒ No   ☐ Yes
If yes, give details in an attached schedule.

RCP-E 74.5 (November 1, 2005)

VALUE OF ASSETS OF ESTATE

Do not include in the total amount: insurance payable to a named beneficiary or assigned for value, property held jointly and passing by survivorship, or real estate outside Ontario.

Personal property	Real estate, net of encumbrances	Total
$ 68,450.00	$ 120,000.00	$ 188,450.00

Is there any person interested in the estate who is not an applicant? ☐ No ☒ Yes

If a person named in the will or a codicil as estate trustee is not an applicant, explain.

The named trustee Bethany Anne Spring predeceased the deceased.

If a person not named in the will or a codicil as estate trustee is an applicant, explain why that person is entitled to apply.
Nominee of the next of kin

If the spouse of the deceased is an applicant, has the spouse elected to receive the entitlement under section 5 of the *Family Law Act?* ☐ No ☐ Yes
If yes, explain why the spouse is entitled to apply

N/A

AFFIDAVIT(S) OF APPLICANT(S)
(Attach a separate sheet for additional affidavits, if necessary)

I, a trust officer named in this application, make oath and say/affirm:

1. I am a trust officer of the corporate applicant.
2. I am 18 years of age or older.
3. The exhibit(s) referred to in this application are the last will and each codicil (where applicable) of the deceased person and I do not know of any later will or codicil.
4. The corporate applicant will faithfully administer the deceased person's property according to law and render a complete and true account of its administration when lawfully required.

5. If the corporate applicant is not named as estate trustee in the will or codicil, consents of persons who together have a majority interest in the value of the assets of the estate at the date of death are attached.
6. The information contained in this application and in any attached schedules is true, to the best of my knowledge and belief.

Name of corporate applicant	Name of trust officer
Algonquin Permanent Trust Company	**Gregory Czyowski**

Address of corporate applicant *(street or postal address)* *(city or town)* *(province)* *(postal code)*
500 Tower Road   **Newmarket** **Ontario**   **L6R 9V2**

Sworn/Affirmed before me at the **City**

of **Newmarket**

in the **Regional Municipality**

of **York**

this .... day of ...., 20 ....

_____
A Commissioner for taking Affidavits *(or as may be)*

_____
Signature of trust officer
Gregory Czyowski

RCP-E 74.5 (November 1, 2005)

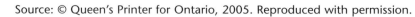

CERTIFICATE OF APPOINTMENT
OF ESTATE TRUSTEE WITH A WILL
Form 74.13
Courts of Justice Act

Court file no.

Ontario
Superior Court of Justice

(insert name)

IN THE ESTATE OF **HENRY JAMES EAST, deceased.**

late of **the City of Toronto in the Province of Ontario ,**

occupation **Retired Dentist ,**

who died on **January 31, 2007 .**

**CERTIFICATE OF APPOINTMENT
OF ESTATE TRUSTEE WITH A WILL**

Applicant	Address	Occupation
Howard Albert East	**19 King Street Brampton, Ontario, L5S 3C8**	**Dentist**
Mary Elizabeth East	**145 William Street Toronto, Ontario, M9C 4S8**	**Retired Nurse**

This CERTIFICATE OF APPOINTMENT OF ESTATE TRUSTEE WITH A WILL is hereby issued under the seal of the court to the applicant named above. A copy of the deceased's last will (and codicil(s), if any) is attached.

DATE: **August** , 20__

_____
Registrar

Address of court office:

**330 University Avenue
7th Floor
Toronto, Ontario
M5G 1R7**

RCP-E 74.13 (November 1, 2005)

Court file no.

Ontario
Superior Court of Justice

at Toronto

IN THE ESTATE OF **HENRY JAMES EAST**, deceased

**CERTIFICATE OF APPOINTMENT
OF ESTATE TRUSTEE WITH A WILL**

*Name, address, telephone number and fax number
of solicitor or applicant:*

**Peter T. Grant
HILL, JOHNSTON & GRANT**
17 Princess Street South, Suite 2501
Toronto ON M8Y 3N5

LSUC Registration No.: 12345G
Tel: (416) 354-9000
Fax: (416) 354-9909

Source: © Queen's Printer for Ontario, 2005. Reproduced with permission.

ONTARIO

SUPERIOR COURT OF JUSTICE

**APPLICATION FOR CERTIFICATE
OF APPOINTMENT OF ESTATE TRUSTEE
WITHOUT A WILL (INDIVIDUAL APPLICANT)**
(Form 74.14 Under the Rules (Page 1 of 3))
Courts of Justice Act

at **Brampton**

This application is filed by *(insert name and address)*
**Peter T. Grant, HILL, JOHNSTON & GRANT
17 Princess Street South, Suite 2501
Toronto ON M8Y 3N5   Tel: (416) 354-9000   Fax: (416) 354-9900**

DETAILS ABOUT THE DECEASED PERSON

Complete in full as applicable

First given name	Second given name	Third given name	Surname
DOREEN	**MARION**		**CLARKSON**

And if the deceased was known by any other name(s), state below the full name(s) used including surname.

First given name	Second given name	Third given name	Surname

Address of fixed place of abode *(street or postal address) (city or town)*	*(county or district)*
1920 Connor Road **Mississauga, Ontario, L3V 5J8**	**Regional Municipality of Peel**

If the deceased person had no fixed place of abode in Ontario, did he or she have property in Ontario? **N/A** ☐ No ☐ Yes	**Last occupation of deceased person** **Accountant**

Place of death *(city or town; county or district)*	**Date of death** *(day, month, year)*
City of Mississauga in the Regional Municipality of Peel	**03 Apr 2007**

Marital Status ☒ Unmarried   ☐ Married   ☐ Widowed   ☐ Divorced

Was the deceased person's marriage terminated by a judgment absolute of divorce, or declared a nullity? If yes, give details in an attached schedule.	☒ No	☐ Yes
Did the deceased person go through a form of marriage with a person where it appears uncertain whether an earlier marriage of the deceased person had been terminated by divorce or declared a nullity? If yes, give the other person's name and address, and the names and addresses of any children (including deceased children) of the marriage, in an attached schedule.	☒ No	☐ Yes
Was any earlier marriage of a person with whom the deceased person went through a form of marriage terminated by divorce or declared a nullity? If yes, give details in an attached schedule.	☐ No	☐ Yes
Was the deceased person immediately before his or her death living with a person in a conjugal relationship outside marriage? If yes, give the person's name and address in an attached schedule.	☒ No	☐ Yes

RCP-E 74.14 (November 1, 2005)

PERSONS ENTITLED TO SHARE IN THE ESTATE

(Attach a schedule if more space is needed. If a person entitled to share in the estate is not a spouse, child, parent, brother or sister of the deceased person, show how the relationship is traced.)

Name	Address	Relationship to deceased person	Age (if under 18)
Karen Alissa Clarkson	14 Leeds Road Vancouver, BC, V7W 4X9	mother	
Jennifer Warner	953 Quarry Stone Road Brampton, Ontario, L4S 3G6	sister	

VALUE OF ASSETS OF ESTATE

Do not include in the total amount: insurance payable to a named beneficiary or assigned for value, property held jointly and passing by survivorship, or real estate outside Ontario.

Personal property	Real estate, net of encumbrances	Total
$ 56,750.00	$ 260,000.00	$ 316,750.00

Explain why the applicant is entitled to apply.

Sister of the deceased and nominee of other next of kin.

RCP-E 74.14 (November 1, 2005)

Source: © Queen's Printer for Ontario, 2005. Reproduced with permission.

AFFIDAVIT(S) OF APPLICANT(S)

(Attach a separate sheet for additional affidavits, if necessary)

I, an applicant named in this application, make oath and say/affirm:

1. I am 18 years of age or older and a resident of Ontario.
2. I have made a careful search and inquiry for a will or other testamentary document of the deceased person, but none has been found. I believe that the person did not leave a will or other testamentary document.
3. I will faithfully administer the deceased person's property according to law and render a complete and true account of my administration when lawfully required.
4. Consents of persons who together have a majority interest in the value of the assets of the estate at the date of death are attached.
5. The information contained in this application and in any attached schedules is true, to the best of my knowledge and belief.

Name *(surname and forename(s))*	**Occupation**		
Warner, Jennifer	Accountant		
Address *(street or postal address)*	*(city or town)*	*(province)*	*(postal code)*
953 Quarry Stone Road	Brampton	Ontario	L4S 3G6

Sworn/Affirmed before me at the **City**

of **Toronto**

in the **Province**

of **Ontario**

this .... day of ...., 20 ....

Signature of applicant
Jennifer Warner

_____
A Commissioner for taking Affidavits *(or as may be)*

RCP-E 74.14 (November 1, 2005)

RENUNCIATION OF PRIOR RIGHT TO A
CERTIFICATE OF APPOINTMENT OF ESTATE TRUSTEE
WITHOUT A WILL
Form 74.18
Courts of Justice Act

Ontario
Superior Court of Justice

(insert name) IN THE ESTATE OF **DOREEN MARION CLARKSON**, deceased.

**RENUNCIATION OF PRIOR RIGHT TO A
CERTIFICATE OF APPOINTMENT OF ESTATE TRUSTEE
WITHOUT A WILL**

(insert date) The deceased died on **April 3, 2007**, without a will.

(insert name) I, **Karen Alissa Clarkson**,

am entitled to apply for a certificate of appointment of estate trustee without a will in priority

(insert name) to **Jennifer Warner**.

I renounce my right to a certificate of appointment of estate trustee without a will in priority

(insert name) to **Jennifer Warner**.

DATE: _____

_____
Signature of witness

_____
Signature of person renouncing
Karen Alissa Clarkson

RCP-E 74.18 (November 1, 2005)

Source: © Queen's Printer for Ontario, 2005. Reproduced with permission.

CONSENT TO APPLICANT'S APPOINTMENT AS
ESTATE TRUSTEE WITHOUT A WILL
Form 74.19
Courts of Justice Act   *Ontario*
                              Superior Court of Justice

(insert name)   IN THE ESTATE OF **DOREEN MARION CLARKSON**, deceased.

CONSENT TO APPLICANT'S APPOINTMENT AS ESTATE TRUSTEE WITHOUT A WILL

(insert date)   The deceased died on **April 3, 2007**, without a will.

(insert name)   I, **Karen Alissa Clarkson**,

am entitled to share in the distribution of the estate.

(insert name)   I consent to the application by **Jennifer Warner**
for a certificate of appointment of estate trustee without a will.

(Delete if inapplicable)   I consent to an order dispensing with the filing of a bond by the applicant.

DATE: _____

_____   _____
Signature of witness   *Signature of person consenting*
                                                Karen Alissa Clarkson

RCP-E 74.19 (November 1, 2005)

Source: © Queen's Printer for Ontario, 2005. Reproduced with permission.

CHAPTER 34

Settling the Estate

OBJECTIVES:

- Describe the steps taken to obtain the documentation required to settle the estate

- Demonstrate an understanding of the procedures to transfer the assets of the deceased

- Use legal precedents to prepare the necessary documents to settle the estate

Once the certificate of appointment of the estate trustee with or without a will has been granted, the solicitors for the personal representative proceed to settle the estate. This includes selling any assets that must be disposed of, transferring specific gifts to named beneficiaries, distributing the proceeds of the assets to the next of kin under an intestacy, paying outstanding debts, applying for the appropriate Canada Pension Plan benefits, and filing an income tax return for the deceased for the year of death. The most common procedures and documents for settling the estate are discussed here, but there may, of course, be others.

NOTARIAL COPIES

To carry out the distribution of the estate, notarial copies of certain documents will be required by third parties. Precedent 34.1 illustrates the special form of notarial certificate used in connection with estate matters.

Make at least five notarial copies of the certificate of appointment of the estate trustee with or without the will and put the original away for safekeeping.

DEATH CERTIFICATE

Several copies of the death certificate of the deceased are usually provided by the funeral home handling the funeral arrangements for the deceased. If that is not the case, or an insufficient number are provided, an application for a copy or copies of the death certificate may be completed and forwarded together with a certified cheque in the appropriate amount to the Minister of Finance. The application form may be obtained at the Ministry of Government Services website (http://www.mgs.gov.on.ca/) under Forms.

ADVERTISING FOR CREDITORS

Although there is no statutory requirement to do so, to be sure that the personal representative of the deceased has notice of all claims against the estate of the deceased before the assets of the estate are distributed, a notice to creditors and others may be placed in a newspaper in the county in which the deceased normally resided or carried on business. The notice sets out the date by which claims against the estate must be sent to the personal representative; this date is usually at least one month from the date of the first appearance of the notice. For many years, the practice was to have this notice appear three times during a one-month period, but now the notice often appears only once. The lawyer will indicate which practice to follow if you are asked to prepare this notice.

There is no prescribed form of notice to creditors. It may be presented in a variety of styles, as reference to the legal column of your local newspaper will illustrate. One acceptable style appears in Figure 34.1.

Two copies of the notice to creditors are prepared, and the original is sent to the newspaper in which it is to appear. In the covering letter, indicate the number of times the notice is to be published and request that, following the final publication

Figure 34.1 Notice to Creditors

NOTICE TO CREDITORS
AND OTHERS

All claims against the estate of **HENRY JAMES EAST**, late of the City of Toronto, Province of Ontario, who died on or about the 1st day of August, 20__, must be filed with the undersigned estate trustees on or before the 11th day of November, 20__; thereafter the undersigned will distribute the assets of the estate having regard only to the claims then filed.

DATED this 10th day of October, 20__.

HOWARD ALBERT EAST and
MARY ELIZABETH EAST
Estate Trustees, by their solicitors
HILL, JOHNSTON & GRANT
17 Princess Street South, Suite 2501
Toronto ON M8Y 3N5

of the notice, the newspaper furnish an affidavit by one of its employees swearing as to the publication of the notice. A copy of the notice will be an exhibit to such an affidavit. Receipt of this affidavit provides proof of advertisement for creditors of the estate.

CANADA PENSION PLAN

Most individuals in Canada contribute to the Canada Pension Plan. Following a contributor's death, both of the following benefits may be payable: a monthly pension to a surviving spouse and for any dependent children and a lump-sum death benefit to the estate of the surviving spouse to help defray funeral expenses.

The application forms are often provided by the funeral home. If not, the information kit and application forms may be obtained from the Service Canada website (http://www.servicecanada.gc.ca/en/home.shtml). Applications for a lump-sum death benefit and survivor's pensions must be supported by the death certificate, the deceased's birth certificate, the deceased's social insurance card, and the statement of contributory salary and wages. Both applications are usually submitted at the same time, using the same material. For a survivor's pension application, the marriage certificate and the surviving spouse's birth certificate and social insurance card are also required.

INCOME TAX RETURN

An income tax return for a deceased taxpayer must be filed by the personal representative for any previous year for which a return has not yet been filed, and a final (known as a *terminal*) tax return is filed to the date of death for the year of death. If the deceased died before November, the return must be filed by April 30 of the next calendar year. If the deceased died in November or December, the return must be filed within six months of the date of death.

There is no terminal tax return; if necessary, use the previous year's T1 General return and change the date that appears in the upper right-hand corner. In complex estates, up to four separate T1 income tax returns may be required for the year of death; for most estates, only one return is necessary. In many estates, a chartered accountant will prepare all required returns; in other estates, the returns are prepared in the office of the solicitor acting for the personal representative.

GOODS AND SERVICES TAX

If the deceased held a personal registration number for the purposes of GST, it may be necessary to file a GST return as of the date of death. The lawyer handling the estate will give instructions on what procedures are to be followed.

ASSETS OF THE DECEASED

Estate Bank Account

If the deceased left cash on hand or uncashed cheques, or if assets of the estate are to be sold, an estate bank account is opened in the name of the personal representative(s). The bank will usually require a notarial copy of the certificate of appointment of estate trustee; however, for very small estates, which need not always involve granting of a certificate, the bank may accept a notarial copy of the will. Funds received that are payable to the estate are deposited in this account, and cheques written on the account are signed by the personal representative in that capacity. When the estate is distributed, this account is closed.

Bank Accounts

If the bank account of the deceased was held jointly with someone who survives him or her, the bank will usually allow such survivor to deal with the account upon presentation of proof of death of the deceased.

If the bank account of the deceased was not a joint account, the account may be closed out by completing the prescribed bank forms and presenting to the bank a notarial copy of the certificate. In the case of a small estate, the bank will often require only a notarial copy of the will. The amounts on deposit are then transferred to the estate bank account.

Automobiles

If an automobile owned by the deceased is to be transferred to a next of kin or beneficiary, an Application for Registration of Motor Vehicle form (available at Driver and Vehicle Licence offices) and the transfer portion of the ownership certificate are completed by the personal representative and taken to a Driver and Vehicle Licence Office with the required transfer fee. If the transfer is to someone other than a spouse of the deceased, a certificate of mechanical fitness is also required.

Government Bonds

If the bonds were held jointly with right of survivorship, a death certificate is provided to the financial institution to have the bonds transferred into the name of the surviving bondholder. If there is no right of survivorship or if the bonds are to be transferred to a beneficiary, the following material is required:

1. Death certificate
2. Notarial copy of certificate of appointment of estate trustee with a will (with a copy of the will attached) or certificate of appointment of estate trustee without a will
3. Bond certificates
4. Government of Canada form (Precedent 34.2). This form must be completed in front of a bank manager who can guarantee the signature or a notary public.

Non-Government Bonds and Shares

When shares or non-government bonds are to be transferred to a beneficiary, this material is furnished to the transfer agent for the company whose shares or bonds were owned by the deceased:

1. Notarial copy of the certificate
2. The original share or bond certificate
3. A declaration of transmission. There is one form for the transmission shares and a separate one for bonds.
4. Power of Attorney to Transfer Bonds-Shares. This form is signed by the personal representative in front of a bank manager or broker who can guarantee their signature.

These forms are available from legal stationers or the financial institutions or brokerage companies themselves. Once the forms are completed, the transfer agent then provides new certificates in the name of the beneficiary.

Insurance

If the assets of the deceased included life insurance policies, the insurance company concerned is advised of the death and requested to furnish the application forms for payment of the proceeds. These forms include a claimant's statement of proof of death, which may be completed by supplying either an original death certificate or a signed physician's statement. The insurance company usually requires that the policy of insurance be submitted when the claim is filed.

Transferring Title to Real Property to Surviving Joint Tenant

If the deceased left real property that was held as a joint tenant with a surviving tenant, title to the property automatically passes by law to the surviving joint tenant. If the property is in the registry system, no action is required until the surviving tenant wishes to transfer title. The transfer/deed given at that time cites the date of death of the deceased joint tenant; either a copy of the death certificate or an appropriate affidavit is registered on title.

If the property is in the land titles system, a survivorship application is registered to delete the name of the deceased joint owner on the register. Precedent 34.3 outlines the steps for creating an electronic Survivorship Application in Teraview. Precedent 34.4 illustrates a printout of an electronic survivorship application in progress.

Transferring Title to Real Property to Others

If the deceased left real property that was not held jointly with others and that he had the right to dispose of, the document prepared will depend on whether the property is in the registry or land titles system.

If the property is registered in the registry system, it may be conveyed to the beneficiary by registering a notarial copy of the will. In some circumstances, a new transfer/deed may be prepared, following the procedures outlined in Chapter 21.

If the property is registered in the land titles system, a Transmission by Personal Representative – Land is prepared and registered electronically through Teraview to register the land in the name (and capacity) of the personal representative before title to the property can be transferred to the new owner. Once the property is in the name of the personal representative, an electronic Transfer by Personal Representative is prepared and registered when the property is transferred. The preparation of electronic transfers is discussed in Chapter 21.

RELEASE BY BENEFICARY

Beneficiaries are asked to execute a release indicating that they have received gifts left to them under the will or their distributive share of an intestate estate. Precedent 34.5 illustrates an example of a form of release of a personal representative. Two copies of the release are prepared, and both are executed. One copy is for the beneficiary, and the other is for the personal representative. Make photocopies of the executed document for the office file.

PASSING OF ACCOUNTS

In some estates in which large amounts of money are involved, the personal representative maintains detailed accounts of receipts and disbursements, which are filed with the court that appointed the personal representative. This procedure is referred to as **passing of accounts**. Accounts are not required to be passed in all estates. They are passed when circumstances require, such as when an infant's share is paid into court or when the beneficiaries make a motion requesting that the personal representative pass the accounts. Because passing of accounts is not a procedure a legal assistant encounters often, the procedures and forms are not detailed here. However, if necessary, such procedures and forms are available in the *Rules of Civil Procedure*.

WINDING UP THE ESTATE

When the personal representative has received the compensation fee to which he or she may be entitled under the *Estates Act* (based on the value of the estate), the estate bank account has been closed, all assets of the estates have been distributed, and releases have been received from all beneficiaries or next of kin, the solicitors for the personal representative have completed their work. The estate is then said to be *wound up*. The solicitor writes a reporting letter to the personal representative, enclosing an account for an amount determined by the size of the estate.

Terms and Concepts

notarial copies in estates
death certificate
advertising for creditors
Canada Pension Plan benefits
income tax return
GST
estate bank account
automobile transfer

bonds and share transfers
life insurance claim
transferring title to real property in land
   titles and registry systems
release by beneficiary
passing of accounts
winding up estate

Review Questions

1. Where can you secure a copy (or additional copies) of the death certificate of a deceased person?

2. How can the personal representative ensure that he or she has a record of all debts of the deceased?

3. How is the Canada Pension Plan involved in the estate of the deceased person?

4. What happens to bank accounts of the deceased person that were
   a. held jointly with another party?
   b. held in his or her own name?

5. What procedures are followed if the deceased left real property that must be sold to settle the estate?

6. What is meant by "passing of accounts"?

7. What do personal representatives receive from beneficiaries when their bequest or share of the estate has been paid? What is the purpose of this document?

8. What procedures are followed to "wind up" an estate?

PRECEDENTS

Precedent 34.1 Notarial Certificate, Estate Documents

NOTARIAL CERTIFICATE OF TRUE COPY

CANADA
PROVINCE OF ONTARIO

(insert name)   I, **PETER T. GRANT,**

a duly appointed notary public for the Province of Ontario, residing at the

(insert city or town and county or district, metropolitan or regional municipality of residence)   **City of Toronto in the Province of Ontario,**

in the Province of Ontario, certify as follows:

1.   I have compared the attached document with a document produced and shown to me and purporting to be the original

(Applicable document)   **Certificate of Appointment of Estate Trustee With a Will in the Estate of HENRY JAMES EAST late of the City of Toronto in the Province of Ontario, deceased, issued out of the Superior Court of Justice at Toronto dated August 3, 2007.**

2.   The attached document is a true copy of the original.

DATE: _____

_____
A Notary Public for the Province of Ontario
PETER T. GRANT

Notarial Seal

Source: Do Process Software Ltd.

*For all provinces **except Quebec***

Redemption of Government of Canada securities or transfer from a deceased registered owner to a beneficiary(ies)

In the matter of the estate of _____ , _____

Full name of deceased   Marital status

I/we _____ am/are the representative(s) for the above-mentioned deceased.

Name

1. The deceased died on the ___ day of _____ , ____ and was domiciled in the Province of _____ .

   Month   Year

2. The following is a list of all the Government of Canada securities which were registered to the deceased at the time of his / her death.

Account/Portfolio Number or Series	S.I.N.	Registration (name)	Amount

Note: If space is insufficient, prepare an attachment **initialed by** the representative(s).

Total Face Value $ _____

*Check **only 1** box (A, B or C)*

3. A) ❑ Letters Probate or Letters of Administration were obtained and I am/we are the estate's legal representative(s). Attached is a **notarial certified copy of** *Letters Probate with copy of Will annexed* or *Letters of Administration*.

   B) ❑ The deceased died **TESTATE**:
   - attached is a **notarial certified copy of the deceased's Will** dated the ____ day of _____ , _____
   - attached is a **Proof of Death** that is acceptable to the Bank of Canada Month   Year
   - **no application for Letters Probate** for the estate of the deceased has been made or is intended to be made in any jurisdiction
   - The following are all of the persons, besides myself (ourselves), who are entitled to a share of the securities according to the Will and have consented to the transfer/redemption of the securities by signing below:

   PLEASE PRINT

Beneficiary(ies)	Age if minor	Relationship to deceased	Signature of beneficiary(ies) (if a minor, the legal guardian must sign)	Signature of witness

   C) ❑ The deceased died **INTESTATE**:
   - to the best of my/our knowledge and belief the undersigned is/are all of the person(s), besides myself (ourselves), who are entitled to a distributive share of the securities under the **laws respecting intestacy of the Province** in which the deceased was domiciled at the time of death
   - attached is a **Proof of Death** that is acceptable to the Bank of Canada
   - **no application for Letters of Administration** for the estate of the deceased has been made or is intended to be made in any jurisdiction
   - the undersigned have consented to the transfer /redemption of the securities by signing below:

   PLEASE PRINT

Heirs (next-of-kin)	Age if minor	Relationship to deceased	Signature of heirs (next-of-kin) (if a minor, the legal guardian must sign)	Signature of witness

2351-05-02   1 of 2   **Continue**

4. I/We hereby ❑ **transfer** and / ❑ or **redeem** to the person(s) named below in the amount(s) indicated:

Series:	Amount: $
Full name:	Address:
S.I.N.:	Date of Birth:
Home phone number :	Business phone number:

Series:	Amount: $
Full name:	Address:
S.I.N.:	Date of Birth:
Home phone number :	Business phone number:

Note: If insufficient space, prepare an attachment **initialed by** the representative(s).

5. All debts of the estate have been or will be fully paid and I/we hereby undertake to be responsible for the same to the extent of the aggregate value of the above mentioned securities.

6. In consideration of the transfer/redemption of the securities as herein requested, I/we agree to save harmless and keep indemnified the Bank of Canada and the Government of Canada against any cost, expenses, fees or indebtedness based upon any claim that may at any time arise as a result of such transfer/redemption.

7. I/We give all right, title and interest in the securities described above absolutely and The Bank of Canada is hereby authorized to make such entries in the books of registration as are required to give effect to such transfer/redemption.

Dated at: _____ _____ _____ _____
　　　　　　　　City, town　　　　　　　　Day　　　Month　　　Year

Affix the signature guaranteed stamp of the Financial Institution*
otherwise a Notary Public's signature is required.

_____
　　　　　　　Signature of authorized representative

Signed before me at _____

this _____ day of _____, _____
　　　　　　　　　Month　　　　　Year

_____
　　　　　　　Signature of authorized representative

_____
　Notary Public's signature and seal properly identified

* Signature of the authorized representative(s) must be guaranteed by a Canadian Financial Institution acceptable to the Bank of Canada or a Medallion guarantee stamp.

2351-05-02   2 of 2

Source: http://www2.csb.gc.ca/eng/pdf/service_eforms_bondholder_transfer-deceased.pdf, Bank of Canada.
Reproduced with the permission of the Minister of Public Works and Government Services Canada, 2008.

To Create a Survivorship Application - Land

Menu Bar   ► Instrument
                   ► Create New…

The Create New Form window will open displaying all document types available in a file directory tree
► Expand the Death of Owner Applications by clicking on the plus sign
► Select Survivorship Application - Land
► OK

Work in Progress window opens as shown here:

Create the document by moving through each branch of the directory shown on the left-hand side.

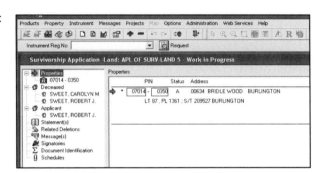

Always expand the directory for each branch by clicking on the plus sign, then click on each subdirectory, and complete the data entry fields as required on the right-hand side, noting the guidelines below:

Properties:
► Click on PIN number (in the directory) and review the information, changing if necessary

Deceased:
► Name of owners should already be prepopulated
► Click on the each name (in the directory) and complete the screens for **each** of the tabs, noting the following:

    Family Law Act and Age Statements – Select statement 603. Double click on NAME in the statement and key in the name of the surviving spouse in the dialog box.

    Other Statements – Select Date of Death; double click on YYYY/MM/DD to open dialog box to insert date of death.

    Writs – Not usually necessary for a survivorship transfer. If required, see Precedent 25.5.

    Address for Service – Insert the Applicant's (the surviving spouse's) address.

    Note: These steps must be completed for **each** name under DECEASED branch.

Applicant:
► Click on New Party (in the directory) and complete the following:

    Name: Key in name of surviving spouse: last name first, followed by a comma, followed by the given name(s).

    Capacity: Select Registered Owner

    Share: Leave blank

    Other Statements: Select the statements: 2906 (not under power of attorney) and
                                           616 (The applicant held the property as joint tenant…)
                                         617 (By right of survivorship…..)

    Address for Service Tab: This will default to the property address; change if necessary

    See Precedent 21.3 for information on the remaining directory items (if required).

Source: Teranet Inc.

**** NOT VALID - TO BE USED FOR TRAINING PURPOSES ONLY ****

This document has not been submitted and may be incomplete.

LRO # 20   **Survivorship Application -Land**

yyyy mm dd   Page 1 of 1

In preparation on 2007 08 03   at 17:11

Properties

PIN	07014 - 0350 LT
Description	LT 87 , PL 1361 ; S/T 209527 BURLINGTON
Address	00634 BRIDLE WOOD BURLINGTON

Deceased(s)

Name	SWEET, CAROLYN M. Acting as an individual
Address for Service	123 Main Street Mississauga ON

Date of death was 2007/07/07

The deceased and Robert J. Sweet, a/the surviving joint tenant, were spouses of each other when the deceased died.

Name	SWEET, ROBERT J. Acting as an individual
Address for Service	

Date of death was 2007/07/07

The deceased and Robert J. Sweet, a/the surviving joint tenant, were spouses of each other when the deceased died.

Applicant(s)   Capacity   Share

Name	SWEET, ROBERT J. Acting as an individual
Address for Service	00634 BRIDLE WOOD BURLINGTON

Registered Owner

This document is not authorized under Power of Attorney by this party.

The applicant(s) held the property as joint tenants with the deceased.

By right of survivorship, the applicant(s) is entitled to be the owner(s), as a surviving joint tenant(s).

NEL

RELEASE OF ESTATE TRUSTEE
(WITH A WILL)

I, KYLE ANDREW EAST, of the City of Toronto, in the Province of Ontario, do hereby acknowledge that I have this day received from HOWARD ALBERT EAST and MARY ELIZABETH EAST, Estate Trustees, of the last Will and Testament of HENRY JAMES EAST, late of 145 William Street, Toronto, in the Province of Ontario, deceased, full receipt and payment of such sum or sums of money and bequests as were given and bequeathed to me under the said last Will and Testament and all interest that may have accrued thereon.

I, KYLE ANDREW EAST, do by these presents remise, release, quit claim and forever discharge the said HOWARD ALBERT EAST and MARY ELIZABETH EAST, his, her or their heirs and estate trustee(s) of and from any and all actions, claims, and accounts whatsoever which I now have or ever had against the said HOWARD ALBERT EAST and MARY ELIZABETH EAST in connection with the Estate of HOWARD ALBERT EAST.

IN WITNESS WHEREOF I have hereunto set my hand and seal the   day of October, 20__.

SIGNED, SEALED AND DELIVERED   )
       in the presence of   )
)
)
)
) _____
)
)
)

GLOSSARY

A

abatement The act of reducing or mitigating an amount.

ab initio From the beginning.

abstract of title A chronological history of the registered **legal instruments** and documents that relate to a specific piece of **real property**.

accept service The receipt, by a lawyer, of an originating document on behalf of his or her **client** to undertake the necessary procedural steps on the client's behalf (see **admit service**).

act A law passed by the federal or provincial government.

action A civil **proceeding** that is not an application and includes a proceeding commenced in the Ontario **Superior Court of Justice** by a **statement of claim, notice of action, counterclaim, third-party claim,** or **crossclaim;** also refers to a civil proceeding commenced in the Provincial Court or Small Claims Court.

addendum An attachment to a written document.

ad hoc For this special purpose.

adjourn To suspend a sitting of a court for resumption at another time or place.

adjudication A **judgment** or decision of the court.

administration bond A legal document in which the **estate trustee** of an **intestate** estate and another person(s) or company (called a **surety**) promise to pay to the court a sum of money if the estate trustee fails to lawfully administer the **estate**.

administration de bonis non administratis See **succeeding estate trustee without a will.**

administrator (male) or **administratrix (female)** Before 1995, the term for a person appointed by the courts to administer the **estate** of a deceased person who died **intestate** or without having appointed an **executor;** now called **succeeding estate trustee without a will.**

admit service To acknowledge receipt of a **true copy** of a **court document** (other than an originating document) prepared for use in a **legal proceeding**.

ad valorem According to the value.

affidavit A written statement of facts in the name of a person by whom it is voluntarily signed and sworn to under oath.

affidavit of bona fides The sworn statement of a party to a legal document as to the genuineness of the transaction covered by the document.

affidavit of condition of will The sworn statement of a witness to a **will** verifying the condition of the will at the time of **execution;** it is made and presented when administering the will.

affidavit of documents An **affidavit** completed by each party in an **action** that outlines material the party has or had relating to the matter in dispute.

affidavit of execution and of legal age
The sworn statement of a witness as to the signing of a legal document, verifying that she or he actually saw the document signed and that she or he is the **age of majority** (formerly known as the *affidavit of subscribing witness*).

affidavit of residence and of value of the consideration See **Land Transfer Tax Affidavit.**

affidavit of service The sworn statement of the person who served a **court document,** verifying the method of service.

affidavit of service of notice In an **estate,** the sworn statement of the person who sent or caused to be sent a **notice of application for certificate of appointment of estate trustee with/without a will** to the **beneficiary**(ies) of the estate.

age of majority The age at which an individual is legally deemed to be an adult; in Ontario this age is 18.

agenda A list of items of business to be transacted at a meeting.

agreement of purchase and sale An accepted **offer to purchase.**

allegation Assertion, statement, or declaration of a party that the party is prepared to prove in court.

alimony See **support.**

alternative dispute resolution (ADR) A process mediated by a neutral third party to assist parties in reaching a settlement without going to court.

amendment A change to a legal document.

amortize To provide for the payment of a debt by periodic, set payments at a rate calculated to repay the debt over a given number of years.

ancillary Auxiliary.

ante Before.

appeal A **legal proceeding** in which the decision of a lower court is brought before a higher court for re-examination or review, reversal, or modification.

appellant The party who brings an **appeal** from the **judgment** of a lower court.

appellate court A court of **appeal.**

applicant A person who makes an **application.**

application A civil **proceeding** asking for the advice, direction, or authority of the court.

a priori From the cause to the effect.

arbitration The settling of a dispute by a party or parties appointed or chosen by the disputing parties.

area municipality A local **municipality** within a **regional municipality,** for example, the District Municipality of Muskoka or the County of Oxford.

arm's length Genuine, open, and **bona fide.**

articles of incorporation A method of incorporating companies; the application form submitted when a corporation is applying for incorporation as an Ontario or federal corporation.

articling The period a student lawyer spends working under the direction of a practicing lawyer to gain practical experience before being called to the bar.

assess To determine the amount of money to be paid as **costs** to the successful or interested parties in **legal proceedings**.

assessment officer A court official who assesses **party and party costs**.

assignee The party to whom a contract is assigned.

assignor The party who assigns a contract.

associate A lawyer who practices law in a law firm under the supervision of one or more partners in that firm.

ats At the suit of.

attendance money Money given to a person who will be a witness at a trial to help cover his or her expenses in attending the trial.

attest To witness an act or event, for example, the signing of a legal document.

attestation clause A clause in a legal document that indicates the document was signed in the presence of a witness.

attorney The American term for a lawyer. In Canada, this term refers to a person who receives authority under a **power of attorney** (see **grantor**).

authority A case cited in support of a legal principle.

authorization A document signed by a **client** that directs a person or company to release information to a lawyer or law firm.

B

back See **backsheet**.

backsheet The last page of a legal document which identifies the nature of the document; see also **endorsement**.

banking forms Documents that must be prepared and executed in order for a corporation to conduct business.

bar admission course In Ontario, the course taken by a student lawyer following completion of law-school training and a period of **articling;** if this is completed successfully, he or she receives a **call to the bar**.

bar of dower The giving up by a wife of her **inchoate** one-third life interest in the **real property** of her husband.

barrister A lawyer who appears in the courts. In Canada, a lawyer is both a barrister and a **solicitor**.

bencher A lawyer elected to serve as a member of the governing body of his or her provincial law society.

beneficiary A person who receives a benefit under a **will** or from an insurance policy.

bequest A gift of **personal property** by **will**.

billable time Time spent by a lawyer or a **law clerk** performing work for which a **client** may be charged.

bill of costs A document in a **legal proceeding** that sets out the claim for **costs** in an **action** or **application**.

bill of sale A legal document covering the sale of **personal property** when the title to—but not physical possession of—the property is conveyed (see **convey**).

blended payment A regular payment on a loan (usually a **charge/mortgage**) of a set amount of money. The monies are applied first against accrued interest on the loan, and second against the unpaid **principal** balance of the loan.

bona fide In good faith, honestly, without fraud.

bond (insurance or guarantee company) A document guaranteeing an amount payable to the **Superior Court of Justice** by a company acting as a **surety** to ensure the faithful administration of an **estate** (see **administration bond** and **guarantee**).

bond (personal sureties) A document guaranteeing an amount payable to the **Superior Court of Justice** by one or more individuals to ensure the faithful administration of an **estate** (see **administration bond** and **guarantee**).

brief A file of **pleadings,** documents, and other memoranda prepared for the use of the lawyer appearing at a trial or other hearing.

brief of authorities A booklet for the use of a **judge** or judges that contains a copy of relevant extracts from authorities intended to be referred to in a **legal proceeding** (also referred to as a **case book**).

by-law A rule or regulation made by a corporation to govern its own affairs or its dealings with others.

By-Law No. 1 The corporate **by-law** that contains the general rules for governing the internal affairs of the corporation.

By-Law No. 2 Usually called the *borrowing by-law*, this corporate **by-law** governs the borrowing transactions of a corporation.

C

call to the bar The ceremony by which graduates of **bar admission courses** are admitted as practicing lawyers in Ontario.

capacity The legal competency to enter into a contract.

capital The contribution of each **shareholder** to the common fund or stock of a corporation.

capital gains tax A form of income tax that applies when property is sold for more than was paid for it.

case book See **brief of authorities**.

case law The decisions of **judges** that establish the law in a given set of circumstances (see **precedent**).

case management Civil procedural rules designed to eliminate delays in civil **proceedings** and thus reduce time and costs for all parties. A case management **judge** is assigned to each case to ensure timely processing of the proceeding.

cause An **action** or other original **legal proceeding** between a **plaintiff** and a **defendant**.

cause of action Facts that give rise to a right of **action**.

caveat A warning.

central divorce registry An office in Ottawa that files all registered **divorce** forms in Canada to avoid duplicate divorce **actions**.

centralized filing system A central location where all law office files are kept.

certificate of appointment of estate trustee with a will The formal document of **authority** and appointment granted by the appropriate court to the **estate trustee** of an **estate** of a deceased person who died **testate;** or when the individual named as **trustee** in the **will** is unable or unwilling to serve; or when there is a will but no trustee is named in it (formerly **letters probate** or **letters of administration with will annexed**).

certificate of appointment of estate trustee without a will The formal document of **authority** and appointment granted by the appropriate court to the **estate trustee** of an **estate** of a deceased person who died **intestate** (formerly **letters of administration**).

certificate of appointment of succeeding estate trustee The formal document of **authority** and appointment granted by the appropriate court to a second **estate trustee** to complete the administration of an **estate** following the death of the originally appointed estate trustee.

certificate of divorce A document **issued** by the local **registrar** of the Ontario **Superior Court of Justice** to certify that a **divorce judgment** is effective.

certificate of incorporation The document certifying that a corporation is incorporated.

certificate of pending litigation A **notice** of pending **action** or application (formerly known as a certificate of **lis pendens**).

cessation of charge A **legal instrument** used until April 1, 1985, to formally acknowledge that the claim against **real property** contained in a **charge/mortgage** had been discharged (see **discharge of charge/mortgage**).

cestui que trust A person who benefits by a **trust account**.

chains and links A term used until 1967 that described the perimeter of a **parcel** of land by chain and link measurements (one chain = 100 links, 66 feet, or 20.12 m).

charge A lawyer's day-to-day record of work performed or **disbursements** used in the **land titles system** until April 1, 1985, to formalize the claim upon title to **real property** as security for a debt or loan (see **charge/mortgage**).

charge/mortgage The legal document used to formalize a loan when **real property** is used as **collateral**.

chargee The party to whom **real property** is mortgaged (see **mortgagee**).

charger The party who gives the **mortgage** or **real property** (see **mortgagor**).

chattel Any property other than **real property;** movable property.

chattel mortgage A **mortgage** of **personal property** as security for a loan or debt.

Children's Lawyer A person appointed by the Ontario government whose main responsibility is to ensure that the rights and interests of a **minor** are protected when the minor becomes involved in a **legal proceeding** (formerly *Official Guardian*).

chose in action A right of **proceeding** in a court of law.

citation In documents, a reference to a decided case or matter; in estates, before 1995, an application to the court in an **estate** matter for an **order** that certain steps be taken **without notice;** now called *orders for assistance*.

cite To refer to a decided case or matter.

client An individual or company that comes to a lawyer for assistance.

client files The normal office records containing copies of correspondence, documents, and so on, sent or received on behalf of a **client**.

client number A numerical or alphabetical identification assigned to a **client**.

closing A meeting of the **solicitors** who represent the **vendor** and the **purchaser** in a real estate transaction to finalize the transaction.

codicil A legal document that amends a **will**.

cohabit To live together in a conjugal relationship within or outside marriage.

cohabitation agreement A contract between two people who are cohabitating or intend to **cohabit** and who are not married to each other (see **marriage contract**).

collateral Security to ensure the performance of an obligation; secured or guaranteed by additional security (see **guarantee**).

collusion A secret agreement or cooperation between two people who appear to have different interests, which is intended to injure a third party or deceive a court.

Commercial Court A division of the Ontario **Superior Court of Justice** that deals with **legal proceedings** in the area of bankruptcy.

commercial document Written legal paper, such as a contract, **will,** or real estate document, that gives formal expression to a legal act or agreement. Formerly known as a **legal instrument** (see also **court document**).

commissioner An **officer** who is authorized to administer oaths to persons coming before him or her to swear to the truth of statements. All lawyers are commissioners.

committee Someone to whom the custody of the **estate** or the person of an individual of unsound mind is committed.

common elements The areas of a condominium, such as halls, elevators, and grounds, owned by individual unit owners as **tenants in common**.

common expenses Normal costs to maintain and repair the **common elements** of the property, jointly shared by all owners of units in a condominium.

common law Law based on unwritten custom and long-established practices.

common shares A class of **shares** of a corporation that usually have no special privileges attached to them but **convey** full voting rights.

conditional sales agreement An agreement covering the sale of **personal property** where title to the property passes to the **purchaser** only when certain conditions (usually the payment in full of the purchase price) have been fulfilled.

condominium Ownership **in fee simple** of a specific unit of space in a multi-unit building, with ownership of **tenants in common** with all other owners of the **common elements**.

condonation Tacit forgiveness of a matrimonial offence by the injured party and the reinstatement of the guilty **spouse** in the marital relationship.

conflict of interest Any inconsistency between the interests of the lawyer and her or his **client**.

conjugal rights The rights of a married person to the society and cohabitation of his or her **spouse**.

connivance The intentional or passive acceptance by the **petitioner** in **divorce** proceedings of the adultery of the **respondent**.

consent A document **filed** with the court in which parties to a **legal proceeding** mutually agree to do or not to do something.

consideration The return given for the property, act, or promise of another.

constitutional law The area of law that deals with the distribution and exercise of power between the federal government and the province.

construction The process of ascertaining the meaning of a written document.

contingency fund The fund contributed to by individual unit-owners in a **condominium** to meet unexpected expenses or to build up a reserve for future major repairs or replacements.

continuing record A booklet or booklets that contain a copy of all the written documents for a **family law** proceeding in an organized and chronological order.

contra Against.

convey To transfer or pass title to **real property** to another person.

conveyancing The act of transferring or passing title of **real property** from one party to another.

co-respondent A term sometimes used to refer to the non-spouse **respondent** in a **divorce** action; usually a person with whom the respondent is alleged to have committed a matrimonial offence. The term is not used in divorce documents.

corner A triangle-shaped picket into which the left-hand corners of pages may be inserted before stapling.

corroboration Evidence that confirms a fact in material evidence.

corollary relief Claims in addition to the claim for **divorce** contained in a divorce petition, for example, a claim for custody of children.

costs Money to which a party may be entitled as partial compensation for the expense of being a party in **legal proceedings**.

counsel A lawyer involved in court work.

counterclaim A separate and distinct claim of the **defendant** against the **plaintiff,** or against the plaintiff and another party or parties, that has nothing to do with the defendant's defence to the plaintiff's claim.

county An **upper-tier municipality** that is a federation of the towns, villages, and townships located within its boundaries; equal to a **district** or a **regional municipality**.

county centre A town or city in a **county, district,** or **regional municipality** in which is located the court house and **land registry office** for the county.

course A term used when the perimeter of a **parcel** of land is described by degrees, minutes, and seconds.

court document Legal paper prepared for use in **legal proceedings** brought before the courts or administrative tribunals.

court file number The **file number** assigned when an **action** or application is commenced in the courts.

Court of Appeal for Ontario Highest court in Ontario; hears **appeals** from lower courts (formerly **Supreme Court of Ontario**).

court of first instance A court of original jurisdiction, which hears a case for the first time.

court of record A court wherein the evidence is recorded by a qualified court reporter.

covenant An agreement that creates an obligation.

crossclaim A separate and distinct claim of one **defendant** against another defendant.

crossclaiming defendant A **defendant** in the main **action** who crossclaims against a codefendant in the action.

crown attorney A lawyer who represents the government through the office of the Attorney General (federally and provincially) in civil, administrative, and criminal **proceedings**.

cui bon To whose advantage.

cy-près The doctrine related to carrying out the intention of a **testator** in a manner as nearly as possible to the way stipulated by the **testator**.

D

damages An amount of money claimed or awarded to a party in a **legal proceeding** as a result of damage done to or suffered by that party because of the actions of the other party.

day book A chronological file of all outgoing correspondence and memoranda (also called a **letter book**).

de bene esse To act in anticipation of a future occasion.

decentralized filing system A file system maintained at each secretary's workstation.

declarant A person who voluntarily declares a **statutory declaration**.

declaration A document registered in a **land registry office** by a **condominium** corporation that sets out the rights and obligations governing the use of the individual units and the **common elements.**

declaration of possession A **deposition** setting out the details of the time the **vendor** has been in possession or control of **real property,** including details about other matters that affect title.

decree The decision of the court in a **divorce** action before June 1, 1986.

decree absolute The **order** of the court before June 1, 1986, terminating a marriage.

decree nisi The **order** of the court before June 1, 1986, terminating a marriage; subject to obtaining a **decree absolute.**

deed A legal document used in the **registry system** up to April 1, 1985, by which title to **real property** was conveyed from one party to another (see **transfer/deed**).

deed to uses A **deed** used before March 1978 that permitted a married man to take title to **real property** in his own name without **dower** vesting in his wife.

de facto In fact; actually.

default judgment A **judgment** given by the court in favour of the **plaintiff** when the **defendant** fails to defend an **action.**

defendant A person against whom an **action** is commenced by a **statement of claim** or a **notice of action.**

defendant to the counterclaim The **plaintiff** against whom the **defendant** in the original main **action** has a **counterclaim** in the **legal proceeding.**

de júre By right.

deliver To **serve** and **file** a document prepared for use in a **legal proceeding.**

demise To grant a **lease** of lands.

de novo Anew.

deponent A person who voluntarily signs an **affidavit.**

depose To swear under oath.

deposition A sworn declaration of facts by an individual or individuals.

devise A gift of **real property** by **will.**

directors Individuals elected by the **shareholders** of a corporation to manage or supervise its operation.

disability A condition that requires a party to a **legal proceeding** to act through a litigation guardian; examples include being a **minor,** mentally incompetent, or incapable of managing one's affairs.

disbursements Expenses, other than for work performed, incurred by the law firm on behalf of a **client.**

discharge of charge/mortgage A legal document used since April 1, 1985, to formally acknowledge that the debt covered by a **charge/mortgage** has been discharged (formerly *discharge of charge* or *discharge of mortgage*).

distance A term used when the perimeter or a **parcel** of land is described in feet and inches or in metres.

district A division of those parts of Ontario that do not have a **county** organization; also known as a territorial district.

District Court The name given until August 31, 1990, to the court that sat in each **county** or **district** in Ontario.

district municipality See **regional municipality**.

dividend A payment made to a **shareholder** out of profits earned by a corporation.

divorce The **action** commenced to terminate a marriage.

divorce judgment The **judgment** of the court in a **divorce** action, which terminates the marriage effective on the thirty-first day of the date of judgment. In Ontario, these are now divorce orders as **proceedings** are by way of application under the *Family Law Rules*.

docket A record of time spent on a case or matter and the **disbursements** incurred.

document general Form 4 under the *Land Registration Reform Act* that is used to **register** all documents related to land except a transfer/deed, **charge/mortgage**, or **discharge of charge/mortgage**.

domestic contract An agreement that outlines property rights, and so on, during marriage or cohabitation, or upon separation.

domicile The place in which a person has his or her permanent home and to which, whenever absent, he or she has the intention of returning.

donatio mortis causa A gift of **personal property** in anticipation of death.

donee See **grantee**.

donor See **grantor**.

double probate Before 1995, the term referring to the grant of second letters probate to an **executor** named in the **will** who was not a party to the original application for letters probate; or the grant of second letters probate to an alternative executor called upon to complete the administration of the **estate;** now called **certificate of appointment of succeeding estate trustee**.

dower Under **common law**, the interest of a widow in one-third of her late husband's **real property,** or the rents or profits therefrom, for her life. Now replaced by **statutes** dealing with matrimonial property.

duces tecum Bring with you; for example, a *subpoena duces tecum* orders a witness to appear and bring certain material.

due date The date by which certain steps are to be taken or completed.

duplicate original A copy of a legal document that is executed as if it were the original.

E

E. & O.E. Errors and omissions excepted.

easement A right enjoyed by the owner of **real property** over lands of another; a right of way.

electronic filing (e-filing) Electronic filing of documents from a personal computer to the appropriate court (litigation and **family law**) or the government office (corporate law).

electronic registration (e-reg) Electronic registration of real estate documents from a personal computer to the appropriate **land registry office**.

eleemosynary Charitable.

eminent domain The right of a government to take private property for public use.

encumbrance A claim or lien upon **real property**.

endorsement The last page of a legal document that sets out the date or the name of the court, the names of the parties, a description of the document, and the name and address of the law firm that prepared it; also known as a **back** or **backsheet**.

engross To do a final copy of a legal paper, usually after such a paper has first been done in draft.

entry A lawyer's day-to-day record of work performed or **disbursements** incurred for a **client;** also called a **charge**.

enure To operate or take effect.

en ventre sa mere A child not yet born.

equity of redemption A right that a **mortgagor** has, upon payment of the total **mortgage** debt and all accrued interest, to redeem the mortgage property after the mortgagor has gone into default and breached the terms of the contract.

erratum; errata (pl) Error(s).

escheat The reversion of land to the Crown.

escrow The holding in trust of a written documentation or monies by a third party until certain conditions are fulfilled.

estate The **real property** and **personal property** owned by a person as of the date of his or her death.

estate trustee A person designated in a **will** to administer the **estate** of a testator according to the terms of the testator's will, or a person appointed by the courts to administer the estate of a deceased who died **intestate** or without having appointed someone to administer the estate (formerly **executor** or **administrator**).

estoppel The doctrine that prevents a person from denying the truth of some statement made by him or her, or of the existence of facts that the person has by words of conduct led others to believe.

estoppel certificate See **status certificate**.

et al. Abbreviation for *et alii*: "and others."

et seq. And those following.

examination for discovery An examination under oath of parties to a **legal proceeding** that is held before the trial or hearing and touches upon the matters in dispute. May also be in writing.

execution Doing what is required to make a legal document valid; usually signing and sometimes sealing it.

executor (male) or **executrix (female)** The former term (although still used in wills) to refer to a person designated in a **will** to administer the **estate** of a testator according to the terms of the testator's will; now called an **estate trustee**.

exhibit An article or material **filed** in the course of a **legal proceeding;** written material referred to in and forming part of an **affidavit**.

ex officio By virtue of office.

ex parte On one side only; by or for one party (see **without notice**).

expropriation When the Crown compulsorily deprives a person of the right to property belonging to him or her in return for compensation.

F

factum The statement of facts and law to be relied on by parties in an application and on certain **motions**.

family assets Assets owned by one or both **spouses** and used and enjoyed by the spouses or their children for household, educational, recreational, social, or aesthetic purposes.

Family Courts of the Ontario Court of Justice Ontario courts that deal with matters involving custody, enforcement of **support** of **maintenance** orders, adoptions, and applications by the Children's Aid Society for the protection of children.

Family Courts of the Superior Court of Justice Ontario courts that deal with all areas of **family law** but operate in certain regions only.

family law The area of legal practice concerned with matters relating to **divorce**, domestic contracts, **support**, and custody of children.

Family Law Motions Court Sittings of a **motions court** in the **Ontario Court of Justice** to deal with matrimonial matters other than **divorce**.

fiduciary One who is placed in a position of trust.

file To **deliver** to the appropriate court office the original or a copy of a document prepared for use in a **legal proceeding**.

file memorandum A memorandum that records, for the file, information that is relevant to the client matter; also called an **inter-office memorandum**.

file number A number assigned to a file when it is opened, or a number for a **docket** when accounting records are maintained numerically.

financial statement A document required in some **family law** proceedings that sets out detailed financial information on a party and on valuations of his or her property.

financing change statement The statement of details of a document that alters the details of a previously registered document in which **personal property** was used as security for a debt.

financing statement The statement that must accompany a document for registration purposes when **personal property** is being used as a security for a debt.

firm account A bank account of the law firm in which it deposits monies belonging to the firm; also called a **general account**.

foreclosure The act of a **mortgagee** that requires the **mortgagor** of **real property** either to pay off the **mortgage** upon its **maturity** or to relinquish his or her interest in the real property.

G

general account See **firm account**.

general damages Those **damages** that the law regards as a direct result of the act resulting in a claim, such as pain and suffering. These are always a round amount.

general heading The heading on a **court document** that sets out the **court file number,** the name of the court, and the title of proceeding (that is, the names and capacity of the parties) in an application. It also includes the statutory or rule authority under which the application is made.

gift tax Income tax paid by the **donor** on gifts made in prescribed circumstances during her or his lifetime.

grantee The party who receives a **power of attorney**—also known as the **attorney** (formerly **donee**); in real estate, the term used a in **deed** to describe the party who received title to **real property** (see **transferee**).

grantor The party who gives the **power of attorney** (formerly **donor**); in real estate, the term used in a **deed** to describe the party who gave title to **real property** (see **transferor**).

guarantee A promise to answer for the debt or default of another.

guarantor A person or company that promises to answer for the debt of another person or company.

guardian ad litem Formerly a person appointed to defend an **action** on behalf of a **minor** (see **litigation guardian**).

H

holograph will A **will** that is entirely handwritten by a testator or testatrix.

I

ibid In the same place.

idem The same.

in camera Any judicial, quasi-judicial, or administrative session conducted in private.

inchoate Begun but not completed.

incorporator A person who signs articles of incorporation.

indenture An agreement in writing, usually in duplicate.

index An alphabetical printed listing or arrangement of material.

in esse In being.

infant See **minor**.

in fee simple A term used to describe absolute ownership of **real property**.

infra Below.

injunction An **order** or decree by which a party to an **action** is required to do or refrain from doing some particular thing.

in loco parentis In the place of a parent.

in personam An act done or directed against a specific person.

in re In the matter of.

in rem An act against the world at large.

inter alia Among other things.

interrogatories A set of questions asked during discovery stage of a **proceeding**.

inter vivos During a lifetime.

interlocutory A term describing an act or decision of a court that is made after a **legal proceeding** commences and is complete in itself before the legal proceeding is complete.

inter-office memorandum See **file memorandum**.

intestacy The state of dying without a **will**.

intestate The state of not having a **will**.

in toto Entirely.

intra vires Within the power.

ipso facto By the mere fact.

issue A person's children, grandchildren, and all other lineal descendants; to sign, seal, date, and assign a **court file number** to a document that originates a **legal proceeding**.

J

joint tenants Two or more parties who hold title to **real property** where each holds the same interest as the other. Upon the death of one party, the surviving co-owner acquires the interest of the deceased tenant.

judge Lawyer appointed by either a provincial or the federal government to hear cases in court.

judgment The final decision of a court in a **legal proceeding**.

judgment creditor A person to whom a **judgment** of the court orders that payment be made.

judgment debtor A person ordered by the court in a **judgment** to make a payment to another person.

judicial district The term used until September 1, 1990, for purposes of the administration of justice to describe a former **county** or **district** that formed or was part of a regional or **district municipality**.

judicial region The term used since September 1, 1990, to describe a group of counties, **districts,** or regional municipalities established as one region for the purpose of the functioning of the **Ontario Court of Justice**.

jurat The ending of an **affidavit** or **statutory declaration** that begins with the word "sworn" or "affirmed" and attests when, where, and before whom the affidavit was sworn or declared.

jurisprudence The philosophy of law.

K

King's Counsel (K.C.) Equivalent to **Queen's Counsel,** if the monarch is a king.

L

laches Negligent or unreasonable delay in putting forward legal rights.

land registrar A person appointed by the government to supervise and administer the registration in a land titles or registry office of documents affecting the ownership of **real property**.

land registry office Office where documents giving **notice** of an interest in **real property** may be **filed** or deposited; may be a land titles or a registry office.

land titles system A system of recording document registrations relating to land. In this system the government maintains the registration records and guarantees the title and specific interests in the land.

Land Transfer Tax Affidavit The sworn statement of the **purchaser** of **real property** setting out the **consideration** paid for the real property.

law clerk An individual who has successfully completed a two-year community college program or the requisite courses provided by the Institute of Law Clerks and works under the supervision of a lawyer to assist in routine legal matters.

law reports The written, published reports of legal decisions in cases of interest before the courts.

lawsuit A **legal proceeding** in a court.

lawyer's docket sheet A form of **docket** record maintained in the **client's** file.

lease A legal document under which one party allows another party to occupy and use **real property** in return for monetary or other **consideration**.

legal assistant An individual who has successfully completed a two-year community college program.

legal document Commercial and court documents (see **commercial document** and **court document**).

legal instrument See **commercial document** and **court document**.

legal proceeding An **action** or application tried or heard in a court.

legal seal A small, red, gummed sticker that is affixed following the signatures of the signing parties to a document, or the seal of a corporation that is stamped over or beside the signatures of the **officers** of a corporation; see also **locus sigilli**.

lessee The party who rents **real property** or **personal property** from another party (**lessor**) for monetary or other **consideration**.

lessor The party who owns **real property** or **personal property** that is rented to another party (**lessee**).

letter book See **daybook**.

letters of administration Before 1995, the term that referred to the formal document of authority and appointment granted by the appropriate court to an **administrator** of an **estate** of a deceased person who died **intestate** (see **certificate of appointment of estate trustee without a will**).

letters of administration with will annexed Before 1995, the term for the formal document of authority and appointment granted by the appropriate court to an **administrator** of an **estate** of a deceased person who died **testate** when the **executor** or executors named in the **will** were unable or unwilling to serve, or when there was a will but no executor was named in it (see **certificate of appointment of estate trustee with a will**).

letters patent A method of incorporating companies; the official document issued by provincial governments that certifies the existence, purpose, and financial structure of a corporation.

letters probate Before 1995, the term for the formal document of authority granted to an **estate trustee** by the appropriate court to carry out the provisions in the **will** of the deceased (see **certificate or appointment of estate trustee with a will**).

lien A **notice** of a security interest on property to secure the payment of a debt or other obligation.

life tenant A person in possession of **real property** during his or her lifetime only.

limitation date The date by which certain **actions** or steps must be taken or the right to do so is lost.

liquidated damages A fixed or readily ascertained amount of money owed by one person to another person due to a breach of a contractual obligation.

lis pendens See **pending litigation**.

litigation guardian A person over the age of majority who acts on behalf of a **minor** or mentally incompetent person in **legal proceedings;** a person appointed by the Ontario government when there is no other person willing or able to act on behalf of a party to a proceeding who is either a minor or is mentally incompetent.

local municipality An incorporated municipal unit, such as a city, town, or village, located in a larger municipal unit, such as a **county, district,** or **regional municipality**. Also called an **area municipality**.

local registrar The chief administrative officer of the **Ontario Court of Justice** in each **county** in Ontario.

locus signilli The place of the seal; abbreviated **L.S.;** appears on copies of a document that are sealed.

lot A small area of land that forms part of a larger area covered by a registered **plan**.

lower-tier municipality See **local municipality** and **area municipality**.

L.S. See **locus signilli**.

M

maintenance See **support**.

mala fides Bad faith.

marriage contract A contract between two people who are married to each other or who intend to marry.

master A lawyer appointed by the Ontario government to assist Ontario **Superior Court of Justice** judges in carrying out their administrative and judicial duties.

matrimonial home Property in which a person has an interest and that is (or, if **spouses** have separated, was at the time of separation) ordinarily occupied by the person and his or her spouse as their family **residence**.

matter number The number assigned to a new matter undertaken by a law firm; **file number**.

maturity The date on which a **charge/mortgage** is due.

mechanic's lien A claim against property for satisfaction of a debt incurred of work done or materials supplied to improve property.

memorandum of law A memorandum that refers in some detail to decided cases on some point at issue, and that may quote from the decisions made in such cases.

mens rea The state of a person's mind.

metes and bounds A description of **real property** that commences with a determinable point and outlines the perimeter of the **parcel** in directions and **distances.**

minor An individual under the age of majority. Formerly known as an **infant.**

minutes The formal, permanent record of decisions made and business conducted at a **shareholders'** or **directors'** meeting of a corporation.

minutes of settlement A **legal document** that is **filed** with the court and that sets out the terms upon which parties agree to settle a **legal proceeding.**

mitigate To make or become less severe. The phrase "mitigation of damages" describes the legal obligation of a party to a **legal proceeding** to take all reasonable steps to minimize the **damages** resulting from another party's action.

mortgage A **legal document** used in the **registry system** until April 1, 1985, to formalize the conveyance of title to the **mortgagee** as security for a debt or loan owed to the mortgagee by the **mortgagor** (see **charge/mortgage**); to **convey** property, upon certain items and conditions, as security for the payment of debt.

mortgagee The term used before April 1, 1985, to describe the party to whom **real property** is mortgaged. Now officially replaced by **chargee,** but still widely used.

mortgagor The term used before April 1, 1985, to describe the party who gave a **mortgage** on **real property.** Now officially replaced by **chargor,** but still widely used.

motion A document that asks the court for an **order** that some step or procedure either be taken or not allowed.

Motions Court A division of the Ontario **Superior Court of Justice** that deals with **motions** brought during the course of a **legal proceeding** (formerly known as **Weekly Court**).

moving party A person who makes a **motion**.

municipality A legally incorporated municipality such as a **county; regional municipality;** township, city, town, or village.

mutatis mutandis The necessary changes being made.

N

net family property The value of all the property that a **spouse** owns on the **valuation date,** after deducting the spouse's debts and liabilities, less the value of property (other than the **matrimonial home**) owned on the date of marriage, after deducting the spouse's debts and other liabilities calculated as of the date of the marriage.

next of kin The closest blood relatives of a deceased person.

nolle prosequi An agreement not to proceed with an **action** or matter in the courts.

nonbillable time See **unbillable time**.

non compos mentis Not of sound mind.

non sequitur It does not follow.

non sui juris Without capacity to manage one's own affairs.

nota bene (N.B.) Note or mark well.

notarial certificate A **legal document** that certifies the authenticity of the copy of the legal paper to which it is affixed.

notary public One who may affirm under notarial seal the **execution** of certain legal writings or the authenticity of a copy of a document or writing. All lawyers are notaries public.

notice A **court document** that advises the court and the **solicitors** for the other party of some procedural step in a **legal proceeding**.

notice of action A **court document** that may be **issued** to originate an **action** and secures additional time to complete the **statement of claim**.

notice of application The document that originates an application.

notice of application for certificate of appointment of estate trustee with a will A document that notifies the beneficiaries named in a **will** of the application to appoint an **estate trustee** to administer the will.

notice of application for certificate of appointment of estate trustee without a will A document that notifies all persons entitled to share in the distribution of an **estate** of the application to appoint an **estate trustee** for an estate lacking a **will**.

notice of examination A **legal document** advising a party in a civil **proceeding**

what documents to bring, and where and when to attend an **examination for discovery**.

notice of motion A **court document** that asks the court to order that something be either done or not done.

nulla bona No goods; the wording of a return to a **writ of seizure and sale**.

nunc pro tunc Now for then.

O

obiter dictum An opinion by a **judge** on **collateral** issues.

offer to purchase An offer signed by a party seeking to purchase the **real property** of another.

offer to settle An offer made by one of the parties in an **action** to settle the action.

Office of the Children's Lawyer See **Children's Lawyer**.

officer An individual appointed by the **directors** of a corporation to carry on its day-to-day operation, such as the president, vice president, secretary, or treasurer.

official examiner A person appointed by the Ontario government to record the questions and answers on an **examination for discovery**.

Ontario Court of Justice Formerly the Ontario Court (Provincial Division).

order The term generally used to refer to decisions of the court, including **judgments,** and specifically used to refer to a decision of the court that does not finally dispose of a **legal proceeding**.

ordinary service Serving a **legal document** by **personal service** or by serving the document on the **solicitor of record** in person, or by mail, fax, document exchange, courier, or e-mail according to the rules of the court that has jurisdiction in the **proceedings**.

originating process The document that commences a **legal proceeding**.

P

paralegal An individual who works directly under the supervision of a lawyer to perform many of the routine legal procedures required to meet the needs of a **client**. In Ontario, paralegals may work independently (not under the supervision of a lawyer) to provide legal services in certain specified areas of legal practice.

parallel citations Many decided cases reported in more than one law report. When citing such cases, the name of the case is set out, followed by each law report in which it can be found. The year of the decision is not repeated with each report and each parallel citation is separated with a comma.

parcel Parts or portions of land; the entire holding of land in one location owned by a registered owner under the **land titles system**.

pari passu Without preference.

parol Verbal; not in writing or under seal.

partial indemnity costs A system of calculating **costs** awarded in **legal proceedings** to partially compensate a party for their legal fees and **disbursements**. Formerly known as **party and party costs**.

partition The act of dividing **real property** in certain proportions among persons who previously owned the property as joint tenants or as **tenants in common**.

party and party costs Costs that arise because of an **order,** a **statute,** or rules (usually because of a court **proceeding**) and paid to or by the **client**.

passing of accounts The procedure of having **estate** accounts approved or "passed" by the court.

paternity agreement A contract between two people who are not married to each other, where there is a child or children of the relationship, in which the man acknowledges that he is the father of such child or children, and which sets out provisions for care, custody, and **support**.

payor A person who is required to pay **support** under a support order.

pendente lite While litigation is pending.

per annum By the year.

per autre vie For another's life.

per capita By head or by the individual.

per diem By the day.

per se By itself; taken alone.

personal property All things or interests that are not land or permanently attached to land; also known as "personalty" or movable property.

personal service Serving a **legal document** by leaving a copy with the individual to be served or by one of the alternatives to personal service stated in the rules of the court that has jurisdiction in the **proceedings.**

per stirpes By family stock, branches, or family representation.

petition for divorce The **court document** that originates a **divorce** action.

petitioner The person who commences a **divorce** action against a **respondent.**

PIN See **property identifier number.**

place of trial The place where a **legal proceeding** is to be tried or heard. Formerly known as the **venue.**

plaintiff The person who commences an **action** by a **statement of claim** or a **notice of action.**

plaintiff by counterclaim A **defendant** in the main originating **action** who counter claims against the original **plaintiff**(s) or the original plaintiff and other parties.

plan A design that covers the division of an area of **real property** into lots.

pleadings Statements delivered by the parties to an **action** that state their case, for example, a **statement of claim** or a statement of defence.

postjudgment interest Interest on an amount owing in a **legal proceeding** from and after the date of **order** or **judgment.**

power of attorney A **legal document** by which one person empowers another to represent her or him or to act in her or his place.

practice management software Software programs, such as PCLaw™, that manage all accounting functions including time **entry** and billing as well as records management, calendaring, and tickler systems, and perform conflict of interest searches.

praecipe See **requisition.**

prayer for relief A paragraph in a pleading that sets out the claim or remedy sought by one party from another party.

preamble An introductory paragraph in **judgments, orders,** and **notices** setting out the events leading up to or the reasons for the document.

precedent A **judgment** or decision of a court of law that is cited as an authority as to what decision should be made by a **judge** in a similar situation.

preferred shares A class of **shares** that usually have some special rights, limitations, preferences, or restrictions attached to them.

prejudgment interest Interest on an amount owing in a **legal proceeding** for the period before the handing down of the **judgment.**

prescribed form A **legal document** whose style and basic content have been established by an act or statutory regulation.

pre-trial conference A meeting of the **solicitors** for the parties in an **action** with a **judge** before the trial to consider matters that might help to dispose of, shorten, or simplify the **proceeding.**

prima facie At first sight; on the face of it.

principal The amount of the **charge/mortgage** upon payment of which, together with any accrued interest, the charge/mortgage is discharged.

proceeding See **legal proceeding**.

pro forma As a matter of form.

prohibition A declaration forbidding some action.

property identifier number (PIN) A nine-digit number used to describe property in Ontario, consisting of a block number and a property number.

pro rata According to the rate of proportion.

prospectus A document setting out the objectives and financial structure of a company, designed to facilitate the sale of the company's **shares** to the public.

pro tem For the time being.

proxy The person appointed to represent a **shareholder** of a corporation at a shareholders' meeting, or the document that confirms such an appointment.

Public Guardian and Trustee A person appointed by the Ontario government, when there is no other person willing or able to act, to administer the **estate** of a mentally incompetent person or act as his or her **litigation guardian** in **legal proceedings**.

purchaser One who buys **real property** or **personal property**.

Q

quaere Query or question.

quantum The amount.

quantum meruit As much as someone has earned or deserved.

quash To discharge or set aside.

quasi As if; as it were.

Queen's Counsel (Q.C.) A lawyer who has been appointed **counsel** to Her Majesty on the recommendation of the attorney general or minister of justice of the federal government or of his or her province.

quid pro quo Something for something.

quit claim To relinquish a claim to **real property**.

quorum The minimum number of **directors** or **shareholders** of a corporation who must be present to hold a valid meeting.

R

R. Rex or Regina (king or queen).

ratio decidendi The decision of a **judge** on the main issue in dispute.

real property The land, buildings, and all permanent attachments thereto; also known as **realty** or immovable property (for example, a tree is real property, but branches cut from the tree are **personal property**).

realty See **real property**.

reasons for judgment A document in which a **judge** sets out his or her reasons for arriving at a particular decision in a court case.

recipient A person who is entitled to receive support under a **support** order.

record A booklet containing a copy of relevant documents **filed** with the court for the use of the **judge** or other court official involved in a **legal proceeding**.

reference plan (R plan) A **plan** of survey of a part of a block, lot, or **parcel** of land on a registered plan of subdivision or a portion of a registered parcel.

regional centre A town or city located in one of the upper tier municipalities making up a **judicial region,** in which the offices of the regional senior **judge** and regional director are located.

regional municipality A **municipality** created by a special act of the Ontario legislature that is a federation of all the local municipalities within its boundaries. District municipalities are basically regional municipalities.

register To **file** notice of an interest in **real property** or **personal property** at the appropriate land registry or land titles office.

registrar The chief administrative officer of the Ontario courts.

registry system A system of recording document registrations relating to land. In this system, the government is responsible only for maintaining the registration records.

regnal year The number of the consecutive year of reign of a British monarch.

regular service Under the *Family Law Rules* in Ontario, serving a **legal document** by leaving a copy with the party to be served or by one of the alternatives to regular service stated in the *Family Law Rules*.

regulations Rules outlining how the provisions of an **act** are to be carried out or administered.

release A legal document or a clause in a legal document in which a person gives up rights or claims in a legal matter.

rent The **consideration** paid for the use of the **real property** or **personal property** of another person.

replevin The remedy of a person whose **chattels** are unlawfully taken from her or him.

requisition A document that requests a court official to carry out a duty.

requisition date The date by which a **purchaser** of real estate may submit any questions to the **vendor** about the validity of title to the property being purchased.

requisition on title Written requests to the **vendor** on behalf of the **purchaser** asking that defects or doubts as to the title of **real property** be removed or otherwise satisfied.

rescission The revocation of a contract.

res gestae The circumstances surrounding a particular act; things that are done.

residuary clause A clause in a **will** that sets out how all the remaining property in an **estate** will be distributed after all the special **devises** have been made.

residue The remaining **real property** or **personal property** in an **estate** after all succession duties, debts of the deceased, and specific legacies and bequests have been paid or distributed.

res ipsa loquitur The thing speaks for itself.

res judicata A thing adjudicated.

residence The home where one normally resides.

respondent A person against whom an application is made or an **appeal** or a **divorce** action is brought.

responding party A person against whom a **motion** is made.

retainer A sum of money received by a law firm from a **client** when the client engages the firm to act for or advise him or her or the document signed by a client employing the lawyer or law firm to take or defend **legal proceedings** on behalf of the client.

right of survivorship In a joint tenancy, the right of each tenant to acquire the interest in **real property** of the other tenant when that tenant dies.

S

search An examination of records and registers by a **purchaser** of **real property** to check the state of the title to the property.

security for costs An amount of money paid into court by a party making a claim against another party in a **legal proceeding** to protect the other party against the **costs** of disputing the claim.

separation agreement A domestic contract signed by two people who are married or have cohabited setting out the terms under which they agree to live separate and apart from each other. Such terms usually include provision for the custody and **support** of any children, division of property, and support obligations.

serve To **deliver** a copy of a **court document** to the opposing party in a **legal proceeding,** or to a person who is not a party but who has an interest in the proceeding. Service may be by mail or by personal delivery, depending on the type of document.

setoff A claim by the **defendant** in an **action** to set off against the claim of the **plaintiff** an amount owed by the plaintiff to the defendant.

share certificate A document under seal that records ownership of a stated number and type of **shares** of a corporation.

shareholder A person who holds **shares** in a corporation.

shares Portions of the capital of a corporation.

sheriff A person appointed by the Ontario government as the chief administrator of the Crown's business in a particular **county** within the province. The sheriff's duties include serving statements of claim and other **court documents,** keeping records of persons against whom there are outstanding **judgments,** and summoning jurors for cases.

sic Indicates an error in quoted material that appears in original material.

simplified procedure Civil procedural rules that eliminate some of the procedures, time, and **costs** for smaller claims.

sine die Indefinitely.

sine qua non A necessary condition.

single-family residence A unit or proposed unit under the Condominium Act, or a structure or part of a structure that is designed for occupation as the **residence** of one family; including dependants or domestic employees of a member of the family.

sittings A session of a court.

sole practitioner A single legal office with one lawyer.

solicitor A lawyer who conducts **legal proceedings** or who advises on legal matters. In Canada, a lawyer is both a **barrister** and a solicitor.

solicitor and client costs Costs incurred by a **client** as a result of engaging the services of a lawyer that are paid by the client to the lawyer.

solicitor of record A **solicitor** who has **filed** the **court documents** for parties in a **legal proceeding**.

special damages Specific amounts of **damages** arising from the act that is the cause of a **proceeding,** such as medical bills, lost wages, or property damage.

special examiner See **official examiner.**

special resolution A resolution submitted to a special meeting of **shareholders** that is called for the purpose of considering it, and passed with or without **amendment** by two-thirds of the votes cast at the meeting or by unanimous **consent** in writing of all shareholders.

specific performance An **order** of the court compelling a person to do that which the person previously agreed to do in accordance with a contractual obligation.

spouse A husband or wife.

standard charge terms Special provisions that apply to a **charge/mortgage** registered with the Director of Land Registration.

stare decisis To abide by decided cases.

statement of adjustments A detailed statement prepared in a real estate transaction that outlines the exact amount of money the **purchaser** must pay when the transaction is closed.

statement of claim The **court document** that originates all **actions** except a **divorce.**

status certificate Certificate obtained from a **condominium** corporation advising on the amount of **common expenses,** any arrears of common expenses by the owner of a unit, the condominium budget statement, reserve funds, insurance particulars, and so on. (formerly **estoppel certificate**).

status notice A document sent by the **registrar** to all **solicitors of record** advising them that they must attend a hearing on the status of an **action.**

status quo The existing state of things at any given time.

statute A law enacted by the federal or provincial legislature.

statute law The **written law** as set out in federal and provincial legislation.

Statute of Limitations The provincial **statute** that sets out time limits within which a **legal proceeding** must be commenced in order to protect a cause of **action**.

statutory declaration A written statement of facts in the name of one or more persons by whom it is voluntarily signed and declared under oath before a **commissioner**.

stipulation An **undertaking** in writing to do a certain thing, usually made when litigation is pending.

style of cause See **title of proceeding**.

subpoena See **summons**.

subrogation Substitution of one person or thing for another.

sub rosa Secretly.

substantial indemnity costs A system of calculating **costs** awarded in **legal proceedings** to compensate a party for its legal fees and **disbursements** at a substantially higher rate than **partial indemnity costs** and only applied in extraordinary circumstances. Formerly known as **solicitor and client costs**.

succeeding estate trustee with a will Since 1995, the term that refers to a new **estate trustee** appointed to complete the administration of an **estate** following the death of the original estate trustee (formerly **administration de bonis non administratis** *with will annexed*).

succeeding estate trustee without a will Since 1995, the term that refers to a new **estate trustee** appointed to complete the administration of an **estate** following the death of the originally appointed estate trustee (formerly **administration de bonis non administratis**).

succession duty A tax formerly levied by the provincial government on persons receiving property from the **estate** of a deceased person.

sui juris Of one's own right.

summary judgment A **judgment** of the court without holding a trial.

summons A document requiring the person to whom it is addressed to be present at a specified time and place and for a specified purpose, usually to give evidence on behalf of a party in a **legal proceeding** (formerly **subpoena**).

Superior Court of Justice The Ontario court that hears all types of criminal and **family law** cases, civil law cases (in which, when they involve the payment of money, the amount must exceed $10,000), and all trials of cases with a jury.

support Monies paid before and after a **divorce** by one **spouse** to the other spouse or on behalf of a child or children of the marriage.

support deduction order An **order** (made by an Ontario court in a **proceeding** in which the court has also made an order providing for payment of **support** on a periodic basis at regular intervals) requiring an income source who receives **notice** of the order to make payments to the Director of the Family Responsibility Office in respect of the payee named in the order.

supra Above.

Supreme Court of Ontario The name used until September 1, 1990, to describe the highest court in the Province of Ontario; now the **Court of Appeal for Ontario.**

surety A person or company that promises to satisfy the obligation of another in the event of the other's default.

T

table of contents The printed listing of contents of a document in the order in which they appear.

tariff A schedule of fees, set out in the *Rules of Civil Procedure*, that may be charged to perform specified legal services.

tenants in common Two or more persons who hold title to **real property** where each tenant may dispose of his or her interest independently of the other by transfer/deed or **will.** There is no **right of survivorship** in such an arrangement.

tenure The mode of holding or occupying land or an office.

term The number of years over which a **mortgage** will be repaid at a specified interest rate.

terms The conditions of repayment of a **charge/mortgage.**

testament Originally, an individual's written statement of how his or her **personal property** was to be distributed after death. The term **will** is now commonly used to refer to disposition of both **real property** and **personal property,** but

the formal instrument begins, "THIS IS THE LAST WILL AND TESTAMENT OF...."

testate The state of having a **will.**

testator (male) or testatrix (female) A person who has a **will.**

testimonium clause The last clause in the body of a traditional **commercial document** or a **will.** The clause begins with "IN WITNESS WHEREOF," "IN TESTIMONY WHEREOF," or "TO EVIDENCE THEIR AGREEMENT."

third party A person who is a stranger to the original **legal proceeding.** Where a **defendant** claims to be entitled to a contribution from a party who is not a party to an **action,** that party is known as the third party.

third-party claim A pleading in an existing **proceeding** to originate a claim by the **defendant** against a party who is not a party to the main **action,** who is or may be liable to the defendant for part of the **plaintiff's** claim.

tickler A note reminding the lawyer of dates by which steps need to be taken in a given matter.

tickler date The date on which a lawyer is to be reminded that specific **actions** or steps are to be taken in a matter.

tickler system A manual or computerized system for tracking dates by which steps need to be taken on a matter; also referred to as a "bring forward" system.

title The right to ownership of property.

title insurance Provides the owners of **real property** with insurance coverage against defects in title and any legal expenses that may arise from these defects.

title of proceeding The names of the parties and their capacity in a **legal proceeding**.

transaction levy surcharge A fee charged by the Lawyers' Professional Indemnity Company to law firms on the registration of an originating document in litigation and on registration of documents that effect title change in real estate. This levy is collected for use in errors and omission insurance for real estate and civil litigation **proceedings**.

transfer A **legal instrument** used in the **land titles system** up to April 1, 1985, by which title to **real property** was transferred from one party to another (see **transfer/deed**).

transfer/deed The legal document used in both the registry and the land titles systems since April 1, 1985, by which title to **real property** is conveyed or transferred from one party to another.

transferee The party who receives title to **real property** under a **transfer/deed**; before April 1, 1985, the party who received title to real property under a transfer.

transferor The party who gives title to **real property** under a transfer/deed; before April 1, 1985, the party who gave title to real property under a transfer.

true copy A photocopy or printed copy of an executed legal document, or a carbon copy of an executed legal document on which the names of the executing parties have been written in ink and in quotation marks, and upon which all other insertions or corrections made at the time of **execution** have been noted.

trust account A bank account of the law firm in which it deposits all monies received in trust for someone else, usually a **client**, or to which the law firm has no claim as payment for services rendered.

trustee A person who holds **real property** and/or **personal property** in trust for another.

U

ultra vires Beyond the power.

unbillable time Time spent by a lawyer or **law clerk** on activities that cannot be charged to a **client**.

undertaking A promise to take some **action** or provide some information at a later date.

unliquidated damages **Damages** that must be determined by the court.

upper-tier municipality A **county, district, regional municipality,** or **district municipality.**

V

v. See **versus**.

valuation date The date on which the value of property is determined. For example, in **family law** proceedings this would be the date of separation or **divorce,** or the day before the death of a **spouse**.

vendor One who sells **real property** or **personal property**.

venue See **place of trial.**

versus Against, abbreviated **v.**

vest To endow with a legal right.

via By way of.

vice versa Conversely.

viva voce By word of mouth.

void Of no legal effect.

voir dire A hearing in a criminal case to determine the admissibility of a confession or statement.

W

waive To renounce or give up a benefit or right.

Weekly Court See **Motions Court**.

will An individual's written statement of how he or she intends his or her **estate** to be distributed after death.

winding up See **wound up**.

without notice A **notice** of **motion** that is considered by the court without a copy of it being served on any other party.

without prejudice A term used in correspondence that deals with a **legal proceeding** to indicate that the contents cannot be used as evidence in the proceeding or be deemed an admission of liability.

wound up The final settlement of the accounts and affairs of an **estate**.

writ of seizure and sale A writ directed to the **sheriff** to reduce a **judgment debtor's** property to money in the amount of the **judgment**.

written law Principles of law set out in provincial and federal **statutes**.

INDEX

borrowing, 541, 558, 573–74
By-Law No. 1, 558, 568–72
By-Law No. 2, 558, 573–74
certified copies, 560
corporations, 528
format, 559–60
general, 541, 558, 568–72
Ontario corporations, 541
paper, 559–60
preparing, 559–60
By-laws, property, 483

C

Calendars, 12
Called to the bar, 3
Canada Legal Directory, 20
Canada Pension Plan, estate settlement, 653
Canadian Bar Association (CBA), 4
Canadian Guide to Uniform Legal Citation, 98
Canadian residency requirement, 533
CanLII, 106
Capital, 524
Capitalization
    in corporate material, 533
    descriptive terms for parties, 23
    government officials, 23
    legal documents, 23–24
    proper names, 24
    titles, of legal papers, 23
    titles, of persons, 24
Case Conference Brief (Form 17A), 361–63
Case conferences, family court, 345, 360–63
Case law, 93, 98
Case management, 172–73, 207
Cash receipts form, example, 82
CBA (Canadian Bar Association), 4
Central Divorce Registry, 313, 343, 348
Centralized filing systems, 42
Certificate and Affidavit of Solicitor, 324
Certificate of appointment of estate trustee
    consent to appointment, 626, 631, 650
    court fees, 632
    renunciation of appointment, 626, 631, 649
    renunciation of prior right, 631, 649
    with a will (testate)
        affidavit of condition of will or codicil, 628–29
        affidavit of execution of will and codicil, 628
        affidavit of service, 626–27, 637–38
        corporate application, 642–43
        definition, 625
        exhibits filed, 629
        exhibit stamping, 630
        individual application, 639–41
        notice of application, 626, 634–36
        obtaining the certificate, 629–30
        precedent (example), 644–45
        required documents, 629–30
    without a will (intestate)
        administration bond, 631, 632
        affidavit of service, 631, 637–38
        application for certificate of appointment, 631
        consent to appointment, 631, 650
        copies, 631
        definition, 625
        Estates Act, 631
        notice of application, 631
        precedent (example), 646–48
        renunciation of prior right..., 631, 649

required documents, 631
Succession Law Reform Act, 630
Certificates
    incorporation, 540–41, 552
    independent legal advice, 312, 324
    solicitor, 238, 257
Certified copies
    by-laws, 560
    resolutions, 566–67
    See also notarial certificates.
Changed names of chargee, 432
Change of Name Act, 311
Chargee
    changed name, 432
    charge/mortgage document, 419–20
    corporate, 431
    deceased, 432
    definition, 383, 411
    discharge of mortgage, 431–32
    individual, 431
    real estate transactions, 383
Charge/mortgage
    adjustments at closing, 462
    amortization schedule, 413
    amortized, 412–14
    assigned mortgage, 429
    assumed mortgage, 411, 429
    blended payments, 412
    chargee/chargor, 411
    definition, 383
    first mortgage, 411
    foreclosure, 411
    maturity, 411–12
    mortgagee/mortgagor, 411
    open mortgage, 412
    parties to, 383
    principal, 411
    renewed mortgage, 429
    repaying, 411–14
    second mortgage, 411
    term (duration of loan), 411
    terms (of repayment), 411
    See also mortgage.
Charge/mortgage, discharge
    address for service, 432
    assignments, 431
    changed names of chargee, 432
    chargee, 431–32
    charge to be discharged, 431
    copies, 432
    corporate chargee, 431
    deceased chargee, 432
    document prepared by, 432
    e-reg (electronic registration), 433, 435–36
    execution, 432
    final partial discharge, 429
    FORM 3 (Discharge of Charge/Mortgage), 387
    full discharge, 429
    individual chargee, 431
    legal description, 430–31
    partial discharge, 429
    PIN (property identifier number), 430
    precedents (examples), 434–36
    preparer, 429
    recitals, 431
    registration, 432
    release of interest in insurance, 433

background information, 118
body, 118–19
corners, 127
corporate seal, 121
declarants, 125–26
definition, 112
definitions, 118
ending, 119–22
heading, 116–17
notarial certificates, 126–27, 136
parties, 116, 118
parts of, 116
precedents (examples)
    agreements, 129–31
    backsheet, 132–33
    notarial certificate, 136
    release, 137
    statutory declaration, 134–35
recitals, 118
releases, 127, 137
signatures, 120–21
statutory declaration, 125–26, 134–35
testimonium clause, 119–20
See also court documents; legal documents; legal material
    preparation guidelines; specific documents.
Commissioners, lawyers as, 3
Commissioners, of affidavits, 123
Common elements, 383
Common expenses, 384, 466
Common law, 93
Common shares, 528–29
Companies and Personal Property Securities Branch
    (CPPSB), 531
Company names, indexing, 40–41
Compass bearing (course), 386
Complimentary close, 56–57
Computers
    automatic document preparation, 151
    search engines, 106
    See also software.
Condominium Act, 383–84
Condominiums
    common elements, 383
    common expenses, 384
    contingency fund, 384
    as corporations, 383–84
    declaration of rights and obligations, 383
    definition, 383
    searches, 482
    status certificate, 458, 482
Conference Notice (Form 17), 360
Conferences. *See* family court, 345, 360–63
Confidentiality agreement, 9–10
Confirmation
    of application, 273
    of conference, 345
    Form 14C (Confirmation), 364
    of motions, 226–27, 234, 346
Confirmation (Form 14C), 364
Conflict of interest, 36–37
Consent
    to act as director, 554
    to act as first director, 540, 551
    to appointment of estate trustee, 626, 631, 650
    copies, 227
    definition, 227
    precedent (example), 235
Consideration, transfer/deed, 397

Consolidated regulations, 96
Consolidations, transfer/deed, 398
Constitution Act, 93
Contingency fees, 69, 71
Contingency fund, 384
Contingency reserve, adjustments at closing, 466
Continuation pages, 50, 57–58
Continuing power of attorney for property, 608, 617–18
Continuing record, 341–42, 350–51
Contracts. *See* commercial documents
The Conveyancer software, 388
Conveyancing real property, 388
Co-ownership, 383
Copies
    accounts, 86
    affidavit of documents, 240
    affidavit of service, 627, 627
    affidavits, 158
    application for certificate of appointment, 628
    application record, 272
    articles of incorporation, 538
    authorizations, 38
    bill of costs, 285
    certificate of appointment, with a will, 626, 629
    certificate of appointment, without a will, 631
    charge/mortgage discharge, 432
    charge/mortgage document, 420
    commercial documents, 115–16
    consent, 227
    counterclaims, 208–9
    crossclaims, 210
    death certificate, 652
    default judgment, 299
    estate settlement, 652, 658
    evidence on application, 269
    factum, 226–27, 272
    financial statements, 319
    judgments, 283
    land transfer tax affidavit, 488
    letters, 58
    memoranda, 50–51
    memoranda of law, 108
    minutes, 565
    motion record, 225, 232
    motions, 223
    NFP (Net Family Property) statement, 319
    notice of action, 170
    notice of application, 269
    notice to beneficiaries, 626
    orders, 283
    reply to action, 207
    responses to actions, 206–7
    retainers, 38
    statement of claim, 169, 171
    third party claims, 210–11
    transfer/deed, 403
    trial record, 244
    undertaking to re-adjust, 467
    wills, 605
    See also certified copies; notarial certificates; specific
        documents.
Copy, definition, 21
Copying documents, charges for, 81
Copying documents, description, 19–20
Copy notations, 58
Corners, commercial documents, 127
Corporate chargee, 431
Corporate seal, 121, 541

H

Heading, document
    actions, 153
    affidavits, 123
    applications, 153
    commercial documents, 116–17
    continuation pages, 57–58
    court documents, 152–54
    See also specific documents.
Hearing motions, 222
Hearings on applications, 271–73
Highest court in Canada, 140
Holograph will, 603, 606
Hourly fees, 69
HST (harmonized sales tax), 71
Hudson's Bay Company, 524
Hydro, adjustments at closing, 465

I

Income tax return, estate settlement, 654
Incorporation
    in Ontario (*See* Ontario corporations)
    purpose of, 524
    See also corporate; corporations.
Incorporators, 539
Independent legal advice, 312, 324
Indexing
    abbreviations, 40
    company names, 40–41
    files, 36
    government departments and ministries, 41
    guidelines, 40–41
    multiple files for same client, 41
    municipalities, 41
    "nothing before something," 40
    personal names, 40
    titles, 40
    See also filing.
Individual chargee, 431
Individuals, party to statement of claim, 166–67
Information for court use form, 171, 186
Information form, 338
Information on first directors, 539
Initial capitals, 23–24
Initial return/notice of charge, 542, 555–56
Inside address, 52–54
Inspection of documents, 240
Instruments, in Teraview, 389
Insurance
    adjustments at closing, 466
    estate settlement, 655–56
    real estate (*See* fire insurance; title insurance)
    release of interest in, 433
Interest charges, unpaid accounts, 86
Interest/estate transferred, 398
Interlocutory proceedings, 221
Internal rules. *See* by-laws
Internet resources. *See* electronic resources; websites
Interoffice memoranda, 50
Intestate, definition, 603
Intestate clients, 622
Issuing share certificates, 585–86
Issuing statement of claim, 169

J

Joint and several, 608
Joint application for divorce, 348
Joint tenants, 383
Joint venture agreements, 532

Judges

Judges, citing, 107
Judges, definition, 144–45
Judgment, trial phase, 249
Judgments
    copies, 283
    definition, 281
    form of, 281–83
    precedents (examples), 288–89
    signed and entered, 283
    See also fees and costs; orders.
Jurat, 124, 157

K

K.C. (King's Counsel), 3
Korbite Inc., 151

L

Land registration
    Land Registration Reform Act, 382–83
    land titles system, 382
    POLARIS, 382–83
    registry system, 381
    statements, 382–83
    Torrens title, 382
    See also real property, describing; titles, real estate.
Land Registration Reform Act, 382–83
Land titles system, 382
Land transfer tax, calculating, 488–90
Land Transfer Tax Affidavit
    authorizing funds withdrawal, 506
    City of Toronto land transfer tax, 489–90
    copies, 488
    e-reg (electronic registration), 505
    format, 487–88
    guidelines for amounts, 487
    land transfer tax, calculating, 488–90
    precedent (example), 504–5
    requirements, 487
    retail sales tax, calculating, 490
Last page of documents. *See* backsheets
Last will and testament. *See* wills
Law clerks, 7. *See also* legal assistants.
Law firms
    administrative assistants, 7
    associates, 5
    law clerks, 7
    legal assistants, 8
    legal secretaries, 7
    letterhead, examples, 6
    LLP (limited liability partnership), 5
    naming, 5
    paralegals, 7
    partnerships, 5
    sole practitioner, 5
    staff positions, 5, 7–8
    technology in, 8 (*See also* computers; software)
Law reports, citing
    abbreviations, 98–102
    bound volumes, 98
    format, 102–4
    guidelines, 98–102
    parallel citations, 105
    pinpoint references, 104–5
    style of cause, 102
    title of proceeding, 102
Laws
    case, 93
    common, 93
    statute, 93–96
    See also regulations; specific laws.

Municipalities
    describing real property, 385
    indexing, 41
    lower tier, 113, 385
    upper tier, 113, 385

N

Name format, parties to statement of claim, 166–67
Names
    acts, 94
    capitalizing, 24
    files, 31
    indexing, 40–41
    law firms, 5
    matters, 31
    Ontario corporations, 536, 538
    of parties, charge/mortgage document, 419
Neutral citations, 105
New file/matter form, 30
New housing rebate, 438, 509
New Upgraded Automated Name Search (NUANS), 536
Next of kin, 624
NFP (Net Family Property), 315, 317–18
NFP statement (Form 13B), 334–36
NFP statements, 318–19, 334–36, 343
Non-amortized payments, 415, 417
Nonbillable time, 69
Non-essential dates, 102
Non-government bonds, estate settlement, 655
Non-offering corporations
    definition, 526
    directors, 527
    incorporating, 538
    proxy form, 576
Non-profit corporations, 524
Notarial certificates
    description, 126–27
    estate documents, 652, 658
    precedents (examples), 136, 658
Notary public, 3. *See also* affidavits.
Notations
    blind copy, 58
    copy, 58
    envelopes, 59
    letters, 52
    mail type, 52
    on-arrival, 52
    Q.C. (Queen's Counsel), 53
    reference initial, 57
    without prejudice, 52
"Nothing before something" rule, 40
Notice of action
    copies, 170
    parties, 165
    precedent (example), 183–84
    preparing, 170
    responses to, 206
    ticklers, 175
    See also originating process; pleadings; statement of claim.
Notice of action to originate an action, 170
Notice of appearance, 270, 277
Notice of application, 267, 269, 275–76
Notice of application for appointment of estate trustee, 626, 631, 634–36
Notice of Appointment for Assessment of Costs, 285
Notice of defence, 212
Notice of estate settlement, 652–53
Notice of intent to defend, 206, 214
Notice of meetings, 575

Notice of motion, 220, 221–23, 231. *See also* motions.
Notice of Motion (Form 14), 365–66
Notice of withdrawal, 302
Notices, 220–21, 230
NUANS (New Upgraded Automated Name Search), 536
Number formats, 24–26
Numbering pages, minutes, 565
Number names for corporations, 536
Number of pages, charge/mortgage, 414
Number of pages, transfer/deed, 396–97
Numbers, in files/matters, 31, 32–33
Numerical filing, 41–42

O

Offering corporations
    definition, 526
    directors, 527
    incorporating, 538
Offer to purchase, 439
Offer to settle, 246
Officer register, 588, 596
Officers of corporations, 527, 589
Official examiner, 241
Omissions, indicating, 27
On-arrival notations, 52
ONBIS (Ontario Business Information System), 542
Online resources. *See* electronic resources; websites
Ontario
    case management system, 172–73
    court system
        Court of Appeal, 142–43
        court offices, 144
        Divisional Court, 143
        Family Court, 143
        family law, 313–14
        Ontario Court of Justice, 144
        Rules of Civil Procedure, 142
        Small Claims Court, 143
        structure, chart of, 142
        Superior Court of Justice, 143
        website, 144
    Family Law Rules, 311
    incorporating in (*See* corporations, Ontario)
    law clerks/paralegals, 7
    simplified origination procedure, 172
Ontario, corporations
    articles of incorporation
        business of corporation, 539
        certificate of incorporation, 540–41, 552
        classes of shares, 539
        consent to act as director, 554
        consent to act as first director, 540, 551
        execution, 540
        incorporators, 539
        information on first directors, 539
        name, 538
        number of directors, 538
        other provisions, 539
        precedent (example), 544–50
        registered office, 538, 589
        restrictions re transfer of shares, 539
        special provisions attached to shares, 539
    by-laws, 541
    corporate supplies, 541
    directors
        consent to act as, 554
        consent to act as first, 540, 551
        information on first, 539
        number of, 538
        resignation of, 541, 553

estate settlement, 656
mortgage (*See* charge/mortgage)
title transfer (*See* transfer/deed)
See also real estate.
Realty tax certificates, searches, 483, 499
Realty tax office, 510
Receipts, 81
Recitals, 118, 431
Records management. *See* filing; indexing
Reference IDs, commercial documents, 114
Reference initial notations, 57
Reference plan, describing real property, 386
Reference resources
Canada Legal Directory, 20
Canadian Guide to Uniform Legal Citation, 98
Gregg Reference Manual, 12
legal directories, 20
Legal Telephone Directories, 20
LexisNexis, 20
Martindale-Hubbell Canadian Law Directory, 20
online (*See* electronic resources; websites)
Ontario Legal Directory, 20
Pitman Office Handbook, 12
postal code directories, 20
telephone directories, 20
See also electronic resources; websites.
References. *See* citations
Regarding (re/Re:), 31
Regional municipalities, 113
Registered office, 538, 587, 589
Registers, 541
Registrar of the court
definition, 145
requests of (*See* requisitions)
Registration
electronic (*See* e-reg (electronic registration))
land (*See* land registration)
Registry system, land registration, 381
Regular service. *See* ordinary service
Regulations
citations, 96–97
citing, 96–97
consolidated, 96
gazettes, 97
revised, 96
Releases
by beneficiary, 656, 663
bonds, 632
description, 127
of interest in insurance, 433
precedent (example), 137
Relief sought, 168
Religious corporations, 524
Reminders. *See* tickler slips
Renewal clause, 418
Renewed mortgage, 429
Rent, adjustments at closing, 466
Renunciation of
estate trustee, 626, 631, 649
prior right to certificate of appointment, 631, 649
Repaying charge/mortgage, 411–14
Reply to action, 207
Reply to service, 344
Reporting letter to purchaser, 510, 514–17
Reporting letter to vendor, 511, 518–20
Requisitions
agreement of purchase and sale, 439
date, 439
for default judgment, 298, 303–6

description, 227–28
precedent (example), 236
on title, 457
re/Re: (regarding), 31
Resignation of directors, 541, 553
Resolutions
certified copies, 566–67
for corporate change, 590, 598
corporations, 528
format, 566
order of, 562
precedents (examples), 580–83
preparation guidelines, 566
shareholder, 566, 582
single director, 566, 583
Respondents
applications, 145, 267
family court, 315–16
motions, 221
Responding party, 221
Responses to
notice of action, 206
notice of applications, 270
originating process
case management, 207
chart of, 205
consent, 220, 227, 235
counterclaim, 208–9
crossclaim, 209–10, 217
demand for particulars, 211
factum, 225–26, 233
motion record, 224–25, 232
motions
confirmation, 226–27, 234
decisions on, 227
notice of motion, 220, 221–23, 231
notice of intent to defend, 206, 214
notices, 220–21, 230
reply, 207
requisitions, 220, 227–28, 236
simplified procedure, 207
statement of defence, 206, 215–17
Statement of Defence and Counterclaim, 208–9, 216
Statement of Defence and Crossclaim, 209–10, 217
third party claims, 210–11
transcript of evidence, 225
statement of claim, 206
Restrictions re transfer of shares, 539
Retail sales tax, calculating on real estate, 490
Retainers, 39, 46–47, 146
Return envelopes, 59
Returning telephone calls, 18–19
Revised regulations, 96
Revised statutes, 94
Right of survivorship, 383
Royal charter, 524
Rule 3 (Time), 146
Rules for corporations. *See* by-laws
Rules of Civil Procedure
estate matters, 622
Ontario courts, 142
regulations, 96
Rule 3 (Time), 146
tariff of fees, 284
time limits, calculating, 146
wills, 603

S

Safekeeping of wills, 607
Sale by chargor, 418